Exploring a Changing World

GLOBE BOOK COMPANY

New York, N. Y. 10010

Exploring a Changing World

MELVIN SCHWARTZ

Principal
New York City School System

JOHN R. O'CONNOR

Principal
New York City School System

Our thanks to Mr. Robert Gritz for reading
the manuscript of this text and making many
helpful suggestions.

Illustrations by Robert Shipman
Four-color maps by Milton S. Venezky and
associates
Two-color maps and pictographs by Dyno
Lowenstein, Pictograph Corp.

Table of Contents

Unit 9: THE PACIFIC WORLD

Conclusion

LIST OF MAPS

LIST OF PICTOGRAPHS

Exploring a Changing World

UNIT I

The Earth

CHAPTER 1

Our World in Maps and Globes

PROBLEM: How can maps show the world as it really is?

1. We live on the planet Earth. It is one of nine planets that travel around the sun. Our planet is shaped like a ball or *sphere*. Since most of us cannot travel into space to look at our planet, the next best way to study it is through maps. The best map of the earth is a *globe*. A globe is round, so it shows us the earth almost as it is. (The earth really is slightly flat at the poles.) It is the only map that shows us the correct size and shape of the land and water areas on the earth.

2. There are some disadvantages to a globe, though. A globe is not easy to carry with you; it can hardly be kept in your pocket. When we are learning about our planet in school, we can't keep a globe inside our book. Therefore, map makers have had to make other maps that show how the earth looks on a flat surface.

3. There are many such maps, some of which are shown in this chapter. All are ways in which map makers have tried to show the roundness of the earth on a flat surface. There is a problem, however. Flat maps cannot be made without some *distortion,* or changing of the accurate shapes of things. For example, a map that can show the correct directions on the earth's surface probably will not show the true size and shape of land areas. If the correct size and shape of land areas are shown, the water areas may not be correct. In any flat map of the earth, the map maker decides which things he wants to show correctly. (The globe photograph is an attempt to show the roundness of the earth on a flat surface.)

4. The *Mercator* map is one of the most common of flat maps. Mercator was a Dutch map maker who lived about 300 years ago. He was interested in making a map that would help sailors. His map uses only straight lines. This map has been useful for sailors. However, it cannot be used if you want to find correct distances. The land and water areas are not shown in their true size. On a Mercator map, the continent of North America looks larger than the continent of Africa, and Greenland is as large as South America. A globe would show that this is wrong.

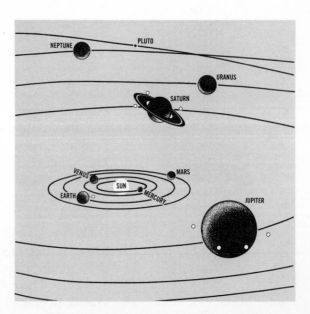

The nine planets of our solar system.

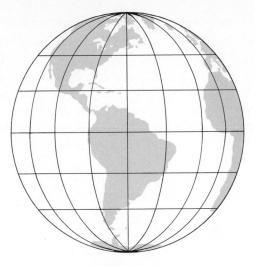

Globe map.

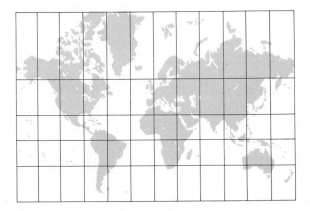

Mercator map.

5. With the coming of the airplane, it became possible to travel over the "top" of the earth rather than "around" it. As a result, distances between certain countries became much less. The *polar* map shows this fact. The North Pole is the center of the polar map. (The North Pole is the northernmost point on the earth. The South Pole is the farthest point south.) The polar map shows clearly how close Europe, Asia and North America are to each other across the Arctic Ocean. On this map, it is easy to mark some of the air routes that connect these continents. However, there are distortions here too. The lands far from the center of the map appear too large and have strange shapes.

6. The *Lambert* projection is sometimes called the "flier's map." This map is good for showing land areas that extend in an east-west or right-left direction. The shapes of these land areas are true. The distances and directions are almost accurate. Therefore, this map is used by pilots.

7. In order to compare the sizes of land and water areas, the *Mollweide* or *equal-area* map is used. This is a map in the shape of an oval. The land and water areas are shown in true size, but the land shapes are not true. To correct this distortion, the oval is broken into several parts. The continents now show their correct shape, but the oceans are distorted. This is called a *broken projection* map.

8. There are many other kinds of maps. There

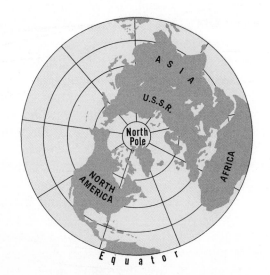

Polar projection.

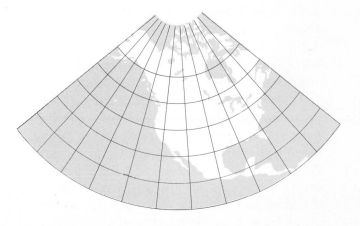

Lambert projection.

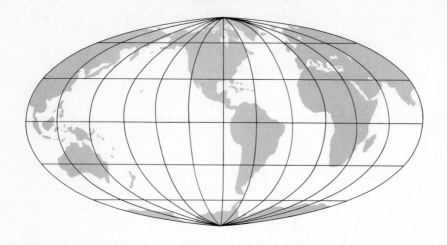

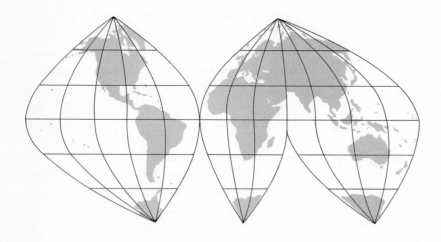

Mollweide equal-area maps.

are maps that show us highlands, lowlands and bodies of water. These are called *physical* or *relief* maps. These maps also show us the altitude or height of land above sea level. (Sea level is the level of the ocean when it is still.) Maps that show the boundaries between countries and states are called *political* maps. *Product* maps show us the things made from a country's resources. *Rainfall* maps tell us how much rain a place receives at certain times. Some maps tell us how many people live in one area. These are *population* maps. *Climate* maps show us the climatic regions of the earth—where it is hot or cold, wet or dry. We will use many of these maps as we study our world.

9. As we have seen, each type of map has its good and bad points. However, we will always need maps, because we cannot study or travel without them. When we travel by car, we need a road map. We may have a large map of a section of the United States, another of the particular state we are interested in, and still another of the city or community in the state. In the subways of our large cities, we must look at a map to find our station. At sea, a ship's captain must use a map to plot the course of his ship. We use maps on planes and in the armed forces. We may even use a map to look for buried treasure, as men have done for hundreds of years. Whatever the reason, maps are a part of our lives. And they make much easier the job of exploring our changing world.

UNDERSTANDING WHAT YOU HAVE READ

As you read *Exploring a Changing World*, you will find some words that you do not know. Sometimes it is easy to tell the meaning of a word from the way the word is used in a sentence. You will often find *clues* to the meanings of words. It is important that you learn to recognize some of these clues.

Let us look for some of the new or difficult words in Chapter 1 and see the clues that tell us what they mean:

In paragraph 1, a new word is *sphere*. The clue to the meaning of sphere is the smaller word before it, *or*. The sentence states that "Our planet is shaped like a ball *or* sphere." The word *or* tells us that sphere means "shaped like a ball." *Or* is therefore one of our clues.

In paragraph 3, the new word is *distortion*. Again, you will notice the use of the word *or* as a clue. The sentence says there is ". . . some distortion, *or* changing of the accurate shapes of things." We know then that *distortion* means "putting out of shape."

Sometimes the clue to the meaning of a word appears *in the sentence before the word*. In paragraph 8, there is an example of this kind of clue. The third sentence tells us about *physical maps*. The sentence before it tells us that these are maps that show highlands, lowlands and bodies of water. Therefore, we know that a *physical map* shows us the surface of the earth.

The clue may appear *in the sentence following the word*. In paragraph 5, the first sentence tells us about a *polar* map. The next sentence states that this map has the North Pole at the center. Thus, the word *polar* refers to the *North Pole*, or to the poles of the earth.

In paragraph 8, there is another example of the clue to the meaning of a word appearing in the sentence before the word. The sentence says, "Some maps tell us how many people live in one area." The next sentence states, "These are population maps." We know, therefore, that the word *population* refers to the number of people living in a certain area.

You will meet other clues to word meanings as you read the other chapters in this book. Some of these clues are explained for your help:

A *dash* (—) is often a clue to the meaning of a word. Example: "The *llama*—a woolly animal of the Andes—can carry heavy loads." The word *llama* is explained by the words set off from the rest of the sentence by dashes.

The meaning of a word may be shown by the use of *parentheses,* ( ). Example: "Inventions brought about many changes in farm *implements* (tools used in farming)." Parentheses ( ) are used to show that "implements" means "farm tools."

The meaning of a word *may be given in a sentence* for you. When that happens, the meaning of the word is very clear. Example: "*Canyons* are long narrow valleys surrounded by high cliffs."

The words *that is* are often good clues. Example: "The earth *revolves, that is,* travels, around the sun." The words *that is* show us the meaning of *revolves*.

In your study, you will often be asked to tell the meanings of words. You will have to know their meanings if you are to understand the important facts about our changing world. Remember the clues that may help you:

1. *Or*
2. *Dash* —
3. *Parentheses* ( )
4. *That is*
5. The *sentence before* the word
6. The *sentence after* the word
7. The *definition in* the sentence

SUMMING UP

Tell whether these statements are true or false. The underlined words make the statement true or false. If the statement is false, what words would you place in the statement to make it true?

1. The only true picture of the earth is the Mercator map.
2. A Mercator map has straight lines.
3. A polar map will show us how close land areas are to the North Pole.
4. A "flier's map" will show us true shapes and land areas.
5. Physical maps will usually show us the number of people living in one place.
6. Boundaries between countries are shown on a political map.
7. Land areas will have strange shapes near the center of the earth on a polar map.
8. Highlands, lowlands and bodies of water are usually shown on a rainfall map.
9. The sizes of land and water areas are best shown on a globe.
10. Another word for "putting out of shape" is distortion.

CHAPTER 2

The Language of Maps

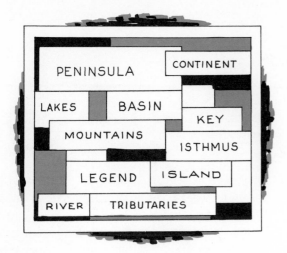

PROBLEM: How do maps show what is on the surface of the earth?

1. No map can show us real things on the earth—farmlands, hills, mountains, rivers, oceans, cities, crops and minerals. Those things are shown on a map by using special marks. These marks are called *symbols*. Most map makers use the same kinds of symbols: lines, dots, special colors and small pictures. No map shows everything, but every map will show a few things.

2. In order to understand what a particular map is trying to tell us, it is necessary to read the map *legend*. The legend, usually found in one corner of the map, explains what the symbols on the map mean. It is sometimes called the *key* to the map. You should first look for the legend before you begin to read any map. The title or name of the map is usually part of the legend.

3. The map on page 10 shows the North American continent and part of South America. A thin black line is used to show where the land and water meet. This line is the symbol for the coastline. The black line can also be called the shoreline. Coastline symbols may be crooked or irregular, showing places for harbors or seaports. (A seaport is a city on the water where people and goods go in and out by boat.)

4. The large land areas on the map are called *continents* or mainlands. There are also smaller land areas on the map. A small land area entirely surrounded by water is an *island*. A *peninsula* is a piece of land *almost* entirely surrounded by water. An *isthmus* is a narrow strip of land joining two larger bodies of land. *Mountains* are shown on maps by little pictures or symbols that look roughly like mountains.

5. There are many kinds of bodies of water on the earth. The largest bodies of water are the *oceans*. Bodies of water are sometimes shown by the use of wavy lines. *Lakes* can be seen easily because they are completely surrounded by land. A thin black or blue line that winds through land is usually a *river*. Still other lines join the river. These are the *tributaries,* or branches of the river. The land that is drained by a river and its branches is called a *basin*.

6. Lines are also used to show the boundaries of countries. Many countries are divided further into smaller areas called states and provinces. (Sometimes these boundary lines are broken lines: - - - -.) The map symbol for a city is a dot. The symbol that stands for the capital city of a country is a star or a dot with a circle around it. The name of the city is usually given with the dot or star to show what the symbol stands for.

7. The map maker also uses colors for many reasons. Colors can be used to show the difference between land and water areas. Water is usually colored blue. Colors also make it easier for the reader to see the boundaries of different countries. Maps that show differences in climate use a color for each kind of climate. The map legend on a climate map will tell you what each color means. The height of land—the elevation above sea level—is shown in color on relief maps. Sometimes different shadings of the same color are used on these maps. Again, you must look at the legend to find out what each color stands for.

8. Map makers use still other symbols. For example, they use dots and circles of different sizes to show the number of people, the amount of cattle, or the kinds of minerals that may be found in the places shown on the map. *Picture symbols* can also be used to show these things. Many of the small pictures look much like the items they represent or stand for. You may see small stacks of wheat or oil wells, horses or lumps of coal, depending on what facts must be given about an area.

Map # 1—Map of Geographic Terms

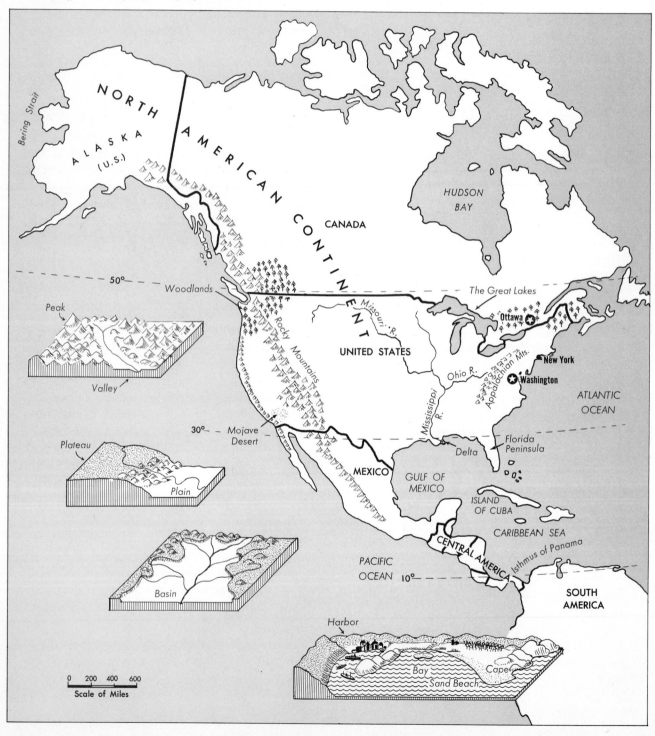

UNDERSTANDING WHAT YOU HAVE READ

I. *Finding the Main Idea*

One of the most important skills you can learn is the ability to find the *main idea* of a paragraph or a chapter. Each paragraph tells us about one main thought. In the chapter, each of the paragraphs helps us to understand the main idea of the entire chapter. The title of the chapter is a clue to the main idea of the chapter. Let us look at Chapter 2 and see if we can find the main ideas of the paragraphs and of the chapter.

The main idea of a paragraph may be expressed in a sentence. This sentence may be at the beginning or end of the paragraph, or it may be in the middle. Sometimes the main idea is not stated, but we can tell what it is if we read all the sentences in the paragraph.

In paragraph 1, we learn that the special marks called symbols are used on a map to show us real things. Is there a sentence that tells us this idea? Yes, the second sentence states, "Those things are shown on a map by using special marks." This is the main idea of paragraph 1.

In paragraph 2, you know after you have read the paragraph that it is about a map legend. We learn what the legend is and how important it is in using a map. The main idea is told in the first sentence, "In order to understand what a particular map is trying to tell us, it is necessary to read the map legend." This sentence contains the main idea of the paragraph.

In paragraph 4, there is no key sentence that tells us the main idea. Read the six sentences in paragraph 4. Each one tells us about a land area on a map. The one idea of the paragraph is that there are different kinds of land forms on the earth. Although no sentence tells us this, we know it because all the sentences are about kinds of land forms on the earth. So we can express the main idea as "the kinds of land forms on the earth."

The main idea of the chapter is the summary of all the main ideas presented in the paragraphs of the chapter. In Chapter 2, we learn about map symbols, the map legend, lines on a map, land forms, colors used on maps and other markings. We know that all of these things are ways in which maps tell a story—ways in which they give us a message. They are the ways that maps *communicate ideas* to us. Therefore, the main idea of the chapter might be stated, "Ways that maps communicate ideas to us." We communicate with each other through language. The title for the chapter, then, is "The Language of Maps."

II. *Knowing Words*

In Chapter 1, you learned how to tell the meanings of words by using clues in each paragraph. Look at each paragraph for the words listed below. Can you tell the meanings of these words in Chapter 2? Can you tell the *clues* you used to know the meanings of these words?

Paragraph 1—symbols	Paragraph 5—tributaries
Paragraph 2—legend	Paragraph 5—basin
Paragraph 3—irregular	Paragraph 6—provinces
Paragraph 4—peninsula	Paragraph 7—elevation above sea level
Paragraph 4—isthmus	Paragraph 8—represent

11

SUMMING UP

In the following, terms and symbols are matched with other words. Some are correctly matched. Some are incorrectly matched. Tell which items are correctly matched.

1. Legend—key to a map.
2. Peninsula—entirely surrounded by water.
3. Isthmus—narrow body of water.
4. Continent—largest land area.
5. Symbols—special map marks.
6. Tributaries—lakes.
7. Political map—shows boundaries of states.
8. Climates—dots of many sizes.
9. Map Symbols:
    a. Dots—cities.
    b. Lines—boundaries of countries.
    c. Dot with a star—harbor.
    d. Winding lines—rivers.
    e. Blue color—mountains.

The Importance of Latitude

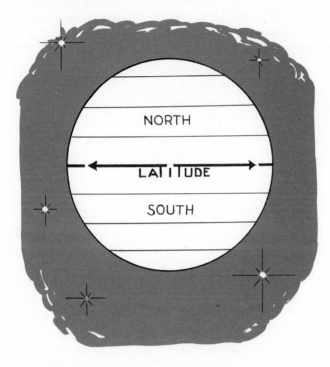

NORTH

← LATITUDE →

SOUTH

PROBLEM: How can we find places on the earth's surface, using latitude?

1. There are three main kinds of information that a map can give you: *location*—where are certain places on the earth?, *distance*—how far is it from one place to another?, and *direction* —what route would you take to get from one place to another?

2. The actual size of any place on the earth cannot be shown on a map. It would be impossible to bring such a map into your home or classroom. Even a map that is made to be 1/100 of the size of a country would be far too large to handle. It would cover as much room as a large city. For a map to be small enough to use, it must be drawn *to scale*. This means that a map is drawn to a definite *propor-*

tion, or part of the true size. For example, one inch on a map might stand for 500 or 1,000 miles. The scale would then be written as 1:500 or 1:1000. This *scale of miles* would be part of the map legend. The scale is a clue to how distant or far one place on the map is from another. It can also be used to find out the sizes of the areas shown.

3. Directions on maps are indicated by the words *north, south, east* and *west,* or combinations of these words, such as *northeast, northwest, southeast* and *southwest.* North means toward the North Pole; south means toward the South Pole. When a person faces north, south is behind him, east is on his right and west is on his left. On most flat maps, north is placed at the top of the map, south is at the bottom, east is at the right and west is at the left. While it is easier to have most maps alike in this way, there is actually no top or bottom to the earth; it is almost a perfect sphere. One could draw a map with any direction at the top and still be correct. (*Down* means toward the center of the earth and *up* away from the earth; they are not the same as north and south.)

4. To show location, map makers use lines that crisscross the map. Some of the lines are drawn across the map in an east-west direction; others go north and south. These lines do not really appear on the earth's surface. They are imaginary lines invented by the map maker. The lines form a pattern called a *grid.* With them, it is possible to locate any place on the earth.

5. The east-west lines on a map are called lines of *latitude.* The imaginary line of latitude that circles the earth at its center is called the *equator.* It goes 25,000 miles around the middle of the earth. It gets its name from the fact that it is half way between, or equally distant from, the North and South Poles. The equator is the longest line of latitude on the earth.

6. The equator divides the earth into two parts, the *northern hemisphere* and the *southern hemisphere.* (*Hemi* means "half," so a hemisphere is half a globe or half a sphere.) The northern hemisphere lies between the equator

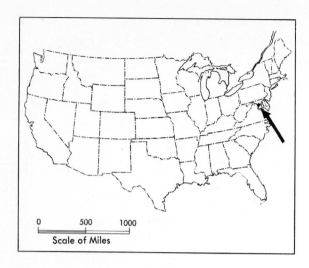

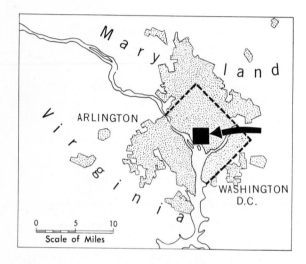

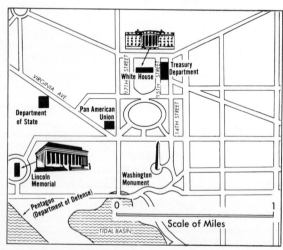

Differently scaled maps—all showing Washington, D.C.

and the North Pole. The southern hemisphere lies between the equator and the South Pole. Most of the land areas of the earth are in the northern hemisphere. Most of the water areas are in the southern hemisphere. (Look at the world map on p. 56, and you will see that this is true.)

7. Lines of latitude are *parallel* to the equator. That is, each line of latitude remains the same distance from the equator for its entire length around the earth. These lines or parallels are numbered. Through the numbers we can tell how far north or south of the equator the lines are. Their numbers are called *degrees*. One degree of latitude is about 70 miles on the earth's surface. (Figure this out by dividing 25,000 miles, the circumference of the earth, by 360, the number of degrees or divisions in any circle or sphere.) Instead of saying that a city is about 70 miles north of the equator, we say that it is one degree north, or 1° N.

8. The lines of latitude or parallels are numbered from 0 degrees to 90 degrees. The equator is 0 degrees, the North Pole is 90 degrees north latitude and the South Pole is 90 degrees south. The numbers of the latitudes grow larger the farther you go from the equator—from 0° to 90°. In writing degrees of latitude, you must add the word "North" (N) or "South" (S) to tell whether the line is north or south of the equator. For example: Seattle, Washington, is located at 47° N. Latitude. Lima, Peru, is at 12° S. Latitude.

9. New York City is about 41° north of the equator. New Orleans is 30° North. Washington, D.C. is about 38° North. We know then that Washington is farther from the equator than New Orleans, but not as distant from the middle of the earth as New York City is. Cities that are 40 degrees north of the equator and cities that are 40 degrees south are the same distance from the equator, but in opposite directions.

10. A few lines of latitude are specially marked on the map. Two of these are 23½° north and 23½° south of the equator. All places between these two lines of latitude have

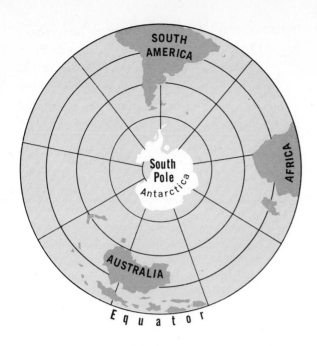

The southern hemisphere.

tor. In the northern hemisphere, 66½° is known as the Arctic Circle. In the southern hemisphere, the same distance from the equator is called the Antarctic Circle. Between the tropics and these lines of latitude are the *middle latitudes*. Beyond 66½° north and south of the equator are the *high latitudes*. The low, middle, and high latitudes do not have completely different climates. Their special parallels are marked to show a separation between areas that get different amounts of sunlight. You will read more about the effect of the sun on these areas when you study the movement of the earth around the sun.

the noonday sun directly overhead twice a year. Places farther north or south never have the direct rays of the sun overhead. The area between 23½° north and 23½° south is called the *tropics*. (These two lines of latitude have names that will give a clue to their meaning: The Tropic of Cancer is north of the equator; the Tropic of Capricorn is south of it.) The tropics is an area of direct sunlight. This same region is often called the *low latitudes*. They are called "low" because they are marked with the lowest numbers, 0 to 23½ degrees.

11. Other special lines of latitude are found at 66½° north and 66½° south of the equa-

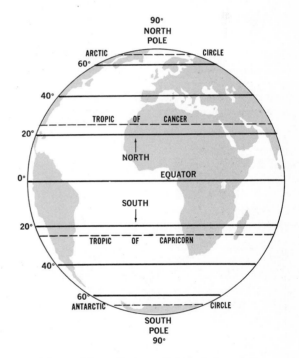

Lines of latitude (parallels) of the earth.

15

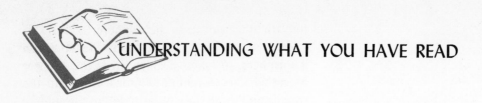
I. *Finding the Main Idea*

In Chapter 2, you learned how to find the main idea of a paragraph or a chapter. This is an important skill, for it helps you to know the important ideas in any lesson. It helps you to remember what you have learned. See if you can answer the following questions about the main ideas of paragraphs in Chapter 3. Is there a sentence in each paragraph that helped you to choose your answers?

1. In *paragraph 2*, the main idea is that:
a. many maps are too large to use in the home.
b. the scale of miles is part of the map legend.
c. maps are drawn to a scale of the true size of an area.

2. The main idea of *paragraph 3* is to describe how:
a. most maps are alike.
b. directions are shown on maps.
c. flat maps are made.

3. The main idea of *paragraph 4* is to describe:
a. the largest line of latitude.
b. lines that crisscross maps.
c. the imaginery lines of latitude.

4. The main idea of *paragraph 8* is to describe:
a. how lines of latitude are numbered.
b. latitude south of the equator.
c. the use of grid lines.

5. The main idea of *paragraph 10* is to describe:
a. the region of low latitudes.
b. places that never get the direct rays of the sun.
c. names for special lines of latitude.

II. *Knowing Words*

Look at each paragraph for the words listed below. Can you tell the meanings of these words in Chapter 3? Can you tell the *clues* you used to know the meanings of these words?

Paragraph 2—proportion
Paragraph 4—grid
Paragraph 5—latitude
Paragraph 5—equator
Paragraph 6—hemisphere
Paragraph 7—degrees
Paragraph 8—parallels
Paragraph 10—tropics
Paragraph 11—middle latitudes

SUMMING UP

Tell whether these statements are true or false. The underlined words make the statements true or false. If a statement is false, what words would you place in it to make it true?

1. You can measure distance on a map by using the scale of miles.
2. Bogotá, Colombia, is 4° North Latitude. This means that it is located in the high latitudes.
3. Lines of latitude on a map are real lines on the earth's surface.
4. Columbia, South Carolina, is located at 34° North Latitude. This means that it is located in the tropics.
5. 0° of latitude is shown on the map by the line called the equator.
6. Between 23½° North Lat. and 23½° South Lat. are the low latitudes.
7. If one inch on the map stands for 500 miles, cities that are 2,000 miles apart would be 3 inches apart on the map.
8. The number of degrees grows higher as we travel away from the equator.

CHAPTER 4

Finding Longitude

PROBLEM: How can we "pinpoint" places on the earth's surface?

1. It was easy to begin at the equator to measure distances north and south. But where do we begin to measure distances in an east-west direction? This beginning line has been placed at Greenwich, Great Britain, by agreement among the nations of the world. Greenwich is near the city of London. Greenwich is the line of 0 degrees (0°) *longitude*. This line is called the *Prime Meridian* or *First Meridian*. All distances east and west of the Prime Meridian are measured in lines of longitude or meridians. These lines are numbered in degrees just as lines of latitude are.

2. Lines of longitude run north and south from North Pole to South Pole. They all meet at the two poles. Thus they are *not* always parallel—that is, the same distance apart for their whole length—as are lines of latitude. At the equator, where the meridians are farthest

apart, the distance of one degree is about 70 miles on the earth's surface, the same as between lines of latitude. Near the poles, the meridians or lines of longitude may be only a few miles apart.

3. Using the map below, place your finger on the line showing 0° longitude that passes through Greenwich. Place another finger on the line to the right or east of 0°. This line is 20° east of the Prime Meridian. Try the same thing in the opposite direction. This line is 20° west of the Prime Meridian. Find Los Angeles, California, on the map on page 19. Note that it is almost 118° west of the Prime Meridian. In reading degrees of longitude you add "East" (E) or "West" (W) to tell whether the line of longitude is located east or west of the Prime Meridian.

4. When we put latitude and longitude together, we can accurately locate any place on the globe. Find St. Louis on the map on page 19. On what line of latitude is it located? Is it north or south latitude? What is its longitude? Is it east or west longitude? We can tell anyone how to find St. Louis on a map or globe of the earth simply by saying that it is at 38° North

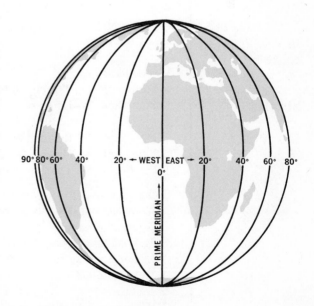

Lines of longitude (meridians) of the earth.

Latitude and 90° West Longitude. Can you imagine the value of these lines to a ship at sea or an airplane in the sky? A ship in trouble can radio its exact position by giving its latitude and longitude. Ships that speed to the rescue will know exactly where the troubled ship is.

5. There are 360 degrees in a complete circle. If you travel half way around the earth from the Prime Meridian, in either direction, you will come to the 180° Meridian. This line is the International Date Line and is located in the middle of the Pacific Ocean. Like the other lines we have studied, it is imaginary, but it is always a "talking point" for travelers who go across the Pacific. You will learn the reasons for travelers' interest in the International Date Line in Chapter 5.

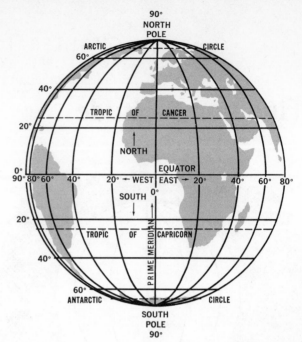

Latitude and longitude on the globe.

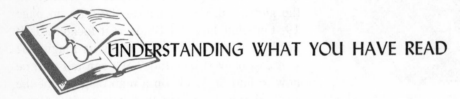

UNDERSTANDING WHAT YOU HAVE READ

I. *Finding the Main Idea*

Below are listed the main ideas of each of the five paragraphs in this chapter. After reading the main ideas, *choose the two best titles* for the chapter from the list of titles that follows.

Main Ideas:
    Paragraph 1—0° Longitude is the Prime Meridian.
    Paragraph 2—Lines of longitude run north and south from North Pole to South Pole.
    Paragraph 3—Reading lines of longitude on a map.
    Paragraph 4—How to use both latitude and longitude.
    Paragraph 5—The International Date Line is the 180th Meridian.

Choose the two best titles:
    1. Measuring Distance from the Equator.
    2. Parallels on a Map.
    3. Longitude and Latitude Equals Exact Location.
    4. Longitude of Large Cities.
    5. Longitude Helps Us to Find Places on the Earth.

II. *Choose the Best Answer*

1. Lines of longitude are called:
    a. meridians.   b. parallels.   c. east-west lines.

2. Lines of longitude:
   a. are always the same distance apart.
   b. are measured from the equator.
   c. run in a north-south direction.
3. 0° longitude is called the:
   a. equator.   b. Prime Meridian.   c. First Parallel.
4. When we know latitude and longitude, we:
   a. can accurately find any place on the map.
   b. know the distance from one place to another.
   c. know areas of sunlight.
5. In paragraph 2, the word *parallel* means:
   a. meeting at the poles.
   b. closer together.
   c. the same distance apart.

DEVELOPING IDEAS AND SKILLS

Map # 2—The United States

1. What are the latitude and longitude of:
   a. Cleveland, Ohio?
   b. Montreal, Canada?
   c. Great Falls, Montana?
2. What cities are located at:
   a. 30° N. Lat. and 95° W. Long.?
   b. 34° N. Lat. and 118° W. Long.?
   c. 42° N. Lat. and 88° W. Long.?
3. Which *two* of these cities are located at 90° West Longitude?
   Cincinnati, St. Louis, Kansas City, New Orleans.
4. Which *two* of these cities are located at 39° North Latitude?
   Baltimore, Denver, Los Angeles, Detroit.

Map # 2—The United States

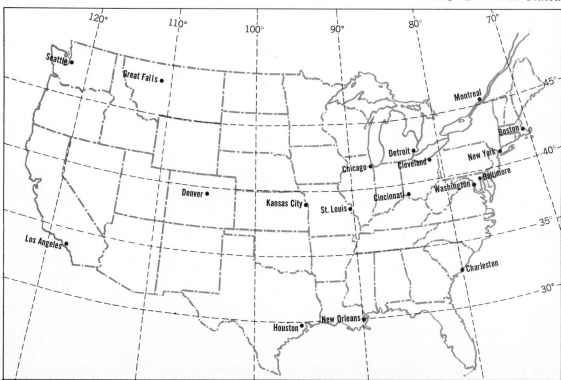

CHAPTER 5

The Spinning Earth

PROBLEM: What are the effects of the earth's movements?

1. The earth is always spinning. It is always turning or spinning in the same direction, from west to east. Of course, only one side of the earth can face the sun at a time. The side of the earth that faces the sun receives light and heat. When that happens, it is day on that side of the earth. On the part of the earth that is away from the sun, it is dark or night. If the earth did not spin, one half of the earth would always be lighted and the other half would always be dark.

2. The earth spins on an *axis,* an imaginary line through the earth from one pole to the other. This spinning of the earth on its axis is called *rotation. The rotation of the earth causes our day and night.* Since the earth makes one complete turn in a 24-hour period, we say that the earth rotates once each day. At the same time that the earth rotates, it is also orbiting or moving around the sun. This movement of the earth around the sun is called *revolution*—the earth *revolves* around the sun. Once every year, 365¼ days, the earth makes a complete trip around the sun. At the same time, it is spinning on its axis, once every 24 hours.

3. If you should someday travel in space, you would see that the earth is not standing straight up and down facing the sun. It is leaning at an angle. The earth leans or tilts at an angle of 23½ degrees. It is always tilted in the same direction. As it revolves around the sun, the earth tilts so that the North Pole points toward the North Star. For part of this revolution, the northern hemisphere is tilted toward the sun and catches the direct rays of the sun. At this time, the southern half of the world gets only the indirect or slanting rays of the sun. This is the period of spring and summer in the northern half of the earth, March 21 to September 22, while the southern hemisphere has fall and winter.

4. As the earth continues on its path or orbit around the sun, the southern hemisphere is then tilted toward the sun and gets the direct rays. At this time, the northern half of the earth receives the slanting rays. It is now spring and summer in the southern half of the earth and fall and winter in the north. The lands near the equator receive the direct rays of the sun dur-

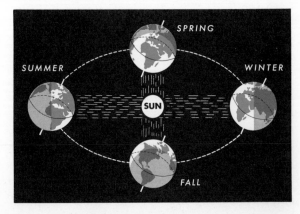

The earth in its orbit.

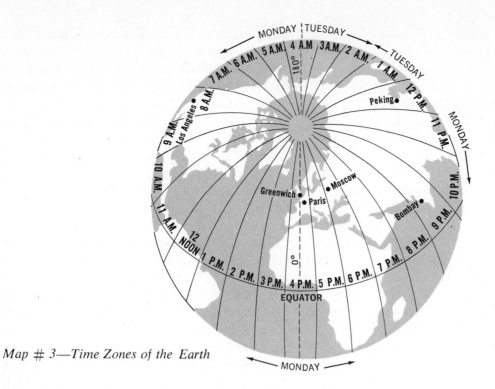

Map # 3—Time Zones of the Earth

ing the earth's entire trip. This is why the tropics are warm all year round.

5. The leaning of the earth and its orbit around the sun cause our four seasons—spring, summer, fall and winter. When the people of New York, Detroit, Chicago and San Francisco are receiving the more direct rays of the sun, the people of Argentina, Chile and Australia are receiving the indirect and weaker rays. Thus, when it is summer in the middle and high latitudes north of the equator, it is winter in the same regions south of the equator. The reverse is also true. If you are a sports fan, you may have noticed that tennis championships are played outdoors in Australia near Christmas time. You may also have heard that the skiing in Chile is excellent in July!

6. On March 21st and September 22nd, days and nights are equal in length all over the earth. At noon the rays of the sun strike the earth directly at the equator. Each of these days is called an *equinox* or equal night. March 21st marks the beginning of spring in the northern hemisphere and the beginning of autumn in the southern hemisphere. On September 22nd, autumn begins in the northern hemisphere and

spring begins in the southern hemisphere.

7. After March 21st, the sun's rays move a little farther north of the equator each day. Summer is on its way to the northern half of the world and winter to the southern half. Since the earth's axis is tilted 23½ degrees, the direct rays move north 23½ degrees to the Tropic of Cancer. They reach this point about June 22nd. This date is the beginning of summer north of the equator. On this date, the rays of the sun strike the earth directly at the Tropic of Cancer. This is the farthest point north at which the sun will shine directly overhead. On this date, too, all places within the Arctic Circle will have 24 hours of sunlight. As you may have guessed, this date also marks the beginning of winter in the southern hemisphere.

8. The movement of the earth around the sun continues. The sun's rays move again steadily south until they reach 23½ degrees south of the equator, the Tropic of Capricorn. This point is reached on December 22, the beginning of summer south of the equator. This is the beginning of winter in the northern hemisphere.

9. Even if you have not traveled you may have noticed a difference in time from one part

21

of the country to another. For example, if you live in Kansas City and want to see a swimming meet on television from Boston, it may start at 9:00 in Boston, but you will see it at 8:00. This difference in time is caused by the *rotation* of the earth. In its spinning on its axis, the earth turns through 360 degrees of longitude in 24 hours. It thus turns 15 degrees of longitude in one hour. (The 360 degrees of the earth divided by 24 hours equals 15 degrees each hour.) Therefore, there is one hour's difference in time between places on earth for each 15 degrees of longitude. The world is divided into 24 time zones about 15 degrees apart from each other. In the United States alone there are six time zones.

10. The earth turns or rotates from west to east. As a result, the sun "rises" or appears earlier at places that lie farther east. For example, when it is 8:00 A.M. in New York City, it is also 8:00 A.M. in Boston, Philadelphia and Cleveland—they are in the same time zone. However, it is then 7.00 A.M. in Chicago and New Orleans because they are 15 degrees *west* of New York City. It is only 6:00 A.M. in Denver and Great Falls because they are 30 degrees west of New York. Los Angeles and San Francisco are still in darkness because they are still farther west. In Fairbanks, Alaska, and Honolulu, Hawaii, it is only 3:00 A.M. People in these cities will not see daylight in summer until three hours after Denver and five hours after New York.

11. The International Date Line, half way around the world from the Prime Meridian, is a special problem. Look at the map on page 21. Starting at Greenwich, Great Britain, where it is 4 o'clock on Monday afternoon, count 12 hours in an easterly direction. You will see that it is then 4 o'clock in the morning on *Tuesday*, at the International Date Line. Now begin at Greenwich again and count 12 hours in a westerly direction. You will see that it is 4 o'clock in the morning on *Monday*. Yes, it is Monday west of the Date Line, but it is Tuesday east of the line. A traveler going west across the Date Line will "skip" a day in his trip, but one who is going east across it will repeat the same day. In September, 1958, General Curtis LeMay piloted a jet airplane from Tokyo, Japan, to Washington, D.C. in 11½ hours. He left Tokyo on Friday at 8 o'clock in the morning, and arrived in Washington at 7:30 Friday morning, Eastern Standard Time. He arrived before he took off!

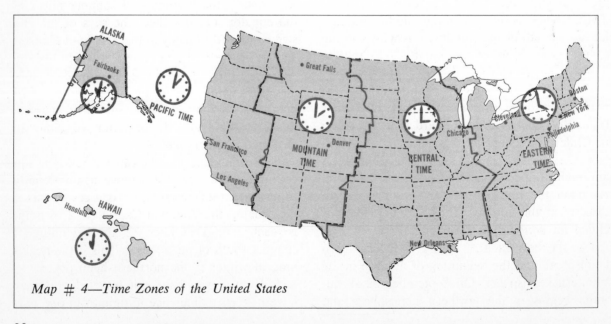

Map # 4—Time Zones of the United States

UNDERSTANDING WHAT YOU HAVE READ

1. The main idea of *paragraphs 5 through 7* is to describe:
   a. why we have differences in seasons.
   b. the reasons for the tilt of the earth.
   c. the results of the earth's rotation.

2. If the earth did not spin:
   a. we would have no seasons.
   b. half of the earth would always be in sunlight.
   c. there would be no summer in the northern hemisphere.

3. The differences in seasons are caused by:
   a. the revolution and tilting of the earth.
   b. the rotation of the earth.
   c. the spinning of the earth.

4. The earth orbits around the sun:
   a. once each day.
   b. once each season.
   c. once each year.

5. The earth rotates on its axis:
   a. once each day.
   b. once each month.
   c. once each year.

6. When do the direct rays of the sun strike the city of Chicago?
   a. on June 22.
   b. on September 22.
   c. never.

7. The earth *orbits* the sun. The best meaning for *orbit* is:
   a. rotates.   b. travels around.   c. spins.

8. Some people say that a storm will take place on the *equinox*. This refers to:
   a. 6 months of daylight at the South Pole.
   b. the time when days and nights are the same length.
   c. the season when the southern hemisphere is tilted toward the sun.

SUMMING UP

Do You Agree or Disagree? Give reasons for your answers.

1. All places north of the equator have summer at the same time.
2. The tropics always receive the most direct rays of the sun.
3. When the sun's direct rays are striking the earth north of the equator, the North Pole is in darkness.
4. High latitude regions never receive the direct rays of the sun.
5. On the hottest day of the year in the middle of the United States the direct rays of the sun are directly overhead.
6. If the earth did not lean on its trip around the sun, sunlight would never reach the poles of the earth.
7. The tropics means low latitudes.
8. The slanting rays of the sun are not as hot as the direct rays of the sun.
9. In our summer, there are more hours of daylight than there are of darkness.
10. At the equator, the length of the hours of sunlight changes greatly during the year.

CHAPTER 6

Land Forms of the Earth

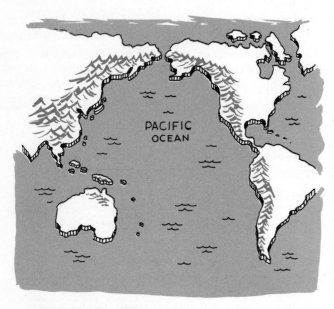

PACIFIC OCEAN

PROBLEMS: What are the varieties of land surface on the earth?

How do differences in land surface affect the ways people live?

1. Although water covers 75 per cent of the earth's surface, the 25 per cent land area is most important to us. The reason, of course, is that we live on the land. Land areas are called either continents or islands, depending on their size. There are six continents on our planet. Asia is the largest and Australia is the smallest. After Asia in size comes Africa, then North America, South America, Europe and finally, Australia. Antarctica is a huge empty mass of land covered with a thick layer of snow and ice.

2. Look at the globe. Look at the earth from the North Pole. Then look at it from the South Pole. You will see that most of the land on the earth is in the northern hemisphere. About 85 per cent of the earth's surface below the equator is water. (You will see that all the oceans are connected here.) The important trade routes of the world are north of the equator. It may not be surprising, then, to find that the most important and powerful nations of the world are in the northern hemisphere.

3. There are four chief kinds of land forms on the earth. These are mountains, hills, plateaus and plains. Most of the land surface of the earth is made up of one of these four land forms. These lands are also crossed by rivers. When geographers write or talk about land forms, they use the word *topography*.

4. *Mountains* are masses of land that rise high above the surrounding areas. They come to a top or peak. Mountains are grouped into ranges or chains. There are two great mountain chains on the earth. One borders the Pacific Ocean. You can trace an almost continuous line of mountains through the lands around the Pacific Ocean. Most of these are high, and many have *volcanoes*. (A volcano is an opening in the earth through which melted rock or lava flows.) The tops of these mountains form islands, such as the Philippines, Indonesia, Japan and the Aleutians. A huge mountain chain extends from Alaska in the north to the southern tip of South America. This mountain system is called the Rocky Mountains in North America and the Andes in South America.

5. The other great mountain chain spreads across Africa and Eurasia. (We group Europe and Asia together and call them Eurasia because they are really one great land mass.) The western end of this chain starts in Spain and North Africa. It stretches across southern Europe as the Alps and the Caucasus. It extends into inner Asia as far as the Himalayas. The Himalayas are the highest mountains in the world. Mt. Everest, the highest peak on earth, is in the Himalayas. These mountains separate India on the south and China and Siberia (Soviet Asia) on the north. Moving eastward, this range begins to spread out. Some mountains run north into Siberia and others stretch eastward across China and southeastward across the Indochinese peninsula.

6. *Hills,* in general, are lower than mountains. It is often hard to tell the difference between high hills and low mountains. Hills are usually no higher than 1,000 feet above sea level. More people live in the hills than in the mountains because hills are lower and flatter. They are easier to reach.

7. Hill and mountain regions are often called highlands. Highlands are not heavily populated. The chief occupations of mountain people are mining, lumbering, cattle raising and sheep grazing. It is difficult to farm hillsides because the soil is thin and rocky and rains wash away the seeds and the soil. In the hilly regions of the Far East and southern Europe, farmers cut *terraces* (steps in the hillsides) to increase the amount of land they can farm.

8. Mountains are a source of *minerals* such as coal, iron ore, lead and manganese. (Minerals are useful materials that can be mined or dug up from the earth.) Streams that tumble down the mountainsides are used to make electric power. However, mountains have often separated people from one another and made transportation difficult. People who live in the highlands of the Andes in South America and of the Himalayas in Asia often know little of what happens outside their villages.

9. *Plateaus* are land forms that rise sharply above the level of the land around them. Many are level on top. They are also called *tablelands* or *mesas.* In the high latitudes, the plateaus are very cold. In the low latitudes, they may have a cool and healthful climate. The Bolivian Plateau of South America is an example of a cool climate in an area that would otherwise be very warm. Some plateaus are surrounded by mountains that shut out rainfall. The plateaus that extend northward from Mexico through the western United States and into Canada are very dry. In the high latitudes, plateaus are likely to be covered with snow and ice. This is true in Greenland and Antarctica.

10. *Plains* are areas of broad level land. The land is never completely flat, but slightly rolling. These land forms are sometimes called lowlands. Plains support most of the world's people. The lowland area of North America reaches from the Gulf of Mexico northward to the Arctic Ocean and from the Appalachian Mountains westward to the Rockies. Another lowland area extends from Great Britain east through Central Europe into Siberia. Although the Far East is hilly and mountainous, there are several lowland areas of good size.

11. Many plains throughout the world have been formed by large rivers. Great numbers of people live in these river valleys because they are usually fertile—that is, good for growing crops. One of the most thickly populated regions on earth is the Yangtze River Valley in China. Great industrial cities are located along the Rhine River in Europe. The Nile River Valley of Egypt is the only fertile area in a land that is mostly desert. The Mississippi drains the great farm lands of the United States. However, the hot lowland of the Amazon River in South America has few people. The great heat, thick jungles, poor soil and millions of insects make it hard for large numbers of people to live there.

12. Our earth is a restless, living thing. It is continually being changed by heat, cold, rain, snow, winds and rushing water. It is disturbed by volcanoes and rumbling earthquakes. (An earthquake is a terrible trembling that causes buildings to fall and great cracks to open in the ground.) There are still glaciers or large masses of ice in the far north of our planet. Because of these forces, our land forms are still changing, sometimes slowly and sometimes quickly.

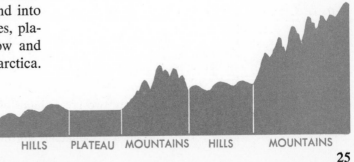

SEA LEVEL

PLAIN   HILLS   PLATEAU   HILLS   PLATEAU   MOUNTAINS   HILLS   MOUNTAINS

25

Making an Outline

An outline is like the bones of the body. It is the skeleton of a chapter. The sentences of each paragraph are like the body built around the skeleton. Once we are able to pick out the main ideas of a paragraph or a chapter, we are able to *outline*. It is as easy as that. Let us see how we can outline Chapter 6. We have to read the chapter first. Then we pick out the main idea for each paragraph. Let us see what these main ideas are:

Paragraph 1—Land is important to us.
Paragraph 2—Most of the land is in the northern hemisphere.
Paragraph 3—There are four chief kinds of land forms.
Paragraph 4—Mountains are masses of land that rise above the land around them.
Paragraph 5—There are great mountain chains on the earth.
Paragraph 6—Hills are lower than mountains.
Paragraph 7—Not many people live in the highlands.
Paragraph 8—Mountains have good and bad features.
Paragraph 9—Plateaus rise sharply above the land around them.
Paragraph 10—Plains are areas of broad level land.
Paragraph 11—River valleys have many people.
Paragraph 12—Our earth is continually changing.

After listing these main ideas, we can easily see the important thoughts of the chapter. These main ideas are a good *summary* of the chapter, too. If you were *taking notes* for this chapter, you would have a fine set of notes simply by listing these main ideas.

In making an outline, we first choose our *headings*. We collect some of the thoughts that are about the same topic and see if we can find one heading for them. The title of the chapter is "Land Forms of the Earth." What does this chapter say about land forms? It tells us that there are four main kinds: mountains, hills, plateaus and plains. We can make these our headings.

A. Mountains   B. Hills   C. Plateaus   D. Plains

Next, we locate the paragraphs that tell us about these headings. You will note from our list of main ideas that paragraphs 4, 5 and 8 tell us about mountains; paragraphs 6 and 7 tell about hills; paragraph 9 is about plateaus and paragraphs 10 and 11 are about plains. (A river valley is a kind of plain.)

Now take one of our headings, "Mountains," and look in the paragraphs about mountains to see what is said about this land form. We can begin our outline with these facts about mountains:

A. Mountains
   1. There are two great chains of mountains.
   2. Some islands are the tops of mountains.
   3. The highest mountains are the Himalayas.

4. Many mountains have minerals.
5. Mountains have made travel difficult.

This can be our outline on mountains. We can then go on and do the same thing with our other headings. When we finish, the rest of our outline may look like this:

B. Hills
    1. Hills are lower than mountains.
    2. More people live in the hills than in the mountains.
    3. Farming is difficult on hillsides.
C. Plateaus
    1. In high latitudes, plateaus are cold; in low latitudes, they are cooler than the lowland around them.
    2. Some plateaus are dry because the mountains around them shut off rainfall.
D. Plains
    1. Most of the world's people live on the plains.
    2. There are great plains areas in North America and in Europe.
    3. Rivers have made large plains.
    4. Fertile soils are often found in plains.
    5. Rivers have brought people together rather than separating them.

This could be your outline. You will find that outlining is not hard if you can pick out main ideas. The outline helps you to jot down important information in such a way that you can remember it. It helps you to take notes when you look for information. It helps you to put the ideas of a chapter into a small form—to make a summary.

SUMMING UP

Tell whether these statements are true or false. The underlined words make the statements true or false. If a statement is false, what words would you place in it to make it true?

1. Most of the land surface of the earth is found south of the equator.
2. The great mountain system of South America is called the Andes.
3. Africa is the largest continent.
4. Most of the world's people live on the plains.
5. Europe and Asia are really one large mass of land.
6. The Nile River flows through a jungle where few people live.
7. The highest mountains in the world are the Rockies.
8. Mountains have often had the effect of keeping people from meeting and exchanging ideas.
9. Farmers often cut steps or terraces into hillsides so that they can farm the land.
10. Another word for plains is mesa.
11. Topography is a word that we use when we talk about land forms.
12. River valleys are very often a source of minerals.

CHAPTER 7

The Waters of the Earth

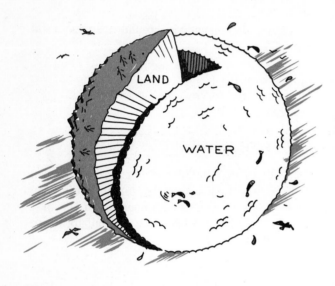

LAND

WATER

PROBLEM: How has man made use of the earth's waterways?

1. You have learned that there is much more water than land on the earth. In fact, if we divided the earth into four equal parts, three of those parts would be made up of water. Therefore, we should know more about the kinds of bodies of water that are found on our planet.

2. The earth's largest bodies of water are called *oceans*. There are five oceans: the Pacific, the Atlantic, the Indian, the Arctic and the Antarctic. The largest of these is the Pacific, separating North and South America from Asia and Australia. The Pacific Ocean covers almost one-third of the whole earth's surface. It covers more area than all the land on earth put together! The Atlantic Ocean is about one-half the size of the Pacific. However, it is more important because of the many trade routes that cross its waters. The smaller Indian Ocean touches Africa on the west, Asia on the north and Australia and Indonesia on the east. The ice-filled Arctic Ocean extends to the North Pole. The Antarctic Ocean surrounds the ice cap of Antarctica, in which the South Pole is located. In every ocean there are many swift-flowing "streams" of water that always move in the same direction. These are called *ocean currents*. You will learn more about ocean currents and how they affect us in Chapter 9.

3. While there are only five bodies of water that are called oceans, there are many other large bodies of water in the world. Most of these are called *seas*. A sea is a body of water almost completely surrounded by land. The Mediterranean Sea has long been important, for it lies between the large land areas of Africa and Eurasia and was once the center of all that was known of the world. The Caribbean Sea, east of Mexico, the Arabian Sea and the Sea of Japan are all important water routes for trade.

4. *Gulfs* and *bays* are also large bodies of water. It is sometimes difficult to tell the difference between a sea, a gulf and a bay. The Gulf of Mexico is really larger than the Sea of Japan or the North Sea. Hudson Bay is also larger than either of them.

5. Rivers are the "lifeblood" of many nations. Rivers are formed by rainfall and melting snow. They begin as small streams. The place where a river begins is called its *source*. The movement of a river is called its *current*. Rivers flow from higher land to lower land. They may be joined by other rivers and streams as they flow "down" into a larger body of water. The place where a river empties its waters is called its *mouth*. Larger rivers usually build a *delta* at their mouth by carrying bits of rock and soil along their course and depositing them. These deltas are often very fertile.

6. It is not easy to tell which rivers are important, or whether one river is more important than another. Each great river is important to so many people. However, as you study the world and the people in it, you will learn about

the rivers listed below. They are among the most important in the world.

River	Region of the World
1. Missouri-Mississippi	Anglo-America
2. St. Lawrence	Anglo-America
3. Amazon	Latin America
4. Danube	Europe
5. Nile	North Africa
6. Tigris-Euphrates	Middle East
7. Congo	Africa, South of the Sahara
8. Ganges	Far East
9. Hwang	Far East
10. Yangtze	Far East

7. Transportation by water has always been important for trade. It was the earliest and cheapest means of moving from one place to another. Water transportation is still used in many places where heavy loads must be moved. When it is possible to go from one body of water to another without unloading, shipping goods is easy.

8. Sometimes, two larger bodies of water are connected by a narrow water passage. This narrow body of water is called a *strait*. In passing from the Atlantic Ocean to the Mediterranean Sea, ships travel through the Strait of Gibraltar. Ferdinand Magellan found a strait in sailing from the Atlantic to the Pacific Ocean at the southern tip of South America. It now bears his name. The Soviet Union and Turkey have argued over control of the Dardanelles for years. This strait provides an opening between the Black and Mediterranean Seas.

9. Man sometimes has to dig his own water passage to connect two larger bodies of water. Such a man-made passage is called a *canal*. There are several important canals in the world. The Suez Canal connects the Mediterranean and Red Seas. It is a sea-level canal. The Suez Canal shortens the trip from Great Britain to India by almost 5,000 miles. Because of the importance of this canal in world trade, it is an often disputed spot in the world. Once controlled by Great Britain, it is now run by Egypt.

10. The Panama Canal was opened in 1914. It connects the Atlantic and Pacific Oceans through the narrow country of Panama. It belongs to the United States. Before it was built, ocean-going ships had to travel all the way

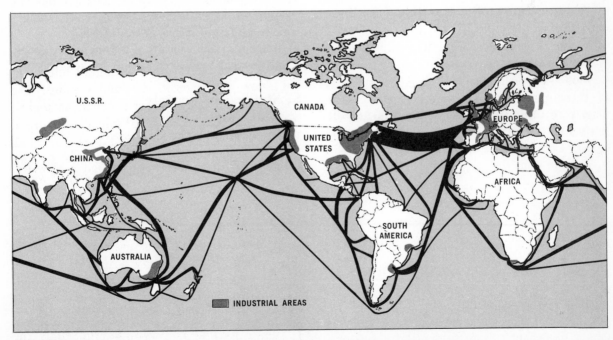

Map # 5—Water Trade Routes of the World

29

around South America to go from New York to San Francisco. Because the Isthmus of Panama is mountainous, locks had to be built to move boats from one level to another. The Soo or Sault Sainte Marie Canals are three canals that connect Lake Superior and Lake Huron at the United States-Canada border. This canal chain carries a huge traffic in iron ore.

11. Not all canals are used for ocean-going ships. There are many important inland canals. In Western Europe, the canal system connects rivers with other rivers. This canal system is an important means of shipping farm and factory goods for short distances. In the Far East, too, canals connect rivers in order to make travel and communication easier.

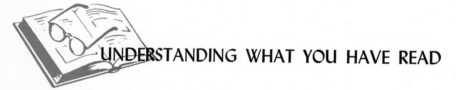

UNDERSTANDING WHAT YOU HAVE READ

1. A good title for *paragraph 8* would be:
a. Making Water Transportation Easy.
b. Important Straits of the World.
c. The Strait of Magellan.

2. The greatest water trade routes of the world are found on the:
a. Pacific Ocean.
b. Atlantic Ocean.
c. Gulf of Mexico.

3. A large body of water that has three narrow entrances to it is the:
a. Mediterranean Sea.
b. Indian Ocean.
c. Caribbean Sea.

4. An example of a canal inside a large continent is the:
a. Soo Canal.
b. Panama Canal.

c. Suez Canal.

5. The largest of the oceans is the:
a. Pacific.   b. Atlantic.   c. Indian.

6. Great inland canal systems are found in:
a. the United States.
b. North Africa.
c. Western Europe.

7. Water transportation has long been important because:
a. it is the fastest means of transportation.
b. it is the cheapest means of moving heavy goods.
c. goods can be delivered directly to factories.

8. Straits and canals are important in water routes because they:
a. are sometimes as large as seas.
b. have the best seaports along their routes.
c. are often short cuts to larger bodies of water.

DEVELOPING IDEAS AND SKILLS

Making an Outline

In Chapter 6, you learned how to develop the outline of a chapter. Now try to make a short outline of part of Chapter 7. From the chapter, choose *one* of these two sections: paragraphs 2 through 4 or paragraphs 9 through 11. Follow the steps you learned in the previous chapter:

1. Find the main ideas of the paragraphs you choose.
2. After you have seen the three main ideas, choose a title for the outline that includes all the main thoughts of the three paragraphs.
3. Use each of the main ideas of the paragraphs as your *headings*: A, B and C.
4. See what *details* there are in each paragraph for each of the headings.
5. List two or three of these details under each heading. Choose the ones that you think are most important.

When you have finished these five steps, you will have made an outline of the paragraphs you selected.

SUMMING UP

Match the statements in Column B with the terms in Column A.

COLUMN A	COLUMN B
1. strait	Swift-flowing streams in the ocean.
2. current	Large body of water almost completely surrounded by land.
3. source	Where a river begins.
4. delta	Soil and rocks piled up at a river mouth.
5. mouth	Man-made waterway.
6. canal	Where a river empties its water.
	Narrow body of water connecting larger bodies of water.

CHAPTER 8

How Climate Affects Us

PROBLEM: How does climate cause differences in the ways people live and work?

1. A class was about to begin a lesson on Latin America. One of the students asked, "Why don't bananas grow in the United States?" When the class looked for answers, they found that bananas need a long growing season. It must be hot and rainy most of the time. There is hardly any place on the mainland of our country where such a climate can be found. Therefore, we must bring bananas in from other lands if we want them. In short, bananas grow where the *climate* is right for them.

2. Climate and *weather* do not mean the same thing. The weather report on the radio or in the newspaper tells you what each day will be or was like. The report tells you how hot or cold it is during a day or over a short period of time. It tells you whether to expect rain or snow. This is weather. Climate, on the other hand, means the kind of weather a region has over a long period of time—year after year.

3. Therefore, when you read about climate in any place on the earth, there are three ques-

tions you should ask: How hot or cold is it over a long period of time? How much rain falls throughout the year? How long is the growing season? The answers to these questions will give you a good idea of an area's climate.

4. The earth is surrounded by a "blanket" of air called the *atmosphere*. This air can be hot or cold. Geographers call the amount of heat or cold in the air *temperature*. Temperature is measured by a thermometer, which is marked in degrees. (Thus, 70 degrees is written as 70°.) Temperatures can change rapidly. It can be very hot in the daytime and cold at night. However, one who studies geography is more interested in temperature throughout a season than in daily changes. For example, the *average* daily temperature of New York City during the winter months is 34°. The average temperature during the summer months is 76°. This tells you that New York City has warm summers and cold winters. In San Francisco, the average winter temperature is 52° and in summer, 63°. You can tell from these temperatures that San Francisco is neither too hot nor too cold the year round.

5. The *average rainfall* of any place is also measured over a long period of time. Rainfall is measured in the number of inches of rain that falls in a given time. Ten inches of rainfall is recorded as 10″. It is possible to measure rainfall during a season or during a year. For example, the average rainfall for six summer months in Charleston, South Carolina, is 30″. The winter average is only 15″. This tells us that the summer months receive a great deal of rain. By comparison, the winters are dry. The average rainfall for the year, then, can also be found.

6. Another factor in climate is the *length of the growing season*. This is the length of time that a place is free from frost. This is very important to the farmer. He can plant only the kinds of crops that can be grown in the particular growing season of his area. He plants his crop after the last frost in the spring and harvests before the first frost in the fall. In general, the farther one travels from the equator, the

shorter the growing season.

7. Throughout your study of our changing world, climate will be mentioned many times. You will find that climate is important in understanding how people live and work. (For example, the people of the Sahara live and think differently from the people who live in the Amazon Basin.) In many cases, people are making good use of a favorable climate. In other regions, they are struggling against the problems caused by a difficult climate.

8. Climate explains, in part, the kind of homes people live in. The Eskimo in northern Canada lives in an igloo made of blocks of ice. People of the cold northern forests live in log cabins. Rain-forest peoples live in huts made of straw and grass. Some people in the dry lands of the earth live in homes made of sun-dried brick or mud.

9. Climate affects the clothes we wear. The desert people of the Middle East wear loose-fitting cotton clothing to keep themselves cool while they travel in the hot desert. In the highlands, shepherds wear clothing made of wool or leather to keep themselves warm. In the Amazon rain forest, the natives wear little clothing because it is always hot and wet.

10. As you have learned, climate also determines the kinds of crops that are grown in an area. Differences in climate mean differences in temperature, rainfall and length of growing season. Some parts of the world have plenty of rain, while other parts are dry. Farmers cannot always grow the same crops in both wet and dry regions. For this reason, you would not find rice being grown in Michigan or oats in Indonesia. If a country is located near the equator, it would be safe to guess that it might export bananas but not furs. Wheat can be grown in a great variety of climates, whereas olives need a dry climate.

11. *Trade* or the exchange of goods among nations is also the result of differences in climate. Our country, except for Hawaii, does not have the climate for growing rubber, coffee or bananas. Thus, we buy coffee from Brazil and Colombia. We get rubber from Indonesia and Malaysia. We may be able to grow silk and olives, but we can grow other crops better, so we import those things as well. We grow what suits our climate best. Hawaii's climate is perfect for growing sugar cane and pineapples. The Midwest of the United States is good for growing corn and wheat. Just as we cannot grow all kinds of products, so do other nations face the same problem.

 UNDERSTANDING WHAT YOU HAVE READ

1. The main idea of *paragraphs 4 through 6* is to describe:
a. the meaning of temperature.
b. how we figure average rainfall.
c. what we mean when we speak of climate.

2. On the mainland of the United States, we do not have the climate to grow:
a. cotton.　　　b. rubber.　　　c. oats.

3. A "growing season" refers to:
a. weather.　　　b. rainfall.　　　c. climate.

4. Growing seasons become shorter as we:
a. travel toward the equator.
b. travel away from the equator.
c. travel toward the Prime Meridian.

5. Climate causes a difference in the:
a. minerals nations have.
b. amount of steel a nation can make.
c. amount of water for farming.

6. When the newspaper says that "Tomor-

row will be cloudy and warm," it is telling us about:

a. weather.   b. climate.   c. rainfall.

7. Which figure refers to rainfall?

a. 30°   b. 25″   c. 61° N. Lat.

8. Climate will affect the kinds of clothing we wear, the crops we grow and:

a. the sports we enjoy.
b. the television programs we see.
c. the newspapers we read.

DEVELOPING IDEAS AND SKILLS

Understanding the Difference Between FACT and OPINION

One of the most important things you can learn as a citizen is to be able to distinguish (to tell the difference) between statements that are *facts* and those that are *opinions*.

A *fact* is a true statement. It can be proven. An *opinion* is what a person or a group of people think about a subject. An opinion cannot be proven to be true. An opinion may tell:

a. what a person thinks *will happen*.
b. what someone thinks *should happen*.
c. the *feeling* that a person has about a subject.
d. what a person *believes* about a subject.

It is from your knowledge of facts that you arrive at a good opinion. There is nothing wrong with having an opinion. Good citizens will think about the facts they know and try to make judgments about problems in their lives. The important thing is that we are able to tell when a thought that is expressed is a fact—is true—and when it is someone's feeling about a subject.

Notice the difference in these examples:

FACT: The Pacific is the largest ocean.
OPINION: The Pacific Ocean will have more trade than the Atlantic Ocean in a few years.

FACT: The United States has taken part in two world wars.
OPINION: The United States should not go to war unless it is attacked.

FACT: Transportation has improved in the last hundred years.
OPINION: It is nonsense to say that we will travel to the moon by 1980.

Now see if you can tell which of these are *facts* and which are someone's *opinion*:

1. Temperatures may change quickly from day to night.
2. Chicago will have more snow than Denver next year.
3. A farmer will plant a crop that he can raise in his growing season.
4. The clothing people wear will depend upon the climate of the place in which they live.
5. Climate is the kind of weather we have over a long period of time.
6. People who live on the desert are not able to govern themselves.
7. The United States should use all the cotton it grows instead of selling some of it to other countries.
8. Some farmers find that they can grow several different crops on the same farm.

CHAPTER 9

Differences in Climate

PROBLEM: What are the reasons for differences in climate?

1. Throughout the world, there are differences in climate from place to place. Even within our own nation, there is a variety of climate. Why is this so? There are five good reasons for differences in climate, and we ought to know them.

2. The most important factor that influences climate is *latitude,* or distance from the equator. If two places in the world are the same in all ways and they are the same distance from the equator, they will have the same climate. At the equator, the sun's rays are direct. Thus, they are stronger and hotter. As you travel away from the equator, the sun's rays slant and become weaker. You will find that it gradually becomes cooler.

3. *Altitude*—the elevation or height of land above sea level—also affects climate. Air grows cooler as we travel upward, away from the surface of the earth. For example, Quito, the capital of Ecuador in South America, has 300,000 people. Yet this city is almost on the equator. Not too far east, the city of Manaus, Brazil, has a lot fewer people. How do you explain the fact that so many people live in one city and so few in another? Part of the answer is that the Andes Mountains cross the equator. Quito is located in the highlands and Manaus is in the lowlands. Quito has a pleasant climate. Manaus is hot and wet. In general, the *higher* a region is, the *colder* it is. Most people prefer to live in a cool climate.

4. *Winds and mountains* also determine climate. If the winds blow in from a warm sea, they will carry moisture with them. Rain will fall when the air cools. If the winds blow from the land out to sea, they will be dry winds because they have had little chance to pick up moisture. The winds that blow from the Pacific Ocean toward the United States are a good example of this factor in determining climate. The Pacific winds carry moisture with them, for they come from the ocean. As the winds meet the mountains along the west coast, the air rises and is cooled. When the air is cooled, the moisture drops as rain on the western side of the mountains. Here are found thick, green forests and fertile land. After the air has crossed the mountains, it is drier. Thus the land east of the mountains receives little rainfall. The rainy side of the mountains is the *windward* side. The dry side is called the *leeward* (or sheltered) side.

5. Not all the winds of the earth blow con-

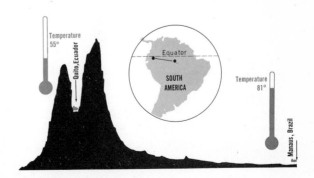

Altitude, as well as latitude, determines climate.

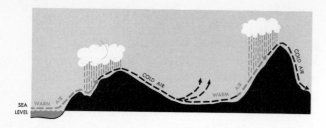

Winds and mountains also determine climate.

tinually from the same direction. There are shifting local winds caused by the heating or cooling of land. The *monsoon* winds of Asia are an example of this. When the winds blow from the land, they are dry and cold. These dry winds cause great hardship for the farmers of India. However, when the winds blow from the Indian Ocean, they are warm and wet, bringing humid weather and heavy rains.

6. *Nearness to water* is another factor that affects climate. Water has the effect of making temperatures "even." Water neither heats nor cools as fast as land. Places near large bodies of water (oceans, seas and large lakes) have a more "even" temperature than other places in the same latitude. When it is a hot summer day and you go swimming to cool off, the temperature of the water may be 20 degrees cooler than the land temperature. At night the sun's rays disappear and the land cools. You can feel the cold and dampness if you lie on the ground. But the water may have dropped only a few degrees in temperature, if it has dropped at all. If you went swimming in the evening, you would find the water almost the same temperature as during the day.

7. This difference in land and water temperature explains the fact that although New York City and Omaha, Nebraska, may have almost the same latitude, there is a difference in temperature throughout the year. Omaha is not near a large body of water. Summer temperatures there often reach 100° and winter temperatures may drop to 10° below zero. New York City is on the Atlantic Ocean. The temperature seldom reaches 100° in the summer or 0° in the winter. Omaha may have a difference of 110 degrees in temperature during a year. New York is likely to have only a difference of 80 degrees throughout the year.

8. *Ocean currents* affect climate in many parts of the world. Ocean currents are like fast-flowing "streams" of water within a larger body of water. Some of these currents are cold and others are warm. The winds that blow over them, therefore, are affected by the temperatures of the currents. The Gulf Stream is a warm current that begins in the warm waters of the Gulf of Mexico. It flows northward along the eastern coast of the United States toward

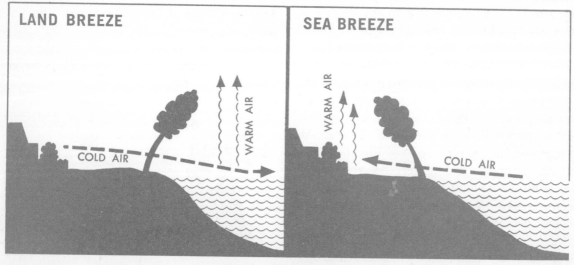

Dry Season.   The Monsoon Climate   *Wet Season.*

Newfoundland. Then it turns eastward across the Atlantic Ocean. This current brings warm waters to the British Isles. The winds blowing over the current are warm winds. These warm winds blow across Great Britain and Western Europe. As a result, the people of those lands enjoy a warmer climate than that of Hudson Bay, Canada. Yet Great Britain is about the same distance from the equator as that cold region of Canada.

9. The Japanese Current is another warm current. Warm winds from this ocean stream make it possible to farm along the southern coast of Alaska. This current also warms the coasts of Oregon and Washington. On the other hand, the Labrador Current brings masses of floating ice from the north polar region into the Atlantic Ocean. When the cold air from the Labrador Current meets the warm air of the Gulf Stream in the North Atlantic, dangerous fogs result. The southwest coast of South America is colder and drier because of the Humboldt Current, which flows northward from the Antarctic Ocean.

10. These, then, are some of the important facts to remember about the causes of different climates:

1. In general, the farther a land is from the equator, the colder its climate.
2. As you climb higher above sea level, temperatures become cooler.
3. As you move farther from large bodies of water, there is a greater difference in temperature throughout the year.
4. Rainfall is greatest where land borders a warm part of the ocean.
5. Winds that blow from the land are dry winds.

UNDERSTANDING WHAT YOU HAVE READ

1. The main idea of *paragraph 7* is to describe:
   a. the weather of cities in the same latitude.
   b. the temperatures of New York City.
   c. how nearness to water affects temperature.

2. When wet winds blow toward mountains, the side that gets the most rain is the:
   a. northern side.
   b. windward side.
   c. leeward side.

3. *Monsoons* are winds of Asia that:
   a. blow from the ocean.
   b. are sometimes wet and sometimes dry.
   c. always blow from the same direction.

4. Midwestern United States has hot summers and very cold winters because:
   a. this land is far from large bodies of water.
   b. the land is thousands of feet above sea level.
   c. cold ocean currents bring cold winds.

5. Large cities, like Quito, Ecuador, can be found in the mountains because:
   a. it is cooler there.
   b. it is the only place with fertile land nearby.
   c. sheep are raised in the mountains and manufacture of clothing is important.

6. Great Britain is warmer than other places of the world the same distance from the equator because of:
   a. its nearness to water.
   b. its altitude.
   c. the warming effects of the Gulf Stream.

7. Our states of Oregon and Washington are warmer in winter than other American states at the same latitude because of the:
a. Japanese Current.
b. warm winds that blow from the east.
c. altitude of land along the coast.

8. The western side of the mountains along the Pacific Coast receives more rain than the eastern side because:
a. the Gulf Stream brings warm winds.
b. the western side is nearer the equator.
c. winds from the Pacific bring rain.

DEVELOPING IDEAS AND SKILLS

Making an Outline
Using the headings below, write at least two topics under each heading for your outline of the factors that affect climate.
   A. Latitude

B. Altitude
C. Winds and Mountains
D. Nearness to Large Bodies of Water
E. Ocean Currents

SUMMING UP

Fact or Opinion Can you tell which of these are facts and which are someone's opinion?

1. The climate of Oregon is better than the climate of South Carolina.
2. Some places in the world get rain during only one season of the year.
3. Ocean currents have changed the climates of many places in the world.
4. As the population of the world grows, lands with cool climates will become crowded, while lands with warm climates will have fewer people.
5. People who live in a cool climate are harder workers than those in a hot climate.
6. There are many different climates in the United States.
7. Farmers can grow crops even in parts of Alaska.
8. No country having a hot climate will ever be a leading nation of the world.

CHAPTER 10

Climatic Regions of the World

PROBLEM: What are the different kinds of climate in the world?

1. There are many kinds of climate in the world. Very rarely does a single country have only one kind of climate. In this chapter, we will make a summary (give the main points) of the different kinds of climatic regions found throughout the world. We have divided the climatic regions into the latitudes at which they will probably appear: low latitudes—0° to 23°, middle latitudes—24° to 66° and high latitudes —67° to the poles.

2. The low-latitude climates are the *rain forest,* the *savanna* and the *desert.* The tropical rain forest is the hot, wet climate of the lowlands near the equator. Large rain forests are located in South America, central Africa and Southeast Asia. In the rain forest, the sun shines overhead all year and it is hot throughout the year. Some rain falls almost every day. Temperatures seldom rise above 90°, but it is always damp and sticky. The thick jungles keep the sun from reaching the ground. If the jungle is cut away, it grows back quickly.

3. North and south of the rain forests are the tropical savannas or grasslands. These are the "lands of two seasons." There is a winter dry season and a summer wet season. During the dry season, the grasses turn brown as the hot sun burns the earth. The water in the streams gets lower and lower. During the rainy season, the rain pours down day after day. River beds fill up with muddy water. After a while, the water floods the land. The ground becomes soft and muddy. Now the climate is like that of the tropical rain forest, hot and sticky. When the rain stops, the process begins again.

4. North and south of the grasslands are the deserts. (The change from the savanna to the desert is gradual, not sharp. This area of change from heavier to very light rainfall is called the *steppe* zone.) These are lands that receive less than 10 inches of rainfall a year. Among the large desert areas of the low latitudes are the Sahara Desert in Africa; Arabia; parts of the Middle East and the desert that covers most of Australia. The Sahara is as large in area as the mainland of the United States. Deserts are the driest and hottest parts of the earth. The difference in temperature between day and night is very great. The land cools off quickly when the sun goes down, and the temperature may drop as much as 50 degrees. Although few people live in the desert, desert soils are not poor. They can come to life if they are irrigated or watered.

5. In the middle latitudes there are several kinds of climate: *Mediterranean, humid-subtropical, humid-continental, marine, steppe* and *desert.* The Mediterranean climate areas are pleasant, sunny lands. Five areas in the world have this kind of climate: the lands that border the Mediterranean Sea, southern California, central Chile, southwestern Africa and southwestern Australia. This type of climate is found on the western coast of countries between 30° and 40° latitude, both north and south. The growing season in these lands is usually twelve months long, with mild winters and hot, dry

The rain forest of Venezuela.

summers. The little rain that falls comes in the winter months. Los Angeles, California, has an average rainfall of less than ⅓ of an inch in the summer months! About 10 inches fall from November through February.

6. The humid-subtropical climate is just what its name tells us. *Sub* means under. This is the moist region just north and south of the tropics. This climate is found along the southeastern coasts of the United States, South America, Australia and mainland China and Japan. All

areas with a humid-subtropical climate are located on the eastern side of their continents. Warm ocean currents flow along these coasts. Winds blowing across these currents bring warm, moist air to the land in all seasons. Summers are long and rainy; winters are short and mild. Many different crops are grown, not once but several times a year. This climatic region supports more people than any other.

7. The marine climate gets its name from its location. Marine, of course, refers to water. Western Europe, the British Isles, our own Pacific Northwest, western Canada, southern Chile and some of the islands of the Pacific have a marine climate. All of these lands are near water or are surrounded by water. The winds that blow from the ocean are warm and wet. They bring a mild, rainy climate to these areas. Summer temperatures in marine lands average below 70°. In the winter, the warming effect of the ocean waters usually keeps the temperature from falling below freezing.

8. The humid-continental climate is the kind of climate found in northern and central United States, the central part of the Soviet Union, northern China and southern Canada. This is the "climate of the four seasons"—autumn,

The desert of Saudi Arabia.

The savanna or dry grasslands of Colombia.

winter, spring and summer. Summers are hot, and winters are cold. As you move inland, away from the coasts, there is a greater difference in temperature throughout the year. It is called humid because there is enough rainfall for a variety of crops. In the areas of the humid continental climate are some of the greatest farm lands in the world. In each of the areas where this climate is found, mining and trading are important.

9. In the interior of large continents like North America and Asia, far from the ocean breezes, are the dry flatlands. These regions are called *prairies* or Great Plains in the United States and Canada. They are called *steppes* in Asia. Summers are hot and winters are cold in these regions as in the humid-continental climate, but there is a big difference. Rainfall is light and uncertain in the steppe climate. Ten to twenty inches of rain a year is normal, falling chiefly in spring and summer. Grass grows where there is enough rain, but there are also deserts where it rains very little. These steppes gradually become deserts as in our own Southwest, the Gobi Desert of Asia and smaller deserts in Peru, Chile and Africa south of the equator.

10. High-latitude climates are of two kinds,

tundra and *taiga*. "Tundra" is a Russian word meaning "marshy plain." This climate is found in the northern areas of Canada, Europe and the Soviet Union. Here winters are very cold. The ground is frozen for most of the year and is mushy during the short summer months. Less snow falls, however, in the tundra than in the eastern United States. Because of the cold, no crops can be raised and few people live there. But although the tundra is empty of human life, it has many land animals and plants that grow during the short summer. (In the very far north and in the far south, it is cold the year round. This is the *ice cap*. There is no summer in Antarctica or Greenland away from the ocean.)

11. South of the frozen tundra is the northern forest region or taiga. "Taiga" is also a Russian word, meaning "forest." The taiga stretches from Alaska and northern Canada across Norway, Sweden, Finland and the Soviet Union. Most of this land is covered with swamps and marshes. Temperatures in the taiga are usually colder in winter and hotter in summer than in the tundra. This is because the taiga is farther from the waters of the Arctic Ocean. Here too the growing season is too short for crops, and few people live here because of the

UNATIONS

The cool highlands of Bolivia, a vertical climate.

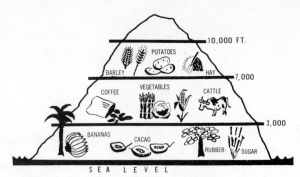

Altitude helps determine what crops can be grown.

extreme climate. But the region is very important in spite of these facts. It contains the largest forest lands in the world. It is also rich in minerals and fur-bearing animals.

12. High mountains form a climate of their own, often different from their surroundings. At the foot of a mountain the climate may be hot and rainy and many lowland crops may be grown. As you go higher up the mountain the air becomes cooler. The climate changes sharply and different activities must be performed, such as growing corn and grazing sheep. At the very top, many mountains have snow on them all year round. This is called a *vertical* climate.

13. You can tell a lot about the climate of any region by knowing what natural plant life or *vegetation* grows in that area. In general, there are three kinds of vegetation: trees, grasses, and bushes. Trees are found, of course, in the forest areas (rain forest, taiga); grasses are found in the grasslands (savanna, humid subtropical, steppe) where there is not enough rain to support too many trees; and bushes and other low plants are found in the deserts and tundras of the earth.

DEVELOPING IDEAS AND SKILLS

Getting Information From Maps

Map # 6—Solaria

There are many ideas and much information that we can find out from maps. It is not even necessary to know the name of the map we are studying. If we know about land forms, latitude, longitude, the factors that affect climate and the ways in which climate influences people, we can gather a great deal of information.

On p. 43 is a map of a land we will call "Solaria." It does not really exist. It is imaginary. Yet we are going to study this map and see how much we can learn about this land.

See if you can answer each question about the map. If you can't, the answer is explained after the question. Check yourself. See how much you can learn from the map without reading the answers.

1. Is the land north or south of the equator?
   Answer: It is north of the equator. The degrees of latitude grow higher as we go north. We know that 0°, the equator, is south of 10°. Therefore, the land must be north of the equator.

2. Is Solaria in the low, high or middle latitudes?
   Answer: The southern part—the smallest part

—is in the low latitudes. Above 23½° is the middle latitudes. Most of the land lies in the region of the middle latitudes. None of Solaria is in the high latitudes.

3. Is Solaria east or west of the Prime Meridian? *Answer:* It is west of the Prime Meridian. 0° longitude must lie to the east of Solaria because the degrees of longitude are increasing as we go west.

4. Where will most of the seaports be? *Answer:* On the west coast, probably. The western coastline is rough—it has many inlets and harbors. The other coastlines are smooth and probably have few harbors.

5. Where will the largest city be? *Answer:* Probably at C. This city is located a small distance below the place where the rivers have joined

to empty into the sea, a good location for trade. The harbor looks as though it will have a wide mouth, and it is sheltered from the ocean.

6. What kind of land form is shown by letter A? *Answer:* An isthmus, a narrow piece of land connecting two larger bodies of land.

7. What land form is shown by letter B? *Answer:* A peninsula—a body of land almost completely surrounded by water.

8. What are the latitude and longitude of city D? *Answer:* About 41° north latitude and 43° west longitude. It is almost at the spot where two marked lines of latitude and longitude meet.

9. What city is located at 35° north latitude and 60° west longitude? *Answer:* E.

10. In which direction does River 2 flow? *Answer:*

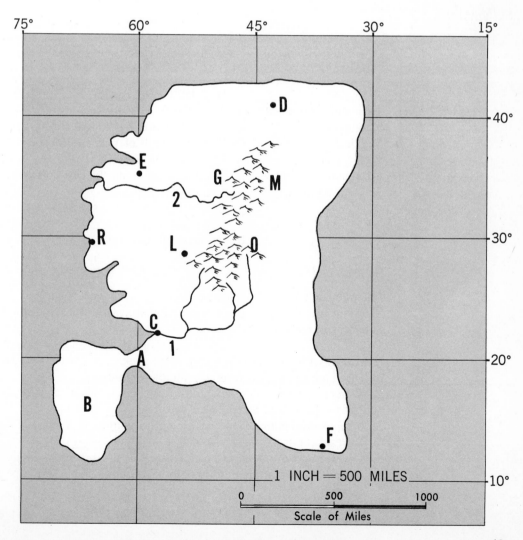

Map # 6—
Solaria

It flows almost directly west. It rises in the mountains and flows to the ocean—to the west.

11. Which side of the mountains will have the most rain? *Answer:* The western side. The winds blow from the west in the middle latitudes, and they have come from the ocean. Therefore, they bring moisture with them. Notice that the rivers are on the western side.

12. What is the difference in climate between cities R and L? *Answer:* City L will probably be hotter in the summer and colder in the winter since it is not near the ocean. Remember that water has the effect of keeping temperatures even.

13. What might keep city F from being a large city? *Answer:* It does not have a good harbor. Also,

it lies in the low latitudes in a lowland. It no doubt has a very warm and wet climate.

14. If you flew in an airplane from E to F, in what direction would you fly? *Answer:* Southeast.

15. If you traveled by air from R to D, how far would you have traveled? *Answer:* Almost 1500 miles. One inch on the map equals 500 miles. From R to D in a direct line is almost 3 inches. Three times 500 is 1500 miles.

16. When it is 8 o'clock in the morning at D, what time is it at C? *Answer:* 7 o'clock. There is a difference of one hour in time for each 15 degrees of longitude. Since the earth is moving toward the east, D has daylight earlier than C. So, D will always be one hour ahead in time.

SUMMING UP

I. *Match the items in Column B with the climatic regions in Column A.*

COLUMN A	COLUMN B
1. marine	a. High-latitude forests.
2. humid-subtropical	b. Sunny lands with dry summers.
3. taiga	c. Grassland north of the rain forest.
4. rain forest	d. Wet, cool lands of Western Europe.
5. savanna	e. Less than 10″ of rain a year.
6. humid-continental	f. Good farm lands on the east coast of continents in the middle latitudes.
7. Mediterranean	g. Climate of the four seasons—cold winters and hot summers.
	h. Always hot and wet.

II. *True or False*

Tell whether these statements are true or false. The underlined words make the statement true or false. If a statement is false, what words would you place in the statement to make it true?

1. Most of Australia is <u>rain forest</u>.
2. The tundra is a climate of the <u>middle</u> latitudes.
3. A great difference in temperature from day to night takes place in the <u>desert.</u>
4. Part of the United States has a <u>Mediterranean</u> climate.
5. A subtropical climate is found along the <u>southeastern</u> coast of China.
6. A great part of the taiga is found in the <u>United States.</u>
7. The wet and dry seasons are a feature of the <u>savanna</u> climate.
8. Temperatures that are mild in both winter and summer are a part of the <u>marine</u> climate.

CHAPTER 11

Gifts of the Earth

PROBLEM: What are natural resources? How are they divided among the peoples of the earth?

1. Our planet Earth has been very good to us. The surface of the earth is covered by water, soil and forests. Beneath the surface of the earth is its crust. In it are rich minerals, such as iron, gold, silver, copper, lead, tin and aluminum ore. The earth's crust also contains layers of coal, petroleum (oil) and natural gas. These are all natural resources. Without the gifts of the earth, man could not live.

2. The *soil* that covers our earth is very valuable to us. The earliest civilizations on earth (China, India, Egypt) started where there was fertile soil—where people could grow crops. The topsoil throughout the world is only about 8 inches deep. This thin layer of topsoil is made up chiefly of minerals and living things. The topsoil contains plants and insects as well as water, air and minerals. The minerals are called

nutrients. As long as the nutrients remain, the land is useful and provides us with food to eat and raw materials for clothing and shelter.

3. There are many different kinds of soil throughout the world. The soils in the rain forests and savannas are very poor. The heavy rains *leach* or wash out the minerals or nutrients from the soil. In the dry lands one finds gray desert soils. These soils are very fertile when irrigated because they have had little rain to wash away the nutrients. (When we irrigate we bring water to dry land through ditches and canals in order to grow crops.) In the humid-subtropical lands, the soils are a reddish-yellow. If they are fertilized they can give rich harvests for many years. (Soil is fertilized when minerals are added to make it richer.) The best farming soils are found inland on the prairies of North and South America and the steppes of the Soviet Union. They are the rich black soils. They have plenty of minerals and need little fertilizer. These "black belts" are the great wheat-growing regions of the world.

4. *Water* is another natural resource that most of us accept without much thought. We need water to drink, to keep us clean and to wash our food. A city of one million people may use as much as 50 million gallons of water a day! We also need water for growing crops. (Where not enough rain falls, we must irrigate dry fields.) Water also gives us a means of travel and carrying goods, and it is an important source of power. Power plants near rivers and waterfalls use water to turn machines called turbines that produce electricity. We call this *hydroelectricity.*

5. *Forests* are one of the valuable resources of the world. They still cover about 1/5 of the earth's surface. Most of the large forests are found in the northern taiga (Canada, Alaska, Norway, Sweden, Finland and Siberia) and in the rain-forest regions of South America, central Africa and Southeast Asia. There are many kinds of trees, from the hardwoods of the rain forest to the evergreens of the taiga. Our forests provide us with raw materials for building homes and for many other things that we use

in our daily lives. Wood is used as fuel for heating and cooking. Trees help save our soil resources. They keep the soil on steep hillsides from being washed away. Newsprint, turpentine, maple sugar, cellophane and many medicines are but a few of the products of our forests. Lastly, forests provide a home for wildlife and a place of beauty and recreation for millions of people.

6. *Coal* is the world's chief source of power. It is important as a heating fuel. But of greatest importance is the fact that with coal we can make steel from iron ore. The largest deposits of coal are found in the United States, Great Britain, West Germany and the Soviet Union. As a result, all of these countries have great mills and factories. Most of the world's known coal deposits are in North America and Europe. Little coal has been found in Africa and South America. In Asia coal has been mined only on a small scale.

7. *Petroleum* or oil provides power for farms and factories. Petroleum is a liquid mineral found in layers of rock deep below the surface

Pictograph # 1—Important Mineral and Food Resources of the World

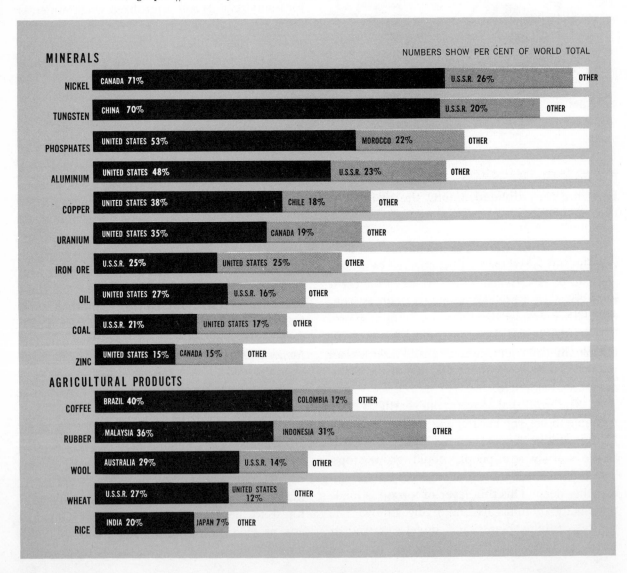

MINERALS — NUMBERS SHOW PER CENT OF WORLD TOTAL

Mineral			
NICKEL	CANADA 71%	U.S.S.R. 26%	OTHER
TUNGSTEN	CHINA 70%	U.S.S.R. 20%	OTHER
PHOSPHATES	UNITED STATES 53%	MOROCCO 22%	OTHER
ALUMINUM	UNITED STATES 48%	U.S.S.R. 23%	OTHER
COPPER	UNITED STATES 38%	CHILE 18%	OTHER
URANIUM	UNITED STATES 35%	CANADA 19%	OTHER
IRON ORE	U.S.S.R. 25%	UNITED STATES 25%	OTHER
OIL	UNITED STATES 27%	U.S.S.R. 16%	OTHER
COAL	U.S.S.R. 21%	UNITED STATES 17%	OTHER
ZINC	UNITED STATES 15%	CANADA 15%	OTHER

AGRICULTURAL PRODUCTS

COFFEE	BRAZIL 40%	COLOMBIA 12%	OTHER
RUBBER	MALAYSIA 36%	INDONESIA 31%	OTHER
WOOL	AUSTRALIA 29%	U.S.S.R. 14%	OTHER
WHEAT	U.S.S.R. 27%	UNITED STATES 12%	OTHER
RICE	INDIA 20%	JAPAN 7%	OTHER

of the earth. It is a heating fuel for millions of homes. After petroleum is refined—that is, its impurities are removed—one of its products is gasoline, the chief fuel for automobiles and airplanes. Chemists have learned how to change petroleum into many useful things. Like other natural resources, petroleum is not found everywhere in the world. Some nations have large deposits of oil, while others have none at all. The great oil countries are the United States, Venezuela, the Soviet Union and the countries near the Persian Gulf (Arabia, Iraq, Iran, Kuwait).

8. *Iron ore* is more valuable than any other mineral. Without iron ore, great industrial nations could never have developed. When iron is smelted or separated from rock and mixed with other minerals, steel is made. Iron ore is often hard to remove from the earth's crust, but in some places it lies near the surface. The ore of the great Mesabi Range of Minnesota is soft and easy to mine. It is simply scooped up by large steam shovels and loaded in railroad cars.

9. About ¼ of the world's supply of iron ore comes from the Lake Superior district of the United States. In Europe, France and Sweden are the chief iron-mining centers. The Soviet Union has large deposits of iron ore, coal and limestone. Large deposits are also found in India, Red China and Indonesia. Other countries have some iron ore, but it is not mined because it is expensive to carry the ore to smelters where it is refined.

10. There are other minerals that are very useful to man. *Copper* can easily be made into wire and can carry electricity. At the present time, the United States is the largest miner and user of copper. A large copper supply also comes from Chile (in South America), central Africa and Canada. The demand for a light, strong metal has made *aluminum* important. Today it is being used more and more in buildings, automobiles, trucks, boats and airplanes. The United States makes more aluminum products than any other nation. The aluminum comes from a mineral called *bauxite*. It must be refined in order to make aluminum. Electric power, chiefly water power, is used to manufacture aluminum. Bauxite is imported from France, Italy, India, Yugoslavia and Surinam.

11. *Tin* is used in cans because it does not rust. We import it from Malaysia, Indonesia and Bolivia. *Uranium* is one of the newest and most important minerals of our time. Leading producers of uranium are the United States and Canada. This ore is the source of our newest form of power, atomic energy!

12. As you study these chapters, you will learn how natural resources differ from region to region throughout the world. You will see that they are not found in the same amounts in every region. Even such large countries as the United States and the Soviet Union do not have all the resources that their people need. You will find out how people make use of natural resources, whether as farmers, miners, fishermen or lumbermen. You will learn how much you depend on these people even though you live far from them. You will learn how people turn to trade in order to provide themselves with the raw materials they don't have.

13. Finally, you will learn that many of these great resources are being used so rapidly that man is searching for new materials to take the place of the ones that are being used up. Every year man is trying to find ways to conserve or save his resources. Conservation is a very important part of our government's responsibilities. The valuable gifts of nature must be used wisely if we hope to keep the standard of living we now enjoy.

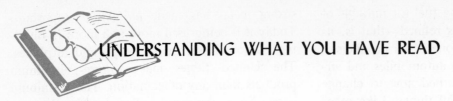

UNDERSTANDING WHAT YOU HAVE READ

1. The main idea of *paragraph 3* is to describe the:

a. great farm regions of the world.
b. different kinds of soil on the earth.
c. problems of rain on soil.

2. Minerals such as iron and coal are usually found in the:

a. earth's crust.   b. topsoil.   c. sea.

3. We get all these products from trees EXCEPT:

a. paper.   b. sugar.   c. cotton.

4. The most valuable minerals for use in industry are:

a. copper and coal.
b. tin and iron ore.
c. coal and iron ore.

5. Uranium is a mineral used in making:

a. atomic energy.   b. steel.   c. aluminum.

6. The United States and the Soviet Union have large supplies of all of these EXCEPT:

a. oil.   b. iron ore.   c. tin.

7. Aluminum has become important in many kinds of work because:

a. it is found almost everywhere in the world.
b. there is a demand for a strong light metal.
c. it can be used as a fuel.

8. Desert lands may still have good soil because:

a. rains have not washed away the minerals from the soil.
b. beneath the surface, there is black soil.
c. they have been farmed for thousands of years.

DEVELOPING IDEAS AND SKILLS

Getting Information From Maps

This is another map of an imaginary land, like the map in Chapter 10. You will be able to get information about this land in the same way that you did in Chapter 10. Study the map. Then see if you can answer the questions that follow. You should be able to find all the answers from information given in the map.

Map # 7—Carmania

1. Is Carmania located in the low, middle or high latitudes?
2. Is Carmania north or south of the equator?
3. Which city is nearest to the Prime Meridian: C, R or O?
4. What is the distance from R to O by railroad: 1050 miles, 1350 miles or 1680 miles?
5. Which city looks as though it would be the biggest seaport: B, R or O?
6. What kind of climate would you expect to find around R: marine, subtropical or rain forest?

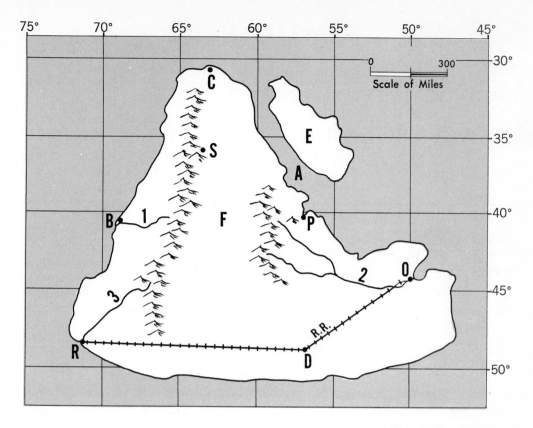

Map # 7—Carmania

7. What kind of climate would you expect to find around F: desert, rain forest or Mediterranean?
8. What city is located at 40° S. Lat. and 57° W. Long.?
9. Which direction is upstream in River 3: north, northeast or southwest?
10. Which city would have the greatest changes in temperature during a year: B, D or O?
11. When it is 3 o'clock in the afternoon at R, what time would it be at E: 2 o'clock, 3 o'clock or 4 o'clock?
12. What do we call A: a peninsula, a strait or an isthmus?
13. Where would you expect to find minerals: P, D or S?
14. Which place is northwest of D: S, E or O?
15. Which place would probably have the most rainfall: F, C or B?

SUMMING UP

Knowing Words   Review the word clues you learned in Chapter 1. Then see if you can find the meanings of these words in Chapter 11. What *clue* helped you to know the meaning of each word?

Paragraph   1—petroleum
Paragraph   2—nutrients

Paragraph   3—leach
Paragraph   3—irrigate
Paragraph   4—turbines
Paragraph   9—smelter
Paragraph   10—bauxite
Paragraph   13—conserve

CHAPTER 12

Machines Have Changed Our Ways of Living

PROBLEM: How have machines changed some nations of the world but not others?

1. The greatest change in the way men use the resources of the earth took place in the seventeenth and eighteenth centuries. This change was called the Industrial Revolution. (A revolution is a basic change that brings about a new way of life for many people.) New kinds of machines were invented and new kinds of power were developed to run these machines. Many goods were now made by machines instead of by hand, in factories instead of at home. New forms of power such as steam began to do some of the work once done by men and animals. This "revolution" changed the face of the earth. It divided the world into those countries that have many industries and those that do not. Let us see what an *industrial society* looks like.

2. With the use of machines it was now possible to produce large amounts of goods of many kinds. These products of the factories could be sold for lower prices than handmade goods because they were cheaper to make. As more and more people came to work in the factories, they earned more money to pay for these goods than they had had before. They became a *market* for the products of the factory. (Factories will not make goods unless there are people who will buy them.)

3. Because the factories made so many more goods, more raw materials to make these goods were needed. Coal and iron ore were needed to make steel. New uses for oil were discovered. As factories grew, there was a demand for more and more workers. Thousands left their farms and moved near the factories. Cities grew around the great industrial centers. In a large city many were factory workers, but many found jobs filling the needs of their neighbors. For every person who worked in the factory, two people could earn a living by working in "services"—storekeepers, teachers, doctors, policemen.

4. How could all these city people be fed? New machines began to be used on the farm. With improved methods of farming and machinery, it was possible for farmers to grow more food with fewer workers. Farmers not only grew food for themselves, but they were able to feed people throughout the nation and the world as well. They now grew *money crops*—crops they could sell at a profit. The farmer was now in business just as much as the factory owner.

5. Steam took the place of wind as the source of power in water transportation, and the great sailing ships were replaced by steam ships. (In time, there were other sources of power: water, oil and atomic energy.) The automobile and airplane were invented; as a result, goods could be carried swiftly and cheaply almost anywhere in the world. The invention of the telephone, telegraph and radio during this period meant that people from one corner of the world to the other could communicate with each other.

6. Today countries like the United States, Great Britain, Canada, Japan, West Germany, France and the Soviet Union are *industrial societies*. An industrial society or region is one in

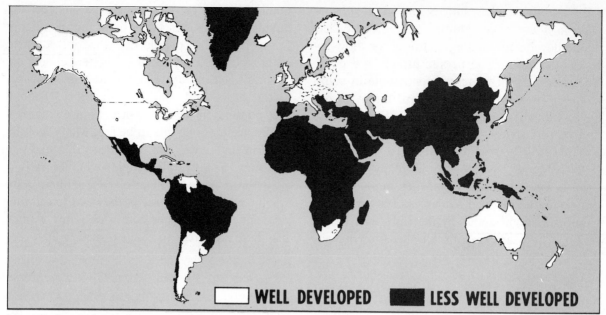

Map # 8—Industrial Development Throughout the World

WELL DEVELOPED   LESS WELL DEVELOPED

which many people make a living by manufacturing or making things in factories. They have power-driven machinery and make great use of the raw materials of the earth. Their factories produce goods for their own people and have enough to sell to other nations as well. They have the means to ship goods from one place to another. Many other countries are also beginning to have mills and factories.

7. On the other hand, there are many countries in the world that the Industrial Revolution still has not reached to any large extent. These countries have not made full use of their natural resources. They still depend on hand labor in the fields and at home. They do not manufacture goods in great amounts and must buy them from other nations at high cost. Many of the people are farmers who work all day just to provide simple food, clothing and shelter for their families. They have nothing left over to

Farmers of Ethiopia turn the soil with simple tools.

A car assembly line in Italy.

UNATIONS

UNATIONS

51

sell to other peoples. This is known as *subsistence farming*. Such countries are often called "underdeveloped" or "agricultural" or "low-income" countries. The people usually are poor. The average yearly income for people in some of these low-income areas is hard for us to believe: Latin America—$300; the Middle East and North Africa—$150; Africa, South of the Sahara—$120; the Far East—$100.

8. However, the people in many of these countries no longer feel that they must be poor and have undeveloped resources. They want the changes brought about by the Industrial Revolution. There are reasons for this growing demand for change. First, such nations feel that having factories will bring them the many comforts of life that people of industrial countries seem to have. They too want better schools and hospitals, electricity, radios and television sets, refrigerators and washing machines. Second, the population of the world is growing fast. There are more people to be fed. Many feel that this means more jobs are needed, chiefly in factories. Finally, all people, whether rich or poor, have pride in themselves and their country. They want to be free of the need to sell their raw materials to other countries. They want to use these resources for their own benefit.

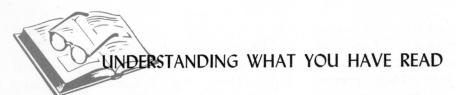

UNDERSTANDING WHAT YOU HAVE READ

1. The main idea of *paragraph 7* is to describe:
a. underdeveloped countries.
b. problems of the Industrial Revolution.
c. poor natural resources.

2. A high standard of living can be found in:
a. most of North Africa.
b. Canada.
c. all of southern Africa.

3. All of these are problems of underdeveloped countries EXCEPT:
a. they have little money to buy goods.
b. they have few people.
c. few people have had an education.

4. A change in farming caused by the Industrial Revolution was that:
a. fewer machines were used on farms.
b. the farmer did not raise food beyond the needs of his own family.

c. fewer workers were needed on farms.

5. Which of these kinds of power was first used?
a. Electric.   b. Oil.   c. Steam.

6. The *Industrial Revolution* refers to the:
a. use of machines to do work once done by men.
b. discovery of oil.
c. rise of independent countries.

7. An *underdeveloped country* is one that has:
a. few water resources.
b. made little use of its natural resources.
c. most of its workers in factories.

8. When there are people who will buy a product or places where it can be sold, we say that the product has:
a. an industrial center.
b. a market.
c. been developed.

DEVELOPING IDEAS AND SKILLS

Making Inferences

Whatever you read, you gain ideas not only from the words you read, but often from what is *not* said. You read "between the lines." This is true in your study of the world, too. You know some things even though they are not stated. You are able to understand because some things are "inferred." One of the skills in reading social studies is to be able to *infer* meanings from what you have read. Here is an example:

"He loved walking with his fishing rod to the edge of the cool stream. The wet grass brushed against his bare feet, making them wet but not uncomfortable. And to think that he didn't have to go back until lunch!"

What do we *infer* from these few sentences? We have gained some ideas without those ideas being put into words. *We know that it is morning*—the grass is wet, and lunch time has not yet come. *We know that it is probably a summer day*—the boy is going fishing in his bare feet. We even know that the sentences are *about a boy,* for walking barefoot in the morning doesn't sound like something a grown man would do.

Another example:

"The five o'clock whistle meant that the rush of workers had begun. Off they went in their shiny cars. Others poured into the subways near by. The bright street lights were already lit."

What can we *infer* from these few sentences? First, *this is probably a city.* There are subways and street lights. *It is probably winter,* too, for the lights are already on at 5 o'clock, the end of the working day. And, *the people probably have a high standard of living,* since the workers have their own cars.

In this exercise, see if you can *infer* from the paragraph whether it is written about low, high or middle latitudes.

1. Across the vast lowland, we see farm after farm. Corn and wheat can be seen for miles. Next to the farms, the hogs and cattle stand out against the green trees in the background.

2. A trip down the river is like going through a fairyland. Coconut palms, banana trees and all kinds of flowering trees and bushes line the shore. The monkeys never seem to stop chattering as they swing through the long vines.

3. The heat goes on and on. It wouldn't be so bad if it weren't for that rain! I'll never come here to build a road again. The bushes grow back as fast as I cut them, and the insects don't stop biting for a moment.

4. It could be worse in these winter months. I don't mind the darkness. After a few weeks you get used to it. I even enjoy melting the ice so that I can wash and make hot coffee.

5. Most of the farms look brown now, but some rain will come soon. The sheep seem to get enough food in the mountains, even though it is winter.

6. All the streams seem to be bordered with trees. The small fields were yellow with grain a month ago. Some workers are weeding potatoes; others are harvesting the ripe oats and wheat.

7. Everything is made of wood here because there is so much of it around. There's no use trying to farm. These trees are our wealth. When the summer comes, the ice will melt and we'll float the heavy logs downstream.

CHAPTER 13

World Regions

PROBLEM: How will we explore our changing world?

1. After Unit One, each unit of this book tells about one of the eight regions of the world. Each region has features that make it a single region. The people and countries may be tied together through climate, land features, history, religion or ways of making a living. One region is made up of only one country, the Soviet Union. The other regions have from a few to a great many countries. Here are a number of questions to guide you as you prepare to study each of the eight world regions:

1. Why are we interested in this region?
2. How do the land and climate of the region explain, in part, the way the people live?
3. How has the geography of the region influenced the history of the people?
4. Who are the people of the region? What are their problems?
5. What are the resources of the region? How do the people make use of these resources?
6. What is the standing of the region in the world community?

2. The first region we will study is *Anglo-America*. This includes the countries of the United States and Canada, two of the largest nations of the world. Only the Soviet Union is larger than Canada. The United States ranks fourth in size after Red China. Both the United States and Canada are located in the middle and high latitudes of the northern hemisphere. They have many things in common. They have the same language and the same ideas of government. They have great industries and a high standard of living. Both countries have been friendly and have cooperated with each other for more than 150 years. They are the richest region of all in natural resources. The people of the United States and Canada make great use of these resources for farming, manufacturing and trading.

3. Our southern neighbors in *Latin America* make up the next region of study. Most of the countries in Latin America were colonies of Spain, Portugal or France. They are studied together because most of them are Catholic in religion and Spanish or Portuguese in the language their people use. This is largely a region of tropical or subtropical climate, although mountains provide a cooler home for many people. Most of the people are descendants of Europeans, Indians and Negroes. Small farms and farming on large estates are the chief kinds of work. The countries of Latin America export many raw materials to other parts of the world.

4. The countries of *Western Europe* (other than the Soviet Union and its satellites) are our next area of study. While Western Europe is the smallest region we will explore, there are a large number of countries within this region. These countries have a marine climate. The leading countries are thickly populated. The people have made good use of their resources —the level and fertile lands, the iron and coal from the earth, the forests and the nearby seas. Their factories make iron and steel goods that are sold all over the world. The

people of Western Europe have a high standard of living. The lands of Europe that border the Mediterranean Sea are poorer. Most people here make a living through farming.

5. The *Soviet Union* will be studied as a separate region. This giant country extends across great parts of Europe and Asia. It is the largest country in the world. Its land has vast plains, many resources and large areas in which few people live because of the cold climate. Since 1917, the Soviet Union has been governed by its Communist Party. This was once a farming nation only, but today it is the second leading industrial nation in the world, following the United States. (The countries of Eastern Europe will be studied here too, since they are under Soviet influence.)

6. The lands of *North Africa and the Middle East* are combined into one region in this book for several reasons. This area, stretching across northern Africa and southwest Asia, is almost all a desert region. Few people live in it because of the lack of water. Except for oil, there are few mineral resources. It is a region of oasis farmers, city people and herdsmen who travel from place to place. Most of the people are Moslem in religion. Many are very poor and unable to read or write. It is divided into many small countries.

7. *Africa, South of the Sahara* is studied as a region apart from North Africa. It is a region of rain forests, grasslands and desert. Much of Africa is underdeveloped. Most of the people are Negro. Since 1945, many small countries in Africa have won their freedom. Although Africa is making much progress, many of the mineral resources have scarcely been used. Most of the people are either poor farmers or herders.

8. The *Far East,* or Orient, has been included as one region. This region is made up of the countries of southern and eastern Asia, including Japan, Indonesia and the Philippines. It is the home of almost half the people of the world! Most of these people live on small farms, on which they grow rice. As in Africa, there are new nations in the Far East. These nations are

UNITED NATIONS

A busy port of Western Europe.

UNATIONS

Bedouin nomads of the Middle East and North Africa.

A rice field in the Far East.

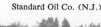

Standard Oil Co. (N.J.)

trying to make better use of their resources, but they face many problems. This region has also seen the rise of another Communist power, Red China.

9. To complete our study of the regions of the world, we will look at the land areas of the *Pacific*. Included in this region are the continent of Australia and the islands that are scattered throughout the Pacific Ocean. Except for Australia, New Zealand and Western Samoa, these islands are governed by other nations. The people of Australia and New Zealand have a high standard of living. They depend largely upon sheep and dairy farming and some manufacturing. Most of the island peoples are simple farmers who depend upon the coconut palm.

UNDERSTANDING WHAT YOU HAVE READ

Match the items in Column B with the regions listed in Column A.

COLUMN A	COLUMN B
1. Anglo-America	___Many islands—simple farming.
2. Latin America	___Large region with large Negro population.
3. Western Europe	___Region of one country.
4. The Soviet Union	___Smallest region; high standard of living.
5. North Africa and the Middle East	___Largely desert and oil.
6. Africa, South of the Sahara	___Half the world's people.
	___Spanish-speaking people; large area of warm climate.
7. Far East	___One of the highest standards of living; divided into many small nations.
8. The Pacific World	___English-speaking people; high standard of living.

Map # 9—The Regions of the World

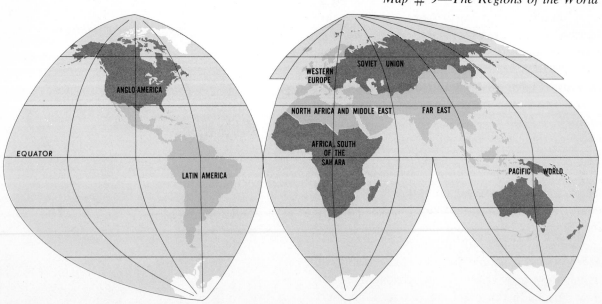

DEVELOPING IDEAS AND SKILLS

Locating Our World Regions

Map # 9—The Regions of the World
Locate each of the regions on the map of the world shown on p. 56. This will help you to prepare for the first region that you are to study.

SUMMING UP

Making Inferences   In our reading, many facts are given to us. From these facts, we draw conclusions. Here are some conclusions or inferences that you might make after reading Chapter 13. Tell whether these conclusions are correct or incorrect. Give reasons for your answers.

Paragraph 2—There will be some places in Anglo-America with very cold climates.

Paragraph 3—Manufacturing is an important work in Latin America.

Paragraph 4—There are large areas of land in Western Europe where few people live.

Paragraph 5—The Soviet Union has large mineral resources, including coal and iron ore.

Paragraph 6—Many cities of millions of people are found in North Africa and the Middle East.

Paragraph 7—The climate and the surface of the land have hurt the development of Africa, South of the Sahara.

Paragraph 8—Much of the Far East is a region of desert, mountains and rain forest.

Paragraph 9—The standard of living of the people of the Pacific islands is rather low.

CHAPTER 14

Understanding Some World Problems

PROBLEM: How can we better understand the problems of other people?

1. As a result of two great wars, the United States has become a leader in world affairs. As our power has grown, so has our interest in all world problems—the spread of communism, the danger of nuclear war, the needs of poorer nations. In order to be a good leader, our nation must have a better understanding of other peoples and their ways of living. With this knowledge, we will be better prepared to help them reach their dreams of freedom and peace. What are some of the things that Americans should know about the rest of the world?

2. First, there is more poverty than wealth in the world. Many people still use wooden plows and other simple tools to farm their land. Some of them do not have enough to eat. Many are sick but cannot get medical care.

3. Second, the population of the world is growing rapidly. This great rise in population is not taking place in only one part of the world; it is world-wide. People are living longer today because more is known about how to keep them healthy. There are more mouths to feed and yet there are millions who do not have enough to eat. It is important that in the future our resources be used wisely to provide for all. If they are not, hunger may drive people to get what they want through violence.

4. Third, there are millions of people in the world who cannot read or write. In the countries of Libya, India and Egypt, eight out of ten people cannot read or write any language. Not every country in the world believes in education for all, or can afford it as we can in the United States. In many nations only the rich or the very bright students go to school. The new independent nations must choose their leaders from a population in which perhaps only one in 1,000 has been to college.

5. Fourth, the races of man are roughly divided into 33% white, 24% Negro and 43% Mongoloid or yellow. (Actually, no pure racial grouping is possible, for over the years all races have mixed in some way.) It is clear, therefore, that there are more "colored" people in the world than "white." Since this is so, we must learn about the contributions of all races to civilization. Every people has its own customs and its own history, its own pioneers and its own patriots. In the United States and other countries, there have been troubles because of misunderstandings between races. Most of the nations in the world have colored people. Therefore, the treatment of any group of people in our own country will decide how these nations look upon our way of life.

6. Fifth, many people in the world have religious beliefs that are different from our own. Most of the people of the United States are Christians, divided into two large groups, Protestant and Catholic. There are also smaller groups of Jews. However, there are many other religions in the world. It is important to know that there are more non-Christian than Christian people in the world. The Middle East and eastern Asia have many Moslems. In India, the

There are more non-Christians than Christians in the world. Here are a group of Moslems at a mosque in Pakistan.

major religion is Hinduism. In China, Buddhism is very strong. There are tribal religions in Africa and on the islands of the Pacific. As a result, ideas of what is right and what is wrong may not be the same throughout the world. Our ways of living are also different. For example, in our country we raise cattle and eat meat and drink milk. In India the cow is sacred and cannot be killed or used for meat.

7. Sixth, we have seen the birth of many new nations since 1945. Most of these nations were once colonies of countries in Europe and America. Colored peoples of Asia and Africa live in most of these new nations. There is a great deal of unrest as they try to solve their problems. They look to the United States for help and support, for we were once a colony ourselves. They also look to the United States for leadership in forming democratic governments. However, the governments of some new nations are made up of a few men who do not allow the people the freedoms we enjoy in this country.

8. Seventh, our world seems to be getting smaller. Today a jet plane can reach any part of the globe in a single day. There are long-

The different races of the world.

African peoples wish for freedom to rule themselves.

range rockets and missiles that can cross oceans and continents in a matter of minutes. Russian and American spacemen have orbited the earth in less than ninety minutes. We can speak to nearly every part of the world in a few minutes by telephone. We can see distant parts of the world through Telstar and Early Bird.

9. Finally, the many peoples of the world are dependent upon one another. We draw upon the industries and natural resources of many countries through trade. (Your own breakfast may include tea from Japan, coffee from Brazil, cocoa from Ghana or bananas from Guatemala.) This means that what happens in one part of the globe affects the people in another. Trouble in the oil fields of the Middle East or in the rice fields of Southeast Asia affects the people of the United States and Western Europe. What you read in the newspapers is not so far from your doorstep as you may think!

UNDERSTANDING WHAT YOU HAVE READ

1. The main idea of this chapter is to describe:
a. the different religions of people in the world.
b. why we are interested in people all over the world.
c. how people have become closer to each other.

2. A large share of the people cannot read or write in:
a. Egypt.   b. Canada.   c. France.

3. The largest race of people in the world is the:

a. Negro.   b. white.   c. yellow.

4. Most of the new nations of the world since 1945 are located in:

a. Asia and Africa.
b. Europe and Africa.
c. South America and Asia.

5. Two great religions of the Far East are:

a. Catholicism and Judaism.
b. Protestantism and Islam.
c. Hinduism and Buddhism.

6. Which of these is closely related to the standard of living of any country?

a. The size and shape of the land.

b. The number of people.
c. How resources have been used.

7. Poverty of people in the world is a problem because:

a. these people will not be able to buy our goods.
b. poor people may turn to violent means to help solve their problems.
c. education cannot help these people.

8. New nations of the world expect the understanding of the people of the United States because:

a. we were once a colony and fought for our freedom.
b. leaders of these nations were educated in the United States.
c. we need their oil resources.

SUMMING UP

Fact or Opinion   Can you tell whether these statements are facts or someone's opinion?

1. The United States has few people of the Moslem religion.
2. Many nations of the world do not have money to provide schools for all children.
3. It is important that we buy as much as we can from poorer nations.
4. Not all people have the same kinds of laws.
5. The needs of poor people in the world are as big a danger to world peace as the spread of communism.
6. Education is the answer to the problems that face the people of the world.
7. Within ten years, there will be a world-wide television system.
8. People all over the world are interested in how our nation treats all its people.
9. The United States depends upon other people for many raw materials.
10. The United States has areas where there is great poverty.

BOOKS FOR UNIT 1

Author	Title, Publisher	Description
1. Barnes, Malcolm, ed.	*The Mountain World,* Rand McNally	The stories of several mountain expeditions.
2. Barnett, Lincoln, and Editors of *Life*	*The World We Live In,* Golden Press	The story of the earth from its beginnings.
3. Brown, Lloyd	*Map-Making,* Little, Brown	The history of cartography.
4. Carson, Rachel	*The Sea Around Us,* Golden Press	How the seas work and move.
5. Doss, Helen	*The Family Nobody Wanted,* Little, Brown	The story of a little "U.N." family.
6. Raisz, Erwin	*Mapping the World,* Abelard-Schuman	The story of maps from their beginning until the present.
7. Rand McNally, Editors	*The Book of Nations,* Rand McNally	Information on geography and history of all nations.
8. Roosevelt, Eleanor, and Helen Ferris	*Partners,* Doubleday	The story of work done by youth and the United Nations.
9. Werner, Jane	*The Living Desert,* Golden Press	The life of desert plants and animals.
10. ——	*Golden Geography,* Golden Press	An exciting and well-illustrated introduction to geography.
11. White, Anne Terry	*All About Archaeology,* Random House	How we learn about ancient civilizations.

BOOKS IN SERIES (useful for many units)

Title	Publisher
1. The "Challenge" Books	Coward-McCann
2. The "First Book of" Series	Franklin Watts
3. The "Getting to Know" Books	Coward-McCann
4. The "Keys to the Cities" Series	Lippincott
5. The "Landmark" Books	Random House
6. The "Lands and Peoples" Series	Holiday
7. The "Let's Read About" Series	Fideler
8. The "Let's Visit" Series	John Day
9. The "Made In" Series	Knopf

10. The "Meet the World" Books	Harper
11. The "My Village" Series	Pantheon
12. The "Other Lands" Series	Life Publications
13. The "Picture Stories of Other Countries" Series	David McKay
14. The "Portraits of the Nations" Series	Lippincott
15. The "World Background" Series	Scribner
16. The "World Neighbors" Series	John Day

UNIT 2

Anglo-America

CHAPTER 1

Northern Giants

PROBLEM: Why do we study the United States and Canada together?

READING FOR A PURPOSE:
1. How large is the United States?
2. How large is Canada?
3. What waterways are part of our common border?

1. Stretching north of Mexico as far as the Arctic Ocean is a vast region that covers nearly all of the continent of North America. It is called Anglo-America. This area is shared by two countries, the United States and Canada. These two countries are called Anglo-America because most of their people speak English. (*Anglo* is the Latin word for "English.") French is also spoken in Canada, but not as much as English.

2. Canada takes up most of the northern half of the North American continent. It covers an area of almost 3,900,000 square miles. As such, it is the second largest country in the world. South of Canada is the United States. It covers more than 3,600,000 square miles, including the Hawaiian Islands in the Pacific Ocean and the state of Alaska northwest of Canada. It is the fourth largest country in the world. Both nations border the two largest oceans, the Pacific Ocean on the west and the Atlantic Ocean on the east.

3. The United States and Canada share a common border that is more than 3,000 miles long. There are no guns or forts along this border. The eastern part of the border is made up of two great waterways—the Great Lakes and the St. Lawrence River. Farther west the border stretches along the 49th parallel until it reaches the Pacific Ocean. For over 150 years, Americans and Canadians have crossed this common border without difficulty. The

Malak Studio

A logger in Canada.

A fishing fleet in British Columbia, Canada.

people of the United States and Canada trade more with each other than they do with any other countries in the world.

4. In many ways the Canadian and American ways of life are alike. Often it is as if there were no border between the two countries. For example, the farming lands just north of the St. Lawrence River are very much like the farming region of our New England states. Along the St. Lawrence River, factories on both sides of the border turn out machinery and manufactured goods.

5. If you were to visit the large cities of Montreal and Toronto, they would remind you of our own large cities. Most of the people speak English. They use many of the same products we do and eat many of the same things. The children go to school and play such games as hockey and baseball. Both peoples, Canadian and American, have a high standard of living.

6. In the Central Plains region there are large wheat farms on both sides of the border. The farmers of both nations use large machinery to plant and harvest their wheat. Farther west, on the prairies, large herds of cattle and sheep are raised. Cowboys on horseback take care of the cattle in both countries.

7. The Rocky Mountains extend north and south through both countries. In both countries miners dig for gold, silver, lead and zinc. Farther west, on the Pacific coast, fishermen on both sides of the border bring in salmon. Lumberjacks cut down trees in the western forests of both the United States and Canada.

8. The relationship between the United States and Canada was very well described by President John F. Kennedy. On a visit to Canada in 1961 he said, "Geography has made us neighbors. History has made us friends. Economics has made us partners; and necessity has made us allies." In the next few chapters, we will explore the meaning of this statement and learn how these two nations are using their great resources for the benefit of both their peoples.

A farmer harvesting corn in Illinois.

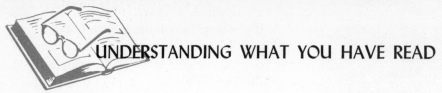

UNDERSTANDING WHAT YOU HAVE READ

1. Which of the following questions are answered in this chapter?
   a. What kinds of work do many people do in the United States and Canada?
   b. What does *Anglo-American* mean?
   c. What two languages do the Canadians speak?

2. The main idea of this chapter is to describe:
   a. the size of the United States and Canada.
   b. the areas where people farm.
   c. things these nations have in common.

3. The United States is the:
   a. largest country in the world.
   b. smallest country in the world.
   c. fourth largest country in the world.

4. On both sides of the St. Lawrence River you are likely to find;
   a. forests.
   b. farms and factories.
   c. fisheries.

5. We are studying the United States and Canada as one region because:
   a. both countries lack natural resources.
   b. most people in both countries are farmers.
   c. English is the language of most people in both countries.

6. People in both countries do much the same kinds of work because:
   a. both are located in the middle latitudes.
   b. both are located in the high latitudes.
   c. both lands are surrounded by water.

DEVELOPING IDEAS AND SKILLS

Map # 10—Anglo-America
Can you answer these questions?
1. Is the region north or south of the equator?
2. Is the region east or west of the Prime Meridian?
3. How far north and south does the region extend?
4. Does the region extend farther from east to west or from north to south?
5. What region or regions are near it?

6. What are the chief bodies of water that border the region?
7. What are some of the important rivers in the region?
8. Are there large rivers that form the boundary line between countries?
9. What is the capital city of each country? How do you know they are the capitals? Is either a sea or river port?

Map # 10—Anglo-America

SUMMING UP

Picture Symbols

The pictures on p. 68 should help you to recall parts of the chapter you have read. Can you tell the main idea of each picture? In what paragraph did you find the answer for each?

FOLLOW UP

Our northern neighbor Canada is often in the news. The class may start clipping articles about Canada from the newspaper. Perhaps one of the pupils has visited Canada. He should report on his experiences there.

CHAPTER 2

Geography Has Made Us Neighbors

PROBLEM: How are the land forms of Canada and the United States alike?

READING FOR A PURPOSE:
1. What mountains are found in the eastern United States?
2. What rivers drain the broad inner plains?
3. What is the Laurentian Shield?

1. In many ways, the United States and Canada share the same topography or land features. Looking at the map on page 73, you will see that a large coastal plain stretches north and south along the Atlantic Coast, around the Gulf of Mexico into Texas. It is narrow in the north but widens in the south. The Atlantic Coastal Plain is bordered along its western side by the Appalachian Mountains. The Appalachians are low mountains whose peaks were smoothed by glaciers. The Appalachians extend northward over most of eastern Canada. These mountains are a great source of wood, coal and water power.

2. Most of the continent between the Appalachians in the east and the Rockies in the west is covered by a vast lowland, the Central Plains. These plains are among the world's richest farming regions. Here the soil is very fertile. The eastern part of this gently rolling land was once covered with forests. West of the 100° meridian, the inner plains become the prairies or dry grasslands. These grasslands begin to rise slowly toward the Rocky Mountains. The plains spread north and northeast through Canada to the Arctic Ocean. They include the St. Lawrence River Valley.

3. The inner plains of the United States are drained by the Mississippi River and its tributaries or branches. The Mississippi River begins near the border of the United States and Canada. As it flows south, the Mississippi is joined by other rivers. Two of these are almost as large as the Mississippi—the Ohio River from the east and the Missouri River from the west. The Mississippi flows southward, emptying into the Gulf of Mexico at Louisiana. The Mississippi and the Missouri together form the longest river system in the world. The lowlands drained by these rivers of the plains form the greatest farming region of North America.

A view of the Great Plains stretching into Canada.

National Film Board of Canada

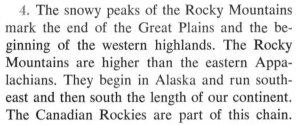

National Film Board of Canada

Part of Canada's Laurentian Shield.

Standard Oil Co. (N.J.)

The Columbia River flows through the western highlands of Oregon.

4. The snowy peaks of the Rocky Mountains mark the end of the Great Plains and the beginning of the western highlands. The Rocky Mountains are higher than the eastern Appalachians. They begin in Alaska and run southeast and then south the length of our continent. The Canadian Rockies are part of this chain.

5. West of the Rockies is a dry, rough area of plateaus and basins. (A basin is a low area in the middle of the mountains.) Great rivers like the Colorado and the Columbia cut across the plateaus, making deep canyons. Many of the streams in this area flow into lakes that have no outlet to the sea. The streams bring salt and other minerals with them. When the water evaporates or dries up, the salt is left in the lakes. The largest and most famous of these lakes is Great Salt Lake in Utah. Many rivers rise in the highlands of the American Rockies. Some flow toward the Atlantic Ocean or the Gulf of Mexico. Others flow westward to the Pacific Ocean. This division is called the Continental Divide. Near the southwestern edge of the Rockies' Great Basin lies Death Valley. This is the driest and hottest desert in North America. It is in the state of California.

6. Farther west are the coastal ranges or mountains that border the Pacific Ocean. They extend southward from Alaska into Mexico. These ranges change names from place to place. Between the coastal ranges are valleys, some of which are very wide. The great Central Valley of California is the largest of these. There is no great coastal plain along the Pacific Ocean as there is along the Atlantic.

7. Canada has one topographical region that is different from any place in the United States. It is called the Laurentian Shield. The Laurentian Shield is an upland that encircles Hudson Bay like a giant horseshoe. It covers more than half of Canada and extends into the United States near Lake Superior. This vast area of hard, old rocks was once scraped by glaciers. As they moved southward from the Arctic Ocean they created valleys, low hills and thousands of lakes and rivers. The Laurentian Shield is rich in forests, minerals and fur-bearing animals. However, only a few people live in this cold northern region. They live mainly by trapping and fishing.

UNDERSTANDING WHAT YOU HAVE READ

1. **Which of the following questions are answered in this chapter?**
   a. How did the glaciers affect the lands of the United States and Canada?
   b. How do the people of Anglo-America use these lands?
   c. What land form is found in Canada but not in the United States?

2. **The main idea of this chapter is to describe the:**
   a. land surface of Anglo-America.
   b. effects of the glaciers.
   c. Laurentian Shield.

3. **The longest river in Anglo-America is the:**
   a. St. Lawrence.   b. Mississippi.   c. Colorado.

4. **The highest mountains in Anglo-America are the:**
   a. Rockies.   b. Appalachians.   c. Ozarks.

5. **Few people live in the Laurentian Shield because:**
   a. the land is filled with streams and lakes.
   b. there is a lack of wood and minerals.
   c. the climate is too cold.

6. **The inner plains of the United States are valuable because:**
   a. they have a wonderful climate for tropical fruits.
   b. the soil is easy to plow.
   c. the land is good for farming and grazing.

7. **A *glacier* is a large mass of:**
   a. ice.   b. land.   c. hardened minerals.

8. **A branch is to a tree as a *tributary* is to a:**
   a. person.   b. river.   c. mountain.

9. **In paragraph 5, the word *evaporates* means:**
   a. "carries salt."
   b. "cuts deeply."
   c. "dries up."

10. **The word *topography* refers to:**
    a. climate.   b. crops.   c. land features.

DEVELOPING IDEAS AND SKILLS

Map # 11—Land Forms of Anglo-America

Tell whether these statements are *true* or *false*. Be able to explain your answers.

1. Plains stretch from north to south through the center of Anglo-America.
2. A great mountain system of Anglo-America lies along and near the western coast.
3. A large lowland area is located along the southeastern coast.
4. A long plain borders the Pacific Coast of Anglo-America.
5. Hills cover much of the eastern part of Anglo-America.
6. When you compare the map opposite with the map of Anglo-America on page 78, you will find that the plains of Anglo-America have the same climate no matter where they are located.
7. Plateaus cover a large area in the western United States.
8. Alaska has a mixture of all four kinds of land forms.

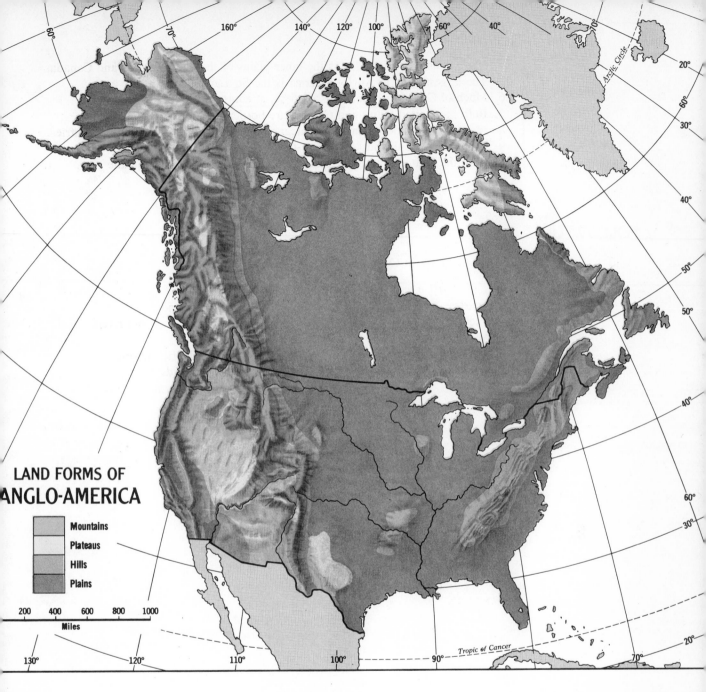

LAND FORMS OF
ANGLO-AMERICA

Mountains
Plateaus
Hills
Plains

200 400 600 800 1000
Miles

Arctic Circle

Tropic of Cancer

SUMMING UP

Do You Agree or Disagree? Give the reasons for your answers.

1. The land forms of both the United States and Canada have been changed by volcanoes.
2. Both countries have chains of low mountains in the east.
3. A vast plateau runs north and south through the heart of North America.

4. The Mississippi River drains the inner plains of the United States and Canada.
5. The largest river in Anglo-America is the St. Lawrence.
6. Much of Canada is a land of old rock, streams and lakes.
7. Both the United States and Canada are bordered by oceans.
8. Many of the same mountains, plateaus and plains are found in both countries.
9. The western highlands cover one-third of the United States.
10. Both the United States and Canada have ports open throughout the year.

FOLLOW UP

Match the items in Column A with those in Column B.

COLUMN A	COLUMN B
1. Prairies	___Western highlands
2. Rockies	___Area of hills, lakes and rivers
3. Appalachians	___Grasslands
4. Laurentian Shield	___Canyons of North America
5. Central Valley	___Eastern highlands
	___Found in California

CHAPTER 3

The Cold and the Warm Regions

PROBLEM: What are the many climates of Anglo-America?

READING FOR A PURPOSE:
1. Where is the taiga in Anglo-America?
2. What climate is found along our southeastern coast?
3. Where are the dry grasslands of Anglo-America?

1. Anglo-America covers a vast area on the earth's surface. Because of its great size it has many different climates. There are a number of reasons for these different climates. The most important reason is latitude, or distance from the equator. All of Anglo-America lies in the middle and high latitudes.

2. In the far north of the continent is the cold, treeless area called the *tundra.* Because of its climate this "upstairs" of Anglo-America is not a desirable place to settle. The tundra stretches across northern Canada from Alaska and the Bering Sea to the Atlantic Ocean, including the island of Greenland. The winds from the Arctic Ocean blow far southward across the tundra, bringing cold air to Canada and the United States.

3. South of the tundra is the *taiga,* or northern forest climate. Forests cover most of northern Canada. The climate of the northern forest land is also harsh. The cold, icy winter lasts from six to seven months a year. In the spring, the snow and ice melt. The surface of the ground thaws or "unfreezes." However, the soil underneath remains frozen so that the water stays on the surface. As a result, swamps and marshes form, making travel in the taiga almost impossible. When summer arrives the weather becomes warmer and many insects appear. The few people who live in this climate depend upon hunting, fishing and trapping for their living.

4. Most of the eastern part of Anglo-America has a *humid-continental* climate. The northeastern part of the United States and the southern border of Canada have this climate. The humid-continental climate is mainly the result of two things: distance from the equator and wet winds that blow from the Atlantic Ocean. Farther

A snowy winter in Vermont, an area of humid-continental climate.

Standard Oil Co. (N.J.)

north in this region the winters are cold. As you go south the summers become warmer and longer. Westward, or inland, the winters are colder and the summers hotter because there are no large bodies of water nearby to "even" the temperature. In the central part of the United States, farthest from the effects of the ocean, temperatures may be as low as 30° below zero in winter and as high as 110° in summer. There is plenty of rainfall in the humid-continental climate. Most of the people of Anglo-America live in this climate area. They live and work in large cities for the most part. However, there are also rich farmlands devoted to corn, wheat and dairying.

5. The southeastern part of the United States has a *humid-subtropical* climate. There is a long, hot summer and a mild winter. Plenty of rain falls throughout the year. The growing season is at least seven months long. No part of Canada has a climate like the humid-subtropical section of the United States. About 25% of our people live here. The area is a rich farmland with fields of cotton, tobacco, peanuts and rice.

6. There is enough rainfall for farming westward as far as the 100° meridian. At this point the climate gradually becomes drier and the prairies or dry grasslands begin. This is the steppe zone of the North American continent. If you travel westward you will find there is less and less rainfall until you reach the deserts of the southwest, where there is almost none at all. The lands west of the 100° meridian are drier because of the Rocky Mountains. The Rockies stop the rain-filled winds as they blow inland from the Pacific Ocean. The rain falls on the western side of the mountains, but the eastern slopes are dry. (The Gulf Coast plains, farther south, have more rainfall because of the winds that blow in from the Gulf of Mexico.)

7. These dry lands make up about one-third of our nation's land area, yet they contain only about 5% of our people. At one time, great herds of buffalo roamed these plains. Now they are shared by cattle and sheep herders and dry farmers. In the highlands, the few who live there work chiefly at mining and raising sheep.

8. The wettest part of Anglo-America is a section along the Pacific coast stretching from northern California to the southern tip of Alaska. This strip of coastal land gets plenty of rain throughout the year, and its winters are cool. A warm current flows along it causing warm winds to blow over the land. The coastal mountain ranges force these winds upward, where they cool and drop their moisture as rain.

The frozen tundra of northern Canada.

The desert climate of the American Southwest.

Bureau of Land Management, N.M.

This is the *marine* climate area of Anglo-America. Because of the heavy rainfall, this land is rich with forests. The many inlets and rivers along its coast are good fishing grounds.

9. While northern California has a marine climate, southern California enjoys the warm, sunny *Mediterranean* climate. In southern California the summers are hot and dry and the winters are mild. Nearly all rainfall takes place in the winter months. The population of California is growing rapidly, partly because the climate is so pleasant. While this climate area covers only 2% of our land, it has 7% of our people. In its irrigated valleys all kinds of crops can be grown.

10. Hawaii has a pleasant climate. Because it is surrounded by the warm waters of the Pacific Ocean, it is always warm. Summer temperatures are always near 80°, and it is never cold in the winter. Like the people of Miami, Florida, Hawaiians need not worry about having heat in their homes. In their fertile fields the farmers of Hawaii raise sugar cane, pineapples and other tropical fruits.

UNDERSTANDING WHAT YOU HAVE READ

1. **Which of the following questions are answered in this chapter?**
a. Why is the Pacific Coast climate so wet?
b. What is the tundra?
c. Where does the Gulf Stream begin?

2. **The main idea of *paragraph 6* is to describe:**
a. the Rocky Mountains.
b. how the Rockies affect rainfall.
c. the wet winds from the Gulf of Mexico.

3. **The Pacific Coast has a:**
a. marine climate.
b. humid-subtropical climate.
c. humid-continental climate.

4. **Most of northern Canada is:**
a. taiga.   b. steppe.   c. desert.

5. **The inner plains have cold winters and hot summers because they are:**
a. close to the equator.
b. open to the winds from the Arctic.
c. far from the effects of the oceans.

6. **The western part of the Great Plains is dry because:**

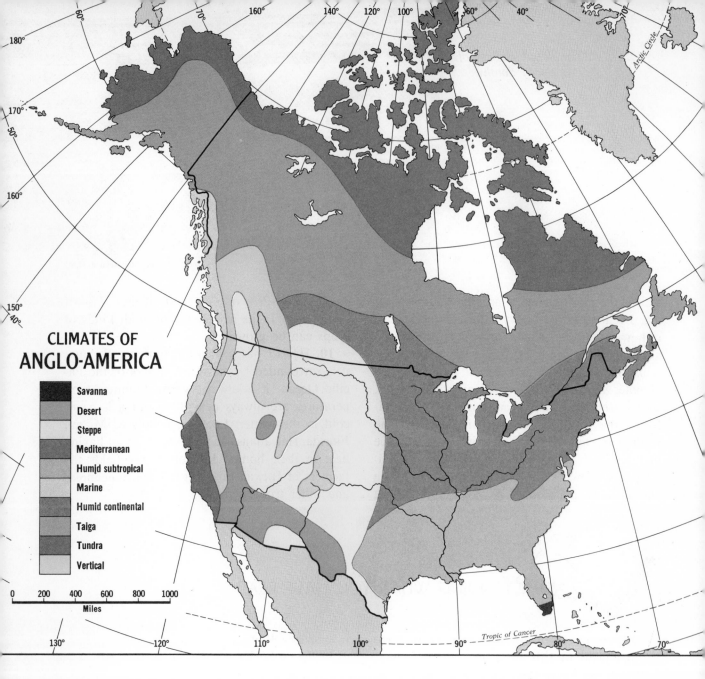

CLIMATES OF ANGLO-AMERICA

- Savanna
- Desert
- Steppe
- Mediterranean
- Humid subtropical
- Marine
- Humid continental
- Taiga
- Tundra
- Vertical

0 200 400 600 800 1000
Miles

a. it lies too far north.

b. it lies near the cold Pacific currents.

c. rain-bearing winds are blocked by mountains.

7. In *paragraph 2*, the expression " 'upstairs' of Anglo-America" refers to:

a. northern Canada.

b. the top of the Rocky Mountains.

c. the winds from the Gulf of Mexico.

8. "The spring *thaw* brings floods to the mountain streams." Refer to paragraph 3. What is the best meaning of *thaw*?

a. unexpected snows.

b. warming of lands.

c. frozen soil.

78

DEVELOPING IDEAS AND SKILLS

Map # 12—Climates of Anglo-America

Do You Agree or Disagree? Give reasons for your answers.

1. All of the taiga lies within the borders of Canada.
2. Both the United States and Canada have an area of vertical climate.
3. The marine climate is located on the western coast of Anglo-America.
4. Large water areas of Canada are found in the tundra climate.
5. The humid-continental climate is found only in Canada.
6. The steppe is found largely west of 100° longitude.
7. The smallest climate area in Anglo-America is the Mediterranean climate.
8. The southeastern coast of the United States has a humid-subtropical climate.
9. The marine climate is found chiefly in the high latitudes.
10. The humid-subtropical climate is found mainly north of 50° latitude.

SUMMING UP

A. Below are the names of seven climatic regions. Tell whether these regions are found in: 1) Canada only, 2) the United States only or 3) both the United States and Canada. Write "C" for Canada, "U.S." for United States or "B" for both. Do not write in this book.

__tundra   __Mediterranean
__humid continental   __taiga
__desert   __humid subtropical
__marine

B. Match the climates in Column A with the items in Column B.

COLUMN A	COLUMN B
__1. marine	a. Cold land without trees.
__2. tundra	b. Wettest part of the United States.
__3. Mediterranean	c. Where most people of Anglo-America live.
__4. humid continental	d. Temperatures are rarely below 80°.
__5. taiga	e. Region of great forests.
	f. Dry summers, mild and moist winters.

FOLLOW UP

Plan a trip to one of these places in Anglo-America: Quebec, Canada; Fairbanks, Alaska; Denver, Colorado; New Orleans, Louisiana; Chicago, Illinois; Los Angeles, California. In your plan, try to include these items:

1. The season in which you would make the trip.
2. The clothes you would take.
3. The sports you would expect to play.
4. Differences in homes that you might see.
5. The best kind of travel, if you went by land.
6. The kind of climate you would find.
7. How people of that area probably make a living.
8. What products could be bought.

CHAPTER 4

History Has Made Us Friends

PROBLEM: How have we grown from colonies to free nations?

READING FOR A PURPOSE:
1. Who were the first people in Anglo-America?
2. What European countries first settled this region?
3. When did the United States reach from coast to coast?

1. Tribes of Indians and Eskimos lived in Anglo-America long before white men came. The Indians lived along the great rivers, on the plains and in the woodlands. The Eskimos lived far to the north along the shores of the Arctic Ocean. As white settlers came from Europe in greater and greater numbers, they pushed the Indians off the land to a point where most Indians now live on small reservations. The Indians could not hold their hunting and farming grounds against the guns and machines of the newcomers. The Indians, however, did make many contributions to farming in Anglo-America. They gave the white man Indian corn or maize, the white potato, tobacco, beans, pump-kins, tomatoes and other foods.

2. When Columbus came to the New World in 1492, the news led other explorers to come to Anglo-America. The first European power to explore the new country was Spain. The Spanish explorer Ferdinand de Soto marched across the southeastern part of the United States in 1539. He discovered the Mississippi River. Francisco de Coronado explored the mountains, deserts and plains of our south-west in 1540. The city of St. Augustine, Florida, was founded in 1565; Santa Fe, New Mexico, was settled in 1609. The Spanish left their ways of living on these and other parts of our country.

3. French interest in the New World began in the sixteenth century. In 1524, Giovanni da Verrazano sailed under the flag of France, exploring the coast of North America. He was looking for a short route to Asia. In 1534, Jacques Cartier sailed up the St. Lawrence River, finding land that was rich in fur-bearing animals. In 1608, Samuel de Champlain founded Quebec, the first permanent French settlement in the New World. The colony was known as New France. The French explored the nearby waterways in search of furs and claimed all the lands surrounding them. In 1682, La Salle reached the mouth of the Mississippi and claimed the river valley for France.

4. Only five years after Columbus' voyage, John Cabot sailed from England and explored the eastern coast of North America. British settlers came to stay in America in the early 1600's. The first settlement was made farther south along the Atlantic Coast in the present state of Virginia. The British gradually established thirteen colonies along the eastern coast of the United States. Most people in these colonies were farmers. The farms were small in the northern part of the colonies, but they were much larger in the South where tobacco was grown. In order to help work the tobacco fields, Negroes were brought to the South in 1619. In 1670, the English explored the land around Hudson Bay in northern Canada. They set up trading posts. They wanted a share of the fur business as well.

Cartier explores the St. Lawrence River.

5. The French built forts and trading posts along the Great Lakes and in the Ohio and Mississippi River valleys. The English colonists also wanted to settle the fertile farm lands of the Ohio Valley. Before long, there was a war between England and France over the Ohio Valley. After several years of fighting, the French lost a great battle to the English near Quebec. This war ended in 1763 with the French giving up their claim to New France, or Canada, and all the territory east of the Mississippi River. Although New France became a British colony, the French settlers were allowed to keep their own language and religion and the laws they brought from France.

6. In 1775, the thirteen American colonies began their fight for freedom from Great Britain. They finally won and a new nation was formed, the United States of America. The Americans thought that Canada would also fight against Britain for its freedom. An American army invaded Canada for this reason but was not successful. At this time, those colonists who remained loyal to England left for Canada. The English-speaking people in Canada now began to outnumber the French.

7. There was peace between the United States and Canada until 1812. At that time some of our lawmakers accused the British in Canada of giving guns to the Indians and urging them to attack our frontier in the West. In the war that followed, the United States forces again invaded Canada, and again they were turned back. Shortly after the war ended, the United States and Canada signed a treaty. They agreed not to build any forts along the Great Lakes. Later this agreement was extended to include the entire length of the 3,900-mile border between the United States and Canada. Such trust and friendship between neighboring nations cannot be found anywhere else in the world.

8. From 1803 to 1853, the American frontier moved westward until it reached the Pacific coast. In 1803, the United States bought the Louisiana Territory from France. In 1819, Florida was acquired from Spain. Great Britain and the United States agreed in 1846 to divide the Oregon Territory at the 49th parallel. Two years later, the United States defeated Mexico

A wagon train on the Oregon Trail.

and gained a large area of land in the southwest. In 1853, the government bought a small strip of land in southern New Mexico and Arizona, the Gadsden Purchase. At that point our westward movement was slowed by the Civil War.

9. After the Civil War, the growth of our nation continued. Everywhere men were busy building factories, railroads and bridges. Steel mills were busy trying to keep up with the demand for steel. The mills were worked by people who had come to this country from other lands. Cities grew larger as people moved to homes near their work. Factories turned out more goods. The United States began to reach beyond her borders. Alaska was bought from Russia in 1867. In 1898, as a result of war with Spain, the United States obtained colonies in the Atlantic and Pacific Oceans.

10. About that time, Great Britain decided to give more freedom to Canada. In 1867, the British government created the Dominion of Canada. This was a union of four eastern provinces—Quebec, Nova Scotia, Ontario and New Brunswick. They joined to form a new nation that had the right to govern itself. The eastern provinces wanted Canada to reach to the Pacific coast like the United States. After a transcontinental railroad was built, more settlers began to move westward. In 1931, Great Britain allowed Canada complete self-government.

U.S. Signal Corps

American forces at the battle of St.-Mihiel, France.

11. The United States and Canada have become fast friends. Soldiers of the two countries fought together in World War I. Canada declared war on Japan when the United States' base at Pearl Harbor was attacked in 1941 and was our strong ally throughout World War II. Both nations are members of the North Atlantic Treaty Organization (NATO). Canada and the United States cooperated in building the St. Lawrence Seaway, which makes it possible for ocean-going ships to reach the Great Lakes. Both nations are working together to keep the Anglo-American region safe from enemy attack.

U.S. Signal Corps

American troops landing in France during World War I.

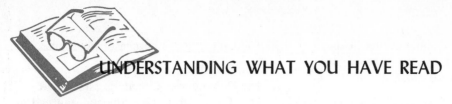

UNDERSTANDING WHAT YOU HAVE READ

1. **Which of the following questions are answered in this chapter?**
   a. Where were the early French settlements in Anglo-America?
   b. Who was John Macdonald?
   c. Why did the first Europeans come to the New World?

2. **The main idea of *paragraph 9* is to describe:**
   a. the growing demand for steel.
   b. how the United States reached the Pacific coast.
   c. the growth of the United States after the Civil War.

3. **The French came to the New World in search of:**
   a. furs.
   b. religious freedom.
   c. a place to build a canal from the St. Lawrence.

4. **The French lost Canada as a result of:**
   a. the American Revolution.
   b. a seven-year war with England.
   c. the War of 1812.

5. **Why did the United States invade Canada during our war for freedom from Great Britain?**
   a. We wanted to annex Canada to the United States.
   b. We wanted complete possession of the St. Lawrence River.
   c. We thought Canada would join us in our fight for freedom.

6. **Canada became a self-governing nation:**
   a. about the same time the United States became independent.
   b. in 1931.
   c. shortly after our Civil War.

7. **Another meaning for *maize* as used in paragraph 1 is:**
   a. corn.   b. guns.   c. vegetables.

8. **In paragraph 10, the word *transcontinental* means:**
   a. long and difficult.
   b. across Canada from coast to coast.
   c. modern and western.

DEVELOPING IDEAS AND SKILLS

Picture Symbols

These pictures should help you to recall parts of the chapter you have read. Can you tell the main idea of each picture? In what paragraph did you find the answer for each?

SUMMING UP

In each group below are listed three events in the history of Anglo-America. Arrange the three events in each *in the order in which they took place*.

A. 1. British and French dispute the Ohio Valley.
2. British gain Canada.
3. British and French fight a war, 1756-1763.

B. 1. The United States acquires Florida.
2. The United States obtains territory from Mexico.

3. The United States purchases Louisiana.

C. 1. Canada gains her full freedom.
2. The Dominion of Canada is established.
3. The Canadian transcontinental railroad is built.

D. 1. The United States buys Alaska.
2. The United States goes to war with Spain.
3. The United States and Canada take part in World War I.

FOLLOW UP

Using a history book or other reference work, find the answers to these questions about the history of the United States and Canada.

1. What European nations explored the east coast of both the United States and Canada?
2. Where in each country are there signs of French ways of living?
3. What ideas about government did both the United States and Canada get from Europe?
4. How did immigrants help each nation grow?
5. How did each nation grow in size? What explorers reached the west coast in each country?
6. How did both countries treat the Indians?
7. How was railroad building helpful to both countries?
8. In what other ways have these two nations cooperated, in addition to those mentioned in this chapter?

CHAPTER 5

The People of the United States and Canada

PROBLEM: Who are the Anglo-Americans?

READING FOR A PURPOSE:

1. How many people live in the United States and Canada?
2. Where do most of the people of Canada live?
3. What standard of living do Anglo-Americans enjoy?

1. There are more than 190 million people living in the fifty states of the United States. Our country ranks fourth in world population. While there are great cities in the Far West and in the South, most of the people live in our northeastern states. Our population is growing very fast today because the high standard of living allows us to live longer. However, our nation is not overcrowded because it is so large.

2. All the people of the United States except the Indians are immigrants or descendants of immigrants. Americans have come from all over the world. They have settled throughout the entire nation. In our Pacific Coast states there are many Chinese and Japanese. In the Southwest and in southern California, people from Mexico have come to live. In the cities of the East are large numbers of people from Puerto Rico. There are 22 million colored people in the United States, most of whom are Negro. There are Protestants, Catholics, Jews—members of every religion.

3. For a long time most Americans lived on farms. Today most of our people (almost 90%) live in towns and cities where they can work in factories, offices and stores. This movement to the cities is called *urbanization*. It has caused many problems. There is a growing need for more housing; many cities have overcrowded slum areas. Many of our colored peoples have been crowded into poor sections of large cities because of discrimination against them in housing and jobs. Enough water must be provided for people to drink and for factories to use. There is a need for more schools. People who are out of work must have help. Much of the air in the cities is poisoned by gases that come from the thousands of autos and factories. Crime is also a serious problem of the cities.

4. The people of the United States have the highest standard of living in the world. Our people are working shorter hours, receiving higher pay and gaining better working condi-

A New York supermarket. People in Anglo-America have a high standard of living.

UNATIONS

National Film Board of Canada

An Eskimo mother with her child.

190 million people living in the United States, which is smaller in size than Canada!

7. Most Canadians live in large cities in the southern part of the country near the U.S. border. The soil is fertile here and the climate warmer than in the rest of Canada. Aside from the land near the United States, Canada is largely a cold wilderness inhabited by a few Indians, Eskimos, fur trappers, loggers, miners and fishermen. All of the large cities of Canada are in the southern part of the country. Toronto, Montreal, Ottawa and Quebec are large cities of the St. Lawrence-Great Lakes region.

8. One-half of Canada's people are of English descent. One-third of the people of Canada are of French descent. Most French-speaking people live in the province of Quebec. Most are Roman Catholics, while the majority of the English are Protestants. The rest of the Canadian people are Indians and immigrants from different countries of Europe. The Indians live on lands set aside for them by the government. In the far north is the land of the Eskimo.

9. More Canadians work in mills and factories than on farms. Many work in mines, in the forests and on fishing boats. The manufacture of wood pulp employs the most workers. Like most Americans, most Canadian people enjoy a high standard of living.

10. Most Canadian boys and girls go to school, as in the United States. Nearly all the people enjoy the benefits of free public education. The

tions. We have more radios and television sets, refrigerators, automobiles, washing machines, telephones and other labor-saving machines than any other nation. We have a great supply of good food of all kinds. Most of our people have enough pure water. Because of our health and medical care, the average person in the United States can expect to live to be 70 years of age.

5. We have free public schools for all our people because we know that a nation governed by its people must have educated citizens. Anyone who does not understand what he is voting for cannot make wise decisions. Schooling is free so that the children of poor families can have the same opportunities as those of rich families.

6. Compared with the United States and most other nations of the world, Canada has very few people. There are slightly more than nineteen million people in Canada. This number is about the same as the number of people in New York State. Compare this, too, with the more than

Education has always been important in the U.S. and Canada.

towns and cities have large modern schools. The subjects taught are like those that a child in the United States might study. In Quebec there are two kinds of tax-supported schools: the Roman Catholic in which the children speak French and the Protestant schools in which English is spoken. Both French and English are official languages in Canada.

UNDERSTANDING WHAT YOU HAVE READ

1. Which of these questions are answered in this chapter?

a. How did the French and English come to settle Canada?
b. What religions are practiced by the people of Anglo-America?
c. Why is free education important to the people of Anglo-America?

2. The main idea of *paragraphs 7 through 9* is to describe:

a. where Canadian people live and work.
b. the religions of the Canadian people.
c. the workers of northern Canada.

3. The United States and Canada are different in that there is a large:

a. French population in the United States.
b. Negro population in the United States.
c. Indian population in Canada.

4. The United States has:

a. a larger population than Canada.
b. a smaller population than Canada.
c. about the same population as Canada.

5. A majority of the people of Canada live near the United States border because:

a. the large cities are located there.
b. the climate is milder.
c. the northern part of Canada has few resources.

6. Education is important to the people of the United States and Canada because:

a. people who have come from other countries have had no education.
b. in the past, only the rich have had education.
c. it is necessary if the people are to run their governments wisely.

7. *Immigrants* are people who:

a. come from other lands.
b. work in factories.
c. work in the government.

8. In *paragraph 3*, the word "discrimination" means:

a. joining together.
b. treated differently.
c. opportunity for.

DEVELOPING IDEAS AND SKILLS

Pictograph # 2—Population, Area and Standard of Living of Anglo-America

1. Is the standard of living in Canada high or low compared with that in the United States?
2. Is Canada as crowded as the United States?
3. Are the people of this region literate?
4. How long may the people of Canada expect to live?
5. What facts tell you the standard of living of the people of Canada and the U.S.?
6. How does Canada compare with the United States in size?

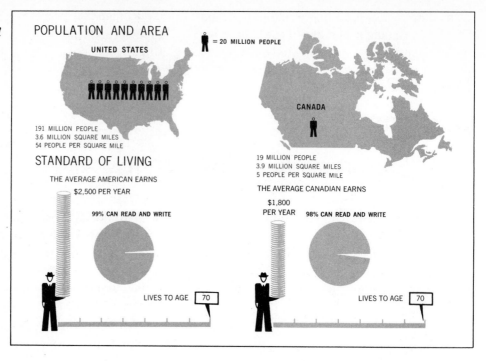

*Pictograph # 2—
Population, Area and
Standard of Living of
Anglo-America*

POPULATION AND AREA

= 20 MILLION PEOPLE

UNITED STATES

191 MILLION PEOPLE
3.6 MILLION SQUARE MILES
54 PEOPLE PER SQUARE MILE

CANADA

19 MILLION PEOPLE
3.9 MILLION SQUARE MILES
5 PEOPLE PER SQUARE MILE

STANDARD OF LIVING

THE AVERAGE AMERICAN EARNS

$2,500 PER YEAR

99% CAN READ AND WRITE

LIVES TO AGE 70

THE AVERAGE CANADIAN EARNS

$1,800
PER YEAR   98% CAN READ AND WRITE

LIVES TO AGE 70

SUMMING UP

Tell whether the following items refer to the *United States only, Canada only* or *both the United States and Canada.*

1. Large population
2. Good medical care
3. Many schools
4. Two official languages
5. Large Negro population

6. High standard of living
7. Many people living in cities
8. Large French population
9. Cities in St. Lawrence Valley
10. Many factory workers

FOLLOW UP

In the following, place before each statement the word that makes the statement correct: *All, Most, Some, A Few.*

1. . . . people in Canada are French-speaking.
2. . . . people of Canada live near the United States border.
3. . . . children go to school in Canada.
4. . . . people of Canada live in the northern provinces.
5. . . . people in our western states are Chinese or Japanese.
6. . . . people in Canada live in towns and cities.
7. . . . colored people in the United States are Negroes.
8. . . . people in Canada and the United States may expect to live to be 70 years of age.
9. . . . people of Canada are members of the Catholic religion.
10. . . . people in the United States work on farms.

CHAPTER 6

Two Democratic Governments

PROBLEM: How are the United States and Canada governed?

READING FOR A PURPOSE:
1. How is Canada governed?
2. What is a prime minister?
3. How are the powers of the United States government divided?

1. Canada is divided into ten provinces and two territories, the Northwest Territory and the Yukon Territory. Each province has its own government. The capital of the Canadian national government is the city of Ottawa. While our government is based on our Constitution, Canada's form of government is based on the British North America Act of 1867 and its changes since then.

2. The laws for the people of Canada are made by Parliament. The Canadian Parliament is made up of two lawmaking houses. One of these is called the Senate and the other is the House of Commons. The House of Commons is the more powerful body. Its members serve for five years unless an election is called sooner. Their chief duty is to make laws. Members of the Senate are named for life by the prime minister. They have little power in making laws.

3. The chief officer of the Canadian government is the prime minister. The House of Commons chooses the prime minister. He is usually the leader of the political party that has the most members in the House. The prime minister selects members of his party to be his advisors, his "cabinet." They plan most of the bills that are brought before Parliament. In this and other ways they are not like an American President's cabinet.

4. The prime minister stays in office only so long as most of the members of the House of Commons support him. If a majority of the House votes against him, he and his cabinet must resign or leave office. He can call for a new election; then the Canadian people may vote for new representatives in the House of Commons or re-elect the same members. Most of the time the prime minister can depend on the support of Parliament. (A President of the United States cannot always count on the support of Congress to pass the laws that he wants.)

5. The courts of Canada explain and uphold the laws and protect the rights of the people. The highest court in Canada is the Supreme Court. It meets at Ottawa. Each province has its own governor and its own lawmaking bodies.

6. While Canada has its own government and makes its own laws, it is also a member of the British Commonwealth of Nations. The king or queen of Great Britain is also king or queen of Canada. The people of Canada are citizens of both Canada and the British Commonwealth. The Queen appoints a governor-general who represents her in Parliament. He has little power.

7. The United States is divided into fifty states. Each state has its own government. The capital of our national government is Washington, D.C. The basis for our government is the Constitution, which was written in 1787. It set up a *federal* system that divided power between the national government and the states. Unlike

A Vermont town meeting, where the people make their opinions known to their lawmakers.

the Canadian government, the powers of our national government are divided among three separate branches: the legislative, the executive and the judiciary. Each branch has certain powers.

8. The President is the head of the *executive* or law-enforcing branch of the U.S. government. He is elected for a term of four years. He may be elected only twice. The executive branch enforces the laws passed by Congress. The President is Commander-in-chief of the Army, Navy and Air Force. He may either sign or veto (disapprove) bills passed by Congress. He is helped in his duties by a cabinet, which he appoints. The members of the cabinet do not have to be members of Congress.

9. Congress is the *legislative* or lawmaking branch of the government. As in the Canadian Parliament, there are two houses of Congress, the Senate and the House of Representatives. There are two Senators from each state. They hold office for six years. Every two years, one-third of the Senate is elected. The House of Representatives has many more members. They are elected for two-year terms. Congress has some very important powers, such as the power to tax, the power to borrow money and the power to declare war.

10. The third branch of our national govern-

ment is the *judiciary*. This branch is made up of the Supreme Court and lower courts. They help explain the laws passed by Congress and protect the rights of the people. Each state also has its own lawmaking bodies and courts.

11. Both peoples, American and Canadian, believe in democracy. Our citizens have the right to choose the officials who make our countries' laws. Each citizen has the right to speak out without fear. He can worship God in a church of his own choice. His children can go to free schools. He can choose his own job and his own home. This is the opposite of a *totalitarian* government. A totalitarian government is run by a few men who control the activities of the people. Under such a government the individual is important only as he serves the state. He does not have many of the rights that we have.

The Parliament Building in Ottawa, capital of Canada.

UNDERSTANDING WHAT YOU HAVE READ

1. Which of the following questions are answered in this chapter?
   a. How can our Constitution be changed?
   b. How does the Canadian government work?
   c. What are the powers of the President of the United States?

2. The main idea of this chapter is to describe:
   a. the powers of the prime minister.
   b. how power is divided among different branches of government.
   c. how the United States and Canada are governed by their people.

3. The head of the Canadian government is the:
   a. Queen of Great Britain.
   b. governor-general.
   c. prime minister.

4. The lawmaking branch of the Canadian government is called the:
   a. Congress.   b. Parliament.   c. Supreme Court.

5. How are the powers of the prime minister of Canada different from the powers of the President of the United States?
   a. The prime minister is the chief executive of his country.
   b. The prime minister is a member of the lawmaking body of his country.
   c. The prime minister appoints his own cabinet.

6. Why are both the United States and Canada called "democratic" countries?
   a. In neither country can the national government tax the people.
   b. In both countries the national government has little power.
   c. In both countries the people vote for the officials who make their laws.

7. Canada is divided into *provinces.* These are somewhat like our:
   a. states.   b. cities.   c. counties.

8. *Parliament* is the branch of government that:
   a. makes the laws.
   b. explains the laws.
   c. enforces the laws.

DEVELOPING IDEAS AND SKILLS

Pictograph # 3—The Government of the United States
Tell whether these statements are true or false.
1. Our national government is divided into three parts.
2. The President is the head of the branch that enforces the laws.
3. The President has twelve departments to help him.
4. The Senate has more members than the House of Representatives.
5. The Supreme Court is our highest court.
6. The Senate and the House of Representatives make the laws.
7. The powers of our government come from the people.
8. Matters concerning war and preparations for war are handled by the Defense Department.

Pictograph # 3—The Government of the United States

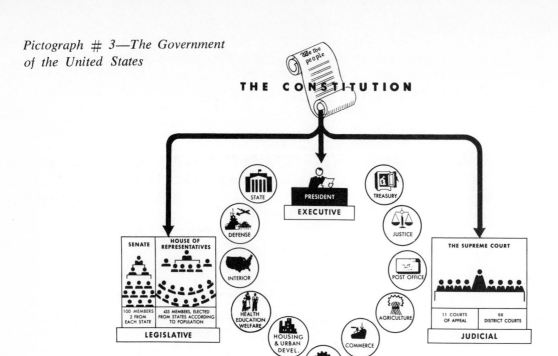

Pictograph # 4—The Government of Canada

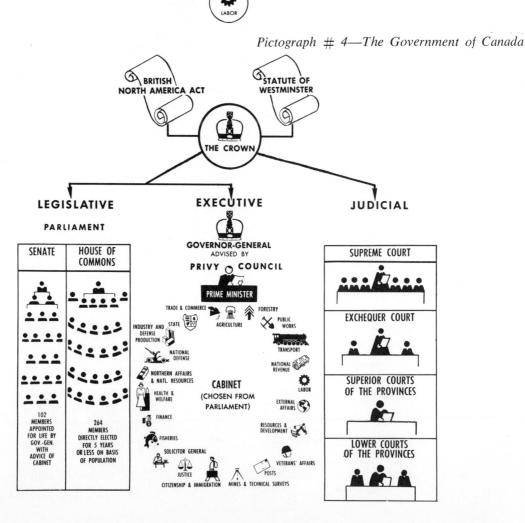

Pictograph # 4—The Government of Canada
Tell whether these statements are true or false.
1. The working head of the Canadian government is the prime minister.
2. Canada's Supreme Court has more members than the Supreme Court of the U.S.
3. Both the Senate and the House of Commons share in making laws.
4. Members of the prime minister's cabinet cannot be members of Parliament.
5. Members of the Senate are probably closer to the people and their needs than members of the House of Commons.
6. The cabinet of the prime minister has fewer departments than our President's cabinet.
7. Members of the House of Commons may serve terms of less than five years.
8. Of the entire Canadian government the highest authority is the ruler of Great Britain.

SUMMING UP

Fact or Opinion   Decide which of these are statements of fact and which are someone's opinion.
1. All nations should have the same form of government as we have in the United States.
2. The President is the head of the government of the United States.
3. Canada should not continue as a member of the British Commonwealth.
4. The Canadian system of electing the prime minister is better than our method of electing the President.
5. The Canadian governor-general has less power than the prime minister.
6. Only people who are able to read and write should be allowed to vote.
7. The powers of our national government are divided among three separate branches.
8. The provinces of Canada and the states of the United States have the power to make their own laws.

FOLLOW UP

Complete the following chart in your notebook.

		UNITED STATES	CANADA
1.	Chief Executive		
	a. Term of office		
	b. How he is chosen		
	c. How cabinet chosen		
2.	Lawmaking Body		
	a. Houses		
	b. How chosen		
3.	Highest court		
4.	Capital		

CHAPTER 7

Sources of Our Strength

PROBLEM: How did the United States become the industrial leader of the world?

READING FOR A PURPOSE:
1. Where is our chief iron mining region?
2. How is oil used in the United States?
3. Where are our remaining forest lands?

1. About 160 years ago, the United States was a country of farms, villages and towns. Most Americans were farmers living in small cabins. The whole family worked hard all day to provide the things that were needed. Today the United States is the most industrialized nation in the world. The American people have the highest standard of living in the world. Let us look at some of the reasons for this change.

2. First, we have many raw materials for industry, such as minerals and forest lands. The United States is first in the production of such minerals as iron ore, copper, lead, zinc and sulphur. Our greatest sources of iron ore are the open-pit mines of the Mesabi Range, near Lake Superior in Minnesota. This ore is easy to re-

move because it is near the surface of the earth. Alabama and Michigan are other iron-ore-producing states. But we use so much iron that we must import more from Canada, Venezuela and Sweden as well.

3. The United States produces about a third of the world's copper. Major copper mines are in Arizona, New Mexico, Utah and Montana. Lead, zinc, gold and silver are found in the Rocky Mountains. Most of our sulphur comes from two southern states, Texas and Louisiana. We also have large quantities of phosphate and potash, useful in making fertilizer. The United States is the world's leading manufacturer of aluminum. This modern metal is made from an ore called bauxite. The ore is imported from the South American countries of Surinam (Dutch Guiana), Guyana and Venezuela.

4. Those who live in our great cities may not realize just how much of the United States is still covered with forests. When America was

The workers of America.

Am. Iron and Steel Institute

A great open-pit iron ore mine of Minnesota.

An oil field in Texas.

settled, its great forests were cut down as the need for farm land grew. Wood was used for homes, ships and furniture. Despite this rapid removal, forests still cover almost a third of the country! Our richest forest lands are found in the Pacific Northwest, the South and New England. Most of the wood is used to make paper, plastics, furniture and houses. We use so much lumber for these products, however, that we must import more from our northern neighbor, Canada.

5. Second, the United States has many resources that provide power for its machines: coal, oil, natural gas and falling water. The United States produces more coal than any other nation except the Soviet Union. Most of our coal is mined in the Appalachian Mountains of Pennsylvania, Ohio, West Virginia and Kentucky. Coal is used to heat homes and to supply power for factories. It is used to smelt iron ore in the manufacture of steel. The leading nations of the world are those that are able to make large amounts of steel products.

6. Our chief source of power is oil. The United States has long led the rest of the world in oil production. About a third of the world's oil comes from the United States. This oil is found mainly in Texas, California, Oklahoma and Louisiana. Oil must be treated after it comes from the ground in order to remove the impurities in it. This process is called refining. One of the products of refining is gasoline.

Gasoline is used, of course, to power automobiles, trucks and airplanes. Diesel locomotives, which pull our long freight trains, are fueled with oil. In spite of our great supply, we need more than we produce in our own country. We import oil from Venezuela and the Middle East to make up the difference.

7. From the oil fields also comes our great supply of natural gas. When this gas first appeared along with the oil, it was wasted. Now, however, giant pipelines bring the gas from the southwestern states all the way to the northern and eastern parts of the country. Homes in Chicago and New York are heated with natural gas that comes from thousands of miles away.

8. The first factories in our nation were run by the waterfalls of New England. Since that time we have built dams on our leading rivers in order to make greater use of the power of falling water to make electricity. (The invention of turbines and generators has made it possible.) The TVA (Tennessee Valley Authority) has built a series of dams on the Tennessee River to provide electricity for people in seven states. The great Hoover Dam on the Colorado River has brought electric power to western states. On the Columbia River, the Grand Coulee and Bonneville Dams produce electricity for the farmers of the Northwest. The Niagara Falls Power Project is just one of the many hydroelectric plants throughout the country that provide light and heat for our great cities.

Hoover Dam on the Colorado River.

9. Since World War II, another source of power has been developed. This is the atom. Atomic energy comes from a mineral called uranium. The United States has been a leader in the development of atomic energy. The United States now has ships and submarines that use atomic power instead of oil, gasoline or electricity. These ships can travel for months without coming into port for refueling. Industries are now trying to find ways to use atomic power in manufacturing. We can expect that in the future our cities will be lighted and heated with power from the atom. This new source of energy will make our industrial strength even greater.

10. A third reason for our industrial leadership is the American people. They are the people who have invented our machines and have shown us how to make good use of our resources. They are the people who have provided money to build factories, buy machinery and start new businesses. They are the skillful men and women who work in the factories, in mines and on the farms to turn out the goods we need. They are the men who build and run our system of railroads, airlines and highways and make it possible to distribute our raw materials and finished goods. Lastly, they are all of us who buy the goods that are sold in our stores and supermarkets and thus keep our industries going.

UNDERSTANDING WHAT YOU HAVE READ

1. **Which of the following questions are answered in this chapter?**
   a. How is iron made into steel?
   b. What are our most important minerals?
   c. Where are our great water power projects?

2. **The main idea of *paragraphs 6 through 9* is to describe:**
   a. the importance of water power.
   b. the widespread use of oil and oil products.
   c. our great power resources.

3. **Our greatest source of iron ore is found in the:**
   a. Mesabi Range.
   b. Appalachian Mountains.
   c. Rocky Mountains.

4. **The United States leads the world in the production of:**
   a. tin.   b. coal.   c. oil.

5. Our great oil fields are located largely in the:

a. Northeast.　　b. Southwest.　　c. Southeast.

6. The United States is a leading steel-manufacturing nation because:

a. coal and iron ore are found near each other in this country.

b. we produce more coal than any other nation.

c. we had an early start in the use of water power.

7. Our water resources are useful because:

a. they are a source of power for homes, farms and factories.

b. they are a source of floods.

c. they are a source of atomic energy.

8. When oil is *refined*:

a. it is made into plastics.

b. impurities are removed.

c. it is used as fuel.

9. A *turbine* turns falling water into:

a. ice.　　b. steam power.　　c. electricity.

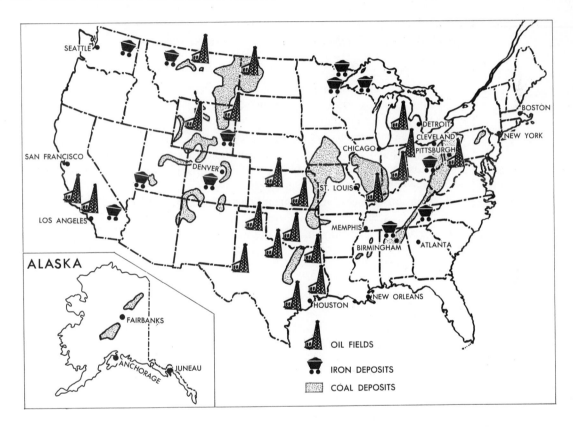

Map # 13—Iron, Coal and Oil Resources of the United States

DEVELOPING IDEAS AND SKILLS

Map # 13—Iron, Coal and Oil Resources of the United States.

Tell whether these statements are *true* or *false*.

1. The largest deposits of iron ore are found near the Great Lakes.
2. The chief coal fields are east of the Mississippi River.
3. The largest oil fields are in the Southwest.
4. There are no oil fields on the West Coast.
5. Coal is found in almost every state in the nation.
6. Texas has large reserves of both iron and oil.
7. Large amounts of iron are found in the Southeast.
8. Many coal fields are found in mountain regions.
9. Most of the large cities are near mineral resources.

SUMMING UP

Complete the following outline in your notebook. Enter *three* topics under each of the headings.

How the United States Became a Leading Industrial Nation

A. The United States has great natural resources.
B. Our sources of power are highly developed.
C. Human resources are our great strength.

FOLLOW UP

Tell whether these statements are true or false. The underlined words make the statements true or false. If a statement is false, what words would you place in it to make it true?

1. Our leading gold and silver mines are located in the Appalachian Mountains.
2. Aluminum is made from an ore called bauxite.
3. Oil must be smelted to get gasoline.
4. Giant hydroelectric plants have been built along the Tennessee River.
5. The United States imports much wood and wood products from France.
6. Most of our coal is mined in the western highlands.
7. Our chief source of power is oil.
8. Iron ore and coal are most important in manufacturing steel.
9. Our greatest iron ore pits are found in the state of Pennsylvania.
10. Arizona is a leading state in the production of copper.

CHAPTER 8

Getting and Spending

PROBLEM: How do we satisfy our needs and wants? How is our economic life organized?

READING FOR A PURPOSE:
1. What is capitalism?
2. What is profit?
3. How does the government help us to get the goods we need?

1. Raw materials, much power and skilled workers are needed for manufacturing. But these alone would not make the United States the leading industrial nation of the world. With only 6% of the world's people and 7% of the world's resources, we produce more goods and make greater use of our resources than any other people in the world. We believe this is caused by our way of making and selling goods to satisfy needs and wants. Our way of doing this is called *capitalism* or *free enterprise*.

2. Under capitalism the land, mines, factories and resources of the nation are owned by individuals—not by the government. They are *private property*. The person who owns property uses it as he sees fit, provided he does not interfere with the rights of others. He may buy any goods he wants. He may sell any goods he produces. The prices he pays for the goods, and the prices at which he sells the goods, are decided by agreements he makes with other persons. The government does not tell him the cost of the goods he uses.

3. The American people have a *freedom of choice* in the kinds of work they want to do. A person may run his own business or work for another person. He may try to become a doctor, a lawyer, a plumber or a carpenter. The choice is his to make. He can quit his job, and he does not have to give any reason for doing so. This freedom to choose one's life work is not found everywhere in the world.

4. Capitalism is a way of life in which a person runs a business or a shop with the idea of making a *profit*. Workers in a capitalist system try to get the most money for their labor. Owners of land and buildings try to get the best rentals. Businessmen try to sell their products for more than it cost to produce or obtain them. Americans believe that the desire to make a profit encourages people to work hard, to invent better methods of doing many kinds of work and to discover new products that people will buy.

5. When many people are working to make the same goods, *competition* is the result. For example, many factories make the same kind of product. Each manufacturer wishes to sell his product. These factories are in competition with each other. Americans believe that competition results in goods of high quality and low price. (The manufacturer who makes radios and sells them at a higher price than other manufacturers ask will not sell many radios. Either he must take less profit or he must learn how to make them at a lower cost. This helps the people who buy products.) Manufacturers *advertise* their goods because they want people to buy them. Our radio, television and billboard advertising are all attempts by manufacturers to sell their products. Advertising is necessary to the capitalist system.

6. Capitalism also depends upon *mass production*. This is a method that makes use of the *assembly line, division of labor* and *standardized parts*. Let us look at a modern automobile factory to see how mass production works. A line or belt runs from one end of the building to the other. At the beginning of this line are the frames of cars. The line is moving. As each car moves along, new parts are added to it by the workers. By the time the car reaches the end of the line, it has been put together or "assembled." Each worker along the assembly line has a separate job to do. This is called "division of labor," since the work is "divided up" among workers. In mass production the parts for a particular model of car are exactly alike for each car. These are called standardized parts. Today,

most factories use the methods of mass production to make all kinds of goods. It is the fastest and cheapest way to make many things.

7. Because of mass production, America's workers are paid more than those in any other country. For example, if a worker is paid $40 a day for an eight-hour day and turns out a hundred items, he is actually a cheaper worker than one from West Germany who is paid $20 a day and turns out forty items. In the first case the cost of each item is 40¢; in the second it is 50¢. American workers turn out more and cheaper goods because of their skill and greater use of machines. With higher wages, they are able to buy more goods.

8. Capitalism has also succeeded because of government help to different groups. From the

An assembly line in New Jersey. Our system depends on mass production.

beginning our government placed a tariff or tax on goods brought into the country. There are no taxes, however, on goods moving from one state to another. As a result there is a free flow of goods from one part of the nation to another. In the nineteenth century, the government encouraged railroad building. The government makes sure that all agreements or contracts are kept. In recent years, farmers have been paid to control their crop production. The government protects the rights of workers to join labor unions in which they can fight for better wages and working conditions.

9. At the same time the government has passed laws that affect the practices of industry. Laws have been passed to protect the American people from unsafe foods and medicines. The government has passed laws to end children's working in factories and to establish a basic level of wages. The communications industries such as radio, movies and television are carefully watched for fairness and decency. In this sense, free enterprise is not as "free" as one might think. It is not free to harm the people living under it.

10. As you can see, there is no one reason for our country's becoming the greatest manufacturing country in the world. We have a rich store of natural resources, power, skillful and inventive people and a vast system of transportation. All of these are brought together through capitalism.

UNDERSTANDING WHAT YOU HAVE READ

1. Which of the following questions are answered in this chapter?
a. What is mass production?
b. How is planning carried out in the United States?
c. What is meant by "freedom of choice"?

2. The main idea of this chapter is to describe:
a. how capitalism works.
b. how resources have made our nation strong.
c. the freedoms that Americans have.

3. Our workers are able to turn out many goods because of the greater use of:
a. machinery.
b. atomic energy.
c. hand labor.

4. Goods flow freely from one state to another because of:
a. government planning.
b. lack of tariffs.
c. airlines.

5. Our workers receive high wages because they:
a. are highly skilled.
b. have private property.
c. hope to make a profit.

6. Mass production is important because:
a. more goods are now made at home.
b. new minerals have been discovered.
c. more goods are produced at lower prices.

7. Another example of *competition* as described in paragraph 5 would be:
a. actors preparing to put on a play.
b. two basketball teams playing against each other.
c. workers doing different jobs on an assembly line.

8. Under *capitalism* there is:
a. private profit and competition.
b. government control over prices of goods.
c. control over manufactured products by the government.

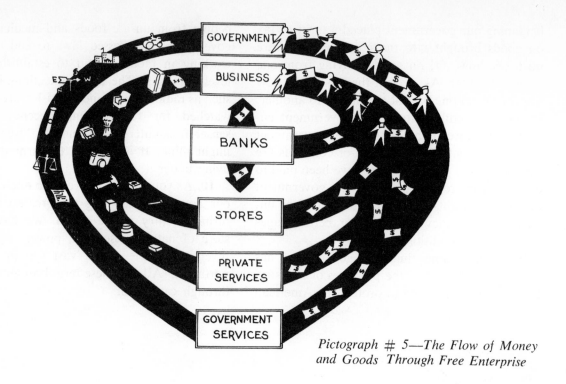

Pictograph # 5—The Flow of Money and Goods Through Free Enterprise

DEVELOPING IDEAS AND SKILLS

Pictograph # 5—The Flow of Money and Goods Through Free Enterprise

1. In this pictograph, people are receiving money as wages from government and business. The people must then give part of the money to the government. This is called paying _____.
2. What government services do we receive in exchange for the money we pay the government?
3. What private services can we buy with our money?
4. Businesses make goods that people want. How do the people obtain these goods?
5. What part do banks play in helping businesses and stores?
6. Where do banks get their money?

SUMMING UP

Pictograph # 6—The United States and the World

Tell whether these statements are true or false.

1. The United States has about half of the world's land area.
2. The United States has about 5% of the world's people.
3. The United States has more telephones and automobiles than the rest of the world.
4. The United States produces twice the amount of oil that the rest of the world does.
5. The United States has as much coal as all other countries in the world combined.
6. The United States has less than half of the possible electric power in the world.
7. The United States is a nation of both farms and factories.
8. For its size, the United States has a small share of the world's resources.

THE UNITED STATES AND THE WORLD

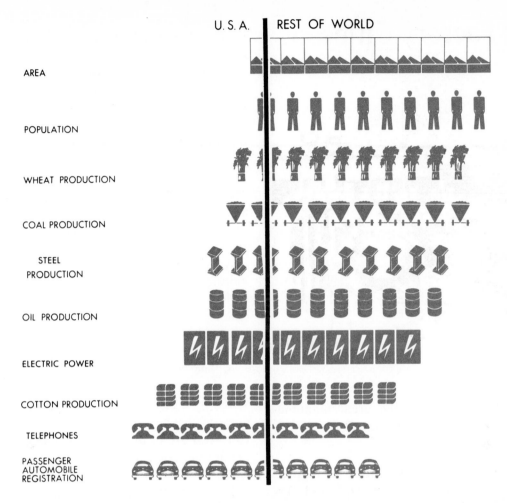

EACH SYMBOL EQUALS 10% OF TOTAL

Pictograph #6

FOLLOW UP

Making Inferences In our reading, many facts are given to us. From these facts we can draw conclusions. The following are some conclusions or inferences that you might make after reading this chapter. Tell whether these conclusions are correct or incorrect. Give reasons for your answers.

1. A storekeeper may keep his workers from joining a union.
2. There is one chief reason why the United States has the greatest factory system in the world.
3. Any person may start a factory on his property if he wants to do so.
4. Nearly all of our soap products are made by one large company.
5. The United States has a small share of the world's resources, but it has made greater use of its resources than any other nation.
6. The government cannot keep a person from becoming a doctor if he wants to be a doctor.
7. Freedom of choice does not always exist in a totalitarian society.
8. Many inventions are the result of a person's desire to make a profit.

CHAPTER 9

Our Factory Cities

PROBLEM: Where are the great manufacturing areas of the United States?

READING FOR A PURPOSE:
1. Where is our leading industrial region?
2. Why are cities like New York and Birmingham important?
3. What are our chief imports and exports?

1. As you have learned, an industrial region is an area in which many people make their living by manufacturing or turning raw materials into useful goods. The largest and most important manufacturing area in the United States—and in the world—is in the Northeast. This area reaches from Illinois to the Atlantic coast. In it are some of the largest coal mines in the world. In nearby Minnesota are the world's greatest iron mines. Throughout this area are supplies of coal and falling water for power. In addition, oil and natural gas are easily obtained from the Southwest.

2. The great manufacturing region of the Northeast has wonderful transportation facilities. The area is crisscrossed by highways, railroads, rivers, canals and lakes. (More than half the railroad track in the country is in the Northeast. The Great Lakes/St. Lawrence Seaway and the Ohio and Mississippi Rivers are great water highways.) Boats, barges and freight trains carry raw materials from mines to factories. Motor trucks, trains and riverboats carry the products of farms and factories to the cities and towns.

3. For all these reasons, there are both "heavy" industries and "light" industries in this area. (Iron and steel mills, auto and other factories that turn out heavy goods are known as "heavy" industries. Industries in which the products are light and not bulky are known as "light" industries.) The products of the factories in this region are almost endless: farm machinery and children's toys, railroad cars and finished clothing, ocean-going ships and pocket-sized cameras.

4. The largest cities in the United States are located in the Northeast. There are always reasons why a city grows up in a certain place; it does not happen by accident. The cities in the Northeast are of different kinds. Some are mining towns, some are factory cities or trading cities, some are capital cities and some are so large that they have many purposes. A few of the great industrial cities in the Northeast are New York, Chicago, Detroit, Cleveland and Pittsburgh. Farther south is Baltimore, while to the west is St. Louis.

5. New York is the largest city in the nation. It has the busiest harbor in the world. Because of its location on the Atlantic Ocean it has long been the best place to bring in goods from many parts of the world. From New York the products are carried to all parts of the nation by river, railroad or airplane. In addition to its being a great trading center, New York is a leading factory center. The chief industries in New York are printing and the manufacture of clothing and leather goods.

6. In the Northeast, Pittsburgh, Chicago and

Cleveland are leaders in the making of steel. Pittsburgh, where the Ohio River begins, is the greatest iron and steel center in North America. Most of its iron ore comes from Minnesota by huge ore boats and rail; coal is mined close by in the Appalachian highlands and is brought by river barges to the mills of Pittsburgh. The Chicago-Gary area, located on Lake Michigan, is another great iron and steel center. Iron ore and coal are brought to these cities over the Great Lakes. Because it is near the corn, wheat and cattle regions, Chicago is also a leader in flour milling and meat packing. From that city, grain, livestock and farm machinery are sent (usually by railroad) to all parts of the nation.

7. Cleveland, on Lake Erie, is a heavy steel producer. More iron ore is brought into Cleveland each year than into any other city in the world. Its coal comes from the Appalachians. Baltimore, on Chesapeake Bay, has one of the largest harbors in the world. The Appalachians supply the coal, but iron ore is imported. It is the only seacoast center that is also a leader in iron and steel manufacture. Detroit is the "auto city." It makes more than half the cars of the entire world! Detroit is located on the Detroit River, which is part of the Great Lakes water-

The steel mills at Dearborn, Michigan.

ways. Heavy materials like coal, iron and steel can be moved cheaply to Detroit by water.

8. Another important industrial region in the United States is in the South. The South has many advantages for industry. It has cheap

New York City.

water power, plenty of workers and large supplies of minerals such as coal, iron and oil. For a long time, there have been iron and steel mills in Alabama. Birmingham, Alabama, is sometimes called the "Pittsburgh of the South" because coal, iron and limestone for making steel are found nearby. There are also many new textile factories that turn the raw cotton of the South into ready-to-wear clothing. Many articles are also made of rayon, a silk-like fiber made from cotton and wood pulp. There is a growing number of chemical plants, oil refineries and other factories around the Gulf Coast. The chief cities in this area are Houston and New Orleans. Cotton, oil, rice and sugar cane are among the many products shipped from the port of New Orleans. Along its docks can be found banana and coffee boats from Latin America and oil tankers from the Middle East.

9. The western region of the United States, between the 100th meridian and the Rocky Mountains, is large in area but has few people because it is so dry. Since mining and cattle and sheep grazing are the chief occupations, there are few cities of great size. Denver, Colorado, at the foot of the Rocky Mountains, is the largest city in the area. Because of the ways people make a living near this city, Denver's industries include flour milling, meat packing and the manufacture of mining equipment and tools.

10. When we think of California we think of the "movies." Hollywood, a section of Los Angeles, is the center of the motion-picture industry. However, aircraft factories and oil refineries are also located in Los Angeles. California is now the third largest oil-producing state. Farther north is the great port of San Francisco. This city with its famous bay is a leading port for trade with Asia.

11. In the states of Oregon and Washington, forests provide the raw materials for paper manufacture. Fish canneries are found in many cities there and in northern California. Seattle is the leading seaport of the Pacific Northwest. This city is closer than any other large port to the Far East and Alaska.

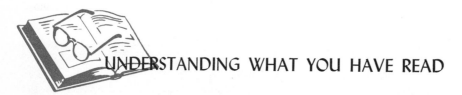

UNDERSTANDING WHAT YOU HAVE READ

1. **Which of the following questions are answered in this chapter?**
a. Why is the northeastern United States important?
b. How have we wasted our resources?
c. Why are industries found in certain places?

2. **The main idea of this chapter is to describe:**
a. the resources of the Northeast.
b. how goods are carried from place to place in the United States.
c. our great manufacturing centers.

3. **The most important manufacturing area** in the United States is located in the:
a. Far West.   b. South.   c. Northeast.

4. **The most important industry in the United States is:**
a. the manufacture of iron and steel products.
b. meat packing.
c. the manufacture of clothing.

5. **The Northeast is an important manufacturing area because:**
a. it is near the Pacific trade routes.
b. it has large deposits of coal, iron and limestone.
c. this is the leading oil and natural gas area of the nation.

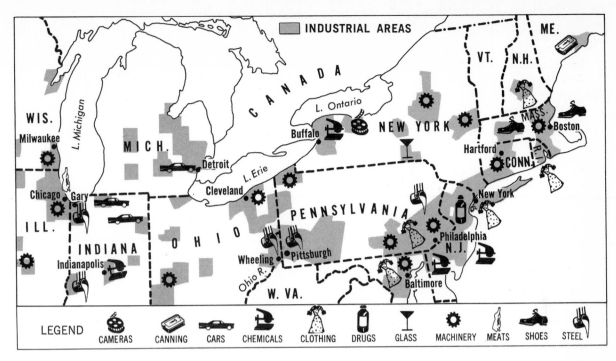

Map # 14—The Northeast: The Leading Industrial Region of the United States

DEVELOPING IDEAS AND SKILLS

Map # 14—The Northeast: The Leading Industrial Region of the United States

Tell whether these statements are true or false.

1. Almost every northeastern state has an important industrial area.
2. One area extends from Massachusetts all the way to Baltimore.
3. Pittsburgh and Wheeling are both steel cities.
4. Auto industry is centered around Philadelphia and Baltimore.
5. Waterways are close to the big industrial areas.
6. Textile manufacturing is most important near Chicago.

Can you answer these questions?

1. Why is machinery manufactured near Cleveland and Chicago?
2. Where are meat-packing plants located in the Northeast? Do you know why they are located there?
3. Where are the centers of the chemical industry?

SUMMING UP

Complete the following outline in your notebook.

The Northeast—North America's Workshop

A. Reasons for manufacturing in the Northeast.

    1.

    2.

    3.

    4.

B. Leading manufacturing cities.
    1.
    2.
    3.
    4.
C. Leading industries.
    1.
    2.
    3.

CHAPTER 10

The American Farmer

PROBLEM: How are the farmlands of the Northeast and South used?

READING FOR A PURPOSE:
1. Where is the corn belt?
2. What is extensive farming?
3. Where is cotton grown?

1. As you know, the United States is so large that the climate and land are not the same in all parts of the country. As a result, there are different farming regions. A farming region does not have a definite boundary like a state. The change from one kind of farming to another is gradual. Because of the differences in climate and soil, there are different ways of living and different farm products.

2. The United States has four main crop-producing regions: the Central Plains, the Great Plains, the southern coastal plains, and the valleys of the Pacific coast. The Central Plains are among the finest farm lands of the world. Many valuable crops are grown in this region. Food from these farms helps to feed people in the United States and in other parts of the world. Some farmers grow wheat; some grow corn; others raise dairy cows.

3. In the eastern part of the Central Plains the chief crop is corn. This is because the growing season is hot and moist. The soil is black and fertile. The almost flat land makes it easy for farmers to use machines to plant, cultivate and harvest their crops. The corn belt extends through the states of Indiana, Illinois, Iowa and parts of Ohio, Missouri, Kansas, Nebraska, South Dakota and Minnesota.

4. The farmer does not sell most of his corn. He feeds it to his animals—hogs and beef cattle. Then he sells the animals. The farmer uses his corn as feed because he expects to make more money from the sale of the meat than from the sale of the corn. Many of the beef cattle may not have been raised on the farms of the Central Plains. They probably came from the grasslands farther west. On the western ranches the cattle feed on grass which makes them grow large and strong. Then they are shipped to the corn belt for fattening. Wheat, oats, soybeans and alfalfa are often grown along with or rotated with the corn. (By rotating his crops, the farmer keeps the minerals in the soil.)

5. In the western part of the Central Plains is the great wheat belt. Here there is less rainfall. The wheat-growing region is divided into two parts. In the southern part of the wheat belt winters are not so cold as they are nearer

Beef cattle are shipped to the Illinois corn belt for fattening.

Standard Oil Co. (N.J.)

Canada. Wheat is planted in the fall, stays in the ground all winter and is harvested in July. This is called winter wheat. Kansas is the center of the winter-wheat belt. In the northern part the winters are very cold. Wheat is planted in the spring and it grows all summer long. This is the spring-wheat belt. The farmlands of North Dakota and Minnesota and the wheat farms of Canada north of these states form the greatest spring wheat area in the world. Wheat farms are much larger than the farms of the corn belt. Farm machinery can be used easily. This is *extensive* farming—farming with machines on a large scale. The United States is second only to the Soviet Union in wheat-growing.

6. Across the northern states, from Minnesota to New England, is a belt of dairy farms. The growing season here is short and cool. This cool, wet climate is good for growing hay. Farmers in this area keep herds of cattle and feed them the hay. As a result, milk, cheese, cream and butter are leading dairy products. Wisconsin alone produces half the cheese in the United States! Large cities in the northeastern states are a giant market for the products of dairy-belt farms.

7. The second of the great farming regions is found along the Atlantic and Gulf Coastal Plain. In the northern part of the Atlantic Plain the soils are rocky and sandy. This has made farming difficult. The early settlers turned to fishing, trading and shipbuilding to make a living. Today New England farmers grow fruit and raise dairy cattle. In the southern part of the plain the days are warmer and the growing season is longer. In the early history of our nation, tobacco, cotton and rice were the chief crops of the southern plain. Tobacco and cotton are still the leading farm crops of the South today.

8. The cotton belt reaches from the Carolinas west to the coastal lowlands of Texas. Cotton is our nation's most valuable cash crop. The best-known cotton farms are the large plantations along the lower Mississippi River Valley and the plains of Texas. Along these lands there is plenty of rain and sunshine, and the soil is fertile. The leading cotton-growing state is Texas. Mississippi and Arkansas rank behind Texas in the South. (California, using irrigated lands, is the second leading cotton-growing state.)

9. For a long time, the large cotton farms of the South were worked by tenant farmers and *sharecroppers*. A tenant farmer paid rent for the use of the land. A sharecropper, however, gave a share of his crops as rent to the owner of the land. The sharecroppers were both white and Negro. Under this system, the land was used year after year for the same crop so that the soil "wore out." Nutrients or minerals used up by the cotton were not replaced. This meant a smaller harvest and poorer crop each year. As

Tobacco being bought at an auction.

Liggett & Myers Tobacco Company

Irrigating young cotton plants in Texas.

Standard Oil Co. (N.J.)

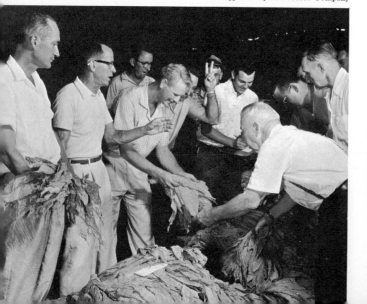

a result, southern farmers had the lowest income among farmers in our country.

10. Today most of the large cotton farms are worked by people who receive wages as in a factory. Large machines such as the "cotton-picker" are used in the fields. The plantation owner uses more fertilizer and plants fewer acres of cotton. In addition to cotton he may plant corn, soybeans, peanuts or other crops. He may also use some of his land as pasture for beef cattle. All these things keep his soil from "wearing out"; they put back the precious minerals so that the land can continue to be used.

11. Southern farmers are learning that they should not depend upon one crop for sale. With one crop, a bad harvest or low market price can bring ruin to a farmer. If he grows more than one crop, his chances for making money are better. Thus, along the hot, rainy coastal lands of Texas and Louisiana, rice and sugar cane are being raised. Tobacco, an important crop since 1619, is still a leading crop in North Carolina, Kentucky and Virginia. Like the cotton plant, tobacco wears out the soil. Therefore, peanuts are often rotated with tobacco. In Florida and southern Texas, large amounts of citrus fruits—oranges, grapefruit and lemons —are raised. With the coming of frozen foods and refrigerated railway cars and trucks, it is now possible to ship the produce of the South to markets thousands of miles away.

UNDERSTANDING WHAT YOU HAVE READ

1. **Which of the following questions are answered in this chapter?**
   a. How is cotton grown?
   b. How is southern farming changing?
   c. How is corn used by the farmers of the Midwest?

2. **The main idea of *paragraph 5* is to describe:**
   a. the winter-wheat areas of the United States.
   b. extensive farming in the United States.
   c. the wheat belt of the United States.

3. **The leading farm crop of the South is:**
   a. peanuts.   b. cotton.   c. citrus fruit.

4. **The leading crops of the inner plains are:**
   a. rice and soybeans.
   b. corn and wheat.
   c. potatoes and sugar beets.

5. **Corn is raised on the Central Plains because:**
   a. there is a warm and moist growing season.
   b. it is the chief food of the American people.
   c. money is made from the sale of corn oil.

6. **Different kinds of wheat are grown in the Central Plains because:**
   a. land is more fertile than it is in the South.
   b. factories that supply machinery are found in the cities of the plains.
   c. there are differences in climate.

7. **A farmer who depends on *extensive farming* will:**
   a. grow one crop.
   b. raise crops and animals.
   c. use a great deal of machinery.

8. **_Citrus fruits_ include:**

a. pears and apples.
b. oranges and grapefruit.
c. peaches and strawberries.

9. In *paragraph 11* a sentence states, "Therefore, peanuts are often rotated with tobacco." This sentence means that:

a. peanuts are planted among the tobacco plants.
b. peanuts are planted in place of tobacco.
c. peanuts are planted some years, tobacco in other years.

DEVELOPING IDEAS AND SKILLS

Photograph Study
This photograph should help you to recall parts of the chapter you have just read. Can you tell the main idea of the photograph? Where in the chapter is it described?

Standard Oil Co. (N.J.)

SUMMING UP

Complete the following chart in your notebook.

Central Plains		Southland
	Climate	
	Chief Crops	
	Methods of Farming	
	Other Products	

FOLLOW UP

Do You Agree or Disagree? Give the reasons for your answers.

1. Corn is the only crop raised on the Central Plains.
2. Most of the wheat and corn grown in the United States is harvested by hand labor.
3. Most of the corn raised in this country is used as food for animals.
4. The lands of the corn and wheat belt are level plains.
5. All the farms in the South are plantations.
6. Most cotton in the South is grown on irrigated land.
7. Cotton is only one of many important crops grown in the South.
8. A sharecropper owns the land that he farms.

CHAPTER 11

The Golden West

PROBLEM: How is farming done on the dry and sunny lands?

READING FOR A PURPOSE:
1. Where is the chief cattle-raising region of the United States?
2. Why is the Central Valley important?
3. How are many western fruit crops harvested?

1. West of the 100th meridian (Central Plains) are the dry grasslands or steppes. Most of the area receives between ten and twenty inches of rain each year. Some parts receive more rainfall than others. The eastern part of the steppes is known as the Great Plains. It extends north and south through the United States and into Canada. On the western edge of the Great Plains lie the Rocky Mountains. Not too many people live in this region because of its dry climate.

2. Since it has so little rainfall, most of the Great Plains is better suited to grazing than farming. Huge herds of cattle roam the Great Plains. The land has been fenced off into ranches. The largest of these ranches are found in the South. Texas is the leading cattle-raising state. There cowboys care for the large cattle herds.

3. There are a few farmers on the Great Plains. The farms are scattered throughout the area. The farmers draw water from rivers and streams that flow from the Rocky Mountains— the Colorado, Arkansas and Platte. The government has built dams along these rivers to hold the water back. Many canals carry water from these reservoirs to the fields. The chief crops grown on these irrigated lands are alfalfa, wheat, sugar beets, vegetables and fruits. The United States is one of the world's leading producers of sugar beets. The Idaho potato is also grown on irrigated land.

4. West of the Great Plains are the drier lands of the Colorado Plateau and the Great Basin, west of the Rockies. This is sheep-raising country. In fact, there are more sheep than people in Montana, Wyoming and Utah! Sheep can get along without much water for long periods of time. Because sheep have "split" lips, they can eat the shorter grasses and shrubs that grow there. Sheep ranches in the highlands are very large because the animals must roam over a larger area in order to find enough to eat.

5. Farther north is the Columbia Plateau. This is a grazing and farming area. Herds of sheep and cattle graze on the grasslands. There are also farmers who raise their crops by two methods, dry farming and irrigation. The dry farmer plants crops that can be raised with little rainfall. He lets some of his fields lie *fallow* (not planted) every year. The farmer waits a year or two before planting a new crop. During the time that a field is fallow, the rain that falls is stored in the ground. Dry farmers usually plant wheat and alfalfa.

6. The fourth great farming region is the coastal area of the Pacific. Because of the different climates, there are two main farming areas, the valleys of California and the rainy lands of Oregon and Washington. In the coastal

valleys of southern California the summers are long, hot and sunny. The winters are mild and rainy. Much of the soil is fertile and many different kinds of crops can be raised. In many places the land is easy to cultivate with machinery because it is almost flat. California has two important farming sections: the Great or Central Valley in the central part of the state and the coastal valleys, mostly in the south.

7. The Great Valley forms an oval 450 miles long. This valley has become one of the richest farming areas in the world. Valley farms get their water from streams rising in the Sierra Mountains. These streams have been dammed. The valley farmers raise almost every crop known in the United States: citrus fruits, nuts, vegetables, grains and cotton. Some farmers specialize in growing grapes that are dried to make raisins.

8. The Imperial Valley in the southernmost part of California was once a desert. It gets practically no rain. However, irrigation from the Colorado River has made it a rich farming land. A great variety of crops is grown here: lettuce, alfalfa, cotton, dates and grapes for wine. A large part of the oranges and lemons eaten in the nation comes from the valleys southeast of Los Angeles. Sugar beets are another product of the irrigated valleys of California.

9. While there are many small farms, most of the fruit is grown on large farms with 1,000 or more acres. They are like "factories in the field." In the past, workers have come from other parts of the nation and from Mexico to help during the busy season. In the winter, these workers may pick lettuce in the Imperial Valley near the Mexican border. In the summer, they may move northward to pick oranges on

Standard Oil Co. (N.J.)

A sheep ranch in Texas.

the ranches near Los Angeles. From there they travel farther north and by fall are returning southward again for the cotton harvest in the Central Valley. The workers take their families with them. The families usually live in a camp set up for them near the farms where they find work. The children have very little schooling because they are always on the move. These people are called *migratory workers.*

10. Farther north along the Pacific coast are the marine lands of Oregon and Washington. While much of the land is covered with mountains and forests, there are fertile farming areas. The cool, rainy climate is good for growing apples and berries and raising dairy cattle. Grains and vegetables are also grown.

11. Some 2,000 miles across the Pacific, the farmers of Hawaii produce two main crops: sugar cane and pineapples. These crops are grown on plantations. The climate is warm all year round and there is plenty of rainfall. Most of the pineapples we eat come from our fiftieth state, Hawaii.

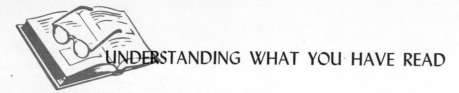

UNDERSTANDING WHAT YOU HAVE READ

1. Which of the following questions are answered in this chapter?
   a. Where are cattle and sheep raised?
   b. How are our dry lands used?
   c. Why are cattle branded?

2. The main idea of *paragraph 9* is to describe:
   a. the life of California families.
   b. cotton-picking in the Central Valley.
   c. the migratory workers of California.

3. The Great Plains are best suited for:
   a. farming.   b. grazing.   c. lumbering.

4. Most of the crops on California's large fruit farms are picked by:
   a. sharecroppers.
   b. migratory workers.
   c. students.

5. The Central Valley of California is important because:

a. desert soils were made fertile through irrigation.
b. a large part of our citrus fruits is raised there.
c. berry-growing has given work to thousands of people.

6. The cattle ranches of the West are large because:
   a. much machinery is used in harvesting crops.
   b. cattle need large areas of land in order to find enough grass to eat.
   c. fences keep cattle from roaming over the plains.

7. A *dry farmer* worries about the problem of:
   a. building terraces on hillsides.
   b. using his animals as a source of labor.
   c. storing water in the soil.

8. A *migratory worker*:
   a. owns his own fruit farm.
   b. moves from ranch to ranch.
   c. works the land for a share of the crops he raises.

Map # 15—Agricultural Regions of the United States

DEVELOPING IDEAS AND SKILLS

Map # 15—Agricultural Regions of the United States

Tell whether these statements are true or false.

1. Irrigation is carried out chiefly in the western part of the United States.
2. The New England states are shown to be a great farming region.
3. Pasture and grazing are found in the drier areas of the United States.
4. Cotton growing is found largely in the southern states.
5. Most of the land in the United States is suited for growing corn.
6. Spring wheat is grown in a cooler climate than winter wheat.
7. Cattle are raised chiefly in the western part of the country.
8. Cotton is the only important crop of the southern states.
9. Fruits are important only in western United States.
10. Dairy farming is located near the area of large cities.

SUMMING UP

Complete the following chart in your notebooks.

Dry Grasslands		California Valleys
	Climate	
	Occupations	
	Farming Methods	
	Source of Water	
	Crops	

FOLLOW UP

Farming Regions Tell whether these statements are true or false. The underlined words make the statements true or false. If a statement is false, what words would you place in it to make it true? (Refer to Chapters 10 and 11 for your answers.)

1. Texas is the leading cattle-raising state in the United States.
2. Cotton is grown on irrigated lands of California.
3. Many workers in the valleys of California have traveled from Canada for the harvesting season.
4. North Dakota is in the heart of the winter-wheat belt.
5. The United States grows more wheat than any other country in the world.
6. Most of the corn grown in the corn belt is used for feeding animals.
7. The dairy belt lies south of the corn belt.
8. Sharecroppers are workers in the cotton fields of the South.
9. Citrus fruits are raised in Florida, California and Arkansas.
10. Sugar beets are a crop grown on irrigated land in the West.

CHAPTER 12

Trade, at Home and Abroad

PROBLEM: Why is trade important to the people of an industrial nation?

READING FOR A PURPOSE:
1. What is trade?
2. How is our country united by trade?
3. Why do people carry on trade?

1. In our society, we do not live on our own work alone. The farmer in North Dakota harvests his wheat with a reaper made in Chicago, Illinois. The rancher in Texas wears a shirt made from Alabama cotton and perhaps manufactured in New York City. The miner in West Virginia takes his family for a drive in an automobile from Detroit, Michigan. We all depend on others in different parts of the country for things we need and want.

2. For example, most of our oil is found in Oklahoma, Texas, the Gulf Coast and California. Coal is mined chiefly in Pennsylvania, West Virginia, Kentucky and Ohio. Iron is taken from the open pits of Minnesota and copper from the mines of Montana. Yet all of these products—in fact, all our products—go to people across the nation who need them.

3. Each section of our country exchanges its riches with another. Millions of North Americans live in cities; they work in factories or stores or provide needed services for other people living there. These people turn the raw materials of our farms, mines and forests into thousands of useful products. The materials for these are supplied by others who work close to our natural resources—the farmer, miner, lumberman, rancher and fisherman. Likewise, those people who make their living far from the city depend on the products and services of city workers. This is called *interdependence*. Our vast, swift system of transportation makes this exchange of goods possible.

4. The exchange of goods is called *trade*. Trade takes place when people produce more goods than they need so that they have some left over to sell. Other people buy goods they need from those who have them to sell. People who use the goods that are grown or made are called *consumers*. (You are a consumer. So are your parents, your friends and everyone else who has ever bought and used anything.) The **process by which goods are sent from producer to consumer is not a simple one.** When you buy a cotton shirt, many people are involved. The product passes from the cotton grower and picker to the baler, shipper, designer, manufacturer, salesman, wholesaler and retail store. And these are only a few of the stops on its journey from raw material to consumer product.

5. Not only is there trade between sections of our nation, but there is also an exchange of goods among nations. Trade with other nations—foreign trade—has several causes. First of all, no nation—not even the United States or the Soviet Union—has all the goods it needs. (We have little tin, for example. We must get this important mineral from countries that mine it.) Second, some countries have the right climate or soil to raise one kind of crop: coffee in Brazil, pepper in Malaysia, and so on. It is cheaper for us to import these products than

it is for us to try to grow them ourselves.

6. Third, people of different nations have developed different skills. The people of Switzerland are famous for making fine watches. They sell their valuable product for goods they cannot get in their own small, mountainous country. Japan, famous for its cameras, toys and instruments, does the same. Fourth, some countries are able to produce more than they need. For example, our farmers grow more wheat and cotton than the people of this nation use. We sell these products abroad. By selling our extra cotton and wheat, we obtain money to buy goods that we need. (When we say that *we* are buying and selling goods, we mean that individual persons or companies are trading, not our national government. Only in countries where there is no free enterprise, such as the Soviet Union, does the government do the actual buying and selling.)

7. The foreign trade of a nation is measured by the amount of its imports (goods bought) and exports (goods sold). The United States is the largest trading nation in the world, followed by West Germany and Great Britain. The greatest amount of world trade is carried on between nations that are industrialized, because people in underdeveloped lands have little money with which to buy. They also have few goods to sell. Therefore, much of our trade is with Canada and the nations of Western Europe. However, we do carry on trade with some underdeveloped areas because they have products we need—tin from Southeast Asia and Bolivia, palm oil from Nigeria, cacao from Ghana.

8. The endless flow of materials and finished goods from one part of the world to another is one of the striking features of our modern world. The needs of any one group in our nation can set in motion businesses, mines and plantations in far corners of the earth. And, as our advances in science increase, the needs of people change. The discovery of how to make nylon almost ended our purchase of silk from Japan. As we have found greater uses for oil, gas and electricity in our daily lives, the coal industry has suffered.

9. Since trade affects our lives in so many ways, it is important that the flow of goods continue without difficulty during a war or when people are not able to buy goods offered for sale. A revolution or change in the government in a foreign country can affect business there. Since our nation is the world's largest seller of goods, we want people to be able to buy them —the more the better. This is another reason why we wish to help improve conditions in underdeveloped nations. Through trade, all people work for each other to achieve a better way of living.

UNDERSTANDING WHAT YOU HAVE READ

1. **Which of the following questions are answered in this chapter?**
a. How does each section of the country help all our people?
b. How does transportation affect trade?
c. What will stop trade among peoples?

2. **The main idea of this chapter is to describe:**
a. our chief imports and exports.

b. why we need a merchant fleet.
c. how people of the world are affected by trade.

3. **Most of our trade is carried on with:**
a. underdeveloped nations.
b. other industrial countries.
c. people who make a living by hunting and fishing.

4. **Goods that are sent out of the country are called:**

a. exports. b. imports. c. free-trade articles.

5. People trade with each other because they:

a. like to travel to different places.

b. have more of some goods than they need and not enough of others.

c. help to develop new products.

6. Trade is important to a nation because it:

a. helps poor nations to receive goods from richer nations.

b. provides the nation with goods that it cannot always produce.

c. makes wars and revolutions less likely to happen.

7. Which of the following best gives the meaning of *interdependence?*

a. A farmer depends upon good soil and rainfall.

b. An underdeveloped nation needs help from an industrial country.

c. People in each section of our country depend upon people in many other sections.

8. *Consumers* are people who:

a. produce goods.

b. use goods.

c. transport goods.

Pictograph # 7

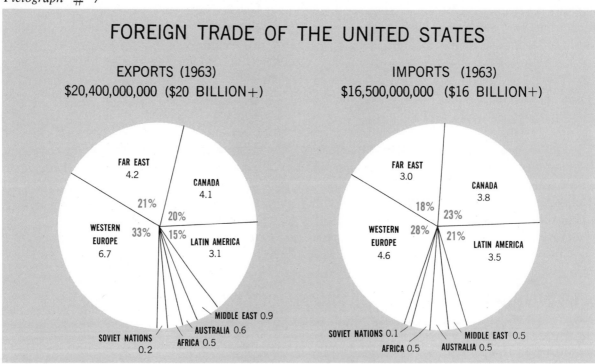

DEVELOPING IDEAS AND SKILLS

Pictograph # 7—Foreign Trade of the United States

If the statement about the information in the graph is true, write T in your notebook; if the statement is false, write F; if no information is given to tell you whether the statement is true or false, write N.

1. Exports of the United States are greater than its imports.

2. The Soviet nations rank lowest of all regions in trade with the United States.

3. We sell more goods to Western Europe than we buy.

4. People of the Middle East have little money to buy our products.

5. The graph shows us our trade with leading countries of the world.
6. More than half our imports come from Canada and Latin America.
7. Our trade with Africa makes up a very small part of our total trade.
8. We probably buy more goods from Great Britain than we do from West Germany.
9. These graphs show us how our trade has grown in the past twenty years.
10. Our trade with the Far East is more than $7 billion a year.

SUMMING UP

Fact or Opinion Decide which of the following are statements of fact and which are someone's opinion.

1. Our country should place taxes or tariffs on all goods coming into the country that are cheaper than American-made goods.
2. No nation has all the goods it needs.
3. The standard of living of the American people depends upon its trade with other countries.
4. The work of scientists often results in the discovery of new products.
5. The United States should trade only with the countries of North and South America.
6. Our nation would have more friends if we bought more goods and sold fewer goods.
7. People of "low-income" countries are the poorest customers for trade.
8. The person who manufactures is the most important person in the process of producing goods for the consumer.
9. One of the important parts of trade is good transportation.
10. It is cheaper for us to buy some products than to try to grow or make them ourselves.

FOLLOW UP

I. If you live in a port city, visit the port and see all the activities of people working there. If you do not live near a port, you might visit a factory that sends goods out of your community. As part of your visit, try to find out the following:

a. Which goods are shipped to foreign countries?
b. Where do the raw materials for them come from?
c. How are the raw materials brought to your community? How are the finished products sent out?
d. Where are the factory products shipped?

II. Look at a mail-order catalog in which goods from foreign lands are advertised. Make your own catalog of goods from other countries: a Japanese camera, French perfume, German binoculars, English china.

a. Why are Americans interested in buying these goods?
b. Why are some foreign-made goods cheaper than our own?
c. Why are these products sold here?
d. Which products are the result of special skills by people in a foreign land?

CHAPTER 13

The Resources of Canada

PROBLEM: What are Canada's resources?

READING FOR A PURPOSE:
1. What are Canada's chief minerals?
2. What are Canada's chief sources of power?
3. Where is Canada's leading industrial area?

1. Like the United States, Canada is rich in natural resources. Minerals are the most valuable of her gifts from nature. Canada supplies most of the world's nickel and asbestos. Iron ore, cobalt, lead, zinc, copper, gold, silver, potash and platinum are other riches of Canadian mines. The discovery of large deposits of uranium has made Canada a leading producer of this valuable ore. Coal, oil and natural gas are also plentiful. Many of these minerals have been found in the Canadian or Laurentian Shield, once thought to be a wasteland.

122

2. Canada leads the world in the production of asbestos. This is a mineral that is made up of fibers. These fibers can be woven into many materials. Asbestos has one important quality —it is fireproof. Therefore, it is used in firemen's suits and in shingles for homes.

3. Before World War II, Canada produced little iron ore. Afterward, valuable iron ore deposits were found near the Quebec-Labrador border. The ore there is easy to mine but at first was not easy to bring to the cities. Then a railroad was cut through the wilderness, and the ore can now be taken to distant industrial centers. Another rich source of iron is located near the northern shore of Lake Superior. The discovery of iron in Canada is important to the United States. There is danger that our own iron reserves may one day be used up. Rich supplies of this mineral in Canada mean that the United States will be able to import iron ore from its neighbor.

4. Canada has many power resources. The most important source of power is falling water. Most of its industries (such as aluminum and paper) are run by hydroelectric power. Water power projects on the St. Lawrence River supply electricity to the nearby parts of Canada and the United States. In 1964, the United States and Canada reached an agreement for building dams on the Columbia River. This project is to provide electricity for new factories in British Columbia, Washington, Montana and Oregon.

5. Two other important sources of power are petroleum and natural gas. Canada once had

Lumber is an important Canadian resource.

National Film Board of Canada

Paper-making is the leading industry of Canada.　　*Catching fish off the shores of Newfoundland.*

to import oil. Now the nation exports it. Discoveries of oil in the Alberta province have made the oil industry in Canada important. Research is still going on to find more sources of oil. Where there is oil, there is usually natural gas. Giant pipelines now carry gas and oil to many parts of the country.

6. Although there are large coal fields in Canada, only a few of the nation's factories use coal. Much of the coal is not very good. Then, too, the coal mines are located far from Canada's mills and factories. Because many of Canada's industries are near the coal fields of the United States, it is often cheaper for Canada to import coal than to mine it.

7. Canada's other resources include the three "F's"—fish, forests and furs. Canada's Atlantic and Pacific coastal waters are among the world's best fishing grounds. The Grand Banks, off the coast of Newfoundland, are the world's richest source of fish. Fishing boats from many nations of Europe use these waters, catching as many fish as the Canadian fishermen do. Cod, herring and lobster are the chief fish of the Atlantic waters. On the west coast, salmon fishing is most important. Canada's many inland lakes and streams provide a large supply of fresh-water fish. Canada's fisheries provide food not only for its own people, but for the people of other countries as well, through export.

8. A great belt of forest land stretches across Canada from the Atlantic to the Pacific. Over half of Canada's land is covered with forest. All ten provinces have forest regions. The most valuable product of the forests is wood pulp, from which paper is made. Nearly all the wood pulp is exported, and the largest buyer is the United States. The western province of British Columbia is the home of the large Douglas fir.

9. Canada was first settled as a fur-trading colony. Fur-bearing animals are still a valuable resource. But fur-trapping is not so important as it was two hundred years ago. Mink, fox, beaver, ermine and other fur-bearing animals are still plentiful in the northern woods. However, many of these animals are now raised more easily on fur farms.

10. Canada is now one of the few industrial nations of the world, even though it has a small population. Its industries draw materials from the nation's mines, forests and fisheries. The greatest industrial region of Canada is found in the provinces of Quebec and Ontario, near the Great Lakes and the St. Lawrence River. Industries are located here for the same reasons as in the United States. Minerals are brought from the Canadian Shield; the nearby Great Lakes and St. Lawrence are useful for transportation; sources of water power are available; and there is a large market for selling goods. Most of the large Canadian cities are found here.

11. Pulp and paper manufacture is Canada's

123

leading industry. The industry depends upon rivers and streams to carry the logs to mills and to furnish power to run the factory machines. It uses about a third of all the electrical power produced in Canada. Another of the great industries of Canada is the production of aluminum. Only the United States manufactures more aluminum products. One of the reasons for this is the great supply of water power Canada has. Canada imports bauxite ore from Latin America and manufactures the aluminum near these sources of water power.

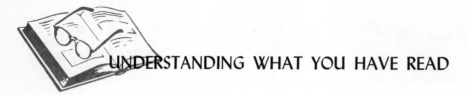

UNDERSTANDING WHAT YOU HAVE READ

1. **Which of the following questions are answered in this chapter?**
a. Why are Canada's forests important?
b. How is paper made?
c. Where are Canada's sources of water power?

2. **The main idea of this chapter is to describe:**
a. the importance of the discovery of oil.
b. how Canada's fisheries are used.
c. the wealth of nature's gifts to Canada.

3. **Canada's most important source of power for industry is:**
a. coal.　　b. water power.　　c. wood.

4. **Canada's storehouse of minerals is located in the:**
a. St. Lawrence River Valley.
b. western highlands.
c. Canadian Shield.

5. **Canada's forests are important as a source of:**
a. wood pulp.　　b. rubber.　　c. asbestos.

6. **Canada imports coal because:**
a. much Canadian coal is not of the highest grade.
b. there is no coal in Canada.
c. its coal mines are found in the frozen north.

7. *Bauxite* **is the ore used in producing:**
a. copper wiring.
b. aluminum.
c. fireproof clothing.

DEVELOPING IDEAS AND SKILLS

Map # 16—The Resources of Canada

Tell whether these statements are true or false.
1. Canada has few mineral resources, except for coal and iron ore.
2. Much of Canada's industry is located in the northern part of the country.
3. Large cities are grouped together near the St. Lawrence Valley.
4. Canada has many forest resources.
5. Little use is made of Canadian lumber.
6. Most of Canada's mineral wealth is found in the far north.
7. A fishing industry is located on both the eastern and western coasts.
8. Wheat-growing is important on the western plains.
9. Wheat fields and oil fields are located in widely separated parts of Canada.
10. Asbestos is found chiefly near Quebec.

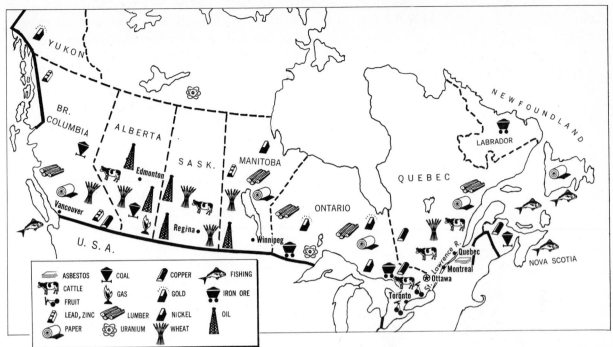

Map # 16—The Resources of Canada

SUMMING UP

Do You Agree or Disagree? Give the reasons for your answers.

1. Canada has few mineral resources.
2. Canada is one of the leading industrial nations of the world.
3. Canada has found little use for its oil reserves.
4. Canada's chief source of power for industry is coal.
5. Canada's forests are rich in fur-bearing animals and wood pulp.
6. Most of Canada's people live on the western coast.
7. Pulp and paper manufacture is the largest industry in Canada.
8. Canada carries on a large trade with the United States.

FOLLOW UP

Tell whether the following items refer to the United States, Canada or both countries. If the item applies to the United States only, use the letters "US"; if the item applies to Canada only, use the letter "C"; if the item applies to both the United States and Canada, use the letter "B."

1. Large area and large population.
2. Great use of coal as power for industry.
3. Large aluminum industry.
4. Fur-bearing animals plentiful in the northern forest.
5. Leading producer of asbestos.
6. Imports large amounts of wood pulp.
7. Resources of oil and iron ore.
8. World's largest producer of nickel.
9. Industrial area near the Great Lakes-St. Lawrence River.
10. Power projects along the St. Lawrence and Columbia Rivers.

Comparing Farming in the United States and Canada

ANGLO-AMERICA

PROBLEM: In what ways are the farms of Anglo-America alike?

READING FOR A PURPOSE:

1. Where are Canada's main farming areas?
2. What are Canada's chief farm crops?
3. Why must some foods be imported to Anglo-America?

1. Only a small part of Canada is useful for farming or grazing. In the north, forest and tundra cover more than half the land. Along the western coast is a chain of high mountains and plateaus as in the United States. Most of the Canadian Shield is too rocky or hilly to be farmed. (As the glaciers moved southward they scraped away the fertile topsoil.) In many parts of Canada the growing season is too short for

raising most crops. Except for the Pacific coast, the farming land of Canada is within a few hundred miles of the United States border.

2. The western plains are Canada's richest farming region. These plains are an extension of the Great Plains of the western United States. The good soil, summer rains and dry harvest season are good for wheat. The farmers of the plains use machines to cut and thresh their crop. Canada is the fourth largest producer of wheat. Farther west, Canadians also graze cattle and sheep on the dry prairies.

3. The other important farming area of Canada is the lowland of the Great Lakes in southern Ontario. The winds from the lakes make it warm enough to grow hay, oats, potatoes and various fruits. Dairy farms provide milk, cream and cheese here and along the St. Lawrence River. Since this is the region of the greatest population in Canada, the dairy products find a good market in the cities of the lowlands.

4. Although only a small part of Canada is useful for farming, Canada is one of the world's great food-producing countries. As you remember, Canada's population is small. Canadian farmers grow much more food than the people need. Therefore, they export the surplus to other parts of the world. For example, Canada leads the world in exporting wheat.

5. What are some of the conclusions we can reach regarding farming in both countries of Anglo-America? In the United States there are vast areas of fertile farm land. The farming area is much smaller in Canada. Nevertheless, both countries raise more than their people need. Both countries are large exporters of food.

6. The farms in both countries vary in size from very small to very large. Most of the farmers own their own land. These farmers live in farmhouses in the middle of their fields. They do not live together in small villages as farmers do in many other parts of the world.

7. In both countries the farmers make great use of machinery, fertilizer, good seed and the latest farming methods. The great use of machinery has made it possible for fewer workers

A snow-covered farm in lower Ontario.

National Film Board of Canada

on a farm to turn out larger crops. Since World War II, science has helped farmers to grow larger and better crops. Without adding to the amount of their land, the farmers of Anglo-America have almost doubled the amount of food they are able to produce. Because the need for farm workers is not so great now, many have left the farms to work in cities.

8. Most farms in the United States and Canada are *commercial* farms, or farms that raise a *cash* crop—a crop for sale. This means that our farmers produce enough for their own needs and still more to be sold in markets in Anglo-America and throughout the world. Many farms specialize—that is, they depend upon one main cash crop. Others raise a variety of vegetables, fruits and grains.

9. Where land is too dry for farming, as on the dry plains, rivers have been dammed to provide water for irrigation. These dams store water until it is needed. A *reservoir* is formed. To get the stored water to the farms, many miles of canals have been built. The sheep and cattle industry is carried on in both nations on the drier lands of the West.

10. Because of the great size of the United States and Canada, a variety of crops is grown. Yet there are a number of crops that cannot be grown in Anglo-America because of its northerly location. These are the tropical crops such as bananas, coffee, cocoa, rubber, spices and tropical vegetable oils. Such crops are imported by the United States and Canada from other nations all over the world.

UNDERSTANDING WHAT YOU HAVE READ

1. Which of the following questions are answered in this chapter?
a. Why is only a small part of Canada used for farming?
b. How are Anglo-American farms alike?
c. Where are apricots grown in Canada?

2. The main idea of *paragraphs 1 through 4* is to describe:
a. the farming regions of Canada.
b. wheat farming on the plains.
c. the growing seasons of Canada.

3. Canada's chief farm crop is:

a. potatoes.　　　b. rice.　　　c. wheat.

4. Canada's chief farming areas are located:

a. in the western highlands.
b. on the plains of the Pacific coast.
c. on the plains of the southern border.

5. Only a small part of Canada can be used for farming because:

a. most of the land is forest and tundra.
b. mining is a more important industry.
c. the government controls the use of land.

6. Canada is a leading exporter of food because:

a. its people have a low standard of living.
b. much of the land is used for farming.

c. Canadian farms grow more food than its people need.

7. When we say that a farmer *specializes*, we mean that he:

a. raises one main crop.
b. divides his land among several crops.
c. uses machinery at harvest time.

8. A *reservoir* is used for:

a. storing food for farm animals.
b. storing water.
c. storing wheat once it has been cut.

9. A *commercial* farm, as mentioned in paragraph 8, is one that:

a. is probably a wheat farm.
b. raises a crop for sale.
c. raises what is needed for the farmer and his family.

DEVELOPING IDEAS AND SKILLS

Photograph Study

This photograph should help you to recall parts of the chapter you have just read. Can you tell the main idea of the photograph? Where in the chapter is it described?

Canada Dept. of Agriculture

SUMMING UP

In the following, place before each statement the word that makes the statement correct: *Many, Much, Some, Few.*

1. _____ land in Canada is not suited for farming.
2. _____ farms in Anglo-America are small in size.
3. _____ wheat farms in Anglo-America use modern machinery.
4. _____ people of Canada are farmers.
5. _____ wheat grown in Canada is exported.
6. _____ bananas eaten by the people of Anglo-America are imported.
7. _____ Anglo-American farmers have learned to irrigate dry land for farming.
8. _____ Anglo-American farmers raise a cash crop.
9. _____ Canadian farmers raise corn.
10. _____ Canadian farms are close to the United States.

FOLLOW UP

Read the statements in the chart below. Then check the correct column in your notebook:

WHY ANGLO-AMERICAN FARMERS ARE SO PRODUCTIVE	YES	NO
1. Extensive use is made of machinery.		
2. Farm plots are very small.		
3. Great use is made of fertilizer.		
4. Most farm lands belong to a few people.		
5. There are large areas of level, fertile soil.		
6. There are no areas of desert.		
7. Rivers are dammed to provide irrigation.		
8. Everything is planned by the government.		
9. Farmers make use of scientific discoveries.		
10. All kinds of fruits can be raised.		

CHAPTER 15

North American Partners

PROBLEM: How do the United States and Canada work together and help each other?

READING FOR A PURPOSE:
1. What are some of the ties that bring Canada and the United States together?
2. What trade is carried on between these two countries?
3. In what ways do the United States and Canada disagree?

1. You have studied many things about the two giant nations of Anglo-America. To make sure that we understand the many ways in which the United States and Canada are alike, let us review the things they have in common.

2. Great Britain was the mother country of both nations. As a result, English is spoken throughout the United States and in most of Canada.

3. Both peoples believe in democratic government. The citizens of each country have the right to elect representatives to make the laws that govern each country. Both believe in such rights as freedom of speech, assembly and religion.

4. Both countries are rich in natural resources. Among the most important are oil, iron ore, coal and falling water. These have been used to make the two nations of Anglo-America leading industrial nations. Much of the work in factories, farms and homes is done by machines.

5. Both peoples, American and Canadian, have a high standard of living. The food, clothing, shelter and general way of life of the peoples of both countries are very much alike. If you were to meet a Canadian for the first time, you could probably not tell him apart from an American.

6. The two countries are tied together by great transportation systems. Autos, trains, trucks and planes travel back and forth freely between Canada and the United States. The good transportation system of Anglo-America makes it possible to exchange many products. The United States imports wood pulp, nickel, uranium, asbestos and fish from Canada. Canada buys farm machinery, fertilizers, textiles, chemicals and household machinery from the United States. More than half of Canada's imports come from the United States. Almost ⅔ of its exports go to the United States.

7. The people of the United States and Canada use their resources to help each other. In 1959, the two countries opened the St. Lawrence Seaway. This made it possible for ocean-going ships to reach ports on the Great Lakes. The St. Lawrence Power Dam provides more electric power than any other plant in the world. In 1964, both countries signed an agreement to use the Columbia River for flood control and electric power.

8. Both the United States and Canada are interested in the Arctic region. The polar map will show you that the shortest route from northern Europe and Asia lies across the frozen

north. With modern planes it is no longer necessary to travel around the North Pole. Now we can fly over it. As a result, the two nations have cooperated in building strings of radar stations across Canada. These stations will give the Anglo-American nations an early warning in the event of an air attack from across the Arctic.

9. While there are many things that we have in common, there are some ways in which the two countries are different. For example, Canada is a large country, but it does not have many people. Therefore, it is not able to raise large sums of money. Many of its industries were started with the help of American money. Because of these investments, Americans now own large parts of Canadian industry. Canadians cannot be pleased that so much of their industry is owned by Americans rather than by Canadians. Because of this ownership a great deal of money leaves Canada and goes to the United States. Canadians do not like to see this money leave their country.

10. There have been some disagreements, too, over foreign policies. Both nations are members of the North Atlantic Treaty Organization (NATO). But they do not always agree on ways to deal with other nations. Canada sells food to Communist China and trades with Castro's Cuba, while we do not.

Canada Industries Ltd.

Working together to build the St. Lawrence Seaway.

UNDERSTANDING WHAT YOU HAVE READ

1. Which of the following questions are answered in this chapter?
a. Why are both Anglo-American nations interested in the Arctic?
b. What products do both countries lack?
c. How are both countries sharing their resources?

2. The main idea of *paragraphs 1 through 6* is to describe:
a. ways in which Canada and the United States are alike.
b. what makes an industrial nation.
c. the standard of living in Anglo-America.

3. Canada trades chiefly with:
a. Latin America.
b. the United States.
c. Japan.

4. In 1959, Canada and the United States opened the:
a. Missouri River Valley Project.
b. World's Fair.
c. St. Lawrence Seaway.

5. Both Canada and the United States are interested in the Arctic region because it:

a. has many minerals.
b. is the shortest route to Asia.
c. is rich in fur-bearing animals.

6. **Canada and the United States are important to each other because:**
a. Canada trades with Communist China.
b. the two nations share many resources.

c. the two nations share the Panama Canal.

7. **In paragraph 9, the word *investments* refers to:**
a. industries in Canada.
b. discoveries of Canadian minerals.
c. money used to begin industry.

DEVELOPING IDEAS AND SKILLS

Cartoon (See page 130.)
1. Who are the two figures at the top of this cartoon?
2. What is happening in the cartoon?

3. Can you give two examples of Anglo-American cooperation?
4. What continents are shown in the cartoon?
5. What is a good title for this cartoon?

SUMMING UP

The United States and Canada   Below are some headings for your *outline*. On the right are topics to be placed under these headings. In your notebook, see if you can make the correct outline.

A. Ways in Which the United States and Canada Are Alike.
B. Common Interests of the United States and Canada.
C. Where Canada and the United States May Disagree.

1. Radar warning stations.
2. NATO.
3. American investments in Canada.
4. Belief in democracy.
5. Standard of living.
6. Building of power projects.
7. Trade with Communist China.
8. Trade of raw materials for manufactured goods.
9. Use of machinery to do man's work.
10. Use of the English language.

FOLLOW UP

Tell whether the following items refer to the United States, Canada or both countries. If the item applies to the United States only, use the letters "US"; if the item applies to Canada only, use the letter "C"; if the item applies to both the United States and Canada, use the letter "B."

1. Two official languages.
2. Members of NATO.
3. Vast Arctic region.

4. Large Negro population.
5. Many pulp and paper mills.
6. Divided into provinces.
7. Most people live in the Northeast.
8. Once a colony of Great Britain.
9. Great Lakes are an important waterway.
10. Trade with Cuba.
11. Great railroad system.
12. Exports textiles.

Toward a Better America

PROBLEM: What are some of the problems facing Anglo-Americans?

READING FOR A PURPOSE:
1. What is the "other America"?
2. What are civil rights?
3. How are we fighting the spread of communism?

1. In comparison with other regions of the world, ours is a land of plenty. Americans as a whole make more money, eat better foods, have more labor-saving machines than any other people in the world. However, not all our people enjoy a comfortable living. There are many poor homes and many poor Americans—unskilled workers, migrant farm workers, coal miners, some of the aged and some of our minority groups. Many of these do not have proper homes, schooling or medical care. There are close to *fifty million* Americans living in this "other America." President Johnson has said that part of America's riches must be set aside to raise the living standards of these people.

2. The largest minority group in the United States is the Negroes. Before the Civil War, many of the nation's Negroes were slaves. In 1863, slavery ended in the United States. However, many states passed laws that kept the Negro a "second-class citizen." He was not allowed to vote; he was kept apart from whites in buses, restaurants, schools and other places. For a long time a number of organizations have fought for equal rights for Negroes. In 1954, the Supreme Court of the United States ordered an end to separate public schools for Negroes and whites. In 1964, a Civil Rights Act was passed by Congress. As a result, all Americans have the right to go where they wish, to eat where they please and to vote if they are qualified.

3. However, unfair laws alone have not kept the Negroes of the United States from gaining a higher standard of living. In our larger cities there are large areas where only Negroes live. This is often because people in other areas will not rent or sell homes to them. Our country faces the problem of integrating *all* Americans in one society. All minority groups must be able to attend schools with their fellow Americans. All must have the chance to obtain jobs for which they are qualified and to raise their standard of living.

4. Canada, too, has a "minority" problem because of the large French population living there, chiefly in the province of Quebec. There are fewer French-speaking people than English-speaking people in Canada. Since 1960, the French people of Canada have been asking for a larger share in the government. Some French in Quebec have talked of making Quebec a separate nation. Although only a third of the Canadians are French, some of their leaders are asking for equal representation in the Canadian Parliament.

5. As in other regions of the world, the population of the United States is increasing rapidly. By 1970, there may be 200 million people living in our nation! This means that there will have to be more jobs, schools, teachers and trained workers. In the future, machines will

do even more of the work now being done by people. Machines will even tell other machines what to do! We call this process *automation*. There will be less need for workers without skills. Our crowded cities will face greater problems—enough homes and fresh water, increased traffic and unclean air and the need for more medical care.

6. As our population continues to grow, we will have to use our great resources more wisely. Up to now we have been wasteful in the way we have cleared our land and used our minerals. We have carelessly dumped wastes into our streams and rivers. The amount of pure water has been reduced a great deal as a result. Yet we need more water than ever! We also may not have enough fuel for our machines. Will we be able to keep a high standard of living as our population grows so rapidly?

7. Of course, our greatest resource is our people. President Johnson, with the help of laws passed by Congress, began a "War on Poverty" in 1965. This "war" is an all-out effort to get rid of the causes of poverty in the United States. If people are to improve their conditions of life, they must have good jobs with good pay. This requires training. Those who have lost their jobs because of the changes in our industrial life are being re-trained in other useful skills. Young people from poor families are given part-time jobs in improving the cleanliness of our cities, growing gardens and helping with work in our schools. Millions of dollars are providing education for children of poor parents, beginning as early as age 3. This early education will help these children get a better start in school—and a good job after they have finished school.

8. Other dangers face Americans and the rest of the world's people alike. There is a danger from nuclear warfare and the testing of nuclear weapons. In 1963, the United States signed a treaty with the Soviet Union. Both nations agreed not to explode atomic bombs in the air or under the water. This has been at least a step in the right direction.

9. To us, one of the greatest of all dangers is the spread of communism. (See Unit 5, Ch. 10.) We feel that the Communists are spreading their way of life in any way they can. In order to prevent the spread of communism, the nations of Anglo-America have joined together with many other countries of the world. The North Atlantic Treaty Organization (NATO) includes the United States, Canada and more than a dozen countries of Europe. The United States is also a member of the Southeast Asia Treaty Organization (SEATO). This organization was formed in an attempt to stop the spread of communism in that region of

Many people live in poor sections of the U.S. Our government hopes to change these conditions.

U.S. Dept. of Agriculture

Through better education, all groups in America can get better jobs.

Scurlock

the world. The United States is also a member of the Organization of American States (OAS, made up of the nations of North and South America, except Canada.)

10. The United States is not only *against* something; it is *for* something. We are eager to help the new nations of Asia and Africa help themselves to improve their standard of living. Workers in these countries have very low incomes. We must help them although many of them have ways of life that are different from ours. We help people because they *are* people. Furthermore, helping them helps us. In this way we gain friends, find other people who wish to trade with us and obtain more help in resisting the growth of communism.

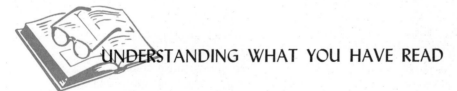

UNDERSTANDING WHAT YOU HAVE READ

1. Which of the following questions are answered in this chapter?
a. Why do we fight communism?
b. Why must we use our resources wisely?
c. What is automation?

2. The main idea of this chapter is to describe:
a. how "other Americans" live in the United States.
b. our efforts to stop the spread of communism.
c. some problems that are not yet solved.

3. The United States has joined with other Western nations to stop the spread of communism. This organization is called:
a. NATO.
b. the Common Market.
c. the League of Nations.

4. The United States has signed a treaty with the Soviet Union to:
a. increase trade between the two countries.
b. help each other in exploring space.
c. stop the testing of nuclear bombs.

5. We must use our resources wisely because:

a. our forests cannot be replaced.
b. our oil reserves have been used up.
c. more people will mean a greater need for resources.

6. **Since the Civil War, the Negroes in the United States have:**
a. enjoyed equal rights with all other Americans.
b. sometimes been forced to attend schools for Negroes only.
c. moved steadily to the farms of the South.

7. **The process by which machines give orders to other machines is called:**

a. division of labor.
b. automation.
c. competition.

8. **The "other America" refers to:**
a. The French people in Canada.
b. people in our large cities.
c. the poor people of America.

9. **In *paragraph 2*, the term "second-class citizen" means:**
a. Negroes did not have the same rights as other citizens.
b. laws were passed by many states.
c. Negroes were forced into slavery.

DEVELOPING IDEAS AND SKILLS

Cartoon (See page 133.)
1. Who is the man in this cartoon?
2. What is happening?
3. What are some of our major problems?

4. What are some plans to overcome some of these problems?
5. What is a good title for this cartoon?

SUMMING UP

Fact or Opinion
Can you decide which are statements of fact and which are someone's opinion?
1. The democratic government is the best form of government.
2. Montreal is the largest city in Canada.
3. Other countries will be our friends if they receive aid from us.
4. The Canadian Shield is an area of low hills, lakes and streams.
5. Both Canada and the United States were once British colonies.
6. By the year 2000, there will be 300 million people in the United States.
7. The new nations of Asia are the most important group in the United Nations.
8. Both Canada and the United States carry on a great deal of trade.
9. Communist countries should not be allowed to be members of the United Nations.
10. Some of the poor people of the United States live near our coal fields.

BOOKS FOR UNIT 2

Author	Title, Publisher	Description
1. Billings, Henry	*All Down the Valley,* Viking	The story of the TVA, told through the life of a family in the valley.
2. Bontemps, Arna	*The Story of the Negro,* Knopf	The history of the Negro people in the United States.
3. Burlingame, Roger	*Machines That Built America,* Harcourt, Brace	The inventions that helped America to grow.
4. Colman, Hila	*The Girl from Puerto Rico,* Morrow	The problems of a Puerto Rican girl living in New York City.
5. Hayes, Florence	*Joe Pole, New American,* Houghton	The story of an immigrant to our country.
6. Judson, Clara	*St. Lawrence Seaway,* Follett	The St. Lawrence River Valley from discovery by Cartier to the completion of the Seaway.
7. Lent, Henry	*Men at Work in New England,* Putnam	Shows the wide range of jobs and skills in this area.
8. ——	*Men at Work in the South,* Putnam	The story of the variety of southern industries.
9. Longstreth, T. M.	*The Scarlet Force,* St. Martins	The first twenty years of the Canadian Mounted Police.
10. McGuire, Edna	*Puerto Rico—Bridge to Freedom,* Macmillan	The interesting story of the small, crowded island southeast of Florida.
11. McNeer, May	*The Canadian Story,* (Ariel) Farrar Straus	The history of Canada from the Vikings to the Seaway.
12. Shippen, Katherine	*The Great Heritage,* Viking	The development of our natural resources.
13. ——	*Miracle in Motion,* Harper	The story of American industry.

UNIT 3

Latin America

CHAPTER I

Our Southern Neighbors

PROBLEM: Why are we interested in Latin America?

READING FOR A PURPOSE:
1. What are the parts of Latin America?
2. Why is this region called Latin America?
3. What products do we get from Latin America?

1. Many of us have used the word "America" or "Americans" in speaking of the United States. This is not accurate. There are others who are Americans, too—the people of Latin America. They often resent our calling ourselves Americans as though the title belonged to us alone. It is common in Latin America to refer to us as "North Americans."

2. Latin America is made up of several parts. South of the United States is the country of Mexico. From Mexico a "bridge" of land extends to the southeast. This land, sometimes called Central America, contains six small coun-

tries. East of Central America is the Caribbean Sea and its many islands. Cuba, Haiti and the Dominican Republic, Puerto Rico, Trinidad and Jamaica are among the largest and most important of the Caribbean islands. Stretching southeast from Central America is the continent called South America. This continent is connected to Central America by a narrow strip of land, the Isthmus of Panama. All of these parts together—Mexico, Central America, the Caribbean Islands and South America—make up Latin America.

3. This region has twenty-three independent nations and small areas that are colonies of nations of Europe. Some are very large, like Brazil. This country is almost as big as the United States. Others are quite small, like El Salvador and the other nations of Central America. Some of the countries are our close neighbors like Mexico or Cuba. Others are a great distance away. Buenos Aires, the capital of Argentina, is farther from Washington, D.C. than any capital of Europe. It is even farther from Washington than is Moscow in the Soviet Union.

4. We call this large region south of us Latin America because the people who first settled there—the Spanish, Portuguese and French—spoke languages that came from Latin. (Latin

Our coffee beans come from Latin America. Here a worker picks coffee on a Colombian farm.

Standard Oil Co. (N.J.)

Census-taking among the Indians of Peru.

was the language of an early Italian people, the Romans.) All but four of the twenty-three republics were once colonies of Spain or Portugal. The four that were not are Haiti, which belonged to France, and Guyana, Jamaica, and Trinidad and Tobago, which belonged to England. Brazil was a colony of Portugal. The other eighteen independent nations were Spanish colonies.

5. We are interested in Latin America for many reasons. First, a friendly Latin America is important to the safety of the United States. If an enemy country had bases in Mexico, Central America or the Caribbean Sea, the United States would be in danger of attack. Likewise, the nations of Latin America know that an attack upon any one of them would be dangerous to the freedom of the others. That is why the United States has joined with the countries of Latin America to form the Organization of American States (OAS).

6. Second, the countries of Latin America send us products that we need. Important minerals such as oil, tin, copper and bauxite come to us from Venezuela, Bolivia, Chile and Surinam. Coffee, sugar, bananas and chocolate are foods that are eaten daily by the people of the United States. We import them from Latin America because they cannot grow in our climate. Beginning with the "Good Neighbor Policy" in the 1930's, our trade with Latin

American countries has grown so that it is now $7 billion a year. Except for Argentina and Cuba, the people of Latin America buy more from the United States than from any other nation in the world.

7. Third, like countries in other parts of the world, the governments of Latin America are trying to raise the living standards of their people. We want to help them in this effort. Young people of our Peace Corps are now working and teaching in Latin America. The "Alliance for Progress," also for this purpose, was started by President John F. Kennedy in 1961. Under this plan, Congress has provided millions of dollars to help the Latin American people. Through this aid it is hoped that Latin America will have more factories, better methods of farming and better schools.

8. Fourth, the Panama Canal is of great importance to the United States. The canal is located on the Isthmus of Panama—in an area or zone we have "rented" from Panama. The canal was completed in 1914 by the United States. It is important to the defense of the United States. With it, warships can move from the Atlantic to the Pacific Ocean in a short time. The United States has built a chain of naval and air bases to protect the canal from attack. In times of peace the canal is open to all the nations of the world.

UNDERSTANDING WHAT YOU HAVE READ

1. Which of the following questions are answered in this chapter?
   a. Why are we interested in Latin America?
   b. What is the "Alliance for Progress"?
   c. How did the "Good Neighbor Policy" begin?

2. The main idea of this chapter is to describe:
   a. how the United States built the Panama Canal.
   b. why we trade with Latin America.
   c. why the American nations need each other.

3. Our nearest neighbor in Latin America is:
   a. Mexico.   b. Brazil.   c. Argentina.

4. All of these Latin American nations are Spanish-speaking countries EXCEPT:
   a. Mexico.   b. Brazil.   c. Argentina.

5. This region is called Latin America because:
   a. the first settlers were Latins.
   b. the people speak Latin languages.
   c. Rome once conquered this part of the world.

6. The Panama Canal is important because it:
   a. shortens the distance between two great oceans.
   b. is a sea-level canal.
   c. is the center of trade between Latin America and the United States.

7. A narrow strip of land connecting two larger bodies of land is a(n):
   a. island.   b. strait.   c. isthmus.

8. In paragraph 2, a sentence reads, "From Mexico a 'bridge' of land extends to the southeast." The best meaning for the words in italics is:
   a. a chain of islands.
   b. land that connects larger areas of land.
   c. wet, swampy land reaching into the ocean.

DEVELOPING IDEAS AND SKILLS

Map # 17—Latin America

Can you answer these questions?
1. Is the region north or south of the equator?
2. Is the region east or west of the Prime Meridian?
3. How far north and south does the region extend?
4. Does the region extend farther from east to west or from north to south?
5. What region or regions are near it?
6. What is the largest country? The smallest?
7. What are the chief bodies of water that border the region?
8. Are there countries that have no outlets to the sea?
9. What are some of the important rivers in the region?
10. Are there large rivers that form the boundary lines between countries?
11. What are the capital cities of each country? How do you know they are the capitals? How many are sea or river ports?
12. Are there any island nations?
13. Are there countries that are located on a peninsula?
14. Are there any lands that are colonies of other nations?

Map # 17—Latin America

143

SUMMING UP

I. In the following, tell which reasons are correct.

We are interested in Latin America because:
1. the Panama Canal is important to us.
2. we get tropical foods from Latin America.
3. most people in this region speak English.
4. we can use Latin America's tin and copper.
5. rich farm lands supply us with corn and wheat.
6. the Latin American people are now fighting for their freedom.
7. we want these people to have a better life.
8. we are Argentina's biggest customer.

II. Tell which of these are *facts* and which are someone's *opinion*.

1. Many countries of Latin America are independent.
2. The United States should buy more products from Latin America.
3. Latin American nations can improve their standard of living without help from the United States.
4. There are many reasons why the United States and the Latin American countries should be friendly.
5. Latin American countries will help the United States in defending the Panama Canal.
6. The United States would surely be attacked if a Communist country were near our borders.
7. Products of Latin America are important to the United States.

FOLLOW UP

Latin American news often appears in our newspapers. You can find many articles and pictures about Latin America in newspapers and magazines. Bring to class the news articles that you find and arrange them in a bulletin-board display. Make several headings for these news items: Government, History, Relations With Other Countries, Problems, Farming, Industry, etc.

CHAPTER 2

The Hollow Continent

PROBLEM: What is the surface of Latin America like?

READING FOR A PURPOSE:

1. How have mountains affected the life of the people of Latin America?
2. What are the chief rivers of Latin America?
3. What are some ways that North and South America are alike?

1. The region of Latin America is about 8,000,000 square miles in area, slightly larger than the United States and Canada together. The continent of South America makes up more than 80 per cent of this land mass. A look at the map on page 143 will show you that nearly all of South America lies southeast of the United States. The eastern bulge of the continent that is part of Brazil brings South America closer to Europe and Africa than to our northeastern states. During World War II, the United States sent planes to Africa by flying them south to Brazil. Then they were flown across the Atlantic to Africa. This was a shorter way of delivering them to the battle areas.

2. The northern part of South America is crossed by the equator. (This is also the widest part of South America.) Therefore, Latin America lies partly in the northern hemisphere and partly in the southern hemisphere. As a result, the seasons in most of Latin America are the opposite of our seasons. When we have winter, the people of Latin America (south of the equator) have summer. When we have summer, they will be having winter. Furthermore, the largest part of Latin America is in the low latitudes. In general, that means that a large part of Latin America has a hot climate. Most of the people of this hot region live along the seacoast or in the mountains where it is cooler.

3. Latin America has many mountains. The Andes Mountains, or western highlands, stretch from the southern border of the United States to the very tip of South America. The Andes are the second highest mountain range in the world. Some of the peaks are more than 20,000 feet high. These mountains are very hard to cross. On the east coast there are lower mountains or hills known as the Guiana and Brazilian highlands. The islands in the Caribbean Sea are

The Andes Mountains of Bolivia.

UNATIONS

really the tops of underwater mountain peaks of these highlands. Because of the mountains, travel by land from one part of South America to another has always been a problem.

4. Between the eastern and western highlands are the great inner plains or lowlands of South America. In Venezuela and Colombia the plains are called the *llanos*. In Argentina, the rich grassy plains are known as the *pampas*.

5. The plains are drained by great rivers. The largest and longest is the Amazon River of Brazil. The Amazon rises in the Andes Mountains of the west. It flows eastward across the continent to the Atlantic Ocean. The Amazon flows through the hot, thick rain forest like a mighty inland sea. The river and its branches are so vast that they drain nearly half of South America. Along its path, the Amazon's shores may be as much as sixty miles apart! The mouth of the Amazon is 200 miles wide. The Amazon is so powerful that the mud that it carries along with it colors the water for fifty miles out into the ocean!

6. Two other great rivers of South America are the Orinoco and the Plata. The Orinoco flows through northern South America. It drains the lowlands of Venezuela. The Rio de la Plata ("River of Silver") is in the southeastern part of the continent. The two branches of the Plata begin in Brazil and flow southward through the pampas. The river empties into the Atlantic Ocean near the city of Buenos Aires, Argentina. For the most part, the rivers of South America are *navigable*. (This means that ships can sail upstream from the ocean for long distances.)

7. In many ways the land forms of North and South America are very much alike. Both continents have high mountains along their western coasts—the Rockies and the Andes. Both have an inner plain drained by mighty rivers. Both have highlands in the east, the Appalachians and the Guiana and Brazilian Highlands. Both have great seaports along the eastern coast.

8. There are also differences between the two continents. First, our largest river, the Mississippi, flows from north to south. The Amazon flows from west to east. The Mississippi flows through the most fertile part of the United States. The Amazon flows through a tropical rain forest where few people live. (We might call the Plata the "Mississippi" of South America. It flows in a north-south direction, through the rich grasslands of the pampas. It is also a great highway for trade like the Mississippi.)

The llanos or plains of Colombia.

Standard Oil Co. (N.J.)

The Magdalena River in Colombia.

Standard Oil Co. (N.J.)

Second, the Rocky Mountains are not as high as the Andes. It has been easier to build roads and railways through the Rockies. (In South America there is no railroad across the continent from east to west because of the mountains.) Third, Anglo-America is blessed with a great inland waterway system, the Great Lakes. There is no such water highway in South America.

9. The geography of South America has caused it to be called the "Hollow Continent." The mountains of South America border the coasts, while inland are the plains. Therefore, the surface of South America makes it "high on the outside, low on the inside." The inland plains are also very hot, and part of the plains is tropical jungle. As a result, most of the people of South America live along the rim or coastline, and little is known about the middle of the continent.

UNDERSTANDING WHAT YOU HAVE READ

1. Which of the following questions are answered in this chapter?
a. Where does the Amazon River begin?
b. How do the mountains affect Latin America?
c. When was South America discovered?

2. The best title for paragraph 5 is:
a. Mighty River of the Rain Forest.
b. Lowland River of South America.
c. The "Mississippi" of South America.

3. A river of South America that flows through fertile land is the:
a. Amazon.   b. Plata.   c. Madeira.

4. The highest mountains in Latin America are the:
a. Rockies.   b. Andes.   c. Guiana Highlands.

5. How have the mountains affected Latin America?
a. Most of Latin America is dry.
b. Most of Latin America is cold.
c. Travel is difficult from one part to another.

6. The large rivers of Latin America are useful because they:
a. provide water power.
b. all drain fertile farm lands.
c. are used by ships for long distances.

7. The *llanos* and the *pampas* are both:

a. mountains.   b. deserts.   c. lowlands.

8. A river that is *navigable* is one that:

a. is used to supply water power.

b. can be used by large ships.

c. carries with it a large amount of soil.

DEVELOPING IDEAS AND SKILLS

Map # 18—Land Forms of Latin America

Tell whether these statements are *true* or *false*. Be able to explain your answers.

1. A high mountain area extends almost the length of South America, from north to south.
2. Hills occupy only a small part of South America.
3. Most of the central part of the continent is mountainous.
4. All of the land at the southern tip of South America is at sea level.
5. The western coast of South America is a broad lowland.
6. Plateaus are located near the northeastern coast.

SUMMING UP

Complete the following outline in your notebooks.

Land Forms of North and South America

A. How They Are Alike	B. How They Are Different
1.	1.
2.	2.
3.	3.

FOLLOW UP

Complete the following sentences in your notebooks.

1. The largest river of Latin America is the _____.
2. The _____ Mountains extend along the west coast of South America.
3. The equator crosses the _____ part of South America.
4. The central part of South America is a vast _____.
5. The river in South America most like our Mississippi River is the _____.
6. The best seaports of South America are on the _____ coast.
7. The Caribbean Islands are really part of the _____ highlands.
8. The continent of _____ makes up most of Latin America.

LAND FORMS OF
LATIN AMERICA

Mountains
Plateaus
Hills
Plains

0   200   400   600   800   1000
Miles

Tropic of Cancer

Equator

Equator

Tropic of Capricorn

CHAPTER 3

A Region of Many Climates

PROBLEM: Why are there differences in climate in Latin America?

READING FOR A PURPOSE:
1. Where is the rain forest?
2. What is a vertical climate?
3. How do the winds affect the climate of South America?

1. If you were asked to plan a trip to Latin America, what clothing would you take with you? For several reasons, this would not be easy to decide. First, Latin America extends over a great distance from north to south. This means there is a great range in latitude. Second, Latin America is mountainous. It may be cold in one place only a few miles from another place that is very hot. Third, because of the differences in wind direction, it may be very rainy or very dry. Fourth, in parts of Latin America the seasons are opposite from ours, so you would have to know whether it is winter or summer at the time you wish to travel.

2. A large part of Latin America is near the equator. This area is hot and wet throughout the year. It is a tropical rain forest. The rain-forest climate is found in the Amazon River Valley, along the Caribbean coast of South and Central America and along the Pacific coast from Ecuador to Panama. The average temperature throughout the year is 80°. It is never as hot as the hottest summer days in the midwestern United States. (In Kansas, Nebraska and South Dakota, temperatures of more than 100° are sometimes recorded in the summer months.) At night one sleeps under a light blanket. But some rain falls almost every day. There is no dry season, and every day is sticky and damp.

3. Knowing that so much of Latin America is in the tropics, you might think that the entire region is hot. This is only partly true. There are differences in temperature between places only a few miles apart, even in the tropics. There are parts of Ecuador, Peru and Bolivia that are very cold, although they are located near the equator. How is this possible? These places are high in the Andes Mountains. Therefore, they have a *vertical* climate. As you have learned, this means that the climate grows cooler as you travel higher up into the mountains, away from the lowland.

4. At sea level the climate is tropical or hot. The people of Latin America call this the *tierra caliente* or hot country. As you go higher, the climate becomes somewhat cooler. You are in the *tierra templada* or cool country. Near the peaks of the mountains you are in the *tierra fría* or cold country. Because mountains are found in many Latin American countries, the vertical climate (up and down) is common.

5. North and south of the rain forest are the tropical grasslands or savannas. There are two seasons in the savannas—wet and dry. The rainy season brings floods and the dry season bakes the land. The soil and grasses of the savannas are tough. There are also many insects that carry diseases. Because of these conditions, few people live in the savannas.

The savanna lands of Colombia.

6. South of the savannas in South America is the humid-subtropical climate. More Latin Americans live in this kind of climate than in any other. Here winters are mild and summers are warm. The pampas of Uruguay and Argentina lie in the humid subtropics. Buenos Aires, Argentina, is about as far south of the equator as Charleston, South Carolina, is north of it. Therefore, you can see that the southeastern part of the United States and the southeastern part of South America have the same kind of climate—although they have opposite seasons.

7. The winds and ocean currents affect the climate of South America as they do that of the United States. In our West, the Rocky Mountains shut off the wet winds from the Pacific Ocean, and the eastern side of the Rockies is dry. In much of South America the rain-carrying winds blow from the Atlantic Ocean. These winds are warm and wet. The West Indies and the northern part of South America get much rain. These winds move westward across South America until they reach the Andes Mountains. There the winds rise; the air is cooled and the rain falls on the eastern side of the mountains. When the air passes to the western side of the mountains it is dry. Therefore, the narrow coastal area on the west has little rain. The Atacama Desert of Peru and northern

A charred tree stump in the rain forest.

Chile is the result. The winds from the Pacific Ocean are of little help either. They blow from the cold Humboldt Current and bring little rain.

8. Much farther south, the winds over South America come from the southwest. These winds travel until they reach the Andes Mountains. The mountains force the winds to rise and rain falls along the coast. East of the mountains it is dry. This causes a dry plain in western Argentina.

9. Chile is a long, narrow country in the southwestern part of South America. Since it is 2500 miles long, it has several kinds of climate. Northern Chile is a desert, the Atacama Desert. South of the desert is a 600-mile strip of Mediterranean climate. Summers are hot and dry and winters are mild and rainy. Most of Chile's people live here. Farther south the climate is marine, like that of the coasts of our states of Oregon and Washington.

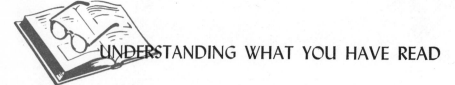

UNDERSTANDING WHAT YOU HAVE READ

1. **Which of the following questions are answered in this chapter?**
a. Why is it cold in some places near the equator?
b. What animals live in the rain forest?
c. Why are parts of South America's west coast a desert?

2. **The main idea of this chapter is to describe:**
a. how the winds affect Latin America.
b. the vertical climate of Latin America.
c. the different climates of Latin America.

3. **The largest part of Latin America is in the:**
a. low latitudes.
b. middle latitudes.
c. high latitudes.

4. **The mountains of Latin America cause a climate that is called:**
a. rain forest.   b. vertical.   c. subtropical.

5. **A reason for the desert of northern Chile is that:**
a. lowland areas in a vertical climate have little rain.
b. the Andes Mountains cut off rain from the east.
c. the seasons are opposite from ours.

6. **Some of the large cities of Latin America are located in the highlands because:**
a. disease-carrying insects are found in all the lowland areas.
b. all of Latin America is near the equator.
c. the climate is more pleasant there.

7. **The best meaning for *subtropical* is:**
a. near the tropics.
b. grassland.
c. rain-carrying.

DEVELOPING IDEAS AND SKILLS

Map # 19—Climates of Latin America

Are these statements true or false?   Give reasons for your answers.

1. There is no marine climate north of the equator in Latin America.

2. Only the rain-forest climate is found along the equator.
3. An area of vertical climate stretches the entire length of South America.
4. The largest region of good rainfall is found along the north and eastern coasts.

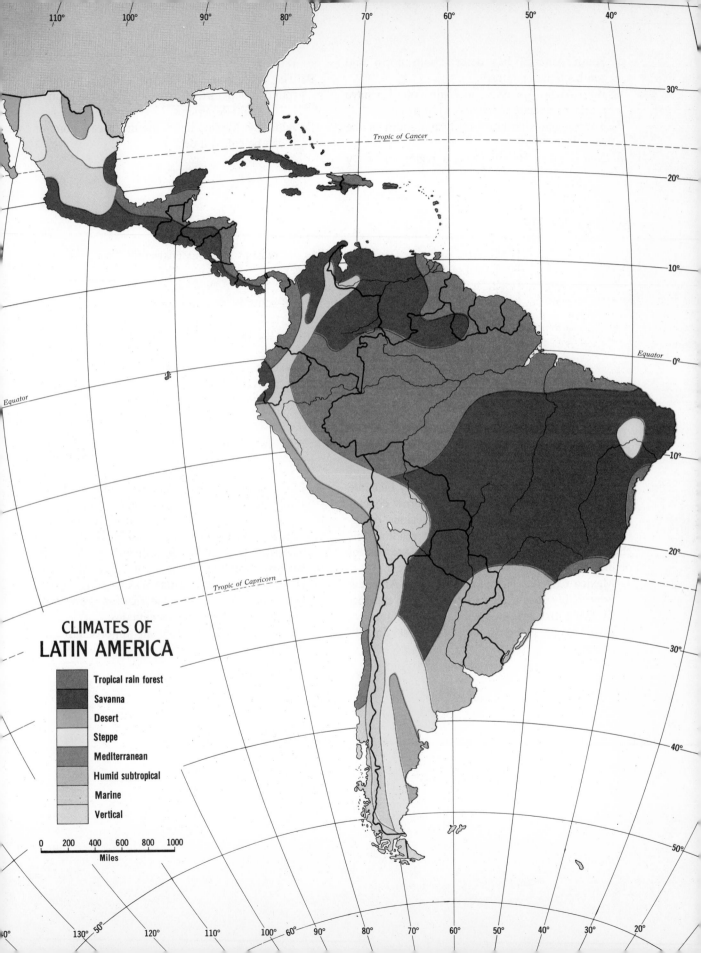

CLIMATES OF
LATIN AMERICA

Tropical rain forest
Savanna
Desert
Steppe
Mediterranean
Humid subtropical
Marine
Vertical

0 200 400 600 800 1000
Miles

110°   100°   90°   80°   70°   60°   50°   40°

Tropic of Cancer

Equator

Tropic of Capricorn

Equator

30°
20°
10°
0°
10°
20°
30°
40°
50°

130° 50° 120° 110° 100° 60° 90° 80° 70° 60° 50° 40° 30° 20°

5. South America has deserts both north and south of the equator.
6. Both Anglo-America and Latin America have a marine climate along the western coast.
7. The savannas lie both north and south of the rain forest.
8. Nearly all of Brazil lies in a region of heavy rainfall.
9. The subtropical climate of Latin America is found much farther from the equator than it is in Anglo-America.
10. Although Mexico has some dry areas, none of it can be called a desert.

SUMMING UP

Do You Agree or Disagree? Give the reasons for your answers.
1. All of Latin America is hot and wet.
2. It is always hot near the equator.
3. Dry grasslands are found north and south of the rain forest.
4. South America has no deserts.
5. Temperatures along the equator are the hottest on the earth.
6. Chile is a land of different climates.
7. Most people live in the tropical lowlands.
8. The Caribbean and Atlantic coasts are dry.

FOLLOW UP

Making Inferences In our reading, many facts are given to us. From these facts we can draw conclusions. The following are some conclusions or inferences that you might make after reading this chapter. Tell whether these conclusions are correct or incorrect. Give reasons for your answers.
1. Mexico City, the largest city in Latin America, is probably located on a lowland near the sea.
2. In flying from New York to Rio de Janeiro, Brazil, your plane would fly almost directly south.
3. Latin Americans grow some crops that we do not have and some that are the same as ours.
4. Latin American countries trade more with Europe and Africa than they do with Australia.
5. There are few cities in the valley of the Amazon.
6. Buenos Aires, Argentina, would have the same kind of climate as Seattle, Washington.
7. Some countries of Latin America can grow crops that are suited to different climates.
8. The airplane has become an important means of travel in Latin America.

CHAPTER 4

From Colonies to Free Nations

PROBLEM: How has Latin America changed in four hundred years?

READING FOR A PURPOSE:
1. Who were the Incas?
2. Which European peoples settled in Latin America?
3. Who was Simon Bolivar?

1. Long before Columbus came to the New World there were people living on the American continents. These were the Indians. The first Americans probably came from Asia. They crossed the Bering Strait into Alaska. Then they moved southward, exploring the land and settling it. Three of the most famous Indian peoples in Latin America were the Mayas, the Aztecs and the Incas.

2. The Maya Indians lived in southern Mexico and Guatemala. They built many beautiful cities in Central America before the arrival of Columbus. They studied the skies and learned about the movements of the sun, moon and stars. They learned to keep time and made a calendar. They built huge pyramids and other buildings of stone. They painted pictures and learned to weave cotton cloth. Finally the Mayas were conquered by other Indian tribes and their way of life disappeared.

3. The Aztecs lived in a valley in the central highlands of Mexico. Their capital city was Tenochtitlan. It was built on islands in the middle of a lake. The Aztecs conquered the other tribes living around them. They forced these tribes to work for them and to pay taxes in gold and silver. Their temples were built on the tops of great stone pyramids. The Aztecs wove cotton cloth and planted corn, beans and potatoes.

4. The Inca empire was in the Andes Mountains, from Ecuador to Chile. The ruler was called the Inca and the people he ruled were called Incas. The leaders lived in stone palaces or fortresses on the tops of mountains. The capital of the empire was at Cuzco, in Peru. The people lived on the hillsides or in the valleys below. They lived chiefly by raising corn, beans and potatoes or by herding llamas and alpaca. The Inca farmers learned to terrace—that is, to build steps on the mountainsides for farming. They irrigated their farm lands with water from the highlands. The Incas were sun worshipers and made many objects in the form of a round golden disk. The Incas were also good road builders.

5. Some of the lands of Latin America were discovered by Columbus while sailing westward from Spain. During his second voyage to the New World, he began the first European settlement there. Before long, both Spain and Portugal claimed lands in America. These countries asked the Pope—the head of the Catholic Church—to divide the New World between them. In 1493, the Pope drew an imaginary line running north and south on the map. This was called the Line of Demarcation. All lands west of this line would belong to Spain. All lands east of this line would belong to Portugal. Because of this settlement, Portugal later claimed the land that is now Brazil.

6. By 1500, there were a number of Spanish settlements in the islands of the West Indies. The Spanish brought horses, cattle and sheep to the New World. From their island forts, soldiers were sent to explore the nearby coasts in search of riches. In 1519, Hernando Cortez landed with a small force on the coast of Mexico. With the help of guns and horses he was able to conquer the Aztec Indians. In 1532, Francisco Pizarro sailed southward along the west coast of South America and discovered the Inca empire. He captured the Inca chief and killed him. The Incas were soon defeated. The Spanish were now masters of two treasure houses in Latin America—Mexico and Peru.

7. By 1600, the Spaniards had explored and conquered most of Latin America. They divided their conquered lands into two kingdoms. The kingdoms were ruled by men called viceroys who were appointed by the King of Spain. The viceroys divided the best lands into huge estates or *haciendas*. These were given to friends of the king. The Indians had to work in the mines or on the farms and ranches. Missionaries arrived also in the New World. They taught the Catholic religion, set up schools and missions and taught the Indians.

8. Brazil was discovered in 1500 by Pedro Cabral, who was sailing for Portugal. The lands along the coast were divided into large farms or *plantations*. Sugar was the chief crop of the plantations. The planters found there were not enough Indians to work in the sugar fields, so they brought Negroes from Africa. The Negroes became slaves on the plantations. As time went on, the Portuguese kept moving westward until they had conquered nearly half the continent.

9. For 300 years Spain ruled its colonies with an "iron hand." The colonies could not make their own laws. But after the success of the American and French Revolutions the colonists wanted their freedom. However, the first revolt in Latin America was not in a Spanish colony. It took place in Haiti, which was ruled by the French. Many Negroes had been brought to Haiti by the French to work in the sugar fields. Toussaint L'Ouverture, a former slave, led them in their fight against French rule. Shortly after his death in 1803 the colony was given its freedom.

10. The ideas of freedom spread throughout Latin America. In 1810, Father Hidalgo, a Mexican priest, led the Mexican Indians in the first revolt against Spain. The Mexicans finally

A stone temple, part of Mayan ruins in Guatemala.

UNITED NATIONS

Simón Bolívar, the "Liberator" of South America.

won their freedom from Spain in 1821. Before long, other people in Latin America began to rebel against Spain. Simón Bolívar, the "George Washington of South America," led the fight for freedom in Venezuela, Colombia, Ecuador and Bolivia. José de San Martín helped to win freedom in Chile and Peru. In 1822, Brazil became free. By 1824, most of the countries in Central and South America were free from Spain and Portugal.

11. For a time, it seemed that the freedom of the new nations might be lost. Some rulers of Europe wanted to give back the nations of Latin America to Spain. The American people were glad to see the Spanish colonies win their freedom. They did not want the powerful nations of Europe helping Spain. In 1823, President James Monroe made a statement concerning the new nations that became known as the Monroe Doctrine. He said that Europe was to keep "hands off" the new governments in the Americas. Any attempt to help Spain to regain its colonies would be thought of as an unfriendly act against the United States.

12. When the people of Latin America became free, they did not unite like the people of the United States. Transportation was poor. It was difficult for people to communicate with each other. Separate little nations were formed. In the beginning, many of the new countries tried to draw up constitutions or plans of government like that of the United States. However, most of the people were poor. They could not read or write and could not understand what their leaders were doing. After a while the new nations came to be ruled by strong men or dictators. The people had few rights even though they were free from their European rulers. We will learn more of the later history of Latin America in Chapter 10.

UNDERSTANDING WHAT YOU HAVE READ

1. Which of the following questions are answered in this chapter?
a. Who was Juárez?
b. How did Spain govern its colonies?
c. How was the New World discovered?

2. The main idea of *paragraphs 9 through 11* is to describe:
a. how the United States treated the countries of Latin America.
b. the Latin American struggle for freedom.

c. the European rule of Latin American colonies.

3. Brazil was settled by the:
a. Spanish.   b. French.   c. Portuguese.

4. The Inca Empire was destroyed by:
a. Cortez.   b. Pizarro.   c. Columbus.

5. The Spanish came to the New World for all of these reasons EXCEPT:
a. the desire for silver and gold.
b. to convert the Indians to the Catholic religion.
c. to get the rich furs from the animals in the forests.

6. Negroes were brought as slaves to Latin America from Africa chiefly to:
a. work in the mines.
b. work in the sugar fields.
c. settle the inland plain of Brazil.

7. A *viceroy* is the same as:
a. a governor.
b. an explorer.
c. a missionary.

8. In a country ruled by a *dictator,* the people:
a. enjoy freedom of speech.
b. choose their own leaders.
c. have little voice in their government.

DEVELOPING IDEAS AND SKILLS

Picture Symbols

These pictures should help you to recall parts of the chapter you have read. Can you tell the main idea of each picture? In what paragraph did you find the answer for each?

SUMMING UP

When Did It Happen? Arrange these events in their proper order in history, according to the headings below.

A. Indian Civilizations
B. Colonies of European Nations
C. Period of Independence
    1. Negroes imported for work on farms.
    2. Land divided into two kingdoms.
    3. Hillsides terraced for farming.
    4. Monroe Doctrine announced.
    5. Cuzco was an important city.
    6. Line of Demarcation established.
    7. Many small nations.
    8. Leadership of Simón Bolívar.
    9. Building of pyramids of stone.
    10. Gold and silver sent to Europe.

FOLLOW UP

Reviewing Chapters 1 Through 4. Which Does Not Belong? Choose the item that does not belong with the others in each group.

1. Reasons for our interest in Latin America:
   a. Panama Canal
   b. trading for each other's goods
   c. source of machinery
   d. source of tropical foods

2. Climates of Latin America:
   a. tundra   b. rain forest   c. vertical   d. desert

3. Land forms of Latin America:
   a. mountains   b. plains   c. plateaus   d. large inland lakes

4. Indians of Latin America:
   a. Incas   b. Seminoles   c. Mayas   d. Aztecs

5. Settlers in Latin America:
   a. Swedes   b. Spanish   c. Portuguese   d. French

CHAPTER 5

The People

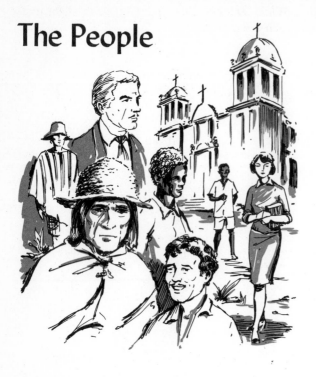

PROBLEM: Who are the people of Latin America?

READING FOR A PURPOSE:

1. What are the main groups of people in Latin America?
2. What languages are spoken in Latin America?
3. How do most people make a living?

1. The population of Latin America is growing at a faster rate than that of any other region of the world. About 230 million people live in the lands south of the United States. There are three main groups of people—Indians, Negroes and Europeans.

2. The Indians were the first people in this region. They were conquered by the Spanish and forced to work in mines and on farms. Today the Indians live mainly in nine of the region's twenty-three countries: Guatemala, Ecuador, Bolivia, Peru, Paraguay, Mexico, El Salvador, Panama and the Amazon valley of Brazil.

3. Negroes were brought to Latin America from Africa in the 16th century. They were the chief source of labor on the large sugar plantations. The Negro population of Latin America is found mainly on the Caribbean Islands and the wet coastal lowlands of Colombia and Brazil. Most of Haiti (90 per cent of the people) and large parts of Cuba and the Dominican Republic are Negro.

4. Most of the "white" people in Latin America are descendants of the early Spanish and Portuguese settlers and other immigrants from Europe. In the 19th century many people came to Latin America from Italy, France and Germany. They settled chiefly in the milder climates of Argentina, Uruguay and Chile.

5. Since the Spanish explorers came to Latin America there has been much mixing among these three groups of people. As a result, a large number of people are a mixture of races. A *mestizo* is a person who is partly Indian and partly white. A *mulatto* is partly Negro and partly white. A *zambo* is partly Indian and partly Negro. Because of this great mixing of races, the people of Latin America have not been greatly concerned with the color of a person's skin.

6. The official language in eighteen Latin American nations is Spanish. In Brazil the people speak Portuguese; in Haiti, French; in Guyana, Jamaica, and Trinidad and Tobago, English. Many Indian tribes in far valleys still speak their own languages. But more people speak Spanish than any other language in Latin America. All languages have been changed slightly. Indian words have been added to the Spanish, and in the south Spanish may also be spoken with Italian words or accent.

7. Religion is another tie that brings Latin Americans together. More than 80 per cent of the people are Catholic. The Spanish and Portuguese brought Catholic missionaries with them to the New World. They converted many of the Indians to the Catholic religion. The Catholic Church is important in the everyday life of the people. Even in tiny Indian villages in the mountains there are churches. While there are

*The large, growing city
of Caracas, Venezuela.*

Protestants and Jews in Latin America, they are small in number compared with Catholics.

8. Most Latin Americans are farmers who work on large farms. These large farms are called *plantations* in the Caribbean Islands. They are called *haciendas* in Mexico, *estancias* in Argentina and Uruguay and *fazendas* in Brazil. Many of the large farms are owned by one man or one family. The farmers who work on the land of other people are called *peons*.

9. Besides the peons, there are many Indians who own their own small farms. They raise corn on small plots of land, farming in the same

An Indian family in Guatemala.

way their ancestors did. They do not speak Spanish. They do not know of the modern inventions that would make their work easier. They have little knowledge of methods of farming that would help them to grow a larger amount of crops on their land. Many herd llamas and sheep on grassy mountain slopes or work in mines.

10. While Latin America is big in size and is growing in population, it does not have a large share of the world's people. Large areas of South America such as the rain forest, the mountains and the dry plains and deserts cannot support many people and are not pleasant to live in. Except for the Caribbean Islands, most Latin Americans live in the eastern and western highlands where it is cooler than in the hot lowlands.

11. One out of three Latin Americans now lives in the growing cities. These cities are modern, and tourists find that they look like cities in the United States. There are wide streets, tall buildings and beautiful homes. There are soft drinks, neon lights and plenty of traffic. The large landowners, the government leaders and the heads of business and industry usually live in the cities as do the growing class of factory workers. Most of the people are of European background. In the cities the children have the best chance for an education. But there are poorer sections of the large cities too.

161

The slums in Latin America are as bad as those in some of our large North American cities.

12. There are ten cities in Latin America with more than one million people. Mexico City has become the largest city among our southern neighbors with almost five million people. Buenos Aires, the capital of Argentina, has almost four million. This is the great port and railroad center of the southeast. São Paulo is another city that has grown fast and is now the largest city in Brazil. It is also the leading industrial city. Rio de Janeiro, once the largest city in Brazil, has one of the most beautiful harbors in the world.

13. The governments in Latin America vary from democracies to dictatorships. The oldest democratic governments are found in the countries of Uruguay, Mexico and Costa Rica. In many others, the people are gaining a greater voice in their governments. Some Latin American countries are dictatorships—ruled by one or a few powerful men. These men have often been supported by the army or by the large land-holders who do not want to share their power.

UNDERSTANDING WHAT YOU HAVE READ

1. **Which of the following questions are answered in this chapter?**
a. What is a mestizo?
b. Where do most Latin American people live?
c. What do the city people of Latin America wear?

2. **The main idea of *paragraphs 1 through 6* is to describe:**
a. the mixture of people in Latin America.
b. people who have come from other lands.
c. the small population of Latin America.

3. **A country with a large Negro population is:**
a. Argentina.   b. Haiti.   c. Mexico.

4. **The great seaport of southeast South America is:**
a. Buenos Aires.   b. São Paulo.   c. Bogotá.

5. **Many people of Latin America live in the highlands because:**
a. there are many winter sports.
b. gold and silver are mined there.
c. it is cooler.

6. **Latin America does not support more people because:**
a. there is a lack of machinery.
b. much of the land is rain forest or mountains.
c. cows and other farm animals cannot live there.

7. **A *peon* is the same as a:**
a. factory worker.
b. tenant farmer.
c. ranch owner.

8. **A *mestizo* is partly Spanish and partly:**
a. Negro.   b. French.   c. Indian.

DEVELOPING IDEAS AND SKILLS

Pictograph # 8—Population, Area and Standard of Living of Latin America
1. Is the standard of living of this region high or low compared with that of the United States? Is it a low-income or underdeveloped area?
2. Is the region as crowded as the United States?
3. Are the people of this region literate compared with the people of the United States?
4. How long may the average person in this region expect to live?
5. What facts tell you the standard of living of the people of the region?
6. How does this region compare with the United States in size?

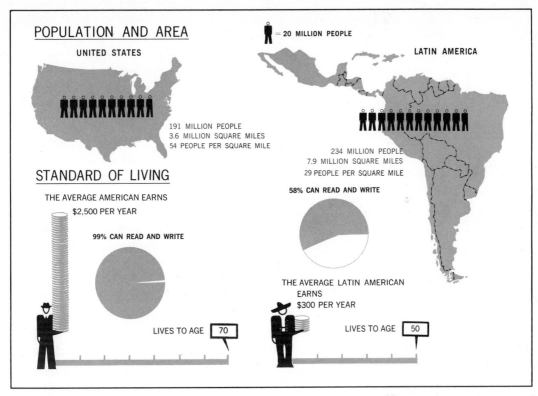

POPULATION AND AREA

UNITED STATES

⬤ = 20 MILLION PEOPLE

LATIN AMERICA

191 MILLION PEOPLE
3.6 MILLION SQUARE MILES
54 PEOPLE PER SQUARE MILE

234 MILLION PEOPLE
7.9 MILLION SQUARE MILES
29 PEOPLE PER SQUARE MILE

STANDARD OF LIVING

THE AVERAGE AMERICAN EARNS
$2,500 PER YEAR

58% CAN READ AND WRITE

99% CAN READ AND WRITE

THE AVERAGE LATIN AMERICAN EARNS
$300 PER YEAR

LIVES TO AGE 70

LIVES TO AGE 50

Pictograph # 8—Population, Area and Standard of Living of Latin America

SUMMING UP

In the following, place before each statement the word that makes the statement correct: *Most, Some, Few.*

1. _____ Latin Americans speak Spanish.
2. _____ people in Latin America have traveled to other countries.
3. _____ Latin Americans are Catholics.
4. _____ people live in large cities.
5. _____ Latin Americans grow coffee.
6. _____ Latin Americans work on farms.
7. _____ people of Haiti speak French.
8. _____ people own their own farms.
9. _____ children in Latin America have a good education.

FOLLOW UP

Complete the following chart in your notebook.

	MY FAMILY	INDIAN FAMILY IN LATIN AMERICA
1. Foods		
2. Clothing		
3. Education		
4. Religion		
5. Occupations		

CHAPTER 6

Village Life

PROBLEM: How do people live in the villages of Latin America?

READING FOR A PURPOSE:
1. How are the houses built?
2. What is the main food of the farmers?
3. What are the problems of the village farmers?

1. In Latin America most farmers do not live on their own farms, but in small villages. The center of the village is usually a small square or *plaza*. Around the plaza may stand the church, the school and a few small stores. The plaza is also the market place.

2. Near the plaza are the homes of the villagers. These homes are built differently throughout Latin America. In the dry climates they may be made of adobe (sun-dried bricks of mud). The roofs of the houses may be covered with tile or straw thatch. In the rainy areas the houses or huts are often made of reeds with thatched roofs. Corrugated iron roofs are also used. In the colder areas of the highlands there are few trees and bushes, so houses are made of stone.

3. Most of the houses are small and simple and have only one room. The furniture may be only a bed, some sleeping mats, a table and a few chairs. There may be no windows in the house. The family spends a lot of time outside, the father working in the fields and the mother cooking, sewing and taking care of the children. There is probably no electricity and certainly no plumbing.

4. The whole family works hard each day to raise the things it needs in order to live. The chief crops are corn and beans. Most of the work is done by hand. The grains of corn are planted by hand. The field is cultivated with a hoe or a digging stick. When the corn is full grown, the ears are gathered by hand. The cornstalks are then cut down with large knives called *machetes*. For several reasons, it is very hard for the farmer to raise more than his family needs. The plot is small. Sometimes the soil is dry; sometimes it is too cold. The farmer has no fertilizer, so the soil wears out. There is no machinery. Many of the farmers have poor seeds. Little is done to stop erosion (the flowing or washing away of the soil).

A market place in an Andean village of Peru.

Standard Oil Co. (N.J.)

Villagers washing clothes in a stream in Colombia.

A street in Cuzco, Peru. Notice the church in the background.

5. Some families may have a vegetable garden and a few fruit trees of their own. These and the corn and beans from the fields provide nearly all that the villagers get to eat. They eat little meat because very few can afford to have large meat animals. The corn flour is often made into flat cakes called *tortillas.* On the islands of the West Indies and in the Amazon Basin, manioc or starch from the root of the cassava plant is eaten. Coffee and tea are favorite drinks. Villagers seldom drink milk, for they do not keep milk cows.

6. Almost everything the people need is made at home, for the family has little money. In most parts of Latin America the farmers and their families wear plain clothes that are made at home. The men wear shirts and trousers of coarse white cotton, and the women wear simple cotton dresses. The women also weave a *rebozo* or shawl that serves as a head covering or baby sling. The men have *serapes.* A serape is a hand-woven blanket with a slit in the center for the head. The farmer uses the serape as both a blanket and a coat.

7. To add to their income many farmers make other things. They make and sell clay pots and bowls, jewelry of silver and turquoise, colorful wool blankets, sandals and straw hats. Many villages may have a shoemaker, a basket weaver, a hat maker and a brick maker to fill the needs of the people.

8. Once a week the people take their handwork, some pigs and chickens and some fruits and vegetables to the nearest market place. They may sell these goods for other things they need. Several times a year there are village *fiestas* where there is plenty of drink, food and dancing.

9. The farmer we have just described is a subsistence farmer. He probably cannot read or write because many of the poor villages or farm areas cannot afford to build schools. Many of his children do not attend what schools there are because they are needed at home to help with the work in the fields.

10. He is probably not well. In many villages there are no sewers, and the drinking water is unhealthy. The water for cooking or washing clothes may come from a ditch alongside the road. The same water may later be used to irrigate a vegetable garden. There are many villages without a doctor or nurse. The people in some villages still go to "village wizards" who use herbs and charms to treat diseases.

165

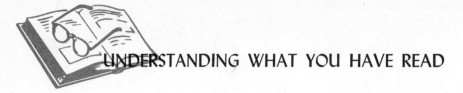

UNDERSTANDING WHAT YOU HAVE READ

1. **Which of the following questions are answered in this chapter?**
a. How does the Latin American farmer live?
b. Why are many farmers in poor health?
c. What games do the children play?

2. **The main idea of this chapter is to describe:**
a. how the village farmer meets his daily needs.
b. goods manufactured in the home.
c. the meals of the small farmers.

3. **The chief crop of the village farmer is:**
a. corn.   b. wheat.   c. rice.

4. **Village people sell their handwork:**

a. to the large department stores.
b. to buyers in the cities.
c. in the nearby market.

5. **Many farm families have poor health for all of these reasons EXCEPT:**
a. lack of sunshine.
b. lack of pure water.
c. poor diet.

6. **Meat is not an important part of the diet of the village farmers because:**
a. the cattle are needed to supply milk.
b. very few meat animals are raised on the farm.
c. farmers sell their meat to the nearby cities.

Standard Oil Co. (N.J.)

DEVELOPING IDEAS AND SKILLS

Photograph Study

The photograph on p. 166 should help you to recall parts of the chapter you have just read. Can you tell the main idea of the photograph? Where in the chapter is it described?

SUMMING UP

Complete the following outline in your notebook.

	SMALL VILLAGE FARMER OF LATIN AMERICA	CORN-BELT FARMER OF THE UNITED STATES
1. Homes		
2. Machinery		
3. Crops and animals		
4. Standard of living		
5. Markets for their products		

FOLLOW UP

In your notebook, match the items in Column A with the items in Column B.

COLUMN A	COLUMN B
1. peon	_____ blanket
2. fiesta	_____ gay party
3. adobe	_____ village square
4. mestizo	_____ farm worker
5. plaza	_____ flat cakes of corn bread
6. tortilla	_____ large knife
7. hacienda	_____ part Indian, part Spanish
8. serape	_____ large estate
	_____ sun-dried brick

CHAPTER 7

The Problem of Land

PROBLEM: How do the people of Latin America make use of the land?

READING FOR A PURPOSE:
1. How do people live in the rain forest?
2. What kind of work is done in the savannas?
3. What is the work of the pampas?

1. In the great region of Latin America only a very small part of the land can be used. Much of the land is covered by mountains, jungle and desert. The Andes Mountains are too high and cold for large-scale farming. The soils of the rain forest and dry grasslands are poor. The deserts cannot support life. Nevertheless, most people in this region make their living by using the land. Let us see how the people of Latin America meet the challenge of these difficult conditions.

2. A large part of Latin America is rain forest. In the forest a few Indian tribes live in villages near the rivers. They are always crowded by trees and plants that grow fast in the hot and wet climate. There are many insects that carry diseases such as malaria. They cannot travel far because there are few paths through the thick jungle. Growing food is a problem because the soil is poor. Keeping the food from spoiling is also difficult in this hot climate.

3. The Indians in the rain forest live simple lives. They grow most of their food in small clearings in the forest. The men clear the land by chopping down trees or burning away the thick brush. Once the land has been cleared, the women start planting. The men go into the forest to get more food by hunting and fishing.

4. The chief foods in the rain forest are bananas, yams and tapioca (manioc). Every two or three years the Indians have to move and make a new clearing because the soil in the old one has worn out. Heavy rains wash out or leach the minerals in the soil that food crops need in order to grow. Most travel is by canoe along the rivers and streams because the forest is so thick.

5. The Indians make nearly everything they use from the products of the forest. They make their houses out of thatch—straw, grass and leaves. These are cone-shaped so as to shed water. The men make fish traps, bows and arrows and blowguns from which they blow or

A rain-forest Indian in his jungle shelter.

A banana plantation in Ecuador.

Opening cacao pods in Colombia.

"shoot" small poisoned darts. They also make canoes or dugouts by hollowing out the trunks of large trees. The women weave clothing, mats and baskets out of grasses and leaves. Some of these are sold.

6. The rain forest has many products that are useful to people in other parts of the world. These products include mahogany and other hardwoods, chicle for chewing gum and cinchona bark from which a medicine called quinine is made. The products are gathered by the Indians and brought to trading posts at Belém or Manaus. (These port cities also supply the people of the rain forest with the things they need from the outside world.) Only a small part of its riches is brought out of the jungle. Few people live there and it is hard to ship goods through the thick forest.

7. As you remember, grasslands are found north and south of the Amazon jungle. Thus, the southern half of Brazil and the llanos of Venezuela in the north have a tropical savanna climate. This means there are two seasons, one rainy and one dry. How do the people make a living in this climate? Cattle raising is very important in the llanos. The land is divided into large cattle ranches or *haciendas*. The cattle are always on the move. The herds are guarded by cowboys called llaneros. These cattle are raised for their hides and rarely for their meat.

8. In the dry season the rivers become little more than streams. Cattle are grazed near the streams where the grass is still moist and green. In the rainy season the rivers flood their banks. Then the cowboys drive the cattle to higher lands or mesas between the swollen rivers. When they have eaten all the grass on one mesa, they wade through the waters to another.

9. The savannas are not the best land for growing crops. The soil is poor because the minerals have been washed out by the heavy rains. However, a number of cash crops are grown in this climate. Sugar cane is the chief crop of the tropical grasslands. The hot weather, the rainy growing season and the dry harvest time are good for growing sugar. Sugar cane is grown on large plantations in the islands of the West Indies, particularly Cuba. Another wet and dry crop is henequen or sisal, from

169

which rope is made. Henequen is raised on the Yucatan Peninsula in Mexico.

10. As you have learned, an important feature of the climate of Latin America is that it is vertical. That is, the climate changes as you travel upward in the mountains. Farming is also vertical. In the hot and damp lowlands of Central America there are plantations of bananas and cacao beans. (Cacao is the bean from which chocolate is made.) These crops need the wet, rainy weather and long growing season of the tropics. Bananas need more than a year to ripen. Most of the workers are Negroes and mestizos. They live on land owned by the plantation or in villages near the plantations.

11. As you travel higher into a cooler climate (tierra templada), the most common crop is coffee. Coffee is grown in the highlands of Brazil and Colombia. In Brazil, coffee is grown on large estates, the fazendas. At first the coffee beans are green. During the hot, rainy summers the little beans turn red and open. During the dry, cooler winters the beans turn brown and are picked. Coffee is the chief export of both Brazil and Colombia. It is our chief import from those countries.

12. Many Indians live in the higher altitudes (tierra fria). They farm on the steep mountainsides. They raise the crops that fill their needs—wheat, barley, beans, potatoes and Indian corn or maize. They graze herds of sheep, llamas and burros. The llamas and burros are used for riding and for carrying heavy loads. The temperature may be from 40° to 50° all year round. Some Indians also work in the tin, copper, lead and zinc mines found at this height.

13. In South America the humid-subtropical area is found along the southeastern coast. This includes part of Brazil, Paraguay and Argentina and all of Uruguay. Because of the climate and soil, the best cattle-grazing lands are found there. There is a long, hot summer and a short, mild winter. The famous grazing lands are the pampas or plains of Argentina.

14. The pampas are divided into large ranches or estancias. The wealthy owners live mainly in Buenos Aires. The cattle are cared for by colorful cowboys called gauchos. Most of them are Indians. The cattle are raised chiefly for their meat. Large amounts of alfalfa are grown on the pampas as food for the cattle. Corn and wheat are grains grown on the rich, black earth. Argentina exports the riches of the pampas—beef, corn and wheat—to other parts of the world. Unlike the rest of Latin America, most of Argentina's trade is with Europe.

15. Two important crops of Latin America are corn and cotton. Corn is a basic food in the diet of millions of Latin Americans. It had been raised by the Indians long before Columbus' voyages. In Mexico, corn is largely eaten by the people. In Brazil it is an important food

Cattle grazing on the llanos in Venezuela.

Standard Oil Co. (N.J.)

for animals. In Argentina it is an export. (You will note that Argentina has large amounts of farm products that are the same as the farm products of our own country. This is because our climates are similar.) Since we grow large amounts of corn and wheat and raise millions of beef cattle, the U.S. cannot be a good customer for Argentina's farm products. Therefore, Argentina looks to Europe to sell her important goods for export.

16. Cotton has become an important product of the dry lands. In her northern deserts, Mexico has used the waters of the Rio Grande to grow cotton. (Mexico ranks first in cotton production in Latin America.) In the desert of Peru cotton is also grown. The water is brought from the mountains near the coast. All over the world it has been found that the finest cotton can be grown in dry areas through water supplied by irrigation.

Pan American Airways

Gauchos tend cattle on the pampas of Argentina.

UNDERSTANDING WHAT YOU HAVE READ

1. Which of the following questions are answered in this chapter?
a. What are the chief crops of Latin America?
b. Why are the pampas good for grazing cattle?
c. How does the banana tree grow?

2. The main idea of this chapter is to describe:
a. the many farming areas of Latin America.
b. how people live in the rain forest.
c. the crops of the vertical climate.

3. The chief crops of the lowland plantations are:
a. rice and pineapples.
b. bananas and cacao beans.
c. palm oil and corn.

4. The chief crops of the pampas are:
a. cotton and coffee.
b. wheat and corn.

c. sugar cane and bananas.

5. A country of Latin America that produces much the same kind of crops as the United States is:
a. Brazil.   b. Chile.   c. Argentina.

6. Life in the tierra fria is difficult because:
a. it is too far above sea level to grow any crops.
b. the forests must be cleared before planting.
c. the steep hillsides must be terraced before planting.

7. A *mesa* is the same as a:
a. lowland plain.
b. small high plateau.
c. mountainside.

8. *Cacao* is a small tree whose beans are used in making:
a. medicine.   b. rope.   c. chocolate.

UNITED NATIONS

DEVELOPING IDEAS AND SKILLS

Photograph Study

This photograph should help you to recall parts of the chapter you have just read. Can you tell the main idea of the photograph? Where in the chapter is it described?

SUMMING UP

Match the items in Column B with the farming regions in Column A. Each farming region may be used several times.

COLUMN A	COLUMN B
A. Rain-forest farming	a. Small clearings in the jungle.
B. Savannas	b. Coffee plantations.
C. Highlands	c. Home of the gauchos.
D. Pampas	d. Houses of straw and grass.
	e. Barley and maize.
	f. Cattle, corn and wheat.
	g. Sugar plantations.
	h. Raising sheep and llamas.
	i. Flood season and dry season.
	j. Banana trees.

FOLLOW UP

Tell whether these statements are true or false. The underlined words make the statements true or false. If a statement is false, what words would you place in it to make it true?

1. Bananas are a product of a <u>hot and wet</u> climate.
2. The chief export of Brazil is <u>coffee</u>.
3. <u>Colombia</u> is a leading exporter of wheat and beef.
4. Very dry lands that have water from irrigation are best for growing <u>cotton</u>.
5. The great farming region of Uruguay and Argentina is called the <u>llanos</u>.
6. <u>Malaria</u> is a disease carried by an insect of the rain forest.
7. A rain-forest Indian may make his house of <u>thatch</u>.
8. One of the hardwoods found in the jungle of South America is the <u>palm</u> tree.
9. Gauchos are the famous cowboys of <u>Mexico</u>.
10. An important part of the diet of the people of Mexico is <u>coffee</u>.

CHAPTER 8

Mining and Manufacturing

PROBLEM: Why have industries grown slowly in Latin America?

READING FOR A PURPOSE:

1. What are the important minerals of Latin America?
2. Where is oil found?
3. Why are there few factories in this region?

1. Compared with the number of people who work on farms in Latin America, there are not many people working in the mines. Yet minerals are an important resource for Latin America. The earliest Spanish explorers found riches in silver and gold. Silver is still mined in Mexico, Peru and Bolivia. Mexico mines more silver than any other country in the world.

2. Even more important than silver and gold are other minerals that play a great part in all our lives. Bolivia has rich tin mines. The tin is located high in the plateaus, more than 10,000 feet above sea level. Working in the tin mines is very difficult. Workers breathe in the dust from the ore. The life of a tin miner is a short one. The Atacama Desert in northern Chile is rich in copper and nitrates. Nitrates are used for fertilizers. The people who work in the desert also lead a hard life. Everything they need must be brought in from the outside—food, clothing and even water. These important minerals—tin, copper and nitrates—are found in areas that are hard to reach.

3. Our entire modern world depends upon oil. One of the richest oil reserves in the world is at Lake Maracaibo in Venezuela. Wells have been sunk into the lake itself. Venezuela is one of the leading oil-producing nations of the world. Much of the oil is sent to the United States. Because of oil, the average income of Venezuelans is higher than that of any other people in Latin America.

4. Since World War II, Venezuela has also become a leading producer of iron ore. And in Peru, iron ore production has grown so that it now ranks second to Venezuela's. Ore deposits are not easy to reach. However, the world needs more and more iron for building and machinery. As a result, foreign countries have supplied Latin America with the money needed

The oil wells of Lake Maracaibo, Venezuela.

Standard Oil Co. (N.J.)

to find this valuable mineral and bring it to factories where it can be used. Steel mills are growing in Latin America. (Steel mills in the United States also import much of Venezuela's iron ore.)

5. Aluminum is much in demand for making airplanes, buildings and hundreds of other products. Aluminum is made from an ore called bauxite. A great share of the world's bauxite is found in Jamaica, Surinam and Guyana. It is shipped to the aluminum mills of the United States and Canada.

6. There are factories in Latin America, but most of them do not make use of the region's mineral wealth. Most of them depend on the products of the farm. For example, there are meat-packing plants near the grazing areas of Argentina. There are textile mills in Mexico and Peru turning out cloth from raw materials nearby. Despite these beginnings, Latin America exports most of the raw materials of its farms and mines to other parts of the world. The United States and the nations of Western Europe are its best customers. In turn, the United States sends Latin America all kinds of machinery.

7. Industry has not grown rapidly in Latin America for various reasons. First, there is a lack of coal. Coal is important as a source of power for mills and factories. It is needed as fuel in the making of steel. There are great possibilities, however, in the use of falling water for power. The heavy rainfall and snows in the mountains provide plenty of water. Less than ten per cent of the possible water power is used, however. This is because the sources of water power are far from the centers of population and industry.

8. Money is also needed. Money used to build factories and power plants is called *capital*. Latin America has lacked capital for several reasons. First, changes in government have taken place often in most of its countries. Businessmen from foreign nations are not eager to invest their money in countries that have "revolutions" all the time. They are afraid that their property will be damaged or taken away. Second, the people who settled Latin America came from Spain and Portugal. These are farming countries. The settlers kept the way of living they had learned in their homeland. Their wealth was measured in how much land they owned. Perhaps some of this wealth will now be used to start factories. Third, the profits that do come from the mines or plantations go outside the country, since they are owned by people

Mining tin high in the Andes Mountains of Bolivia.

UNATIONS

or businesses of foreign countries in many cases.

9. Transportation and communication in Latin America have been poor. Transportation is necessary to bring raw materials to factories. Because of the mountains and jungle, it has been easier to ship raw materials by water or air than to send them overland from one part of Latin America to another. (This meant, of course, that industry in Latin America was held back even more before the coming of the airplane.)

10. Skilled workers are needed for factory work. You have learned that a large number of Latin Americans are unable to read or write. There have been only a small number of schools. However, some improvement has taken place. The leaders of Latin America know that education of the people is most important in bringing them a higher standard of living.

UNATIONS

Making bricks in Bolivia.

UNDERSTANDING WHAT YOU HAVE READ

1. **Which of the following questions are answered in this chapter?**
   a. Why are there so few factories in Latin America?
   b. What power resources does Latin America need?
   c. How is tin mined?

2. **The main idea of *paragraphs 1 through 7* is to describe:**
   a. the mineral resources of Latin America.
   b. the hard work in the mines of Latin America.
   c. Latin American trade with other lands.

3. **Latin America has some minerals, but it lacks:**
   a. coal. b. oil. c. tin.

4. **Venezuela is one of the leading producers of:**
   a. gold and silver.
   b. copper and nitrates.
   c. oil and iron ore.

5. **A reason why Latin America has been slow to develop industry is that:**
   a. most of her trade is with Europe.
   b. lack of rain means that there is little water power available.
   c. there has been a lack of skilled workers.

6. **The desert of Chile is valuable because it is a source of:**
   a. irrigation. b. minerals. c. oil.

7. **"The machinery in the factory was poor because the owner had no *capital* to replace it." The best meaning for *capital* is:**
   a. new property.
   b. money to buy new machines.
   c. useful ideas.

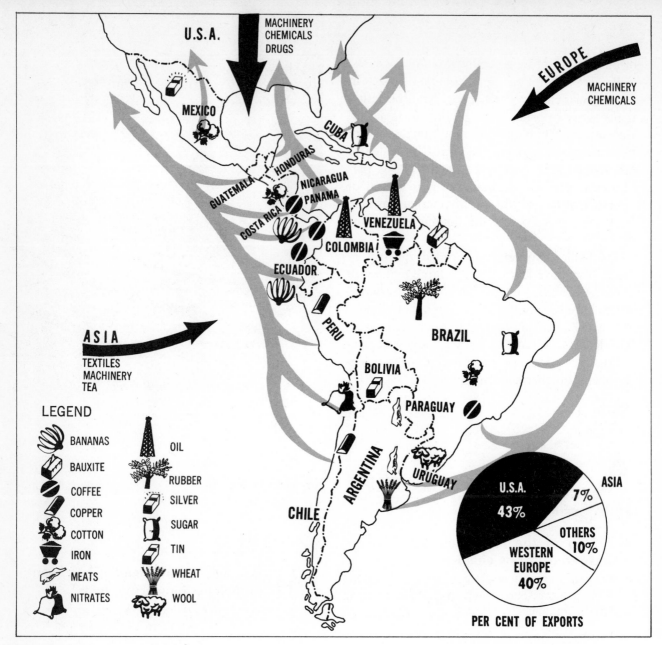

Map # 20—Imports and Exports of Latin America

DEVELOPING IDEAS AND SKILLS

Map # 20—Imports and Exports of Latin America

Tell whether these statements are true or false.

1. The greatest share of Latin American trade is with the United States.
2. Latin American countries import chiefly food from the U.S. and Europe.
3. Bananas are an important export of countries along the east coast of South America.
4. Peru and Chile both have a supply of raw copper.
5. Argentina's exports are chiefly food products.
6. Venezuela is rich in both iron ore and oil.
7. Mexico sends a large share of her exports to the United States.
8. Latin America's trade with Asia amounts to less than 10% of her exports.
9. Chile's resources are largely minerals.

SUMMING UP

A. *Where am I?*

Which country or part of Latin America is described by the person speaking in each of the following paragraphs?

1. "Work here in the highland is hard. My family is poor and I have poor health. If only I didn't have to go back into that mine tomorrow. I cough so much now I know it will never stop. I live in _____."

2. "The ore is near the surface and the machines do the hard work. I'm glad of that because it is so hot every day. My family has a good home. But I wish we weren't so far from other people. If that pipeline breaks, where will we get water? Yet we stay because the United States really wants this mineral. I live in _____."

3. "That sun shines all day, even when it rains. I know it's the rain that makes it seem so hot. And I had to come here in the season of the big rains! It's green all the time, but I can't see the color because the huge trees block out the sun. I am in _____."

4. "It is warm even on the side of the hill. But the sun won't hurt my precious beans here in the shade. I like to look at the rows and rows of trees. The people of the United States can't seem to do without my trees and my family at picking time. I live in _____."

5. "Look at the food on these docks! That wheat and corn will feed a lot of people in Europe. Funny, some people feed that corn to hogs. They should export it as my country does. I live in _____."

B. *Looking Ahead*

In Column I are listed some of the resources that bring wealth to Latin America. In Column II, list the problems that must be overcome to make full use of these resources.

COLUMN I	COLUMN II
1. copper	
2. iron ore	
3. nitrates	
4. oil	
5. tin	

FOLLOW UP

Fact or Opinion Tell which of these are facts and which are someone's opinion.

1. A change in the system of land ownership is the greatest need in Latin America.
2. Mexico has few minerals of value.
3. Latin America has many minerals that the United States can use.
4. Many valuable products cannot easily be brought out of the jungle.
5. Without oil and iron ore, Venezuela would be a poor country.
6. The land system in Latin America will be very slow to change.
7. If it is used, Latin America could have a large amount of electricity from water power.
8. Latin America will never industrialize because it lacks coal.
9. Control over the mines of Latin America is necessary for the safety of the United States.
10. U.S. trade with Argentina will double in the next ten years.

CHAPTER 9

The Needs of Latin America

PROBLEM: What are the problems of Latin America?

READING FOR A PURPOSE:
1. What is meant by "one-crop countries"?
2. How will more factories help Latin America?
3. How have dictators harmed Latin America?

1. The poverty of many people in Latin America is the biggest problem of the region. There are thousands of Indian farmers who live on tiny plots of the poorest land. They are barely able to grow enough food for their families. The money they make from farming each year is very small. Many make less than $100 per year. Their health is poor. They do not eat the right kind of food. Many cannot read and write.

Their needs are simple, but everywhere they are the same: more and better land, pure water, better roads, electricity, public schools and health services.

2. The number of people in Latin America is growing so fast that the population may double in twenty years! Most of this growth in population is taking place among the poorer families. Thus, there will be more mouths to feed where there is the least ability to feed them. There is already a problem of raising enough food for the present population.

3. Much of the fertile land is occupied by huge plantations. Many of these plantations are owned by foreign businessmen or by a few wealthy families of Latin America. The plantations have become like factories. Workers are housed and fed like armies in large buildings. Crops raised on the plantations—coffee, sugar and bananas—are raised for export to other countries. They are not an important part of the diet of the Latin Americans. Therefore, a large amount of food must be imported by these countries for their people.

*Old and new transportation methods
in Latin America.*

UNATIONS

178

More and more machinery is being used, as on this sugar plantation in Colombia.

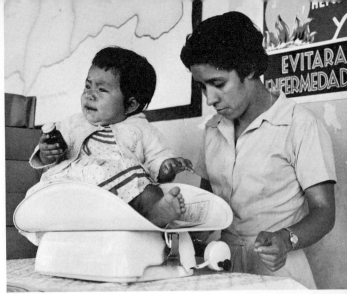

A health center in Guatemala.
Most Latin Americans need better health care.

4. As you learned in Unit 2, the kind of farming that causes a country to depend upon one chief crop may cause problems. Latin America has sometimes been called a region of "one-crop countries." For example, Brazil and Colombia have long depended on one crop—coffee—for their income. The countries of Central America depend upon their sale of bananas. Guatemala and El Salvador get more than half their export sales from coffee. Cuba has depended upon sugar cane. This kind of farming is called "monoculture." If the crop is a poor one or there is a drop in its market price, the whole country suffers greatly.

5. The need for more land for the small farmers is being faced in several ways. Governments are opening new lands for the people. For example, Brasília, the new capital of Brazil, has been built inland to attract people to a new area. There is a growing demand that the large estates be broken up and given to small farmers. People like to own their own land. The chance to have a farm of one's own is the dream of many people all over the world.

6. While the number of large factories is still small, the demand for factories is growing. The new steel mills of Cerro Bolivar in Venezuela are an example of what Latin Americans can

Old and new housing in Costa Rica.

UNITED NATIONS

*The people need to take greater part
in making decisions for their villages.*

do. With more factories the Latin Americans will be able to use more of their own resources for their own benefit. People will be hired to work in these factories. They will receive more pay than they could get from working on the farms. They will be able to buy goods that are manufactured. If they are able to buy more, the factories will make more goods and there will be a need for even more jobs.

7. More jobs and better pay will help a great deal in getting rid of another problem of Latin America. There are two chief classes of people in this region. The wealthy class, usually of Spanish descent, owns much of the land and the factories. The poorer class, usually the Indians and the Negroes, have small farms or work on the large estates. There is no real "middle class." The poorer classes are being heard more often in Latin America. They want more land, more jobs and a better education for their children. They want the opportunity for a higher standard of living for themselves and their families.

8. There have been frequent "revolutions" and changes in government in Latin America. One group after another has tried to gain power in many countries. Many of these revolutions have been supported by the army. Others have been caused by a few strong men who want power. They become dictators. There are still countries in Latin America today that are ruled as dictatorships. Because most of the people have not received an education, it has not been easy to have democratic governments. Education of the people is an important step in the improvement of life in Latin America. It is hoped that as the countries develop, their governments will grow to be the kind that allow the people to make their own laws and choose their own leaders.

UNDERSTANDING WHAT YOU HAVE READ

1. **Which of the following questions are answered in this chapter?**
a. How are some Latin Americans governed?
b. What are the problems of Latin America?
c. How does the United Nations help Latin America?

2. **The main idea of *paragraph 8* is to describe:**
a. revolutions in Latin America.
b. dictators of Latin America.
c. some problems of government in Latin America.

3. **Most Latin American nations obtain money by:**
a. manufacturing goods.
b. selling raw materials abroad.
c. dairy farming.

4. **Which is a correct matching of country and crop?**
a. Brazil—cacao

b. Cuba—sugar

c. Colombia—wheat

5. **Latin American countries import food because:**

a. plantations grow crops for export.

b. Indian farmers grow only for their own needs.

c. corn and wheat are not grown in Latin America.

6. **More factories will help Latin Americans because:**

a. they will provide more raw materials.

b. education will be improved.

c. Latin Americans will be able to use their own raw materials.

7. **In** *monoculture,* **a country depends upon:**

a. exports.

b. one crop.

c. many farm products.

8. **The** *middle class* **refers to:**

a. the very rich.

b. those who are neither rich nor poor.

c. the very poor.

DEVELOPING IDEAS AND SKILLS

Cartoon (See p. 178.)

1. Who is the running figure?

2. What is the meaning of this cartoon?

3. What is monoculture?

4. What is being done to overcome some of the problems shown here?

5. What is a good title for this cartoon?

SUMMING UP

Pretend you are at a meeting of the Organization of American States in which all the Latin American nations are represented. You are the representative of a Latin American country. What would you say were your greatest problems?

If you were a representative of the United States, what kind of help would you offer to Latin America?

FOLLOW UP

Outline   In the following outline, some topics are filled in, but the proper headings are missing. Which headings would you choose for each list of topics in the outline?

HEADINGS

A. _____

   1. Little machinery.

   2. Small plots of land.

   3. Little medical care.

   4. Impure water.

a. One-Crop Countries

b. Problems of Government

c. Land Ownership

d. Need for Education

e. Poverty of the People

B. _____

   1. Colombia—coffee

   2. Brazil—coffee

   3. Honduras—bananas

   4. Uruguay—wool

C. _____

   1. A few people own most of the land.

   2. Peons work on large plantations.

   3. The very rich and the very poor.

CHAPTER 10

The United States and Latin America

AGENDA
• ALLIANCE FOR PROGRESS
• PANAMA
• CANAL
• COMMUNISM

PROBLEM: How can the United States improve her relations with Latin America?

READING FOR A PURPOSE:
1. How did the United States get the island of Puerto Rico?
2. Why have some Latin Americans been unfriendly toward the United States?
3. What is the "Alliance for Progress"?

1. In 1823, President Monroe stated that the United States would defend the freedom of the new countries of Latin America. His statement was greeted with approval by our southern neighbors. However, this friendly feeling toward the United States has changed from time to time.

2. In 1846, the United States went to war with Mexico over the boundary between Texas and Mexico. Many Latin Americans thought that the United States had "picked on" her smaller neighbor. This bad feeling caused by the war lasted for many years.

3. About fifty years later, the United States went to war with Spain, the "mother country" of Latin America. Our people felt that Spain was treating the people of Cuba in a cruel manner. Our people were in sympathy with the Cubans' desire to be free. After the war, the United States gained possession of the island of Puerto Rico from Spain. Cuba was granted her freedom. The United States was to watch over Cuba as her "protector." To this day, the United States has a great naval base at Guantanamo Bay in Cuba, although the leaders of the island country are no longer our friends.

4. In 1903, the United States openly favored Panama's desire to become free from Colombia. Shortly after Panama became free, the United States got permission and land from Panama to build the famous Panama Canal. The canal was important to the United States. A quicker way was needed for ships to go from the Atlantic to the Pacific. There were those in Latin America who felt the United States had used its power to help Panama revolt against Colombia.

5. In 1902, President Theodore Roosevelt sent warships to Venezuela to stop European nations from occupying that country. Venezuela owed money to these countries. President Roosevelt did not want any European nation landing troops in Latin America. Three years later, he sent Americans to Santo Domingo to make sure that that nation paid its debts. At other times, the United States Marines were sent to Nicaragua to keep order and to protect American property there. The people of Latin America did not want this kind of help. They resented the power of the United States. They felt they could take care of themselves.

6. But as early as 1889, an effort was being made to improve relations between the United States and the Latin American nations. The Pan American Union was formed. Twenty-one nations were members. They agreed to settle their disputes peaceably. This Union has grown into the Organization of American States (OAS).

7. President Franklin Roosevelt helped to bring about a better understanding with our

Latin American neighbors. In 1933, he announced the "Good Neighbor Policy." Our troops were brought home from the Caribbean. The United States agreed that it had no right to interfere in the affairs of other countries. The spirit of cooperation grew during World War II. The nations of all the Americas worked together to defeat their enemies. In 1947, at Rio de Janeiro, the American nations agreed that each would help the others in case of attack.

8. At the present time, the Organization of American States is trying to find ways of improving the life of all Americans. The United States has offered to help many Latin American nations. In 1961, President Kennedy announced the Alliance for Progress. Through it, the United States now gives money to Latin America to provide more land, schools and jobs for the people. Our Peace Corps, also started by President Kennedy, is helping farmers in Latin America. Some of its workers are teaching in schools. These workers for peace are trying to help the poorer nations to improve themselves.

9. However, not all the problems in our relations with Latin America have been solved. The control of the Panama Canal is one of these problems. The government of Panama wants to have a greater share in the management of the canal. Some Americans feel that the United States should let Panama run the canal. They feel that this would show our faith in our Latin American neighbors. Besides, we have only leased or rented the Canal Zone from Panama. We may not always be able or want to control it. The canal is already too narrow for use by our largest ships. Travel through it is slow, since it is not a sea-level canal but must use a system of locks. Many feel that the canal cannot be defended in case of an atomic war. Therefore, new routes for another canal are now being studied.

10. Another problem for the United States in Latin America is Cuba. Cuba is an island about ninety miles southeast of the Florida coast. In 1959, Fidel Castro became the ruler of Cuba. In a short time he brought his govern-

The Panama Canal, controlled by the U.S., joins the Atlantic and Pacific Oceans.

ment into close friendship with the Soviet Union and Red China. In October, 1962, it was revealed that the Soviet Union was building missile bases in Cuba. President Kennedy ordered a "quarantine" of the island. Our ships were sent to keep military supplies from reaching Cuba. President Kennedy said that our ships would stay until the missile bases were broken up and the missiles returned to the Soviet Union. The world was close to war. But the Soviet Union agreed to the President's demands and withdrew its missiles. However, there is still great concern over the fact that an unfriendly state is so close to our shores.

11. Castro is hurting our relations with Latin America in another way. He has sent his followers into the countries of Latin America to start revolts. The poor people of Latin America may listen to those who promise them a "quick way out" of their problems. How to make needed changes in the life of the people of Latin America in a peaceful manner is a problem that remains to be solved. In 1965, a civil war broke out in the Dominican Republic. Fearing that the Communists would gain control, President Johnson sent U.S. troops to the island. Not everyone agreed with the President's action. It was hoped that an understanding could be reached through the OAS.

12. Nationalism is growing among the Latin American peoples. (Nationalism is the feeling of pride that one has in his nation and his government.) In all countries, people desire to be free and equal instead of dependent upon others for their safety or their prosperity. This nationalism may take many forms. Latin Americans may resent North Americans who work in their nation or gain profits from it. They may demand that their government take over the mines, factories and plantations that belong to foreign companies. They may demand more land and more schools. It is understandable that this nationalism may take forms with which we do not always agree.

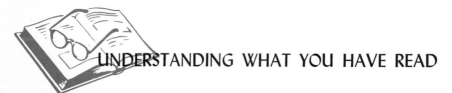

UNDERSTANDING WHAT YOU HAVE READ

1. Which of the following questions are answered in this chapter?

a. Who is Fidel Castro?

b. How did the United States help Mexico in 1864?

c. Why was the Pan American Union formed?

2. The main idea of *paragraphs 6 through 8* is to describe:

a. why some Latin American people did not trust the United States.

b. how the United States has helped Latin America to solve its problems.

c. efforts of the United States to cooperate with Latin America.

3. After the Spanish-American War, the United States obtained:

a. Cuba.   b. the Virgin Islands.   c. Puerto Rico.

4. A plan suggested by President Kennedy was the:

a. Pan American Union.

b. Alliance for Progress.

c. Good Neighbor Policy.

5. The Pan American Union was formed to:

a. improve trade between the United States and Latin America.

b. carry out the defense of the Americas in World War II.

c. work together on common problems.

6. The United States would like another canal through Central America because:

a. the Panama Canal is not fitted for modern transportation.

b. Latin American states have agreed to take over the canal.

c. it is too close to Russian missile bases.

7. President Kennedy's *quarantine* of Cuba means that:

a. ships were kept from reaching Cuba.

b. sugar shipments from Cuba were stopped.

c. the United States sent soldiers to help Cuba.

8. The Pan American *Union* was formed. This means that the countries agreed to:

a. separate.

b. join together.

c. take part in something.

DEVELOPING IDEAS AND SKILLS

Cartoon (See p. 182.)

1. Who are the figures around the table?
2. How many figures should there be?
3. What progress has been made on the problems

they are considering?

4. What other problems would you suggest be added?
5. What is a good title for this cartoon?

SUMMING UP

Below are three headings for your *outline.* Subtopics are listed at the right. In your notebook, make the outline, placing the topics under the correct headings.

HEADINGS:

A. Why Latin America Distrusted the United States

B. Cooperation Between the United States and Latin America

C. Problems in Latin America Today

1. The events of World War II.
2. Panama becomes free from Colombia.
3. Good Neighbor Policy.
4. Poverty in Latin America.
5. The Panama Canal today.
6. The Organization of American States (OAS).
7. Mexican War of 1846-48.
8. Work of the Peace Corps.
9. United States Marines in Nicaragua.
10. Rise of Fidel Castro to power in Cuba.

FOLLOW UP

Special Reports

Now that you have completed your over-all study of Latin America, you should be prepared to make a special report. Select one of the countries of Latin America for special study. In your report, try to answer some of these questions:

1. What does the farmer want in the country you have chosen? What is his day like?

2. What stands in the way of his getting what he wants?
3. What hopes do his children have?
4. What do they know of their country? Of ours?
5. What does the farm family do in its spare time?
6. What part does religion play in its life?

Try to answer the same questions for a factory worker or a large landowner in the country you have chosen.

CHAPTER 11

Mexico — A Neighbor Moving Ahead

PROBLEM: How has Mexico become a leading nation of Latin America?

READING FOR A PURPOSE:
1. Where do most Mexicans live?
2. How do the people make a living?
3. What are Mexico's mineral riches?

1. Much of what we have been learning about Latin America is true of Mexico, the country south of the Rio Grande. Mexico is a mixture of old and new, partly Indian and partly Spanish. There are villages where the Indians live and work much as their ancestors did long ago. Here are the remains of Indian pyramids and temples. One can buy pottery and jewelry made from Indian designs hundreds of years old. The Spanish part of Mexico can be seen in the language, churches, homes and family life in the growing cities.

2. Mexico is one of the larger countries of Latin America, about one-fourth the size of the United States. The country is partly in the low latitudes and partly in the middle latitudes. Most of the land is covered by a broad central plateau or highland. On each side of the plateau

are narrow lowlands. These coastal plains border the Pacific on the west and the Gulf of Mexico on the east.

3. Because of the highlands, much of Mexico has a vertical climate. Northern Mexico is very dry. As you travel southward the land rises; the climate is cooler and there is more rain. This is the *tierra templada*. Still higher, it is colder—the *tierra fria*. The lowlands on the Gulf Coast are hot and rainy. These lowlands are covered with a thick jungle. This is the *tierra caliente*. The Pacific coast is hot, but drier.

4. The central and eastern parts of Mexico were once ruled by the Aztec Indians. The Aztecs were conquered by the Spanish under Cortez in 1519. They were put to work in the gold and silver mines by the Spanish conquerors. Spain ruled Mexico for 300 years.

5. In 1810, Father Miguel Hidalgo led the first revolt against Spain. In 1821, Mexico finally became free. The new government, however, was run by only a few people. The land was divided into large estates called haciendas. Most of the workers on these farms were Indian *peons*. In 1848, Mexico lost a large part of her northern lands in a war with the United States. In 1900, the Indian peons revolted. They wanted a better government that would treat them more fairly. In 1917, a new constitution or plan of government was adopted. Some haciendas were divided up and the land given to the Indian farmers. Also, the people could now vote for their own leaders. (Later Mexican governments have been gradually giving more land to the small farmers.)

6. Most of Mexico's 39 million people live in the plateau around Mexico City, the modern, rapidly growing capital of the country. Most of the people are farmers who live in small villages. They either own their own farms or work lands belonging to the whole village. Most plots of land are small. Many farmers cannot afford machinery. They use oxen or horses to pull their plows. They plant, cultivate and harvest their crops largely by hand. The harvest is small, and most of the food that

Workers making palm furniture in a Mexican village.

is raised must be used at home. The Mexican government is trying hard to encourage the use of more machinery.

7. The chief crops of the highlands are corn, wheat, coffee and tobacco. A favorite food is *tortillas,* flat pancakes made from corn meal. Cotton is grown on the irrigated lands of the north. Bananas, sugar cane and sisal hemp (for making rope) are grown in the tropical lowlands. The drier northern region is also used for growing cattle.

8. The highlands of Mexico are rich in mineral wealth. Mexico exports 40% of the world's silver. It is second to the United States in the production of sulfur. Gold, copper, lead and zinc are other products of its mines. There are large oil fields on the east coast. Mountain streams are used to supply electricity and water for irrigation. Much of this mineral wealth is exported to the United States. In turn, we send Mexico machinery for its mines, farms and factories.

9. Mexico is a changing land. Its leaders are using its resources to build industry. More and more people have moved to the cities where they work in steel mills, chemical plants and oil refineries. There are many new housing projects and office buildings in the big cities. The tourist trade is also becoming a large source of income for the country. Since World War II, the Mexican government has built many schools, both in the cities and in the rural areas. Good roads and railroads are being built throughout the land. The people are taking a greater part in making their government's laws and in choosing their own leaders. Because of these efforts, Mexico is becoming one of the most prosperous nations in Latin America.

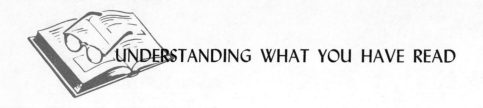

UNDERSTANDING WHAT YOU HAVE READ

1. **Which of the following questions are answered in this chapter?**
a. Who was Juárez?
b. What is the occupation of most Mexican people?
c. How has Mexico made progress since World War II?

2. **The main idea of *paragraphs 6 and 7* is to describe:**
a. farming in Mexico.
b. the lowland regions.
c. the meals of a Mexican family.

3. **Mexico carries on most of its trade with:**
a. Brazil.   b. the United States.   c. Spain.

4. **Mexico leads the world in the production of:**

a. silver.   b. lead.   c. tin.

5. **Most people live in the highlands of Mexico because:**
a. the climate is cooler.
b. large plantations provide work for the people.
c. this is the best grazing land.

6. **Only a small part of Mexico's land is used for farming because:**
a. it is located in the middle latitudes.
b. most people work in mines.
c. much of the land is mountains or desert.

7. ***Tortillas* are:**
a. old Indian temples.
b. hand-made clothing.
c. a kind of corn pancake.

Map # 21a and b—Mexico and the United States

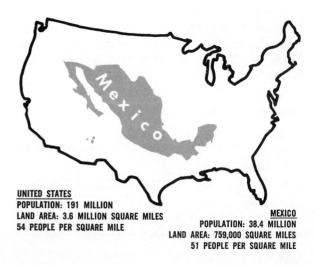

UNITED STATES
POPULATION: 191 MILLION
LAND AREA: 3.6 MILLION SQUARE MILES
54 PEOPLE PER SQUARE MILE

MEXICO
POPULATION: 38.4 MILLION
LAND AREA: 759,000 SQUARE MILES
51 PEOPLE PER SQUARE MILE

DEVELOPING IDEAS AND SKILLS

Map # 21a and b—Mexico and the United States
Can you answer these questions?

1. Does Mexico lie in the high, middle or low latitudes?
2. Does the country extend farther from north to south or east to west?
3. In what part of Mexico are the important cities located? Can you give reasons why this is so?
4. What is the approximate longitude and latitude of Mexico City?
5. Is Mexico as crowded as the United States?
6. How many "Mexico's" could fit inside the territory of the United States?
7. Why do you think there are few large seaports in Mexico?
8. How would you describe the topography of Mexico?
9. What does the latitude of Mexico tell you about its climate?
10. How many degrees of longitude is Mexico City from the community in which you live?

SUMMING UP

Do You Agree or Disagree?   Give the reasons for your answers.

1. Mexico is mostly a mountainous country.
2. Mexico has a civilization that is partly Indian and partly French.
3. Most Mexicans are small farmers who work land near their villages.
4. The chief foods of Mexicans are rice and beans.
5. Mexico is rich in mineral resources; the chief mineral is silver.
6. Mexico has little trade with the United States.
7. Many of the Mexican people make handcrafts.
8. More and more of the Mexican people are living in the cities.
9. Mexico is a changing land whose people live under a democratic government.
10. Much of Mexico's climate is vertical.

FOLLOW UP

Tell whether these statements are true or false. The underlined words make the statements true or false. If a statement is false, what words would you place in it to make it true?

1. The border between Mexico and the United States is the <u>Rocky Mountains</u>.
2. The United States imports <u>minerals</u> from Mexico.
3. Irrigation provides water for crops in <u>northern</u> Mexico.
4. Early Indians in Mexico were the <u>Incas</u>.
5. An important part of life in modern Mexico is an <u>increase in industry</u>.
6. Much of Mexico's power for industry comes from <u>coal</u>.

189

CHAPTER 12

Puerto Rico – Our Pride in the Caribbean

PROBLEM: Why is Puerto Rico important to the United States?

READING FOR A PURPOSE:
1. Where is Puerto Rico?
2. How is Puerto Rico governed?
3. What are the products of Puerto Rico?

1. Puerto Rico is a sunny island about 300 miles southeast of Florida. It belongs to the United States, but the United States is not the only country interested in this beautiful island. People from all over the world come to Puerto Rico to see how her hard-working people have developed their land. Tourists from the United States pour into Puerto Rico for their vacations. The island is a friendly place. The growth of industry changed it from a poor land of small farms to a modern one of small factories and towns.

2. Puerto Rico is a small island, about 100 miles long and 35 miles wide. It is smaller than any of our states except Delaware and Rhode Island. It is located between the Caribbean Sea and the wide Atlantic Ocean. A visitor coming by air to Puerto Rico first notices the green, hilly land. It has a warm, rainy climate throughout the year. The rain-bearing winds blow from the northeast. When the winds hit the mountains, they rise and drop their moisture on the northern half of the island. The southern coastal plain—the leeward side—is drier.

3. Puerto Rico was discovered in 1493 by Columbus on his second voyage to the New World. The Spanish began to settle the island in 1508. They divided the land into large sugar farms, first worked by Indians and then by Negro slaves. Puerto Rico was not rich in gold and silver, but it was still valuable to the Spanish. Because of its location, it helped to guard Spanish treasure houses in the New World.

4. In 1898, the United States went to war with Spain. Spain was defeated and gave up the island of Puerto Rico to the United States. Since that time, the Puerto Rican people have won many rights. In 1900, they gained the right of free trade with the United States. In 1916, Puerto Ricans became American citizens. By 1947, the people were electing their own governor and making their own laws. Luis Muñoz Marín was the first native governor elected by the Puerto Ricans. In 1952, the people adopted their own constitution and set up a "commonwealth" with ties to the United States. Under this form of government, the Puerto Rican people have remained Americans. But they have wide powers in making their own laws.

5. This is a crowded island. There are about 2½ million people in Puerto Rico. There are over 650 people for each square mile of land —one of the most crowded lands in the world. For hundreds of years, most of the people were small farmers. Now many are moving to the cities for jobs in the new factories. Many have left the island for the mainland of the United States in order to find better jobs. While most of the people are Catholics, there are also a large number of Protestants. Most Puerto Ricans are white, Negro or of mixed descent.

6. The Puerto Rican people are proud of their Latin and Spanish culture. Spanish is the language used in schools. But all Puerto Rican children are taught English as a second language. It is not surprising, therefore, to find that so many Puerto Ricans speak two languages. Puerto Ricans are proud of their families too. The family is very important in the life of the people. The family is expected to take care of all its members.

7. Under Spanish rule, most of the land in Puerto Rico was owned by a few persons who raised sugar cane, tobacco and coffee. Today, more people own their own small farms. However, two of the chief crops are still sugar cane and tobacco. While some coffee is grown, land is now being used more for dairy farming. As the people move to cities like San Juan and Ponce, the demand for fresh milk for the city people grows. Citrus fruits and pineapples are grown too. Nevertheless, Puerto Ricans must still import much food from the mainland of the United States.

8. Puerto Rico has no oil, coal or iron ore, but this has not stopped it from becoming a land of small factories. Puerto Rican leaders have used what they have: water power for electricity, and their hard-working people. Because of low taxes, factories were encouraged to come to the island. These factories turn out textiles, paper, cigars, cement and other products. Puerto Ricans also advertise their wonderful climate, beaches and modern hotels and have a successful tourist trade.

9. Their next most important resource, besides themselves, has been their relationship with the United States. The Puerto Ricans, as American citizens, can move to the mainland if jobs are scarce on the island. American armies protect the island. We have helped them work out a democratic form of government. American businessmen have invested money to help develop industry. The people of the island do not have to pay taxes to the United States government. They can trade with the United States without paying tariffs on their imports.

10. Today, through their own efforts and their relations with the U.S., many Puerto Ricans are healthy, go to school and have good jobs on farms and in factories. They have pure water and electricity throughout the island. While many people once lived on a diet of corn, beans and dried meat, today the people eat more wholesome foods. They enjoy radio and television. Low-cost houses are being built in the cities and in the country. All children go to school and receive free lunches daily. The standard of living of Puerto Ricans has risen until it is one of the highest in all of Latin America.

11. What will the future bring to the island? Most people want to keep their present relationship with the United States. There are those who want the island to become a state in the Union, although this would mean paying federal taxes. There are other Puerto Ricans who want complete independence from the United States, despite the loss of free trade and other forms of aid from the United States.

12. Puerto Rico is important to the United States for various reasons. We have military bases there, and they are more important now that there is an unfriendly government in Cuba. However, Puerto Ricans are more important as Latin Americans who are successfully raising the standard of living in their country. In this manner, the Puerto Ricans are pioneers in an experiment that may affect all the Americas.

Cutting sugar cane in Puerto Rico.

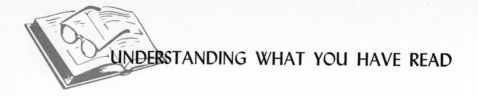

UNDERSTANDING WHAT YOU HAVE READ

1. Which of the following questions are answered in this chapter?

a. Who is Luis Muñoz Marín?

b. How was Puerto Rico acquired by the United States?

c. Why have some Puerto Ricans left the island?

2. The main idea of *paragraphs 9 and 10* is to describe:

a. how Puerto Rico has used its resources.

b. the tax problem of Puerto Ricans.

c. trade between Puerto Rico and the United States.

3. The chief cash crop of Puerto Rican farms is:

a. coconut.　　b. sugar cane.　　c. citrus fruits.

4. Puerto Rico is now:

a. a commonwealth.

b. a state of the Union.

c. an independent country.

5. Puerto Rico is important to the United States because it:

a. supplies our factories with raw materials.

b. is rich in mineral resources.

c. guards the United States from the Caribbean.

6. Many Puerto Ricans have come to the mainland of the United States to:

a. look for better jobs.

b. find religious freedom.

c. work on the farms of our Southwest.

7. In paragraph 2, the *leeward* side means the side that:

a. receives the wind.

b. is away from the wind.

c. receives the winds from the sea.

Map # 22a—Puerto Rico

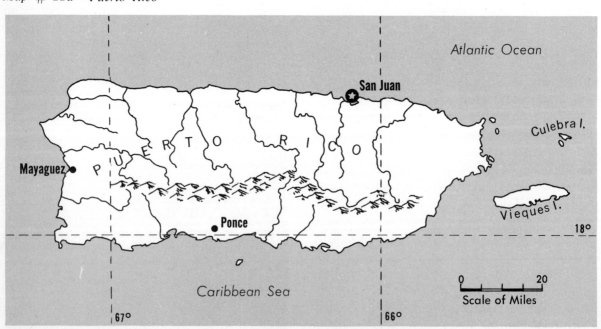

DEVELOPING IDEAS AND SKILLS

Map # 22a and b—Puerto Rico and the United States

Can you answer these questions?

1. Does Puerto Rico lie in the high, middle or low latitudes?
2. How wide is Puerto Rico at its widest point? How long is the island?
3. Where are the most important cities on the island located? Why do you think this is so?
4. What is the approximate latitude and longitude of the city of Ponce?
5. Why do you think San Juan is the largest city on the island?
6. In what direction do the streams of Puerto Rico flow? Can you give reasons for this?

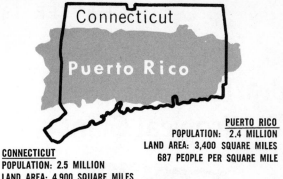

PUERTO RICO
POPULATION: 2.4 MILLION
LAND AREA: 3,400 SQUARE MILES
687 PEOPLE PER SQUARE MILE

CONNECTICUT
POPULATION: 2.5 MILLION
LAND AREA: 4,900 SQUARE MILES
510 PEOPLE PER SQUARE MILE

Map # 22 b—Puerto Rico and the United States

7. Which has the greater population, Puerto Rico or the state of Connecticut?
8. Which is more crowded, Puerto Rico or Connecticut?

SUMMING UP

Making Comparisons Choose the correct word for each statement.

1. Puerto Rico is (larger, smaller) than the state of New York.
2. Since World War II (more, fewer) people have come from Puerto Rico to the United States than before World War II.
3. (More, Less) rain falls on the northern half of the island than on the southern half.
4. The standard of living of the Puerto Rican people is (higher, lower) than that of most of the people of Latin America.
5. Puerto Rico has (greater, fewer) mineral resources than Mexico.
6. (More, Fewer) people are members of the Catholic religion than of any other religion.
7. The climate of Puerto Rico is (cooler, warmer) than that of our southeastern states of Georgia, North and South Carolina.
8. Puerto Rico is (closer to, farther from) Florida than it is from Texas.
9. (More, Fewer) Puerto Rican children attend school now than did in 1940.
10. (All, Some) Puerto Rican people speak two languages.

FOLLOW UP

November 19th is observed by our fellow Americans in Puerto Rico as the anniversary of Christopher Columbus' discovery of the island on his second voyage. To mark this event, prepare:

a. a chart of the second voyage showing the lands he discovered and the names given to them;

b. a map showing the regions of the island of Puerto Rico and their products;

c. letters to pupils in a school in Puerto Rico telling them how you are going to celebrate their Discovery Day.

CHAPTER 13

Brazil: The Tropical Giant

PROBLEM: How has geography limited the growth of Brazil in spite of her great riches?

READING FOR A PURPOSE:
1. How large is Brazil?
2. Why do most of the people live along the coast?
3. What are Brazil's chief resources?

1. Brazil is the giant country of South America. Brazil has more farm land than all of Western Europe. It is rich in minerals, and forests cover more than half the land. It has a large, hard-working population. Yet much of the land is empty and many of the people are poor. Let us see the reasons for this condition.

2. With an area of more than 3 million square miles, Brazil occupies half the continent of South America. It is the fifth largest country in the world. Only the Soviet Union, Canada, Red China and the United States are larger. (Brazil would be larger than the United States if Alaska were not included.) Every nation in South America except Chile and Ecuador borders this giant country. To the east, Brazil faces the Atlantic Ocean. The equator crosses the northern part of the country. Most of the nation lies in the low latitudes. The country is so large, however, that the southern part extends into the middle latitudes.

3. Along the Atlantic Coast, there is a narrow lowland that stretches from the Amazon River south to Uruguay. West of the coastal strip are the Brazilian Highlands, reaching far inland to the Amazon Basin. These highlands are made up of hills, low mountains and large areas of plateau. The other major land form is the lowland of the Amazon. The huge plain of the Amazon reaches from the Atlantic Ocean into Peru and Colombia. It is fed by a thousand rivers and drains almost two-thirds of the nation. The Amazon can be used by ships as far as Peru. Except for this mighty river, most of the rivers of Brazil have rapids and are not useful for transporting goods.

4. Along the low coastal area and in the valley of the Amazon, the climate is hot and rainy throughout the year. It is the rain forest. Inland, where the land is higher, the climate is cooler, but it is still warm. This is the savanna climate with its wet and dry seasons. In the southern part of the country the humid subtropical climate is found—mild winters and long, warm and rainy summers.

5. In 1500, Brazil was claimed by Portugal. The colony was set up to grow sugar cane on large plantations worked by Negro slaves. In the 18th century, sugar was replaced by gold as the main source of riches. Brazil led the world in gold production for a hundred years before the supply ran out. When the world first needed natural rubber, Brazil's forests filled the need. Today the chief crop is coffee.

6. In 1822, Brazil won its freedom from Portugal. However, the country continued to be ruled by an emperor until 1889. Negro slavery was ended in Brazil in the same year and the country became a republic with an elected president and congress. Despite the rule of a few "strong men" and several revolutions,

Brazil still has a government under a constitution. Because Brazil was settled by Portugal, the people of Brazil today speak Portuguese and are largely Catholic. Brazil is the largest Roman Catholic country in the world!

7. Brazil's government is like ours in many ways. There is a president, and the lawmaking body is made up of two houses. Everyone past the age of 18 years who can read and write can vote. The president is elected every five years. The capital is now located in Brasília, about 500 miles in the interior. The capital was built there in the hope that people would move to the inland areas and help to develop them.

8. With over 77 million people, Brazil is the eighth largest country in the world in population. There are a large number of whites, descendants of immigrants from Portugal and other countries of Europe. Indians and Negroes also make up much of the population. The Negro population is the largest of any South American country. There has been much intermarriage among these groups, so the color of one's skin is not important in Brazil. Eight out of ten people live in the narrow lowland along the Atlantic Coast. Most of the people make a living from the land. Because the inland region is a difficult place in which to live, workers have crowded into the cities. São Paulo, Rio de Janeiro and Recife are the largest cities.

9. Brazil has many riches. There is fertile land on which to grow crops and feed animals. Around São Paulo are the large plantations or *fazendas* where coffee is grown. Brazil grows and sells more coffee than any other nation in the world. In addition, Brazil is the world's second largest grower of sugar cane. Brazilians also raise cotton, cacao, bananas, tobacco, corn and rice. In the southeast, there are large cattle ranches tended by cowboys on mules.

10. The highlands produce many minerals, chiefly iron ore and manganese. Brazil has some of the largest deposits of iron ore in the world. As in most Latin American countries, however, coal is lacking. There are good supplies of chromium, nickel, tungsten and bauxite—important metals for the modern world. Large iron and steel plants are located near Rio de Janeiro. São Paulo is the leading industrial city and is one of the fastest-growing cities in the world.

11. Forests cover about half the country of Brazil. Hardwoods are a product of the Amazon rain forests. There are great pine forests in the milder south. Carnauba wax is obtained from the oil palm. This product is used in our finest waxes and in coating phonograph records. Brazil nuts are also gathered in the tropical forests.

12. In spite of its resources, Brazil is still a poor country. Only 4 per cent of its farm land is used. Much of its mineral wealth has not

Drying coffee beans on a fazenda in Brazil.

UNATIONS

The harbor of Rio de Janeiro, Brazil.

been mined. Industry has been slow to develop, although since 1950 manufacturing has been growing at a rapid rate. What are the problems that slow the development of this nation? Transportation along the coast is very good, but there are not enough highways and railroads that lead inland. Secondly, Brazil has depended for a long time on one product for its income—coffee. Thirdly, many people cannot read or write and do not receive proper medical care. Many others have not been trained for skilled jobs. In an industrial nation, people with skills and knowledge are necessary. In the fourth place, a country with little coal needs other sources of power. Brazil has great water resources. But the rivers must be dammed to produce electricity for industry. Finally, there is a need for leaders who are willing to take steps to use the resources of the nation properly.

13. Relations between the United States and Brazil have been friendly. During World War II, Brazil fought on our side. Its airfields were used by the United States to send planes to the war areas of Africa and the Middle East. In the first years of the Alliance for Progress, the United States sent more than a half-billion dollars in aid to Brazil. Our trade with Brazil is greater than our trade with any other South American nation. We import coffee, cacao, waxes, hides and manganese from Brazil. The nation buys our machinery, autos, trucks, wheat, oil and coal. At times the government of Brazil has not been stable, yet our businessmen have invested much money in its industries. The giant of South America has a long way to go to reach its goals. But there is little reason why Brazil cannot become a great source of riches for its own people and for the rest of the world.

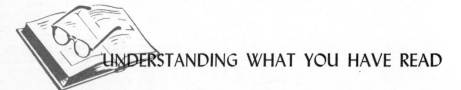

UNDERSTANDING WHAT YOU HAVE READ

1. **Which of the following questions are answered in this chapter?**

a. What produced wealth for Brazil early in its history?

b. What are some problems that face Brazil?

c. Where are cacao and sugar cane grown?

2. **The main idea of this chapter is:**

a. Brazil has great resources, yet it is a poor land.
b. Brazil has a democratic form of government.
c. forest products are Brazil's greatest wealth.

3. The chief industrial city of Brazil is:
a. Brasília.　　b. Recife.　　c. São Paulo.

4. The chief export crop of Brazil is:
a. coffee.　　b. wheat.　　**c. sugar.**

5. One reason why industry has been slow

to develop in Brazil is that:
a. the small population means few workers.
b. the country has almost no minerals.
c. transportation inland is poor.

6. Forests are valuable in Brazil because they:
a. provide wood for the shipbuilding industry.
b. are a source of hardwoods, waxes and nuts.
c. are the world's only source of rubber.

DEVELOPING IDEAS AND SKILLS

Map # 23a and b—Brazil and the United States

Can you answer these questions?
1. Does Brazil lie in the high, middle or low latitudes?
2. How wide is Brazil at its widest point?
3. What is the approximate longitude and latitude of the city of Manaus?
4. In what direction would you be traveling if you flew from your community to the city of Belém?
5. In what parts of Brazil are large cities located? Can you give reasons for this?

6. Which direction is *upstream* on the Amazon River?
7. Which city would have the greatest differences in temperature from one part of the year to another—Brasília or Manaus?
8. What countries on the map border Brazil?
9. How can you explain the large number of rivers in central Brazil?
10. Would it be possible to fit all of Brazil inside the boundaries of the United States?
11. Which is the more crowded country, Brazil or the United States?

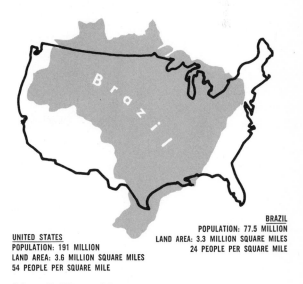

UNITED STATES
POPULATION: 191 MILLION
LAND AREA: 3.6 MILLION SQUARE MILES
54 PEOPLE PER SQUARE MILE

BRAZIL
POPULATION: 77.5 MILLION
LAND AREA: 3.3 MILLION SQUARE MILES
24 PEOPLE PER SQUARE MILE

Map # 23a and b—Brazil and the United States

SUMMING UP

In which region would you find the following? (Refer to the map of Brazil on p. 197 and to the climate map on p. 153.)

_____ 1. cattle ranches.

_____ 2. hardwood and rubber trees.

_____ 3. cacao and sugar plantations.

_____ 4. world's largest river.

_____ 5. coffee plantations.

_____ 6. manufacturing cities.

_____ 7. iron-ore mining.

_____ 8. cotton growing.

FOLLOW UP

I. Choose one of the following topics. Refer to the books in your library for information about the topic. Use these questions as guides.

1. _Coffee_—Where is it grown? What care is given the coffee trees? What happens to the beans after they are picked? Where do most of the coffee-drinking people of the world live?

2. _Rubber_—How is it grown? How is the rubber collected? Why are Brazilian rubber trees no longer so valuable?

3. _Cotton_—Where is it grown in Brazil? Why is it grown there? How can the crop be developed further? How can it improve the life of the Brazilians?

4. _Iron_—Where is it found? Why is it not more fully developed? How will steel change the ways of living in Brazil?

II. Can you fill in the missing words?

1. The capital city of Brazil is _____.

2. Brazil was first explored and settled by people from _____.

3. Brazil is thought to have some of the world's largest deposits of _____.

4. Most of the cities are located along the _____ coast.

5. Most of the people of Brazil belong to the _____ religion.

6. Most of Brazil's coffee is exported to _____.

7. The _____ River flows through Brazil's rain forest.

8. Most of Brazil lies in a _____ direction from the equator.

9. In general, the people of Brazil have a _____ standard of living.

10. The head of Brazil's government is the _____.

BOOKS FOR UNIT 3

Author	Title, Publisher	Description
1. Baker, Nina B.	*He Wouldn't Be King,* Vanguard	The story of Simón Bolívar, South America's "Liberator."
2. Clark, Ann	*Santiago,* Viking	The adventures of an Indian boy in Guatemala.
3. ——	*Secret of the Andes,* Viking	The story of a young boy in Inca land in modern Peru.
4. Considine, Robert	*The Panama Canal,* Random House	How the great canal was built.
5. Kenworthy, Leonard	*Brazil,* Holiday	Brazil's history, including the importance of the Amazon and its products.
6. Kepple, Ella H.	*Three Children of Chile,* Friendship Press	The adventures of young people in Santiago, Chile.
7. Niggli, Josephina	*A Miracle for Mexico,* New York Graphic Society	The history of Mexico as a Spanish colony.
8. Nye, Harriet	*Destination Danger,* Westminster	A story of courage during a hurricane in Mexico.
9. Radau, Hanns	*Illampu,* Abelard	Excitement on a long and dangerous search for a llama in Bolivia.
10. Richardson, Tracy	*Nicho of the River,* Greene	Trouble on a journey by canal through the jungles of Nicaragua and Honduras.
11. See, Ingram	*Jungle Secret,* Doubleday	The story of a rubber plantation in Brazil.
12. Shippen, Katherine	*New Found World,* Viking	The people and nations of Latin America.
13. Waldeck, Theodore	*The White Panther,* Viking	Adventure in the jungles of British Guiana (now Guyana).

UNIT 4

Western Europe

CHAPTER I

The Little Giant

PROBLEM: Why is Western Europe important to the United States?

READING FOR A PURPOSE:
1. Where is Europe?
2. What parts make up Europe?
3. Why do we need Western Europe?

1. The map of the world does not show a separate land area called Europe. Europe is really part of a great land mass called Eurasia. If you look closely at a map, you can see that Europe is a large peninsula on the west of this vast stretch of land. As such, it is bordered by the Mediterranean Sea on the south, the Arctic Ocean on the north and the Atlantic Ocean on the west.

2. There are eighteen independent countries in what we call Western Europe. All of these nations together make up an area that is less than half the size of the United States! France, the largest nation of Western Europe, is not as large as Texas. Great Britain is about the same size as Oregon. Belgium is only half the size of West Virginia!

3. The nations of Western Europe fall into two groups. There is an outer circle of nations that are chiefly agricultural. The northern part of this circle is sometimes called Northern Europe or Scandinavia. It includes the countries of Norway, Sweden, Denmark and Finland. The southern part of this circle is sometimes called Southern or Mediterranean Europe. It includes Portugal, Spain, southern France, southern Italy and Greece.

4. In the center of the circle is a group of nations to whom manufacturing is most important. These "inner" countries are sometimes called Western Europe. This area includes Great Britain and Ireland, France, the Netherlands, Belgium, Luxembourg, West Germany and northern Italy. Austria and Switzerland are landlocked countries whose customs and standards link them with the countries of Western Europe. Hereafter, when we speak of Western Europe, we refer to *all three* parts, north, south and west. There is another group of countries located in Eastern Europe. They will be studied in the unit on the Soviet Union.

5. For hundreds of years, the countries of Western Europe were the leaders of the world. While this leadership is now shared with other regions, Europe is still a very important area to the United States. Let us find out why.

6. First, our way of life owes much to Europe. The United States was settled largely by people who came from Great Britain and other parts of Europe. They brought their ways of living and learning to our land. As a result, Americans speak English, live under a democratic form of government and are mostly Christians.

7. Second, Western Europe is a center of music, art and literature. The books written by authors of Western Europe are read all over the world. Millions of tourists from the United States visit Europe each year to see its art galleries, museums and cathedrals.

8. Third, the Industrial Revolution that became so important in the United States first

D. & M. Wilkes

*The Louvre Museum in Paris, one of
the most famous in the world.*

British Information Services

*Western Europe has some of the
most skillful workers in the world.*

began in Great Britain and spread throughout Europe. Over the years, the people of this region developed a high standard of living. Because of their high standard of living, the people of Western Europe can afford to buy many things. Today they are the best customers for our goods —more than four billion dollars' worth a year. We also buy more from these countries than from any others.

9. Finally, we thought that the Atlantic Ocean would keep us of out of European wars. But two world wars have ended this belief. We now realize that what happens in Western Europe affects us in America. Today we oppose the spread of communism throughout the world, and particularly throughout Western Europe.

We need a friendly Western Europe as a place for military bases and other defenses against communism. We also need Western Europe because it is still the second greatest industrial area in the world. It has many natural resources. It is a leader in making steel. It has great factories and many goods, and its people are among the most skilled in the world. If Western Europe should fall to communism, the Communist bloc would be the mightiest power on earth.

UNDERSTANDING WHAT YOU HAVE READ

1. Which of the following questions are answered in this chapter?

a. Why is a free Europe important to the United States?

b. Why are we interested in the people of Western Europe?

c. What are the important cities of Europe?

2. The main idea of this chapter is to describe:

a. the many countries of Europe.

b. how the people of Western Europe live.

203

c. why we are interested in the countries of Western Europe.

3. **The largest country of Western Europe is:**
a. France.　　　b. Belgium.　　　c. Spain.

4. **The northern part of Europe is called:**
a. the Alpine region.
b. Scandinavia.
c. Benelux.

5. **To Western Europe we owe:**
a. our style of buildings.
b. our public schools.
c. our form of government.

6. **We have a large amount of trade with Western Europe because:**
a. there are no tariffs in Europe.
b. these countries use our money system.
c. their people have money to buy goods.

7. **In an *agricultural* region, people make their living through:**
a. farming.　　　b. mining.　　　c. fishing.

8. **In an *industrial* region, people make their living through:**
a. lumbering.
b. farming.
c. making goods in mills and factories.

DEVELOPING IDEAS AND SKILLS

Map # 24—Western Europe

Can you answer these questions?
1. Is the region north or south of the equator?
2. Is the region east or west of the Prime Meridian?
3. How far north and south does the region extend?
4. Does the region extend farther from east to west or from north to south?
5. What region or regions are near it?
6. What is the largest country? The smallest?
7. What are the chief bodies of water that border the region?
8. Are there countries in it that have no outlets to the sea?
9. What are some of the important rivers in the region?
10. Are there large rivers that form the boundary lines between countries?
11. What are the capital cities of each country? How do you know they are the capitals? How many are sea or river ports?
12. Are there any island nations?
13. Are there countries that are located on a peninsula?
14. Are there any lands that are colonies of other nations?

SUMMING UP

Check the appropriate column in your notebook.

WHY WESTERN EUROPE IS IMPORTANT TO US	YES	NO	WHY WESTERN EUROPE IS IMPORTANT TO US	YES	NO
1. much trade			5. democratic governments		
2. source of oil			6. large in size		
3. skilled people			7. source of tin and aluminum		
4. presence of an important canal			8. leader in making steel		

Map # 24—Western Europe

FOLLOW UP

Western Europe is always in the news. Bring in newspaper or magazine articles relating to Europe. Look for answers to these questions in particular: What are the Nobel Prizes? Who are the leaders of Western Europe? Why is Western Europe important to us?

205

Water, Water Everywhere

PROBLEM: How does Europe's topography explain the activities of the people?

READING FOR A PURPOSE:
1. What is a peninsula?
2. What seas border Western Europe?
3. What is the Great European Plain?

1. As you remember, Europe is a huge peninsula on the great land mass known as Eurasia. Reaching out from Europe's mainland are a number of smaller peninsulas. These peninsulas of Europe are the most striking feature of Europe's shape. Spain and Portugal, Italy, Denmark and Scandinavia are all peninsulas. If you look closely you will see that these peninsulas have even smaller peninsulas! As a result, the coastline of Western Europe is very long and is broken into bays and smaller seas. These bays are fine natural harbors for ships.

2. Almost all the people of Western Europe live near water. No part of the entire region is more than a day's automobile drive from the sea. Therefore, it should not surprise you to learn that the nations of Western Europe have been great sea powers. They have explored distant lands. Some of the nations—Great Britain, France, Spain, Belgium and the Netherlands—have owned colonies in almost every corner of the world. As you might also expect, many people of Western Europe make their living through sea trading, fishing and boatbuilding.

3. There are important bodies of water around Western Europe. The Mediterranean Sea in the south was an important waterway long before America was discovered. The Italian cities of Venice and Genoa were great trading centers for products from the Far East. This sea is still the center of water travel from Western Europe to the countries of eastern Asia. The narrow Strait of Gibraltar at the western end of the sea controls the entrance to the Mediterranean from the Atlantic Ocean.

4. The North Sea is a busy trade route from Great Britain to the Scandinavian countries and the Baltic Sea. The Baltic Sea is the main trading route for Sweden, Finland, Poland and East Germany. Most of the Baltic Sea freezes, however, during the winter months and is not as useful for trade as the more southerly Mediterranean. The English Channel, scarcely 25 miles wide, separates Great Britain from the mainland of the continent. This narrow stretch of water has saved the island from invasion for 900 years.

5. Although all parts of Western Europe are near the sea, not every country has an entrance to the large bodies of water. Switzerland, Austria and Luxembourg are "landlocked." That is, they have no coastline. For Switzerland this has been a blessing. There is no entrance to Switzerland except through the mountains. This tiny nation has therefore been able to avoid war for hundreds of years.

6. Much of Western Europe is a great lowland or plain that stretches from southern Great Britain across the Germanies, Poland and the Soviet Union. It grows wider toward the east.

British Information Services

A busy port in Great Britain. The country depends on its fleet to bring raw materials and carry away finished goods.

It is known as the Great European Plain. North of the plain are highlands or mountains that stretch from northern Great Britain through the countries of Scandinavia.

7. South of the plains the land is also hilly and mountainous. The mountains of southern Europe are high and rugged. The Pyrenees Mountains separate Spain from France. They extend from the Atlantic Ocean to the Mediterranean Sea. The Alps and Balkans stretch across southern France to Yugoslavia and Greece. These mountains separate Southern Europe from the rest of the region.

8. There are many rivers in Western Europe. The most important ones rise in the Alps—the Rhine, Rhône, Po and Danube. Compared with other rivers we have studied, the Mississippi and the Amazon, these rivers are small. However, the rivers are generally navigable. They are joined by many canals to help carry goods such as iron ore from mine to mill. Except for the Rhine, these rivers flow south or east. The Rhône flows into the Mediterranean; the Po leads into the Adriatic Sea; the Danube flows east into the Black Sea. Each runs through fertile valleys where many people live. Many of Western Europe's great cities and seaports are located on these rivers.

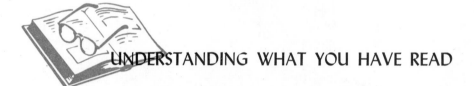

UNDERSTANDING WHAT YOU HAVE READ

1. **Which of the following questions are answered in this chapter?**
a. Why did Western Europeans turn to the sea?
b. What is the topography of Western Europe?
c. How long is the Danube River?

2. **The main idea of this chapter is to describe:**
a. how people of Europe use the sea.
b. the land forms of Western Europe.
c. the southern chain of mountains.

3. **Much of Western Europe is a:**
a. plateau.　　b. desert.　　c. plain.

4. **Most of the rivers of Western Europe rise in the:**
a. Pyrenees Mountains.
b. Alps.
c. northern highlands.

5. **"There are many bays and seas . . ."**

This tells you that:
a. there are many harbors.
b. people travel a great deal.
c. there are many sandy beaches.

6. **The rivers of Western Europe are useful because:**
a. goods are shipped on them between ports and inland cities.
b. most of them flow toward the east.
c. they are a source of minerals.

7. **Land that is surrounded by water on three sides is called:**
a. a peninsula.　　b. an isthmus.　　c. an island.

8. **Venice was a great *trading center*. This means that the city was well known for:**
a. training soldiers.
b. printing books.
c. buying and selling goods.

LAND FORMS OF
EUROPE

Mountains

Plateaus

Hills

Plains

0   100   200   300   400   500
Miles

Arctic Circle

DEVELOPING IDEAS AND SKILLS

Map # 25—Land Forms of Europe

Tell whether these statements are *true* or *false*. Be able to explain your answers.

1. Almost every country of Western Europe may be described as a plateau.
2. The islands of Western Europe are chiefly lowlands.
3. Plains make up a small part of the far northern part of Western Europe.
4. Mountains are found in both the northern and southern parts of this region.
5. Some mountains appear to separate Western Europe from countries along the Mediterranean Sea.
6. Italy and Spain in southern Europe are chiefly one vast plain.
7. Most of Western Europe is part of a large lowland area.
8. In the far north, mountains line the Atlantic Coast.

SUMMING UP

Complete the following chart in your notebook. You may find it helpful to use an atlas or an almanac to find some of the information.

	Comparing Rivers			
	MISSISSIPPI	AMAZON	RHINE	DANUBE
1. Length:				
2. Body of water it flows into:				
3. Area drained:				
4. How it is used by the people around it:				

FOLLOW UP

Tell whether these statements are true or false. The underlined words make the statements true or false. If a statement is false, what words would you place in it to make it true?

1. Europe has great areas of deserts.
2. Central Europe has a broad inner plain.
3. The Mediterranean Sea is an important water route south of Europe.
4. Almost all of the people of Western Europe live in mountain areas.
5. The coastline of Europe provides few harbors.
6. The Alps separate Spain and France.
7. Europe is actually a peninsula on the vast land area of Eurasia.
8. Switzerland is one country that has no outlet to the sea.
9. The rivers of Europe are useful for trade among nations.
10. The main trading route for countries of northern Europe is the Baltic Sea.

CHAPTER 3

Green Lands Near the Sea

PROBLEM: How does Western Europe's climate help to explain its high standard of living?

READING FOR A PURPOSE:
1. Where is Western Europe located?
2. What ocean current reaches Western Europe?
3. Why is Southern Europe's climate different from that of the rest of Western Europe?

1. Nearly all of Western Europe is nearer the North Pole than the United States is. Rome is farther north than New York. London is almost as far north as Hudson Bay in Canada. These cities ought to be very cold, but they are not. The countries in Western Europe have a mild and rainy climate. They have a marine climate.

2. The climate of Western Europe is much warmer than we would expect because of a current of warm water known as the North Atlantic Drift. The Drift begins far away in the warm waters of the Gulf of Mexico. There it is called the Gulf Stream. The Gulf Stream travels eastward. As it nears Europe it becomes wider and weaker. Eventually, the Gulf Stream current becomes the North Atlantic Drift. The Drift moves eastward until it reaches the shores of the British Isles and much of Western Europe.

3. The winds that blow over the countries of Western Europe come from the west. Because these winds blow over the Drift, they bring its warmth to Western Europe. Since no part of the region is more than 400 miles from the sea, the warm winds are felt through much of Western Europe. Farther inland the winds begin to lose their warmth. The winters become colder and longer and snow falls. The summers are shorter. But the presence of water on all sides of Western Europe still tends to keep the winters milder and the summers cooler than they would be otherwise. Because of the rainy winds, the plains of Europe are green with crops.

4. Southern Europe has a Mediterranean climate. The southern coast of France is about the same latitude as Montreal, Canada. Yet this coastal area, far from being cold, has long hot summers. The winters are mild. Rain falls mainly during the winter. Why is this climate so different? The Alps keep out the blasts of cold air from the north. The winds that blow over Southern Europe come from the deserts of Africa. They are hot and dry. As a result, the climate is the same as that of southern California. The long growing season makes it possible to grow all kinds of citrus fruits. Vegetables grown in Southern Europe are sent to the colder areas farther north.

5. Much farther north is the taiga or northern forest lands. The taiga extends through Norway, Sweden and Finland—lands of the "midnight sun." Here summers are short and winters are long and very cold. During the cold winter days there are only a few hours of sunlight. Rivers and lakes are icy, and the ground is frozen. While the soil is poor and stony, there are many evergreen forests.

The green lands of Great Britain.

 UNDERSTANDING WHAT YOU HAVE READ

1. Which of the following questions are answered in this chapter?

a. Why is Western Europe mild and rainy?

b. How are fogs caused?

c. Why do many tourists visit Southern Europe?

2. The main idea of this chapter is to describe:

a. the climates of Western Europe.

b. the effects of the westerly winds.

c. the farm crops of Western Europe.

3. Most of Western Europe is:

a. farther from the equator than New York City.

b. in the region of the taiga and the tundra.

c. about the same distance from the equator as the United States.

4. The Gulf Stream begins:

a. at the Arctic Circle.

b. in the Gulf of Mexico.

c. in the Pacific Ocean.

5. Much of Western Europe has a mild, rainy climate because:

a. it is near the equator.

b. the winds are warm and wet.

c. high mountains shut off the eastern winds.

6. Southern Europe has a sunny climate because:

a. it is located far from large bodies of water.

b. it is located near the Atlantic Ocean.

c. cold northern winds are blocked by the Alps.

211

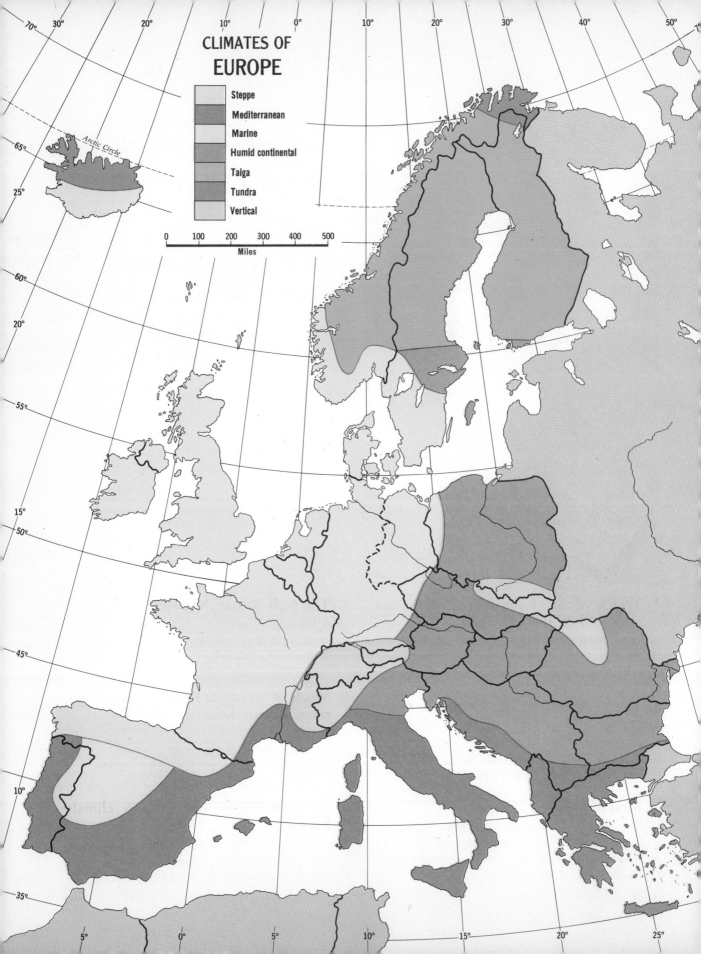

CLIMATES OF EUROPE

	Steppe
	Mediterranean
	Marine
	Humid continental
	Taiga
	Tundra
	Vertical

Miles
0 100 200 300 400 500

Arctic Circle

7. **A feature of the Mediterranean climate is:**

a. frequent rain and fog.
b. a long growing season.
c. hillside farming.

8. **Winters are longer and colder inland because:**

a. the land receives breezes from Africa.
b. the mountains bring cold winds to the plains.
c. these lands are far from the effects of the ocean currents.

DEVELOPING IDEAS AND SKILLS

Map # 26—Climates of Europe

Do You Agree or Disagree? Give reasons for your answers.

1. The taiga occupies all of Western Europe north of 50° latitude.
2. The marine climate reaches north into the high latitudes.
3. Spain and Italy are the only countries in Western Europe with an area of Mediterranean climate.
4. The climate of central Europe is like the climate of the northeastern United States.
5. Nearness to large bodies of water has an effect on the climate of much of Western Europe.
6. All the lands of Western Europe that are near water have a marine climate.
7. The northern part of this region probably has the fewest number of people for each square mile of land.
8. The greatest part of Western Europe lies in an area of marine climate.
9. There is no region in Western Europe where cocoa, cane sugar or rubber can be grown.
10. Mountains have an effect on the climate of all the countries of Western Europe.

SUMMING UP

Obtain travel posters from a travel agency in your community, from an airline or from a steamship line. Plan a trip to Western Europe, keeping in mind the following questions:

a. Where are the places described on the posters?
b. How would you travel to each place?
c. How long might your trip take?
d. What kind of clothing would you take with you?
e. What kind of work do the people do in each place?

FOLLOW UP

Tell whether these statements are true or false. The underlined words make the statements true or false. If a statement is false, what words would you place in it to make it true?

1. The rain-bearing winds blow from the <u>east</u>.
2. The North Atlantic Drift is a <u>cold</u> water current.
3. A <u>Mediterranean</u> climate is found on the southern coast of France.
4. Plenty of rain and mild winter temperatures are found in a <u>marine</u> climate.
5. Lands of the "midnight sun" have a winter in which there is almost continuous <u>sunlight</u>.
6. The northern countries have a <u>short</u> growing season.
7. Much of Europe has a <u>southerly</u> location.

CHAPTER 4

Growth of Modern Europe

PROBLEM: How have the people of Europe changed the world?

READING FOR A PURPOSE:
1. What is feudalism?
2. How did the Industrial Revolution begin?
3. How did the United States help Western Europe after World War II?

1. The lands around the Mediterranean Sea were once part of the great Roman Empire. Even before this huge and powerful empire broke up, people settled wherever there was a good piece of farm land. Later, when Roman rule was replaced by *feudalism,* these settlements were called *manors.* Under feudalism, a lord controlled the life of the manor from his castle. *Serfs* worked for the lord. They lived on the crops they raised on the land. They gave part of their crops to the lord in return for the protection he gave them. These farmers were not free to come and go as they pleased, but had to stay on the land where they were born.

2. In time this way of life changed. As people began to travel and meet other people, trade began and cities grew. The growth of the cities helped to weaken the power of the lords. Sometimes the people in the cities paid the feudal lord for their freedom. Some lords became stronger than others. Wars were fought for control of a large territory. The stronger lords began to call themselves princes or kings. This was the beginning of the nations of Europe.

3. Countries like France and England were brought together by strong lords. The people who lived in the territory of a strong lord or king came to think of themselves as part of his "kingdom"—his nation. At the beginning this feeling of belonging to a nation was weak. By the end of the 19th century it had become very strong. This feeling of belonging to a nation, and of pride in that nation, is known as *nationalism.*

4. One of the reasons for the development of strong nations was the great period of exploration and discovery. After Columbus made his famous voyage, France, Holland, Great Britain, Spain and Portugal all sent explorers to every corner of the world. The coasts of Africa and the islands of the Far East were explored. Because of these voyages Europe became rich from the gold, silver, furs and foods found in these lands.

5. As a result of these and later travels, the lives of millions of people in the New World, Africa, the Far East and Australia were changed. The early settlements in the Americas and Australia were made by people from Europe. The European nations set up trading posts along the coasts of Africa to supply the New World with Negro slaves. This traffic in slaves uprooted the African tribal world for 300 years. In the islands of the Far East, Europeans set up plantations to get more of the products they wanted.

6. At the same time there was a great religious change in Europe. Some kings and princes who were Catholics changed their religion. In the 16th and 17th centuries new churches were

214

started. Because these new churches were started in protest against some of the teachings of the Catholic Church, they were called "Protestant." One of the leaders of this Protestant movement was Martin Luther of Germany.

7. While some learned more about the land and waters of our earth, others studied the heavens. In 1543, Copernicus of Poland stated that the earth revolved around the sun. For thousands of years men had believed the opposite. They had believed that they were the center of the whole universe. Now Copernicus said that they were wrong. Other men looked at the stars and developed new instruments for the study of *astronomy*. Men like Galileo and Sir Isaac Newton tested or experimented with such new ideas as gravity. Many facts concerning the world were discovered. This was the beginning of modern science.

8. The advances in science also led to the Industrial Revolution. This great change from man-made to machine-made goods began in England during the early 1700's. It began first

Galileo demonstrating the telescope.

in the making of cloth. New machines for spinning and weaving cloth were invented. Goods could be made faster by machine, so they became cheaper. Factories grew and people moved near them to get jobs. Cities grew where there were sources of power to run the machines. At first machines were run by water power. Then the coal-fed steam engine was invented. In it, coal was burned to heat water to make the steam for power. The steam engine caused a change in methods of manufacturing and transportation. Britain, where the steam engine and other machines were invented, soon became the first great industrial nation. Its ships carried goods from its factories to people all over the world.

9. At the same time, a different kind of revolution was taking place in France. In 1789, the people of France overthrew their king. The new government divided the large estates of the nobility among the peasants. A few years before, in 1776, there had been a revolution in America out of which the United States was formed. Both revolutions were part of what is called the

Martin Luther.

The beginning of the French Revolution, July 14, 1789.

Democratic Revolution. Before these revolutions most people had few rights. The desire of men to be treated equally was one of the causes of the revolutions. The Democratic Revolution is still going on today. It is based on the desire of all men for the right to "Life, liberty, and the pursuit of happiness."

10. The Industrial Revolution spread to other countries of Europe and to the United States. The machines proved to be "hungry." No one country seemed to have all the resources it needed to feed the machines. Then, too, the goods had to be sold. So industrial nations began to look for materials and markets in other parts of the world. Africa and Asia proved to be areas where the nations of Europe could find the materials they needed. In the 18th and 19th centuries, European countries took control of some of these lands. This was called *imperialism* or *colonialism*.

11. It was bound to happen that in the race for colonies one nation would desire the territory another country wanted. Wars over colonies became frequent. Large armies and navies were built. Finally, in the 20th century, two great world wars were fought on the European

continent. The great world-wide power of the Western European nations was broken. Winners and losers both gave up their colonies, one by one. The United States and the Soviet Union became the most powerful nations in the world.

12. After World War II in 1945, the United States tried to help the nations of Europe recover from the damages of war. Secretary of State George Marshall announced his plan to lend money to the nations of Europe. The Marshall Plan restored farm lands and rebuilt railroads and factories in Europe. In a few years the factories and mills of Western Europe were busy again. In 1949, the United States and some of the countries of Western Europe formed NATO, the North Atlantic Treaty Organization. These nations agreed to help each other in case of attack. The nations of Western Europe also learned another lesson. They found that only by working together could they achieve the best life for their people. Through the Common Market they have begun to cooperate with each other in supplying needed raw materials and products to each other at low tax rates. By this and other means they have built up their industries, their trade and their standard of living.

UNDERSTANDING WHAT YOU HAVE READ

1. **Which of the following questions are answered in this chapter?**
   a. Why did Western Europe want colonies?
   b. Who was Adolf Hitler?
   c. How did the nations of Europe become rich after 1492?

2. **The main idea of this chapter is to describe how:**
   a. the Marshall Plan helped to restore Europe.
   b. Europe has influenced the history of the world.
   c. changes in science began.

3. **One of the leaders of the early Protestants was:**
   a. Martin Luther.
   b. Mohammed.
   c. Copernicus.

4. **The Industrial Revolution began in:**
   a. the Soviet Union.
   b. France.
   c. Great Britain.

5. **One of the causes of the French Revolution of 1789 was that:**
   a. the King of France wanted to explore in America.
   b. people did not have religious freedom.
   c. the people of France wanted more rights.

6. **One of the most important reasons why European nations wanted colonies in the 19th century was the need for:**
   a. raw materials for factories.
   b. large armies and navies.
   c. spreading the idea of equality throughout the world.

7. **Under *feudalism*, wealth was measured in:**
   a. factory-made goods.
   b. land.
   c. water power.

8. **When a country obtains colonies as a source of raw materials, this is known as:**
   a. imperialism.   b. feudalism.   c. liberalism.

DEVELOPING IDEAS AND SKILLS

Picture Symbols

These pictures should help you to recall parts of the chapter you have read. Can you tell the main idea of each picture? In what paragraph did you find the answer for each?

SUMMING UP

In each group there are three events in the history of Europe. Arrange the events in each group *in the order in which they took place.*

1. Feudalism develops.
   Kings begin to form nations.
   The Roman Empire ends.
2. The Industrial Revolution begins.
   New scientific discoveries are made.

Nations want colonies in distant lands.
3. The race for colonies with raw materials begins.
   Two world wars are fought.
   European nations lose their leadership in the world.
4. Columbus discovers the New World.
   Nations find riches in gold and silver.
   Settlements are made in Africa.

FOLLOW UP

Which Does Not Belong? Select the item that does not belong with the others in each group.

1. Feudalism
   a. wealth gained through buying and selling.
   b. serfs work the land.
   c. lord protects the serfs.

2. Colonialism
   a. weaker lands occupied by stronger nations.
   b. African people have self-government.
   c. large nations control raw materials.

3. Industrial Revolution
   a. growth of cities takes place.
   b. new sources of power are found.
   c. greater use of hand labor is made.

4. Democratic Revolution
   a. more people can vote.
   b. new constitutions are written.
   c. fewer newspapers are printed.

5. Revolution in Science
   a. new ideas are tested.
   b. the sun revolves around the earth.
   c. new inventions are made.

6. Protestant Reformation
   a. Catholic religion spreads throughout Europe.
   b. new religions are formed.
   c. Martin Luther announces his beliefs.

7. 20th Century Wars
   a. great loss of life and property.
   b. European nations grow in strength.
   c. United States and Soviet Union become leading powers in the world.

8. Plans for Recovery of Europe after World Wars
   a. NATO is organized.
   b. Marshall Plan is put into effect.
   c. Industrial Revolution begins.

CHAPTER 5

The Busy People

PROBLEM: Who are the people of Western Europe?

READING FOR A PURPOSE:
1. Where do the people live?
2. How do the people make a living?
3. How are the people governed?

1. Western Europe is the smallest of all the regions in our study, but it is one of the most heavily populated. Over 300 million people live there. This is more than in Anglo-America or Latin America. Only in the Far East are people more crowded together. In Belgium and the Netherlands there are about 700 people for each square mile of land. In West Germany and Great Britain there are over 500 people for each square mile of land. By comparison, the United States has 54 people per square mile. Only in Scandinavia, where the northern winters are cold, are there areas of few people.

2. Because of the large population there is very little empty land in crowded Europe. Europeans try to make use of every part of their land.

Throughout Western Europe swamps have been drained and soil improved by careful fertilizing. In the Netherlands the people have built dikes, pumped out sea water and added thousands of new acres of rich soil to their country.

3. Most of the people (three out of five) live in or near large cities. In Great Britain, 80% of the people are city dwellers. In West Germany, 70% of the people live in cities. Millions of people work in factories making goods that are sold all over the world. The workers of Western Europe are highly skilled. Even before the beginning of factories and the use of machines, the people of Western Europe were making goods to sell. Others work in offices, warehouses and docks, preparing goods for shipment to distant parts of the world.

4. In many ways, the life of the people of Western Europe is like that of the people of the United States. Except for Southern Europe, the standard of living is very high. Western Europeans eat and dress much as we do. Potatoes, cheese, milk, butter and rye bread are important in their diet. They eat more fish and less meat than we do. Automobiles, telephones, radios and television sets are a growing part of their daily living.

5. Education is important to Europeans and most children attend school. In Sweden and

Going to market in France. Many people travel by bicycle in Europe.

Standard Oil Co. (N.J.)

Denmark, over 99% of the people are literate —that is, able to read and write. This is a higher percentage than in the United States! The people of Europe are great readers. More books and magazines are printed in Western Europe than in any other region in the world, including our own.

6. The health care of many Europeans is very good. There are modern hospitals served by well-trained doctors and nurses. Government support of medical services is common in Western Europe. This means that both the poor and rich may enjoy good health care.

7. Many different languages are spoken in this region. Most of the languages come from two main sources. The *Romance* languages come from Latin. These are the languages of France, Spain, Portugal, Italy and parts of Belgium and Switzerland. (Different languages may be spoken within the same country. In Switzerland, French, Italian and German are each spoken in a different area.) After the fall of Rome, many German tribes occupied different parts of Europe. They left their *Germanic* languages in such countries as West Germany, Austria, Luxembourg, parts of Switzerland and Belgium, the Netherlands, Great Britain and Scandinavia.

8. There are many different religions in Europe, but most of the people are Christians. The Christians are divided into two main groups: Roman Catholics and Protestants. Ireland, France, parts of Switzerland, Italy, Spain, Portugal and southern Germany are largely Catholic. Scandinavia and Denmark, Great Britain, northern Germany, the Netherlands and part of Switzerland are largely Protestant. For some time, many Jewish people lived in Western Europe. But during the rule of Adolf Hitler in Germany, millions of Jews were killed. Thousands have since moved to Israel and the United States.

9. Most countries in Western Europe have established democratic governments. In most, the laws are made by representatives of the people. In these nations the people enjoy the same freedoms as Americans—freedom of speech, religion and the press. Although kings and queens still "rule" such nations as Great Britain, Norway, Sweden and Belgium, they have little or no real power.

10. The *parliamentary* form of government is most common among the nations of Europe. In such a government there are two lawmaking bodies, but one "house" has most of the power. (In our country both houses of Congress have great power.) They may have presidents, but, except for France, these presidents have little power. The chief officer is the prime minister. He and his cabinet are the real leaders of the government. In most of these governments the prime minister and his cabinet are members of the parliament. They take part in passing and carrying out laws. (In our country there is a separation of the powers held by the President and Congress.)

Nôtre Dame Cathedral, Paris.

D. & M. Wilkes

Great Britain's Parliament, in London, has been a model for democratic governments throughout the world.

British Information Services

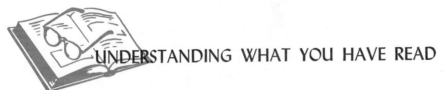

UNDERSTANDING WHAT YOU HAVE READ

1. **Which of the following questions are answered in this chapter?**
   a. What do the people of Western Europe eat?
   b. What are the crowded countries of Europe?
   c. Who is the ruler of Spain?

2. **The main idea of *paragraph 3* is to describe:**
   a. the kinds of work in Western European cities.
   b. how Western Europeans use machines.
   c. the importance of trade in the life of the people.

3. **The religion to which most of the people of Western Europe belong is:**
   a. Christianity.   b. Judaism.   c. Islam.

4. **Dikes have been built to reclaim land in:**
   a. France.   b. the Netherlands.   c. Norway.

5. **Many Jews have left Western Europe because:**
   a. they seek adventure.
   b. many were killed during the time of Hitler.
   c. they cannot receive an equal education.

6. **The people of Europe must use their farm land wisely because:**
   a. there is little fertile land.
   b. there is a need to feed a large population.
   c. Europe exports food to other nations.

7. **The majority of the nations of Western Europe:**
   a. have parliamentary governments.
   b. are ruled by kings or queens.
   c. are governed by dictators.

8. **The title of the chapter, "The Busy People," refers to the fact that:**
   a. Europeans are chiefly farmers.
   b. Western Europe has a high standard of living.
   c. the people work hard and are highly skilled.

9. **In the last sentence of paragraph 10, the term "separation of powers" means that:**
   a. the President and Congress have different powers.
   b. our President has more power than Congress.
   c. the President and Congress have the same powers.

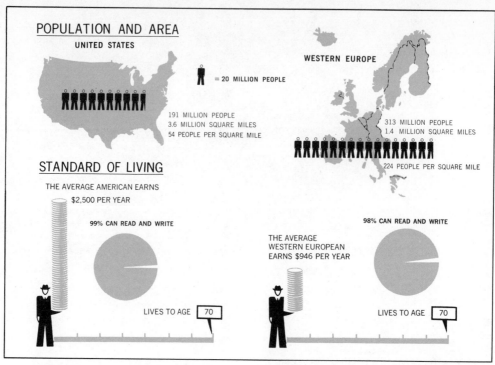

POPULATION AND AREA

UNITED STATES

👤 = 20 MILLION PEOPLE

191 MILLION PEOPLE
3.6 MILLION SQUARE MILES
54 PEOPLE PER SQUARE MILE

WESTERN EUROPE

313 MILLION PEOPLE
1.4 MILLION SQUARE MILES
224 PEOPLE PER SQUARE MILE

STANDARD OF LIVING

THE AVERAGE AMERICAN EARNS
$2,500 PER YEAR

99% CAN READ AND WRITE

LIVES TO AGE 70

THE AVERAGE
WESTERN EUROPEAN
EARNS $946 PER YEAR

98% CAN READ AND WRITE

LIVES TO AGE 70

Pictograph # 9—Population, Area and Standard of Living of Western Europe

DEVELOPING IDEAS AND SKILLS

Pictograph # 9—Population, Area and Standard of Living of Western Europe

Can you answer these questions?

1. Is the standard of living of this region high or low compared with that of the United States? Is it a low-income or underdeveloped area?
2. Is the region as crowded as the United States?
3. Are the people of this region literate compared with the people of the United States?
4. How long may the average person in this region expect to live?
5. What facts tell you the standard of living of the people of the region?
6. How does this region compare with the United States in size?

SUMMING UP

Do You Agree or Disagree?   Give reasons for your answers.

1. Western Europe is a region small in size and population.
2. A visitor from one of our large cities would be "at home" in Great Britain.
3. The farm lands of Europe cover a vast area, much like our midwestern states.
4. Owning a book store would be a good business in Sweden.
5. The health standards of Western Europeans are probably very high.
6. Most people in Western Europe live and work in cities.
7. The religions of the people of Europe are much like the religions of the people of the United States.
8. The Prime Minister of Great Britain and the President of the United States have the same powers.

CHAPTER 6

A Workshop of the World

PROBLEM: Why is Western Europe a great industrial area?

READING FOR A PURPOSE:
1. Where did the industries of Europe start?
2. What are Western Europe's chief sources of power?
3. Where are coal and iron found?

1. Western Europe is one of the world's workshops. Many raw materials for manufacturing are found in the countries of this region. What they do not have, Europeans import from all over the world. Their factories turn these raw materials into machinery, textiles and chemicals. Great ships carry these goods to markets everywhere. With the profit from the sale of manufactured goods, Western Europe can pay for the food needed by her large population.

2. There are many reasons why industry became so important in Western Europe. This group of nations had an early start. The Industrial Revolution began in Great Britain. The first machines and factories were built by Eng- lishmen. By the early 1800's, the use of machines and the factory system spread across Western Europe. Only in the 20th century has the change from man-made to machine-made goods become important in the Soviet Union, India, China and Africa.

3. The people of Western Europe are highly skilled. For a long time, Europeans made things to sell at home or in small shops. When the first factories were started, these people were able to work at the new machines.

4. Western Europe is rich in the sources of power for factories. Europe mines about 45% of the world's coal. Coal is the chief source of power in Great Britain, West Germany, France and Belgium. Other European nations depend upon water power. Western Europe has about one third of the world's developed water power. France, Switzerland, Sweden, Italy and Norway make the greatest use of this power source. Oil is also used, but it must be imported from the fields of the Middle East.

5. There are great amounts of coal and iron in the region for making steel. Although most countries in Western Europe have some coal or iron ore, the main mining areas are in France, Great Britain, West Germany and Sweden. The richest coal and iron area is a small triangle of land that includes Belgium, northern France and southwest Germany.

6. Western Europe has an excellent transportation system. This region is like a spider's web

Mining coal in Belgium.

The steel mills of the Ruhr in the Vital Triangle.

of rivers, canals, highways and railroads. The chief rivers for trade—the Rhine, Rhône and Elbe Rivers—are connected by canals. It is therefore possible to carry goods easily to any inland city or seaport. Moreover, Western Europe's long, irregular coastline provides many ports. Ocean-going ships can pick up Europe's products close to where they are made or grown.

7. There is another reason for Western Europe's early industrial development. Whatever the nations of Europe did not have, they could get from their colonies. Western Europe has no cotton, no rubber and little oil. But Great Britain, France, Germany, the Netherlands and Belgium used to have great colonies in far-off lands. They depended on their colonies to supply the raw materials they needed for their factories. Moreover, profit from this trade gave the Europeans money to build more factories. It also helped to supply them with machinery and equipment.

8. Workers from the northeastern United States feel at home when they visit the great cities of Western Europe. This is because the making of steel and mining are the chief industries. There are two main centers of steel manufacture and mining in the region. Great Britain is one, and the area of the continent known as the Vital Triangle is the other. Britain's great iron and steel district is located in the Midlands in central England. Birmingham and Sheffield are two of the great steel cities in Great Britain.

9. The Vital Triangle, continental Europe's most famous steel area, includes the Lorraine Valley of northern France, parts of Belgium and Luxembourg, and the Ruhr and Saar Basins of West Germany. Here the iron ore deposits and the coal mines are close to each other. There are many rivers, canals and railroads within the Triangle. They connect the iron ore, coal and steel centers with the nearby seaports. These great steel mills with their huge furnaces and smokestacks supply steel not only to Europe, but also to the rest of the world.

10. Europe's factories make use of this steel to produce many goods. Machine tools, farm machinery, electrical equipment, ships, barges and automobiles are only a few of the products. In addition, there are textile and chemical industries. All these goods are carried to world markets by Western European ships. These many products tell the story of Europe's leadership in manufacturing.

A laboratory in Great Britain. The chemical industry is very important in Western Europe.

UNDERSTANDING WHAT YOU HAVE READ

1. Which of the following questions are answered in this chapter?
   a. What is the Vital Triangle?
   b. Why is Western Europe a leader in manufacturing?
   c. How is steel made?

2. The main idea of this chapter is to describe:
   a. how Western Europe makes use of its resources.
   b. the chief industries of Western Europe.
   c. why Western Europe's workers are skillful.

3. Western Europe's chief industry is the making of:
   a. steel.
   b. paper and paper products.
   c. food products.

4. Western Europe is called a "workshop of the world" because this region:
   a. turns raw materials into finished goods.
   b. makes nearly everything by hand.

   c. ships goods to all parts of the world.

5. The chief source of power in Western Europe is:
   a. oil.   b. natural gas.   c. coal.

6. The Ruhr Valley has become a center of industry because:
   a. rich coal mines are located there.
   b. it has good transportation.
   c. farm land is too poor and people have moved to the cities to live.

7. In paragraph 6, the term "a spider's web of rivers" means that:
   a. ships rush back and forth over many great waterways.
   b. rivers bring goods far inland.
   c. the rivers seem to flow out in all directions.

8. In paragraph 10, "chemical industries" might include the manufacture of:
   a. cotton goods.   b. light bulbs.   c. fertilizer.

Map # 27—The Vital Triangle

DEVELOPING IDEAS AND SKILLS

Map # 27—The Vital Triangle
Read each of the following statements about the map of the Vital Triangle. Write *true* if the statement is correct. Write *false* if the statement is wrong. Write *not given* if the map does not give you the information needed to decide on the statement.

Map # 27—The Vital Triangle

COAL
IRON ORE
STEEL PRODUCTION

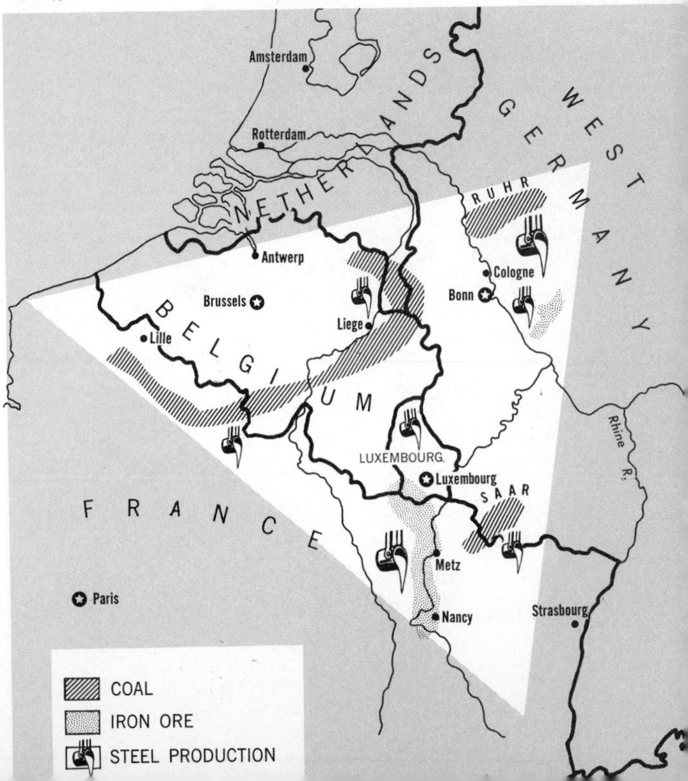

1. Belgium has much coal but little iron ore.
2. The high production of steel in Western Europe is the result of great coal fields.
3. Coal and iron ore are found near each other around the border of France and West Germany.
4. Aluminum production has been growing and steel production has been falling in Western Europe.
5. Most of the Netherlands but only a small part of Belgium lies in the Vital Triangle.

SUMMING UP

Manufacturing in Western Europe   Use these three headings to make an *outline* of the industries of this region. From what you have read, enter three statements under each of the headings.

A. Reasons for the Growth of Industry
B. Resources of Western Europe
C. How Europe's Resources are Used

FOLLOW UP

Tell whether these statements are true or false. The underlined words make the statements true or false. If a statement is false, what word or words would you place in it to make it true?
1. The Vital Triangle is an important area of steel manufacturing.
2. Western Europe does not have a supply of rubber.
3. The chief source of power in Italy and Switzerland is water.
4. One of the mining areas of the Vital Triangle is located in Sweden.
5. Most manufactured goods in Western Europe are made from copper.
6. The Industrial Revolution began in Great Britain.
7. Britain's great manufacturing district is located along the northeastern coast.

CHAPTER 7

His Farm Is His Garden

PROBLEM: How does the European farmer use his land?

READING FOR A PURPOSE:
1. How does the farmer use his land in marine Europe?
2. What is a cooperative?
3. How does the farmer use his land in Southern Europe?

1. The skill of the European farmer matches the skill of the worker in Europe's factories. But in most of the Western European nations only a small part of the population lives on farms. France has an almost even balance between those who farm and those who live in cities. Ireland is one of the few nations that has a large majority of farmers. But in Great Britain, West Germany, Belgium and the Netherlands, not even one person in four is a farmer.

2. Most farmers in Europe own their own land. They do not work for others. They live in villages near the fields. Each farmer works his small lands with great care. That is why we often say that his farm is his garden. He cares for his land much as an American might care for his garden crops. Because most farms are small, most of the work is done by hand or animal labor. However, the European farmer is gradually using more machinery.

3. Because great care is given to the land, an acre will provide a greater yield or amount of crop than in other regions. The European farmer raises about three times as much wheat on an acre of land as the American farmer! Because there is a shortage of good farm land, every acre that can be farmed is put to use. In the Netherlands, much land has been reclaimed from the flooding sea. The great dikes that hold back the Atlantic Ocean have given Netherlands farmers a large area of fertile soil that they could not otherwise have had.

4. Science, hard work and experience have also helped the farmer of Western Europe to grow large amounts of food. He rotates or changes his crops from year to year. He uses fertilizer to enrich his soil. He cultivates the land carefully. He plants crops that grow best in a marine climate. The chief crops are root crops like potatoes, sugar beets and turnips. They are rotated with wheat, rye and barley. (Rye bread or dark bread is more common among the Europeans than white or wheat bread. Barley soup and potatoes are an important part of the diet of many Europeans.)

5. Marine Europe is also one of the great dairying regions of the world. The cool, wet summers provide grass for pasture. The mild winters mean that there is grass for the animals throughout the year. Oats, hay and sugar beets are also used as food crops for the animals. As a result, many countries have an important dairy industry in which cows are raised for milk, butter and cheese. The Netherlands and Denmark are leaders in this area. Switzerland is an example of the good use of mountain land. Despite its mountains, more than three-fourths of the land is used for crops or pasture for cattle, sheep and goats. (Where grass is plentiful and land is flat, cattle are raised. Sheep are found in

227

areas of shorter grass and hillier land. Where grass is thinnest and land is very rugged or mountainous, the hardier and more sure-footed goats are raised. Goat's milk and goat cheese are very popular in many parts of Europe!)

6. Many European farmers raise hogs, chickens and sheep. Sheep are raised in especially large numbers. Great Britain alone has almost half as many sheep as the United States. The sheep supply both wool and meat for the people of Europe.

7. As rich as the farms are, and as carefully as they are worked, they cannot feed all the millions of city dwellers. Western Europe must depend upon other regions for food. Wheat, corn, animal and vegetable fats, cane sugar, cocoa, coffee and tea are a few of the foods that are imported. More wool is imported too.

8. Many European farmers have joined together to form *cooperatives*. These are organizations of farmers who agree to sell their farm crops together. A cooperative sells all the crops at a certain price. Each farmer who is a member of the cooperative shares in the costs and the profits. The cooperatives also buy goods in large quantities to supply cheaply the farmers' needs for fertilizers, feed, tools and clothing.

By buying in large amounts, the farmers can save money. In the Scandinavian countries, almost all farmers belong to cooperatives.

9. In the countries of Southern Europe— Spain, Portugal, Italy and Greece—most of the people are farmers. Farming is different here from that of marine Europe. There is little rainfall during the summer. Much of the land is rough and hilly. Because of this, the Mediterranean farmer has a more difficult time in raising good crops.

10. The average farm family along the Mediterranean is poor. There are many farmers and not enough good farm land. The farms are small and machinery is seldom used. Some of the farming methods have not changed in hundreds of years. Wooden plows, hoes and hand sickles are used. The farmers of the Mediterranean are also "gardeners" because they cultivate their small plots of ground very carefully. Most of the crops are grown for their own use.

11. The farmers of Southern Europe have learned how to farm the steep hillsides. At sea level they grow citrus fruits, if there is water from irrigation. Higher up they build terraces or steps on the sides of the hills. Terracing cre-

Farm lands in France.

Sheep grazing in the northern highlands of Great Britain.

British Information Services

ates more usable farm land. The olive trees and grape vines that are planted here do not need much water or very rich soil. Their roots reach far down into the ground for water. (More than any other crop, the olive tree is a sign of the lack of water.) Wine is used for drinking instead of water and olive oil is used instead of animal fat and for cooking. Wheat and vegetables are also planted among the vines and trees. On the higher rocky slopes, sheep and goats graze in pastures.

12. The seas of Western Europe are another source of food. Fish are an important part of the diet in lands of the marine climate. Fish and fish oils contain vitamins and other things necessary for good health. The North Sea in particular has many shallow waters and narrow areas. These fishing banks are rich in tiny plant and animal life. The larger fish come here to feed on the plants and smaller animal life in the water. Herring, cod and mackerel are found here. The fishermen of Western Europe catch thousands of tons of fish every year. Some is eaten by Europeans, and the rest is sold to other regions of the world.

UNDERSTANDING WHAT YOU HAVE READ

1. **Which of the following questions are answered in this chapter?**
a. Why does the Western European farmer use little machinery?
b. How are the hillsides farmed in Southern Europe?
c. What foods are important in the diet of the Europeans?

2. **The main idea of this chapter is to describe:**
a. the importance of fishing.
b. how Europeans get their food.
c. the importance of dairying.

3. **Important crops of the farms of Europe are:**
a. sugar beets and potatoes.
b. rice and beans.
c. cotton and tea.

4. In Mediterranean countries, farmers face the problem of:
a. little rainfall.
b. unbearable heat.
c. heavy summer rains.

5. Western European farmers are able to raise large crops per acre because:
a. dikes are used for irrigation.
b. machinery is widely used.
c. fertilizing and crop rotation are practiced.

6. Olives, grapes and wheat are farm products of which of these regions?
a. Italy. b. Ireland. c. Belgium.

7. A good farmer *rotates* his crops—that is, he:
a. waters them daily.
b. changes them from year to year.
c. uses minerals to enrich the soil.

8. In an agricultural *cooperative*:
a. people work with others on the farm.
b. farmers buy and sell goods together.
c. people rent machinery to their neighbors.

DEVELOPING IDEAS AND SKILLS

Photograph Study

This photograph should help you to recall parts of the chapter you have just read. Can you tell the main idea of the photograph? Where in the chapter is it described?

SUMMING UP

Complete the following chart in your notebook.

	Farming in Western Europe	
	MARINE EUROPE	SOUTHERN EUROPE
1. Climate		
2. Surface of land		
3. Chief crops		
4. Farm animals		
5. Methods of farming		

FOLLOW UP

Do You Agree or Disagree?   Give reasons for your answers.
1. Most European farmers live on their own farms.
2. The skill of the European farmer matches the skill of the worker in Europe's factories.
3. The countries with a marine climate have a large dairying industry.
4. There are few animals on European farms.
5. France is probably better able to provide all the needs of her people than any other country of Western Europe.
6. The farmers of Western Europe have been slow to join farm cooperatives.
7. The farmers of Southern Europe have learned to farm the hilly lands along the coast.
8. The seas around Western Europe provide much food for the large population.

Great Centers of Trade

PROBLEM: Why does Western Europe need trade with other regions?

READING FOR A PURPOSE:

1. How much does the United States trade with Western Europe?
2. What are Western Europe's chief imports?
3. What is a tariff?

1. Western Europe depends upon trade more than any other region in the world. There are not enough farmers to raise food for all the people of this small region. There are not enough raw materials and minerals to feed the "hungry" machines. All of these things must come from other parts of the world. Many of them come from the United States. Our trade with the nations of Western Europe amounts to ten billion dollars a year!

2. Among Western Europe's important imports are oil from the Middle East, South Amer-

ica and the United States; wheat from Canada and Argentina; cotton from the United States and Egypt; tin and rubber from Malaysia and copper from Chile. In return, ships carry away coal, machinery, automobiles, chemicals and farming tools. The rest of the world benefits from the factories of Western Europe, for they get the finished products in return for their raw materials. Western Europe shows how people help each other through trade.

3. Nearly everywhere you look in Western Europe there are busy harbors. Among the largest and most important are London and Liverpool (Great Britain), Belfast (Ireland), Copenhagen (Denmark), Marseille (France) and Genoa (Italy). Paris (France), third largest city in Europe, is a busy trade and fashion center on the Seine River. Amsterdam and Rotterdam (Netherlands), Antwerp (Belgium) and Hamburg (West Germany) are also important. Day after day shiploads of raw materials are unloaded at these ports. The empty ships are reloaded with goods to be shipped all over the world. The many bays and harbors of Western Europe have helped the people to use the nearby waters as highways for trade.

4. The leading nation in trade in Western Europe is West Germany. Together the countries of Western Europe account for almost half of the world's trade. (While the United States leads the world in foreign trade, we are only one nation.) The imports of foods and raw materials are usually balanced by the export of manufactured goods. If it should happen that the Europeans import more than they export (buy more than they sell), the difference is sometimes made up through the millions of dollars spent by tourists.

5. Still, there are trade difficulties in Europe. The countries are small. None of them is as large as the state of Texas. (In some cases, a trip of less than 100 miles will take you all the way across one country and into another!) There are differences in language and money systems. Passports are needed as you move from one country to another. There are tariffs or taxes on goods going from one nation to another.

232

6. In the United States these difficulties do not exist. A manufacturer in New York can sell his goods in California with little trouble. There is no tax, no passport, no difference in money from one state to another. An American who drives from coast to coast, almost three thousand miles, has few problems. But if you drove from Italy to Belgium (just a few hundred miles) you might pass through three different countries. Oranges can be shipped from Florida to Illinois more easily than from Spain to Belgium, even though the distance is greater. Iron ore from Minnesota is carried over the Great Lakes to Cleveland quite easily. Iron from the Lorraine district in France must cross at least one border to get to the Ruhr Valley where it is used. By the time these goods reach the customer in a European country they are higher in price because of the tariffs.

UNITED NATIONS

The busy port of Hamburg, West Germany.

7. As you can see, Western Europe has a problem in using its resources wisely. The resources are divided among so many nations and must support so many people. In the next chapter, we will see what is being done to overcome this difficulty.

UNDERSTANDING WHAT YOU HAVE READ

1. Which of the following questions are answered in this chapter?

a. Why is the Suez Canal important to Western Europe?

b. Why have many cities in Western Europe become important?

c. What does Western Europe export?

2. The main idea of this chapter is to describe:

a. how Western Europe depends on trade.

b. imports and exports of Western Europe.

c. how many people there make a living.

3. Western Europe imports large quantities of:

a. machinery.　　　b. coal.　　　c. oil.

4. Food imports to Western Europe are paid for by:

a. the sale of manufactured goods.

b. the sale of food products.

c. income from tourists from foreign countries.

5. Western Europe imports food because:

a. the quality of farm products is higher in the United States.

b. the food is bought in order to carry on trade.

c. farms in the region cannot raise all the food the people need.

6. There are difficulties in trading among the nations of Europe because:

a. the mountains are too high to cross easily.

b. there are many tariffs to pay.

c. there is a lack of good transportation.

7. A tariff is a tax on:

a. imports.

b. exports.

c. goods made and sold within the country.

8. In paragraph 2, the term "finished products" refers to:

a. highly polished goods.

b. high-priced goods such as linens and watches.

c. manufactured goods of all kinds.

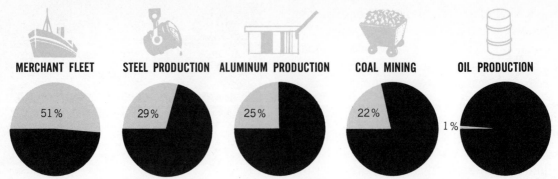

WESTERN EUROPE'S SHARE (IN PER CENT OF WORLD TOTAL)

MERCHANT FLEET — 51%
STEEL PRODUCTION — 29%
ALUMINUM PRODUCTION — 25%
COAL MINING — 22%
OIL PRODUCTION — 1%

Pictograph # 10—Western Europe and the World

DEVELOPING IDEAS AND SKILLS

Pictograph # 10—Western Europe and the World

Read each of the statements at the right about the graph of industry in Western Europe. Write *true* if the statement is correct. Write *false* if the statement is wrong. Write *not given* if the chart does not give you the information needed to decide on the statement.

1. Western Europe depends heavily on trade.
2. Western Europe's chief source of power is oil.
3. Many people in Western Europe work in coal mines and steel mills.
4. The U.S. produces more steel and aluminum than Western Europe.
5. Boats from the nations of Western Europe can be seen in harbors all over the world.

SUMMING UP

Indicate whether the following items are *imports* or *exports* of **Western Europe**.
1. oil
2. fish
3. dairy products
4. wheat
5. meat
6. textiles
7. machinery
8. rubber
9. bananas and pineapples
10. chemicals

FOLLOW UP

In the countries of Western Europe there are many choices of occupation. Complete the following statements, giving the correct reasons for each.
1. Fishing is important because—
2. Trade is important because—
3. Manufacturing is important because—
4. Farming is important because—
5. Mining is important because—
6. Science is important because—
7. City services are important because—

CHAPTER 9

The Common Market

PROBLEM: How have some European nations planned to overcome some of their problems in trade with each other?

READING FOR A PURPOSE:
1. Why was the Common Market started?
2. How does the Common Market work?
3. Who are the Outer Seven?

1. As you learned in the last chapter, Western Europe is divided into many small nations. Each nation has different resources. For example, France has iron and West Germany has coal. By the time the iron ore and coal are brought together in a steel mill, the price of steel is higher because of tariffs. Since World War II, however, the nations of Western Europe have learned that their resources can be used more wisely if they cooperate with each other.

2. After World War II, the power of Western European countries in world affairs had declined. The people were exhausted from the wars that had divided and ruined them. They realized that the United States and the Soviet Union were the new powers in the world. They knew they could not be important in world affairs unless they regained their strength. The idea of sharing their resources through free trade spread in Western Europe.

3. The agreement to lower tariffs among nations has become known as the Common Market. This movement may have started in 1948. At that time, Belgium, the Netherlands and Luxembourg formed a trade union. These nations are called the Benelux Nations because their beginning letters are BE-NE-LUX. Through the plan, each country was able to send its goods to the others without paying a tax or tariff. Trade grew so quickly that the idea began to spread. Other countries decided to try it also.

4. In 1957, Jean Monnet and Robert Schuman of France drew up a plan for pooling Western Europe's coal and iron resources. Six countries accepted this plan: the Benelux countries, France, Italy and West Germany. All of these nations had been hurt in World War II. All of them were willing to give up a little of their national power to join the plan. This plan grew into the idea of the Common Market. The leaders of the plan looked to the day when the countries of Western Europe would be united as a single nation.

5. These countries became known as the Inner Six countries. They began to lower tariffs on goods going back and forth among their nations. Trade could flow as though there were no borders between them. This meant that a manufacturer in France would make things not only for the people of France, but also for the people in all six countries of the Common Market. For purposes of trade, these countries would be one nation.

6. The results of the Common Market have been pleasing to all members. The trade among the member nations has doubled. Tariffs have dropped lower and lower. Businessmen do not think only of the sales they can make within their own nation. They think in terms of six na-

A ferry across the Rhine, the border between France and West Germany.

tions—a market of about 180 million people. The standard of living in all countries has risen. People have more money and are able to buy more goods. The Common Market countries are buying more foreign goods than ever before.

7. Because the Common Market plan has been so successful, other nations of Europe decided to try the same idea. A bloc or group of nations formed another trade alliance called the Outer Seven. The members of this group are Great Britain, Austria, Denmark, Norway, Sweden, Portugal and Switzerland. Great Britain once asked to withdraw from this group to join the Common Market. However, France blocked her request for membership. Each country that is a member of these groups has the right to veto or prevent the admission of new members.

8. The continued success of the Common Market has certain advantages for the United States. It should certainly encourage friendships among the nations of Western Europe. This would reduce the chances of war. It should make them stronger and better able to resist communism. West Germany is now an active member of a group of democratic nations. Since the people have more money to spend, it is also likely they will buy more goods from the United States.

9. At the same time, there are certain disadvantages to the United States. For example, a businessman in France can sell his goods in Italy by paying a small tariff. However, an American businessman selling the same products must pay a higher tariff. Consequently, Europeans may buy fewer articles from the United States because they may be more expensive than the ones made in Europe. The United States must decide how to meet this problem. In the long run, every tariff cut by Common Market countries will affect other nations that depend upon trade—the United States, Japan and Great Britain.

UNDERSTANDING WHAT YOU HAVE READ

1. Which of the following questions are answered in this chapter?

a. Who is Jean Monnet?

b. What are the benefits of the Common Market?

c. Why did France block Great Britain's entry into the Common Market?

2. The main idea of this chapter is to describe:

a. how the Common Market is changing Western Europe.

b. how the Common Market affects the U.S.

c. the work of Monnet and Schuman.

3. How many countries belong to the Common Market?

a. 3.　　　　b. 6.　　　　c. 7.

4. The Common Market began:

a. after World War I.

b. after World War II.

c. at the urging of the United Nations.

5. The Common Market was formed to:

a. share water power resources among the member nations.

b. increase trade with the Soviet Union.

c. share resources and skills of Western Europe.

6. The Common Market has been successful in that:

a. fewer farms are needed.

b. more and cheaper goods are available.

c. tariffs on exports have been raised.

7. The best meaning for the word *bloc* in paragraph 7 is:

a. "group."　　b. "members."　　c. "nations."

8. The best meaning for the term "trade alliance" in paragraph 7 is:

a. a group of nations with the same problems.

b. nations joined together to exchange goods.

c. nations buying foreign goods.

Map # 28—The Common Market

DEVELOPING IDEAS AND SKILLS

Map # 28—The Common Market

Tell whether these statements are *true* or *false*. Be able to explain your answers.

1. Austria is a member of the Common Market.

2. Czechoslovakia and Yugoslavia are part of the Common Market.

3. The Common Market nations have more people than do the Outer Seven countries.

4. France is the largest nation in the Inner Six.

5. Spain is not a member of either the Common Market or the Outer Seven.

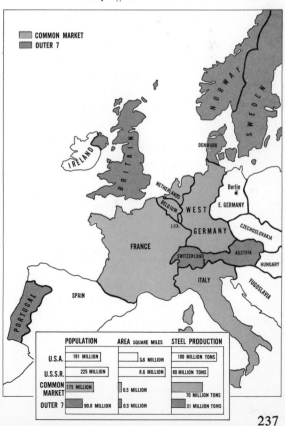

	POPULATION	AREA SQUARE MILES	STEEL PRODUCTION
U.S.A.	191 MILLION	3.6 MILLION	100 MILLION TONS
U.S.S.R.	225 MILLION	8.6 MILLION	80 MILLION TONS
COMMON MARKET	175 MILLION	0.5 MILLION	70 MILLION TONS
OUTER 7	90.8 MILLION	0.5 MILLION	31 MILLION TONS

SUMMING UP

Complete the following *outline* in your notebook.

The Common Market
A. How It Started
   1.
   2.
   3.
B. How It Works
   1.
   2.
   3.
C. Results
   1.
   2.
   3.

FOLLOW UP

Making Inferences   In our reading, many facts are given to us. From these facts we can draw conclusions. The following are some conclusions or inferences that you might make after reading Chapters 6, 7, 8 and 9. Tell whether these conclusions are correct or incorrect. Give reasons for your answers.

1. (Chapter 6)   Many of the stoves in the kitchens of Western Europe are probably gas stoves.
2. (Chapter 6)   In many parts of Western Europe, water takes the place of coal in making electricity.
3. (Chapter 6)   Coal mines, factories and large cities of Western Europe are often found in the same place.
4. (Chapter 6)   Western Europeans have made good use of their rivers and have developed a large system of canals.
5. (Chapter 7)   Wheat bread or white bread is commonly found on the dinner tables of Europeans.
6. (Chapter 7)   Europeans eat many kinds of soups made from vegetables, barley and potatoes.
7. (Chapter 8)   Europe has a great many large cities on a small area of land.
8. (Chapter 9)   At the present time there is a movement of the small nations of Europe to join together to solve common problems.
9. (Chapter 9)   A manufacturer in Europe can succeed in business by selling his goods only within his own country.
10. (Chapter 9)   As a result of World War II, the ability of Western Europe to produce a great amount of goods was weakened.

Europe Divided

PROBLEM: Can Western Europe solve its problems and become strong again?

READING FOR A PURPOSE:
1. How was Germany divided?
2. Where is the city of Berlin?
3. What is NATO?

1. You know that Western Europe is a region of many mills and factories. These factories use raw materials. The raw materials come from Europe or abroad. Oil, rubber, tin, cotton and copper are a few of the raw materials that have always been imported. However, Western Europe is using up its own natural resources, such as iron and coal, at a rapid rate. More and more, these must be imported at high cost from other regions of the world in order to keep the factories going.

2. The Industrial Revolution led Western Europe to obtain colonies all over the world. The raw materials from the colonies helped to feed the great factories. Moreover, Western Europe could sell the products of the factories to their colonies. After World War II, the colonies in Asia and Africa were freed. These new nations want to develop their own resources and use more of the goods for themselves. They are trading less with their "mother countries" and more with such countries as the United States and Japan. In short, the nations of Western Europe have lost many of their former markets to other parts of the world.

3. The countries of Southern Europe—Italy, Spain, Portugal and Greece—are different in many ways from the countries of marine Europe. These nations are poorer than their neighbors to the north. Their populations are growing and their small areas of fertile land are hard pressed to produce enough food for the growing population. When the people are poor, the governments are also poor. There is not enough money to provide the public schools, hospitals and health services that are needed. Moreover, the people of Spain, Portugal and Greece have had less chance to take part in democratic governments than their brothers to the north.

4. One of the big problems facing Western Europe and the entire world is the division of Germany. After World War II, Germany was divided into four parts. The Soviet Union occupied Eastern Germany. England, France and the United States occupied Western Germany. Berlin, located in the Soviet zone, was occupied by all four nations. In 1948, the three Western nations combined their zones of occupation into one. One year later, a new government of West Germany was formed with Bonn as its capital. The Soviet Union followed by establishing the "German Democratic Republic" in East Germany. Whether or not Germany will be reunited into one nation is a problem facing Western Europe and the world.

5. Berlin has been a big problem for the West. It lies about 100 miles inside the Soviet zone. Two million people live in the sections occupied by England, France and the United States. They depend upon West Germany for the goods they need in order to live. These goods must be brought through part of East Germany. In 1948, the East Germans, supported by the Soviet

239

Union, closed the roads leading from the West to Berlin. No food or fuel could come into the city. The United States decided to fight the blockade. Food and supplies were sent into Berlin entirely by air. This airlift was a success. The East Germans gave up the blockade after a year.

6. However, in 1961, the East Germans built a wall in Berlin to stop their people from going over to the West. It is still an aim of the Communists to add all of Berlin to their own territory. They do not like to see a free city inside their territory. However, the United States has made it clear that Berlin is part of the Free World and that we will not give up our rights there.

7. Events in Berlin aroused the Western nations. They feared the spread of communism from Eastern Europe into their nations. In 1949, the United States, Canada and ten nations of Europe formed the North Atlantic Treaty Organization or NATO. These nations agreed to help each other in case of attack. They formed a NATO army. Dwight D. Eisenhower was the first commander of the NATO forces. There are now fifteen nations in NATO. Two NATO member nations, Greece and Turkey, have been having a dispute over Cyprus, a small island in the eastern Mediterranean.

8. As the Western European nations continue

U.S. planes deliver food during the Berlin Airlift.

to grow in strength through the Common Market, they will follow a course of their own choosing. This has worried many people in the United States. Our nation would like Western Europe to follow the same policies that we do. However, we know it is more important that Western Europe be strong. A strong Europe standing between us and the Soviet Union is in our interest, even if there is not always complete agreement. Freedom in Western Europe helps the people of America to remain free.

NATO headquarters in Paris.

UNDERSTANDING WHAT YOU HAVE READ

1. **Which of the following questions are answered in this chapter?**
   a. Why is Berlin important to the free world?
   b. How is Spain governed?
   c. What are Western Europe's chief problems?

2. **The main idea of this chapter is to describe:**
   a. the spread of communism in Europe.
   b. the current problems of Western Europe.
   c. how Western Europe lost its colonies.

3. **At present, Germany is divided into:**
   a. four parts.   b. three parts.   c. two parts.

4. **Berlin is located in:**
   a. West Germany.
   b. East Germany.
   c. Switzerland.

5. **NATO was formed because:**
   a. there was a fear of the spread of communism in Europe.
   b. the United States needed support in Europe.
   c. the United States wanted to increase her trade in Europe.

6. **The loss of colonies hurt the countries of Western Europe because:**
   a. immigrants no longer came.
   b. markets for goods were lost.
   c. raw materials were no longer needed.

7. **In paragraph 2, the term "mother countries" refers to:**
   a. England, France and the Netherlands.
   b. China, India and Japan.
   c. the United States and Canada.

8. **In paragraph 6, the term "Free World" refers to:**
   a. a united Germany.
   b. the United Nations Organization.
   c. nations that are opposed to communism.

DEVELOPING IDEAS AND SKILLS

Cartoon (See p. 239.)
Can you answer these questions?
1. What are some problems dividing Western Europe?
2. For what reason was NATO formed?
3. How is the Common Market helping to overcome some of these problems?
4. When was the Berlin Wall put up?
5. What is a good title for this cartoon?

SUMMING UP

Fact or Opinion   Can you decide which are statements of fact and which are someone's opinion?
1. The United States should join the Common Market.
2. Western Europe is divided into many small nations.
3. Warm ocean currents give Western Europe a mild, rainy climate.

4. The United Nations can guarantee the freedom of the city of Berlin.
5. Manufacturing is more important to the people of France than it is to the people of the United States.
6. The nations of Western Europe are going to unite into one large nation in a few years.
7. The division of Germany presents a problem that threatens the peace of the world.
8. The United States should not trade with any Communist country.

FOLLOW UP

Reviewing Western Europe Complete the following statements by using the words or phrases listed below.

Vital Triangle northerly   finished goods
factories   large cities   food and raw
peninsula   Common Market materials
food   coal and iron North Atlantic
natural harbors rivers and canals Drift

1. Europe is a _____ on the land mass of Eurasia.
2. Europe has many fine _____.
3. The coast of Western Europe is warmed by an ocean current, the _____.
4. Europe has great mineral wealth in _____.
5. The great steel-making area of Western Europe is known as the _____.
6. Western Europe is a web of _____.
7. Western Europe imports _____; in turn, it exports machinery and other _____.
8. Most people in Western Europe work in _____ and live in _____.
9. Six nations of Western Europe have increased their trade through the _____.
10. The farms of Western Europe do not supply enough _____ for the people.

CHAPTER 11

Great Britain: The Island Nation

PROBLEM: How has Great Britain become a world power despite its small size?

READING FOR A PURPOSE:

1. How does Great Britain compare in size with the United States?
2. How do the British people get their food?
3. What mineral resources does Britain have?

1. Great Britain is a narrow island west of the mainland of Europe. It is made up of three parts: England, Scotland and Wales. A fourth part of the nation lies on the northern coast of Ireland. Great Britain is 94,000 square miles in area, a little smaller than our state of Oregon. The population is about 54 million. This makes Great Britain one of the world's most densely populated countries. Generally, ten times as many people live on each square mile in Britain as on each square mile in the United States.

2. The northern and western parts of Great Britain are hilly and mountainous. The eastern part is a lowland plain. This is part of the Great European Plain. The coastline is long and irregular. There are many fine harbors.

3. The island of Great Britain has a marine climate. This mild, rainy climate is caused by the warm current (North Atlantic Drift) and winds that come from the west. The weather of London is much like the weather of Seattle, Washington, and other cities of our Northwest. The ocean winds bring rain. The heaviest rains fall on the western side of the island. The fogs of London are world-famous. We sometimes talk about fogs so thick that we can hardly see in front of us. In London this is often true!

4. The British have always used the seas around them. In the 17th and 18th centuries they began to build a great empire. They planted colonies in the New World, India, Africa and Australia. At the same time the Industrial Revolution was taking place. The British were the first to use machines run by steam engines. Their colonies furnished raw materials. The machines turned these raw materials into finished goods. The goods were shipped to all parts of the world. The sea has meant life to the British people.

5. After World War I, four of Great Britain's former colonies—Canada, Australia, New Zealand and South Africa—joined with Great Britain in a new relationship called the British Commonwealth of Nations. They agreed to help one another by lowering tariffs on goods sent to each other. During World War II, Great Britain fought with the Allies against Nazi Germany. Germany was defeated, but Great Britain had used up much of its resources in the process. Later, Britain had to give up colonies in Asia and Africa. Many joined the Commonwealth as free and equal partners.

6. Most Britons live in cities and towns. The largest city is London, the capital, home of 8 million people. Many of the British ways of living are like those of the people in the United States. Our language came from Great Britain.

Our clothing is in the same fashion. We use many British products. Britons go to the movies, listen to the radio and watch television as much as we do. Almost everyone can read and write. Medical care is given to the people as a government service. The British standard of living is among the highest in the world.

7. Most of our ideas of law and government came from Great Britain, although in Britain there is no written constitution. The king or queen is the head of state, but holds little power. The lawmaking body of the British government is Parliament. Parliament is divided into two houses, the House of Lords and the House of Commons. The chief official is the prime minister. He is the leader of the political party that has the most representatives in the House of Commons. He chooses his cabinet to help him pass and carry out laws. (You will recall that Canada's government is a parliamentary one too.)

Great Britain is experimenting with atomic energy as a source of power.

8. The Britons depend on their farm lands and surrounding seas for part of their food. The best farm land is on the eastern part of the island. Here farmers plant wheat and barley. Machinery is used where it is possible, and the yield per acre is high. In the northern highlands they also raise dairy cattle and sheep. The wool is used in the textile factories. Besides their farm and grazing land, the British obtain a large supply of herring, cod and other fish from the nearby waters.

9. The farms and seas do not provide enough food for Great Britain's millions of people. The British must, therefore, buy more food from abroad. To pay for this food, Great Britain turns to her factories. Raw materials are imported. The raw materials are turned into finished goods and sold in world markets. These goods pay for the materials and foods that must be imported.

10. Great Britain has become a leading manufacturing nation for many reasons. Because Britain is surrounded by water, it has been able to avoid invasions from Europe for centuries. Thus, it has been left alone to develop its industries without interference. Its people are hard-working, skilled and inventive. It has had great resources of coal and iron ore. (Many British are miners. Coal is the chief source of power. The chief coal and iron fields are in Wales and eastern England.) Using these resources, Britain's skilled workers turn out a great variety of products: woolen and cotton goods, steel products of all kinds, automobiles, airplanes, farm machinery, chemicals, electrical equipment and films.

11. These manufactured goods are Britain's exports. Because of its great need for trade, Britain has long been a leading shipbuilding nation. Its ships sail the seas, trading with nations all over the world. Its greatest trade is with the members of the Commonwealth of Nations. However, Great Britain has also long been one of our best customers.

12. Great Britain has a number of problems. Its well-being depends upon its selling goods abroad. This is becoming harder because of the growing number of industrial nations that

British Information Services

Using machines on a farm in Great Britain.

Pan American Airways

Trafalgar Square in the heart of London.

want to sell goods abroad—the United States, Japan and the countries of the Common Market. The loss of colonies after World War II means that Great Britain no longer controls the raw materials or markets in these former colonies. However, the Commonwealth nations still supply it with some raw materials and buy a large share of its manufactured goods.

13. Great Britain lacks some important resources. It does not have oil, copper, cotton or wood pulp. It must import food at high cost. Its coal resources also may be "wearing out." The United States, Soviet Union and West Germany have now passed it in steel production. The British have been trying to develop a cheaper source of power. They were the first people to use atomic energy to operate machines.

14. Despite its weakened resources, Britain still plays a leading part in world affairs. It is a member of the NATO alliance with the United States and nations of Western Europe. It is a member of SEATO (Southeast Asia Treaty Organization) with the United States, Australia and New Zealand, among others. It has joined with Turkey, Iran and Pakistan in forming CENTO (Central Treaty Organization). All of these agreements with nations in many parts of the world have one chief purpose—to stop the spread of communism.

UNDERSTANDING WHAT YOU HAVE READ

1. Which of the following questions are answered in this chapter?
a. How are the British people governed?
b. Where are the coal mining areas?
c. What are some of Great Britain's problems?

2. The main idea of *paragraph 10* is to describe:
a. the variety of British products.
b. how Britain became a great industrial nation.
c. the skill of British workers.

3. Most of the British people work:

a. on farms.
b. in mines.
c. in industry and trade.

4. The leader of the British government is the:

a. prime minister.
b. premier.
c. chancellor.

5. Britain has become a leader in manufac-

turing for all of these reasons EXCEPT:

a. it had an early start.
b. it has a large supply of cotton.
c. there have been large coal and iron resources.

6. Some of Britain's problems are now caused by:

a. the loss of population since World War II.
b. the loss of former colonies.
c. problems of wheat farmers on the island.

DEVELOPING IDEAS AND SKILLS

Map # 29a and b—Great Britain and the United States

Can you answer these questions?

1. Does Great Britain lie in the high, middle or low latitudes?
2. What is the distance from the coast of Britain to the coast of France?
3. How do you explain the presence of the large cities of Liverpool, London, Glasgow, Dublin and Belfast?
4. If you flew from your community to London, you would fly in which direction? How do you know this without looking at a world map?
5. Can you locate the Prime Meridian? It is near which city?
6. Can you name any cities that are not seaports?
7. How many different bodies of water can you find on the map?
8. How does the map tell you that the climate of Great Britain will be milder than the mainland near it?
9. Which is larger, Oregon or Britain?
10. Which is more crowded, Oregon or Britain? The United States or Britain?

Map # 29a—Great Britain

SUMMING UP

Great Britain   Use these four headings to make an outline of the important facts and ideas concerning Great Britain. From what you have learned, write three statements under each heading.

A. How Great Britain Compares With the United States in Size and Population
B. How Great Britain Compares With the United States in Government and Life of Her People
C. Sources of Great Britain's Strength
D. Britain's Weaknesses and Problems

FOLLOW UP

Cause and Effect   In Column A are six statements. In Column B are some results of the facts stated in Column A. See if you can match the effects or results in Column B with the causes in Column A.

COLUMN A
1. Warm ocean winds
2. Coal and iron resources
3. Need for raw materials
4. Lack of farm land
5. Fear of communism
6. Need for trade

COLUMN B
___ gave an early start in the manufacture of steel.
___ caused the development of atomic energy.
___ led to growth of shipbuilding.
___ bring rain and fog to the island.
___ led to defense agreements with nations all over the world.
___ led to a great empire of colonies.
___ led to the sale of manufactured goods in trade for food.

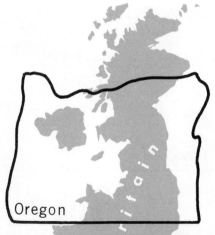

Oregon

OREGON
POPULATION: 1.8 MILLION
LAND AREA: 96,200 SQUARE MILES
18 PEOPLE PER SQUARE MILE

GREAT BRITAIN
POPULATION: 53.8 MILLION
LAND AREA: 93,900 SQUARE MILES
573.1 PEOPLE PER SQUARE MILE

Map # 29 b—Great Britain and the United States

CHAPTER 12

Spain:
Poor Land of
Southern Europe

PROBLEM: Will Spain be able to regain her place as a world leader?

READING FOR A PURPOSE:
1. Where is Spain located?
2. What do most Spanish people do for a living?
3. What are some of Spain's resources?

1. Spain occupies the Iberian Peninsula, sharing it with the small country of Portugal. The Pyrenees Mountains in the north separate her from the rest of Western Europe. Portugal and the Atlantic Ocean form her western boundary. Aside from the mountains in the north, all of the remaining boundaries are water—the Bay of Biscay on the north and the Mediterranean Sea on the east. Her long coastline of 1500 miles is regular and provides few natural harbors. The narrow Strait of Gibraltar separates Spain from North Africa.

2. Spain's 31 million people live in a land somewhat larger than California. Unlike the people of most of Western Europe, most Spaniards are poor. Their yearly income of $275 per person is the second lowest in Western Europe. Moreover, they do not have a democratic form of government; they are ruled by one man, Francisco Franco, who makes the laws.

3. Most of Spain is a wide, treeless plateau called the *meseta* (or little table). The plateau is crisscrossed by low hills and mountains called *sierras*. Madrid, the capital, is in the middle of the meseta. A number of small rivers, such as the Ebro and Guadalquivir, drain the plateau. In the north, the high Pyrenees have few passes through them to France.

4. Spain's climate is varied. In the north it is cool and rainy—the marine climate. The central plateau is hot and dry in the summer and very cold in the winter. Along Spain's Mediterranean coast the summers are hot and dry, but the winters bring some rain.

5. About 2000 years ago, Spain was part of the Roman Empire. The Romans controlled this land for about 600 years. They gave the Spaniards Christianity and the Roman language, Latin. The Moors, a Moslem people from North Africa, then crossed the Strait of Gibraltar and

The Alhambra, former palace of the Moors, in Granada.

D. & M. Wilkes

ruled most of Spain for 800 years. They were finally driven out in 1492.

6. In that same year Christopher Columbus, sailing for Spain, discovered the New World. Spanish conquistadors—de Soto, Cortez, Pizarro, Coronado—soon explored and claimed large areas of this New World. Magellan made his famous voyage around the globe and claimed Guam and the Philippines. Spanish ships brought in gold and silver from Mexico and Peru and silks and spices from the Orient. Spain became the richest nation in Europe!

7. In 1588, Spain's great navy or Armada lost a great sea battle to England. After that, Spain began to lose its power. By 1825, most of its colonies in the New World had won their freedom. Then it suffered a defeat by the United States in the Spanish-American War of 1898 and lost more territory. Cuba became independent. Puerto Rico and the Philippines were given to the United States.

8. A terrible civil war from 1936 to 1939 ruined Spain. More than a million people were killed as Spaniard fought Spaniard. The winners were the "Nationalists" led by Francisco Franco. Franco became the ruler of the nation.

9. Although there is a lawmaking body called the Cortes, the real power in Spain is Franco. He is the head of the government, the armed forces and the Falange, the only political party. Spain did not take part in World War II. Since 1953, the United States has given help to Spain in return for the right to build air bases on Spanish soil. In 1955, Spain became a member of the United Nations.

10. Most of the Spanish people are farmers or herders. They live mostly in the irrigated river valleys and along the coasts where there is more rainfall. The Catholic religion is the official religion of the country. There is no separation of Church and government as in our nation. Madrid, Barcelona and Seville are the large, important cities of Spain. Only Madrid has more than one million people. In the cities a large number of people are poor. Farmers, too, show the poverty of Spain.

11. Most Spanish farmers rent their land from

Pan American Airways

Downtown Madrid.

wealthy landowners. They live in small villages of adobe (sun-dried brick). Most of the country people are not able to read and write. Their farm work is done by hand or with the simplest tools, a wooden plow drawn by a donkey. Unlike most of the farmers of Western Europe, the Spaniards do not use a great amount of fertilizer, nor do many rotate their crops. As a result, harvests are small.

12. The chief farm crop is wheat. However, not enough is raised to feed the people, so more must be imported. There is so little rainfall in some wheat-growing areas that farmers plant their fields only once in two years. In this way they use the rainfall gathered in two seasons for one crop. Much of the meseta is also used for grazing sheep. Large herds of goats graze in the foothills of the Pyrenees as well. (When a country raises large numbers of goats—as in Spain, Italy and Greece, for example—it is often a sign that the land is poor.)

13. Olives and grapes are the chief export crops of Spain. Both of these crops can grow in land that is rocky and where there is little water. These crops are grown on the hillsides along the Mediterranean coast in the south and east.

Farming in southern Spain.
Lettuce is planted under the olive trees.

UNITED NATIONS

Spanish farmers also raise oranges near the city of Valencia.

14. Spain is rich in minerals but has few large industries. Iron ore is mined along the Atlantic Coast. It is the chief mineral export of Spain.

Copper, zinc, silver and lead are also mined. Spain is one of the world's chief sources of mercury, a silver-colored metal used in thermometers. The chief industrial region lies in the north and northeast near the city of Barcelona. The main source of power is falling water, because coal and oil are lacking in large amounts.

15. Although it has valuable minerals, Spain has remained a poor country. Much of the land is in the hands of a few wealthy people. Farming methods are old-fashioned and the lack of water is a problem. The government has been run by one man for many years. However, Spain is "coming to life." New factories have been built to make use of the country's own iron. Dams are being built to irrigate more land. Electricity from these dams is now being brought to more villages. Spain is also trying to build its tourist business, and more people from Europe and the Americas are visiting the country every year.

UNDERSTANDING WHAT YOU HAVE READ

1. **Which of the following questions are answered in this chapter?**
a. What are Spain's chief crops?
b. Who are some of Spain's great writers and artists?
c. Where do most of the Spanish people live?

2. **The main idea of *paragraphs 5 through 7* is to describe the:**
a. government of Spain.
b. great power that was once held by Spain.
c. history of Spain.

3. **Spain was once ruled by people called the:**
a. Mongols.   b. Moors.   c. Mayans.

4. **Most of the land in Spain is:**
a. a fertile river valley.
b. a dry, treeless plateau.
c. covered with high, rugged mountains.

5. **Farms of Spain do not produce a great amount of crops because:**
a. the land is poor and it is worked by hand.
b. there are few farm workers.
c. there are few farm animals.

6. **Olives and grapes are grown because they:**
a. do not need much water.
b. grow best in the cool highlands.
c. are easy to take care of.

7. *Adobe* **refers to:**
a. the lawmaking body of the Spanish government.
b. shawls worn by Spanish women.
c. sun-dried brick.

8. **In paragraph 15, the expression "coming to life" means:**
a. going to be old-fashioned for a long time.
b. giving birth to new ideas.
c. beginning to develop industries.

DEVELOPING IDEAS AND SKILLS

Map # 30a and b—Spain and the United States
Can you answer these questions?

1. What countries border Spain?
2. How would you describe the land formation of Spain and Portugal?
3. How is Spain separated from France?
4. Is your community farther north or south than the city of Madrid?
5. Why do you think there are few large seaports in Spain?
6. The Strait of Gibraltar separates Spain from which continent?
7. Which direction is *upstream* on the Ebro River?
8. What is the distance from the Pyrenees Mountains to the Strait of Gibraltar?
9. How does Spain compare in size with the United States? with the state of California?
10. Which is more crowded, Spain or California?

CALIFORNIA
POPULATION: 18.1 MILLION
LAND AREA: 156.500 SQUARE MILES
103 PEOPLE PER SQUARE MILE

SPAIN
POPULATION: 31.1 MILLION
LAND AREA: 194,900 SQUARE MILES
159.5 PEOPLE PER SQUARE MILE

Map # 30a and b—Spain and the United States

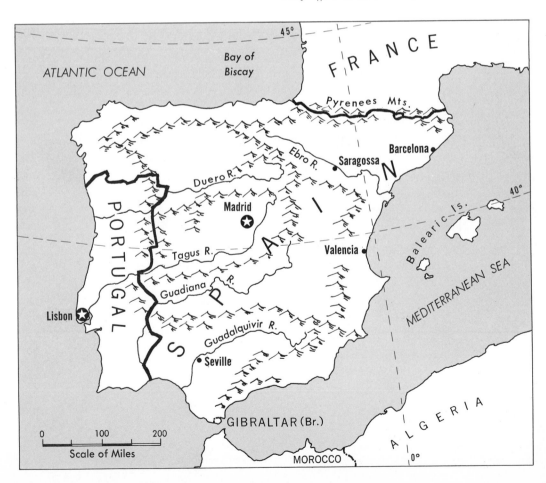

251

SUMMING UP

Complete the following chart in your notebook.

	SPAIN
1. Size	
2. Population	
3. Location	
4. Land Forms	
5. Climate	
6. Occupations	
7. Chief Crops	
8. Industry	
9. Government	
10. Problems	

FOLLOW UP

Tell whether these statements are true or false. The underlined words make the statements true or false. If a statement is false, what words would you place in it to make it true?
1. Spain is located in Southern Europe.
2. The Bay of Biscay separates Spain from North Africa.
3. Since 1939, Spain has been ruled by Francisco Franco.
4. The chief grain crop of Spanish farm lands is rice.
5. Sheep are grazed on the plateaus.
6. The chief export crops of Spain are olives and grapes.
7. The chief industrial region is near Barcelona.
8. The capital of Spain is Seville.
9. Puerto Rico was once a Spanish colony.
10. The Pyrenees Mountains separate Spain and Portugal.

CHAPTER 13

Norway, Sweden, Finland: Lands of the "Midnight Sun"

PROBLEM: How have the people of these lands reached such a high standard of living in spite of their problems of climate and topography?

READING FOR A PURPOSE:
1. Where are these countries located?
2. Who were the Vikings?
3. What are the resources of these northern lands?

1. Norway, Sweden and Finland are northern lands. Except for Sweden, these countries have few minerals. Much of their soil is poor. Yet in all three countries the people have made good use of the resources they have. They have a very high standard of living. Let us see why.

2. Norway and Sweden share the Scandinavian Peninsula. To the east is Finland, a country with many of the same problems. To the west is the Atlantic Ocean; to the south are the Baltic and North Seas and to the east is the Soviet Union. These three countries are among the northernmost nations on earth. They are about as far north as Alaska. About one-fourth of each country is above the Arctic Circle. As a result, the sun shines 24 hours a day for about two months in the summer. That is why this area is sometimes called "Land of the Midnight Sun." During the winter the sun does not appear at all for about two months. The lands lie in almost total darkness during these winter months.

3. Compared with other countries of Western Europe, Norway, Sweden and Finland are both big and little countries at the same time—large in size but small in population. Sweden's 7½ million people live in an area slightly larger than California. Finland's small population of 4½ million occupies an area about the size of the state of New Mexico. Norway is slightly smaller than Finland and has a little more than 3 million people.

4. Most of Norway is mountainous. To the east of these highlands is rough, hilly Sweden. Sweden's land ranges from rolling plains in the south to rugged mountains and plateaus in the north and northwest. Much of Finland is a low plateau. All three countries have countless lakes, rivers, streams and canals. The Atlantic coast of Norway is lined with inlets called *fiords*. These narrow bodies of water reach far inland and are surrounded by high banks. They were carved out of the mountains ages ago by glaciers and are very beautiful. There are still glaciers in the mountains.

5. The climate of these northern countries is not as cold as you might think. The Atlantic coast of Norway and the southern parts of Sweden and Finland have milder climates than the rest of this region. During the summer the temperature is like that of San Francisco. During the winter it is as cold as Chicago or Detroit. The mild climate is due to the Gulf Stream, which brings warm waters and winds from the ocean. Much of Sweden and Finland, however,

is shut off from the warm, westerly winds by the mountains. Because of this the winters there are much colder than in Norway.

6. The Scandinavian peninsula was once the home of a fierce people, the Vikings. Between 800 and 1000 A.D., the Vikings raided and occupied many parts of Western Europe. They settled Iceland and Greenland and some believe they may have reached North America about 1000 A.D. By the 14th century, Norway, Sweden and Finland were ruled by Denmark. Sweden gained its freedom and had a period of power ending shortly after 1700. Sweden and Norway were united for a while until Norway became free in 1905. Russia controlled Finland until the Russian Revolution of 1917. Now all three nations are free and, except for fighting between Russia and Finland in 1939 and in World War II, they have kept their freedom in peace.

7. Norway and Sweden both have governments in which a king rules but a parliament makes the laws. The prime minister is the chief officer of the government. The parliaments are elected by the people. Finland also has a democratic form of government. Finland, however, has no king. Its chief officer is a president.

8. The remarkable thing about these countries is their high standard of living. Schooling is important and the people are wide readers. They live long, healthful lives. They enjoy most of the comforts that we have—radios, telephones, automobiles and electric kitchen appliances. Until 1900, most people were farmers, fishermen and woodsmen. Today most people work in industry. Most live in the southern part of their countries where the climate is milder. Their largest cities are the capitals—Oslo, Norway; Stockholm, Sweden; Helsinki, Finland. Most of the people follow the Protestant religion.

9. Above the Arctic Circle lives a small tribe of people called the Lapps. They live in the bare northern parts of all three nations. The Lapps are nomads. They raise reindeer and follow their animals as they move from place to place in search of food. The reindeer provide Lapps with meat, milk and hides for tents and clothing.

10. Except for Sweden, few mineral resources are found in these northern countries. Only Sweden has iron ore. Coal and oil, two power resources, are lacking. There is little fertile farm land and the growing seasons are short. Despite this lack of resources and favorable climate, the people have learned to make the best use of what they have: the forests, the swift-flowing streams and the fishing

Stockholm, Sweden.
Pan American Airways

A Lapp woman in the far north of Finland.
UNITED NATIONS

A Norwegian fishing fleet.

grounds. All three countries are rich in forests. For years the swift streams have been used to float logs and run saw mills. Today the rivers are more important as a source of electricity for industries. Wood pulp and paper are now the leading exports of all three countries.

11. Because the land and climate make farming difficult, Norway has long turned to the sea for food and for a living. The nation borders the Atlantic Ocean. The ocean waters are filled with cod and herring. Fishermen of Norway are famous as whale-hunters as well. The modern whaling ships are like floating factories. The whale is caught and prepared for market right on the ships. Norway catches more fish than it can use and the surplus is exported. Because of this interest in the sea, Norway has one of the largest fleets of ships in the world. Fishing is less important to Sweden and Finland.

12. Lacking coal and oil, these northern countries have made great use of the electricity provided by waterfalls. This electricity is a source of power for their factories. Factories use the products of Scandinavia's mines, forests and seas. Sweden uses its own iron ore to make fine steel goods. In Finland, copper from its mines is made into wire. In Norway, there are plants for refining copper and nickel.

13. The amount of fertile farm land in each country is small. The growing season lasts only a few months. Yet the people have done remarkable things with what they have. Swedish farmers get very high yields from each acre of land. Finland's farmers have shown the world how to grow wheat in the coldest climates. The chief crops are hay, rye, wheat, barley and oats. All three countries are now raising more dairy cattle. Sweden is one of the great milk-producing nations of the world. While the use of machinery and great care of farm land have brought good crops, Sweden and Norway must still import food for their people.

14. Because these nations need to import food and raw materials from other countries, they must depend upon foreign trade. Their chief exports are paper, wood products, fish, steel and iron ore. Norway's ships may be found all over the world.

15. These three countries of northern Europe are located between the Soviet Union and the Free World. The three nations have tried to remain neutral in world arguments. Only Norway has joined NATO. Neither Sweden nor Finland has joined NATO or the Common Market of Europe. They do not want to give the Soviet Union any reason to distrust them.

255

UNDERSTANDING WHAT YOU HAVE READ

1. **Which of the following questions are answered in this chapter?**
   a. What is the climate of Norway, Sweden and Finland?
   b. What are the Nobel Prizes?
   c. Why do the three nations of Northern Europe depend upon foreign trade?

2. **The main idea of this chapter is to describe:**
   a. the land and climate of the Scandinavian Peninsula.
   b. how the Lapps live.
   c. how the people of three northern nations use their resources.

3. **A good description of these northern lands would include mention of:**
   a. rivers cutting through plains.
   b. mountains covered with great forests.
   c. cold, treeless tundra with large areas of fertile farm land in the north.

4. **The source of food of the Lapps is the:**
   a. reindeer.   b. goat.   c. buffalo.

5. **A reason why farming is difficult in Scandinavia is that:**
   a. the growing season is short.
   b. there is a small population.
   c. there is a lack of water.

6. **These nations carry on much foreign trade because:**
   a. their lumber supplies materials for shipbuilding.
   b. they do not have much to sell.
   c. they need to buy food and raw materials.

7. **A *fiord* would be most important to a:**
   a. sailor.   b. miner.   c. farmer.

8. **When a nation has a *surplus* of goods, it has:**
   a. more goods than are needed for its own use.
   b. large industries using coal and iron.
   c. farm products grown on small farms.

DEVELOPING IDEAS AND SKILLS

Map # 31a and b—Norway, Sweden, Finland and the United States

Can you answer these questions?

1. Do the Scandinavian countries lie in the high, middle or low latitudes?
2. Locate the capital cities of each country on the map. What do all these cities have in common?
3. If you flew from your community to Norway, in what direction would you be traveling?
4. What city is located at 60° N. Lat. and 5° E. Long.?
5. About how far is the distance from Copenhagen in Denmark to Stockholm in Sweden?
6. Where are the large cities of Norway located? Why is this so?
7. Into what body of water do the great number of streams in Finland flow? In Sweden?
8. Why do you think the Gulf of Bothnia is not so important a waterway as the North Sea?
9. What country borders Finland on the east?
10. The city of Hammerfest in the extreme north is located in what country?
11. Which is more crowded, the United States or Scandinavia? How does the map help to tell you why this is so?

Map # 31a and b—Norway, Sweden, Finland and the United States

UNITED STATES
POPULATION: 191 MILLION
LAND AREA: 3.6 MILLION SQUARE MILES
54 PEOPLE PER SQUARE MILE

FINLAND, NORWAY, SWEDEN
POPULATION: 15.8 MILLION
LAND AREA: 428,600 SQUARE MILES
37 PEOPLE PER SQUARE MILE

257

SUMMING UP

Do You Agree or Disagree? Give the reasons for your answers.

1. All three of these northern nations are mountainous.
2. Part of each nation lies above the Arctic Circle.
3. The climate of the three countries is affected by the North Atlantic Drift.
4. Norway, Sweden and Finland have many mineral resources.
5. The northern frontier of Scandinavia is settled by nomads called Eskimos.
6. These northern lands are closer to the United States than they are to the Soviet Union.
7. Much of the land is covered with forests and rapid mountain streams.
8. Rich soils make these nations the greatest wheat-growing countries of Europe.
9. Sweden has rich iron-ore deposits.
10. Electricity is a great source of power in these northern lands.

FOLLOW UP

In your notebook, place the following items under three headings: *Norway, Sweden* and *Finland.*

1. The largest population of the three.
2. The largest nation of the three.
3. Owner of one of the world's largest fleets of merchant ships.
4. Headed by a president.
5. Famous for whaling ships.
6. Large producer of iron ore.
7. Successful in wheat-growing.
8. Fiords are part of the coastline.

BOOKS FOR UNIT 4

Author	Title, Publisher	Description
1. Benary-Isbert, M.	*The Ark,* Harcourt, Brace	The story of a divided family in the Germanies.
2. Bishop, Claire	*The Big Loop,* Viking	Taking a bicycle tour of France.
3. Booth, Arthur H.	*The True Story of Sir Winston Church-ill, British Statesman,* Children's Press	The biography of a person often called the "greatest man of the 20th century."
4. Clément, Marguerite	*In France,* Viking	France's history, people and their ways of living.
5. Corley, Anthony	*The True Story of Napoleon, Emperor of France,* Children's Press	The story of a famous general and ruler of France.
6. Daly, Maureen	*Spanish Roundabout,* Dodd	The history and geography of Spain.
7. DeJong, Meindert	*Wheel on the School,* Harper	The life of children in a Dutch fishing village.
8 Flender, Harold	*Rescue in Denmark,* Macfadden	How Denmark saved the Jews from the Nazis.
9. Rothery, Agnes	*Scandinavian Roundabout,* Dodd	The story of Norway and Sweden.
10. Shirer, William	*The Rise and Fall of Adolf Hitler,* Random House	The story of Nazism and World War II.
11. Thorne-Thomsen, G.	*In Norway,* Viking	How the people live and think in this northern country.

UNIT 5

The Soviet Union

CHAPTER 1

The Global Giant

PROBLEM: Why should we know about the Soviet Union?

READING FOR A PURPOSE:
1. What is the full name of the Soviet Union?
2. How is the Soviet Union governed?
3. Why is the Soviet Union a powerful nation?

1. The Union of Soviet Socialist Republics, or U.S.S.R., stretches across two continents, Europe and Asia. We often refer to this vast nation as the Soviet Union, or simply as the Soviet. What does the name of the country mean? "Soviet" is the Russian word for "council" and "socialist" means that the government owns all the land, resources and industries of the country. (A Soviet citizen may own such personal property as a car or a home.) It is incorrect today to use the name Russia when referring to the Soviet Union because Russia is only a small part of the Soviet. It is only the part west of the Ural Mountains.

2. There are many reasons why we should know about the Soviet Union. The Soviet is the largest nation in the world. Reaching from Europe through Asia, it takes up about one-sixth of the land surface of the earth. The western part of the country is called Soviet Europe, while the eastern part is known as Soviet Asia or Siberia. This huge country is closer to us than most people think. Alaska, our northernmost state, is only about 55 miles from Siberia! And only Canada lies between the United States and the Soviet Union across the North Pole.

3. There are about 230 million people in the Soviet Union, making it the third largest nation in the world in population. Its people are made up of many different races and national groups. (A national group is any group of people who share the same customs, language and traditions.) Most of the people live in Soviet Europe.

4. Since World War II, the Soviet Union has become one of the two most powerful nations in the world. One of the reasons for its great growth in strength is that it has a wealth of nat-

Volgograd (formerly called Stalingrad), a major city in Soviet Russia.

Ewing Galloway

ural resources. Much of the land is covered by vast forests. There is a fertile farming belt in Soviet Europe, and modern farming methods are being extended into Soviet Asia. The Soviet is a storehouse of minerals for use in the manufacture of steel. The Communist Party is using these resources to turn the Soviet Union into a land of mills and factories. Today, the Soviet government keeps one of the world's largest armies. Like our own forces, this huge army is equipped with all the terrible weapons of modern warfare—tanks, missiles, rockets and atom bombs.

5. The Soviet Union has a government that is very different from that of the United States. This government was begun in 1917. The government is controlled by members of the Communist Party. This is the only political party in the nation. In a Communist state, the government runs all the factories and farms. It decides what goods are made. It controls the schools and all the means of communication, such as newspapers, radio and television. In a Communist nation, people are taught that they live to serve the government. In a democracy, the government is formed to serve the people.

6. The leaders of the Soviet Union have tried to spread their way of life throughout the world. At the end of World War II, the Soviet Union occupied many countries in Eastern Europe— Poland, Hungary, Rumania, Bulgaria, Yugoslavia and East Germany. Communist governments still rule these countries, as well as Albania and Czechoslovakia.

7. In the United Nations, the Soviet Union has used its "veto" to block action by that organization more than 100 times. (Each of the five permanent nations who are members of the Security Council has this power, but no other nation has used it nearly so often.) The country has been "difficult" in other ways as well. In 1948, the Soviets blockaded Berlin to try to

Ewing Galloway

Farm workers of Soviet Asia.

force the Western nations out of that city. In 1961, a wall of concrete and barbed wire was built in Berlin to keep the people of East Germany from fleeing to West Berlin. And in 1962, the Soviet Union established missile bases in Cuba, only 90 miles from our shores. What's more, in Vietnam and Laos in the Far East, the Communist forces have the support of Soviet leaders.

8. The spread of communism in Eastern Europe, in the Western Hemisphere and in the Far East has caused much concern among the people of the Free World. The government of the Soviet Union is controlled by a few powerful men. It is hard for us to know what they think, how they will act and how much they will use the great strength of their nation to spread their political ideas. Do they want to bring Communist rule to more peoples of the world? Are they interested in putting more nations under the control of the Soviet Union? The future of our country and of the world may depend to a large extent upon the answers to these questions.

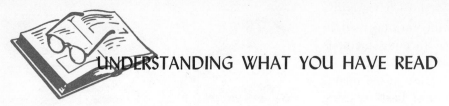

UNDERSTANDING WHAT YOU HAVE READ

1. Which of the following questions are answered in this chapter?
a. Are there forests in the Soviet Union?
b. Why is the Soviet Union important in the thinking of Americans?
c. Who are the leaders of the Soviet Union today?

2. The main idea of this chapter is to describe:
a. the spread of communism.
b. the need to know more about the Soviet Union.
c. how the Soviet Union is governed.

3. The Soviet government first took power in:
a. 1917.   b. 1946.   c. 1964.

4. The Soviet Union placed missiles in:
a. the Congo.   b. Cuba.   c. Spain.

5. The Soviet Union is a powerful nation today because it has:
a. a large standing army.
b. the most power in the United Nations.
c. the largest navy in the world.

6. Communism has spread to all these countries EXCEPT:
a. Poland.   b. Hungary.   c. India.

7. In a *Communist* state:
a. the government owns all the farms and factories.
b. there are many political parties.
c. the people choose their own leaders.

8. "The President *vetoed* the bill; everybody was disappointed." The word *vetoed* means:
a. "approved."   b. "disapproved."   c. "delayed."

DEVELOPING IDEAS AND SKILLS

Map # 32—The Soviet Union and Eastern Europe

Can you answer these questions?

1. Is the region north or south of the equator?
2. Is the region east or west of the Prime Meridian?
3. How far north and south does the region extend?
4. Does the region extend farther from east to west or from north to south?
5. What region or regions are near it?
6. What is the largest country? The smallest?
7. What are the chief bodies of water that border the region?
8. Are there countries in it that have no outlets to the sea?
9. What are some of the important rivers in the region?
10. Are there any island nations?
11. Are there countries that are located on peninsulas?
12. Are there any lands that are colonies of other nations?

Map # 32—The Soviet Union and Eastern Europe

SUMMING UP

Below are some headings for your *outline* on communism. There are also some topics on the question. In your notebook, place the topics under the correct heading.

COMMUNISM

Headings

A. What the Soviet Union Is
B. The Communist Government
C. How Communism Has Spread

Topics

1. Factories and farms are owned by the government.
2. Largest nation in the world.
3. War against the government of South Vietnam.
4. Building of the Berlin Wall.
5. Only one political party is allowed.
6. Soviet Europe and Siberia.
7. Control of European nations occupied during World War II.
8. People are assigned to jobs by the state.
9. Missile bases established in Cuba.
10. Controlled by a few people.

FOLLOW UP

The Soviet Union is in the newspapers daily. Keep a scrapbook of newspaper clippings about events that are taking place in the world in which the Soviet Union is involved.

CHAPTER 2

The Heart of Eurasia

PROBLEM: How does the nature of the land affect the Soviet Union?

READING FOR A PURPOSE:
1. How large is the Soviet Union?
2. What is the surface of the land like?
3. How do the rivers affect the nation?

1. The Soviet Union is more than twice the size of the United States. It covers 8,700,000 square miles. From the border of Poland on the west to the Pacific Ocean on the east is a distance of almost 6,000 miles, or nearly twice the distance across the United States! This is about twelve hours' difference in time from one side of the Soviet Union to the other. (In the United States, there is three hours' difference in time from the Atlantic to the Pacific coast.) Thus, when the sun is "rising" on the Baltic Sea in the Soviet Union, it is already "setting" over the Bering Strait. The Soviet borders twelve different nations and has the longest coastline of any nation in the world. (Much of it is useless, however, because it borders on the frozen Arctic Ocean.)

2. This huge country is located a great distance north of the equator. The southernmost point of the country is only 35° north latitude. This means that the *entire nation* is farther north than our cities of Memphis, Tennessee and Los Angeles, California. Moscow, the capital and largest city, is as far north as Hudson Bay, Canada!

3. A vast part of the U.S.S.R. is a lowland plain. This plain, part of the Great European Plain, stretches across Europe and into Asia as far as the Yenisei River in Central Siberia. The Ural Mountains divide the plain between Europe and Asia. These mountains are low, like the Appalachians of the eastern United States, and are easy to cross. The lowland of Soviet Asia is one of the flattest in the world, and much of it is swampy.

4. West of the Yenisei River, the land rises to the plateaus and mountains of the Far East. In the south, a range of high mountains and plateaus runs from west to east across the Asian continent. These mountains separate the Soviet

Barges on the Amur River.

Ewing Galloway

Novosti from Sovfoto

*The countryside of northern Soviet Europe, part of a vast plain.
The building is an ancient church.*

Union from its southern neighbors. Soviet Asia is landlocked on the south.

5. The Soviet Union has many large rivers. The longest rivers are in Siberia, or Soviet Asia. These are the Ob, Yenisei, Lena and Amur. The Ob is much the longest river in the Soviet Union. These rivers rise or begin in the higher lands to the south. Except for the Amur, they drain toward the ice-filled Arctic Ocean in the north. This means that ships cannot travel down the rivers to the ocean and to ports around the world. The Amur is the only river that reaches the warmer waters of the Pacific Ocean. This lack of warm-water trade routes is an important problem for the Soviet Union.

6. West of the Ural Mountains, the lowland drains mainly to the south. The largest rivers are the Dnieper, the Don and the Volga. The Volga is the longest river in Europe. It empties into the Caspian Sea, which is really a land-locked "lake." The Dnieper and Don Rivers empty into the Black Sea. However, the Black Sea is separated from the busy Mediterranean Sea by narrow straits called the Dardanelles. These straits are controlled by Turkey. Another outlet for Soviet shipping is the Baltic Sea. However, this body of water is partly frozen during much of the year.

7. As you can see, the Soviet Union is really isolated from the great trade routes of the world even though it is the largest nation in the world.

In the southern part of Soviet Asia, high mountains separate the nation from warmer lands. In the north, the icy waters of the Arctic Ocean make the rivers almost useless for trade. Furthermore, the Baltic Sea is partly ice-bound. The Black Sea is separated from the Mediterranean by straits controlled by a foreign country. And the ports on the Pacific Ocean are far from the major trade routes of the world, and from Soviet industries.

The Yenisei River, one of the mighty rivers of the Soviet Union.

L. Polikashin

UNDERSTANDING WHAT YOU HAVE READ

1. **Which of the following questions are answered in this chapter?**
   a. Why are the Soviet rivers not very useful for trade?
   b. Which countries border the Soviet Union?
   c. Why is the Soviet called a landlocked country?

2. **The main idea of *paragraphs 4 through 6* is to describe the:**
   a. use of Soviet water resources.
   b. rivers of the Soviet Union.
   c. problems of the inland seas.

3. **The vast Soviet lowland plain is divided by the:**
   a. Caucasus Mountains.
   b. Ural Mountains.
   c. Alps.

4. **The chief rivers of Siberia flow toward the:**
   a. south (mountains).
   b. north (Arctic Ocean).
   c. east (Pacific Ocean).

5. **Why are the rivers of Siberia not highly useful for trade?**
   a. They are very short in length.
   b. Rapids prevent boats from using them for long distances.
   c. They empty into frozen waters.

6. **The Ural Mountains:**
   a. make travel from Europe to Asia almost impossible.
   b. guard the Soviet against invasion from the south.
   c. are low and easily crossed.

7. **A *landlocked* country is one that:**
   a. is surrounded by land.
   b. is large in area.
   c. borders the seas.

8. **"In spite of its size, the Soviet Union is very much *isolated*." The word *isolated* means:**
   a. "borders few countries."
   b. "its geography keeps it apart from other countries."
   c. "there are few varieties of land forms."

DEVELOPING IDEAS AND SKILLS

Map # 33—Land Forms of Eastern Europe and the Soviet Union

Tell whether these statements are *true* or *false*. Be able to explain your answers.

1. Comparing the climate map of the Soviet Union on page 275 with the map of land forms on page 270, you will see that nearly all the tundra is mountainous.
2. The eastern part of the Soviet Union has several different land forms.
3. The western part of this region is largely lowland.
4. The Great Plains of the Soviet Union cover thousands of miles from east to west.
5. The plateau is the most important land form along the southern border.
6. Most of the mountains of this region are near its outer edges.

269

LAND FORMS OF
**EASTERN EUROPE
AND THE SOVIET UNION**

| | Mountains | | Hills |
| | Plateaus | | Plains |

0   500   1000   1500
Miles

SUMMING UP

Complete the following chart in your notebook. You may have to refer to your
earlier notes on other countries for some information.

COUNTRY	SIZE	LOCATION	LAND FORMS
Soviet Union			
United States			
Canada			
Brazil			

FOLLOW UP

Tell whether these statements are true or false. The underlined words make the statements true or false. If a statement is false, what word or words would you place in it to make it true?

1. Three large rivers of Soviet Asia flow toward the Arctic Ocean.
2. The best "warm-water" outlet for the Soviet Union is the Bering Strait.
3. Soviet Asia is landlocked on the southern border.
4. The Volga River flows into the Caspian Sea.
5. The longest river of the Soviet Union is the Don.
6. The Soviet Union is so wide that there is six hours' difference in time from east to west.
7. The great plain across the Soviet Union is divided by the Ural Mountains.
8. The nearest part of the United States to the Soviet Union is the state of Alaska.

CHAPTER 3

The Cold Land

PROBLEM: How is Soviet life affected by its climate?

READING FOR A PURPOSE:
1. Why do few people live on the tundra or taiga?
2. Where is the good farm land of the Soviet?
3. Where are the warmer lands of the Soviet Union?

1. In general, the climate of the Soviet Union is much like that of Canada. This cold climate has helped the Soviet people on many occasions. For example, the cold winters have turned back invaders. In 1812, the armies of Napoleon had to retreat after a bitter winter in Moscow in which thousands of soldiers froze or starved to death. In World War II, the winter again proved to be a terrible enemy for the armies of Adolf Hitler. However, not all of the Soviet Union has a cold climate. Because of its vast size, the country has many climatic regions.

2. In the far north of the Soviet is the *tundra*. It extends along the Arctic coast as much as several hundred miles inland. This land is flat and treeless. Cold winds from the Arctic Ocean blow across it and reach the lands farther south. The year-round temperature of the tundra is always low, with temperatures below freezing as much as eight months of the year. The ground is never completely warm. As a result, there is a layer of frozen ground a few inches beneath the surface all year long. This frozen ground is called "permafrost." The permafrost allows only a short growing season for crops and prevents trees from growing on the tundra.

3. The land of the tundra climate is a place where few people live. Those who do live there make their living by hunting, fishing and herding reindeer. These people move from place to place as their reindeer herds graze the tundra. The reindeer furnish the people with nearly everything they need. They eat reindeer meat and drink the milk. They make tents and clothing from reindeer skins. The reindeer also carry burdens on their backs. Many wild animals such as the ermine and fox are hunted in the tundra for their valuable furs.

The tundra region of the Soviet Union.
G. Makarov

About a third of the Soviet is covered by the taiga.

4. South of the tundra are the forest lands or taiga. *Taiga* is a Russian word for forest. The Soviet Union has more acres of forest than any other nation in the world. The Soviet taiga is about as large as the whole United States! It has many rivers, lakes and ponds. A greater range of temperature is found here, for the land is farther from the waters of the Arctic Ocean.

(As you remember, large bodies of water help to keep the climate even.) Sixty degrees below zero is common in the winter. During the summer the temperatures may reach eighty or ninety degrees. At that time the frozen waters melt and the land becomes soft and marshy. Few people live in the taiga because of the very cold winter climate.

5. South of the taiga is the humid-continental climate. It is similar to the continental climate of the United States, but colder. Temperatures are lower in the winter, and it is not as warm in the summer. The large, important Soviet cities —Moscow, Leningrad and Kiev—have this climate. The soil is fertile and much of the land has been cleared for farming. The growing season lasts five months or longer.

6. Southward the climate is drier and the summers are longer and warmer. Here the dry grasslands are found. The Russians call this area the *steppes*. The steppes reach from the Black Sea eastward into central Asia. Rainfall is only from ten to twenty inches a year. Despite this lack of rain, the steppes are a great farming area. The soil is rich and black. Part of the western steppes lies in the Ukraine, the great wheat belt of the Soviet. The steppes may be compared with the dry prairies of the United

The Mediterranean climate near the Crimea.

States that are west of the 100th meridian.

7. In the south, from the Caspian Sea eastward to Lake Balkhash, the land is largely a desert. There is little rain and it is very hot. The mountains provide water for irrigation so that cotton and tobacco can be grown. As you can imagine, few people live here because it is very hard to make a living from the dry land.

8. In the northern part of the Black Sea lies the Crimean Peninsula. This peninsula has a climate like that of the Mediterranean countries and southern California. It is the great vacation spot of the Soviet Union. There are hot, dry summers and mild, wet winters. Many fruits are grown here—oranges, figs and grapes. Large hotels provide for thousands of tourists. Because of the extreme cold in much of the nation, this warmer spot is a favorite vacation land for many people.

9. As you can see, most of the Soviet land consists of frozen wastelands, forests and mountains. Much of the Soviet Union is free from frost and snow for only about 150 days a year. This is too short a growing season for many crops. There are many areas in which there is not enough rain for farming. For these reasons, there is much unsettled land in the Soviet. Most people are crowded into the few areas that are fertile and more comfortable to live in.

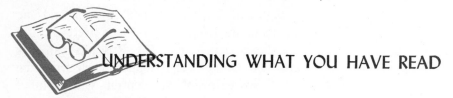

UNDERSTANDING WHAT YOU HAVE READ

1. **Which of the following questions are answered in this chapter?**
a. Why is most of the Soviet Union cold?
b. In what climatic region are the large Soviet cities?
c. What crops are grown on the steppes?

2. **The main idea of this chapter is to describe:**
a. how people live in northern lands.
b. the different climates of the Soviet Union.
c. where the steppes are located.

3. **The best farm lands of the Soviet are found in the:**
a. taiga.   b. steppes.   c. irrigated desert.

4. **The people of the *tundra* herd flocks of:**
a. reindeer.   b. llamas.   c. caribou.

5. **The Soviet Union has no climate in which the farmer can grow:**
a. wheat.   b. cotton.   c. bananas.

6. **The summer climate near the city of Moscow is:**
a. warmer than that of New York City.
b. colder than that of Chicago.
c. much like the climate of New Orleans.

7. **A *taiga* is a:**
a. treeless plain.
b. northern forest.
c. tropical rain forest.

8. **On a *steppe*, people usually make a living by:**
a. farming.   b. fishing.   c. lumbering.

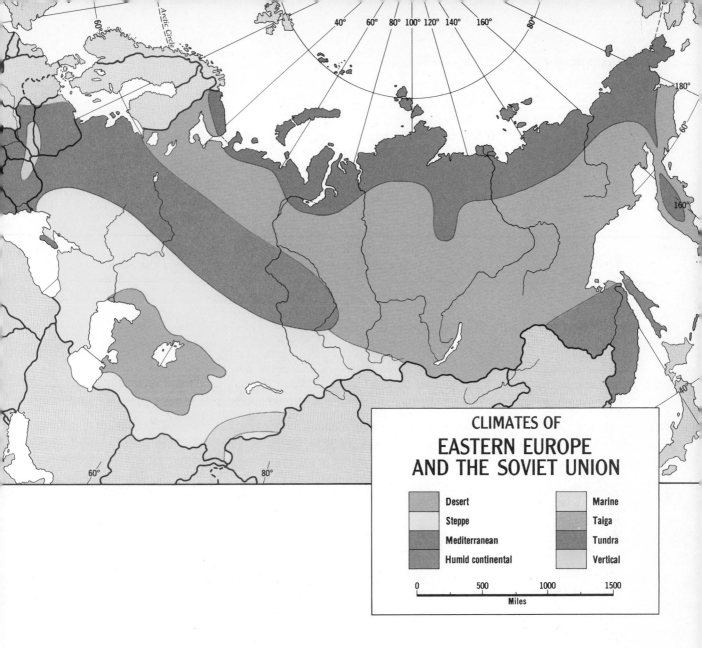

CLIMATES OF
**EASTERN EUROPE
AND THE SOVIET UNION**

Desert   Marine
Steppe   Taiga
Mediterranean   Tundra
Humid continental   Vertical

0   500   1000   1500
Miles

DEVELOPING IDEAS AND SKILLS

Map # 34—Climates of Eastern Europe and the Soviet Union

Do You Agree or Disagree? Give reasons for your answers.

1. The great distance in the Soviet Union from east to west causes great differences in climate throughout the country.
2. The largest climatic region in the Soviet Union is the taiga.
3. The best farm lands are located in the western part of the Soviet Union.
4. The 180° longitude of the eastern part of the Soviet Union has a great effect on its climate.
5. Only a small part of the Soviet Union has a Mediterranean climate.
6. Altitude has little effect on the climate of most of the Soviet Union.
7. Most of the eastern part of the region has a climate much like our states of Oregon and Washington.
8. Most people in the Soviet Union probably live between 120° and 150° longitude.

275

SUMMING UP

Are these statements true or false?   Give reasons for your answers.
1. The tundra has many people.
2. The people of the tundra depend on the reindeer for many things.
3. Most of the Soviet Union is hot.
4. The tundra and taiga climates are found in most of the Soviet Union.
5. The Soviet Union has no deserts.
6. The Soviet Union has a great deal of fertile land.
7. People from California would feel "at home" in the Crimea.
8. The Ukraine is the great farming area of the Soviet Union.
9. Even the cold Arctic Ocean may warm the lands near it.
10. Rubber, cocoa and sugar cane are leading farm crops of the Soviet.

FOLLOW UP

Most people like to travel to far-off places. Plan an imaginary trip to the Soviet Union. As part of your plan, try to answer these questions:
1. Which part of the Soviet Union would you like to visit? Why?
2. What clothing would you take with you?
3. Would you be able to get a part-time job in any occupation? Which would you choose?

CHAPTER 4

How Russia Became the Soviet Union

PROBLEM: How did Russia grow in size and strength?

READING FOR A PURPOSE:
1. When did the Russians reach the Pacific?
2. Who were the serfs?
3. When did Russia become the Soviet Union?

1. Some of the earliest settlers of Soviet Europe were Slavic-speaking people. About the 9th century, these Slavic peoples were conquered by the Vikings from the north. The Vikings set up a kingdom near the city of Kiev. They became Christians. In the 13th century, this kingdom and other lands were overrun by Mongols who came from Central Asia.

2. The Mongols ruled the small Russian kingdoms for 300 years. In the 15th century, Ivan the Great, ruler of a small kingdom near Moscow, began to fight the Mongols and enlarge his kingdom. The new country thus beginning was called Russia. Ivan was the first Russian ruler to be called czar, which means "caesar" or "emperor." The next great ruler, Ivan IV, destroyed the Mongol settlements in the Volga River valley. Now the Russians were able to push on to the Ural Mountains.

3. As early as 1581, Russian soldiers, traders and merchants moved into Siberia. They were looking for gold and furs. They built forts and trading posts along the rivers. By 1639, the Russians had reached the Pacific Ocean. One hundred years later, the Danish explorer Vitus Bering crossed the narrow strait from Siberia to Alaska (now called the Bering Strait). He had been hired by Russia to find out if there was a land connection between Asia and North America. Next the Russians turned south along the Pacific Coast almost to San Francisco Bay. By 1812 they had established trading posts in California. However, these posts were hard to reach, so the Russians gave them up. In 1867, Russia sold Alaska to the United States.

4. Two other rulers continued to extend the land of Russia. Peter the Great (1682-1725) fought a long war against Sweden, gaining some territory on the eastern shore of the Baltic Sea. There he built a new city called St. Petersburg as his capital and chief seaport. Today this city is called Leningrad. Peter wanted to make his country modern, so he brought thousands of skilled craftsmen from Western Europe to Russia. He even wanted his people to dress and act like Westerners. Catherine the Great (1729-1796) moved the Russian boundaries farther south and west. In the south, a war against the Ottoman Turks gained land on the coast of the Black Sea. Russian ships were now free to sail to the Mediterranean. In the west, Catherine took part in dividing Poland, adding more territory to Russia's growing empire.

5. The czars were the supreme rulers of Russia from the 17th century to the 20th century. Most of the land was owned by nobles or friends of the czars. Most of the people were poor peasants called serfs. They had to live and work on the land of the nobles and pay them taxes. Serfs had little education. They could not leave the land on which they were born and were often

The Granger Collection

Catherine the Great of Russia.

gary and their allies. The Russian armies were beaten badly. In three years, almost two million Russians lost their lives. The people had had enough. They did not want to continue the war. They wanted peace, food and land of their own. In 1917, Czar Nicholas gave up the throne when a revolt threatened. A republic was formed.

8. The new government wanted to continue the war, but the soldiers and the people at home were tired of fighting. In November, 1917, the Revolution came. It was led by a party called the Bolsheviks, or Communists. Nikolai Lenin was their leader. Lenin is known as the "Father of Communism" in the Soviet Union. The Communists gradually ended the private ownership of land, factories, mines, banks and railways. The name of the country was changed to the Union of Soviet Socialist Republics.

9. Lenin died in 1924. Joseph Stalin followed him as the leader of the Soviet until 1953. During his long rule, Stalin directed the building of the great industrial system of the Soviet. He had one aim—to make the power of his nation second to none in the world.

10. In 1939, Stalin signed a treaty with Adolf Hitler, the ruler of Germany. They agreed not to attack each other. When Hitler invaded Poland in 1939, Stalin occupied the eastern part of the divided country. He also fought a war against Finland. He brought the Baltic countries (Estonia, Lithuania and Latvia) under Soviet rule.

11. The Soviet-German friendship did not last long. Without warning, Hitler's armies in-

taken to serve in the czar's armies. Meanwhile, the Industrial Revolution was taking place in Western Europe and changing life for the people there. The West was moving ahead. Russia was standing still.

6. In 1904-5, Russia was defeated in war by Japan. The defeat made the Russian people see how backward their rulers were. The Russians demanded a greater voice in their government. For a time the czar allowed a law-making body to be formed. However, this was soon forgotten. The people felt they were helpless.

7. World War I brought about a change in the Russian government. The nation was not prepared for the war when it started in 1914. Nevertheless, Russia joined Great Britain and France to fight against Germany, Austria-Hun-

An attack on the Winter Palace during the Russian Revolution, 1917.

vaded the Soviet Union in 1941. The Germans were very successful at first. But with the help of the United States, the Soviets stopped the German armies. The Battle of Stalingrad marked the end of the German advance. After that the Russians pushed the Nazis back. In 1945, the Russian army met the Allies crossing Germany in the opposite direction, and the war was won.

12. After World War II, the Communists remained in the Eastern European countries they had occupied during the war. In a short while there were Communist governments in Poland, Rumania, Hungary, East Germany, Bulgaria, Yugoslavia, Czechoslovakia and Albania. Much of what went on in this region was kept secret. Winston Churchill, Prime Minister of Great Britain, called this secrecy the "Iron Curtain" around Communist lands. In the years that followed, the Soviet Union and the United States drifted further apart. (This later history will be discussed in Chapter 10.)

The Granger Collection

Nikolai Lenin and Joseph Stalin.

UNDERSTANDING WHAT YOU HAVE READ

1. **Which of the following questions are answered in this chapter?**
a. How did Russia reach North America?
b. Why was there a revolution in 1917?
c. How was Russia ruled by the Mongols?

2. **The main idea of *paragraphs 5 through 7* is to describe:**
a. how the Russians marched eastward in the 16th century.
b. Russia under the rule of the czars.
c. Russia's defeat in World War I.

3. **Russia was ruled for many years by nomadic herdsmen called:**
a. Mongols.　　b. Bedouins.　　c. Huns.

4. **In 1904-5, Russia was defeated by:**
a. China.　　b. Japan.　　c. France.

5. **Russia left the First World War in 1917 because:**
a. Czar Nicholas wanted peace.
b. many Russians had been killed.
c. a new government was formed.

6. **Life was hard for many people under the czars because:**
a. the land was owned by a few nobles.
b. people objected to changes made by the Communists.
c. people had to work long hours in factories.

7. **A *czar* is the same as:**
a. a representative.
b. an explorer.
c. an emperor.

DEVELOPING IDEAS AND SKILLS

Picture Symbols

These pictures should help you to recall parts of the chapter you have read. Can you tell the main idea of each picture? In what paragraph did you find the answer for each?

SUMMING UP

List these events in your notebook. After each, write *Before the Revolution of 1917* or *After the Revolution of 1917*.

1. Invasion of the Mongols—
2. Russian conquest of Siberia—
3. Rule of Lenin and Stalin—
4. Poland has a Communist government—
5. Russian war with Japan—
6. Battle of Stalingrad—
7. Great Russian industries—
8. Rule of Peter the Great—

FOLLOW UP

Who Am I?   Below are statements about some famous people. Can you tell who is described in each statement? Choose your answers from the list of names below.

Bering	Stalin	Lenin
Ivan the Great	Khrushchev	Peter the Great
a Mongol	a Viking	Czar Nicholas

1. I was the first czar of Russia. I broke the power of the Mongols. I am _____.
2. I led the Russian Revolution in 1917. I took Russia out of World War I. From that time, the Communist Party has been in power. I am _____.
3. I liked the ways of the West and tried to bring them to Russia. I defeated Sweden and built a new capital city. I am _____.
4. I ruled as a dictator for many years. I helped to build the great industries of the Soviet Union. I am _____.
5. I was the last czar of Russia. I was overthrown during World War I. I am _____.
6. I was one of many who invaded Russia long ago. My people ruled for hundreds of years. Many of us still live in the Soviet Union. I am _____.
7. I discovered a narrow waterway separating Asia from North America. Many Russian traders crossed into North America over this waterway. I am _____.

CHAPTER 5

The People of the Soviet Union

PROBLEM: Who are the Soviet people?

READING FOR A PURPOSE:

1. How many people live in the Soviet Union?
2. Where do the people of the Soviet Union live?
3. What changes are taking place in the Soviet population?

1. The Soviet Union is made up of fifteen Soviet republics. These Soviet republics are based on racial or national groups. (Our states are simply divisions of land.) Some of the republics are large and others are very small. The largest is the Russian Soviet Federated Socialist Republic, which covers three-fourths of the land area of the Soviet Union. Moscow is the capital of this republic, and of the Soviet Union as a whole. Other important republics are the Ukraine and Byelorussia or White Russia. These republics have votes in the United Nations in addition to that of the Soviet Union.

2. There are about 230 million people living in the Soviet Union today. It is a country of many races in which more than eighty languages are spoken. Most of the people, however, speak Russian or a Slavic language. The rest are descendants of the Mongols and other tribes that came from Central Asia. These different national groups are allowed to speak their own languages and practice their own customs. But all school children must study Russian too. If one desires to "get ahead" in Soviet society, it is necessary to know the Russian language well.

3. The population of the U.S.S.R. is not distributed evenly. Some areas, as in Soviet Europe, are thickly settled. In Soviet Asia, however, vast areas are too mountainous, too cold or too dry for many people to live. Most of the people live in a "triangle" of land stretching from the Black Sea to the Baltic Sea to Novokuznetsk (Stalinsk) in Siberia. This is called the Fertile Triangle because it is the region of the best farm land. It is only a small part of the land area, but it has three-fourths of the Soviet people. There are more than twenty cities in the Triangle with at least a half-million people. The largest cities are Moscow, Leningrad and Kiev.

4. In 1930, Magnitogorsk in the Ural Mountains was a tiny village. It could scarcely even be called a village then. Today, it is a city of more than 300,000 people. The growth of this village and others like it shows clearly what is happening in the Soviet Union. The popu-

People of Uzbek, Soviet Asia.

Ewing Galloway

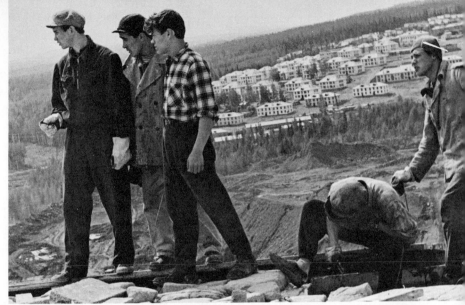

*Workers from a new town
in the rapidly growing
industrial area of the Urals.*

*Grapes being harvested by young girls
in Azerbaijan.*

lation is growing and it is spreading out. In the years since World War II, large cities have sprung up in Soviet Asia near new sources of farm land or minerals. The growth of cities where none had existed is one of the important features of the Soviet Union today. Moreover, this nation in which most people once lived on farms has changed so that half the people now live in cities!

5. While the standard of living of the people is rising, it is still far from the high living standard of the American people. Few Soviet farms have electricity or running water. Farmers are seldom able to spend an evening of recreation in the nearest town. A suit of clothes for a factory worker costs a month's wages. A shirt costs a full day's pay. A worker will labor for a week to buy a pair of shoes. There are probably only one million cars in the Soviet, compared with more than sixty million in the United States. The Soviet has somewhat more than 2½ million television sets compared with the sixty million in our country.

6. As more and more people work in factories, another new occupational group is growing in the Soviet. Over the years the Soviet government has built a great many factories. In order to run these factories, people with special training are needed: engineers, scientists, managers. These people receive much

higher pay than factory workers. They can afford to buy homes, automobiles, refrigerators and washing machines. They tend to give strong support to the Soviet system because their jobs and way of life depend upon it. They are the new Soviet middle class.

7. The Communists are against all religion. Despite this policy there are still many religious people in the Soviet Union. Most of the religious believers of the Soviet are Christians who belong to the Greek or Russian Orthodox Church. There are also a few Roman Catholics and Protestants. For a long time the Communists closed most of the churches. This practice has not been as strict in recent years. However, church leaders cannot say anything against the Communist government, and a man who practices his religion may find it difficult to "get ahead" in the Communist world.

8. The second largest religious group in the Soviet Union is the Moslems. Most of the Mongol groups are Moslem. They are allowed to have their own schools and houses of worship. There is also a large group of Jews. Since 1960, the Soviet Union has not allowed the Jews much freedom to practice their religion. Their temples or houses of worship and their schools have been closed. Jews and other religious groups in the United States have made strong protests to the Soviet leaders about this lack of freedom of worship.

UNDERSTANDING WHAT YOU HAVE READ

1. **Which of the following questions are answered in this chapter?**
a. How do the Soviet farmers live?
b. How many Soviet republics are there?
c. What do the Communists think of religion?

2. **The main idea of this chapter is to describe:**
a. the religious beliefs of the Soviet people.
b. the people of the Soviet Union.
c. the growing cities of Soviet Asia.

3. **The capital of the Soviet Union is:**
a. Kiev.   b. Leningrad.   c. Moscow.

4. **Most people in the Soviet Union live:**
a. in the Fertile Triangle.
b. in the northern regions.
c. along the Pacific coast.

5. **People of the Soviet Union are moving to new areas because they:**
a. feel they are pioneers.
b. are using new resources.
c. want to gain riches from using better farm lands.

6. **Why is there a growing middle class in the Soviet Union?**
a. Industries need people with special skills.
b. New political parties are being formed.
c. There is an increase in farm production.

7. **New large cities of the Soviet Union are appearing in:**
a. the Crimea.   b. the Ukraine.   c. Soviet Asia.

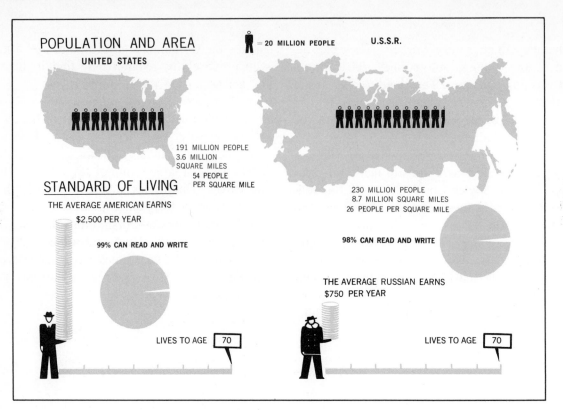

POPULATION AND AREA

= 20 MILLION PEOPLE   U.S.S.R.

UNITED STATES

191 MILLION PEOPLE
3.6 MILLION
SQUARE MILES
54 PEOPLE
PER SQUARE MILE

230 MILLION PEOPLE
8.7 MILLION SQUARE MILES
26 PEOPLE PER SQUARE MILE

STANDARD OF LIVING

THE AVERAGE AMERICAN EARNS

$2,500 PER YEAR

99% CAN READ AND WRITE

98% CAN READ AND WRITE

THE AVERAGE RUSSIAN EARNS
$750 PER YEAR

LIVES TO AGE 70

LIVES TO AGE 70

Pictograph # 11—Population, Area and Standard of Living of the Soviet Union

DEVELOPING IDEAS AND SKILLS

Pictograph # 11—Population, Area and Standard of Living of the Soviet Union
Can you answer these questions?
1. Is the standard of living of this region high or low compared with that of the United States? Is it a low-income or underdeveloped area?
2. Is the region as crowded as the United States?
3. Are the people of this region literate compared with the people of the United States?
4. How long may the average person in this region expect to live?
5. What facts tell you the standard of living of the people of the region?
6. How does this region compare with the United States in size?

SUMMING UP

Do You Agree or Disagree?   Give reasons for your opinion.
1. The largest cities of the Soviet Union are in the European part of the country.
2. Most of the Soviet leaders are very religious people.
3. More and more of the Soviet people are living in cities.
4. The population of the Soviet Union is rising.
5. Most of the Soviet people are crowded into a small region of fertile land.
6. Most of the Soviet people are able to read and write.
7. Most of the people speak one language and are of the same race.
8. A drive in the country on Sunday is a common recreation of the Soviet people.
9. Moscow is probably one of the fashion centers of the world.
10. The factories in the Soviet Union are owned by the government.

FOLLOW UP

Select the item that *does not belong* with the others in each group.

1. **We should know more about the Soviet Union because:**
   a. it has a huge area.
   b. it has a favorable climate.
   c. it has many resources.
   d. it has strong armed forces.

2. **Soviet land forms include:**
   a. a vast lowland plain.
   b. a far eastern frontier of mountains.
   c. few rivers.
   d. low mountains.

3. **Climates of the Soviet Union include:**
   a. rain forest.
   b. tundra.
   c. steppe.
   d. desert.

4. **Czars who have ruled Russia are:**
   a. Peter.
   b. Nicholas.
   c. Lenin.
   d. Ivan.

5. **Among the people of the Soviet Union:**
   a. there is a rising standard of living.
   b. the number of farm workers is increasing.
   c. a growing middle class has developed.
   d. new settlements in Siberia have sprung up.

CHAPTER 6

The Communist Dictatorship

PROBLEM: How is a small group able to control the people?

READING FOR A PURPOSE:
1. What is the Supreme Soviet?
2. Who are the real rulers of the Soviet Union?
3. Why is the Communist Party able to control the Soviet Union?

1. Communist rulers like to call their governments "democracies." This is a deception used over and over again. In Red China the government is called the "People's Republic." East Germany is called the "Democratic Republic." Actually, the people have little to do with running the government in Communist countries. In all Communist countries there is an "acting" government and a "real" one. The Soviet Union is ruled by a few highly placed members of the all-powerful Communist Party.

2. Like the United States, the Soviet Union has a written constitution. It was drawn up in 1936. It sets up a union of fifteen republics. The constitution promises certain rights to all citizens. Many of these promises have not been kept. There is no free speech, free press or right of assembly. There is no freedom of religion. Although it is a federal government of fifteen republics, the national government has most of the power. The republics have less power than our fifty states.

3. The Supreme Soviet is the lawmaking body. Like our Congress, it has two "houses." One is elected on the basis of population, like our House of Representatives. The other has representatives from each republic, as our Senate has separate representatives from each state. The members of the Supreme Soviet are elected every four years by all citizens over eighteen years of age. It meets twice a year for only a few days at a time. Only members of the Communist Party or people approved by the Com-

A meeting of the Supreme Soviet.

Sovfoto

A young man asking to become a member of the Communist Party.

Sovfoto

munist Party may hold office in the Supreme Soviet.

4. Since the Supreme Soviet doesn't meet often, the real work of the government is carried on by two small committees or groups. One is called the Presidium; the other is the Council of Ministers. The Presidium makes the laws and the Council of Ministers carries out the laws and directs the government. There is no separation of powers in the Soviet government.

5. There is a Supreme Court. The judges of this court and the lower courts ("people's courts") are chosen mainly by the Supreme Soviet. There is no jury system. The judges decide all cases. They deal very harshly with persons who talk or act against the government.

6. You have read about the Soviet officials that are "elected." The "real" government, however, is the Communist Party. Unlike the United States, the Soviet Union has only one political party—the Communist Party. In our country you may join any of several political parties, or change from one party to another as you wish.

7. In the Soviet Union you are *asked* to be a member of the Party. You must have a period of training before you can be accepted. Only the most able people are chosen. As a result, there are only about nine million members of the Communist Party in a total population of 230 million. If you become a member of the Party and do not follow the rules, you may lose your membership.

8. Despite its small size, the Communist Party is able to rule the Soviet Union. There are several reasons why this is so. First, once a decision has been reached by the Soviet rulers, all Party members must carry it out. This is called "following the Party line." Second, Party members are placed everywhere. Every important organization, every state farm, every factory has some members. In the third place, the Communist Party is the only political party. No one can gain high office unless he is a member or is approved by the Party. Fourth, the Party controls what is taught in schools and what is said in the newspapers, on radio and on television. The Party also controls the army. Finally, the Communists have secret police that watch everyone. A person whose behavior is not approved may suddenly "disappear." A country such as this, where everything is controlled by the government, is known as a *totalitarian* state.

287

UNDERSTANDING WHAT YOU HAVE READ

1. Which of the following questions are answered in this chapter?
a. How is a law made in the Soviet?
b. Why are there so few members of the Communist Party?
c. Why are there secret police?

2. The main idea of this chapter is to describe:
a. how the Supreme Soviet works.
b. how one becomes a Communist.
c. how the Soviet people are governed.

3. What is the lawmaking body of the Soviet Union?
a. Congress. b. Parliament. c. Supreme Soviet.

4. Who holds the "real" power in the Soviet government?
a. Scientists.
b. Army officers.
c. The Communist Party.

5. There are only a few members in the Communist Party because:
a. there are few privileges.
b. most people want to join many of the other parties.
c. only the most reliable people are chosen.

6. Citizens of the Soviet are careful in what they say about their government because:
a. they fear the secret police.
b. everyone may be a member of the Communist Party.
c. they are eager to have friendship with other nations.

7. A *totalitarian* government is the opposite of a:
a. dictatorship. b. democracy. c. monarchy.

8. In the first paragraph, the word *deception* means:
a. "trickery." b. "method." c. "comfort."

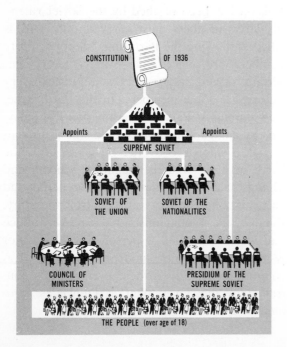

Pictograph # 12a and b—The Government of the Soviet Union

DEVELOPING IDEAS AND SKILLS

Pictograph # 12a and b—The Government of the Soviet Union

Tell whether these statements are true or false.
1. The Soviet Union has no written plan of government.
2. The Council of Ministers is elected by the people.
3. The chief lawmaking body of the Soviet Union is the Supreme Soviet.
4. Only Communist Party members are allowed to hold high office in the Soviet Union.
5. Different nationalities can elect their own representatives.
6. The Supreme Soviet is elected by all the people.
7. Women are not allowed to vote in the Soviet Union.
8. There are two houses in the Supreme Soviet.
9. This pictograph tells us how a law is made in the Soviet Union.
10. The Secretary of the Communist Party may be the most powerful person in the Soviet Union.

SUMMING UP

Complete the following chart in your notebook.

Comparing Governments		
	UNITED STATES	SOVIET UNION
1. Plan of government:		
2. Branches of government:		
3. How laws are made:		
4. Freedoms allowed:		
5. Political parties:		

FOLLOW UP

Tell whether each of these statements applies to a *democratic* or a *totalitarian* state.
1. We believe in a strong government controlled by a few people.
2. We believe that the law should treat all men equally.
3. We believe that people should be educated to believe only what their rulers want them to believe.
4. We believe that everyone must work for the state.
5. We believe that each person has certain rights that no one can take from him.
6. We believe in the use of secret police.
7. We believe that no one should criticize the government.
8. We believe that newspapers should print the truth.

CHAPTER 7

The Soviet Farmland

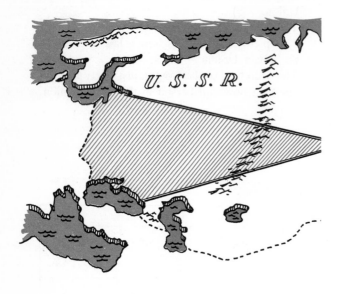

PROBLEM: How is Soviet farm life organized?

READING FOR A PURPOSE:
1. What is a collective farm?
2. Where is the chief farming area of the Soviet?
3. What are the chief farm crops?

1. In the Soviet Union, the government owns all the land. It may not be bought or sold by an individual farmer. Like everyone else in the country, the Soviet farmer is dependent upon and is controlled by the Communist Party. This is the complete opposite of the farmer's position in the United States. The American farmer can own his own land. He can decide what he wants to grow on his land. He can hire others to work for him. He can sell his land if he chooses.

2. There are two kinds of farms in the Soviet Union—the state farm and the collective farm. A state farm is very large. It is called a *sovkhoz*. The state farm is used by the government to

find better methods of raising crops and animals. It is very much like a factory. Each worker does a certain job on the farm and is paid for his work.

3. The collective farm or *kolkhoz* is also large, but not as large as a state farm. On an average collective farm, there may be one hundred farm families. The farmers work together, tilling the soil and harvesting the crops. Because the farms are large and the land is generally flat, machinery can be used. The harvest is sold to the government. Expenses for machinery and seed are paid. After that, each farmer gets a share of the remaining profits from the harvest. The size of each farmer's share depends upon the amount of work he has done. If the harvest is large, he receives a good reward.

4. Soviet farmers live in villages near their fields. Each farmer owns his own house and tools. He may also own a small garden plot on which he grows vegetables and fruits. He may keep a cow, goats and some chickens. He is allowed to sell whatever he does not need from his garden and keep the profits. The farmer's diet generally consists of black rye bread, beet soup (called *borscht*), cabbage, potatoes, salt pork, buckwheat and tea. He does not get as much meat, milk and eggs as we do because there are fewer farm animals in the U.S.S.R. than in the United States. The collective may have radio and television, but the individual farmer will not. A member of the Communist Party lives among the farmers. He plans the

A state farm in Soviet Asia.

Ewing Galloway

290

Threshing barley on a Soviet collective farm.

Grazing sheep in the dry lands of the south.

work of the collective with them.

5. The greatest farming area in the Soviet Union is the "Fertile Triangle." This belt of farm land begins near the Black Sea. It stretches across the Ukraine eastward to the southern Ural Mountains and beyond. This is the heartland of Soviet farming. The soils are rich and black. The area is flat and suitable for the use of machinery. The major crop of this black earth belt is wheat. The Soviet Union is the world leader in the production of wheat.

6. Besides wheat, the chief farm products are rye, barley, potatoes, cotton and wool. Rye is second only to wheat as the important grain product of the Soviet. It can be grown farther north where the climate is cooler. It is used in the black bread that is eaten by Soviet farmers. White potatoes, also important in the Russian

A Communist Party committee discusses farm production on a Soviet collective.

diet, are also grown in the cooler areas. This is another food product in which the Soviet Union leads the world.

7. Very fine cotton is grown in scattered oases (fertile areas) in the dry lands east of the Caspian Sea. The Soviet Union has become a world leader in production of cotton, and nearly all of it is produced in the dry regions of Asia. Textile mills are fed with the wool from thousands of sheep. The main grazing lands are found along the border of the steppes and the southern Caucasus Mountains. These are the old grazing grounds of the Mongol tribes. Only Australia produces more wool than the Soviet Union.

8. Soviet leaders and planners once thought that the collective farm would bring huge crops because tractors and other farm machinery could be used. But it has not worked out this way. There are often food shortages in the U.S.S.R. There are several reasons for this. First, the Soviet farmer has little desire to grow a large amount of crops or try new methods because he does not own the land. Second, despite the size of the Soviet Union, there is less fertile farm land than in the United States. Too much of the country is too cold or too dry for crops. To increase farm production, the Soviet government is now giving the farmer more freedom to sell for a profit the foods he grows in his garden. Also, more lands in Soviet Asia are being opened for farming than ever before.

291

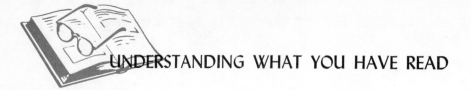

UNDERSTANDING WHAT YOU HAVE READ

1. Which of the following questions are answered in this chapter?
a. Why did the government "collectivize" the farms?
b. Why is most of the Soviet land not good for farming?
c. Where is cotton grown?

2. The main idea of *paragraphs 1 through 4* is to describe:
a. what is grown on Soviet farms.
b. how Soviet farms are organized.
c. the use of machinery on Soviet farms.

3. What is the most important crop of the Fertile Triangle?
a. Potatoes.   b. Rice.   c. Wheat.

4. On a state farm the farmers work for:
a. a share of the crops.
b. wages.
c. the profits from their own gardens.

5. Part of the food problem in the Soviet Union is caused by a lack of:
a. machinery.   b. seed.   c. fertile land.

6. In the Soviet Union, as in many parts of the world, cotton is grown in dry areas because:
a. cotton needs little water during the growing season.
b. water is supplied through irrigation.
c. cotton needs only a small amount of labor at picking time.

7. On a *collective* farm, people:
a. own the lands together.
b. sell the crops to the government and share the profits.
c. gather the crops from nearby farms for sale.

8. On a *sovkhoz* and *kolkhoz*, people make a living through:
a. farming.   b. mining.   c. factory work.

DEVELOPING IDEAS AND SKILLS

V. Yakovlev

The photograph on page 292 should help you to recall parts of the chapter you have read. What is the main idea of the photograph? Where in the chapter is it described?

SUMMING UP

Complete the following chart in your notebook.

Comparing Farmers		
	AMERICAN	SOVIET
1. Ownership of land:		
2. Kinds of farms:		
3. Farming methods:		
4. Crops:		
5. Animals:		
6. Standard of living:		

FOLLOW UP

Tell whether these statements are true or false. The underlined words make the statements true or false. If a statement is false, what word or words would you place in it to make it true?

1. The farms of the Soviet Union are owned by individual farmers.
2. The greatest farming area is called the Vital Triangle.
3. The chief grain crops of the Soviet are wheat and rye.
4. The Soviet Union has more fertile farm land than the United States.
5. A large Soviet farm on which many families live is called a collective farm.
6. Work on a collective farm is divided among the workers by a committee of farmers.
7. The Soviet Union leads the world in the production of wheat.
8. A Soviet farmer will most likely have coffee with his meal.

CHAPTER 8

The Soviet Factories

PROBLEM: How did the Soviet Union become a leading industrial nation?

READING FOR A PURPOSE:
1. How has the Soviet government helped the growth of industry?
2. Where are the main Soviet industrial regions?
3. Where is oil found?

1. Before the Revolution of 1917, Russia was largely a farming nation. While countries of Western Europe were building large factories, Russia had few. In 1928, the government of the Soviet Union began planning the use of its natural resources. Since then, the Soviet Union has changed from a farming nation to a land of mills and factories second only to the United States.

2. There are several reasons for this change. First, the Soviet Union has a greater variety of mineral resources than any other nation in the world, including the United States. There are large deposits of coal, iron ore, copper, manganese, platinum, bauxite and other mineral ores. Second, there are many sources of power: coal, oil and peat—a soft, cheap, coal-like material dug near the surface of the ground. Water-power resources are being developed. In the Soviet are four of the five largest hydroelectric plants (producing electricity by the power of falling water) in the world, and more projects are now being built. There is also uranium, from which atomic power is developed.

3. Third, the Soviet government owns most of the natural resources and factories in the nation. As a result, the use of these resources is planned by the government. Planners can decide how many houses, dams or factories are to be built. Wherever possible, factories and cities are located near the source of the raw materials. These areas are called "industrial regions." Factories are built and run by the government, and the Soviet leaders decide how and where the goods are to be sold.

4. As a result of this system, there is almost no unemployment in the Soviet Union. Everybody works for the government because all the property is owned by the government. All factory workers do not receive the same pay, but are paid according to their skills and the amount of work they do. It is often very difficult to leave a job without the permission of the government. There are labor unions, but they can-

A power station on the Dneiper River.

Ewing Galloway

Ewing Galloway

The Lenin Iron and Steel Works in the Ukraine.

A fully automated Moscow factory

Novosti Press Agency

*A fully automated Moscow factory
where roller bearings are made.*

not strike. The unions can only discuss working conditions with the Communist "boss." Each worker receives a pension when he retires. In addition to the regular working force, the Communists have often used forced or slave labor. These workers are people who have been arrested by the secret police and are kept in lonely camps. Slave labor has been a large part of the working force used in building roads and

A lathe operator in a Russian factory.

UNATIONS

railroads in distant and rugged parts of the country.

5. There are four important industrial regions in the Soviet Union: the Donets Basin in southeast Ukraine; the Kuznetsk Basin in south-central Siberia; the Ural region just east of the Ural Mountains and the Moscow-Leningrad region in Soviet Europe. The development of these regions has been greatly encouraged by Soviet planners.

6. The most important industrial region in the Soviet is the Donets Basin or Donbas, located in the Ukraine. This basin is one of the richest parts of the Soviet Union. Coal, iron ore and manganese are found here. The Donets coal field supplies fuel for the steel mills. Dams on the Dnieper River provide electric power. All these things together make this region very much like the Vital Triangle in Western Europe and our U.S. steel centers in the Northeast. Kiev is the capital and chief city of the Ukraine.

7. The Soviets began to develop the Urals as an industrial region before World War II, partly for military reasons. This was a blessing for the Soviets. When the German armies overran the Ukraine, they hardly touched the iron and steel

295

production of the Urals. The mountains are rich in iron, copper, manganese, bauxite and platinum. Oil and natural gas are found on the western side of the mountains. (Oil fields are also located near the Caspian Sea. Pipelines carry the oil directly to ports on the Black Sea.) Coal is brought by rail from newly found deposits in Karaganda, about six hundred miles to the east. Magnitogorsk is the leading iron and steel city in this region.

8. The Kuznetsk Basin or Kuzbas is about 1200 miles east of the Ural Mountains. It is also very rich in coal. At first Kuzbas coal was taken by rail to the Urals and iron ore was brought from the Urals. This two-way shipment of coal and iron between the two regions made both of them leading iron and steel centers. However, the steel was very expensive because of the long shipping distances involved. Luckily, iron ore has since been discovered near Kuzbas and coal discovered at Karaganda, a city much closer to the Urals. Novosibirsk is the great steel city of the Kuznetsk.

9. The Moscow-Leningrad area is one of the oldest industrial regions. It got its start because it had many people and was a transportation center. It is connected by railroad, river and canal to the needed sources of raw materials. The Black, Caspian and Baltic Seas all have water routes leading to the Moscow region. As a result, goods flow steadily in and out of the Moscow-Leningrad area. The region is known for both *heavy* (automobiles, machinery, etc.) and *light* (textiles, shoes, etc.) industries.

10. There have been handicaps in the development of Soviet industry also. In general, too much government planning and control has hurt the output of the factory as it has the farm. The manager of a factory often has little desire to try new methods. Lately, the Soviet government has been trying a new policy. It is giving the manager more freedom in deciding what goods to make and how to make them in order to bring about more profits for the factory. Second, the Soviet transportation system is weak. While the country has the second largest railroad system in the world, the nation is vast and many places are far from railroad lines. There are few highways and only a few trucks carrying goods over these highways. Many of the rivers and canals are frozen over much of the year. Finally, coal and iron deposits are not always found near each other. Transporting these heavy materials by rail is expensive. Because of the high cost of transportation the government would like to make each industrial region as self-supporting as possible. This means that each region is encouraged to produce as much of the things it needs as it can.

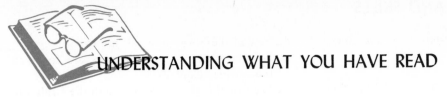

UNDERSTANDING WHAT YOU HAVE READ

1. **Which of the following questions are answered in this chapter?**
   a. Why are steel goods expensive?
   b. What are the Five-Year Plans?
   c. How rich is the Soviet Union in natural resources?

2. **The main idea of this chapter is to describe:**
   a. working conditions in the Soviet Union.
   b. how planning is used.
   c. the resources and industries of the Soviet Union.

3. **The chief source of power in the Soviet Union is:**
   a. coal.   b. water.   c. atomic energy.

4. **The Soviet Union is one of the leading producers of:**
   a. tin and rubber.
   b. manganese and platinum.
   c. nitrates.

5. **Many steel goods are expensive because:**
   a. high wages are paid to workers.
   b. there is a lack of machinery in the factories.
   c. iron ore and coal are often far from each other.

6. **The Soviet Union is a leading industrial nation because:**
   a. it has many useful resources.
   b. factories are owned by individuals who make a profit.
   c. there has been great use of water power in Soviet Asia.

7. **In an *industrial* region there are:**
   a. farms.   b. mines and factories.   c. fisheries.

8. **In paragraph 10, the term "self-supporting" means:**
   a. "increasing production."
   b. "not depending on others."
   c. "following the state plan."

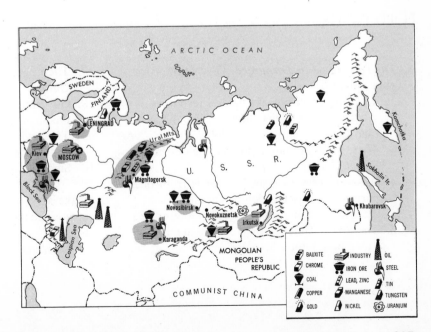

Map # 35—Industrial Resources of the Soviet Union

DEVELOPING IDEAS AND SKILLS

Map # 35—Industrial Resources of the Soviet Union

If the statement is correct, write *true*; if the statement is incorrect, write *false*; if no information is given in the map so you can decide whether the statement is correct or not, write *not given*.

1. The Ural Mountains have a large variety of important minerals.
2. Great oil fields are found near the Caspian Sea.
3. All the important iron and coal fields are located in the European part of the Soviet Union.
4. Few of the Soviet minerals are exported.
5. All the Soviet industrial centers are found in the warmer climates.
6. We would find steel mills in both the Urals and the region near Kiev.
7. In order to make steel, coal must be brought to the Karaganda district.
8. Railroad lines lead from Novosibirsk in all directions.
9. Minerals are found in the northern part of Siberia.
10. Uranium is mined west of the Ural Mountains.

SUMMING UP

The Soviet Union is almost like a pyramid. See if you can name the parts, using the headings below:

factory workers
farm workers
slave labor
Communist Party leaders
middle class

FOLLOW UP

A. *Do You Agree or Disagree?* Give reasons for your opinion.
   1. The Soviet Union lacks natural resources.
   2. Workers in the Soviet Union receive different salaries, depending on their jobs.
   3. There are four main industrial regions in the Soviet Union.
   4. It is very easy to transport goods from one part of the Soviet Union to another.
   5. The Soviet Union has large deposits of oil.
   6. The Soviet Union is making greater use of water power for electricity.
   7. There are no labor unions in the Soviet Union.
   8. Government planning is very important in the Soviet Union.
   9. The Soviet Union trades a great deal with the rest of the world.
   10. Siberia is a storehouse of mineral riches.

B. Make a list of the *advantages* and *disadvantages* of government planning. Then use this outline to write a brief statement about the importance of government planning in the Soviet Union.

CHAPTER 9

Nation in a Hurry

PROBLEM: How do the city people live?

READING FOR A PURPOSE:
1. What are Soviet homes like?
2. Where do people shop for their goods?
3. How are Soviet children educated?

1. The Soviet Union has shown its great power to the world in recent years. The nation has a standing army of two million men. It has exploded some of the most powerful bombs known to man. Its Sputnik, launched in 1957, was the first satellite to orbit the earth. It has also sent a rocket to the moon. It placed the first woman in space and sent three men around the earth together in the same space ship in 1964. Yet it has a standard of living lower than that of the United States, Canada and many countries of Western Europe. Its people have little freedom. Great deeds have been accomplished by the nation, but the ordinary people have received little benefit from them.

2. Since 1928, Communist leaders have been eager to prove to the world that communism can work. They have planned to produce much machinery and iron and steel goods. Collective farms were supposed to make Soviet farm production equal to that of any other nation. They announced their aim of matching the United States and passing us in many areas. But despite their great advances they have not done so. In the Soviet's effort to produce industrial and farm products, the Soviet people have been left behind. Few goods have been produced for them, and little attention has been paid to their wants.

3. For example, living in the growing cities is hard. Most apartments are crowded, for there is a housing shortage. If the worker lives in an old building he may have one room for himself and his family. He may have to share a kitchen or a bathroom with other families. Newer apartment buildings are going up at a great rate throughout the country. But they do not provide enough apartments for families' needs.

4. Most people in the Soviet have enough clothing to keep them warm and healthy. But the usual clothing is drab in color, poorly made and poorly fitted. The city dweller buys his food in government stores. These stores sell just about everything he needs, if he can afford to buy it. There are more goods available now than there were ten years ago. Still, a traveler

A counter in a Moscow department store.
Ewing Galloway

Shoppers in GUM, Moscow's largest department store.

A geography lesson in a Soviet school.

was told by many Soviet people what they wanted most that they didn't have: an automobile, a cottage in the country, a refrigerator and a television set.

5. Medical treatment for Soviet citizens is supplied by the government. There are many trained doctors. Doctors are even sent to the far regions of the Soviet Union. As a result of the efforts to improve medical service, the Soviet death rate is now below that of the United States. Health resorts are located near the Black Sea. A citizen may make use of these resorts at little or no cost.

An atomic reactor in Kiev.

6. All children are expected to go to school. Boys and girls at the age of seven years attend classes six hours a day, six days a week. The homework is heavy, for the government wants an educated population. Most children attend school for eight years. After that only qualified pupils continue their studies. Those who go on to college study for three more years; science and mathematics are the important subjects.

7. All schools are free for the students who qualify for them. Examinations are required before a student can enter college. Students who are members of working families or members of the Communist Party are most often picked first. The Soviet invites students from foreign countries, chiefly the new countries of Africa and Asia. The aim of the college is to graduate scientists and engineers—to help the Soviet Union become stronger.

8. The Soviet Union has also placed a great emphasis on making women equal with men in job opportunities. Women have the same chance for education as men and are admitted to any job on the same basis. It is not unusual to see women building roads, driving buses and trucks and working in factories.

9. Most forms of communication are considered by the Soviet government to be ways of "educating" the people. Plays in the theater, operas, dances and musical shows are controlled by the state. Teachers are trained by the Communist Party. Writers of popular books must be

careful that they do not offend the Communist leaders. The press is not free. Children are taught from their earliest years that communism is the best system of government. They are told that the people of the Soviet Union are the happiest people in the world—that they enjoy the greatest freedoms and have the most advanced scientists. They are always reminded of the contributions of the Communist Party to their well-being.

10. There is no doubt that the Soviet Union is making progress. The leaders have placed great importance on the education of the people. They want the best engineers and mechanics. Their achievements in exploring space continue to be outstanding. The standard of living of the people is rising slowly but steadily. It is hoped that some of these things will lead to better understanding between the people of our countries.

UNDERSTANDING WHAT YOU HAVE READ

1. **Which of the following questions are answered in this chapter?**

a. How are women treated in the Soviet Union?
b. How important is education to the Soviet government?
c. What is propaganda?

2. **The main idea of *paragraph 9* is to describe:**

a. Soviet control over means of communication.
b. the problems of writers in the Soviet Union.
c. Communist education.

3. **The Soviets were the first to:**

a. develop atomic energy.
b. start a system of free education for all.
c. send a satellite into space.

4. **Soviet citizens receive free:**

a. housing.   b. medical care.   c. clothing.

5. **As the Soviet Union planned for progress in industry:**

a. farm machinery was not produced.
b. there was little interest in space exploration.
c. comforts for the people were not thought to be important.

6. **In which way has the Soviet Union become a world leader?**

a. It has made many achievements in science.
b. The people have many freedoms.
c. Their houses are models for the rest of the world.

7. **In paragraph 8, the words "placed a great emphasis on" mean:**

a. "continued to."
b. "made progress."
c. "considered to be important."

8. **The title of the chapter, "Nation in a Hurry," refers to:**

a. the desire of the U.S.S.R. to equal the United States as soon as possible.
b. the need for free schools for all people.
c. equal rights for women.

DEVELOPING IDEAS AND SKILLS

Picture Symbols

These three pictures should help you to recall parts of the chapter you have read. Can you tell the main idea of each picture? In what paragraph did you find the answer for each?

SUMMING UP

Do You Agree or Disagree?   Give reasons for your opinions.

1. Most Soviet citizens own their own homes.
2. The Soviet citizen has free medical care.
3. Most Soviet people cannot read or write.
4. The aim of Soviet schools is to encourage loyalty to the Communist way of life.
5. Most forms of communication in the Soviet Union allow individual freedom.
6. So far, the Soviet Union is behind the rest of the world in achievements in science.
7. Some of the great Soviet achievements have been in space exploration.
8. Women are hired equally with men for most jobs.

FOLLOW UP

If you live in a large city you may be able to plan one of the following trips to get more information about Soviet life:

a. visit a movie theater showing a Soviet film;

b. visit the Soviet embassy;
c. visit an exhibition of Soviet art or culture;
d. visit a restaurant specializing in foods of the Soviet Union.

CHAPTER 10

The Growing Communist World

PROBLEM: How has communism spread throughout the world?

READING FOR A PURPOSE:
1. What is the Cold War?
2. What is NATO?
3. What is happening in Southeast Asia?

1. During World War II, the United States and the Soviet Union were allies. However, when the war ended, real peace did not result. As soon as the war was over, the nations of the West and the Soviet Union moved far apart. The Soviet Union had occupied many countries in Eastern Europe in the march toward the heart of Germany in 1945. After the war, the Soviet refused to give up control of the countries it had occupied—Poland, Hungary, Rumania, Bulgaria and Yugoslavia. These countries' farms and factories were turned over to the state. Those who fought the Communists

were killed or sent to labor camps. It was said that an "Iron Curtain" was being placed around Eastern Europe. This was the beginning of the "Cold War." Although there was a kind of peace, there was also a feeling that fighting could start again at any time.

2. The first efforts by the United States to stop the spread of communism came in 1947. The Soviet Union had made moves toward Greece and Turkey in an attempt to gain control of the valuable Dardanelles. President Truman said the United States would give aid to Turkey and Greece in order to stop the Communist threat in these countries. This policy became known as the Truman Doctrine. Later in the year, the United States loaned money to the nations of Europe to help them recover from the damages of World War II. This was called the Marshall Plan. The money was used to restore farm land and to rebuild railroads and factories in Europe. The Marshall Plan played a great part in keeping some of the nations of Europe from turning to communism to solve their problems.

3. Germany has been a "trouble spot" since 1945. After the war, Germany was divided into four parts called zones of occupation. The Soviets occupied eastern Germany; England, France and the United States placed troops in western Germany. Berlin, in the Soviet zone, was occupied by all four nations. In 1948, the three Western nations combined their zones of occupation into one. At once, the Soviet Union cut off shipments of supplies on all roads and railroads leading to the city of Berlin. They hoped this blockade would force the Allies to give up their occupation of the city. The Soviet Union did not want even part of a free city inside Communist territory.

4. Berlin lies about 100 miles inside the Soviet zone. More than three million people live there. They depend upon West Germany for the goods they need in order to live. They depend upon the Allies for their protection. With the blockade, the people of West Berlin found themselves without food, medicine and other necessary goods. The United States de-

303

cided to break the blockade. American planes began to bring supplies into Berlin. This "Berlin Airlift" was a success; the Soviet Union gave up the blockade after a year. However, in August, 1961, the Soviet built the Berlin Wall to stop East Germans from crossing to the West. Now the Communist section of Berlin is locked behind the Iron Curtain by a wall of concrete.

5. Early in 1948, the Communists overthrew the democratic government of Czechoslovakia. The Berlin Blockade and the spread of communism to Czechoslovakia aroused Western nations. Believing that Western Europe was in danger, twelve nations met in 1949 to sign a treaty. They formed the North Atlantic Treaty Organization or NATO. These nations agreed to help each other in case of attack. The members of NATO also set up an army to defend their countries. By 1955, there were fifteen nations in NATO.

6. In Asia there were also great changes after World War II. The British colony of India was divided into two self-governing countries, India and Pakistan. Great Britain also gave up its other colonies in Asia. The Communists gained control of China in 1949. Indonesia was formed into an independent state. The little country of Korea was occupied in the north by the Soviet Union and in the south by the United States. The people of South Korea then held elections and established their own government. In North Korea, the Soviets set up a Communist state.

7. In June, 1950, the North Koreans invaded South Korea. President Truman ordered American troops to fight. The United Nations sent other forces to help South Korea. The Soviet Union did not support the United Nations in stopping the invasion. When the United Nations army drove the North Koreans back almost to the border of Manchuria, the troops of Red China entered the battle. This "seesaw" war lasted three years. The end of the fighting did not bring victory for either side. Korea is still divided, but the action of the United States and other members of the United Nations saved the independence of South Korea.

8. French Indochina suffered too from the spread of communism. The Communists supported a revolt against French rule. The French then divided the country into three separate states—Cambodia, Laos and Vietnam—and gave the people more self-rule. But this did not end the fighting. Despite American aid, the French could not stop the northern part of Vietnam from becoming Communist. Vietnam was divided into two parts, North and South. The peace of the world has been seriously threatened by the war now being waged in Vietnam.

9. Because of the advance of communism in Asia, the United States has entered into many military agreements with countries in that region. A peace treaty was made with Japan in 1951. In 1952, the Senate of the United States approved treaties with the Philippines, Australia and New Zealand. In 1954, the United States

East German soldiers guard the Brandenburg Gate at the Berlin Wall, symbol of the Cold War.

Eastfoto

joined six other nations in the Southeast Asia Treaty Organization or SEATO. The purpose of this treaty was to help the nations of Southeast Asia resist communism.

10. Communism has spread all over the world in the years since World War II. The Cold War has spread from Europe and Asia to Africa and Latin America. In July, 1960, Belgium gave independence to its African colony, the Congo. Trouble developed in the new republic as soon as Belgium withdrew. The United States wanted to give help through the United Nations, but the Soviet Union would not agree.

11. In Latin America, the ruler of Cuba is Fidel Castro. He has been very friendly with the Soviet Union. The Soviet has supplied Cuba not only with food but also with arms. In 1962, it was reported that there were Soviet missile bases in Cuba. They remained there until President Kennedy demanded that the missiles be sent back to the Soviet Union. He set up a naval blockade around Cuba to see that this was done. In all, the struggle between the Communist world and the Free World has caused much

A collection of Soviet-made weapons captured in the fighting in South Vietnam.

trouble. The United States faces the problem now of meeting the Communist threat around the globe.

UNDERSTANDING WHAT YOU HAVE READ

1. Which of the following questions are answered in this chapter?
   a. What is the Marshall Plan?
   b. How did the Communists win control of China?
   c. Why were United States troops sent to Korea?

2. The main idea of this chapter is to describe:
   a. how Germany was divided after World War II.
   b. how the Korean War ended.
   c. the Cold War in Europe and Asia.

3. The main purpose of the Marshall Plan was to:
   a. sell our coal and steel at lower prices.
   b. help European countries after World War II.
   c. build air bases in Asia.

4. NATO was formed to:
   a. develop new weapons of war.
   b. unite North and South America against enemy attacks.
   c. unite Western nations against the spread of communism.

5. The Berlin Airlift was necessary because:
   a. tourists could not enter the city.
   b. Britain's railroads had been damaged.
   c. goods could not be brought into Berlin by land.

6. We are interested in Asian affairs because:
   a. we want to keep communism from spreading.

b. much of the continent is still unexplored.

c. large parts of our navy are stationed there.

7. "The navy moved to *blockade* the island." "Blockade" means:

a. "bombard."

b. "bring food."

c. "keep ships from going in and out."

8. The "Iron Curtain" separates:

a. European nations from Africa.

b. African nations from Asia.

c. Communist nations from the rest of the world.

9. A nation that is under the control of the Soviet Union is called:

a. a colony.   b. a satellite.   c. an ally.

DEVELOPING IDEAS AND SKILLS

Cartoon (See p. 303.)

Can you answer these questions?

1. What is happening in this cartoon?
2. What is the Cold War?
3. Can you suggest other incidents of the Cold

War not shown in the cartoon?

4. Why must we put an end to the Cold War?
5. What is a good title for this cartoon?

SUMMING UP

The World Since 1945 Below are three headings for an *outline*. Following them are some topics to be placed under these headings. In your notebook, write your outline using the headings and topics listed.

Headings:

A. Events in Europe

B. Events in Asia and Africa

C. Events in Latin America

Topics:

1. The Korean War
2. United States aid to Greece and Turkey
3. Congo independence
4. The Berlin Wall
5. Division of Vietnam
6. NATO
7. Soviet satellite nations
8. Freedom for India and Pakistan
9. The Marshall Plan
10. Soviet missiles in Cuba

FOLLOW UP

Tell whether these statements are true or false. The underlined words make the statements true or false. If a statement is false, what word or words would you place in it to make it true?

1. Cambodia, Laos and Vietnam were once colonies of Spain.
2. The dictator of Cuba is Marshal Tito.
3. NATO is a group of nations united to defend themselves against communism.
4. One of the important members of SEATO is the United States.
5. Two divided countries today are Germany and Korea.
6. The United States broke the Berlin Blockade by sending supplies into the city by train.
7. Japan is now the leading Communist nation of Asia.
8. Hungary is a satellite of the Soviet Union in Europe.
9. Berlin is located in the Soviet part of Germany.
10. At the present time, ten nations are members of NATO.

CHAPTER 11

Balance Sheet

PROBLEM: How strong is the Soviet Union?

READING FOR A PURPOSE:
1. What is the Iron Curtain?
2. What are some Soviet strengths?
3. What are some Soviet weaknesses?

1. It is not often easy to tell what is going on inside the Soviet Union. For many years the "Iron Curtain" of secrecy has made it hard for the world to know the truth about the Communist world. Much of the news the world receives is what the Soviet government wants the world to know. Unlike what happens in the free world, failures are seldom reported. Visitors to the Soviet generally see what the rulers want them to see. However, times are changing somewhat. More people are being encouraged to visit the Soviet Union and even to talk with the Soviet people.

2. As a result, we are better able to learn some facts about the Soviet Union than before. A summary of what we have learned about the U.S.S.R. will help us to get a better picture of this vast Communist country and its standing in the world:

a. The Soviet is the second leading industrial nation in the world. It has made a great effort to raise its production of iron and steel goods, oil, water power, machinery and machine tools—everything that makes a nation strong.

b. The Soviet Union has powerful armed forces. The army is large and well trained. Soviet jet planes are respected by military experts everywhere. The Soviet Union possesses the largest and most destructive types of bombs and has tested them so that the world would know this fact. Its missiles are also among the best.

c. To many of the new nations in Asia and Africa, the Soviet Union seems to be a success. The Communist government has changed it from a backward farming country to a highly industrialized nation in about thirty-five years. These new nations are chiefly farming nations. They would like to change their countries into nations of mills and factories as soon as possible. In some cases, the Soviet Union has offered to help them. Soviet help often means Soviet control.

d. The countries of Eastern Europe are under Communist control and supply raw materials to help the industries of the Soviet. Red China, in Asia, is also a Communist country. This nation of 700 million people may not agree with the Soviet Union on a number of policies, but it is under a Communist government. It remains to be seen whether the split between the two giant Communist nations will be healed.

3. There are weaknesses as well as strengths in the Soviet Union. Let us look at some of the problems that exist:

a. The cold climate and great amount of frozen and desert land mean that large areas of the Soviet Union have few people and are little used. The rivers flow into the frozen Arctic or into lakes that have no outlet. (Compare this with the great river system of the United

States and its mild climatic region.) The Soviet has the same problems with its cold climate as Brazil in South America has with its hot climate.

b. The trade of the Soviet Union is largely within its own borders or with its "satellite" nations. It does not wish to depend upon other nations for its needs. Trade builds friends. The Soviet Union may wish some day it had opened its borders to more trade with other nations.

c. The Soviet Union is ruled by a small group of men, the Communist Party. Their rule covers many areas that in our country are left to the individual—jobs, schooling, where to live. Freedom of religion, press and speech as we know it is not allowed in the Soviet Union. While most of the people in the country can read, they have not been able to read books and newspapers of their own choice. The people of the U.S.S.R. cannot learn the complete truth about people in other countries.

d. While the Soviet Union is making greater use of its resources, many of its people still live poorly compared with the farmers and factory workers in our own country. In the United States a worker can earn in a few days enough money to buy a suit of clothes, a shirt and a pair of shoes. In the Soviet Union a worker must labor about six times as long to buy the same amount of clothing. The Soviet people work chiefly to produce goods for the government. The worker has little reason to work hard and well. The Soviet citizen wants more goods for his own use, not for the state's.

e. The Soviet Union has been using much of its resources and the labor of its people in building up its armed forces. Keeping a large army and making war materials such as bombs, tanks, jets and missiles are expensive. As a result, the people do not have many of the comforts that we enjoy. They are beginning to resent this. They would like better clothing, better homes and more television sets, radios and cars.

f. The Soviet transportation system is weak. The waterways are often icebound. Although the Soviet Union has many railroad lines, most of the country—particularly Siberia—has poor railway transportation. Large sections are far from any railroads at all. There are not many highways in the Soviet Union, nor are there many cars or trucks to travel them. In most areas, limited air service is the only means of transportation to make up for the lack of railroads and highways.

g. The rise of Red China in Asia threatens the power of the Soviet Union in the Communist world. The rulers of China do not believe that communism and democracy can live together side by side. The Red Chinese exploded their first atomic bomb late in 1964. If Red China becomes another nuclear power, how will it affect the Soviet

Union? Some people feel that Red China will no longer follow the lead of the Soviet Union. Moreover, Red China is one of the most heavily populated countries in the world. Just across its northern borders lie the vast uncrowded lands of Siberia. The Red Chinese may desire a part of this land. There are signs of growing differences between Communist China and the Soviet Union.

4. The Soviet Union is one of the most interesting countries in the world. It occupies a vast space on the earth's surface and its people's ideas are very different from those of citizens of the United States. It has great strengths and great weaknesses. The control of this vast nation is in the hands of a few men. Do you re-

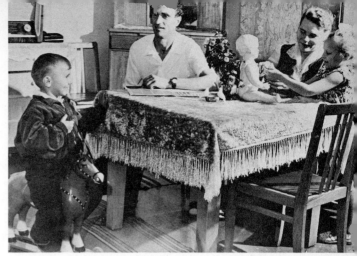

Ewing Galloway

A Soviet family at home.

member the questions that were asked in Chapter 1 of this unit? Now that you have studied the Soviet Union, see if you can provide some answers to these questions.

UNDERSTANDING WHAT YOU HAVE READ

1. **Which of the following questions are answered in this chapter?**
a. What does the Soviet Union import?
b. Why is the Soviet Union a strong nation?
c. Why do the Soviets help the new nations of Asia and Africa?

2. **The main idea of this chapter is to describe:**
a. the needs of the Soviet people.
b. relations between Red China and the Soviet Union.
c. some strengths and weaknesses of the Soviet Union.

3. **One of the chief weaknesses of the Soviet Union is lack of:**
a. good transportation.
b. armed forces.
c. natural resources.

4. **The largest Communist country in Asia is:**
a. Yugoslavia.   b. China.   c. Indonesia.

5. **Why are there differences between the Soviet Union and the Free World?**
a. The Soviets desire to introduce their form of government to other nations.
b. The Soviet Union does not have enough land.
c. The United States refuses to trade with the Soviet Union.

6. **Why do some people want to leave areas controlled by the Soviet Union?**
a. They lack work.
b. They have a desire for adventure.
c. They lack freedom.

7. **The best meaning for the term "nuclear power" in paragraph 3g is:**
a. "military force."
b. "nation able to build and use atomic bombs."
c. "source of electrical power."

8. **In paragraph 3a, "lakes that have no outlet" means that:**
a. boats are not able to travel on these lakes.
b. lakes are frozen for long periods of time.
c. lakes do not connect with larger bodies of water.

DEVELOPING IDEAS AND SKILLS

Cartoon (See p. 307.)

Tell whether these statements are true or false.
1. The Soviet Union has many political parties.
2. The Soviet Union is rich in natural resources.
3. The Soviet Union has no problems.
4. The people of the Soviet Union have a high standard of living.
5. From this cartoon it can be seen that the Soviet Union is a powerful nation.
6. A good title for this cartoon is "Strengths and Weaknesses of the Soviet Union."

SUMMING UP

Fact or Opinion Can you decide which are statements of fact and which are someone's opinion?
1. The Soviet Union must change its form of government.
2. The population of the Soviet Union is growing.
3. The Soviet Union should not be allowed to be a member of the United Nations.
4. New nations of Africa will follow the leadership of the Soviet Union.
5. The Ukraine is one of the rich farming regions of the world.
6. In order to keep peace in the world, the Soviet Union will have to stop building atomic weapons.
7. The Ural Mountains are a known storehouse of minerals.
8. The control of the government of the Soviet Union is in the hands of a few people.

FOLLOW UP

Complete this *outline* in your notebook. Use the headings shown at the right. From what you have read, place *three* statements under each of the headings.

The Soviet Union

STRENGTHS	WEAKNESSES
1.	1.
2.	2.
3.	3.

CHAPTER 12

Eastern Europe: The Satellite Nations

PROBLEM: Why does the Soviet Union keep control of the satellite countries?

READING FOR A PURPOSE:
1. Which are the satellite nations?
2. What is the topography of Eastern Europe?
3. What crops are grown in Eastern Europe?

1. Eastern Europe is the belt of land stretching from Poland southward to Czechoslovakia, Hungary, Rumania, Bulgaria, Yugoslavia and Albania. Except for Yugoslavia, these are all Soviet satellite states. After World War II, the U.S.S.R. gradually took over complete control of these countries. (It was also in control of Yugoslavia until 1948. In that year Marshal Tito, the Yugoslav leader, broke away from Soviet rule. Yugoslavia is still a Communist country today, but it is an independent one.) The combined area of these countries is smaller than that of our state of Alaska. Poland is the largest

country, about the size of our state of New Mexico.

2. Most of Eastern Europe is made up of hills, mountains and plains. The southern part of the region is hilly and mountainous. The most important plains are in northern and central Poland. They are a continuation of the Great European Plain. The second plains area is found in Hungary. This plain stretches into Czechoslovakia, Yugoslavia and Rumania. The greatest river of Eastern Europe is the Danube. It is the second longest river in Europe. It flows through Czechoslovakia, Hungary, Yugoslavia, Rumania and Bulgaria and is navigable for most of its length. The Danube is much used by the nearby peoples to carry their goods to market.

3. Most of Eastern Europe has a humid-continental climate, like that of our Northeast. Although the winters are cold, the summer growing season is long and warm. There is also plenty of rainfall for the crops. As a result, most people earn their living by farming or herding cattle, sheep and pigs. The main crops are grains such as wheat, rye, barley and oats. Potatoes and sugar beets are also grown. There are also mineral resources—oil (Rumania), iron ore (Czechoslovakia and Poland) and coal (Poland), for example.

4. There are approximately 120 million people living in this area. Most people speak a Slavic language. However, the people of Hungary speak Magyar, a language they learned from Mongolian invaders from Central Asia. The Rumanians speak a Latin language, while Albanians speak Albanian. The people of Poland, Hungary and Czechoslovakia are mainly Roman Catholic in religion. Bulgaria's people belong to the Greek Orthodox Church. Albania is largely Moslem. Many of the people cannot read or write, but this is changing rapidly.

5. Under the influence of the Soviet Union, the ways of living in Eastern Europe are changing. Except in Poland, collective farms have spread throughout the area. There has been a great drive to build industry in these nations. Many workers are leaving the farms to work in the new factories in the cities. It must be re-

Yugoslav women bringing goods to market. They are passing a power station.

membered that part of the farm produce is sent to the Soviet Union. Many of the raw materials also go to the Soviet Union to strengthen its war machine and industry.

6. Since World War II, Eastern European governments have been modeled after the government of the Soviet Union. The people had little experience in free government before this time, so it was easy for the Communists to establish their form of government. For a long time after, Soviet leaders took strong measures to keep control over these countries. Most signs of revolt were speedily crushed. In 1956, the people of Hungary started a revolt. This uprising was crushed by Soviet tanks and troops. In recent years, Albania, Poland and Rumania have shown a little independence of the Soviet Union. Nevertheless, millions of people in Eastern Europe are still ruled by governments not of their own choice.

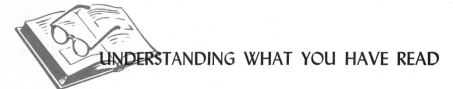

UNDERSTANDING WHAT YOU HAVE READ

1. Which of the following questions are answered in this chapter?
a. Why is the Danube River important to the people of Eastern Europe?
b. Why does the Soviet Union need Eastern Europe?
c. Which countries are landlocked?

2. The main idea of this chapter is to describe:
a. trade in Eastern Europe.
b. the lands and people of Eastern Europe.
c. how the satellite countries are ruled.

3. Which country is *not now* a satellite of the Soviet Union?
a. Czechoslovakia.   b. Bulgaria.   c. Yugoslavia.

4. Most of the people of Eastern Europe make a living through:
a. lumbering.
b. fishing.
c. farming and herding.

5. Why does the Soviet Union need Eastern Europe?
a. It is a source of food and raw materials.

b. The workers are highly skilled.

c. These nations are the chief source of oil for the Soviet Union.

6. Why is there unrest in Eastern Europe?

a. The people may want to be free from foreign control.

b. These nations are becoming poorer.

c. These countries are not members of the United Nations.

7. Most of Eastern Europe's trade is with:

a. European nations along the Mediterranean Sea.

b. nations of Western Europe.

c. the Soviet Union.

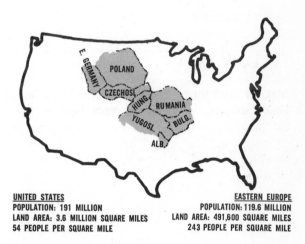

UNITED STATES	EASTERN EUROPE
POPULATION: 191 MILLION	POPULATION: 119.6 MILLION
LAND AREA: 3.6 MILLION SQUARE MILES	LAND AREA: 491,600 SQUARE MILES
54 PEOPLE PER SQUARE MILE	243 PEOPLE PER SQUARE MILE

Map # 36 a and b—Eastern Europe and the United States

DEVELOPING IDEAS AND SKILLS

Map # 36 a and b—Eastern Europe and the United States

Can you answer these questions?

1. How many countries do we include in Eastern Europe?

2. Which of these countries border the Soviet Union?

3. How many of these countries are landlocked, without outlets to the sea?

4. Locate the capital cities of each country. Which ones are sea or ocean ports?

5. Locate the Danube River. Through how many countries does it flow?

6. The Danube forms the boundary or part of the boundary between which countries?

7. In which direction does the Vistula River in Poland flow?

8. The United States is how many times as large as the entire region of Eastern Europe?

9. How does Eastern Europe compare with the United States in the density of population?

10. Which countries share outlets on the Black Sea with the Soviet Union?

SUMMING UP

Do You Agree or Disagree? Give the reasons for your answers.

1. The countries of Eastern Europe are largely farming countries.
2. The Danube River is an important "highway" of trade in Eastern Europe.
3. This region has few mineral resources that modern nations can use.
4. Most of the people of this region are followers of the Moslem religion.
5. The people of Eastern Europe speak a variety of languages.
6. The Eastern European farms and factories are established, in part, to serve the needs of the Soviet government.
7. These countries have more freedom than other countries under the control of the Soviet Union.
8. The people of Eastern Europe have had a long history of democratic government.
9. A visitor from Seattle, Washington, would find the climate of Eastern Europe much like that of his home city.
10. None of the satellite nations have made an effort to break away from Soviet control.

FOLLOW UP

Make a brief list of the ways in which the Soviet Union uses the people of Eastern Europe. Then use this list, or outline, to write a short summary of the relationship between the Soviet and Eastern Europe.

BOOKS FOR UNIT 5

Author	Title, Publisher	Description
1. Abramov, Fyodor	*One Day in the New Life,* Praeger	A clear picture of life on a collective farm.
2. Bartos-Höppner, B.	*The Cossacks,* Walck	A description of the war against the Tartars.
3. Braumann, Franz	*Gold in the Taiga,* Watts	The story of robbers in the dark pine forests of the taiga.
4. Baker, Nina Brown	*Lenin,* Vanguard	The story of the leader of the Russian Revolution of 1917.
5. ——	*Peter the Great,* Vanguard	The story of the czar who brought the ways of the West to Russia.
6. Caldwell, John	*Communism in Our World,* Day	The history of communism and its spread.
7. Footman, David	*The Russian Revolutions,* Putnam	The history of revolution in Russia from 1825 to the mid-1920's.
8. Roosevelt, Eleanor	*On My Own,* Harper and Row	An account of her travels in the Soviet Union including her own ideas of Soviet leaders.
9. Scherman, Katharine	*Catherine the Great,* Random House	The story of an empress who extended the power of Russia.
10. Vandivert, Rita	*Young Russia,* Dodd, Mead	A picture for American children of what it is like to grow up in Russia.
11. Westbrook, Robert	*Journey Behind the Iron Curtain,* Putnam	An American teen-ager describes his trip to the Soviet Union.

North Africa and

UNIT 6

the Middle East

CHAPTER I

The Crossroads of the World

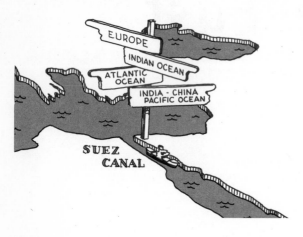

EUROPE
INDIAN OCEAN
ATLANTIC OCEAN
INDIA - CHINA PACIFIC OCEAN
SUEZ CANAL

PROBLEM: Why are the Middle East and North Africa important to us?

READING FOR A PURPOSE:
1. How are the lands of North Africa and the Middle East alike?
2. What is the main resource of this region?
3. What religions had their beginning in the Middle East?

1. Many books have been written and movies have been made about the Middle East and North Africa. These usually show the region to be a land of mystery, adventure and romance. The true picture is far different, however. In the lands of North Africa and the Middle East, water is in short supply. This is a region of great poverty, hunger and illiteracy. The incomes of most people here are among the lowest in the world.

2. The region known as North Africa and the Middle East begins on the west coast of northern Africa. It stretches across North Africa and southwestern Asia to the mountains of Central Asia. It may be divided into two parts, the "Middle East" and "North Africa." The Middle East includes the Asian countries as far north as Turkey (which is partly in Europe too), as far east as Iran and as far south as the Indian Ocean. It includes Egypt, which is located mostly in Africa. North Africa includes the countries west of Egypt—Libya, Tunisia, Algeria and Morocco.

3. These lands are studied as one region because they are alike in several ways. The climate of the region is generally hot and dry. In fact, much of the land is barren desert. Getting enough water just for everyday needs is a problem. Most of the people are poor farmers, town dwellers or nomads. Most of them speak the Arabic language and follow the Moslem religion.

4. The United States has a great interest in North Africa and the Middle East. First, the Middle East is rich in oil. Most of the oil is used by our friends in Europe for their homes and factories. We want to make sure that they will always be able to get this oil. American oil companies have long taken part in exploring and drilling for oil in the Middle East. We also want to make sure that we are able to use the oil of the Middle East.

5. Second, this region is sometimes called the "crossroads of the world." The countries of North Africa and many of those in the Middle East border the Mediterranean Sea. This is one of the busiest trading routes in the world. The Suez Canal is found here. It connects the Mediterranean Sea and the Red Sea. The Suez shortens the distance from Western Europe to India by almost 5,000 miles. More ships pass through this canal than any other canal in the world. The countries of Western Europe and the United States send their products to Asia and Africa through the Suez. In turn, oil, rubber, tin and other raw materials from far-off lands are shipped through the canal to our factories. The countries of the Middle East control the land and sea routes at the eastern end of the Mediterranean Sea. We want to make sure that they are always open to us and our friends.

6. Third, three of the world's great religions

The Suez Canal, one of the busiest waterways in the world.

—Judaism, Christianity and Islam—began in this part of the world. The religious beliefs and customs of millions of Americans began in this area on the eastern side of the Mediterranean Sea. Jesus, the founder of Christianity, lived, taught and died in the lands around Jerusalem. This area, now the states of Israel and Jordan, is thought of as the Holy Land by Christians, Jews and Moslems.

7. Fourth, the Soviet Union has always been interested in the Middle East. The countries of the Middle East lie south of the Soviet Union. It is no secret that the Soviet would like to be able to control the rich oil fields of the Middle East. The Soviet is interested, too, in reaching the busy trade routes of the Mediterranean Sea. But to get from the Black Sea to the Mediter-ranean Sea, Soviet ships must pass through the Dardanelles, the narrow straits controlled by Turkey. The United States is concerned about this Soviet threat to the Middle East.

8. Finally, the Jewish state of Israel stands in the middle of the Arab countries of this region. Israel was formed in 1948, largely through the help of the United Nations. Israel is a democracy in a region where most people have little voice in their governments. Since the little country was formed, Arab nations have wanted to get rid of Israel. A war was fought between them in 1948, and from time to time, border fights still break out between Israel and her Arab neighbors. The United States fears these outbreaks could lead to a larger war.

UNDERSTANDING WHAT YOU HAVE READ

1. **Which of the following questions are answered in this chapter?**
a. Why is this region important to the United States?
b. Why is the Suez Canal important?
c. Who owns the city of Jerusalem?

2. **The main idea of this chapter is to describe the:**
a. resources of the Middle East.
b. reasons why we should study this region.
c. importance of religion in the lives of the people.

3. **Most of the people in North Africa and the Middle East are:**
a. Christians.   b. Jews.   c. Moslems.

4. **The greatest need of people living in this region is:**
a. water.   b. wood.   c. a home.

5. A reason why North Africa and the Middle East are important to the United States is that:

a. their coal and iron are needed for our factories.

b. the United States has agreed to protect the Arab nations.

c. this region is the birthplace of three great religions.

6. The Suez Canal is an important waterway because it:

a. gives the Soviet Union an outlet to the Mediterranean Sea.

b. connects two great oceans.

c. carries a great amount of trade between Europe and the Far East.

7. The *Middle East* is a region in:

a. southwestern Asia.

b. central Africa.

c. northwestern Africa.

8. The *Dardanelles* is a narrow strait connecting the Mediterranean Sea and the:

a. Atlantic Ocean.   b. Red Sea.   c. Black Sea.

DEVELOPING IDEAS AND SKILLS

Map # 37—North Africa and the Middle East

Can you answer these questions?

1. Is the region north or south of the equator?
2. Is the region east or west of the Prime Meridian?
3. How far north and south does the region extend?
4. Does the region extend farther from east to west or from north to south?
5. What region or regions are near it?
6. What is the largest country? The smallest?
7. What are the chief bodies of water that border the region?
8. Are there countries in it that have no outlets to the sea?
9. What are some of the important rivers in the region?
10. Are there large rivers that form the boundary lines between countries?

Map # 37—North Africa and the Middle East

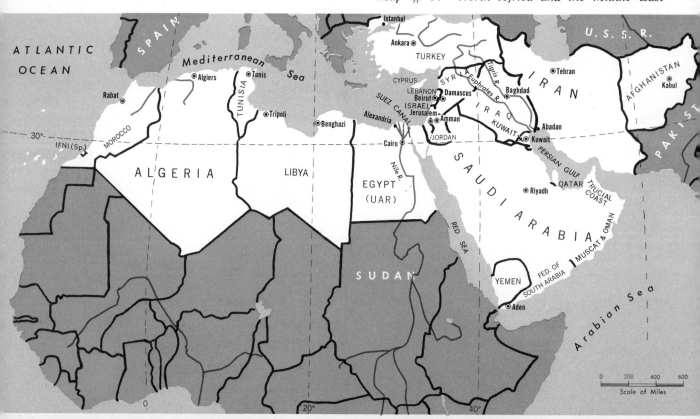

11. What are the capital cities of these countries? How do you know they are the capitals? How many are sea or river ports?
12. Are there any island nations?
13. Are there countries that are located on peninsulas?
14. Are there any lands that are colonies of other nations?

SUMMING UP

Comparing North Africa and the Middle East with Western Europe

In your notebook make the following chart. Check the column that shows the region to which each statement applies. Check both columns if the statement applies both to North Africa and the Middle East and to Western Europe.

	NORTH AFRICA AND MIDDLE EAST	WESTERN EUROPE
1. There are large deposits of oil.		
2. Factories are most important.		
3. There are rich stores of coal and iron.		
4. Great religions had their beginnings here.		
5. A large population is found in nearly the entire region.		
6. Important waterways provide trade.		
7. The Mediterranean Sea makes trade and travel easy.		
8. Most of the land has a mild, wet climate.		
9. A great desert covers most of the land.		
10. A high standard of living is found in nearly all countries.		

FOLLOW UP

The region of North Africa and the Middle East is in the newspapers and magazines daily. You should note news items that apply to this region and bring them with you to class. Start a bulletin-board display or scrapbook that shows the important events taking place in North Africa and the Middle East. You should find clippings that show *why we are interested in this region; areas where there is trouble; statements by our leaders concerning this region.*

321

CHAPTER 2

Warm, Dry Lands

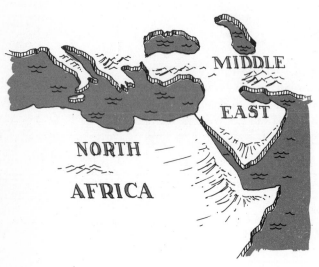

PROBLEM: How does the geography of the region affect the life of the people?

READING FOR A PURPOSE:
1. What is it like on the desert?
2. Why are the mountains important?
3. How does the Nile benefit Egypt?

1. North Africa and the Middle East are a region of desert. There are mountains and plateaus as well, but the desert most affects the life of the people. The largest desert area is the Sahara in North Africa. The Sahara is almost as large as the United States, without Alaska. It reaches from the Atlantic Ocean eastward to the Red Sea. Beyond the Red Sea there is desert again! The Arabian peninsula, large parts of Iran, Jordan and southern Israel are all desert. Thus, a dry region extends for 5,000 miles from the Atlantic to the Indian Ocean! Except for the coastal areas and the area around a few rivers, fertile land is scarce.

2. Some people have mistaken ideas about deserts. For example, some believe that the desert is all sand. This is not true. While there are large "hills" of sand (called sand dunes),

most of the desert is either bare rock or is covered with small pebbles and sandstones. Some also believe that the desert is flat. In some places the desert *is* a large, flat plain. However, in other areas there are mountains and high peaks. Some people believe that the desert is always hot. This is partly true. During the day, the sun bakes the sand and bare rock until they are very hot. At night, however, the earth cools quickly and may become very cold. Thus, temperatures may range from 100° or hotter during the day to 40° at night—a change of sixty degrees in a single day!

3. Life on the desert is very difficult. The hot sun bakes the earth and the winds blow continually. There is almost no rain. Except for small animals like lizards and snakes, there is very little life. There is not enough grass to support life, not even the herding of animals. Humans living on the desert move from one oasis to another. (An oasis is a fertile spot in the desert where water can be found. Some of the oases are quite large and support many crops.)

4. Parts of the Middle East and North Africa are hilly or mountainous. The highest mountains are found in northern Turkey and Iran. These are the Taurus, Elburz and Zagros Mountains. In northwestern Africa are the Atlas Mountains of Morocco and Algeria. They lie between the desert and the Mediterranean Sea.

5. The mountains are very important to the people of this region. What little rain there is falls in the mountains. Water trapped by the mountain peaks travels for hundreds of miles underground. In some places it comes to the top of the earth in springs. In others it is reached by digging wells at the base of the mountains.

6. Because of the water from the mountains, there are two great river systems: the Tigris and Euphrates Rivers in Iraq and the Nile River in Egypt. The Tigris and Euphrates Rivers rise in the northern mountains of Iraq. The Euphrates is west of the Tigris River. The two rivers flow almost parallel or next to each other as they wind through Iraq. They finally join together and empty into the Persian Gulf. Where the rivers almost meet on their flow

The Sahara Desert in Libya.

southward, the ancient city of Baghdad is located. For thousands of years the people living along these rivers have used the waters to irrigate their lands.

7. The Nile is the longest river in the world. It begins south of Egypt in the highlands of Central Africa. The Nile River is joined by other streams that rise in Ethiopia and East Africa. This giant river flows northward through Egypt until it reaches the Mediterranean Sea, over 4,000 miles from its source! The river brings both water and rich soils to the people of the Nile Valley. Without the Nile, few people could live in Egypt. Beyond the waters of the Nile there is desert. Thus you can see that Egypt is truly the "Gift of the Nile."

8. While most of the Middle East and North Africa is hot and dry, the lands along the Mediterranean Sea have a more pleasant climate. This is the Mediterranean climate that we found in California and southern Europe. The summers are long, hot and dry; the winters are mild and moist. Because there is more rainfall, more crops can be grown. Olives, fruits and grapes are grown on the hillsides of the coastal lands. This area has a mild climate because of the surrounding mountains, the warm Mediterranean waters and the hot winds from the desert.

UNDERSTANDING WHAT YOU HAVE READ

1. **Which of the following questions are answered in this chapter?**

a. Why are the rivers of this region important?

b. Why is this region largely a desert?

c. How do people live in the desert?

2. **A good title for *paragraph 2* would be:**

323

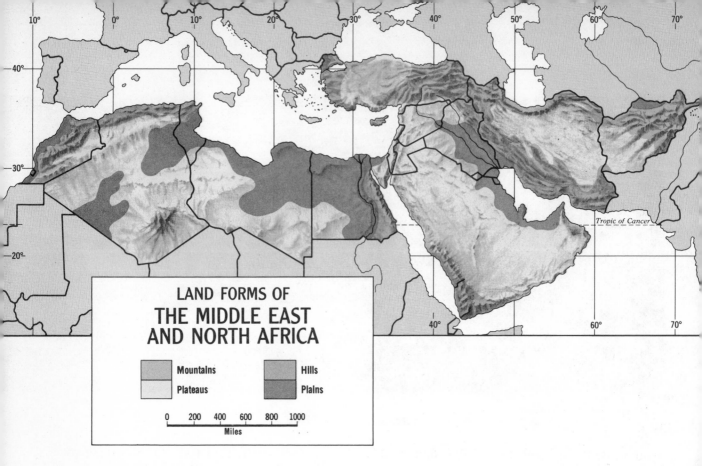

LAND FORMS OF THE MIDDLE EAST AND NORTH AFRICA

Mountains   Hills

Plateaus   Plains

0 200 400 600 800 1000
Miles

a. Hot and Cold Regions.
b. Clearing Up Some Ideas About Deserts.
c. Traveling in the Sand.

3. The largest desert in the world is the:
a. Atacama.   b. Gobi.   c. Sahara.

4. The Nile River flows in which direction?
a. South.   b. North.   c. East.

5. Mountains are important in the Middle East because they:
a. are the source of rivers.
b. are rich in minerals.
c. block the cold winds.

6. More crops can be grown along the coast of the Mediterranean Sea because:
a. there is greater rainfall.
b. the dry winds from the desert pick up moisture over the Mediterranean Sea.
c. some of the world's richest soils are found there.

7. An *oasis* is a:
a. mountain spot where water is collected.
b. place where rivers flow into the sea.
c. place in the desert where water can be found.

8. "Rivers *parallel* each other." This statement means that the rivers:
a. touch each other.
b. flow next to each other for a long distance.
c. rise in the same mountains.

DEVELOPING IDEAS AND SKILLS

Map # 38—Land Forms of the Middle East and North Africa

Tell whether these statements are *true* or *false*. Be able to explain your answers.

1. Most of the desert of North Africa may be called plains.

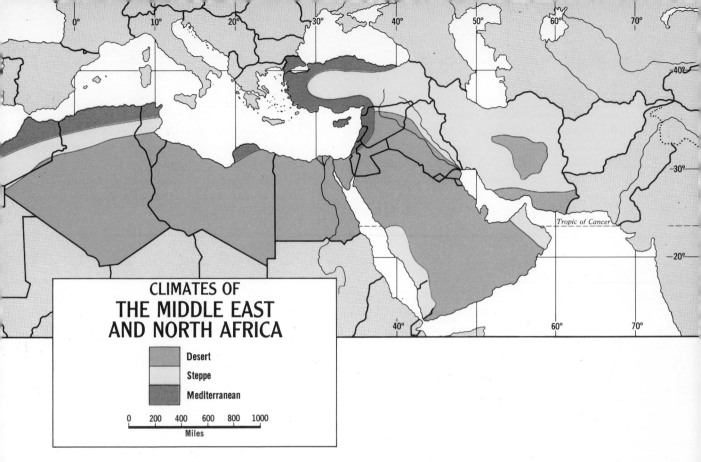

CLIMATES OF
THE MIDDLE EAST
AND NORTH AFRICA

Desert
Steppe
Mediterranean

0   200   400   600   800   1000
Miles

2. Nearly all the land around the Mediterranean Sea is a lowland plain.
3. Mountains guard the western end of the Mediterranean Sea.
4. The Red Sea lies in the middle of a low plateau.
5. Highland is found even in desert areas.
6. There is little lowland in the area known as the Middle East.

Map # 39—Climates of the Middle East and North Africa

Do You Agree or Disagree? Give reasons for your answers.

1. The small number of climatic regions here is caused partly by a very narrow range of latitude.
2. Only North Africa has a Mediterranean climate.
3. The desert is the largest climatic region in the Middle East and North Africa.
4. All three climatic regions are found in both the Middle East and North Africa.
5. All of the climates of the region are climates of the low latitudes.
6. No part of this region receives heavy rainfall.
7. If it were not for the Red Sea, the desert would continue unbroken from Africa to Asia.
8. The desert borders the Nile River only on the western side.

325

SUMMING UP

Tell whether these statements are true or false. The underlined words make the statements true or false. If a statement is false, what word or words would you place in it to make it true?

1. The Sahara is located in <u>northern</u> Africa.
2. The Tigris and Euphrates Rivers flow through <u>Iraq</u>.
3. <u>Potatoes</u> are a major crop near the Mediterranean Sea.
4. Egypt has fertile soil because of the <u>Nile River</u>.
5. There <u>are two</u> great river systems in this region.
6. On the desert, groups of people have gathered to live near the <u>tin mines</u>.
7. The Nile River flows into the <u>Persian Gulf</u>.
8. Some of the highest mountains in this region are found in <u>Egypt</u>.

FOLLOW UP

Making Inferences In our reading, many facts are given to us. From these facts we can draw conclusions. The following are some conclusions or inferences that you might make after reading Chapters 1 and 2. Tell whether these conclusions are correct or incorrect. Give reasons for your answers.

1. In the United States, farmers can grow many kinds of crops that the farmer of North Africa and the Middle East cannot grow.
2. Because water is so scarce, much of the available water will be used to supply power for factories.
3. The largest number of people live near rivers.
4. In order to develop its resources, this region will need the help of other countries.
5. European nations have little interest in the problems of the people of the Middle East.
6. Corn, potatoes and pineapples would be an important part of the diet of the people of this region.
7. Irrigation is necessary if the farmers of the Middle East are to grow enough food to supply the needs of the people.
8. Lumbering must be an important industry in North Africa.

CHAPTER 3

Where Civilization Began

PROBLEM: How has this region contributed to a changing world?

READING FOR A PURPOSE:
1. Where were the first civilizations in this region?
2. What have Egypt and Babylonia given to the world?
3. Who was Mohammed?

1. This is a region with a very long history. Many of the farm animals we now use—oxen, sheep, goats, pigs and dogs—were first tamed by the early hunters and farmers of the Middle East. They also tamed wild horses and camels and used these animals to cross the desert. They also knew where to find water in the desert and how to grow crops on the oases. Some of the crops that first came from this part of the world are rye, wheat, barley and beans. The region also gave us figs and dates.

2. Farmers settled early in the great river valleys of North Africa and the Middle East. They noticed that the rivers flooded the land every year at a certain time. They learned how to dam the water when it flooded and how to let it out when they needed it. They made up rules for the use of the water. Before long, they had the first government in which laws were being enforced. The first civilizations we know of began in the river valleys of the Nile and the Tigris and Euphrates.

3. Babylonia was one of the great civilizations along the Tigris-Euphrates valley. The people of Babylonia and Egypt learned to do many things. They learned how to grow crops and irrigate their farm lands. They lived in cities. Both had a form of picture writing. The Egyptians wrote on the treated leaves of the *papyrus* plant. (We get our word *paper* from *papyrus*.) The Egyptian writing was called *hieroglyphics*. The Babylonians used a chisel to "write" on clay tablets. The Egyptians built great tombs, burial places for their rulers. These were called *pyramids*. The Babylonians built great temples. The Egyptians used a calendar of 365 days. The people around the Tigris and Euphrates Rivers were the first to count in units of sixty. From them comes our method of counting sixty seconds in one minute and sixty minutes in one hour.

Gathering dates from a date palm.
Standard Oil Co. (N.J.)

A peasant farm in Egypt within sight of the pyramids.

4. The Jews also contributed to the civilizations of the Middle East. The Jewish people lived in Palestine, much of which is now called Israel. Their religion taught for the first time the belief in one God. This is called *monotheism*. The history of the Jewish people and their religious beliefs are written in the world's most famous book, the Bible.

5. The Middle East was ruled at different times by the Persians, the Greeks and the Romans. While the little land of Palestine was under Roman rule, a new religion, Christianity, began. Its founder, Jesus, lived and taught in this land. He also taught the belief in one God. He taught that men should love one another. His followers spread Christianity to all parts of the world.

6. About 570 years after Jesus, a man named Mohammed was born at Mecca in Arabia. As a young man, he was a trader or merchant. Later he came to believe that he was a prophet or messenger of God. He taught a new religion that he called Islam. Mohammed gradually *converted* the tribesmen of Arabia and united them. Inspired by their new faith, the Moslems (followers of Islam) began to spread eastward and westward, overrunning many lands.

7. Within 200 years, the Moslems controlled a vast area extending from Spain across North Africa to India. The Arab lands became centers of a great civilization. In time, most of the people of these lands became followers of Mohammed and used the language of the Arabs. Arab traders carried the goods and ideas of the Far East throughout their lands into Europe. They became the "middle men" between the civilization of the Far East and the civilization of Europe. Arabic words such as *soda, alcohol, coffee, algebra* and *magazine* became part of our language. Near the end of the 8th century, the Arab empire began to weaken. First it was conquered by the Turks (who later became Moslems). About 500 years later, Mongol tribes from Central Asia invaded Arab lands and destroyed their cities. By 1500, the people of Europe had found an all-water route to the riches of the Far East and could bypass the overland routes controlled by the Arabs. Therefore, the Arab traders were no longer so important as they once were.

8. Europe became very much interested in North Africa and the Middle East in the middle of the 19th century. In 1869, a French company built the Suez Canal, greatly shortening the distance between Europe and the Far East. The British soon gained control of the canal. Other European nations began to take parts of the empire that had conquered the Arabs. France took Algeria in 1830 and Tunis in 1881. Italy obtained Libya after a war with Turkey in 1912.

9. During World War I, the Arabs helped

Great Britain and the Allies. When the Allies won, the Arabs hoped that their lands would be made free. However, after the war the League of Nations was formed. The League gave some of the Arab lands to the Allies, who were to govern them until the Arabs were ready for self-government. These Arab territories were called *mandates*. Among the governing nations, France was given Syria and Lebanon. Great Britain became the protector of Iraq, Palestine and Jordan. Egypt did become free in 1923.

10. The fact that some of their lands were held by nations of Europe made the Arabs want their freedom even more. This dislike of foreign nations has carried over to the present day. It is true that France and Great Britain built dams and railroads, schools and hospitals in the lands they held. It is also true that they probably knew more about good government than the Arabs. But this did not stop the desire of Arab people to govern themselves. During World War II, Syria and Lebanon gained their independence. Since that war, independence has been granted to Jordan, Libya, Morocco, Tunisia, Algeria and Israel.

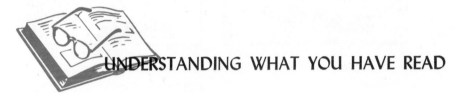

UNDERSTANDING WHAT YOU HAVE READ

1. Which of the following questions are answered in this chapter?
   a. How did Islam begin?
   b. How did world wars change this region?
   c. How was the Suez Canal built?

2. The main idea of this chapter is to describe:
   a. the results of World War I and World War II.
   b. the ways of life in ancient Egypt and Babylonia.
   c. the changing world of North Africa and the Middle East.

3. The Suez Canal was built by:
   a. a French company.
   b. the British government.
   c. the United States.

4. *Both* of the old civilizations along the Nile and Tigris-Euphrates Rivers had:
   a. a system of writing.
   b. the Christian religion.
   c. great trade with the countries of Western Europe.

5. The Arab civilizations have been important in world history because:
   a. they started the belief in one God.
   b. Arab traders brought goods and ideas from East to West.
   c. they first developed a system of reading and writing.

6. The contributions of the old civilizations of the Middle East include all of these EXCEPT the:
   a. use of gunpowder and printing thousands of years ago.
   b. beginning of cities and governments.
   c. discovery of methods to irrigate land.

7. A *monotheist* believes in:
   a. one God.   b. no gods.   c. many gods.

8. "Many Arabs were *converted* to Islam." The best meaning for *converted* is:
   a. "changed their beliefs."
   b. "opposed something new."
   c. "spoke roughly about."

9. The best meaning for *mandate* in paragraph 9 is:
   a. "order given by a ruler."
   b. "backward territory."
   c. "lands taken care of by other nations."

DEVELOPING IDEAS AND SKILLS

Picture Symbols

These pictures should help you to recall parts of the chapter you have read. Can you tell the main idea of each picture? In what paragraph did you find the answer for each?

SUMMING UP

In each group are three events in the history of the Middle East and North Africa. Arrange the events in each group *in the order in which they took place*.

1. Beginning of Judaism.
   Founding of Islam.
   Beginning of Christianity.
2. Building the Suez Canal.
   Freedom for Egypt.
   End of World War I.
3. Algeria wins freedom.
   End of World War II.
   Some Arab countries made mandates.
4. Mohammed born in Mecca.
   Arab trade with Europe important.
   Islam spread over parts of Africa and Asia.

FOLLOW UP

The history of North Africa and the Middle East is filled with so many interesting events and people that you will want to know more about it. Special reports may be made on many of the following:

1. How have ancient ruins given us a knowledge of life in: Egypt, Babylonia, Israel?
2. The contributions of these civilizations include great buildings and statues. Find out about the: pyramids, sphinx, Hanging Gardens of Babylon.
3. The building of the Suez Canal and the traffic through the canal make a great story. Find out what you can about this great waterway and report to the class.
4. The religious leaders of this region have been very important in its history. Report to the class on one of them. You will also be interested in such political leaders as: Lawrence of Arabia, David Ben-Gurion, Kemal Ataturk, Gamal Abdel Nasser.

CHAPTER 4

How the People Live

PROBLEM: Who are the people of the dry lands?

READING FOR A PURPOSE:
1. Where do most Arab people live?
2. How do people live in the cities?
3. Who are the nomads?

1. About 160 million people live in the Middle East and North Africa. Except for those in Israel and Lebanon, most are Moslems. However, they do not all speak the same language. In Arabia, Syria, Lebanon, Jordan, Iraq, parts of Egypt and most of North Africa the people speak Arabic. In Turkey and Iran, other languages are spoken. In parts of North Africa, there are people who have come from Europe. As a result, European languages and customs may be found in this area. (Remember, the nations of North Africa were once European colonies.)

2. The people are scattered unevenly throughout the Middle East and North Africa because of the lack of water. Where there is water, there are people. Many live along the shores of the great rivers, the Nile and the Tigris-Euphrates. (For example, nearly all of Egypt's 29 million people are crowded around the Nile River.) Others live near the borders of the seas or at the foot of mountains where there is more rainfall. The farmers in these mountain areas dig tunnels to catch the streams. These tunnels carry water into the desert. Along the tunnels are farm villages that depend on this method of getting water.

3. Finally, other farmers live near a well or spring that will give them the water they need for growing crops. Such a green place in the middle of the desert is called an oasis. In the oasis is a farm village. The fields are planted for grains. Date palms also grow. There is even grass for sheep and goats.

4. About seventy-five per cent of the people in the Middle East are peasants who till the soil. About twenty per cent are city dwellers, and the rest are nomads who wander about the desert. The farmer, the townsman and the nomad live very different lives. Few farmers own their own land. The landowner supplies them with water, farm tools and work animals. In return for his work on the land, the farmer keeps a small part of the crop. Many farmers are in poor health and cannot read or write.

5. The second largest group of people live in towns and cities. These cities are very different from the small villages of the farmer. Arab cities are a fascinating mixture of the old and the new. There are new buildings and "old quarters" with narrow streets and crowded, dingy houses. Automobiles and camels fill the streets. Modern Western dress is seen along with the long, flowing cotton robes that Middle Easterners have worn for years. There are modern schools and hospitals, but many of the women still wear veils to cover their faces. There are television antennas, radio stations and newspapers. Some of the largest and most important cities are: Cairo and Alexandria, Egypt; Tehran, Iran; Istanbul, Turkey; Tel Aviv and Haifa, Israel; Damascus, Syria and Baghdad, Iraq.

6. The towns and cities are the homes of fac-

A market place or bazaar in Morocco.

tory workers, government officials, doctors, merchants and craftsmen. The factory workers are often farmers who have moved to the cities in search of a better life. The craftsmen are the people with special skills who make all kinds of beautiful and useful things. They turn cotton into cloth, wool into rugs, skins into leather and silver into jewelry. Their articles are sold by merchants in the market place, called the *bazaar*. The bazaar is the meeting place where goods are sold or exchanged with the oasis farmer and other workers. It is also the place where ideas from the outside world reach the Moslem world.

New apartment buildings are everywhere in the modern Israeli city of Tel Aviv.

D. & M. Wilkes

A leather craftsman in Morocco.

7. Although many people think of Arabs only as nomads who live in the desert, they are the smallest group of people in the region. The nomad tribes are always traveling over deserts and dry grass lands in search of food for their sheep, goats and camels. They live in tents of tanned skins or cloth. They carry all their belongings with them. The camel is their chief means of transportation and provides many other things as well. Milk from goats, sheep and camels is the most important food of the nomads. They weave the hair of camels into robes and make their hides into sandals. The nomads exchange their wool and camel's hair for grain, rice, tea and other crops raised by the farmers.

UNDERSTANDING WHAT YOU HAVE READ

1. Which of the following questions are answered in this chapter?
a. How do the Arab people make a living?
b. How do the nomads use their animals?
c. Who are the rulers of the Arab countries?

2. A good title for *paragraphs 5 and 6* would be:
a. The Bazaar—Meeting Place of the World.
b. Booming Factories of the Middle East.
c. The Cities—Where the Old Meets the New.

3. Most of the people of this region are:
a. farmers.   b. city dwellers.   c. nomads.

4. The people get most of their water from:
a. rainfall.   b. the ocean.   c. springs and wells.

5. Some people have moved to the cities to:
a. learn about the modern world.

b. find work in factories and mills.
c. be near the oil fields.

6. Nomads are always moving because they are:
a. looking for minerals.
b. warlike people.
c. looking for water and pasture.

7. *Craftsmen* earn a living through:
a. making goods by hand.
b. working in the oil fields.
c. building irrigation ditches.

8. "The lady purchased some pots at the *bazaar*." A *bazaar* is a place where:
a. clothes are washed.
b. goods are bought and sold.
c. movies are shown.

DEVELOPING IDEAS AND SKILLS

Pictograph # 13—Population, Area and Standard of Living of the Middle East and North Africa

Can you answer these questions?
1. Is the standard of living of this region high or low compared with that of the United States? Is it a low-income or underdeveloped area?
2. Is the region as crowded as the United States?

3. Are the people of this region literate compared with the people of the United States?
4. How long may the average person in this region expect to live?
5. What facts tell you the standard of living of the people of the region?
6. How does this region compare with the United States in size?

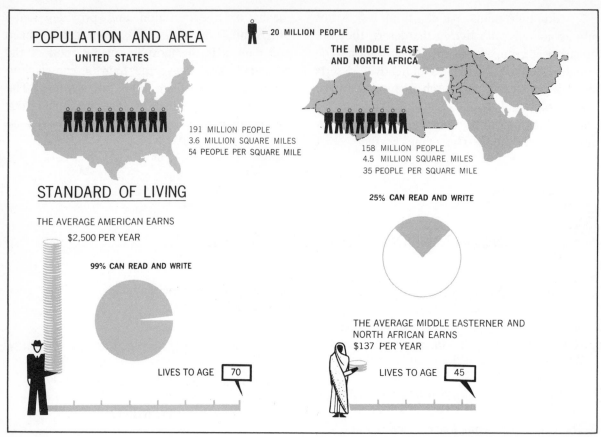

POPULATION AND AREA

UNITED STATES

= 20 MILLION PEOPLE

THE MIDDLE EAST AND NORTH AFRICA

191 MILLION PEOPLE
3.6 MILLION SQUARE MILES
54 PEOPLE PER SQUARE MILE

158 MILLION PEOPLE
4.5 MILLION SQUARE MILES
35 PEOPLE PER SQUARE MILE

STANDARD OF LIVING

THE AVERAGE AMERICAN EARNS $2,500 PER YEAR

99% CAN READ AND WRITE

25% CAN READ AND WRITE

LIVES TO AGE 70

THE AVERAGE MIDDLE EASTERNER AND NORTH AFRICAN EARNS $137 PER YEAR

LIVES TO AGE 45

Pictograph # 13—Population, Area and Standard of Living of the Middle East and North Africa

SUMMING UP

Complete this chart in your notebook. Place a check (✔) in the column to which each statement applies. (A statement may apply to more than one column.)

	FARMER	NOMAD	CITY DWELLER
1. His home is a tent.			
2. He lives in the oasis.			
3. He visits the bazaar.			
4. People are organized into tribes.			
5. Herding is his chief occupation.			
6. Land and water are his wealth.			
7. He has a better chance for schooling.			
8. He may trade, work for the government or weave beautiful rugs.			
9. He depends upon camels and horses for much of what he needs.			

	FARMER	NOMAD	CITY DWELLER
10. He may wear the Western style of dress.			
11. His chief work is raising crops.			
12. The greatest number cannot read or write.			
13. He is probably a Moslem.			
14. He may speak a European language.			

FOLLOW UP

In the following, place before each statement the word that makes the statement correct: *All, Most, Some, A Few.*

1. . . . people are farmers who live in small villages.
2. . . . nomads wander from place to place.
3. . . . people have a high standard of living.
4. . . . people are able to read and write.
5. . . . people speak the Arabic language.
6. . . . people live in cities.
7. . . . people of Egypt live near the Nile.
8. . . . farmers own their own land.
9. . . . people live where water can be found.
10. . . . people work in factories that make cotton goods.

CHAPTER 5

Islam — Religion of the People

PROBLEM: How does the Moslem religion unite the people of the Middle East?

READING FOR A PURPOSE:
1. How did Islam begin?
2. What are the chief duties of Moslems?
3. What is the Koran?

1. In the Middle East and North Africa, the Moslem religion is an important part of the life of the people. Except in Israel, Turkey and Lebanon, most people in this region are Moslems—followers of Mohammed—and speak Arabic. (It is a mistake to believe that all Arabs are Moslems. Lebanon is an Arab-speaking country, but half its people are Christians. In Turkey, the people do not speak Arabic, but most of them are Moslems.) Since the Moslem religion affects almost everything the people do, we should know something about it.

2. The Moslem religion was founded by Mohammed early in the 7th century. Mohammed lived in Mecca, Arabia, a city that is holy for Moslems all over the world. Mohammed called his religion Islam. Islam means "surrender to the will of God." Those who follow Mohammed's religion are called Moslems, or "surrendered ones." It is not correct to call them Mohammedans, for Mohammed did not put himself before his people as God. He said that he was a prophet or messenger from God.

3. Mohammed taught that there was only one God. He called that God "Allah." There could be no images or idols of Allah. Mohammed set up some rules that all Moslems had to follow, and that they still follow today. First, all Moslems believe in one God, Allah. Second, each Moslem must pray five times a day. (When Moslems pray, they turn toward Mecca, the holy city.) Third, Moslems are expected to fast (go without food) from sunrise to sunset during the holy month of Ramadan. Fourth, they are required to give help to the needy and poor of the community.

4. Finally, each member of the Moslem faith must make a trip to the sacred mosque, or

A mosque or Moslem house of worship in Damascus, Syria.

UNITED NATIONS

336

temple of worship, at Mecca. This religious trip is called a pilgrimage. This pilgrimage should be made once during the life of each Moslem. Every year, thousands of Moslems from different parts of the world travel to Mecca to fulfill this duty.

5. After his death, Mohammed's followers put his words and beliefs into a book called the Koran. This holy book is considered by Moslems to be the word of God. It is the book used by most Moslem children in learning to read.

6. Moslems believe that theirs is the only true religion. Each Moslem city has a mosque or temple of worship. Every morning the Moslem is awakened by a call to prayer from the mosque. Every Friday, the faithful Moslem goes to the mosque and listens to a reading from the Koran. There are no idols or images in the mosque, and no one may enter who is not a Moslem. The religious beliefs that Moslems

Arabian American Oil Company

Camels wait patiently while their Arab masters turn toward Mecca and pray.

share have brought them close together. These beliefs have been carried over into their day-to-day living and into their forms of government.

UNDERSTANDING WHAT YOU HAVE READ

1. **Which of the following questions are answered in this chapter?**
a. How does Islam differ from other religions?
b. What is a mosque?
c. What is the meaning of "Islam"?

2. **The main idea of this chapter is to describe the:**
a. Moslem religion.
b. duties of Moslems.
c. life of Mohammed.

3. **The holy city of the Moslems is:**
a. Rome. b. Jerusalem. c. Mecca.

4. **Mohammed lived in:**
a. Egypt. b. Arabia. c. Turkey.

5. **The Moslem religion is important in the Middle East because it:**
a. affects the actions of the people in all walks of life.
b. forces members to travel great distances.
c. is the religion of all Arabs.

6. **Islam, Judaism and Christianity are alike in that they:**
a. have many statues and holy pictures.
b. teach belief in one God.
c. require their members to make a pilgrimage to a holy city.

7. **"The people visited a *mosque* to pray." A *mosque* is like:**
a. a church. b. a school. c. an office.

8. **"The old man went on a *pilgrimage* to see the Holy Land." A *pilgrimage* is a trip taken for:**
a. health. b. study. c. religious reasons.

DEVELOPING IDEAS AND SKILLS

Picture Symbols

These pictures should help you to recall parts of the chapter you have read. Can you tell the main idea of each picture? In what paragraph did you find the answer for each?

SUMMING UP

Complete the following chart in your notebook.

	JUDAISM	ISLAM	CHRISTIANITY
1. Founder			
2. Holy Book			
3. Name of Place of Worship			
4. Idea of God			
5. Day of the Week for Special Worship			

CHAPTER 6

The Oasis Farmer

PROBLEM: How does the farmer use his land to meet his needs?

READING FOR A PURPOSE:
1. What is life like on a Middle Eastern farm?
2. How do the members of the family help?
3. What are the products of the farms?

1. Three out of four people in the Middle East and North Africa are small farmers. The farmers in this region are often called *fellahin,* an Arabic word that means "peasants." Most of the farmers live in villages. Where there is plenty of water (as in the Nile Valley), the villages are close together. Where there is little water, the villages are farther apart. Most villages are small—ten to fifty families. A large village may have electricity. The fields are outside the village.

2. The Middle Eastern peasant is a subsistence farmer. Everyone in the farm family works in the fields. The average farmer turns his soil with a wooden plow drawn by a buffalo or an ox. He harvests his crops with a hand sickle. He also threshes his grain by hand or uses his animals to trample it. His sons help him in the never-ending job of drawing water. Because of poor soil and simple tools, the farmer raises barely enough to feed his family.

3. The farmer and his family usually live in a two-room hut of dried mud. The house shelters not only his family but also his animals—water buffalo, goats or chickens. He owns little clothing and knows few comforts. Because wood is scarce, his house has it only in the door frames or windows, if at all. The house has little furniture. The family usually eat and sleep on mats and rugs on the floor.

4. The farm family eats little meat. Their chief foods are bread, goat's cheese, fruits and vegetables. The girls of the family help their mothers prepare the food. They milk the family goats and make the cheese. They grind the wheat or millet into flour for bread.

An Arabian boy using a bucket to get water for his father's fields.

Standard Oil Co. (N.J.)

Irrigated farms and fisheries in Israel's Jezreel Valley, once desert and swamp land.
The barren hills of Syria are in the background.

5. Most of the peasants are always in debt. Nearly all the land in an Arab village belongs to a rich landowner, who most likely lives in the city. The landowner also owns the water that the village uses. In return for the use of the land, water, seed and sometimes fertilizer, the village farmer must turn over most of his crops to the landlord. There have been promises of land reform in some countries, but changes are slow in coming. This problem of land ownership is one of the chief problems of this region.

6. The main crops of the Middle Eastern farmer are cereals such as wheat, barley and millet. Corn and rice are also grown. Rice must be grown on irrigated land, for there is not enough rain to produce it otherwise. The most important cash crop is cotton, which is raised in the irrigated fields of the Nile Valley. The waters of the Nile River and the warm climate have made Egypt a leader in the growing of cotton.

7. Poverty causes many problems in the villages. There are not enough teachers and schools in the thousands of scattered villages. As a result, only a few boys and girls learn to read and write. While the cities might have good drinking water, only a few villages can afford pure water. The few sources of water are used by the women of the village not only for cooking and drinking, but for bathing their children and washing their clothes as well. Also, the farmers throw their garbage into the irrigation ditches. As a result, many villagers suffer from diseases of many kinds.

8. Farming in Israel is different, however. Most of the Jewish families have come from Europe and America and know how to use modern machines and good farming methods. As in the rest of the Middle East, many Israeli farmers live in villages. But the land is not owned by wealthy landowners; it is owned by the people in the villages. These people work together and share in the goods and services of the community. This community is called a *kibbutz* or cooperative farm.

UNDERSTANDING WHAT YOU HAVE READ

1. **Which of the following questions are answered in this chapter?**
   a. Why is the Arab farmer poor?
   b. Why is fertilizer important?
   c. Why are Arab families often sick?

2. **The main idea of this chapter is to describe:**
   a. the simple tools of the village farms.
   b. land ownership in the Middle East.
   c. the life of the village farmer.

3. **Most of the farmers in North Africa and the Middle East:**
   a. own their own farms.
   b. rent their farms.
   c. work on land belonging to the government.

4. **The chief crop of the small farm is:**
   a. wheat.   b. corn.   c. rice.

5. **Cotton is grown in the Nile River Valley because:**
   a. the climate of Egypt is different from the rest of the Middle East.
   b. a warm climate and irrigated land are best for growing cotton.
   c. farmers in Egypt are richer than farmers in the rest of the region.

6. **Farmers are poor in the Arab world for all of these reasons EXCEPT:**
   a. farm lands are too small to use much machinery.
   b. there is little demand for fine cotton.
   c. few farmers own their own land.

7. **On a *kibbutz*, people make a living by:**
   a. farming together.
   b. drilling for oil.
   c. mining.

8. **When a farmer *threshes* his grain, as described in paragraph 2, he:**
   a. removes the weeds.
   b. gathers it into a shed.
   c. separates the grain from the straw.

DEVELOPING IDEAS AND SKILLS

Photograph Study
This photograph should help you to recall parts of the chapter you have just read. Can you tell the main idea of the photograph? Where in the chapter is it described?

SUMMING UP

Complete the following chart in your notebook.

	AMERICAN CORN-BELT FARMER	MIDDLE EAST FARMER
1. Who owns the farm land?		
2. What kinds of tools are used?		
3. What are the chief crops?		
4. What does the farmer do with the crops he grows?		
5. What animals are on the farm?		
6. What is the size of the farm?		
7. What is the climate of this farm region?		
8. What comforts does the farm family have?		

FOLLOW UP

Do You Agree or Disagree? Give the reasons for your opinions.

1. Farmers of Morocco face the same problems as farmers in Arabia.
2. A television set would often be found in a farm home in Algeria.
3. Wheat can be grown only in a region of heavy rainfall or where irrigation is used.
4. Millet is a cereal that can grow in a dry climate.
5. Few people in North Africa and the Middle East would find work in lumber mills.
6. A farmer in a kibbutz would have little use for a tractor.
7. A large number of Arab farmers grow a cash crop.
8. The best chance for a boy or girl in the Middle East to get an education is to live in one of the large cities.
9. You would probably not want to drink the water in an Arab village.
10. Most countries of North Africa and the Middle East need land reform very badly.

CHAPTER 7

A Disappearing Traveler

PROBLEM: How does the nomad make use of his few resources?

READING FOR A PURPOSE:
1. How does the nomad make a living?
2. What are the different kinds of nomads?
3. Why are the nomads disappearing?

1. Beyond the village fields and the oasis farms of North Africa and the Middle East are the dry, lonely lands of the desert. The people who live in these desert lands are different from the farmers. They are the nomads, the wanderers. They live in tribes that roam over the dry lands in search of water and pasture for their herds of sheep, goats and camels. The nomads have learned how to use the scarce resources of the desert. They are expert at finding water. The nomad tribesmen make up about five per cent of the people of this region.

2. There are two kinds of nomadic tribes. The first group are those who live in and around the mountains. In the winter, they graze their herds in the valleys. In the summer, they move the herds into the mountains to find grass. The second group of nomads are those who live in the desert. They move every few days or weeks in search of grass and water. These desert nomads are called *Bedouins*. The Bedouin tribes often split into smaller groups because the pastures they find are too small to feed all their animals. When water is found, the group settles down to enjoy its new-found riches for a short time.

3. Because he is always on the move, the nomad has few goods besides his cooking pots, his loose, flowing clothes, his rugs and his blankets. He lives in a tent. He sleeps and eats on rugs. The men and boys of the family live in one half of the tent, and the women and girls in the other half. When the tribe is ready to move, the tents are folded up and packed on the camels along with the other belongings.

4. The animals—sheep, goats and camels—provide the nomad with all he needs. Goat's milk and cheese are his main foods. Like the farmer, he rarely eats meat. His blankets, his tent and most of his clothes are woven from the hair of goats or camels. Leather from the hides of the animals is used to make baskets and sandals. Whatever his animals do not supply,

A nomadic tribe of Iraq.

UNITED NATIONS

Standard Oil Co. (N.J.)

Bedouin tribesmen and their animals camp near a well in the desert.

the nomad buys when he reaches an oasis. He also may have horses, which are useful for faster travel. His wealth is judged by the number of camels and horses he owns.

5. During the hot summer months when his desert wells are dry, the Bedouin goes to an oasis. Here he exchanges his camels, wool and woven rugs for dates or flour raised by the farmer. He buys other goods that he needs—knives, tea, clothing, sugar and coffee.

6. In the past, the herders of the desert were the rulers of the Middle East. They crossed and recrossed borders as they pleased. They were able to conquer the oasis farmers because they could attack swiftly on their horses and camels. The farmers were forced to give their crops to the desert nomads. Today, only a few tribes remain on the desert. The others have settled down on oases or in the cities. Many of the tribal rulers (*sheiks*) are now large landowners.

UNDERSTANDING WHAT YOU HAVE READ

1. **Which of the following questions are answered in this chapter?**
a. Why does the nomad live in a tent?
b. Why is the camel important to the nomad?
c. Why is the nomad's way of life disappearing?

2. **The best title for *paragraph 6* would be:**
a. Herders of the Oases.
b. Dashing Horsemen of the Desert.
c. Border Leaders.

3. **Animals of the nomads are used for all of these purposes EXCEPT:**
a. meat.   b. milk.   c. hides.

4. **A rich Bedouin is one who owns:**
a. camels and horses.
b. oil fields.
c. water rights and land.

5. **"Bedouins wear loose, white clothing." This tells you that the Bedouins:**
a. dislike suits.
b. live where the temperature never changes.
c. have clothing that protects them from the sun and sand.

6. **Nomads go to the oases because:**
a. it is too hot in the desert at certain times.
b. they wish to trade with the farmers.
c. they want to buy land.

7. **A *herdsman* makes a living through:**
a. grazing animals.   b. farming.   c. fishing.

8. **A *sheik* is a:**
a. skilled weaver of rugs.
b. landowner of Israel.
c. leader of a desert tribe.

DEVELOPING IDEAS AND SKILLS

Photograph Study

This photograph should help you to recall parts of the chapter you have just read. Can you tell the main idea of the photograph? Where in the chapter is it described?

Standard Oil Co. (N.J.)

SUMMING UP

Complete the following chart in your notebook.

HOW DO NOMADS LIVE IN THE DESERT?	
1. Sources of Wealth	
2. Housing and Home Furnishings	
3. Clothing	
4. Diet	

FOLLOW UP

Reviewing Chapters 6 and 7   Which Does Not Belong?

Choose the item that does not belong with the others in each group.

1. *Crops grown on an oasis*—dates, olives, sugar cane.
2. *Animals of the nomad*—goats, horses, chickens.

3. *Farm tools*—sickle, thresher, wooden plow.
4. *Needs of the village*—rugs, furniture, drinking water.
5. *Occupations*—farming, herding, lumbering.
6. *Farming in Israel*—large landowners, cooperative farms, use of machines.
7. *Belongings of the nomad*—camels, land, skins.
8. *Education of boys and girls*—public schools, the Koran, teaching by parents.

CHAPTER 8

Oil Is King

PROBLEM: Why is oil so important in North Africa and the Middle East?

READING FOR A PURPOSE:
1. Where are the large oil fields located?
2. How is oil carried to the seaports?
3. Why are there few factories in this region?

1. At one time it was thought that the deserts of the Middle East were almost worthless. But with the discovery of oil under the desert sands, this region has become one of the most important in the world. In the Middle East are almost two-thirds of the world's entire oil reserves! Most of the oil comes from the countries around the Persian Gulf. Some oil is also found in Egypt, Israel, Turkey and in the Sahara region of Algeria and Libya. There are those who believe that the Sahara may hide one of the world's largest areas of oil.

2. Most of the oil fields in the Middle East are owned by oil companies from Europe or the United States. In return for working the oil fields, these companies share their profits with the governments of the Middle East. The governments of these Middle Eastern countries, then, control much of the world's supply of oil. Four countries—Saudi Arabia, Iran, Iraq and Kuwait—produce 95 per cent of the oil from the Middle East. Kuwait, on the Arabian peninsula, is no larger than the state of Connecticut. It has about the same population as Richmond, Virginia, or Des Moines, Iowa. Yet this tiny state has about one-sixth of all the oil reserves in the world!

3. Oil must be *refined* before it can be used. Seven hundred gallons of water are needed to refine one barrel of oil. Since water is lacking in the Middle East, little of the oil is refined there, or used there. The oil is carried by pipelines to seaports along the Mediterranean Sea and the Persian Gulf. Every few miles along the lines there are pumps to keep the oil moving to the sea. Ocean-going ships called tankers carry the oil from the Middle East to ports all over the world. Much of the oil goes to the na-

A worker at an oil refinery in Iraq.

UNITED NATIONS

A U.N.-sponsored school in Iraq.

UNITED NATIONS

tions of Western Europe and to the United States. It is used in many forms in homes, automobiles and factories.

4. Oil has brought about great changes in the Middle East. Oil profits have made some of the Middle Eastern rulers very rich. In some cases, the money has been used to build schools, hospitals and railroads and to increase the water supply. In other cases, the rulers have spent the money on themselves. The peasant who works his poor lands has gained little from the wealth brought by oil.

5. The oil companies have provided a large number of new jobs for the people of the Middle East. Men whose fathers were poor farmers or nomads now work in the oil fields. They live better lives. They have concrete houses instead of tents or mud huts. They make more money. Their children go to school and receive medical care. They can buy goods in supermarkets. There are electric power plants in the oil settlements. There are good roads across the desert. The ways of life in Europe and America have come with the oil companies and have changed the lives of many people in the region.

6. Except for oil, there are few mineral resources in this region. There is very little iron ore. Turkey alone has a useful supply of coal. Turkey also has some iron ore, copper and chromium. In the western part of North Africa there are rich deposits of phosphates, used in manufacturing fertilizer. Fuels and power resources are very small indeed. Because there are few trees, there is little wood.

7. There are some factories in North Africa and the Middle East. These make such items as clothing, flour and cement for new homes. Israel has a larger percentage of its people working in factories than any of the other nations. There are not enough factories in the rest of the region to meet the needs of the people. (Many of the goods of this region—leather products and rugs, for example—are made at home or in small shops. They are called *handicrafts.*) Most of these nations' leaders would like to have more factories. However, the change from workshops to factories will take place slowly for several reasons. First, the countries of North Africa and the Middle East lack coal and iron. Second, most of the people cannot read or write; they have not been trained to work with machines. Third, there is little money within the region to build factories and power plants. Fourth, the great numbers of people are too poor to buy manufactured goods. The products of the mines, mills and factories, however few, must be shipped to other parts of the world.

348

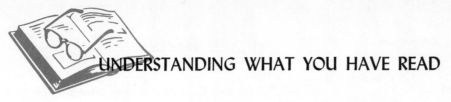

UNDERSTANDING WHAT YOU HAVE READ

1. Which of the following questions are answered in this chapter?
   a. Why is oil important in the Middle East?
   b. How are oil wells drilled?
   c. Why are there few factories in this region?

2. The main idea of *paragraphs 4 and 5* is to describe:
   a. the oil pipelines of North Africa and the Middle East.
   b. the little benefit that the common people have received from the riches in oil.
   c. how oil has changed ways of life in this region.

3. Most of the oil fields have been developed by:
   a. foreign companies.
   b. national governments.
   c. fellahin.

4. Factories have become important in which nation?

   a. Israel.   b. Libya.   c. Saudi Arabia.

5. This region has been slow to develop industries because:
   a. the oil fields keep so many people busy.
   b. there are few fuel and power resources.
   c. trading with other nations is more important.

6. Little oil is refined in the Middle East because:
   a. there are few electric plants.
   b. the leaders of the governments are against it.
   c. refining oil requires a large amount of water.

7. *Tankers* used to carry oil from the Middle East travel by:
   a. land.   b. air.   c. sea.

8. *Phosphates* may be described as:
   a. minerals used in refining oil.
   b. minerals from which hard steel is made.
   c. salts used in making fertilizer.

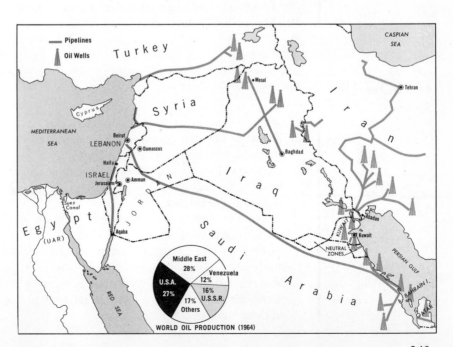

Map # 40—Oil Fields and Oil Pipelines

DEVELOPING IDEAS AND SKILLS

Map # 40—Oil Fields and Oil Pipelines
Tell if these statements are true or false.

1. The United States produces more oil than any other region in the world.
2. The Persian Gulf lies almost in the center of oil fields.
3. Most Middle Eastern oil is piped to the Red Sea for export.
4. Venezuela is one of the world leaders in oil production.
5. Among the other nations that produce oil, Egypt ranks high on the list.
6. Important pipelines run through Lebanon and Syria.
7. All Middle Eastern countries have rich oil reserves.
8. All pipelines leading from the Persian Gulf area connect on their way to seaports.
9. Almost no oil is produced by countries bordering the Mediterranean Sea.
10. Iran, Iraq and Saudi Arabia are three of the biggest producers of oil in the Middle East.

SUMMING UP

Tell whether the following items refer to the United States, the Middle East, or both regions. If an item refers to the United States only, use the letters US; if the item refers to the Middle East only, use the letters ME; if the item refers to both regions, use the letter B.

1. Large amounts of oil are used within the region.
2. Much oil is exported.
3. Much oil is produced.
4. There are many large oil-refining plants.
5. Great pipelines carry oil to ports.
6. Tankers are used in shipping oil.
7. Many engineers from foreign countries help in the oil fields.
8. There is a large supply of coal along with oil.
9. Profits from oil make government leaders rich.
10. Much water is used in refining oil.

FOLLOW UP

Choose one or more of the following activities.

1. Report to the class on this subject: "How Oil Is Changing the Lives of People in North Africa and the Middle East."
2. Prepare a classroom debate on one of these topics:
   RESOLVED: That unrest in the oil fields may cause difficulties in Western Europe and the United States.
   RESOLVED: That Arab nations have too few resources ever to become leading nations of the world.
   RESOLVED: That without foreign help, the Middle East would never produce much oil.
3. Many American families have gone to work in the oil fields of the Middle East. As a class project, write a letter or send a tape recording to a boy or girl in one of these families.

CHAPTER 9

Staying Alive

PROBLEM: How are the people of this region facing their problems?

READING FOR A PURPOSE:
1. Why are the village farmers poor?
2. How are some countries increasing their water supply?
3. Why is sickness common in this region?

1. Except for Israel, Turkey and Lebanon, the great majority of farmers in the Middle East are poor and are likely to remain that way. There are reasons why this is so. Egypt and Iran have made some attempts at land reform. But most farmers still do not own their own land. They must still give part of their crops to the large landowner for the use of his land and seed. Although the farmers work very hard, their crop yields are low. This is because the same crops are raised year after year. The soil wears out, since there is little money to buy fertilizer. Thus, the lack of land, small plots, poor soil and high rents keep most of the farmers in extreme poverty.

2. Besides these problems, the farmer of this region must always worry about his water supply. Important as oil is in the Middle East, water is still more important. Water is the most needed natural resource of the region. The future of the Middle East and North Africa depends upon the full use of its scarce water resources.

3. The Aswan Dam on Egypt's Nile River was an early effort to make use of water in a desert land. This dam "saves" or holds back a part of the Nile's yearly flood. The water is then used for irrigation. The first Aswan Dam was built in 1902. The government of Egypt is now building a higher dam at Aswan. This dam will hold back an even larger supply of water and will create new farm lands through irrigation. The water spilling over the huge dam will also provide electric power for areas that never had it before. Using a different method to solve its problems, Kuwait has one of the world's largest plants for removing salt from sea water and making it into fresh water. A little more than three gallons of salt water can be converted into a gallon of fresh water. The Kuwait plant produces millions of gallons of fresh water daily.

4. Israel would also like to increase its water supply. Most of southern Israel is a desert. The Jordan River forms part of the boundary between Israel and Jordan. Under the Jordan River Plan, the Israelis hope to build dams and canals that will bring more water to their desert region. They wish to share this development with the Arab country of Jordan, but so far Jordan has refused to join them, or to agree to Israel's going ahead alone. The Israeli government has taken control of all water resources within the country. As a result of careful planning of wells and pipelines and strict control of all water resources, only a small percentage of Israel's population does not have pure running water for at least part of each day.

5. Many of the people of North Africa and the Middle East are in poor health. Because the rivers and irrigation ditches are used for bathing and washing, pure drinking water is scarce. In the waters of irrigation canals are

An Iranian farmer using a wooden plow and donkeys to till his soil.

snails that carry tiny worms. These worms enter the skin of barefoot farmers and weaken their bodies. Such diseases as snail fever, trachoma, malaria, typhoid fever and hookworm are common in the farming villages. Most Arab countries are trying to solve this problem of poor health among their people. However, it is difficult to get the villagers to follow such simple health measures as wearing shoes, washing their hands before eating or boiling drinking water. Villagers feel that they have no money to buy shoes and that water is too scarce to be used only for washing.

6. Lack of money presents many problems for the Arab governments. Without money the nations of North Africa and the Middle East must depend upon foreign countries to develop their resources. (Foreign money has developed the oil fields. The Soviet Union is helping Egypt to build the great Aswan Dam.) Money is needed in order for the people to be able to buy the goods made in their factories. Money is needed to build power plants and more factories. The governments of Middle Eastern countries want foreign help, but they want this aid without losing the freedom to govern themselves.

7. Not only are so many of the people poor and hungry, but they also cannot choose their own leaders or make their own laws. Most of the countries in this region are ruled by kings or military men. Only in Turkey, Israel and Lebanon are elections held and people able to vote for their leaders. This is another reason why there is often unrest in the Middle East.

Women from a Moroccan village do their laundry.

UNDERSTANDING WHAT YOU HAVE READ

1. Which of the following questions are answered in this chapter?
a. Who are the rulers of the Middle Eastern countries?
b. Why are dams important in North Africa?
c. Why is there often unrest in the Middle East?

2. The main idea of this chapter is to describe:
a. the problems of people in North Africa and the Middle East.
b. the need for more electricity.
c. how land can be divided among the peasants.

3. Of these, the country with the highest standard of living is:
a. Israel.   b. Egypt.   c. Algeria.

4. The new Aswan Dam will bring water and power to the people of:

a. Saudi Arabia.   b. Lebanon.   c. Egypt.

5. A big problem in government in this region is that:
a. only men are allowed to vote.
b. few leaders are elected by the people.
c. Arab nations believe in communism.

6. Water is called the most important resource of this region because:
a. so much water is needed for refining oil.
b. it is needed merely to stay alive and in good health.
c. without water power, the people could not improve their standard of living.

7. In paragraph 1, "crop yields" means:
a. profit gained.
b. amount produced.
c. time saved.

DEVELOPING IDEAS AND SKILLS

Cartoon (*See p. 351.*)
Tell whether these statements are true or false.
1. The Middle East has few problems.
2. It is hard to make a living in the Middle East.
3. Many Middle Eastern peoples cannot read or write.

4. Better use must be made of the water resources of this region.
5. Much of the region is desert.
6. The people have a voice in making the rules of the government.

SUMMING UP

Do You Agree or Disagree?   Give reasons for your answers.
1. Fertilizer is widely used by North African farmers.
2. Farmers in some of the nations of North Africa and the Middle East now own their own land.
3. Although three religions began here, Christianity is the center of life for most people.
4. Arab countries of the Middle East are friendly with Israel.
5. There is little democracy in North Africa and the Middle East.

6. A lack of many natural resources helps to cause the poverty in this region.
7. Factory work has taken the place of farming as the chief occupation in some countries in the Middle East.
8. Many different ways of saving water are being tried in the countries of the Middle East and North Africa.

FOLLOW UP

Comparing   Many events and ideas of North Africa and the Middle East may remind you of something similar in another region you have studied. See if you can choose the correct answer from each of these, based upon what you have already studied in other regions.
1. The *problem of land ownership* in the Middle East and North Africa is much like the problem of the people of: a. Western Europe.   b. Latin America.   c. Anglo-America.
2. The *low income* of many people of North Africa and the Middle East is also a problem faced by a large number of people in: a. Western Europe.   b. Latin America.   c. Anglo-America.
3. *Dams* built for irrigation and electric power are found also in: a. the Netherlands.   b. the United States.   c. Argentina.
4. The Jordan-Israel border problem over the Jordan River is much like a problem solved by: a. the United States and Canada.   b. Norway and Sweden.   c. the Soviet Union and Red China.
5. Foreign businessmen investing money in Middle Eastern oil fields is like foreign businessmen investing in the: a. tin mines of Bolivia.   b. oil fields of the United States.   c. coal fields of Belgium.
6. Much of North Africa and the Middle East is wasteland, in the form of desert. This problem of wasteland is also faced by: a. France.   b. Great Britain.   c. Canada.

CHAPTER 10

The Restless Arab World

SINAI PENINSULA

PROBLEM: Why are the problems of North Africa and the Middle East so important to the peace of the world?

READING FOR A PURPOSE:
1. Who controls the Suez Canal today?
2. What is meant by "Arab nationalism"?
3. Why is the Soviet Union interested in the Middle East?

1. The presence of the Suez Canal alone would make the Middle East and North Africa one of the most important regions of the world. The canal is one of the busiest of all water routes. For years, Great Britain controlled the canal. In 1956, Egypt seized it. Now the Suez Canal brings money to Egypt. It also enables Egypt to control a great part of the world's shipping, for Egypt could refuse to allow ships to go through the canal. Most countries want to make sure that the canal is always open for their ships.

2. Nationalism—the pride that a person has in his country—is growing stronger within the Arab nations. For years, this region was under the control of foreign nations, chiefly Great Britain and France. Syria, Lebanon, Jordan and Libya have all become independent since the beginning of World War II. Morocco became free in 1956, Tunisia in 1957 and Algeria in 1962. Many of the people now feel that they can make a better life for themselves. But they are bitter about the years spent under foreign rule. Western nations are often blamed for all the troubles of the Arab people.

3. There has been a strong feeling among some Arab leaders that there should be a single Arab nation. The "Arab League" was formed in 1945 in order to bring the Arab states closer together. But the League has not grown into a single nation of Arab peoples. Leaders of the Arab nations are not eager to give up their newly won power to a larger central government. In 1958, President Nasser of Egypt led his nation into a union with Syria that was called the United Arab Republic. This union lasted only three years.

4. Probably no other single problem in North Africa and the Middle East causes as much

King Saud of Saudi Arabia and President Gamal Abdel Nasser of the United Arab Republic.
Wide World Photos

An Arab refugee camp operated by the U.N.

Wide World Photos

trouble as the dispute over the state of Israel. Israel was formed in 1948 as a homeland for the Jews. The Arab nations invaded Israel soon after but were thrown back. The two sides agreed to a truce—a stopping of the fighting. This truce was arranged by Ralph Bunche of the United Nations. However, the Arabs still say that they want to destroy the Jewish state, and there are outbreaks of fighting from time to time.

5. Another problem resulted from the Arab-Israel war. This is the problem of the refugees. During the fighting of 1948, thousands of Arabs fled or were forced to leave Israel. Today, more than one million of these people still live on the borders of Jordan and Egypt. They are called refugees. The Arab nations have refused to find homes and jobs for them within their borders. They say the refugees belong to Israel and should return to that country. Israel says these people cannot return because they are unfriendly. The United Nations has been supporting camps for them until the issue is decided.

6. The Soviet Union also has a deep interest in the Middle East. The history of Russia is filled with efforts made by that nation to extend its power toward the Persian Gulf and Mediterranean Sea. Soviet troops were in Iran during most of World War II. In 1946, the

U. N. had to step in before the Soviet would remove the troops. Egypt has received great help from the Soviet Union in building the second Aswan Dam. About one-half the aid that the Soviet has given to poorer countries has gone to this region, chiefly Egypt and Syria.

7. In order to prevent the Soviet Union from gaining control over the oil resources and trade routes of this region, the United States has taken action. In 1947, when the Soviet began to threaten the Dardanelles, President Truman announced that aid would be sent to Greece and Turkey to help them fight the spread of communism. In 1955, Iran, Iraq, Turkey and Pakistan joined with Great Britain in an alliance for their protection. The United States supported this organization, although we did not join it. (Iraq has since withdrawn.) The name of this group of nations is CENTO, or Central Treaty Organization.

8. In 1957, President Eisenhower said that the United States would send help to governments whose freedom was threatened by communism. In support of this, the United States sent marines to Lebanon in 1958 when that government asked for help. When the fears of the Lebanese government passed, the marines returned home.

9. It is hoped that cooperation between the United States and this poor and troubled region

will increase. The United States wants the Arab nations to know that we have no desire to control them as they have been controlled before. The North African and Middle Eastern nations need help in many ways. They are trying to find the respect among the nations of the world that they have not had for so long. They face great problems caused by the nature of their land and climate. People of the United States must know the deep problems of this region in order to help its people.

UNDERSTANDING WHAT YOU HAVE READ

1. **Which of the following questions are answered in this chapter?**
a. How is the Suez Canal operated?
b. Why have Arab nations worked together in world affairs?
c. Why is the United States interested in this part of the world?

2. **The main idea of this chapter is to describe:**
a. why the Suez Canal is important to the whole world.
b. the freedom of the Arab nations.
c. how affairs of the Middle East affect the rest of the world.

3. **In 1956, the Suez Canal was seized by:**
a. Egypt.   b. Great Britain.   c. Israel.

4. **The last country in this region to gain freedom was:**
a. Egypt.   b. Israel.   c. Algeria.

5. **Arabs left Israel in 1948 because:**
a. war broke out between Israel and the Arab states.
b. new farm land was opened near the Red Sea.
c. freedom came to the people of Arabia.

6. **The United States has sent troops to the Middle East to:**
a. collect money from oil companies.
b. keep Lebanon free from communism.
c. stop the Arab-Israeli War.

7. **When nations agree to help each other, they form:**
a. a government.
b. an alliance.
c. a political party.

8. **Persons who leave their homes to escape danger are called:**
a. pioneers.   b. traitors.   c. refugees.

DEVELOPING IDEAS AND SKILLS

Cartoon (*See p. 355.*)
Can you answer these questions?
1. What problem is raised by the people in the lower left corner?
2. What problem is raised by the people in the lower right corner?
3. Where are these problems taking place?
4. How do these problems affect us in the United States?
5. What is a good title for this cartoon?

SUMMING UP

Fact or Opinion

Which of these statements are fact and which are someone's opinion?

1. The Soviet Union has the same right as the United States to be interested in the Middle East.
2. The United States should not send arms either to Israel or to the Arab nations.
3. The Suez Canal is one of the most important waterways in the world.
4. Many Arab refugees live on the borders of Israel and Jordan.
5. The independence of the nations of North Africa and the Middle East will bring the needed improvements to the region.
6. The United States helped Greece and Turkey in 1947 because of the threat of the spread of communism.
7. Arab states wish to destroy the state of Israel.
8. A single Arab nation may solve most of the problems of the region.

FOLLOW UP

In the following, match the statements in Column B with the items in Column A.

COLUMN A	COLUMN B
1. Turkey	a. tiny, oil-rich country.
2. Kuwait	b. some minerals besides oil.
3. Islam	c. has great influence throughout the region.
4. Egypt	d. mountains of North Africa.
5. Aswan	e. important dam on the Nile River.
	f. ruled by President Nasser.

1. wheat	a. chief product of Iran.
2. cotton	b. valuable product of the Nile Valley.
3. dates	c. big import from Western Europe.
4. oil	d. found on the oases of the desert.
5. coal	e. very little supply in the Middle East.
	f. chief food of the small farmer.

CHAPTER 11

Egypt: Land of the Pharaohs

PROBLEM: Why is Egypt called the "Gift of the Nile"?

READING FOR A PURPOSE:
1. Why is the Nile River so important to the people of Egypt?
2. What is Egypt's chief crop?
3. Who is Gamal Nasser?

1. It has been said that Egypt is the Nile, and the Nile is Egypt. Without the Nile, this North African country would be a vast desert. Except for a few scattered nomads, nearly all of Egypt's 29 million people live and work in the Nile Valley. It has always been so in Egypt. The Nile has been the center of Egyptian life for thousands of years. One of the earliest civilizations in the history of the world grew up around this great river.

2. More than 5,000 years ago, the Egyptians had learned to irrigate the land in the Nile Valley and raise crops. They built large stone temples to their gods. The great pyramids, one of the wonders of the ancient world, were huge stone burial places for their rulers, the *pharaohs*. The pyramids have lasted to this day. In the 8th century, the Egyptians were conquered by the Arabs. They became Moslems then and were ruled by Moslem kings or sultans for more than a thousand years.

3. In 1869, the Suez Canal was built on Egyptian land. In time, Great Britain gained control of the canal. The government of Egypt grew weaker and in 1952 it was overthrown. A new government was formed by Gamal Nasser. When Great Britain withdrew her soldiers from guarding the canal in 1956, Nasser seized it. The armies of France, Britain and Israel attacked Egypt after this act. The United Nations forced these nations to remove their troops and Nasser kept control of the canal. As a result of this action regarding Suez, Egypt is still angry with the West.

4. Egyptians today, like Egyptians long ago, depend upon the Nile. It is the longest river in the world, flowing from central Africa through the Sudan and Egypt into the Mediterranean Sea. Each year there are heavy summer rains in the mountains to the south. As a result, the Nile floods its banks each fall, bringing rich soil to the lands near it.

5. The Egyptian farmers no longer depend upon the yearly flood alone to water their land. In 1902, the first Aswan Dam was built. This dam holds back the water of the Nile until it is needed. When the water is released, it is carried by a system of canals to the fields. In this way, water is available for irrigation throughout the year and can cover more distant farms. With enough water and a warm climate the Egyptian farmer can grow two or three crops a year. Egypt's chief crops are cotton and wheat. Growing two or three crops a year, however, "wears out" the soil. And the poor farmer has little money to buy fertilizer.

6. The Egyptian farmer or *fellah* lives in one of the many small villages that lie in the Nile Valley. If he is lucky, he owns his own farm. Otherwise he rents land from a large landowner

These ancient Egyptian temples must be moved to avoid being flooded by the waters of the new Aswan Dam.

or works for others. He uses simple tools and yet he produces a great deal on his small plot. Still, he does not make enough to feed his family. He earns about $100 a year from the sale of cotton or wheat. An Egyptian farmer's chief foods are corn and vegetables. His animals provide a little milk and cheese. He rarely eats meat. Because of the small amount of food and poor sanitary conditions, most farm families are often sick. Many of the farmers and their children cannot read or write.

7. Though Egypt is mainly a farming country, it has some large and well-known cities. Cairo, its capital, is the largest city in all of Africa! The city of Cairo marks the beginning of the delta of the Nile. Northwest of Cairo is Alexandria, second largest city in Africa. It is Egypt's chief seaport.

8. The cities of Egypt contain both the old and the new. There are new shops, offices and apartment buildings, large hotels and department stores. There are both factories and smaller workshops. There are schools and several universities. But the older sections have dark, narrow streets, dried brick houses and small shops. These sections are crowded with fellahin who can neither find jobs in the city

nor obtain land in the country.

9. Like other nations in North Africa and the Middle East, Egypt is a poor country. There is not enough fertile land for all its people. Secondly, many of the people suffer from sicknesses and have little education. However, this is changing. When the new dam at Aswan is finished, a larger amount of land will be irrigated than ever before. More electricity will be provided for the villages. Pure water will become available. Although there is a shortage of mineral resources, new industries are being started. More children are going to school than could in the past. Under the present government, the amount of land that a person may own is being limited so that more peasants can own land.

10. Egypt's chief imports are cloth, machinery and iron and steel goods. These must always be imported by a farming country without large industries. Egypt pays for the goods by the sale of cotton. As in Latin America, this dependence upon one export crop can cause trouble. A drop in the price of cotton throughout the world will seriously hurt the Egyptian farmer, and the income of the nation.

11. With all its problems, Egypt is still im-

portant in the world because it owns the Suez Canal. Unlike the Panama Canal, the Suez is a sea-level canal. It needs no locks. It is about 100 miles long and is wide enough for two ships side by side. A great part of the world's trade passes through the canal. Not only does Egypt get income from the canal, but it can also control ship traffic from Europe to the Far East. This is a very powerful position to be in.

12. There are no free elections in Egypt and little freedom of speech. The leader of the nation is President Gamal Nasser. He wants to see Egypt grow into a strong and powerful nation. He would like the entire Arab world to unite around his leadership. Israel is his main target. He would like to destroy that country. The future of Egypt, one of the world's poorest nations, may largely depend upon the ambitions of this man.

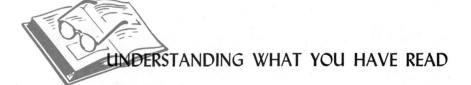

UNDERSTANDING WHAT YOU HAVE READ

1. **Which of the following questions are answered in this chapter?**
   a. How long is the Nile River?
   b. Where is the source of the Nile?
   c. Why does the Nile River flood?

2. **The main idea of *paragraphs 4 through 7* is to describe:**
   a. how the Suez Canal has changed the government of Egypt.
   b. improvements in irrigation along the Nile.
   c. how people live along the Nile.

3. **The Nile River begins in the:**
   a. Mediterranean Sea.
   b. highlands of east and central Africa.
   c. Sahara Desert.

4. **Most people of Egypt live:**
   a. along the route of the Suez Canal.
   b. in the valley of the Nile River.
   c. in the cool southern mountains.

5. **Dams are of great importance to the people of Egypt because:**
   a. electric power is provided in this way.
   b. farmers will be able to use the water in the fall.
   c. a larger amount of land can be used for grazing cattle.

6. **Egypt's income from selling goods is never certain because:**
   a. her machinery often breaks down.
   b. the Suez Canal can easily be closed to ships.
   c. she depends largely upon the sale of cotton.

7. **A *pharaoh* is the same as:**
   a. a king.   b. a soldier.   c. an engineer.

8. **A *fellah* is the same as a:**
   a. fisherman.   b. teacher.   c. peasant.

DEVELOPING IDEAS AND SKILLS

Map # 41 a and b—Egypt and the United States
Can you answer these questions?
   1. What is the distance from the Mediterranean Sea to the southern border of Egypt?
   2. What bodies of water are connected by the Suez Canal?
   3. What direction is *downstream* on the Nile River?
   4. To what continent is the Sinai Peninsula connected?
   5. What continent lies north of the Mediterranean Sea?

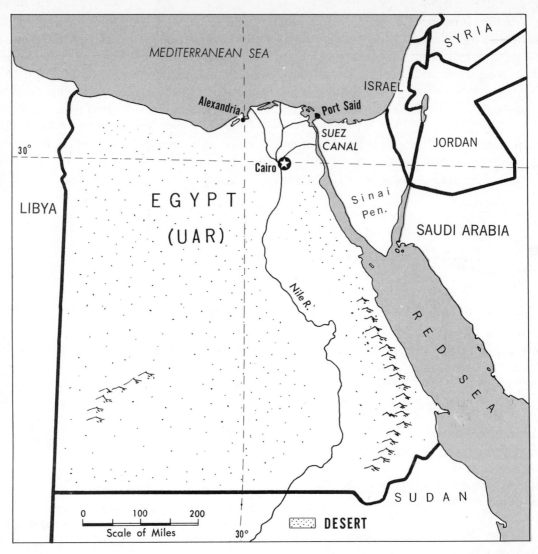

Map # 41 a and b—Egypt and the United States

6. How would you describe the topography of Egypt?
7. Where do you think most of Egypt's 29 million people live?
8. How would you compare Egypt with Texas in size and population?
9. What city is located at 31° N. Lat. and 30° E. Long.?
10. What countries border Egypt?

TEXAS	EGYPT
POPULATION: 9.6 MILLION	POPULATION: 29 MILLION
LAND AREA: 262,800 SQUARE MILES	LAND AREA: 386,100 SQUARE MILES
36 PEOPLE PER SQUARE MILE	75.1 PEOPLE PER SQUARE MILE

SUMMING UP

Tell whether these statements are true or false. The underlined words make the statements true or false. If a statement is false, what word or words would you place in it to make it true?

1. Egypt is located on the continent of <u>Africa</u>.
2. Until 1956, the Suez Canal had been controlled by <u>Great Britain</u>.
3. Egypt looks upon its neighbor <u>Libya</u> as an enemy to be destroyed.
4. The Nile River flows <u>north</u> through Egypt.
5. An Egyptian farmer and his family usually have a meal of <u>meat</u> and vegetables.
6. The largest city in Africa is <u>Alexandria</u>, the capital of Egypt.
7. Egypt's chief export crop is <u>wheat</u>.
8. Most of Egypt's land is <u>desert</u>.

FOLLOW UP

Which of these statements are fact and which are someone's opinion?

1. The new Aswan Dam will make Egypt one of the most powerful nations in the world.
2. Egypt's people are poor because there is not enough farm land to feed all the people.
3. Dams along the Nile will provide more water for irrigation.
4. Most of Egypt's land is too dry to grow crops.
5. It is said that Egypt will soon lead a union of Arab states.
6. The Nile River will always be important in the life of the people of Egypt.
7. President Nasser's leadership has made Egypt the leading state in the Middle East.
8. Great Britain waits for a chance to regain control of the Suez Canal.

CHAPTER 12

Israel: The Desert Reclaimed

PROBLEM: Can Israel continue to grow in the Arab world?

READING FOR A PURPOSE:
1. When was Israel formed?
2. Why is the Jordan River important?
3. Why is Israel important to the world?

1. Israel is a tiny land (about 8,000 square miles in area) at the eastern end of the Mediterranean Sea. Israel has the same desert climate as the other nations in the Middle East. Nevertheless, Israel is different from them in several ways. First, its people are Jews rather than Moslems. Second, most Israelis live in towns and cities rather than in farm villages. Many work in factories. Third, Israel has one of the few democratic governments in this region. Fourth, most of its people can read and write. It is a land of newspapers, books, schools and modern hospitals.

2. This tiny nation is bordered by four countries: Lebanon on the north, Syria on the north-east, Jordan on the east and Egypt on the south. To the west lies the Mediterranean Sea. At its southernmost end, Israel comes to a sharp point at the Red Sea. Despite its small size, this country is important to the United States. It lies close to the Suez Canal. An important pipeline runs through it. And it is a bridge for three continents, Europe, Asia and Africa.

3. Israel has a fertile plain along the Mediterranean Sea. East of the plain, the land rises and then drops sharply to the valley of the Jordan River. Much of this valley is below sea level. Part of the river valley lies outside Israel and belongs to Jordan. The Jordan River flows south and empties into the Dead Sea, the lowest spot on earth. The waters of the Dead Sea are very salty because they do not flow out of the sea. South of the sea is the Negev Desert. It is by far the largest part of Israel.

4. Along the coast, the climate is Mediterranean, very much like that of southern California. In the summer it is hot and dry; in the winter it is milder. The winter season is the season of rain. However, much of Israel is desert—the Jordan Valley and the Negev.

5. Israel was once called Palestine. It was

Israelis laying pipes to bring the waters of the River Yarkon to the dry Negev.

UNITED NATIONS

the home of the Jewish people for centuries until the Romans destroyed it in 70 A.D. Then most of the Jews left and were scattered throughout the world. As one nation or another conquered Palestine, the Jewish people became a people "without a country." In many countries they were forced to live apart in sections of cities called *ghettos*. They dreamed of returning to their homeland. In the 19th century, a Hungarian Jew named Theodor Herzl urged the Jews to return to Palestine. His followers were called Zionists.

6. Palestine became a mandate of Great Britain after World War I. With the permission of Britain's government, Jews began to settle in Palestine alongside the Arabs. (The Arabs also had been living there for many centuries with their own religion and customs.) The number of Jews in Palestine grew yearly. The largest number came from 1933 to 1945, when the Nazi government of Germany carried out Hitler's terrible program to destroy the Jewish people. During this time, more than six million Jews were killed by the Nazis in Europe. Many of those who escaped fled to Palestine. The Arab leaders wanted this movement of Jews to the Middle East to stop.

7. When Great Britain gave up its control of Palestine after World War II, the United Nations wanted to settle the problem growing in Palestine. It was suggested that Palestine be divided into two states, one Jewish and one Arab. In 1948, the nation of Israel was formed. This started a war. The Arab nations invaded Israel, but they were defeated by the small nation. In 1956, Israel, Britain and France invaded Egypt after Egypt seized the Suez Canal. However, they had to withdraw. There is still no real peace between the Arabs and the Jews.

8. The Israelis have set up a government like that of Great Britain. The lawmaking body is called the Knesset and is elected by the people. The Knesset chooses a president who has little power. The chief officers are the prime minister and the members of his cabinet. David Ben-Gurion, prime minister for many years, has been the most famous leader of Israel since

D. & M. Wilkes

This ship and others like it smuggled Jews into Palestine during Nazi persecutions in Europe.

1948. The new government has made great progress in building a modern nation in a short time.

9. The people of Israel have come from many different parts of the world—Europe, Asia, North Africa and even America. They speak different languages and have different customs. Some are highly skilled; others cannot even read or write. Some are from poorer lands; some come from rich, industrial nations. Some were farmers; others were factory workers. The only thing they have in common is that they are Jews. (But while Israel is a Jewish state, there are still 250,000 Moslems and some Christians living in the country.)

10. Like other places in the Middle East, Israel is short of water and fertile land. Despite these difficulties, more and more land is being reclaimed through irrigation. However, Israel cannot make greater use of the waters of the Jordan River because part of this important river is located in Jordan.

11. Most Israeli farms are found along the fertile coast and on the "reclaimed" land—land made useful again—of the desert. The chief crops are olives, grapes and citrus fruits (lemons and oranges). The farms do not produce enough food for all the people, however, so much must be imported. In the more distant parts of Israel, the people live in small villages

Haifa, a modern Israeli port city.

or *kibbutzim*. (In a kibbutz the land belongs to the people who live there. They not only farm, but they also have the job of patrolling the border between Israel and her hostile neighbors.)

12. There are many small factories in Israel, despite the fact that it lacks coal and iron. These factories depend upon the skills of the people, such as watchmaking, metal work or diamond cutting. By bringing water to the Negev, Israel is now able to mine there. Near the southern tip are the copper mines first worked by King Solomon more than 3,000 years ago. The Dead Sea is also rich in minerals used for fertilizer.

13. Israel's cities have grown in size with the increase in factories. The cities are different from the border settlements. The largest city, Tel Aviv, is only fifty years old, yet it has over 400,000 people. Northward along the Mediterranean Sea is Haifa, the main seaport. Haifa is at the western end of an oil pipeline. The capital of Israel is Jerusalem. This very old city contains the holy places of three religions—Juda-

ism, Christianity and Islam. It is also the home of the famous Hebrew University. The city of Jerusalem is divided between Israel and Jordan.

14. One of Israel's most serious problems is the hatred felt by its Arab neighbors. The Arab states feel that Israel belongs to them because they have lived there for so long a time. They refuse to trade with Israel. Egypt won't let Israel use the Suez Canal. The Arab leaders have said that they will destroy this new and tiny nation. As a result, Israel must keep a large army. This is a great expense for the small country.

15. The citizens of Israel are showing the world how people from many lands can live together. They are also proving that a skilled and hard-working people can develop even the poorest land. This has brought respect for Israel from other new nations in Asia and Africa. And in Israel there is a democratic way of life, unlike the other nations of North Africa and the Middle East.

UNDERSTANDING WHAT YOU HAVE READ

1. Which of the following questions are answered in this chapter?
a. Why is there trouble between the Arabs and the Jews?
b. What are Israel's problems?
c. How large is Israel?

2. The main idea of this chapter is to describe:
a. how Israel began.
b. Israel's growth.
c. Israel's farms.

3. The name of the lawmaking body of Israel is the:

a. Congress.   b. Knesset.   c. Parliament.

4. The founder of Zionism was:

a. Ben-Gurion.   b. Einstein.   c. Herzl.

5. Israel is important in this region because it:

a. has the highest standard of living in the region.
b. is located near the oil fields.
c. has the only river near the Mediterranean.

6. The Arab states of the Middle East dislike Israel because:

a. in Israel are the only iron and coal resources of the region.
b. Israel has a large and modern army.
c. they feel Israel is a state on land that belongs to the Arabs.

7. If a farmer *reclaims* a swamp, he has:

a. made it into useful land.
b. watered it.
c. sold it.

8. A section of a city in which people of a particular race or religion live apart from others is often called a:

a. ghetto.   b. slum.   c. province.

DEVELOPING IDEAS AND SKILLS

Map # 42a and b—Israel and the United States

Map # 42a and b—Israel and the United States
Can you answer these questions?
1. How long is Israel in a north-south direction?
2. What kind of land is found in the Negev?
3. What river is important to the people of Israel?
4. Is Israel in the high, middle or low latitudes?
5. How does Israel compare with the United States in density of population?
6. What countries border Israel?
7. Where are the large cities of Israel located? Why?

SUMMING UP

Do You Agree or Disagree? Give reasons for your answers.
1. People of many different religions are visitors to Jerusalem.
2. To support a growing population, Israel must irrigate more land.
3. Arab nations will cooperate with Israel to make use of the waters of the Jordan River.
4. The land along the Mediterannean coast provides much of Israel's food.
5. The people of Israel have little use for the Suez Canal.
6. Israel is a fairly new state in the Middle East.
7. The Dead Sea is a source of water for future irrigation.
8. The people of Israel have in common religion, customs and skills.

FOLLOW UP

Tell whether the following items refer to Israel, Egypt or to both countries. If the item applies to Israel only, write the letter I; if the item applies to Egypt only, write the letter E; if the item applies to both Israel and Egypt, write the letter B.

1. Oil pipelines.
2. Suez Canal.
3. Export of cotton.
4. Most people live in cities.
5. Coastline on the Mediterranean Sea.
6. Many skilled workers.
7. Much of the land is desert.
8. People have come from many countries.
9. Larger than the state of Texas.
10. Fertile river valley.
11. Most people of the Moslem religion.
12. Dependence on one export crop.

BOOKS FOR UNIT 6

Author	Title, Publisher	Description
1. Copeland, Frances	*The Land Between,* Abelard-Schuman	Ways of life and customs of four countries of the Middle East.
2. Cottrell, Leonard	*Land of the Pharaohs,* World	The story of early civilization in Egypt.
3. ——	*Land of the Two Rivers,* World	The story of early civilization in Mesopotamia.
4. Edelman, Lily	*Israel: New People in an Old Land,* Nelson	Ways of living in Israel.
5. Ekrem, Selma	*Turkey, Old and New,* Scribner	The story of a young woman who grows up in Turkey.
6. Ellis, Harry B.	*The Arabs,* World	Describes Arabian history and ways of living.
7. Gidal, S. and T.	*My Village in Israel,* Pantheon	Life in Israel today.
8. Kaufmann, Herbert	*Adventure in the Desert,* Obolensky	A story of danger in the Sahara.
9. Lengyel, Emil	*They Called Him Ataturk,* Day	The story of the man who founded modern Turkey.
10. Najafi, N., and Helen Hinckley	*Persia Is My Heart,* Harper	The home life of a Moslem girl.
11. Russcol, Margalit	*Achmed, Boy of the Negev,* Putnam	A young Bedouin faces the hardships of life on the desert.
12. Stinetorf, Louise	*The Shepherd of Abu Kush,* Day	A story that shows the differences between the Arabs and Jews in Israel.
13. Thomas, John	*The True Story of Lawrence of Arabia,* Children's Press	The story of the man who led Arabs against Turks in World War I.

UNIT 7

South of the Sahara

CHAPTER 1

The New Africa

PROBLEM: Why are we interested in Africa?

READING FOR A PURPOSE:
1. How does the Sahara divide Africa?
2. Why is Sub-Sahara Africa important to the world?
3. How can unrest in Africa affect the world?

1. Nigeria, Kenya, Ghana, Mali, Tanzania! A few years ago, these names were unknown to most Americans. Now they appear almost daily in our newspapers. These are only a few of the new nations in Africa. In our changing world, no other region is changing as much as Africa —the giant continent. Africa is over 11 million square miles in area, larger than either North or South America. It is more than three times the size of the United States!

2. Africa's geography really makes it two regions. In the north is the vast Sahara Desert. Stretching eastward from the Atlantic Ocean to the Red Sea, it divides Africa in two. North of the Sahara, the people have a way of life much the same as that of Middle Eastern peoples. South of the Sahara, the people are largely Negroes whose ways of living are different from their northern Arab neighbors. Africa, South of the Sahara—or Sub-Sahara Africa—is the region we are going to learn about now.

3. There are several reasons why the United States is interested in Africa, South of the Sahara. First, since World War II, many nations have won their freedom in this part of Africa. In some nations, the struggle for independence was as hard as was our fight for independence from Great Britain. These new nations want to take their place among the older nations of the world. They want to do in a few years many things that took us 200 years. They want to set up stable governments, develop their natural resources and give their people a better way of life. They want new roads, factories and schools. In these tasks, they need help. The United States gives much aid to the nations of Africa. Also, through such projects as the Peace Corps and "Operation Crossroads Africa," young Americans are going to Africa to help these new nations reach their goals.

4. Second, Africa, South of the Sahara is rich in mineral resources. No one knows just how great these resources are, for it has been difficult to explore and develop the region up to now. We do know that gold, diamonds, uranium, copper, bauxite and manganese can be found in this part of Africa. All of these minerals are important to the modern world. Many of them are part of our daily lives.

5. Third, U.S. businessmen have invested large amounts of money in the development of Africa's resources. Although we do not trade as much with this region as with some others, still our trade with the nations south of the Sahara amounts to more than one billion dollars a year! The Firestone Rubber Company owns millions of rubber trees in Liberia. Plans for aluminum plants in Ghana have been formed by several American companies. One of our large chemical firms has a plant in Nigeria. The United States Steel Corporation has invested

Railroad building in Gabon. Africans are trying to do the work of 200 years in only a few.

UNITED NATIONS

millions of dollars in producing manganese in Gabon.

6. Fourth, the forming of so many new nations in Sub-Sahara Africa has made that region important in the affairs of the world. The African nations now have the largest vote of any group in the United Nations General Assembly. This large vote is one reason why the United States and the Soviet Union want to hold their friendship.

7. Fifth, there is still unrest in the African world. A few nations, such as the Congo, have had trouble in setting up stable governments. In some cases, larger tribes have made war on smaller tribes. The world is worried that a small war in Sub-Sahara Africa could easily grow into a world war.

8. Finally, the rise of new independent nations in Africa is a source of pride and interest to Negro-Americans, who make up ten per cent of our population. What's more, the African Negro is interested in how Negroes in the United States are treated. We cannot talk equality to the peoples of Africa and practice inequality in the United States. In the age of the Cold War, it is important that the new African nations look upon our democracy as a real one.

UNDERSTANDING WHAT YOU HAVE READ

1. Which of the following questions are answered in this chapter?

a. How many people live in Africa, South of the Sahara?

b. What is the great change taking place in Africa?

c. Why should we know more about Africa?

2. The main idea of this chapter is to describe:

a. Africa's needs.

b. Africa's resources.

c. why Africa is important to us.

3. The continent of Africa is divided into two parts by the:

a. Sahara Desert.

b. Atlas Mountains.

c. Congo River.

4. Most of the people living in Sub-Sahara Africa are members of the:

a. white race.   b. Negro race.   c. yellow race.

5. Africa, South of the Sahara is important to us because:

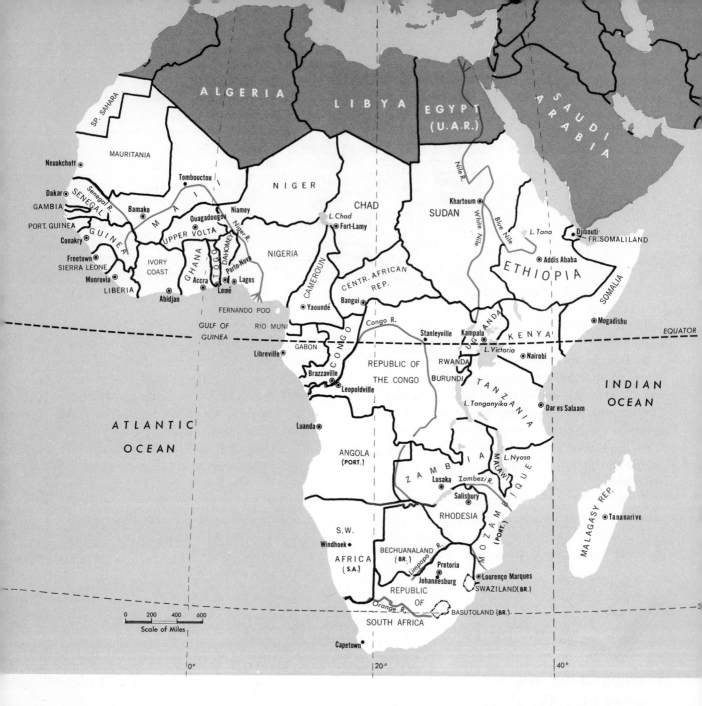

Map # 43—Africa, South of the Sahara

a. it is rich in mineral resources.

b. it is our biggest source of trade.

c. there are many highly skilled workers.

b. want to be admitted to the United Nations.

c. need help in developing their resources.

6. New nations of Africa need our help because they:

a. lack natural resources.

7. In *paragraph 7*, the term "stable government" means a government that is:

a. new.   b. lasting.   c. changing.

374

DEVELOPING IDEAS AND SKILLS

Map # 43—Africa, South of the Sahara

Can you answer these questions?
1. Is the region north or south of the equator?
2. Is the region east or west of the Prime Meridian?
3. How far north and south does the region extend?
4. Does the region extend farther from east to west or from north to south?
5. What region or regions are near it?
6. What is the largest country? The smallest?
7. What are the chief bodies of water that border the region?
8. Are there countries in it that have no outlets to the sea?
9. What are some of the important rivers in the region?
10. Are there large rivers that form boundary lines between countries?
11. What is the capital city of each country? How do you know they are the capitals? How many are sea or river ports?
12. Are there any island nations?
13. Are there countries that are located on peninsulas?
14. Are there any lands that are colonies of other nations?

SUMMING UP

Do You Agree or Disagree? Give reasons for your answers based on what you have read in Chapter 1.
1. In North Africa and Sub-Sahara Africa we find different ways of living.
2. Equal treatment for all people in our country is important to the people of Sub-Sahara Africa.
3. Africa has many mineral resources the United States can use.
4. African nations have a long history of governing themselves.
5. New African nations cannot become world leaders without the help and understanding of older nations in the world.
6. Many of Africa's resources could be more greatly developed.
7. The people of Africa, South of the Sahara have little interest in events taking place in the United States.
8. African nations are an important voice in the United Nations.

FOLLOW UP

Collect materials on the people of Africa from current newspapers and magazines. Arrange them in a scrapbook or make a display for your class bulletin board. Make several headings for the items you collect: National Leaders, Problems of the People, Farming, Industry, Interest of Other Countries.

CHAPTER 2

The Unknown Continent

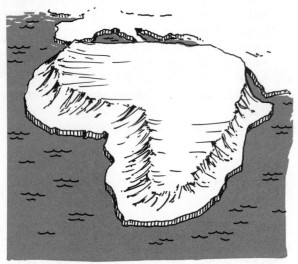

READING FOR A PURPOSE:
1. Where does the equator cross Africa?
2. What are the chief rivers of Africa, South of the Sahara?
3. What are the problems of Africa's rivers?

1. Africa was once called the "Unknown Continent." While today it is no longer unknown to us, there are still parts of Africa about which the world knows little. The mystery of Africa is caused partly by the geography of the continent. In this chapter, we are going to learn some of the reasons why Africa was not well known by the rest of the world for so long.

2. Most of Africa is a plateau. There is very little coastal plain for lowland. The land rises sharply near the coast. The plateaus vary from 1,000 to 5,000 feet above sea level. The surface of the continent is very much like a saucer. Near the coasts, the land rises and then dips toward the center.

3. The plateaus of Africa below the Sahara are drained or hollowed by three large rivers: the Congo, the Zambezi and the Niger. Because the rivers begin on high ground, they flow rapidly "downhill" toward the narrow coastal plains. In this drop there are many rapids and falls. Travel on the rivers is possible, but boats must stop at the rapids. Travelers must then go by land to the next place where they can board a boat. The Congo is more widely used for transportation than the other large rivers. Some of the rivers also form muddy deltas or sand bars at their mouths.

4. On the eastern coast, there is a range of mountains that extends from South Africa northward to Ethiopia. In this range there are many high peaks. Mount Kilimanjaro is over 19,000 feet high. Mount Kenya is over 17,000 feet above sea level. Both of these mountains are located almost on the equator. Yet they are so high that they are covered with ice and snow. In the mountains the largest number of Europeans are found. They prefer to live where it is cooler. The largest cities are also located in these eastern highlands.

5. Some huge lakes have been formed in the deep valleys of the African highlands. The snow from the very high mountains has provided the water for these lakes. Lake Victoria is the largest lake. It is almost the size of Lake Superior, the largest of the North American Great Lakes. Lake Tanganyika and Lake Nyassa are other important lakes in the highlands. These lakes also can be compared in size to our Great Lakes. But the Great Lakes of North America are busy water routes. The lakes of Africa are hardly used for trade at all.

The Cape Peninsula in the Republic of South Africa. Most of Sub-Sahara Africa rises sharply near the coast.

South African Information Service

UNITED NATIONS

Mount Kilimanjaro, the highest peak in Africa.

UNITED NATIONS

One of Africa's many falls, this is at Lake Tana in Ethiopia, the source of the Blue Nile.

6. Why was Africa, South of the Sahara so hard to explore? First, the Sahara made it nearly impossible to reach central Africa by land from the north. Second, the African coastline is regular so that there are few harbors. (Africa has fewer miles of coastline than Europe, which is one-third its size.) Third, many of Africa's river mouths are difficult to enter because of the deltas and sand bars. Transportation up the rivers is not easy because of the falls and rapids. Fourth, in the 17th and 18th centuries, many Africans were taken as slaves. As a result, African tribes were often unfriendly because they were afraid the Europeans were looking for slaves. This made exploration even more dangerous.

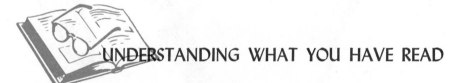

UNDERSTANDING WHAT YOU HAVE READ

1. Which of the following questions are answered in this chapter?

a. What is the Great Rift?

b. Why was Africa unknown for so long?

c. Where do most Africans live?

2. The main idea of this chapter is to describe:

a. the rivers of Sub-Sahara Africa.

b. African land forms.

c. the mountains of Sub-Sahara Africa.

3. Most of Africa is a:

a. lowland.   b. plateau.   c. rain forest.

4. Most of Africa's highlands are located in the:

a. east.   b. north.   c. west.

5. Africa's rivers are often of little help in transporting goods because:

a. there is a lack of boats.

b. most of the rivers flow inland.

c. many of the rivers have falls and rapids.

6. Most Europeans live in the highlands because:

a. the best farm land is found there.

b. the mountains are rich in minerals.

c. the climate is cooler.

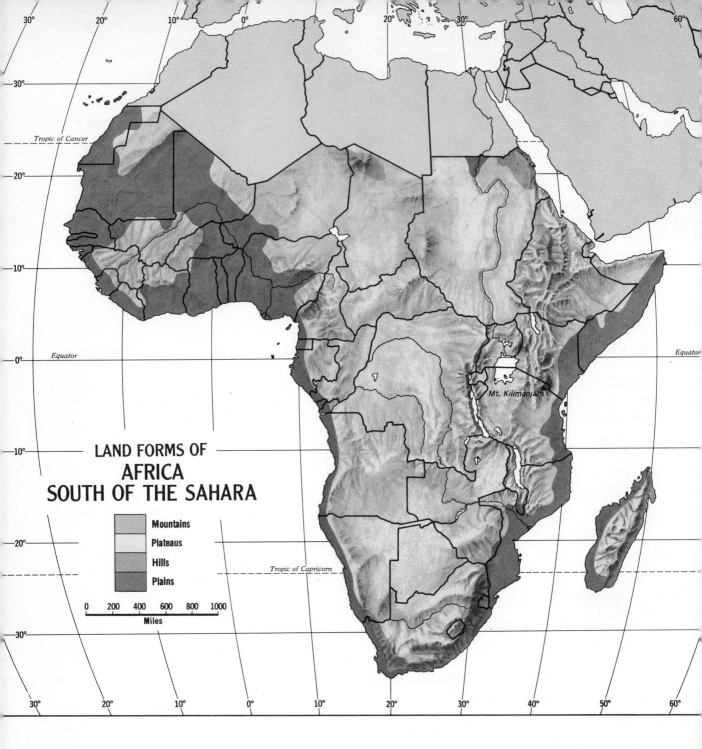

LAND FORMS OF
AFRICA
SOUTH OF THE SAHARA

Mountains
Plateaus
Hills
Plains

0 200 400 600 800 1000
Miles

Tropic of Cancer

20°

10°

Equator

10°

20°

Tropic of Capricorn

30°

Mt. Kilimanjaro

Equator

DEVELOPING IDEAS AND SKILLS

Map # 44—Land Forms of Africa, South of the Sahara

Tell whether these statements are *true* or *false*. Be able to explain your answers.

1. A vast plain stretches completely across the continent of Africa at the equator.
2. Plateaus are an important land form in southern Africa.
3. Chains of mountains stretching more than a thousand miles are located in this region.
4. The western part of this region north of the equator has more lowland area than the part south of the equator.
5. The lowlands along the southeastern coast extend inland for 500 miles.
6. Most of the land in Africa, South of the Sahara is highland.

SUMMING UP

In your notebook, place an X next to the reasons that explain why Africa was unknown to the people of Europe for so long.

___ 1. a vast desert in the north
___ 2. thick forests and heavy rains
___ 3. southern tip near the cold southern ocean
___ 4. few openings into the land for harbors
___ 5. lack of natural resources
___ 6. unfriendly natives
___ 7. not near other continents
___ 8. large inland lakes
___ 9. disease-carrying insects
___10. cliffs and mountains near the coasts

FOLLOW UP

True or False Tell whether these statements are true or false. The underlined words make the statements true or false. If a statement is false, what word or words would you place in it to make it true?

1. The Sahara Desert crosses the <u>middle</u> of Africa.
2. Most of Sub-Sahara Africa is a <u>plateau</u>.
3. One of the large rivers of Sub-Sahara Africa is the <u>Congo</u>.
4. <u>Rapids and falls</u> cause troubles in water transportation.
5. Mud piled up at the mouth of a river is called its <u>source</u>.
6. <u>Lake Victoria</u> is the largest lake of Africa.
7. The large cities of Sub-Sahara Africa are found in the <u>highlands</u>.
8. Early Europeans came to Africa in search of <u>slaves</u>.

CHAPTER 3

The Hot Continent

PROBLEM: What are the climates of Africa?

READING FOR A PURPOSE:
1. Where is Africa's rain forest?
2. What is the tsetse fly?
3. Where do Africa's large animals live?

1. The equator runs through the middle of Africa. This means that most of the continent lies in the low latitudes. (Even in the tropics, however, it is not always hot. Where there are highlands it is always cooler than it is at sea level.) No part of Africa is as far from the equator as New York or Chicago. Thus, it is easy to remember the climate of Africa, South of the Sahara with the simple statement, "Africa is warm, but some places are warmer than others."

2. Near the equator in Africa is a large rain forest. It extends from the Gulf of Guinea on the west to the highlands of East Africa. The rain forest of the Congo is very much like the rain forest of the Amazon River in South America. It is always hot and rainy. Winds of more than ten miles an hour are almost unknown. The growth of the jungle is thick. It is crowded with birds, snakes, monkeys, fish and apes. The rain forest is full of mosquitoes that carry malaria and yellow fever. Sleeping sickness is carried by the tsetse fly. This is one of the most deadly diseases of Africa.

3. Most of tropical Africa is not a rain forest, but a dry grassland called a *savanna*. The savannas lie north and south of the rain forest. Here summer is the rainy season and the winters are dry and dusty. It is always hot. During the dry season the grasses turn brown. Cattle and people grow thin as food becomes scarce. During the rainy season the earth is green again and grain grows. Cattle and people become healthier as more food can be found. Most of Africa's large animals—the antelope, lion, elephant, giraffe and zebra—live on the savannas.

4. North and south of the savannas are the deserts. The great Sahara Desert occupies nearly all the northern part of the continent. In south-

A tropical jungle forest of mahogany trees.
UNITED NATIONS

The dry lands of southwest Africa.

ern Africa is the smaller Kalahari Desert. (This desert is only as large as the whole of Western Europe!) The edges of the desert may receive as much as ten inches of rain a year, but most of this area rarely has rainfall.

5. You will remember from your study of North Africa that the lands of the northern coasts border the Mediterranean Sea. They have the sunny climate of the Mediterranean. The same climate is found in southwestern Africa near Capetown. The summers are almost rainless. Whatever rain there is comes during the winter months.

6. On the southeastern coast is the region of the humid-subtropical climate. Can you remember the sections of North and South America that have the same climate? Southeastern Africa is about 35 degrees from the equator and is on the east coast of a large continent. This is the climate we find in other regions with the same conditions—Argentina and Uruguay in South America, and our own southeastern states.

7. Rainfall is a problem in most of Africa. Some parts get too much, while others get too little. The savannas and the Mediterranean regions both have very dry seasons. One year the rains may come early and soak the earth. In other years they may be too late and too scarce. There are few ways of storing water for the dry season. What is worse, the heavy rains wash important minerals out of the soil.

8. As you study the geography of Africa, you are probably thinking that Africa is like South America in many ways. This is true. The shapes of the two continents are very much the same. Both have a large mass of land in the north and a narrower section of land in the south. Both have large rain forests. (The one in South America is much larger, however.) Both have deserts, although the Sahara in Africa is much larger than any in South America. On both continents it is hard to travel because of the thick forests, deserts and mountains. In both areas, most of the people are farmers and raise food chiefly for themselves only. (South America has one great farming region, however—the pampas. There is no section like it in Africa.) Only now are the people of both regions beginning to manufacture goods for themselves.

A low-rainfall area during the dry season.

UNDERSTANDING WHAT YOU HAVE READ

1. **Which of the following questions are answered in this chapter?**
   a. Why isn't it always hot in the tropics?
   b. Where is the Kalahari Desert?
   c. Why is life difficult in Sub-Sahara Africa?

2. **The main idea of this chapter is to describe:**
   a. the climate of Sub-Sahara Africa.
   b. the animals of Africa.
   c. how people live south of the Sahara.

3. **Most of Africa has the climate of the:**
   a. rain forest.   b. savanna.   c. desert.

4. **The tsetse fly causes:**
   a. malaria.   b. sleeping sickness.   c. smallpox.

5. **One reason why life is hard in parts of Sub-Sahara Africa is that:**
   a. it is too cold in the mountains.
   b. there are many sandstorms.
   c. diseases are common.

6. **Water is a problem to many Africans because:**
   a. the peope can't store it during dry seasons.
   b. rains cause frequent floods.
   c. too much water is used to provide electricity.

DEVELOPING IDEAS AND SKILLS

Map # 45—Climates of Africa, South of the Sahara
Do You Agree or Disagree? Give reasons for your answers.

1. Mountains have a great effect on the climate of all of Sub-Sahara Africa.
2. The savannas are located both north and south of the equator.
3. The African rain forest extends from one coast to the other.
4. No part of the southern tip of Africa receives enough rainfall for good farming.
5. Great differences in latitude are one reason for the different climates of the region.
6. At the equator the climate is the same across the continent.
7. Most of Africa, South of the Sahara is rain forest.
8. Considering the entire continent of Africa, the same climatic regions are found north and south of the equator.
9. High mountains are located in eastern Africa.
10. The rain forest is found within ten degrees' latitude north and south of the equator.

SUMMING UP

I. Complete the following outline in your notebook.

   AFRICA AND SOUTH AMERICA

   A. Ways in which these two continents are *alike*.
      1.   3.
      2.   4.

   B. Ways in which these two continents are *not alike*.
      1.   3.
      2.   4.

II. *Fact or Opinion* Using the information you have gained in Chapters 1, 2 and 3, tell whether the statements on the next page are fact or opinion.

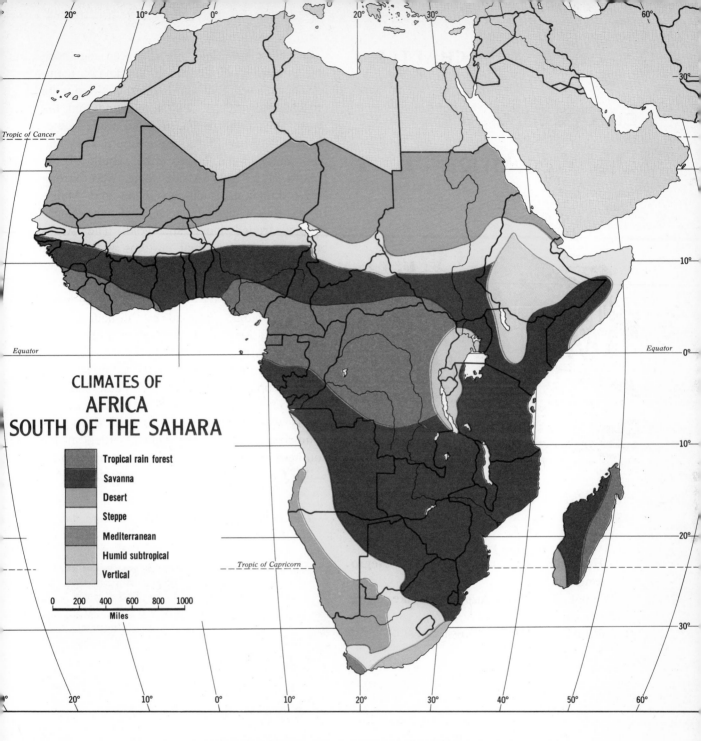

CLIMATES OF AFRICA SOUTH OF THE SAHARA

- Tropical rain forest
- Savanna
- Desert
- Steppe
- Mediterranean
- Humid subtropical
- Vertical

0 200 400 600 800 1000
Miles

1. The Peace Corps should be extended so that all Africans receive proper medical care.
2. Africa today is not the same as it was 100 years ago.
3. The lakes of Africa have not been very useful in providing transportation.
4. Communism cannot affect the people of Africa.
5. There are few good harbors in Africa because of the regular coastline.
6. The largest animals of Africa do not live in the rain forest.
7. Some climates of Africa are like those in the United States.
8. Africa, South of the Sahara cannot be as highly developed as North Africa.

383

CHAPTER 4

Europeans Discover Africa

PROBLEM: How did Europeans gain control of Africa?

READING FOR A PURPOSE:
1. How did the Arabs reach the Negro kingdoms?
2. What did the Europeans take from Africa?
3. Who was David Livingstone?

1. Africa, South of the Sahara was almost completely unknown to the people of Europe until the late 1400's. Then the rulers of Portugal began a search for an all-water route from Europe to India. They were interested in trade. The Portuguese sea captains sailed along the west coast of Africa, each time going farther and farther south. They traded with the African tribes and returned with shiploads of gold and ivory. Finally, in 1498, Vasco da Gama rounded the southern tip of the continent, turned north and sailed on to India.

384

2. Before this time, no European had been able to learn much about the African continent. It was believed that the Sahara could not be crossed. However, it was now found that the Arabs of the north had opened trade routes across the narrow parts of the desert. They had met some of the Negro tribes south of the Sahara. (In West Africa there were strong Negro kingdoms such as Ghana and Mali.) In return for figs, dates and salt, the Negro peoples traded ivory and gold. The Arabs brought with them their customs and ways of living. Many of the Negro tribes became Moslem.

3. After Vasco da Gama found the all-water route to India, Portugal established trading posts or stations along the eastern and western coasts of Africa. Africans brought goods that the Portuguese wanted to these trading stations. Other peoples besides the Portuguese soon set up African trading posts. The land along the coasts was divided up by several European countries. In 1652, the Dutch settled at the southern tip of the continent in what is today called Capetown. This southern settlement sup-

The Zimbabwe ruins of Rhodesia were built about 1,000 years ago by early Negro peoples.

plied Dutch sailors with food and water.

4. In the 1500's, the European nations wanted slaves for their colonies in the New World. In 1619, Dutch ships brought the first Negroes to the English colonies. The Europeans did not go into Africa's interior for their slaves. The slaves were captured and brought to the coastal stations by strong Negro tribes who raided other villages. While they were waiting, the Europeans kept themselves supplied with food by planting New World crops such as maize, peanuts, tobacco, potatoes and tomatoes. These crops were later adopted by African farmers.

5. The great inland explorations did not begin until the 1800's. Mungo Park, an explorer from Scotland, traveled the route of the Niger River in western Africa. John Speke and Samuel Baker discovered Lake Tanganyika in East Africa. But the two most famous explorers were David Livingstone and Henry Stanley.

6. Livingstone first came to Central Africa as a missionary in 1840. For 16 years, he explored the regions of East Africa. He discovered the Zambezi River and Victoria Falls, the source of the Nile River. He fought the slave trade and won the friendship of many African people. In 1866, Livingstone disappeared. In 1869, a New York newspaper sent Henry Stanley to find the missing missionary. Stanley found Livingstone two years later near Lake Tanganyika. He was very sick. When he recovered, the two men continued exploring in East Africa. Livingstone died in Africa in 1873. Stanley remained and explored along the Congo River.

7. Stanley and Livingstone opened Africa for other missionaries. These men came to Africa to help the natives and to teach them the Christian religion. They opened schools, hospitals and churches for the African people. The reports of Stanley and Livingstone also gave the world information about the riches of Africa: gold, ivory, animal skins and fine tropical woods. The news reached Europe at a time when European nations were looking for raw materials for their factories. They also wanted places to sell their manufactured goods. Great Britain, France, Belgium, Germany and Italy soon divided most of Africa into colonies.

8. For a time, Ethiopia and Liberia were the only independent countries on the entire continent. Liberia, on the west coast, had been started by the United States as a home for its former slaves. In 1910, the Union of South Africa gained self-government. For most purposes, Egypt gained freedom in 1922, but it was under the protection of Great Britain until after World War II. This situation remained unchanged in Africa until after World War II. Since that time, the world has seen the great movement of African peoples to free themselves of their European rulers and establish their own governments.

UNDERSTANDING WHAT YOU HAVE READ

1. **Which of the following questions are answered in this chapter?**

a. Who explored Africa?

b. Who was Cecil Rhodes?

c. Why were Europeans interested in Africa in the 1600's?

2. **The main idea of this chapter is to describe:**

a. the exchange of goods between Europe and Africa.

b. how missionaries opened Africa.

c. the exploration of Africa, South of the Sahara.

3. **A great explorer of Sub-Sahara Africa was:**

a. David Livingstone.

b. James Cook.

c. John Cabot.

4. The search for a route around Africa to India was begun by:

a. Portugal.   b. Great Britain.   c. Italy.

5. Europeans became interested in Africa in the 1600's because they:

a. needed raw materials for factories.

b. wanted slaves and ivory.

c. wished to make the land safe for missionaries.

6. Europeans had a great interest in Africa in the 1800's because they:

a. were looking for a new route to India.

b. wanted more fertile farm land.

c. wanted raw materials for factories.

7. People who went to Africa to teach the Christian religion were:

a. sea captains.   b. traders.   c. missionaries.

DEVELOPING IDEAS AND SKILLS

Picture Symbols

These pictures should help you to recall parts of the chapter you have read. Can you tell the main idea of each picture? In what paragraph did you find the answer for each?

SUMMING UP

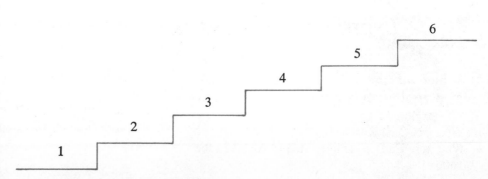

Steps in the Exploration of Africa

In your notebook, place the following explorations in the order in which they happened. The first step is No. 1. The next event is No. 2, etc.

Europeans sailed along the western coast and set up trading posts.
Livingstone explored East Africa.
Arabs crossed the Sahara.
Europeans divided Africa into colonies.
Stanley explored the Congo.
Mungo Park explored the Niger River.

FOLLOW UP

Complete the following sentences, using the names listed below.

Arabs	Dutch sailors	Vasco da Gama
European nations	Missionaries	David Livingstone
Slave traders	Portuguese sailors	Henry Stanley
Egypt		

1. _____ crossed the Sahara to trade with Negro tribes.
2. _____ began searching for an all-water route around Africa to India.
3. _____ went as a missionary to central Africa.
4. _____ reached India by rounding the southern tip of Africa and then sailing northward.
5. _____ divided Africa into many colonies.
6. _____ was sent to Africa to find a missing missionary.
7. _____ brought the first Negroes to the English colonies.
8. _____ did much good by building schools and hospitals in Sub-Sahara Africa.

CHAPTER 5

The Tribal World

PROBLEM: Who are the peoples of Africa?

READING FOR A PURPOSE:
1. What groups of people live below the Sahara?
2. What is a tribe?
3. What is a tribal religion?

1. Africa is not a crowded continent; about 240 million people live in Africa, South of the Sahara. As you have learned, much of tropical Africa is either too wet or too dry. Africa below the Sahara is Negro Africa—the home of people with brown or black skin. Most of the Negro peoples are Bantus or Sudanese (which means black). The Bantu-speaking peoples live south of the equator. The Sudanese live in the grasslands between the Sahara and the tropical rain forest. Both of these peoples are divided into hundreds of tribes.

2. There are three important smaller Negro groups in Sub-Sahara Africa. The Pygmies, averaging about 4½ feet tall, are found mainly in the rain forest of the Congo Basin. They live by hunting wild game. The Bushmen live in the Kalahari Desert in southwest Africa. They hunt and gather food for a living. The Hottentots live on reservations in southwest Africa. These people are herdsmen who raise sheep, goats and long-horned cattle.

3. Besides the Negro peoples, there are smaller groups of Asians and whites or Europeans living in this region. The Europeans number only about four million of the total population. Most of them live in the Republic of South Africa, Rhodesia and Kenya. (The eastern highlands and southern plateaus of these countries appeal to them because the climate is cooler and free of tropical diseases.) Despite their small numbers, the Europeans have been the rulers of the continent since colonial times. They have controlled the governments. They have been the professional people, the traders, the owners of farms and mines. The hard work has been done by the native Africans.

4. Many Africans live in the world of the *tribe*. A tribe is a group of people who live together in a single place, united by their own

A young mother and child from Senegal.

A Ghanian chief with members of his tribe. Many Africans still belong to tribes.

customs and their own language. (Many of the tribal languages have not been written down, making it difficult for one tribe to understand another.) Each tribe has its own chief. While the chief has great power, he usually rules by the customs of his people. The land that a family farms and uses for cattle does not belong to the family. It belongs to the tribe. Many of the tribes are so large that they include a million or more members. The tribes differ from each other in many ways.

5. It is up to the parents to teach their children the laws and customs of the tribe. The boys learn to hunt, fish, tend cattle, make weapons and be brave in battle. The girls are taught to cook, farm and keep house. Much is learned through songs, stories and dances. Some children live and work with the craftsmen of the tribe. They are taught to make tools, masks and jewelry. The tribe cares for its members throughout their lives.

6. While many Africans are Christians, Moslems or Hindus, most follow the religion of the tribe. Many tribal people believe that each thing or object has a spirit. These spirits are either good or evil. The African tries to please these spirits so they will help him. Each tribe has medicine men or witch doctors who try to make the spirits bring good fortune to the tribe.

7. In general, tribal Africans are always "on the go." If they are hunters they move about in search of game. If they are herdsmen they are always looking for better pasture lands. If they are farmers they want better land. The soils of Africa are not good. The heavy rains of the rain forest wash away the valuable minerals. After two or three years the farmer must move on to find a new plot of ground. The farmer grows only what he needs for food or to trade for the things he cannot grow.

8. The tribal African has lived most of his life in a world of sickness. From the time he was born he has probably had many diseases. You will recall that the insects of the wet regions bring yellow fever, malaria and sleeping sickness. The tribesman's diet of starches causes his bones to be poorly formed. Pure drinking water is seldom found. He has depended on the tribal medicine men to cure his diseases with strange mixtures or with "magic."

9. In many places the tribes still carry on their old ways of living. In other places Afri-

Dr. Albert Schweitzer.

Brown Brothers

cans have welcomed the changes brought by Europeans. Missionaries have done a great deal for the people as teachers, doctors, nurses and ministers. They have worked to build schools and hospitals. One of the most famous of modern missionaries was Dr. Albert Schweitzer. He came to Africa because he felt that the African people needed doctors more than the people of Europe did. He built a hospital in the jungles of Gabon near the equator. In 1952, he was awarded the Nobel Peace Prize for his work in helping others. He died in 1965 after fifty years of service to the people of Africa.

10. The life of the African is changing rapidly. A short time ago, many Africans lived in tribal villages and used only simple tools. Now more and more own their own farms or work in the city, using modern machinery and earning wages. The cities are places where Africans of many different tribal backgrounds meet and exchange ideas. There is a growing number of schools for those who want to learn. There are modern hospitals and other signs of a new Africa. More and more, the African is preparing himself to take part in his new nation.

UNDERSTANDING WHAT YOU HAVE READ

1. **Which of the following questions are answered in this chapter?**
a. How do Africans live?
b. How do African children learn tribal ways?
c. How do Africans communicate with each other?

2. **The main idea of this chapter is to describe:**
a. how the African uses his land.
b. the religions of African people.
c. the importance of the tribe in African life.

3. **Most Africans are:**

a. miners.
b. herders and farmers.
c. factory workers.

4. **Most Africans still live:**
a. in cities.
b. on tribal lands.
c. on their own farms.

5. **Tribal Africans seem to be always "on the go" because they:**
a. search for better farm lands.
b. move from one kind of factory work to another.
c. are driven from their land by wild animals.

6. New African nations may have some trouble in uniting all their people because:

a. there is a big health problem.
b. much of Africa is too dry for a large population.
c. many people are loyal to many different tribes.

7. A *tribe* is:

a. one family.

b. a large number of families.
c. all the people of a certain race.

8. Most of the sickness of members of a tribe is taken care of by:

a. European doctors and nurses.
b. the women of the tribe.
c. witch doctors.

DEVELOPING IDEAS AND SKILLS

Pictograph # 14—Population, Area and Standard of Living of Africa, South of the Sahara

Can you answer these questions?
1. Is the standard of living of this region high or low compared with that of the United States? Is it a low-income or underdeveloped area?
2. Is the region as crowded as the United States?

3. Are the people of this region literate compared with the people of the United States?
4. How long may the average person in this region expect to live?
5. What facts tell you the standard of living of the people of the region?
6. How does this region compare with the United States in size?

Pictograph # 14—Population, Area and Standard of Living of Africa, South of the Sahara

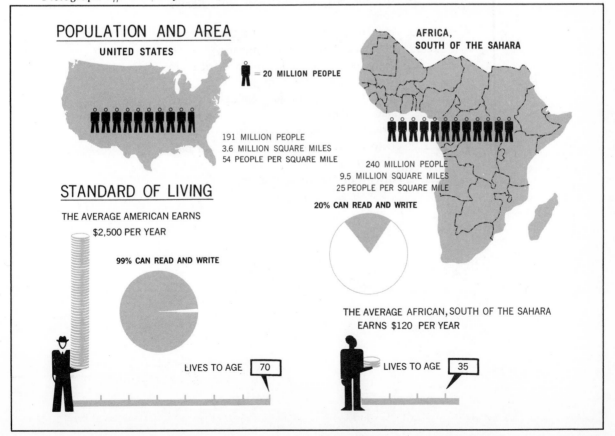

SUMMING UP

Compare the standard of living of a tribal family with that of your own family.

YOUR FAMILY		AFRICAN TRIBAL FAMILY
	Means of Education	
	Health Care	
	Occupations	
	Religion	
	Kind of Community	

FOLLOW UP

In the following, place before each statement the word that makes the statement correct: *Most, Some, Few*.

1. _____ Europeans in Sub-Sahara Africa live in the highlands.
2. _____ Africans are members of a Christian religion.
3. _____ Africans are members of the Pygmy group.
4. _____ Africans are members of the Negro race.
5. _____ tribes speak the same language.
6. _____ Negro people in Sub-Sahara Africa are owners of farms and mines.
7. _____ small farmers grow just enough to feed their families.
8. _____ Africans now work in the cities.
9. _____ doctors and nurses have come from outside Africa.
10. _____ African tribes are very large.

CHAPTER 6

The Rain-Forest Farmer

PROBLEM: How does the African farmer meet his needs?

READING FOR A PURPOSE:
1. How do the rain-forest people live?
2. What is migratory farming?
3. What is plantation farming?

1. As you have learned, much of the climate in Sub-Sahara Africa is either rain forest or savanna. These climates are not good for farming. Despite this fact, most people in Africa, South of the Sahara are either farmers or herders of cattle. Most of these people use whatever they raise for their own needs. Starting with the rain forest, let us see what kind of farming is carried on by the people who live there.

2. The rain-forest people live in small villages near a stream or river. The village huts are small and dark. They have cone-shaped roofs made of grass and leaves. The shape of the roof allows the rain to run off quickly. Around the village are the clearings for the main food crops,

such as bananas, yams, rice and manioc. (Manioc is a plant with a root like a potato. It is the source of the bread of all rain-forest peoples.) Besides these crops, the natives also grow fruits and vegetables in small garden plots.

3. The women farm the clearing with simple tools like the hoe and digging stick. The yields from their fields are very low. The men fish and hunt, but meat is hard to get. There are few cows in the rain forest because they die of the tropical diseases. When the crop or the hunt is good, there is plenty to eat. However, the food cannot be kept long because it spoils in the heat. When the crops are poor, the problem of having enough food is serious. Some men earn money by gathering palm-oil nuts or rubber to sell to traders. Others work on plantations.

4. Rain-forest people are always moving because the soil is so poor. They do not have modern methods of farming. It is easier to change a clearing and start over in a new field. The trees are cut down, but the stumps remain. The thick undergrowth is cut and burned. The ashes enrich the soil. Crops are planted among the tree stumps. These crops grow well for about two or three years, but after that time, the thick brush returns. Rather than fight it, the tribe moves out and looks for a new place to clear. This kind of farming is called *migratory* farming because it involves moving from place to place. The same kind of farming is also found in the Amazon rain forest.

5. Most rain-forest people are subsistence farmers. However, plantation farming is also found in the rain forest. Many of the plantations are owned by foreigners but are worked by Africans. Two of the leading plantation crops in the rain forest are palm-oil nuts and cacao beans. Lately, there has been a growing number of farms and plantations owned by Africans.

6. The palm nut, from which oil is made, is one of Africa's leading products. The soap you use today may be made from Africa's palm oil. This same oil is important in the manufacture of cosmetics. The oil palm grows wild in the Congo rain forest. Plantations are also located along

Homes in the rain forest of Mali.

the river valleys. Africa produces ninety per cent of the world's supply of palm nuts. The nuts are shipped to Europe for processing— that is, changing into oil products. The leading producer of palm nuts is Nigeria.

7. Americans love chocolate. Most likely the chocolate you eat comes from the cacao trees of Africa. Ghana and Nigeria produce about

half the world's total supply of cacao beans. The cacao trees grow best in the tropical climate. Natives gather the pods from the trees and remove the beans. Then the beans are carried to the trading stations located along the rivers. They are shipped to the United States and Europe where they are made into chocolate.

UNDERSTANDING WHAT YOU HAVE READ

1. **Which of the following questions are answered in this chapter?**
a. Why is the oil palm important?
b. How do the native people work with iron?
c. What crops are raised on plantations?

2. **The main idea of this chapter is to describe:**
a. how the African makes use of wood products.
b. the major products of the rain forest.
c. how rain-forest people travel.

3. **The chief plantation crops of the African rain forest are:**
a. palm nuts and cacao beans.
b. olives and oranges.
c. corn and millet.

4. **The chief foods of the rain-forest people are:**
a. proteins, like meat and beans.
b. starches, like manioc and yams.
c. sugars, like chocolate and oranges.

5. **Farming is difficult in the rain forest because:**
a. the land is hilly.
b. weeds grow rapidly.
c. soils are poor.

6. **The oil of the palm nut is important because:**
a. Africans use it for heating their homes.
b. it is used to make machinery run more smoothly.
c. it is an important export crop.

7. *Migratory* farmers:

a. use irrigation canals.

b. move from place to place.

c. build terraces on hillsides.

8. "The factory *processes* wool and turns out beautiful cloth." *Processes* means:

a. "buys directly from herders."

b. "imports from distant lands."

c. "changes raw material into finished goods."

DEVELOPING IDEAS AND SKILLS

Photograph Study

This photograph should help you to recall parts of the chapter you have just read. Can you tell the main idea of the photograph? Where in the chapter is it described?

SUMMING UP

Compare the life of the people in the Congo and Amazon regions.

AMAZON	*How People Live*	CONGO
	Location and Climate	
	Main Foods	
	Main Occupations	
	Transportation	
	Important Crops	
	Problems	

FOLLOW UP

Making Inferences In our reading, many facts are given to us. From these facts we can draw conclusions. The following are some conclusions or inferences that you might make after reading this chapter. Tell whether these conclusions are correct or incorrect. Give reasons for your answers.

1. Farmers of the rain forest use little fertilizer on their land.

2. Wheat bread is little known to rain-forest families.

3. At night, after a hard day's work, rain-forest families probably spend some time reading.

4. When an African goes to the city, he will prob-ably look for other people from his own tribe.

5. Cotton plantations are probably found in the rain forest.

6. Some customs of American women might change if we did not trade with Ghana and Nigeria.

7. The African jungle grows back almost as fast as the natives can clear it away.

8. Drier areas of Africa usually have the greatest number of insects.

9. Most people in the rain forest have plenty to eat.

10. Most rain-forest people live near rivers.

CHAPTER 7

The Savanna Farmer and Herder

PROBLEM: How does the African adapt himself to the wet and dry lands?

READING FOR A PURPOSE:
1. How does a Hausa farm?
2. What is the Masai's chief form of wealth?
3. What are some farming problems in Africa?

1. Africans of the savannas are usually farmers or herders. In the northern grasslands of western Africa live the Hausa tribe. They are farmers who live in huts of dried mud thatched with grass. Like most African farmers, the Hausa use only a hoe or digging stick. They build ridges on their farm land to catch the water during the rainy season and hold it for the dry season. Their chief crop is corn. They use the grain for food and the stalks for roofs and fences. They also grow wheat, millet and yams. The Hausa grow crops to feed themselves and their families. However, they may grow a cash crop such as peanuts to get money for other goods.

2. Some of the farming peoples of western Africa are also herders. However, raising cattle is difficult in this area. Good cattle cannot be grazed on the western savannas because of the disease-carrying tsetse fly. The cattle are thin, particularly in the dry season. The little milk they give is used to make butter and cheese. When the animals die, their hides are sold and tanned to make clothing.

3. In the highlands of eastern Africa, safe from the tsetse fly, herding is the chief occupation. Two typical herding tribes are the Masai of Tanganyika and the Karamojong of northeast Uganda. The Masai wander with their herds. They are nomads like the Bedouins of the Middle East. The Masai measure their wealth in cattle. They rarely kill their animals for food or use them to provide fertilizer. Their chief use for cattle is their milk. The Masai often drink the blood of the cow with the milk. They believe it gives them strength.

4. During the rainy season, the Masai herder keeps his cattle in the valley. During the dry season, he moves to the highlands where there is more rain and more grass. The cattle have a hump of fat on their backs. When there isn't enough food to eat during the dry season, the cattle "use" the fat they have stored. In this, they are like the camels of North Africa. The Masai have so many cows on the grazing lands that the grass is soon killed and the soil is washed away when the rains come. While the men are away, the women care for any crops that are planted.

Cattle grazing in the highlands of East Africa.

Belgian Gov't. Photo from UNATIONS

South African Information Service

A Zulu kraal or village in South Africa.

UNITED NATIONS

Sisal, Tanzania's chief export crop, drying in a factory.

5. The Masai live in a village called a *kraal*. They live in round thatched huts. The thatched huts form a large circle with only one entrance. Inside the circle are many cattle pens. There is a special pen for the chief's herd. Each morning, the men of the tribe drive the cattle out onto the grazing land. They are watched carefully during the day and returned to the kraal at night. Whenever there is need for a new pasture, the village is given up by the herders. The village is surrounded by a fence of thorny brush to protect it against wild animals and enemy tribes.

6. The Masai believe that God gave cattle only to the Masai. This seems to give them the right to raid other tribes and steal their cattle. When the Masai marry, they pay a "bride price." This means that a man pays to the girl's father a certain number of cattle. This payment is to make up for the father's loss—the work done by the girl around the home.

7. The Karamojong live on a plateau. They also live in thatched villages near wells or a river bank where they can raise crops as well as tend herds of cattle, goats and sheep. The men and boys take care of the herds. The women and girls tend the fields, grind the grain, fetch the water and collect the firewood. The chief food is a grain called *sorghum*. It is planted in the dry season and ripens in the rainy season. It is eaten with sour milk or vegetables. During the dry season the men move the cattle far from the village in search of grass and water. As with the Masai, guarding cattle is the Karamojong way of life. The animals make it possible for the tribesmen to marry and support their families. When they are away with their herds, they also live on blood and milk.

8. As you have learned, most of Africa's people are herders or subsistence farmers. As such, their income is low and they cannot buy many goods. (Ghana has the highest average income of the new nations of Sub-Sahara Africa—about $150 per year per person.) In recent years, however, there has been an increase in the number of "cash crops" such as cacao, coffee, sisal, palm oil, peanuts and cotton. These crops are grown on both small farms and plantations.

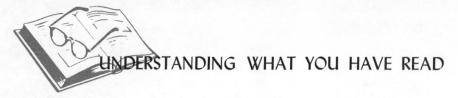

UNDERSTANDING WHAT YOU HAVE READ

1. **Which of the following questions are answered in this chapter?**
a. What is a kraal?
b. How do peanuts grow?
c. Why do herding tribes move?

2. **The main idea of this chapter is to describe:**
a. how the African uses the dry grasslands.
b. the customs of the Masai.
c. life in African villages.

3. **The chief form of wealth of the Masai is their:**
a. water rights.   b. camels.   c. cattle.

4. **An important food crop of the grasslands is:**
a. palm oil.   b. peanuts.   c. corn.

5. **Masai tribes are always on the move because they:**
a. fear attacks by other tribes.
b. need to find new pastures.
c. are looking for fertile farm land.

6. **Few cattle are grazed in certain parts of the grasslands because:**
a. there is no grass.
b. Africans have little use for cattle.
c. the tsetse fly kills many of the cattle.

7. **A *kraal* is a native:**
a. village.   b. drum.   c. boat.

8. **All of these are food *grains* grown in the grasslands EXCEPT:**
a. yams.   b. sorghum.   c. millet.

DEVELOPING IDEAS AND SKILLS

Photograph Study
This photograph should help you to recall parts of the chapter you have just read. Can you tell the main idea of the photograph? Where in the chapter is it described?

SUMMING UP

Complete the following chart in your notebook.

MASAI HERDSMEN		BEDOUIN TRIBESMEN
	Wealth	
	Use of Land	
	Foods	
	Clothing	
	Shelter	
	Goods for Trade	

FOLLOW UP

Below are some headings for your *outline*. Following them are some topics. In your notebook, place the topics under the correct headings.

HEADINGS
A. Farmers and Herders of Western Africa
B. The Herders of East Africa
C. Problems of African Farming

TOPICS
Use ridges to hold water.
Raise corn and wheat.
Believe cattle are a gift from God.
Sorghum and milk are products.
Low income per person.
Measures his wealth in cattle.
Problem of the tsetse fly.
Storage of water during the dry season.
Live in a kraal.
Few "cash crops" for sale.

CHAPTER 8

Unlocking the Resources

PROBLEM: Why has Africa gone so long without making full use of its resources?

READING FOR A PURPOSE:
1. What are some resources of Africa?
2. What is Africa's chief industry?
3. What fuels does Africa lack?

1. Africa, South of the Sahara has many resources: animals, forests, minerals and falling water. There are more different kinds of wild animals in Africa than in any other region. The animals have both helped and harmed the African. Many tribes of the forest still depend upon hunting for their meat supply. However, some of the animals, such as leopards and lions, wander near the villages and destroy property and human life. The wild animals are becoming fewer in number, though, as place after place is cleared for settlement.

2. Of equal importance to the people of Africa are the trees and plants. Great forests still cover more than one-third of Sub-Sahara Africa. From certain trees come the raw ma-terials for many waxes and medicines. In the rain forests are valuable hardwood trees: mahogany, ebony and many others. Yet, few of the trees are cut down because of the difficulty in getting the wood to the seaports. Before the forests can be used fully, more railroads and highways will have to be built.

3. The land contains great mineral riches. The most important industry in Africa is mining. Many of the mineral deposits are found in the highland areas. One of the world's richest mining areas is the southeastern part of the Congo and the new nation of Zambia. The Katanga Province of the Congo leads all regions of the world in the mining of industrial diamonds. (Because diamonds are so hard, they are used in high-speed drills in factories.) The Congo and Zambia are also leading copper producers. More copper is mined here than in any other area of the world except the United States. Cobalt, used in the manufacture of special steel, is also mined.

4. Important mining areas also extend south into Rhodesia and the Republic of South Africa as well. South Africa has long been famous for its gold and diamonds. These diamonds are large and very beautiful. They are made into jewelry. Gold mines are located near the city of Johannesburg. For this reason it is sometimes called the "City Built on Gold." Uranium, now one of the world's most important minerals, is also mined in South Africa. Uranium is used in producing atomic power.

5. In West Africa, Ghana has large deposits of manganese, gold, diamonds and bauxite. The small nation of Guinea may have the world's largest supply of bauxite, from which aluminum is made. Nigeria has rich supplies of tin. Iron ore deposits are found in Guinea, Liberia and Sierra Leone.

6. Mining is big business in Africa. Thousands of workers are needed in the mines. Mining companies bring Africans from a wide area to live in the villages built by the mining companies. The Africans come because more money can be earned in the mines than on the farms. The movement of people from the farms to the

mines has done much to change the life of the African. More and more, he works for wages and has new needs.

7. Most of Africa's riches are not fully used. There are several reasons for this. First, until recently, most mines were directed by foreigners, and most of the profits went back to owners in Europe and America. While Africa's new leaders still allow foreigners to develop their resources, Africans keep a bigger share of the profits. In this way they are raising money for the needs of their people.

8. Second, fuels used to supply power are scarce. Except in the Republic of South Africa, there is little coal for fuel. There is almost no oil in the entire region. In many places water power could be used, for Africa has the greatest water-power resources in the world. However, this source has been touched very little because of the difficulty in reaching streams and water-falls.

9. Third, factories need skilled workers. However, a great number of Africans have not had the opportunity to go to school. African leaders today recognize the need for education and are trying to provide schools for their citizens.

10. Fourth, there are few good highways and railroads in Sub-Sahara Africa. What railroads there are do not connect with other roads to form a large transportation system. Early in the twentieth century, Cecil Rhodes, the great developer of South Africa, announced a plan for a railroad from Capetown, South Africa, to Cairo, Egypt. It is still a dream. Then too,

Hippopotamuses in South Africa's Kruger National Park, one of the world's largest game reserves.

Miners at work in Zambia.

Africa's rivers have many falls and rapids that make them difficult to navigate. The coastline has few good harbors. Transportation improvement is a goal for modern Africa.

11. Fifth, the local market for African products has been small. Most of the people do not have the income to buy the products of the farms and mines. Foods and minerals have been shipped to Europe or America, where they were sold. Now, however, there is a growing number of factories to make use of the products of the continent. Processing plants will use the oils of the palm and coconut. Refineries will use the raw tin, copper, bauxite and manganese. Textile mills will produce cotton goods.

12. The new nations of Africa are receiving aid from other countries in order to help them develop their rich resources. The Free World gave forty billion dollars to the new nations in the ten years before 1963. Most of this aid came from the United States. (Workers of America's Peace Corps are also helping several African nations.) Many large American companies are investing their money in new plants and power projects in Africa. The Soviet Union and Red China are also offering assistance to the African people. As a result of this help, new dams have been built to supply water

401

A copper smelting plant in Elisabethville, Republic of the Congo.

for power and irrigation. Besides the aid from individual nations, Africa is also receiving assistance from the United Nations. In time, Africa's resources will be "unlocked."

UNDERSTANDING WHAT YOU HAVE READ

1. Which of the following questions are answered in this chapter?
a. How has mining changed the life of the African?
b. Why are Africa's riches not fully used?
c. How are the minerals brought to the coast?

2. The main idea of this chapter is to describe:
a. how Africa trades with the world.
b. how Africans work in the mines.
c. the variety of riches in Africa.

3. The Congo leads in the production of:
a. nickel.   b. gold.   c. industrial diamonds.

4. Most of Africa, South of the Sahara has little:
a. coal and oil.
b. gold and diamonds.
c. copper and tin.

5. The Congo has been an important section of Africa because:

a. it lies along the trade routes from north to south.

b. its mines have copper and diamonds.

c. it has the only oil processing plants in Africa.

6. Africa's forests are useful because:

a. soils are fertile.

b. they contain good grazing lands.

c. they provide raw materials for furniture, waxes and medicine.

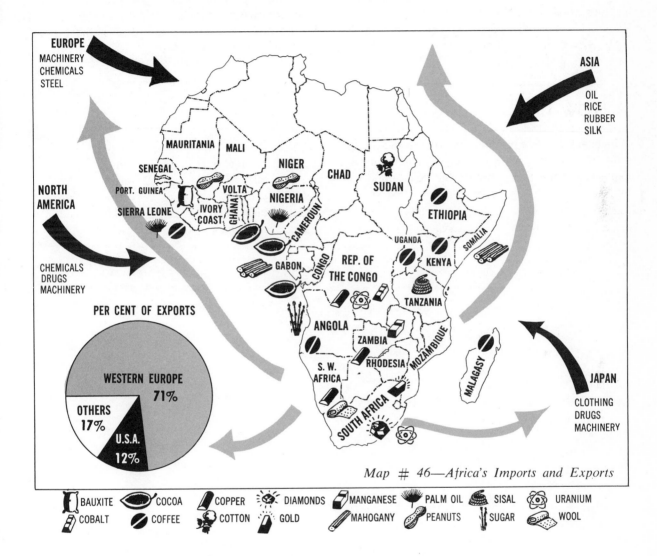

Map # 46—Africa's Imports and Exports

DEVELOPING IDEAS AND SKILLS

Map # 46—Africa's Imports and Exports
Tell if these statements are true or false.

1. Africa sends most of its goods to the United States.

2. Africa exports chiefly raw materials and imports mostly finished goods.

3. The leading copper-producing nations are the Republic of the Congo and Zambia.

4. Most mineral wealth is found along the western coast.

5. Palm-oil nuts are exported by Nigeria.

6. Africa lacks oil and iron ore.

7. Several countries grow coffee for export.

8. We get much of our chocolate from Africa's rain forest.

9. South Africa is rich in gold and diamonds.

403

SUMMING UP

Making an Outline of Chapter 8

1. Review the steps in making a good outline in Chapter 7 of Unit I.
2. Then, choose the main ideas or headings for your outline as follows:
   a. The main idea of paragraphs 1 through 6.
   b. The main idea of paragraphs 7 through 11.
   c. The main idea of paragraph 12.
3. Choose a title for the outline that includes all the main ideas you have chosen.
4. See what information (details) there is in each of these paragraphs that you want to include under each main idea.
5. List three or four of these details under each main idea in the outline.

FOLLOW UP

Which way do these products go, to or from Africa? In your notebook, write *EX* for each item that is exported from Africa, and *IM* for items imported by Africa.

_____ palm oil   _____ peanuts
_____ automobiles _____ cacao

_____ tin   _____ copper
_____ machinery   _____ candy
_____ oil   _____ radios
_____ gold   _____ cotton cloth
_____ diamonds   _____ building materials
_____ medicines

CHAPTER 9

The Freedom Explosion

PROBLEM: Can the new nations survive?

READING FOR A PURPOSE:
1. How did the European powers change Africa?
2. Who is Kwame Nkrumah?
3. What are some problems facing Africa's new leaders?

1. In 1950, only four nations in Africa were free. Today, 37 nations are independent and others expect to be free soon. A true "freedom explosion" has taken place, ending the colonial empires of Africa. The European nations themselves have been partly responsible for this change on the African continent. It is important to understand how this came about.

2. As you remember, Europeans became very interested in Africa in the 1870's. Explorers had found great riches there. The leading countries in Western Europe needed raw materials. Because of this, almost all of Africa was divided into colonies. Three nations—Britain, France and Germany—had the most colonies. Belgium,

however, gained possession of the valuable Congo.

3. When the Europeans first came to Africa, they found they had to teach the Africans their way of doing things in order to bring out the riches of the mines and forests. They built roads and railroads to bring the ore and other products to the sea. They brought schools and better health to many Africans. They trained Africans to run the railroads and to work in the offices. They educated Africans for a certain amount of leadership. This system is sometimes described as *imperialism* or *colonialism*.

4. Great Britain and France did the most to prepare the African people for their freedom. As more and more Africans became educated, they realized that it was possible for them to govern themselves. During World War II, many Africans served in the armies of the Allies. After the war they saw that other people were gaining their freedom—India, Indonesia and the Philippines. Africans wanted a share of freedom to make a better life for themselves.

5. The year 1957 was the beginning of the great freedom movement south of the Sahara. Ghana was the first Negro colony to become independent, and native-born Kwame Nkrumah became the first prime minister of the new government. After Ghana, freedom came rapidly to many other nations. Guinea was given its freedom in 1958. In 1960, a total of seventeen new nations were formed. Some of the nations in this group were: Cameroun, Nigeria, Republic of the Congo, Malagasy (the island of Madagascar), Niger, Congo, Chad and Gabon. Tanganyika and Kenya achieved independence in 1961. Gambia, the 37th free state, became free in 1965. In 1965, Rhodesia declared itself independent from Great Britain. You will have to examine the map of Africa very carefully to find all the changes since 1950.

6. The new nations of Africa face many problems before their governments can work well. Some countries have been better prepared for self-government than others. In Nigeria and Ghana, governments were quickly formed. In the Congo, however, the Belgians left few Afri-

Young people of Rwanda celebrate the independence of their country.

cans who were trained in running a government. Fighting broke out when the Republic of the Congo became free. That fighting has continued from time to time ever since.

7. The new national governments of Africa are troubled by the fact that many people are still loyal to their tribes. Within any one country there may be many tribes, each with its different customs and languages. These tribes may have many members. The tribal chiefs do not want to give up any of their power to the head of a new national government.

8. Another problem of the new nations is that many of their boundaries are artificial. When the European nations divided Africa in the nineteenth century, they took what they could get without war. Boundary lines were placed almost anywhere. As a result, a tribe may have members in two different nations. The Somali people of East Africa are divided in this way. Some tribes wish to break the national boundaries that now exist and form new countries along tribal lines.

9. There is also the problem that a dictator

In changing Africa, hardly a person is not aware of Western goods.

may gain control of a new government. The new African nations would like to set up democratic governments. This is not done overnight. At the same time, they must fill the growing desire of their people for more comforts. Millions of Africans know of and want Western clothes, cars, radios and television sets. If the needs of the people cannot be met quickly, there is always the danger that a popular leader will be able to seize power and rule as a dictator. The new nations need help from the "richer" nations of the world in order to meet the problems of their early years of freedom.

10. One of the most important problems is how to build greater cooperation between Africans and Europeans. For a long time, African Negroes worked in mines or on farms owned by Europeans. They worked for the Europeans to develop the natural resources of Africa. Today, however, Negroes control most of the governments of Sub-Sahara Africa—and the resources of these nations. What kind of governments will develop? Will there be a place in Africa for the smaller white groups?

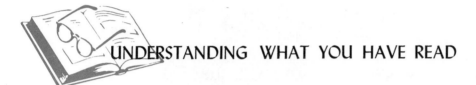

UNDERSTANDING WHAT YOU HAVE READ

1. Which of the following questions are answered in this chapter?
a. What did European countries do for their colonies?
b. What happened when the Republic of the Congo became free?
c. What are the leading tribes of Africa?

2. The main idea of this chapter is to describe:
a. the problems of new African nations.
b. how Africa changed from colonies to independence.
c. why European countries were interested in Africa.

3. Much of Africa in 1920 was controlled by:
a. Great Britain and France.
b. Spain and Portugal.
c. the United States and the Soviet Union.

4. In 1965, most African territory was:
a. colonized by European nations.
b. the mandate of European nations.
c. free and independent.

5. Some leaders of new nations are having difficulties in organizing their new governments because:
a. The United Nations will not admit them as members.
b. the tribal chiefs still have much power.
c. the people want their old governments.

6. A big problem facing new nations of Africa is that:
a. the new governments are ruled by Europeans.
b. tribes have given up their old customs.
c. few people have had the opportunity for an education.

7. "They seemed almost real, but when he looked more closely, he saw that the roses were *artificial*." *Artificial* means the roses were:
a. fresh from the garden.
b. not real.
c. natural.

8. An *imperialist* believes in:
a. obtaining colonies.
b. self-government.
c. keeping tribes together.

DEVELOPING IDEAS AND SKILLS

Map # 47—Africa in 1914

Tell whether these statements are true or false.

1. Most of Africa was free in 1914.
2. Much of the continent was made up of colonies of Great Britain and France.
3. The United States had colonies in Africa.
4. All the African colonies were ruled by European countries.
5. There were four independent African nations in 1914.
6. English colonies stretched in an unbroken line from north to south.
7. Much of the French territory was desert.
8. Germany had colonies in some of the hottest parts of Africa.

EGYPT

FRENCH WEST AFRICA

ANGLO-EGYPTIAN SUDAN

ETHIOPIA

LIBERIA

BELGIAN CONGO

S.W. AFRICA

SOUTH AFRICA (Dominion)

■ FREE COUNTRIES
▩ ITALIAN COLONIES
▦ FRENCH COLONIES
▨ ENGLISH COLONIES
≡ GERMAN COLONIES
▨ PORTUGUESE COLONIES
□ SPANISH COLONIES
▨ BELGIAN COLONIES

Map # 47—Africa in 1914

SUMMING UP

How Was African Life Changed by Colonialism?   Copy this chart and check the correct column in your notebook.

	YES	NO
1. People began to move from native villages to new cities.		
2. Standards of living were raised for some people.		
3. Self-government was encouraged.		
4. Wealth stayed in the region.		
5. There was a more rapid development of natural resources.		
6. People found new jobs and got more pay.		
7. Many new factories were started.		
8. Roads, schools and hospitals were built.		

FOLLOW UP

Who Am I?   What person is speaking in each of these paragraphs? Choose your answer from the list of people below.

Leader of a new   Tribal chief
   African nation   African miner
Rain-forest farmer   European plantation owner
Masai herder   Missionary

1. "I have had power over thousands of people for a long time. I don't intend to give up this power. I want to have some say in the new government, too. My people will stick together." _____ .

2. "The new government doesn't interest me very much. I am too busy watching my animals and trying to make a living. How can the new government bring water to my land?" _____

3. "I work hard for the minerals everyone wants. I'd like to have a share in the profit my work brings. I'd like our resources to be used for my benefit, too." _____

4. "I want this nation to be for the African people. I want all Africans to act like free men. We must all unite to make our government work." _____

5. "I still have work to do in the new Africa. There is still a need for more schools and hospitals." _____

CHAPTER 10

Developing Africa

PROBLEM: What are Africa's chief needs?

READING FOR A PURPOSE:

1. Why does Africa support so few people?
2. Why are many Africans poor?
3. How is the new Africa meeting its problems?

1. Africa has many resources. Its gold, diamonds and copper already play an important part in world affairs. Yet, people ask, why is Africa so poor? (The average income in most African countries is about $100 a year.) Why do so few people live there? By this time, we should be able to supply some of the answers to these questions.

2. First, life is hard in much of Africa. Much of the land is dry. The Sahara is as large as the United States, and the dry lands in the south are as large as most of Western Europe. Much of the continent is hot. In the heart of Africa is the steaming rain forest. North and south of the tropical jungle is the savanna area, with its wet and dry seasons. The tsetse fly and other insects are present in much of these areas.

3. Second, the heat and rainfall affect every-

thing. The possessions of the African family often rust or rot. The climate makes it hard to get a good "set" in chocolate, so that Ghana must export its cacao beans in their raw form. Many kinds of cattle cannot be raised in this heat. Those that are raised give little milk and less meat. The climate makes it difficult to raise crops like peas and beans, which the people of the middle and high latitudes depend on for body growth. (Rain-forest people must depend on starchy foods such as bananas, yams and manioc.)

4. Third, from the voyage of Vasco da Gama to recent times, the world's main interest in Africa was in taking things out of the continent. European nations seized and divided among themselves the vast lands of the continent. They profited from the slaves, gold, ivory and raw materials that Africa provided. As a result, Africa remained underdeveloped for hundreds of years.

5. "Underdeveloped" means that most Africans must make a poor living by simple farming methods. The hand hoe is the main tool. They have few work animals to help them and little or no fertilizer. The result, of course, is low crop yield. In some places, Africans do not even produce enough food to feed themselves. There is also a lack of water at certain times.

6. "Underdeveloped" means the poor use of

Wash day along the shores of the Senegal River.

UNITED NATIONS

410

A Nigerian railroadman drives a new diesel locomotive past a village of mud huts.

An English class in a small village in Cameroun.

human resources. Until now, most Africans were not taught how to read and write. Part of this failure can be traced to the colonial governments that did not provide enough schools. However, there is a strong drive to change this situation at once. Aware of the need to read and write, many of the new African governments are setting aside more and more money to build elementary schools for their children. Africans feel that schooling will help them to be better farmers, to operate machines in factories, to run railroads or pilot airplanes. (Ghana, for example, has its own airline with native pilots.) It will help them to learn how government works.

7. As we have learned, "underdeveloped" means poor health for most Africans. Good health for all the people is another important goal of African leaders. Diet is being improved. Through the use of DDT, mosquitoes that carry diseases are being killed. The brush and jungle where the tsetse fly breeds are being burned. More children are being vaccinated. Hospitals are being built so that there will be doctors for the people. The power of the witch doctor is dying out. People are moving to the cities where modern comforts are available. The "old Africa" is slowly being limited to the villages far inland.

8. "Underdeveloped" also means few factories. Most African countries export their raw materials. For example, Ghana produces half the world's cacao beans. Yet, if a child of Ghana wants chocolate candy, it must come from abroad. Africans want to process their own goods and materials at home and then ship them abroad. Water power must also be developed. Where once people traveled over jungle trails and down streams, many miles of roads must be built. Already, air transportation has become an important factor in African trade. These are some of the things that must be done to lead Africa into the modern world.

African doctors examine specimens from cases of sleeping sickness in Togo.

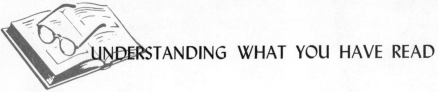

UNDERSTANDING WHAT YOU HAVE READ

1. **Which of the following questions are answered in this chapter?**
a. How can we help African nations solve their problems?
b. How is the health of Africans being improved?
c. What are Africa's major problems?

2. **The main idea of this chapter is to describe:**
a. the greatest needs of the African people.
b. the effect of climate on the African people.
c. Africa's relations with the rest of the world.

3. **One of the chief needs of African nations today is to:**
a. export food.
b. encourage home manufacturing.
c. begin a factory system to use their resources.

4. **The main tool of the African farmer is the:**

a. tractor.　　b. bulldozer.　　c. hand hoe.

5. **Africa supports such a small population because:**
a. few minerals are found anywhere.
b. most of Africa is desert, rain forest and dry grasslands.
c. mountains line the coast of the oceans.

6. **Africa has remained underdeveloped for so long because:**
a. it lacks mineral resources.
b. there is little use for electric power.
c. raw materials are not used at home.

7. *Underdeveloped* **means all of these EXCEPT:**
a. people work in factories and shipping.
b. people have little opportunity to trade goods.
c. people follow a simple way of life.

DEVELOPING IDEAS AND SKILLS

Cartoon (*See p. 410.*)
1. Who is the main figure?
2. What are some of the major problems facing Africa today?

3. Why was the figure of the tsetse fly used?
4. How can we help the nations overcome some of their problems?
5. What is a good title for this cartoon?

SUMMING UP

Fact or Opinion　Tell whether these are statements of fact or merely someone's opinion.

1. Almost every part of Africa is changing in some way today.
2. Africans are not able to govern themselves.
3. Water power will become more important in Sub-Sahara Africa.

4. Most African nations depend upon a small number of crops for export.
5. The best medical care should be provided for all Africans, rich and poor.
6. The tsetse fly has discouraged the grazing of cattle in the grasslands.
7. Africans will find that living in the cities is much different from village life.
8. Every part of Africa must be free if resources are to be developed.

FOLLOW UP

I. *Underdeveloped Lands* Are these statements about underdeveloped lands *true* or *false?* Give reasons for your answers.

1. The climate is too difficult for the people to raise their standard of living.
2. The average income of the people is low.
3. South America has some countries that can be called underdeveloped.
4. Only a small number of the world's people live in underdeveloped lands.
5. The greatest number of people in Africa are poor.
6. Most Africans have the opportunity to become leaders in their governments.
7. Canada has large areas that can be called underdeveloped.
8. All underdeveloped nations are near the equator.

9. African farmers use little machinery.
10. People are chiefly concerned with raising crops for sale.

II. *Who's Who* See if you can identify the following people connected with the history of Africa. Use an encyclopedia or biographical dictionary to find out about names you don't already know.

David Bruce	Haile Selassie
David Livingstone	Moise Tshombe
Albert Schweitzer	Jan Smuts
Cecil Rhodes	Alan Paton
Patrice Lumumba	Lobengula
Kwame Nkrumah	Albert Luthuli
Jomo Kenyatta	Ian Smith

Republic of South Africa: A Land Divided

PROBLEM: Why is this richest of southern African lands troubled?

READING FOR A PURPOSE:
1. What are the resources of the Republic of South Africa?
2. Who were the Boers?
3. What is apartheid?

1. To some it may seem that the Republic of South Africa is one country that is not aware of the "freedom explosion" in Africa. This nation became independent in 1910. The white people in the republic make up only one-fifth of the population. More than two-thirds of the people are Negroes. Yet South Africa's Negroes have almost no share in the government of their country. In spite of the freedom movement among its African neighbors, the Republic of South Africa has not changed its policy of keeping Negroes from having equal rights with its white citizens.

2. The Republic of South Africa is located at the southern end of the African continent. It is made up of four provinces and a "trust territory" to the west called Southwest Africa. It is the only country on the continent that is almost entirely in the middle latitudes. Except for a narrow belt of lowland along the coast, the country is a great plateau. The western and northern parts of the plateau are desert. The rest is a grassy prairie land known as the *veld*. The winds from the Indian Ocean provide this area with enough rain for farming and grazing.

3. The Dutch were the first European settlers in South Africa. In 1652, they set up a small trading post at Capetown. In the early 1800's, the British occupied Capetown and the Dutch moved north, away from British rule. The Dutch settled on the veld and called their new homelands the Orange Free State and Transvaal. While they were moving north, they defeated Bantu tribes who were moving south.

4. The Dutch farmers and herders on the veld became known as *Boers*. When gold and diamonds were discovered in the lands of the Boers (1886), the British moved into their land. Before long, a war broke out between the Dutch descendants and the British. After several years of fighting, the Boers were defeated. All the provinces were united into a new self-governing part of the British Commonwealth. Today the Republic of South Africa is completely independent. In 1961, South Africa left the British "family" of nations because the British opposed its policy toward Negroes.

Capetown, chief seaport of the Republic of South Africa.

South African Railways

414

The landing of the Dutch at Capetown in 1652.

5. Because of its natural resources, South Africa has become the richest country in Africa. Gold and diamonds are mined, and these industries are very important. The gold fields near Johannesburg are the richest in Africa. South Africa also has iron and coal. There are many factories that produce textiles, chemicals and automobiles. There is a modern transportation system. This republic has the highest standard of living on the continent—for its white people. It has the largest cities in Sub-Sahara Africa. Johannesburg has a population of more than a million. Other large cities are Capetown, Durban and Pretoria, the capital.

6. Despite the fact that it is the richest nation on the continent, the Republic of South Africa has a serious problem. The policy of the government is *apartheid,* or separation of races. The government does not want equality between Negro and white. As a result, the Bantu natives of South Africa live on *reserves* that have been set aside for them. The soil and pasture land in the reserves are poor and it is hard for the native people to make a living. Many leave the reserves in search of a better living. Some move to the large cities, others to farms and mines owned by Europeans. When the Bantus move to the cities, they must live apart from the white people. Many of their homes are in slum areas. Now there are about six million Bantus living in the cities. Many

are forgetting their old tribal ways of living.

7. What does apartheid mean to the Negro people of South Africa? It means that they live in two worlds. During the day, they work in the white world of skyscraper offices, department stores, factories and warehouses. When night comes, they must return to the all-black world of the Bantu reserve or section of the city. It means that they receive lower wages than white workers. Many are probably unable to read and write, for little schooling is provided for them. They are not able to vote and cannot take an active part in the government. When they move from one part of the city to the other, they are forced to have a special pass.

8. To Americans, and to most other people all over the world, apartheid is wrong and should be ended. But the white people of South Africa think differently. They believe that South Africa is theirs because they have worked and lived in it for many years. They feel they have the right to control the land and its resources. They feel that if Negroes vote, they will lose their rights because there are more Negroes than whites.

9. The Negro Africans do not like apartheid, for they feel that it is close to slavery. There have been many protests. Some of the demonstrations have led to bloodshed. The policy of the government toward South African Negroes has brought criticism from other parts of the world. The United Nations has asked South Africa to end apartheid and to give up its colony of Southwest Africa.

Africans coming into Johannesburg to go to work.

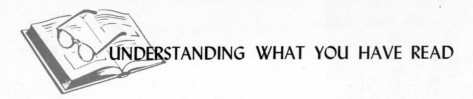

UNDERSTANDING WHAT YOU HAVE READ

1. Which of the following questions are answered in this chapter?
   a. Why do we say that the Republic of South Africa is rich?
   b. Where do many native people live?
   c. How are the people governed?

2. The main idea of this chapter is to describe:
   a. the meaning of apartheid.
   b. the large cities of South Africa.
   c. ways of living in South Africa.

3. Most of the people of South Africa are:
   a. Negroes.   b. Europeans.   c. Asians.

4. The only city in Sub-Sahara Africa with more than one million people is:
   a. Nairobi.
   b. Leopoldville.
   c. Johannesburg.

5. We call the Republic of South Africa a rich country because:
   a. it has many natural resources.
   b. there is a great deal of fertile farm land.
   c. it has a democratic form of government.

6. There is unrest in the Republic of South Africa because:
   a. the government has changed often.
   b. the policy of apartheid separates people.
   c. there is no religious freedom.

7. A policy of *apartheid* means:
   a. equal rights.
   b. separation of races.
   c. religious persecution.

8. The Bantu tribes live on *reserves.* "Reserves" are:
   a. crowded sections of cities.
   b. river boats.
   c. lands set aside for farming and herding.

DEVELOPING IDEAS AND SKILLS

Map # 48a and b—Republic of South Africa and United States
Can you answer these questions?
1. In which direction is the equator from the Republic of South Africa?
2. Is the Republic of South Africa in the high, middle or low latitudes?
3. The Orange River flows into which body of water?
4. Are there any independent countries bordering the Republic of South Africa?
5. What is the latitude and longitude of the city of Durban?
6. Why do you think there are only a few large seaports in the Republic?
7. How does the map show you why early settlers remained near the coast?
8. The United States is how many times as large as the Republic of South Africa?
9. If you flew from your community to Capetown, in which direction would you be traveling?
10. Why has a large city grown inland at Johannesburg?

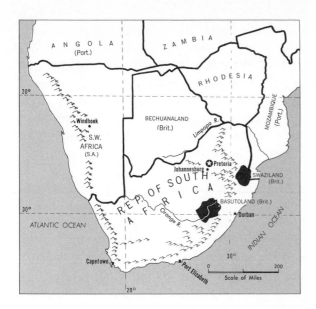

UNITED STATES
POPULATION: 191 MILLION
LAND AREA: 3.6 MILLION SQUARE MILES
54 PEOPLE PER SQUARE MILE

REP. OF SOUTH AFRICA
POPULATION: 17.1 MILLION
LAND AREA: 472,400 SQUARE MILES
36 PEOPLE PER SQUARE MILE

Map # 48a and b—Republic of South Africa and United States

SUMMING UP

Complete the following chart in your notebook.

	REPUBLIC OF SOUTH AFRICA
1. Location	
2. Size	
3. People	
4. Resources	
5. Problems	

FOLLOW UP

Tell whether these statements are true or false. The underlined words make the statements true or false. If a statement is false, what word or words would you place in the statement to make it true?

1. The largest city in South Africa is <u>Capetown</u>.
2. The first white settlers of South Africa were <u>French</u>.
3. The <u>veld</u> is the farming and grazing land of South Africa.
4. The separation of races is known as <u>apartheid</u>.
5. The greatest number of people in the Republic of South Africa are the <u>Dutch</u>.
6. South Africa is bordered on the east by the <u>Indian Ocean</u>.
7. Most of the Republic of South Africa is located in the <u>middle</u> latitudes.
8. Before it became free, South Africa was ruled by <u>Great Britain</u>.
9. One of South Africa's great riches is <u>oil</u>.
10. The <u>Boers</u> were Dutch farmers in South Africa.

CHAPTER 12

Ghana: Africa Awakening!

PROBLEM: Can Ghana become one of Africa's leading nations?

READING FOR A PURPOSE:
1. When did Ghana win its freedom?
2. How is Ghana governed?
3. What are Ghana's chief exports?

1. Ghana was the first Negro nation in Africa to win its freedom from its European rulers. Ghana's people today are working hard to develop their land. There are many schools, fine roads, new hospitals and airfields, radios, telephones and modern buildings in its cities. The people are greatly interested in making their new government work. How have these changes come about?

2. The nation of Ghana is not far north of the equator. It lies almost in the center of the countries along the Gulf of Guinea. It is not a crowded country. Its population of about seven million lives in an area about the size of our state of Wyoming. Except for the sandy coast in the south and plateau in the north, most of Ghana is low forest-covered hills. Many rivers and streams crisscross the plateau. The chief river is the Volta. It rises in the country of Upper Volta to the north and flows southeastward to the sea.

3. There are heavy rains in the southwest of Ghana—as much as 100 inches a year. This is the rain forest. Most of Ghana, however, has a savanna climate. The savanna woodlands lie north of the rain forest. There are two seasons, wet and dry. During the wet season—the summer—the woodlands turn green and the rivers overflow their banks.

4. Portuguese sailors reached this part of Africa at the end of the 15th century. They were looking for gold, ivory, spices and slaves. So much gold was found and taken out that this country was called the Gold Coast. The Portuguese traders became so rich that the English, French, Dutch and Germans followed. In 1886, the coastal area became a British colony. The British gradually extended their power and territory northward.

5. When the British first came to the Gold Coast, they found they had to do certain things to get the raw materials out of the forests. They needed men to work in offices. They had to build schools and train people for jobs. They educated many Africans for leadership. These educated Africans gradually became unhappy with the rule of the British. During World War II, they fought on the side of the British, but they came back after the war filled with new ideas. They had fought for freedom; now they wanted it for their own land. In March, 1957, the Gold Coast became independent of Great Britain. The name of the country was changed to Ghana, the name of an ancient and powerful Negro kingdom. Ghana's "father of independence" was Kwame Nkrumah. Ghana is a member of the British Commonwealth of Nations.

6. Ghana has a written constitution. It pro-

Wide World Photos

Ghana's Kwame Nkrumah speaking to the U.N. General Assembly.

vides for a strong central government. The head of the government is the president. He has more powers than our president. The chief lawmaking body is the National Assembly, elected every five years by the people. There is only one house and only one political party. Under this form of government, the tribal chiefs have little power. There is a greater control over the life of the people by the government. Kwame Nkrumah has said that Ghana will remain neutral in the Cold War. However, there are some who believe that the country is more friendly with the Soviet Union than it is with the West.

7. Most Ghanian people are Negroes. The most powerful of the country's many tribes is the Ashanti. While English is the official language, many of the tribes speak their own languages. The religion of most Ghanians is the religion of their tribe, although there are many Christians and Moslems. Ghanians wear the most colorful dress in Africa. Their native dress is a many-colored robe called the "kenti." Modern dress is worn in the cities, but visitors will see many people in the gay colors of the kenti. The chief city and capital is Accra.

Most of Ghana's people are small farmers who own their own lands. The chief crop is cacao. It makes up seventy per cent of Ghana's exports. Palm oil, nuts, coconuts (copra) and cotton are also exported. For food, the people grow cassava, maize, yams and plantains (a fruit like a banana). Most villagers raise sheep, goats and chickens as a source of meat. Fishing and cattle-raising are growing in importance. The government is also setting up a number of state farms. The average income of a Ghanian worker is about $150 per year.

9. Before Ghana became free, most of its wealth came from its farms, chiefly from the growing of cacao. Today, the government is trying to develop other resources. Timber is being cut from the forest lands. Minerals such as gold, industrial diamonds, bauxite and manganese are being mined and exported. With the help of money from the United States, Ghana has built a dam on the Volta River. Opened in 1965, it provides water for irrigation and electric power. The electric power will be used to change bauxite into aluminum. Every month, new plants are opened for the production of such items as matches, paper, tobacco products and insecticides (insect killers).

A school in Ghana open to children of all races.

UNITED NATIONS

A health worker in Ghana sprays a village to destroy disease-carrying mosquitoes.

10. Independence has done much for the people of Ghana. Although schools had been started by the British government and missionaries, it is the new nation that is ending illiteracy through education for all. There are two fine universities, and a third one is planned. With the help of the Peace Corps, leaders are being trained for the government. Hospitals and clinics are being built to improve health conditions. Doctors are fighting sleeping sickness, malaria and tuberculosis, the three chief killers.

11. In Ghana, as in many nations of Africa, most new industries have been started by the government. Leaders no longer want their resources to be controlled by outsiders. Despite this development, however, much of Ghana is still influenced by Great Britain and the United States. Many of the government officers were educated in Britain. English books and magazines and American films, foods and clothing are plentiful. English is the language of business, government and the schools. Ghana still has strong ties with the Western world.

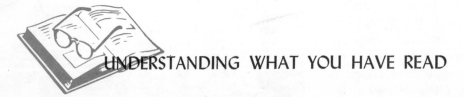

UNDERSTANDING WHAT YOU HAVE READ

1. Which of the following questions are answered in this chapter?
   a. Which Negro kingdoms once ruled Ghana?
   b. What are the chief minerals of Ghana?
   c. Who is Kwame Nkrumah?

2. The main idea of *paragraph 6* is to describe the:
   a. power of Kwame Nkrumah.
   b. nation's system of government.
   c. place of Ghana in the "Cold War."

420

3. **The main idea of *paragraph 9* is to describe:**

a. the Volta River dam.

b. the importance of the sale of cacao.

c. other resources of Ghana.

4. **The old name for Ghana was:**

a. Gold Coast.   b. Mali.   c. Upper Volta.

5. **One of Ghana's farm problems is that:**

a. the land is not owned by the people.

b. the rain forest is of little use.

c. there is too much dependence on cacao.

6. **Ghana's freedom was important in the history of Africa because:**

a. Ghana was the first nation in the world to become free after World War II.

b. Ghana was the first Negro colony to become free.

c. Ghana's freedom ended British rule in Africa.

7. **The government of Ghana has built the Volta River dam to:**

a. provide more electric power.

b. increase the importance of ocean-fishing.

c. change the course of the river.

8. **If *homicide* means "to kill a human being," then *insecticide* means:**

a. "to kill insects."

b. "man-eating insects."

c. "plants that live on insects."

Map # 49a and b—Ghana and the United States

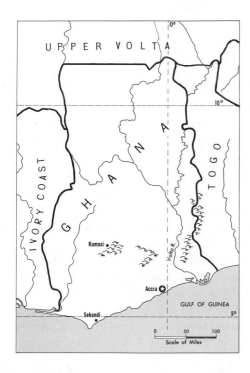

WYOMING
POPULATION: 0.3 MILLION
LAND AREA: 97,400 SQUARE MILES
3 PEOPLE PER SQUARE MILE

GHANA
POPULATION: 7.3 MILLION
LAND AREA: 91,800 SQUARE MILES
79.5 PEOPLE PER SQUARE MILE

DEVELOPING IDEAS AND SKILLS

Map # 49a and b—Ghana and the United States
Can you answer these questions?

1. Is Ghana north or south of the equator?

2. Is Ghana located in the high, middle or low latitudes?

3. What does the location of Ghana tell you about its climate?

4. What is the important river of Ghana? In what direction does it flow?

5. What is the distance from the northern border to the southern border?

6. What is the capital city of Ghana?

7. Which is more thickly populated, Ghana or our state of Wyoming? Ghana or the United States?

8. How would you describe the topography of Ghana?

SUMMING UP

Complete the following chart in your notebook. Head it, "Some New Nations of Africa." Use an almanac, an encyclopedia or an atlas to get additional facts.

NEW NATION	CLIMATE	LAND	PEOPLE AND GOVERNMENT	RESOURCES
Ghana				
Ivory Coast				
Nigeria				
Kenya				
Zambia				

FOLLOW UP

I. *True or False*   The following statements are true or false. The underlined words make the statements true or false. If a statement is false, what word or words would you place in it to make it true?

1. Most of Ghana has a desert climate.
2. The first Europeans to be interested in Ghana were from France.
3. Ghana's "father of independence" is Kwame Nkrumah.
4. The chief export crop of Ghana is copra.
5. Most people of Ghana are Negroes.
6. The capital of Ghana is Accra.
7. Most of the power of the government is in the hands of the president.
8. The official language of Ghana is French.
9. Ghana was a member of the British Commonwealth of Nations.
10. Most Ghanians are small farmers.

II. *Fact or Opinion*   Can you decide which are statements of fact and which are someone's opinion?

1. Kwame Nkrumah has done more for Ghana than the British did.
2. Some of the tribes would like to have more power in the government.
3. The education of the people is improving year by year.
4. The new Volta Dam will make Ghana the richest nation in western Africa.
5. Ghana is a member of the United Nations.
6. Ghana would become richer if the cotton industry were developed.
7. Only a small part of Ghana borders the sea.
8. Ghana cannot stay neutral in the "Cold War" for very long.

BOOKS FOR UNIT 7

Author	Title, Publisher	Description
1. Ames, Sophia	*Nkrumah of Ghana,* Rand McNally	A biography of the leader of Ghanian independence.
2. Arnold, Richard	*The True Story of David Livingstone, Explorer,* Childrens Press	The story of the missionary doctor who mapped the unknown regions of central Africa.
3. Busoni, Rafaello	*Stanley's Africa,* Viking	How the "Dark Continent" was opened to the world.
4. Gatti, Attilio and Ellen	*The New Africa,* Scribner	The birth of the new nations in modern Africa.
5. Gibbs, Peter	*The True Story of Cecil Rhodes in Africa,* Childrens Press	The Englishman who dreamed of an empire in southern Africa.
6. Kenworthy, Leonard	*Leaders of New Nations,* Doubleday	A report of the men who lead the new Africa.
7. Mennett, John	*Albert Schweitzer, Humanitarian,* Childrens Press	The story of the doctor who devoted his life to helping the people in West Africa.
8. Mirsky, Reba	*Seven Grandmothers,* Follett	Life among the Zulu people of Africa.
9. Nevins, Albert	*Away to East Africa,* Dodd	The everyday life of the peoples of East Africa.
10. Plimpton, Ruth	*Operation Crossroads Africa,* Viking	The story of young American volunteers in Africa.
11. Spencer, Cornelia	*Claim to Freedom,* John Day	The awakening of new nations in Africa and Asia.
12. Turnbull, Colin	*The Peoples of Africa,* World	A description of the hunters, herdsmen and farmers of the continent.
13. Waldeck, Theodore	*Lions on the Hunt,* Viking	A story of the South African veld.

UNIT 8

The Far East

CHAPTER 1

Lands of the Rising Sun

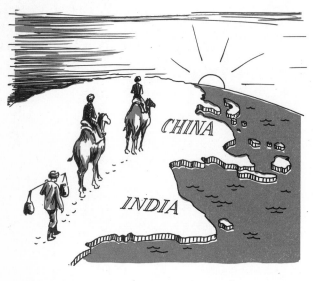

PROBLEM: Why are we interested in the Far East?

READING FOR A PURPOSE:
1. What do we mean by the Far East?
2. Why is this area called the Far East?
3. When did mainland China become Communist?

1. The Far East is the home of *half* the people of the world. Many of them are poor and hungry. These billion-and-a-half people live in a vast region extending over 4,000 miles, from Pakistan on the west to the Philippine Islands on the east. What's more, the Far East is a region of great change. Most of the people live under new governments whose leaders are hopeful of providing them with a better way of life. Millions of people throughout Asia and the rest of the world are watching to see how these new nations will develop.

2. The Far East is often divided into three parts. First, there is the Indian peninsula, which is so big that it is sometimes called a subcontinent—that is, almost a continent. This area includes the countries of India, Pakistan and Ceylon, an island nation. Eastward are the smaller nations of Southeast Asia, the second part. This includes the island republics of Indonesia and the Philippines and a Texas-sized peninsula divided among the countries of Burma, Thailand (Siam), Malaysia and the countries of what was Indochina (Cambodia, Laos, North and South Vietnam). Northward in the third part are the countries of eastern Asia: China, North and South Korea, and the easternmost islands of Japan and Taiwan (Formosa).

3. The whole region is called the Far East because it lies far to the east of Europe. These lands were visited by Marco Polo in the thirteenth century. When he returned to Europe, he described the riches of these far-away lands. The term "Far East" was used by early merchants who traveled to these lands in search of the goods described by Marco Polo. Part of this region is called the Orient, because the word means "the East." It is also called "Land of the Rising Sun" because the sun "appears" first in this part of the world.

4. The Far Eastern countries vary in size. The largest country in the region is Red China, which is the third largest nation in the world. The second largest country in the Far East is India. Together with Pakistan, this *subcontinent* is about half the size of the entire United States. Indonesia is not much larger than our state of Alaska, but its many islands extend

A village market in India. The Far East contains more than half the world's people.

Unloading bales of jute in Pakistan.

over 3,000 miles from east to west. The Philippines is not much larger than our state of Colorado, but its islands reach about 1,100 miles north and south. Japan, the richest country of the Far East, is about as large as our state of Montana.

5. The United States is interested in the Far East for many reasons. First, we get many valuable raw materials from the people of the Orient—tin, rubber, silk, quinine, spices and jute. In exchange, we send them the manufactured goods of our factories. Our trade with Japan is greater than our trade with either Great Britain or West Germany.

6. Second, the United States is concerned about the growing power of Communist China in the countries of the Far East. The Communists took over China in 1949. The former Nationalist government of Chiang Kai-shek moved to the island of Formosa or Taiwan. Now about 700 million people live under the rule of the Communist Party in China. This government is not recognized by the United States. In 1964, Red China became the only Asian nation to explode an atom bomb.

7. Red China is using its growing power throughout the region. In 1950, Chinese soldiers fought United Nations troops in Korea. In 1962, they battled Indian soldiers along the Himalayan border. They are giving support to local Communists and to "civil wars" in the smaller countries of Southeast Asia.

8. While Red China, North Korea and North Vietnam have Communist governments, other Asian nations are trying to develop a democratic way of life. These are the nations of India, Japan, the Philippines and some of the nations of Southeast Asia. (The Philippines was given its independence by the United States in 1946.) They need time to develop their resources and to give their people a better way of life. If they fail, much of the Far East will be closed to the people of the free world. American soldiers and arms have been sent to Southeast Asia to help keep South Vietnam free of communism.

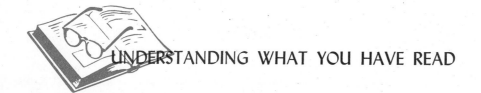

UNDERSTANDING WHAT YOU HAVE READ

1. Which of the following questions are answered in this chapter?
a. Why are we interested in the Far East?
b. What were the results of the Korean War?
c. What government has headquarters on Formosa?

2. The main idea of this chapter is to describe:
a. how the new nations of the Far East have won their freedom.
b. why the Far East is important to us.
c. the growing power of Red China.

3. The largest country of the Far East is:

a. India.   b. Indonesia.   c. Red China.

4. Most of the countries of the Far East are part of the continent of:

a. Asia.   b. Australia.   c. Africa.

5. Why are these lands called the Far East?

a. They lie far to the east of Europe.

b. The sun rises in the east.

c. The Pacific Ocean is east of the mainland.

6. Why are India, Japan and the Philippines of unusual interest to us?

a. All are island groups off eastern Asia.

b. All have had civil wars in the past few years.

c. All are trying to make democratic governments work.

7. The *Orient* is the same as the:

a. West.   b. East.   c. North.

8. A *subcontinent* is:

a. like an archipelago.

b. land "below" the equator.

c. a body of land almost as large as a continent.

Map # 50—The Far East

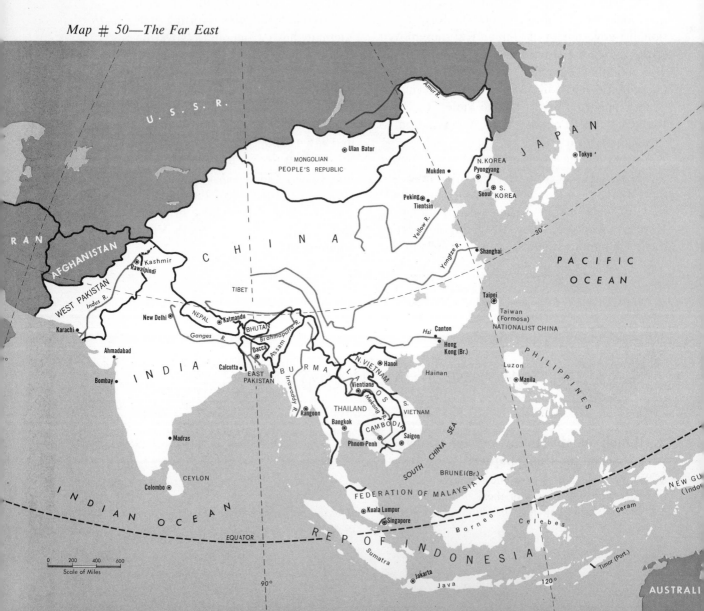

DEVELOPING IDEAS AND SKILLS

Map # 50—The Far East

Can you answer these questions?

1. Is the region north or south of the equator?
2. Is the region east or west of the Prime Meridian?
3. How far north and south does the region extend?
4. Does the region extend farther from east to west or from north to south?
5. What region or regions are near it?
6. What is the largest country? The smallest?
7. What are the chief bodies of water that border the region?
8. Are there countries in it that have no outlets to the sea?
9. What are some of the important rivers in the region?
10. Are there large rivers that form boundary lines between countries?
11. What is the capital city of each country? How do you know they are the capitals? How many are sea or river ports?
12. Are there any island nations?
13. Are there countries that are located on peninsulas?
14. Are there any lands that are colonies of other nations?

SUMMING UP

Reasons for Our Interest in the Far East In your notebook, copy the following and place a check (✔) next to those items that are reasons for our interest in this region.

___ The power of communism is spreading in the Far East.

___ Half the people of the world live there.

___ The Suez Canal is an important waterway.

___ Our troops are fighting in the Far East.

___ These people are customers for our manufactured goods.

___ Many Far Eastern nations have won their freedom lately.

___ There are many raw materials there that we need.

___ In this region the Industrial Revolution began.

FOLLOW UP

Match the items in Column B with the countries in Column A.

COLUMN A	COLUMN B
1. Red China	a. Government of Nationalist China.
2. Japan	b. Island republic that once belonged to the United States.
3. Formosa	c. Center of a civil war supported by Communists.
4. India	d. Largest Communist country.
5. Vietnam	e. Carries on greatest trade with the United States.
6. The Philippines	f. Negro republic.
	g. Occupies a subcontinent.

CHAPTER 2

Crowded Islands and Valleys

PROBLEM: What is the topography of the Far East?

READING FOR A PURPOSE:
1. What are the highest mountains in the world?
2. What are the great rivers of the Far East?
3. What is an archipelago?

1. Much of the Far East is mountainous. The inner highlands of the Far East are the highest in the world. In the south are the Himalaya Mountains. These mountains extend east and west for 1500 miles, separating India from the countries to the north. Mount Everest, in the Himalayas, is the highest mountain peak in the world. In the middle of these great mountains is the lonely Plateau of Tibet. This plateau, about 16,000 feet above sea level, is sometimes called the "roof of the world."

2. Ranges of high mountains continue from Tibet southward across the Malay Peninsula.

There they drop below the surface of the seas and appear again above water to form the main islands of Southeast Asia. Another mountain range runs eastward through the center of China, dividing it into two regions. In general, however, the land slopes downward from the inner highlands until it reaches the great Chinese plains in the north and the Pacific Ocean in the south.

3. Many rivers rise in the mountains of the Far East and form plains as they flow toward the oceans. The lowlands formed by these rivers are bordered by hills and low mountains. Millions of people in the Far East are crowded into these river valleys, working the fertile land. The rivers bring the rich soil of the mountains into the valleys and supply water to irrigate the crops.

4. Three major rivers rise in the Himalayas —the Ganges, the Brahmaputra and the Indus. The Ganges flows across northern India, forming a great lowland plain. It flows southeastward and empties into the Indian Ocean near the city of Calcutta. The Brahmaputra flows southwestward from the northern mountains and joins the Ganges in East Pakistan. The Indus flows through the dry lands of West Pakistan and empties into the Arabian Sea.

5. China has three great rivers that rise in

A fertile terraced area in a Philippine valley.
UNATIONS

The Himalayas of northern India.

the mountains to the west. The Hwang, or Yellow, River begins in the Plateau of Tibet and flows through northern China to the sea. (The region through which it flows is covered with a fine yellow dust called *loess*. As it flows through the loess hills, the river picks up the yellow dirt. Thus, it has been given the name of Yellow River.) The Hwang is not a deep river. When there are heavy rains, the river overflows its banks and floods the land. For this reason it is sometimes called "China's Sorrow."

6. The Yangtze, the fourth longest river in the world, is China's longest and most useful river. It rises in Tibet and flows eastward to the sea near the city of Shanghai. The Yangtze is comparable to our Mississippi. Along this waterway, one-tenth of all the world's people live. The Yangtze is connected to the Hwang by a canal. Farther south is the Hsi River, flowing into the sea near the city of Canton.

7. Several large rivers also flow southward across the vast peninsula of Southeast Asia. The Irrawaddy, Mekong and Red Rivers rise in the Himalayas. They form broad valleys and deltas as they flow toward the sea. These valleys are separated by rugged mountain ranges.

8. Off the mainland of southern and eastern Asia are thousands of islands. These groups of islands are called *archipelagoes*. The main archipelagoes are Japan, the Philippines and Indonesia. A large number of these islands have volcanoes. The lava from the volcanoes has kept the soil of some of these islands very fertile.

9. Finally, one of the most striking features of this region is that, like Western Europe, there

A small fishing village on the Mekong River, Cambodia. Many people in the Far East live in river valleys.

are so many peninsulas. India is almost completely surrounded by water as it reaches out into the ocean. The Malay-Indochina peninsula is very heavily populated. It is near the important trade routes that lead to the great city-state of Singapore. The Korean peninsula has long been a center of dispute between Japan, China and the Soviet Union. Many of these peninsulas are near much-traveled bodies of water and are therefore important in world trade.

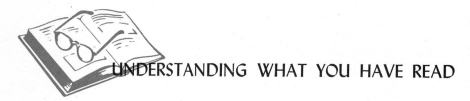

UNDERSTANDING WHAT YOU HAVE READ

1. **Which of the following questions are answered in this chapter?**
   a. Why are the rivers of Asia important?
   b. When was Mount Everest first climbed?
   c. How does the Yellow River cause sorrow?

2. **The main idea of this chapter is to describe:**
   a. the topography of the Far East.
   b. the chief rivers of the Far East.
   c. the mountains of the Far East.

3. **The highest mountain chain in the world is the:**
   a. Rockies.　　b. Andes.　　c. Himalayas.

4. **The city of Calcutta is located near the mouth of which river?**
   a. The Ganges.
   b. The Yangtze.
   c. The Mekong.

5. **The rivers are important to the people** of the Far East for all these reasons EXCEPT:
   a. they furnish rich soil for farming.
   b. they serve as boundaries between countries.
   c. they provide water for irrigation.

6. **Rivers are said to have the opposite effect of mountains because:**
   a. rivers are a source of great mineral wealth.
   b. mountains have kept people apart; rivers have brought people together.
   c. the mountains of the Far East have the best soils.

7. **The word *loess* would have most meaning to a:**
   a. farmer.　　b. factory worker.　　c. fisherman.

8. **A group of islands surrounded by a large body of water is:**
   a. a continent.
   b. an archipelago.
   c. a peninsula.

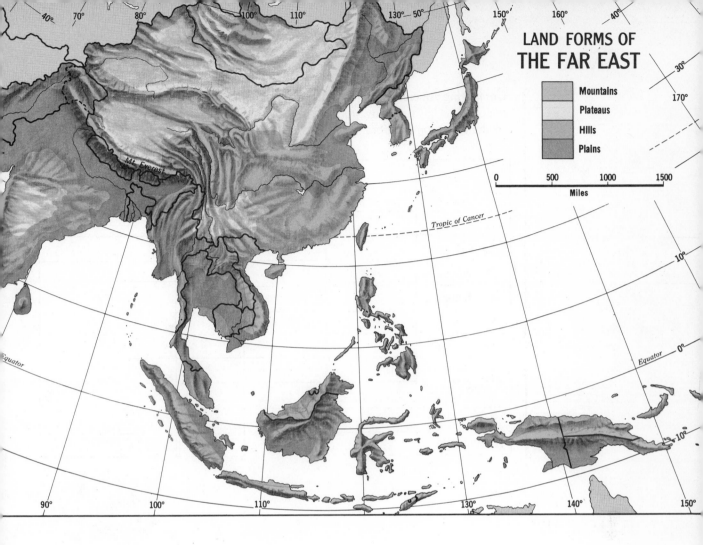

LAND FORMS OF
THE FAR EAST

Mountains
Plateaus
Hills
Plains

0   500   1000   1500
Miles

DEVELOPING IDEAS AND SKILLS

Map # 51—Land Forms of the Far East

Tell whether these statements are *true* or *false*. Be able to explain your answers.

1. Much of the Indian peninsula is a plateau.
2. Mountains are found on all the important islands of the Far East.
3. Japan has more lowland area than any other land form.
4. Lowland makes up a small part of the total land area of China.
5. A long, narrow plain stretches from north to south along the eastern coast of Asia.
6. There are fewer plains in the Far East than any other land form.

SUMMING UP

Comparing Rivers   Complete the following chart in your notebook. Refer to the regions you have already studied. If you need more information, use an almanac in the classroom or library.

RIVER	CONTINENT	LENGTH	MOUTH	KIND OF REGION THROUGH WHICH IT FLOWS
1. Yellow				
2. Yangtze				
3. Ganges				
4. Mekong				
5. Mississippi				
6. Amazon				
7. Nile				
8. Congo				
9. Danube				
10. Ob				

FOLLOW UP

Complete the following sentences in your notebook.

1. The _____ are the highest mountains in the world.
2. The Plateau of _____ is sometimes called the "roof of the world."
3. A great number of the island mountains are ____.
4. The great northern plain of India is formed by the _____ River.
5. Most of the people who live in the river valleys make a living by _____.
6. Two large archipelagoes of the Far East are Japan and _____.
7. The great port of _____ is located at the southern end of the Malay Peninsula.
8. The island of _____ is located at the southern end of the Indian peninsula.

CHAPTER 3

Monsoon Asia

PROBLEM: How do the climates of the Far East affect the way people live?

READING FOR A PURPOSE:
1. Where is the Asian rain forest?
2. What are the monsoons?
3. Where is the Gobi Desert?

1. As you might guess, a region as large as the Far East has many kinds of climate. The Far East extends from the equator a great distance north. From Indonesia in the south to the Chinese-Soviet border is a distance of more than 60 degrees! This is the same distance as from the tropics of Brazil to Newfoundland, Canada. In the second place, much of the region is mountainous. Also, many of the land areas border or are surrounded by large bodies of water.

2. The equator passes through the southern part of this region. Indonesia, Malaysia, Ceylon and much of the Philippines, Southeast Asia and southern India are all within fifteen degrees of the equator. Indonesia, Malaysia and the Philippines are hot and rainy the year round. (Mountains provide some relief from the heat.) There is thick jungle and a year-round growing season. The heavy rains wash minerals from the soil. This is the same kind of climate as is found in the Amazon Basin in South America and the Congo in Africa; it is the rain forest.

3. In many ways, however, the rain forest of Southeast Asia is different from the others we have studied. One of the chief differences is caused by the land itself. The Amazon and Congo forests are within the hearts of their continents. In Southeast Asia, this climate is found largely on islands off the mainland. Again, in the Amazon and Congo, the land is largely lowland plains. The Asian rain-forest lands are mountainous. Around the mountain "centers" of the islands is a narrow belt of hilly lands, next to which are the coastal plains.

4. The rain forests of Asia support a huge population. Some of the fertile areas of rain forest in Southeast Asia have more people for each square mile of land than any other farming area in the world! These people have cleared more land in the Asian forests than have the people of either the Amazon or the Congo. The example that the people of Southeast Asia have set gives hope that the Amazon and Congo rain forests will some day contain more people and be more productive.

5. North of the rain forest, the tropical savanna climate is found. As in other savanna regions, there is a wet and a dry season. This climate is found in most of India, Ceylon, Burma, Thailand and the new countries of Southeast Asia. These lands are affected by winds called *monsoons*. The monsoons are winds that blow steadily either from the water or from the land for several weeks at a time. During the summer, the winds blow from the ocean to the land; they are hot and rainy. During the winter, they blow from the land to the sea; they are dry and cold.

6. The reasons for the monsoon winds are easy to understand. Land heats more quickly than water. During the summer months, the hot

A Philippine rain forest cleared for farming. The stumps will be burned for fertilizer, but the heavy rains will wash it away with the topsoil.

rays of the sun beat down on the lands of Southeast Asia. The air is also heated. The warm air then rises because it is lighter. Because the ocean waters are cooler than the land, the ocean air remains cool and heavy. When the warm land air rises, the cool air over the oceans rushes toward the land to take the place of the rising warm air. It brings rain to the land. This rainfall takes place from May to October. During the winter months, the monsoon winds change because the land becomes cooler than the water. The air over the ocean is then warmer than the air over the land. The warm ocean air rises and the cooler land air moves in to take its place, making dry winds. These blow from November to March.

7. The people of Southeast Asia cannot get along without the monsoons. In May, they begin to watch the skies for the coming of the summer monsoons. The summer winds bring rain and the land becomes green again. Without this rain, the crops would fail. The farmers try to save some of the water in small tanks or reservoirs. If there is too little or too much rain, or if it is too late, farmers can be ruined.

8. In southeastern China and in parts of Japan, the climate is humid subtropical. This region is much like our southeastern states. The summers are long, hot and rainy. The winters are mild and there is less rain. This makes for a long, moist growing season. Southern China is a rice-growing region. (You will remember that rice can also be grown in our southeastern states from South Carolina to Louisiana.)

9. Farther north in China and Japan, the climate is like that of the northeastern United States. Peking, China, is the same distance from the equator as New York City is, while the boundary between North and South Korea is 38° North Latitude. There are long, cold winters, hot summers, and enough rainfall to support crops. Near the sea, the temperatures are milder throughout the year. In the mountains, the cold of winter is very severe. The lower rainfall in the north has made this an area of wheat growing.

10. Most of western China lies in the dry regions of Asia. Almost half of this land is desert; the other part is a region of grassy steppes. (Grass will grow where the rainfall is at least ten inches a year.) The desert areas are almost completely surrounded by mountains, which keep out the rain-bearing winds. The Gobi Desert of northwestern China is one of the loneliest places on earth. Few people live there. In West Pakistan there is another vast dry region. The Indus River is important, for it provides water for irrigation.

UNDERSTANDING WHAT YOU HAVE READ

1. **Which of the following questions are answered in this chapter?**
   a. When was the Asian rain forest cleared?
   b. What causes the monsoon winds?
   c. Why is the Gobi Desert such a dry place?

2. **The main idea of this chapter is to describe:**
   a. the effects of the monsoons.
   b. the various climates of the Far East.
   c. how mountains affect climate.

3. **The climate of many lands of Southeast Asia is affected by the:**
   a. monsoons.
   b. Himalayas.
   c. winds from Siberia.

4. **Southeastern China has a climate like that of:**
   a. Oregon and Washington.
   b. Massachusetts and New York.
   c. South Carolina and Georgia.

5. **Monsoons are important to the people of the Far East because they:**
   a. bring rain for crops.
   b. bring cool weather.
   c. bring fine soil from the interior.

6. **The Asian rain forest is more important in our changing world than the Amazon rain forest because it:**
   a. is a wonderful place for visitors to spend their vacations.
   b. is drained by a great river.
   c. supports a greater population.

7. **People in *monsoon* lands have:**
   a. rain throughout the year.
   b. a wet and dry season.
   c. only ten inches of rain a year.

Map # 52—The Monsoons

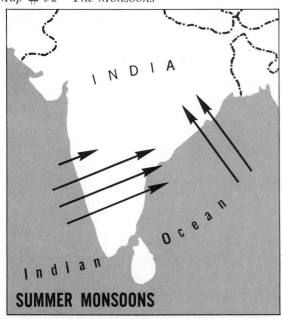

SUMMER MONSOONS

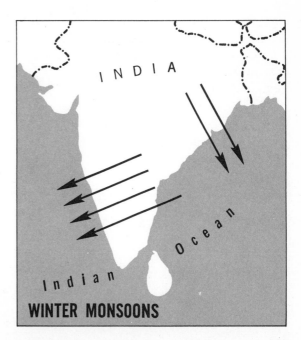

WINTER MONSOONS

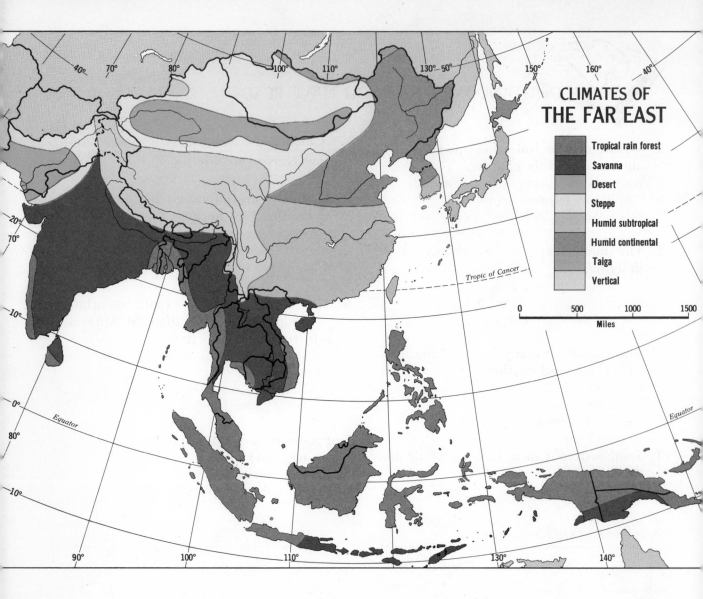

CLIMATES OF
THE FAR EAST

- Tropical rain forest
- Savanna
- Desert
- Steppe
- Humid subtropical
- Humid continental
- Taiga
- Vertical

0   500   1000   1500
Miles

Tropic of Cancer

Equator

DEVELOPING IDEAS AND SKILLS

Map # 52—The Monsoons

Can you answer these questions?

1. From which direction do the winds blow in the summer?

2. From which direction do the winds blow in the winter?

3. Which monsoons bring rain?

4. Which are the dry monsoons?

5. Do you know why this changing of wind direction takes place in India?

Map # 53—Climates of the Far East
Do You Agree or Disagree? Give reasons for your answers.

1. Almost all of the islands of Southeast Asia are located in the region of the rain forest.
2. Japan and the Philippines have climates that are very much alike.
3. Mountains cause some changes in the climate of the islands of Southeast Asia.
4. No Mediterranean climate is found in the Far East.
5. Colder areas are found in central Asia.
6. Most of the climatic regions of the Far East are in the low latitudes.
7. Nearly all of India is rain forest.
8. The differences in climate along the eastern coast of China are caused chiefly by changes in latitude.
9. This region is unusual in that deserts are located in the low latitudes.
10. The climate of northeastern China is like that of northern Canada.

SUMMING UP

Complete the following outline in your notebook.

Comparing Rain Forests—Amazon, Congo and Asian

I. How They Are Alike.
   1.
   2.
   3.

II. How the Asian Rain Forest Is Different.
   1.
   2.
   3.

FOLLOW UP

Making Inferences In our reading, many facts are given to us. From these facts we draw conclusions. The following are some conclusions or inferences that you might make after reading Chapter 3. Tell whether these conclusions are correct or incorrect. Give reasons for your answers.

1. The farmers of Indonesia and the Amazon River Valley could grow the same crops.
2. On the Gobi Desert, life would be very different from that on the Sahara in Africa.
3. A large part of the population of West Pakistan probably lives near the Indus River.
4. In Indonesia and the Philippines, temperatures throughout the year might vary from 20° to 100°
5. Throughout China, farmers will grow rice.
6. If the wet monsoon should arrive later than usual, millions of Asian people might starve.
7. The growing season in Indonesia is shorter than the growing season in northeastern China.

CHAPTER 4

Early History

PROBLEM: How did people live in the ancient lands of China and India?

READING FOR A PURPOSE:
1. Why was a government needed in the river valleys?
2. Who were the Aryans?
3. How did the Mongols affect China?

1. The ancient Chinese were almost completely shut off from the outside world by natural barriers. To the east lay the great Pacific Ocean. To the south was a dense tropical forest where elephants, tigers and other wild animals lived. The high Himalayas and the highlands of Tibet shut off the ancient people on the west. The only opening into China was through the Gobi Desert to the north. As a result, these ancient people developed their own way of life.

2. Some of the earliest civilizations known to man started in the Far East. It is believed that the art of government first began in the valley of the Yellow River and spread southward to the Yangtze River Valley. (The early Chinese people had to have laws in order to share the work of fighting floods and building canals.) It was near the Yangtze that rice became the main food of the ancient Chinese people. The rice-growers changed the land. They built terraces on the hillsides. They divided the land into hundreds of small, diked fields.

3. For much of its history China was ruled by powerful families. These ruling families were called *dynasties*. The founder of a dynasty would take and hold power over the people by means of a strong army. Over the years, the strength of his dynasty would become less and a new family would take its place. In time, another man would build up a powerful army and set up a strong government, and then his dynasty would rule for a while. This happened many times.

4. The history of China is also the history of many invasions. On the northern steppes were tribes of nomads who raised goats and sheep. These nomads often moved southward in search of better pastures for their herds. The Chinese built a great wall along their northern border to keep the nomads out. The wall did not succeed. Again and again, Chinese armies had to battle invaders from the north. Finally, a very strong tribe called the Mongols overran large parts of Asia and Russia. Their leader was Genghis Khan. About 1260, his grandson, Kublai Khan, became the ruler of all China.

Samurai warriors dressed this way in feudal Japan.

Japan Tourist Association

The Angkor ruins of Cambodia, built around 1100 by a people who lived in the rain forest.

5. The stories of Marco Polo tell us much of the size and riches of the great empire of the Mongols. Marco Polo went to the Far East with his father and uncle and lived in Cathay, as China was called, from 1275 to 1292. He was amazed to see the beauty and wealth of China. When he returned to Europe, he described what he had seen. Marco Polo told the people of Europe about such Chinese inventions as printed money, gunpowder, the compass and a counting machine. He described how the Chinese made silk and paper and printed by wood blocks and movable type.

6. Chinese civilization did not remain within the borders of that country. It spread to Korea and later to Japan. The Japanese, over a period of years, imitated the Chinese in many ways. They used their system of writing. They adopted their religion and copied their form of government. In time, the Japanese people were taught to obey their emperor because he was supposed to have descended from the gods.

7. There were other early civilizations in the Far East, as we know from certain ruins that still exist. We are just beginning to learn that in India there was a civilization as old as that of China. A dark-skinned people had settled in the river valleys of the northern plain. About 2,000 years before the time of Christ, they were invaded by wandering herders from the northwest. These nomads were a light-skinned people called Aryans (from the language they spoke). The Aryans pushed the earlier people slowly toward the south. Under the Aryans, the Hindu religion began to develop.

8. India was invaded many times. In 327 B.C., Alexander the Great of Greece reached India. In the tenth century, Moslems from Central Asia invaded India through the Himalayas and overran much of the land. India was ruled during the next few centuries by Moslem dynasties. In the thirteenth century, the Mongols (who were also Moslems) began their invasion of India. The invasions by Mongol tribes continued for several hundred years, during which the Mongol chiefs ruled India.

9. Meanwhile, the ships of Europe were beginning to come to the Far East. Since the time of Marco Polo, the people of Europe wanted the precious jewels, cloth and spices of the Orient. Most of these goods were reaching Europe over land routes. The kings of Europe wanted an all-water route that would be quicker, safer and cheaper. This all-water route was found in 1498 by the Portuguese explorer Vasco da Gama, who sailed around Africa. After the Portuguese established a colony in India the English, Dutch and French followed the same route and set up their own trading posts in the Orient.

The beautiful Taj Mahal, built by a Moslem ruler of India in the 17th century.

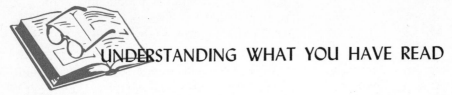

UNDERSTANDING WHAT YOU HAVE READ

1. **Which of the following questions are answered in this chapter?**
   a. Why did the Chinese build a great wall?
   b. Why did Europeans want an all-water route to the Far East?
   c. Who built the Taj Mahal?

2. **The main idea of *paragraphs 2 through 5* is to describe the:**
   a. early history of China.
   b. importance of Mongol invasions.
   c. journeys of Marco Polo.

3. **The Koreans and Japanese can trace their civilizations to the:**
   a. Aryans.   b. Chinese.   c. Greeks.

4. **An early invader of India was:**
   a. Kublai Khan.
   b. Vasco da Gama.
   c. Alexander the Great.

5. **The Chinese built a great wall to:**
   a. keep out nomad tribes.
   b. keep their people from moving west.
   c. stop trade with European nations.

6. **Europeans wanted an all-water route to the Far East because they:**
   a. wanted more knowledge of the oceans.
   b. wanted the spices and jewels of the Orient.
   c. were looking for adventure.

7. **A *dynasty* is in many ways like:**
   a. a democracy.
   b. the dictatorship of a few men.
   c. a royal family or monarchy.

8. **In *paragraph 6*, the phrase, "descended from the gods," means:**
   a. "following a tribal religion."
   b. "the gods were his ancestors."
   c. "ruled according to the teachings of the Bible."

DEVELOPING IDEAS AND SKILLS

Picture Symbols

These pictures should help you to recall parts of the chapter you have read. Can you tell the main idea of each picture? In what paragraph did you find the answer for each?

SUMMING UP

Which Does Not Belong?   Select the item that does not belong with the others in each group.

1. What the ancient Chinese discovered: a. printing, b. use of gunpowder, c. a calendar of 365 days.
2. How China was shut off from the world: a. Mediterranean Sea, b. Gobi Desert, c. Pacific Ocean.
3. People who came to China: a. Mongols, b. Aryans, c. Marco Polo.
4. European nations that settled in the Far East after 1498: a. Portugal, b. France, c. Italy.
5. People who came to India: a. da Gama, b. Alexander the Great, c. Kublai Khan.
6. How the Japanese imitated the Chinese: a. trade with Europe, b. followed the religion of the Chinese, c. used the Chinese system of writing.

FOLLOW UP

Some of the people who are outstanding in the history of the Far East had interesting lives. In your class or school library, find out more about these famous people in the history of the Far East:

Alexander the Great   Marco Polo
Genghis Khan   Asoka
Kublai Khan   Akbar

CHAPTER 5

Years of Struggle

* RUSSO-JAPANESE WAR 1904
* CHINESE REVOLUTION 1911
* CHINA INVADED 1931
* WORLD WAR II 1941
* CHINESE CIVIL WAR 1949
* KOREAN WAR 1950
* VIETNAM 1965

PROBLEM: How did the lands of the Far East win their freedom?

READING FOR A PURPOSE:
1. What was the Open Door Policy?
2. Who was Sun Yat-sen?
3. What happened to the European colonies after World War II?

1. After Vasco da Gama's voyage, the European nations rushed to obtain the riches of the Orient. Gradually, they gained control of many lands in the Far East. By 1858, Great Britain had won control over the lands that are now India and Pakistan. The Dutch ruled the Netherlands East Indies. The French were powerful in Indochina, the lands of the southeast peninsula. Portugal never became as strong as the others and held only small territories.

2. The nations of Europe and North America knew very little about China and Japan. China was ruled by an all-powerful emperor and a strong army. Japan was divided among powerful landowners called feudal lords. Each lord ruled over the peasants who worked his fields. The most powerful lord, or *shogun,* was stronger than the emperor who ruled the land. The Chinese emperor and the Japanese shogun kept their lands shut off from the rest of the world.

3. The Western nations, however, were beginning to produce great amounts of goods by machine. They became interested in the Far East as a place to sell their goods. They began to force the Chinese nation to allow trade with them. At the same time American sailors reported that they were badly treated if they were shipwrecked on Japanese shores. To protect American sailors, Admiral Perry was sent in 1853 to make a treaty with Japan. The Japanese agreed not to harm American sailors and to let the United States trade in several of their harbors.

4. The Japanese rulers saw that they could no longer keep their country shut off from other nations. The government decided that the people must change their ways of living. Within a short time Japan built up a strong army and navy. It learned to make use of the machines of European nations. Factories were started. Japan became the strongest nation in the Far East. It attacked China and occupied Formosa and Korea.

5. At the same time China was growing weaker. The British, French, Russians, Germans and Japanese soon gained control over parts of the country. In order to help China and to protect American trade with that country, the United States announced the "Open Door Policy" in 1899. By this, we meant that China should be open to all nations that wished to trade or do business there. For a time, nations stopped dividing China among themselves.

6. In 1911, the Chinese people overthrew their weak ruler and formed a new government. The revolution was led by a young doctor named Sun Yat-sen. His government was called the Nationalist government. Sun Yat-sen died in 1925, before he could unite China. He was followed by General Chiang Kai-shek. From the beginning, Chiang fought to rid his government

of Communists. He drove them to hideouts in northern China.

7. Japan was becoming warlike. The Japanese wanted to extend their control over the entire Far East. They wanted the rich natural resources of Southeast Asia. In the 1930's Japan again attacked China, took away Manchuria, and occupied much of the east coast. The United States protested these conquests of Japan. On December 7, 1941, Japan made a surprise attack on the American naval base at Pearl Harbor in Hawaii. The United States was now in World War II!

8. For a time, Japan was successful. Japanese armies overran many of the lands of Southeast Asia and came close to landing in Australia. In the Pacific, World War II lasted almost four years. The Japanese were finally defeated. Toward the end of the war the United States used a new weapon, the atomic bomb, to destroy two cities on the Japanese mainland. Japan lost all that it had gained by conquest as a result of the war. Instead of an empire, Japan's rulers brought only hardship and suffering to their people.

9. Following the war, the colonies of European nations demanded their independence. India, Ceylon, Pakistan and Burma broke away from Great Britain and became self-governing. Civil war broke out again in China between the Nationalists and the Communists. By 1949, the Communists under Mao Tse-tung had defeated the Nationalists of Chiang Kai-shek and become rulers of mainland China.

10. Chiang moved his Nationalist government to the island of Formosa (Taiwan). France's possessions in Indochina were broken up to form the new nations of Cambodia, Laos and Vietnam. The Philippines, a possession of the United States, was given its freedom in 1946. Korea, which was taken from Japan, was divided into North and South Korea. Indonesia became free after a long struggle with the Netherlands.

11. In June, 1950, North Korea invaded South Korea. The United States and other members of the United Nations sent armed forces to help South Korea. The Chinese Communists helped the North Koreans. The end of fighting did not bring victory for either side. Korea is still divided as before, but the action of the United States and the United Nations saved the independence of South Korea.

12. There is still no peace in the Far East. Vietnam has been divided into two parts. The northern part is Communist. It is trying to force Communist rule on South Vietnam. United States soldiers are in that country trying to prevent it from being taken over entirely by the Communists.

Matthew Perry arriving in Japan in 1853.

The New-York Historical Society

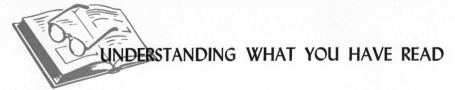

UNDERSTANDING WHAT YOU HAVE READ

1. **Which of the following questions are answered in this chapter?**

a. Why did Europe become interested in the Far East?
b. How did India become British?
c. How did Japan become a modern nation?

2. **The main idea of this chapter is to describe:**

a. how Europeans ruled many lands in the Far East.
b. Japanese attacks on the mainland of Asia.
c. how events led to the Far East of today.

3. **The first nation in the Far East to develop large industries was:**

a. China.   b. Japan.   c. India.

4. **India was ruled for a long time by:**

a. the Netherlands.
b. Great Britain.
c. Japan.

5. **European nations established colonies in Asia in the nineteenth century because they:**

a. needed lands for their growing populations.
b. wanted to try out their new ideas of government.
c. wanted markets for their goods.

6. **The United States announced the Open Door Policy because it wanted:**

a. to keep China open to trade.
b. to obtain land in China.
c. the friendship of the Japanese.

7. **In *paragraph 7*, a sentence states, "The United States protested these *conquests* of Japan." *Conquests* means:**

a. "attacks."   b. "controls."   c. "victories."

DEVELOPING IDEAS AND SKILLS

 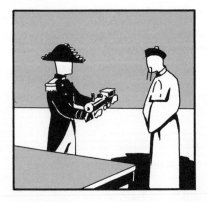 

Picture Symbols

These pictures should help you to recall parts of the chapter you have read. Can you tell the main idea of each picture? In what paragraph did you find the answer for each?

SUMMING UP

Match the items in Column A with the periods of time listed in Column B. Show that you know the time in which each of these events took place.

COLUMN A
1. French obtain colonies in Indochina.
2. Chinese build a great wall.
3. The Philippines obtains independence.
4. War in Korea.
5. Alexander the Great invades India.
6. The Open Door Policy is announced.
7. Mongols invade China.
8. United States begins trade with Japan.
9. Japan invades Manchuria.
10. Chinese Nationalist government moves to Formosa.
11. The Chinese revolution changes the government.
12. Indochina is divided into many small nations.

COLUMN B
A. Before Vasco da Gama's Voyage.
B. From Vasco da Gama to 1900.
C. From 1900 to World War II.
D. Since World War II.

FOLLOW UP

Who Am I? Who is described in each of the following statements? Choose your answer from the names below.

a rice farmer   Marco Polo   Sun Yat-sen
Aryans   Chiang Kai-shek   Admiral Perry
Kublai Khan   Vasco da Gama   John Hay
Mongols

1. We invaded India from the north. We forced out the darker-skinned peoples. We started the religion of Hinduism. We are _____.
2. I visited Japan in 1853. I made a treaty protecting American sailors and opening trade. I am _____.
3. I fought the Communists for control of China. I left China in 1949 and moved the Nationalist government to Formosa. I am _____.
4. I terraced the hillsides of the river valleys to get more land. I divided the valley land into small, diked fields. I am _____.
5. I found an all-water route to India by sailing around the southern tip of Africa. I am _____.
6. I was the ruler of Cathay in the thirteenth century. I was a descendant of the Mongols who invaded that country. I am _____.
7. I wrote an account of my travels in Cathay. As a result, the people of Europe were eager to get the goods of the East. I am _____.
8. I led the overthrow of the Chinese kingdom in 1911 and started a new government. I did not live to see a united China. I am _____.

CHAPTER 6

The People
of the Orient

PROBLEM: Who are the people of the Far East?

READING FOR A PURPOSE:
1. What do most people of the Far East do for a living?
2. What are the chief racial groups of the Far East?
3. What are the chief cities in the Far East?

1. The Far East has about one half the people of the world. China, with about 700 million people, and India, with about 480 million people, are the two most populous countries in the world. Since a great part of the Far East is covered with either mountains or desert, most people are crowded into the fertile river valleys and coastal plains. The fertile island of Java in Indonesia has nearly 1,100 people for each square mile of land. In Japan there are 670 people for each square mile. Compare these figures with our own country, which has about 54 people for each square mile!

2. The Far East is the home of many racial groups. In China, Korea and Japan live the "yellow" or Mongoloid peoples. Caucasians or "whites" are found mainly in India and Pakistan. It is believed that they came from the northwest a long time ago. Many of these "white" peoples are actually dark-skinned. The Malays or "brown-skinned" peoples make up the majority of the population in Southeast Asia (including Indonesia and the Philippines). However, people from India and China have lived in Southeast Asia for centuries. At one time there were so many Chinese living in Indochina that it was part of the ancient Chinese empire.

3. Most of the people of the Far East are poor farmers. The farmers live in thousands of small villages, not in widely separated houses as in our country. The farmers have a deep love for their fields. Most of the work is done by hand on small, scattered plots. The main crop in the warm areas is rice. Many of these farmers cannot read or write, and they are sick much of the time. Since most families raise barely enough food for themselves, they cannot afford to pay taxes to build schools or hospitals.

4. Even where schools have been built, children are often kept at home. Many parents believe that their children can't help but grow

A rice farmer of Burma.

UNATIONS

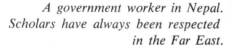
A basketmaker in a Cambodian village.

*A government worker in Nepal.
Scholars have always been respected
in the Far East.*

up to be poor farmers like themselves and therefore do not need an education. In many villages there is no pure water. People use the water of village "ponds" and tanks where animals are brought to drink. Poor diet, over-crowded houses, dirt and disease-carrying insects are a few other reasons why many people of the Far East are sick and die at a young age.

5. In addition to the many villages, there are also large cities in the Far East. In Japan, the majority of the people live in cities. Tokyo, its capital city with over ten million people, may be the largest city in the world. Other large cities in the Far East are Shanghai, Peking and Tientsin, Red China; Bombay and Calcutta, India; Osaka, Japan; Jakarta, Indonesia and Manila in the Philippines. Each year more and more people come to live and work in the cities. Not all of them find the better way of life they are looking for. In many cities of India, people must sleep and eat in the streets, for they have no other place to go.

6. Not only are there different racial groups in the Far East, but many languages are spoken

*The modern Philippine city
of Manila.*

as well. As a result, it is difficult for the people of various countries to understand each other. People often speak different languages within the same country, as in India and Indonesia.

7. Family life is important in the Far East. Boys and girls in thousands of villages are taught to think of their families before themselves. Families are usually large. When a daughter marries, she joins the family of her husband. The father is the head of the family and is respected by all. All members of the household share what the family owns. Each family is expected to look after its own affairs and help each of its members. It is not unusual to find whole villages made up of one or two families, with all the relatives living together.

UNDERSTANDING WHAT YOU HAVE READ

1. Which of the following questions are answered in this chapter?
a. How many people live in Japan?
b. How do people feed themselves in the Far East?
c. Why do so few children there have schooling?

2. A good title for *paragraphs 3 through 6* would be:
a. Home of the Yellow Race.
b. Crowded Cities of the Orient.
c. Oriental People and Their Problems.

3. The country in the world with the most people is:
a. India.
b. the Soviet Union.
c. Communist China.

4. Most people in the Far East are:
a. fishermen.   b. farmers.   c. factory workers.

5. There are few schools in many Far East- ern countries because:
a. newer nations have little interest in schools.
b. there is little money to support schools.
c. the villages are too far apart.

6. In Japan and Indonesia:
a. people are more crowded together than in the United States.
b. the climates are the same as those of the United States.
c. there are more people in each country than there are in the United States.

7. Members of the *Caucasian* race have:
a. yellow skins.   b. black skins.   c. white skins.

8. A *majority* of the people of the Malay peninsula are brown-skinned. *Majority* means:
a. "all."
b. "more than half."
c. "less than half."

DEVELOPING IDEAS AND SKILLS

Pictograph # 15—Population, Area and Standard of Living of the Far East
Can you answer these questions?
1. Is the standard of living of this region high or low compared with that of the United States? Is it a low-income or underdeveloped area?
2. Is the region as crowded as the United States?
3. Are the people of this region literate compared with the people of the United States?
4. How long may the average person in this region expect to live?
5. What facts tell you the standard of living of the people of the region?
6. How does this region compare with the United States in size?

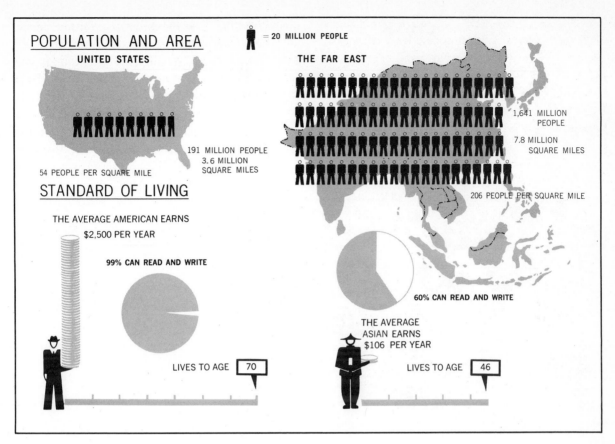

Pictograph # 15—Population, Area and Standard of Living of the Far East

SUMMING UP

Making an Outline of Chapter 6
Review the steps in making a good outline in Chapter 7 of Unit I. Select three *main ideas* of the chapter as your headings. (If you wish, you may choose more than three headings.) Then select the important facts that should be placed under each heading.

FOLLOW UP

Which Does Not Belong?   Select the item that does not belong with the others in each group.
1. *Our interest in the Far East:* a. source of raw materials, b. spread of communism, c. many canals, d. important trade routes.
2. *Land forms of the Far East:* a. highest mountains in the world, b. few harbors, c. fertile river valleys, d. islands.
3. *Climates of the Far East:* a. rain forest, b. wet and dry seasons, c. tundra, d. steppes and deserts.
4. *History of the Far East:* a. ruling families, b. control by European powers, c. invasions by nomadic tribes, d. exploration of the coast of Africa.
5. *People of the Far East:* a. one language in each country, b. overcrowded lands, c. rice farmers, d. low standard of living.

CHAPTER 7

Religions of the Far East

PROBLEM: What are the chief faiths of the Oriental peoples?

READING FOR A PURPOSE:
1. What do Hindus believe?
2. Who was Buddha?
3. What is the Confucian way of life?

1. In the United States, most people are members of the Christian religion. This is not true of the Far East. The Far East is the home of religions little known to us. Four of these together—Hinduism, Buddhism, Confucianism and Islam—have more followers than Christianity. These religions have played a great part in the history of the Far East and in the lives of the people. To understand the people of the Far East and how they live, we must know something of their religious beliefs.

2. The religion of the great majority of people in India is Hinduism. The Hindus worship many different gods or spirits. They believe that certain pools and rivers, like the Ganges,

are sacred. Two of their most important beliefs are the ideas of *caste* and *reincarnation*. The caste system is no longer legal in India. It was based on the belief that a person was born into the same "class" or caste as his father. He could not leave that class and was expected to do the same work his father did. (Certain work could only be done by certain castes.) There were four main castes. The highest caste was that of the priests or Brahmins. The second caste was made up of the warriors. The third caste was that of the craftsmen, traders and farmers. The lowest caste were the unskilled workers.

3. These four main groups were divided into many smaller castes. These were formed as new jobs were needed in the village or town. Each caste had its own rules by which its members lived. Members of one caste did not eat with or marry members of another caste. They did not mix at social affairs. Lower than the fourth caste were those people who were called "untouchables." They belonged to no caste and did all the jobs no one else would do.

4. Through the caste system the people of the village lived and worked together. In each village there were people of every caste to do the jobs needed. Because of caste rules, the villagers were sure they would be treated fairly for their services and products. One of the worst things that could happen to a Hindu was to break the rules and be put out of his caste. For a long time, as you have learned, the Hindu people of India were ruled by Moslem kings. They had little to do with the government except to pay taxes. However, they were held together by their beliefs about the Hindu gods and the way men should live, i.e., the caste system. Although the constitution of the new India has forbidden the caste system, the old ways of living are hard to change overnight.

5. Another major belief of Hinduism is reincarnation. According to this belief, a person's soul never dies. After death, the person can be born again. The kind of life a person can expect after he is reborn depends how he has lived before. If he has worked hard and followed the rules of his caste, he will be rewarded. If a per-

son was evil and broke the rules of his caste, he might be reborn into a lower caste, as an untouchable or even as an animal. This explains, in part, why Hindus do not harm living creatures or eat meat. A Hindu believes that a person can be reborn many times until he learns to lead a good life.

6. Islam is another religion of the Indian subcontinent. Islam was brought to India by the followers of Mohammed. When this land was ruled by Great Britain, the Hindus and Moslems lived side by side. Now the subcontinent is divided into two countries, India and Pakistan. Today, India is largely Hindu, while Pakistan is largely Moslem. However, millions of followers of each religion live as a minority in both of these countries. Indonesia is another large Moslem country in this part of the world.

7. When the followers of Hinduism and Islam lived together in British India, there were many disputes because of their different beliefs. Hindus worship many gods; Moslems believe in one God. Moslems have one sacred book, the Koran; Hindus read many sacred texts. The Moslems have no images or idols in their mosques; the temples of the Hindus are filled with them. The Moslems eat meat; the Hindus worship the cow and often will not eat other animals either. Islam has only a few rules that all must follow; Hinduism has many rules. The Hindus follow a caste system. The Moslems believe that all are equal if they follow Mohammed. There are many holy places in the Hindu religion; in Islam, there is only Mecca. When a Hindu dies, he is burned and his ashes are scattered in a sacred river. When a Moslem dies, he is buried with his face toward Mecca.

8. Buddhism began in India more than 2,500 years ago. It was started by a young prince called Gautama. He decided to spend his life helping others. The Buddhists have no God such as is found in Christianity, Islam or Judaism. Buddhism teaches that man has many desires that lead to evil. He must fight himself to drive away these desires and do what is right. The best way to do this is to forget yourself and help others. Buddhism spread throughout Asia. Millions of people in China, Tibet, Japan and Southeast Asia are Buddhists. A Buddhist temple is sometimes called a *pagoda*.

9. While Buddhism and other religions became part of Chinese life, it was really the teachings of a wise man called Confucius that guided the every-day life of the Chinese people. Confucius lived in the 6th century B.C. and began his teachings about the same time as Gautama in India. He did not teach about a life after death but about how to live on earth. He believed that man should be more concerned about his responsibilities than his rights. These responsibilities included respect for learning, love and obedience to parents and family, loyalty to the emperor and understanding one's "place" in society. As a result of Confucius' teachings,

A Hindu temple in Nepal.

The Ganges River is sacred to the people of India.

A Buddhist shrine or pagoda in Burma.

the Chinese form of government developed: power was in the hands of a small, educated group while the majority of the people worked hard, lived simply and loyally supported them. This way of life lasted far into the twentieth century.

10. There are other groups of people who follow different religious beliefs in the Far East. Lao-tse was another famous teacher in China. The book of Tao contains many of his teach-ings. In time, Taoism became a religion with many gods, priests and colorful ceremonies. There are many Christians in the Far East, too, although they are few in number when compared with the number of people of other religions. The Filipinos are a Christian people. Their early Spanish rulers brought Christianity to the islands. Christian missionaries are teaching in many of the Far Eastern countries. About ten million people in India are Christian.

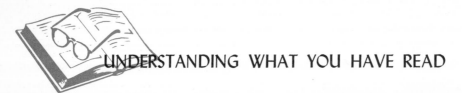

UNDERSTANDING WHAT YOU HAVE READ

1. Which of the following questions are answered in this chapter?
a. Why don't Hindus eat meat?
b. What is Shintoism?
c. How do Hinduism and Islam differ?

2. The main idea of this chapter is to describe the:
a. beliefs of Oriental people.

b. importance of Buddha.
c. teachings of Confucius.

3. Most of the people of India are:
a. Hindus.   b. Buddhists.   c. Moslems.

4. The Christian religion was brought to the Far East by:
a. nomads.   b. explorers.   c. missionaries.

454

5. Confucianism is not a religion in our sense of the word because there are:
a. no beliefs in God or an afterlife.
b. no ways of worship.
c. no sacred books.

6. There have been disputes between Hindus and Moslems because they:
a. are both warlike people.
b. try to spread their beliefs throughout the world.
c. have different religious beliefs.

7. Under a *caste system*, people are:
a. united. b. divided. c. enslaved.

8. *Reincarnation* is the belief in:
a. many lives after death.
b. one God.
c. help to needy people.

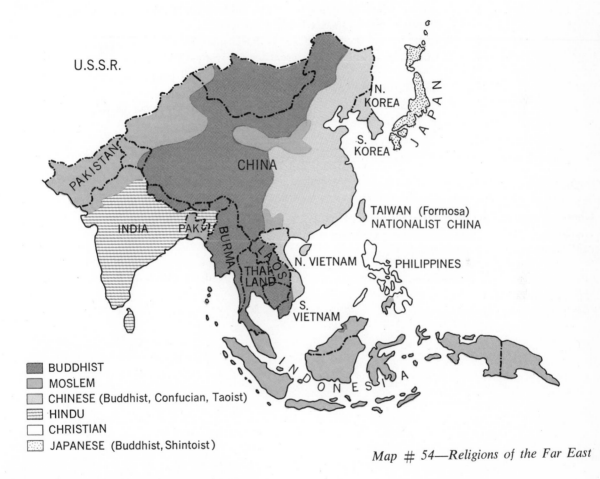

BUDDHIST
MOSLEM
CHINESE (Buddhist, Confucian, Taoist)
HINDU
CHRISTIAN
JAPANESE (Buddhist, Shintoist)

Map # 54—Religions of the Far East

DEVELOPING IDEAS AND SKILLS

Map # 54—Religions of the Far East
Tell whether these statements are true or false.
1. All the people of India are Hindus.
2. Most of the people of Indonesia and Pakistan are Moslems.
3. The Philippine people are chiefly followers of Christianity.
4. Large numbers of people in both Japan and China are Buddhists.
5. People in Southeast Asia practice religions that are different from those of their neighbors in China.

Can you answer these questions?
1. How did the Philippines become Christian?

2. Where did Buddhism begin?

3. How did Islam reach the Far East?

4. How did Confucianism begin?

SUMMING UP

Do You Agree or Disagree?   Give reasons for your answers.

1. Most of the people of the Far East belong to one of three great religions.
2. All religions of Far Eastern peoples have a belief in one God.
3. India is the only Far Eastern country in which cattle are raised for their meat.
4. There are more Christians than non-Christians in the world.
5. The caste system has divided the Indian people into various groups.
6. Hindus believe in sacred rivers and pools.
7. In Buddhism the main belief is that a man may be born again several times.
8. Confucius is known as a great teacher rather than as a religious leader.
9. Since the caste system was ended in India, all people are considered equal by their fellow Indians.
10. Because Buddhism was founded by an Indian prince, its followers are found only in India.

FOLLOW UP

Choosing either Hinduism, Buddhism or Confucianism as your subject, complete the following outline about a Far Eastern religion.

Title: _____

I. How it began.
  1.
  2.

II. Major beliefs.
  1.
  2.

III. How it affects the lives of the people.
  1.
  2.

CHAPTER 8

Farmers of the Far East

PROBLEM: How do most Asians meet their daily needs?

READING FOR A PURPOSE:
1. How does the farmer use his land?
2. How is farming carried on in the rain forest?
3. What is a commune?

1. Good land is like a precious gem in the Orient. This is because so much of the land is not suited for farming. Most of the people in the Far East live in thousands of small villages. Each of these villages is a little world of its own. Its people take care of their own needs. They use nearly everything they raise and rarely have any products left over for sale. As a result, little is brought into the village from other areas. In most villages there is probably no electricity, school or movie. There are few roads to the big cities.

2. The farmer's fields are outside the village. These may be a dozen or more scattered plots, seldom larger than four or five acres. The farmer tends these small plots of land very carefully. He does almost everything by hand: planting the seeds, removing the weeds and harvesting the crops. Since much of the region is hilly, it is not unusual to find the farmer and his family working on terraces carved out of the hillsides. The plots are too small to use machinery. Because of his methods of farming, the yields per acre are higher than those of the American farmer. This kind of farming is called *intensive* farming. It is much like the farming practiced in Western Europe.

3. Except for a few pigs and chickens, the Far Eastern farmer does not raise animals for food. He must use all of his land to raise food for his family; he cannot afford to graze animals on it. As a result, the people of the Far East eat less meat than we do. (While India has more cattle than any other nation, the people cannot eat them because it is against their religious beliefs.)

4. Despite their hard work, farmers of the Far East have low incomes. Many farmers do not own their own land, but rent it from large landowners. The tenant farmer pays his rent with the crops he raises. If it is a good year, he has enough to pay his debts to the village moneylender or to the government. If he is very lucky, he may have enough left over to buy a water buffalo or some fertilizer.

5. In the monsoon region, water is as precious as land. Every effort is made to save it during

Farming in the Far East is done chiefly by hand, as in this rice paddy.

UNITED NATIONS

Most farmers depend on irrigation canals, like this one in East Pakistan, for water.

the dry season. In some places the fields are irrigated by water brought from the rivers through canals. In other places there are wells. In India there are many ponds or "tanks." For some villages, these tanks are the only source of water. The people wash their clothes in the tanks and bring their cattle to them to drink.

6. Besides the subsistence farmer, there is both primitive and commercial (plantation) farming in the rain forest. The "primitive" farmer goes about his work much the same as the rain-forest farmer in central Africa or South America does. To clear a field, he first burns the thick underbrush. Then he digs holes in the ground with a stick and drops in his seeds.

When the crop ripens, he picks it. After two or three years, the farmer leaves his field and goes on to another. This migratory farmer finds that it is easier to prepare a new field than to continue with one that is no longer fertile.

7. There are also many plantations scattered throughout the rain forest. Each plantation raises a cash crop such as rubber, tobacco, coffee, tea or sugar cane. These crops are not grown for use by the people in the home countries. They are exported to other lands throughout the world. Plantations are big businesses with directors and hundreds of workers. Many have stores and shops, a school, a hospital and a water and electric plant on the plantation property. Many of the plantations are owned by people in Europe and North America.

8. In China, as in other countries, most people are farmers. However, the Communist Chinese have introduced a new way of farming to the Far East. In 1958, they started to force their people into large state farms or *communes*. The commune is very much like a factory. The people work in the fields ten hours a day, six days a week. As on a Soviet state farm, they receive wages. The crops belong to the Communist government. The workers live in villages scattered throughout the commune. Despite this change, the production of foods is not great enough to feed the huge and growing population of China.

Laotian women pound rice with a wooden mortar. Many tools used by Far Eastern farmers are simple.

458

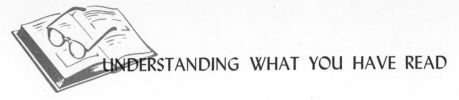

UNDERSTANDING WHAT YOU HAVE READ

1. **Which of the following questions are answered in this chapter?**
   a. Why does the Far Eastern farmer get a high yield from his land?
   b. Why is the Far Eastern farmer poor?
   c. Why don't Oriental peoples eat much meat?

2. **The main idea of this chapter is to describe:**
   a. a new kind of farming in Red China.
   b. how the farmer of the rain forest meets his needs.
   c. different kinds of farming in the Far East.

3. **The chief farm animal of the Far East is the:**
   a. camel.   b. water buffalo.   c. horse.

4. **Most of the work on Far Eastern farms is done by:**
   a. hand.   b. machinery.   c. animals.

5. **There are few farm animals in the Far East because:**
   a. there is a lack of water for them.
   b. religious beliefs forbid owning animals.
   c. farmers use all the land to raise food for their families.

6. **In the Far East, farm machinery has not been widely used because:**
   a. the religions are against it.
   b. the farms are too small.
   c. climates are not favorable for use of machines.

7. **In *intensive* farming, the farmer:**
   a. uses machinery and plants his crops a distance apart.
   b. uses hand labor and plants seeds close together.
   c. gets a smaller amount of grain from each acre planted.

8. **A *commune* may be best compared with:**
   a. a state farm in the Soviet Union.
   b. a coffee plantation in Latin America.
   c. a corn-belt farm in the United States.

DEVELOPING IDEAS AND SKILLS

Photograph Study

This photograph should help you to recall parts of the chapter you have just read. Can you tell the main idea of the photograph? Where in the chapter is it described?

UNITED NATIONS

SUMMING UP

Comparing Farmers   Complete the following chart in your notebook.

WESTERN UNITED STATES		FAR EASTERN VILLAGE
	Size of farm	
	Crops raised	
	How work is done	
	Yield per acre	
	Land ownership	
	Homes of farmers	
	Saving resources	

FOLLOW UP

Choose the correct answer.

1. Terraces are used by Far Eastern farmers chiefly because of:
   a. the favorable climate.
   b. overcrowded land.
   c. the lack of machinery.

2. In the warm lands of the Far East, the chief food crop is:
   a. tea.   b. wheat.   c. rice.

3. Most of the farmers in the Far East may be called:
   a. commercial.   b. subsistence.   c. communal.

4. Most of the farmers of the Far East live:
   a. in small villages near their farms.
   b. on their individual farms.
   c. in houses owned by the state.

5. A pond or "tank" on an Indian farm might be called a:
   a. canal.   b. dam.   c. reservoir.

Using the Good Earth of Asia

PROBLEM: How does the Asian farmer make use of his lands?

READING FOR A PURPOSE:
1. How is rice grown?
2. What are the important forest products?
3. Why are the seas important?

1. Wherever the climate of the Far East is warm and wet, rice is the chief crop. Rice is a way of life for millions of people in this region. There are many reasons why this is so. First, in a region where there are many people and little fertile land, rice provides more food for each acre planted than any other grain. Second, in a hot climate, rice can be stored without spoiling. Third, rice has many uses. It is the Orientals' substitute for bread, potatoes and even milk and cheese. When boiled, it is eaten with meat or fish. It can be used to make wine. Animals can also be fed rice straw.

2. The rice plant is grown in small fields called *paddies*. The paddy is surrounded by dikes or walls made of earth. While the rice seedlings are growing, the paddies are flooded with water. The dikes control the supply of water. On the hillsides, terraces are built for the paddies.

3. The farmer first plants his rice seeds in a small plot of ground. As the plants start to grow, he clears the rest of his land. He uses a wooden plow pulled by a water buffalo or carabao. The fields are flooded by means of the dikes. When the young rice plants are about six inches high, he transplants or moves them to the flooded fields. (In a monsoon area, there may not be enough rainfall. Therefore, the farmer gets water by digging ditches from nearby streams or pumping water from a well.) In four months the rice plants are fully grown. The water is then drained from the paddy and the rice is cut and threshed. (Burma, Thailand and the countries of the Malay peninsula are known as the "rice bowl." The farmers there produce more rice than they need. Much of it is sold to their neighbors, China and India.)

4. The warm, rainy climate of the Far East is good for other crops as well. Scattered throughout the rain forest are many plantations on which are grown special crops such as rubber, tea, coconuts, tobacco, coffee and sugar cane. Southeast Asia is the largest rubber-pro-

Transplanting young rice plants in Indonesia.
UNITED NATIONS

*A Malaysian worker collects latex
on a rubber plantation.*

ducing area in the world. The rubber is gathered by hundreds of native workers. The worker first makes a cut in the tree. The sap of the rubber tree, *latex,* drips out of this cut into small pails. The latex is collected and then processed or turned into rubber. It is then shipped to factories all over the world.

5. The rain forest has other valuable products. *Quinine,* a medicine used to treat the disease of malaria, is obtained from the bark of the cinchona tree. *Kapok* is a light waterproof fiber used to fill mattresses and life preservers. Wood from the *teak* tree is used in making furniture. *Rattan* is a palm that is made into baskets, chairs and furniture. *Bamboo* is a tall grass with hard stems. It is used to make poles, furniture and even houses. And then there are spices. Indonesia produces more than half the pepper used by Americans. *Cinnamon* comes from the inner bark of a tree grown in Ceylon and India.

6. *Jute* is a wet-season crop grown in India and Pakistan. It is a fiber that is made into burlap bags and rope. In the Philippines, *abacá,* another rope fiber, is grown. This product is often called Manila hemp and is used in making the strongest kind of rope.

7. China, India and Pakistan are leading growers of cotton. Indian cotton was among the first products to be introduced to the countries of the Western world. The silk products of China and Japan have long been famous. Silk is obtained from a worm that eats the leaves of the mulberry tree. A great amount of labor is needed to care for the mulberry trees. Silk is not as important in world trade as it once was. The discovery of nylon, dacron, orlon and other such products has reduced the demand for silk throughout the world.

8. Where it is too cool or dry for rice to grow,

Picking tea in Ceylon for export.

such grains as wheat, barley, millet and corn are raised. China ranks third after the United States and the Soviet Union in wheat production. Spring wheat is planted in northern China and Manchuria where the climate is cooler. China is also a world leader in growing corn. Corn is used chiefly as a food for the people. Manchuria, in northern China, is a leading producer of *soy beans*. This vegetable has many uses. It provides flour and breakfast food, and its oil is used for cooking. Soups and sauces are also made from it. The plant is valuable, too, for it can be used to feed animals. The soy bean plant enriches the soil where it is grown, restoring minerals to the earth.

9. As you have learned, the Far Eastern farmer eats little meat because he lacks the land to raise large animals. Therefore, the peoples along the coast have turned to the sea for other sources of food. Fish is more important in the diet of many Far Easterners than meat. Thousands of little fishing boats sail along the coasts of China and Japan every day to catch fish. Japan has some of the finest fishing grounds

Japan Tourist Association

A Japanese fisherman displays his catch.

in the world. Not only do small boats go out, but Japan also has very modern fishing boats that can sail far from land. The fish are not only caught aboard these boats, they are also prepared for sale on board ship.

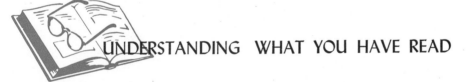

UNDERSTANDING WHAT YOU HAVE READ

1. **Which of the following questions are answered in this chapter?**
a. What is a "paddy"?
b. What is jute used for?
c. Why does India import rice?

2. **The main idea of this chapter is to describe:**
a. how the Oriental uses the seas.
b. the products of the rain forest.
c. how the Oriental people make use of their land.

3. **The warm, rainy climate is suited to the growing of rice and:**
a. millet.　　b. tea.　　c. olive trees.

4. **The Asian rain forest has plantations that grow:**

a. rubber.　　b. bananas.　　c. corn.

5. **How does the Asian farmer provide water in the dry season?**
a. He depends upon dams.
b. He draws water through canals.
c. He plants only in the highlands.

6. **Wheat and corn are grown instead of rice where:**
a. the growing season is longer.
b. the growing season is shorter.
c. rainfall is steady throughout the year.

7. **A *paddy* is important to the:**
a. rice farmer.
b. fisherman.
c. rubber planter.

8. Many of our modern paints for the home are "rubber-based" paints. These are called:

a. enamels.   b. flat paints.   c. latex paints.

Standard Oil Co. (N.J.)

DEVELOPING IDEAS AND SKILLS

Photograph Study
This photograph should help you to recall parts of the chapter you have just read. Can you tell the main idea of the photograph? Where in the chapter is it described?

SUMMING UP

In your notebook place the items listed below in the proper columns.

I	II	III
AMAZON RAIN FOREST	CONGO RAIN FOREST	ASIAN RAIN FOREST

A rice paddy   A cow dead of sleeping sickness
A smoking volcano   A woman making palm oil
A tea plantation   An Indian eating manioc
A Pygmy village   A Bantu growing sorghum
A farmer with a water buffalo   A native collecting cacao pods
A man cutting bamboo and teak   A worker picking spices
A man picking bananas

Match the statements in Column B with the Far Eastern products listed in Column A.

COLUMN A	COLUMN B
1. wheat	___ Indonesia has more than half the world's supply.
2. tea	___ Plantation crop of Ceylon.
3. cotton	___ From trees grown on plantations of Southeast Asia.
4. jute	___ Chinese crop of many uses.
5. rubber	___ Grain grown in northern China.
6. soy beans	___ Chief farm crop of the Malay peninsula.
7. pepper	___ Special fiber found in Japan.
8. rice	___ India has been a leader in exporting this fiber.
9. silk	___ Produced in Pakistan and used in making rope.

CHAPTER 10

Industrial Resources of the Far East

PROBLEM: Will the people of the Far East be able to develop large industries?

READING FOR A PURPOSE:
1. Which is the leading industrial nation of the Far East?
2. What are the chief mineral resources of the Far East?
3. Why has this region been slow to industrialize?

1. The population of the nations of the Far East is continuing to grow rapidly. Since much of the land is not farmed, the problem of feeding this growing population becomes more and more serious. In most cases, food must be imported. In order to buy food from abroad, a country must have goods to sell. These are products of the nation's mines, fields or factories. The island of Japan was the first nation in the Far East to realize it could not depend on its land alone to feed its large population. As a result, it changed its ways of living.

2. The change in Japan came rapidly. The Japanese bought machines from the West and built factories. They imported raw materials from other nations. They used their small amount of coal and their swift-flowing mountain streams as sources of power for their factories. The country's large population provided plenty of workers for the factories. They were sent to schools and trained for their new jobs.

3. In time, Japan became the leading industrial nation in the Far East. Its goods are now sold throughout the world. Our shops and stores are filled with products marked "Made in Japan." The Japanese have exchanged these finished goods for rice and other foods needed to feed themselves. Japan has the 4th largest merchant fleet in the world. This fleet brings to the islands the needed food and raw materials from all over the world.

4. Other countries in the Far East must now face the problem of how to industrialize. They would like to increase the production of their mines and factories. As far as we know, the Far East has the power resources and raw materials needed to do this. India has good supplies of iron and coal. In addition, it has reserves of manganese, bauxite, gold, chromite and other minerals. While lacking oil for power, the Himalaya Mountains are a good source of water power to produce electricity. Some dams are now being built there. India also has the raw materials of its farms and plantations—cotton, tea, jute and sugar cane. And there are millions of people to do the work needed.

A camera assembly line in Japan.
Japan Tourist Association

A cotton mill in India.

5. Communist China is also rich in natural resources. Only three nations in the world have more coal than China. It also has iron ore, manganese, tungsten, antimony and other minerals. These are all useful in the manufacture of fine steel products. Red China's huge population can supply all the workers needed in factories and mines. Under Communist rule, China has made tremendous gains in the production from her mines and factories.

6. Southeast Asia has other riches. Malaysia, Thailand and Indonesia mine great amounts of tin. Almost two-thirds of the world's supply of tin comes from this region. Indonesia has oil, but it is not enough to supply the needs of the Orient. President Sukarno of Indonesia announced in 1965 that he was taking over the oil fields that had been owned by foreign oil companies. He wanted to use the oil resources to increase the wealth of Indonesia rather than that of oil companies in Europe and North America.

7. In spite of the resources of some nations in the Orient, there are several reasons why these nations may not develop industries as quickly as Japan did. Millions of people in the Far East cannot read or write. They must be trained in schools before they can work the machines in factories. Many do not want to work in factories. They prefer to work at home,

making things by hand for people they know. Most of the people are poor. They cannot afford to buy the goods made in factories. Since there are few "markets"—little demand for machine-made goods—factories are not built. Money is also needed to start factories and businesses.

8. Transportation throughout much of the Far East is poor. Japan has a fine network of railroads. India has a large railway system too. When the British ruled India they built railroads in what are now India and Pakistan. Throughout much of the Far East, however, there are few good highways. The mountains, jungle and desert make roads very difficult to build and maintain. In Red China, most people use the rivers for travel. (We know that the Communist government is now improving the transportation system inside China.) Good transportation is needed if raw materials and manufactured goods are to flow back and forth between buyers and sellers in the Far East. Without good transportation, the cost of moving goods is very high.

9. Most Far Eastern nations trade with each other. Japan alone carries on a heavy trade with the United States. Indonesia sells oil to Japan and Indian cotton supplies Japanese mills. Rice

A tin mine in Malaysia, the world's largest producer of tin.

from Burma and Thailand is sent to China and India. Most nations trade more with Western Europe than they do with the United States. But the United States is a good customer for the tin, rubber and spices of the Far East.

10. Two of the greatest seaports in the world are centers of trade in the Far East. Both are islands. The island of Singapore is located off the coast of the Malay peninsula. Trade from the Indian Ocean to the Pacific Ocean passes through the straits near Singapore. Hong Kong lies off the coast of southern China. This island is still owned by Great Britain. Visitors from all over the world travel to Hong Kong; it seems to be a meeting place of East and West. The city is crowded today with thousands of people who have fled from Communist China.

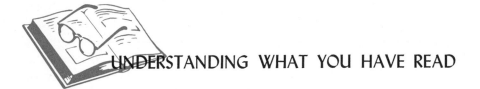

UNDERSTANDING WHAT YOU HAVE READ

1. Which of the following questions are answered in this chapter?
a. What is Japan's chief source of power?
b. What are the resources of Southeast Asia?
c. Why did Japan go to war in 1941?

2. The main idea of this chapter is to describe:
a. problems of transportation in the Far East.
b. the resources of Communist China.
c. the reasons why industry has been slow to develop in this region.

3. Communist China has a large supply of:
a. oil.   b. coal.   c. copper.

4. The most industrialized country in the Far East is:
a. Japan.   b. China.   c. India.

5. One reason why India has been slow to develop industry is that it has:
a. almost no railroads.
b. no good source of power.
c. few skilled workers.

6. In spite of the great population of this region, there is no great market for factory goods because:
a. too many people work in the mines.
b. people have little money to buy goods.
c. schools train people for office work rather than factory work.

DEVELOPING IDEAS AND SKILLS

Photograph Study
This photograph should help you to recall parts of the chapter you have just read. Can you tell the main idea of the photograph? Where in the chapter is it described?

SUMMING UP

Developing Industry in the Far East   Place a check before each item that is *true* about the Far East.

___ 1. Good water power resources.
___ 2. Coal reserves in every country.
___ 3. Enough oil for the entire region.
___ 4. Few trained workers for factories.
___ 5. Many raw materials to sell.
___ 6. Money to invest in new industries.
___ 7. Good seaports.
___ 8. Large population.
___ 9. Iron ore deposits in India.
___ 10. Large, modern highway system.
___ 11. Minerals that other nations need.
___ 12. More trade with the United States than with any other region.

FOLLOW UP

Tell whether these statements are true or false. The underlined words make the statements true or false. If a statement is false, what word or words would you place in it to make it true?

1. The United States trades more with <u>India</u> than with any other Far Eastern country.
2. <u>Tin</u> is a leading product of Indonesia.
3. A good railway system is found in <u>Malaysia</u>.
4. <u>Singapore</u> is an important seaport near the mainland of China.
5. <u>Japan</u> is the leading industrial nation of the Far East.
6. One of the problems of the Far East is that many countries must import <u>food</u>.
7. India must import <u>cotton</u> for her people's needs.
8. Most people in the Far East work <u>in factories</u>.

CHAPTER 11

Toward a Better Way of Life

PROBLEM: What are some of the needs of the Far East?

READING FOR A PURPOSE:
1. What are the chief needs of the Far Eastern peoples?
2. Why is a change in land ownership needed?
3. What are the problems of the cities?

1. Despite the fact that they are hard-working, many of the people of the Far East are poor and hungry. The farms are too small, and many peasants do not own their own land. They cannot grow enough food. The farmer is often in debt to the village moneylender or large landowner. They have few of the comforts of life that we enjoy. A way must be found for farmers to own more land and to learn how to use it wisely.

2. In Japan, most people can read and write. Red China claims that more than ninety per cent of its children are now going to school. India, Indonesia and the Philippines are all building more schools. However, in much of the Far East, many people cannot read or write. They know little about the rest of the world. In the villages far from the cities, most farmers do not have radios or television sets. They have probably never been on a train, traveled in an automobile or seen a motion picture.

3. Many of the people are in poor health, and death at an early age is common. Many of the countries are trying to improve the health of their peoples through better water supplies, vaccination and the use of insect-killers. United Nations teams have visited many of the small villages, giving medical help and advice. As health improves, however, the population grows at an even faster rate. This raises a new problem—namely, will the growing of food keep pace with the growing population?

4. There is a need to improve the water supply in the monsoon lands. In many of the countries affected by the monsoon, there is either too little or too much water. More reservoirs and tanks must be built so that rain water can be stored during the wet season for use during the dry season. There is a need for more dams to hold back water and provide irrigation for the dry lands. If more water is available, more food can be raised for the fast-growing populations of Far Eastern countries.

A classroom in Burma.

Protecting Burmese children against malaria.

Young Burmese scientists investigate causes of disease in cattle.

5. Because fertile land is scarce and the population is growing, many people are leaving their villages to go to the cities in search of work. Cities are growing at a faster rate than farm lands. Yet while some people find work in the cities, millions of others are jobless. The movement of the people to the cities increases the need for more homes and better health care. It is not unusual to find people living and sleeping in the streets in some cities of India. Calcutta has some of the worst slums in the world.

6. Many of the nations—India, Pakistan, Burma, Malaysia, the Philippines, Indonesia, Ceylon and others—are new. Until recently, their people lived under foreign rule. Their leaders are now setting up stable governments and are trying to solve the problems of hunger and illiteracy that face many of their people.

7. At the same time, communism is spreading in the Far East. The mainland of China, North Korea and North Vietnam are now under Communist rule. President Sukarno of Indonesia has been friendly with Communist China and even took his country out of the United Nations. The leaders of the new nations need to remain free so that their governments have time to grow in strength. We fear that their people may listen to the Communists and their promises of more food and land. Democracy is in danger in the Far East if the new nations cannot work out their problems.

Building new irrigation canals in India to provide more grain land.

UNDERSTANDING WHAT YOU HAVE READ

1. **Which of the following questions are answered in this chapter?**
   a. Why are people moving to Far Eastern cities?
   b. Why are all nations in the Far East over-crowded?
   c. What are the problems that face new nations?

2. **The main idea of this chapter is to describe:**
   a. the greatest needs of the Far Eastern peoples.
   b. conditions in the crowded cities.
   c. the plans of India and China to improve the life of the people.

3. **The greatest problem of nations in the Far East is the:**
   a. need for food for a growing population.
   b. lack of foreign aid.
   c. the use of the sea for transportation.

4. **The most powerful nation in the Far East is:**
   a. Indonesia.
   b. Red China.
   c. the Philippines.

5. **Land ownership is a problem in the Orient because:**
   a. the government owns the farms in all countries except Red China.
   b. most of the land is owned by foreign business-men.
   c. many farm lands are rented from large land-owners.

6. **We can help the new nations of South-east Asia by:**
   a. supplying atomic bombs for their defense.
   b. providing help in the form of men, money, machines and medicines.
   c. withdrawing our troops from Vietnam.

DEVELOPING IDEAS AND SKILLS

Cartoon (See p. 469.)
1. Who is the main figure in this cartoon?
2. What is the meaning of the cartoon?
3. Which countries in the Far East have democratic governments and which are Communist?
4. Where are civil wars taking place in this region?
5. What is a good title for this cartoon?

SUMMING UP

Fact or Opinion

Which of the following statements are *fact* and which are merely someone's *opinion?*
1. Red China will be recognized by the United States because we cannot ignore 700 million people.
2. Some of the problems facing the Far East today have existed for hundreds of years.
3. The spread of communism is the greatest danger facing the Far East today.
4. Red China should not be allowed to become a member of the United Nations.

471

5. The resources of Southeast Asia are needed by other nations.
6. Most of the people of the Far East are farmers who barely make a living.
7. Some Far Eastern countries have improved the literacy of their people.
8. Nationalism is an important force in the Far East today.

FOLLOW UP

Making Comparisons   Choose the best answer.
1. Which country has the largest population? a. Red China. b. the Soviet Union. c. the United States.
2. Which country of Europe is most like Japan in its dependence upon foreign trade?   a. France. b. Great Britain. c. Spain.
3. Germany is divided into a Communist and a "Free" section; so is which of these Far Eastern countries? a. Pakistan. b. Korea. c. Burma.
4. The equator crosses the Congo Republic, Brazil and which of these Far Eastern nations? a. Indonesia. b. India. c. Japan.
5. Which part of the Far East has a climate like that of our southeastern states? a. Indonesia. b. Malaysia. c. Southeast China.

CHAPTER 12

Japan: Workshop of the Far East

PROBLEM: How has this small land become one of the leading nations in the world?

READING FOR A PURPOSE:
1. What are Japan's climates?
2. How do the Japanese people make a living?
3. What are some of Japan's problems?

1. Off the eastern coast of Asia is the archipelago of Japan. Japan has four main islands, all of which are very mountainous. While only about a fifth of the land is good for farming, the Japanese have used their resources wisely and have the highest standard of living in the Orient. Japan's 96 million people live in a country smaller than our state of Montana; its farmland is less than half the area of New York State.

2. While Japan is narrow, it extends for a long distance north and south—as far as the distance from Vermont to Alabama! In the northern islands the climate is humid continental, like that of our northeast. In the winter, cold air from Asia blows over these islands and brings heavy snows. In the southern islands the climate is milder or humid subtropical. Rainy winds from the Pacific Ocean blow across Japan. Like Great Britain, Japan is surrounded by water and is affected by a warm ocean stream, the Japanese Current. This current starts north of Indonesia and warms the southern coast of Japan. Therefore, Japan's year-round temperatures are milder than those of lands in the same latitude on the Asiatic mainland.

3. The modern history of Japan began a little more than a hundred years ago. In 1853, an American fleet under the command of Matthew Perry came to Japan. Soon the Japanese were forced to trade with Europe and the United States. After seeing the inventions of the Western world, Japan decided it had to copy Western ways in order to grow strong and remain free. Before long, the Japanese built factories and made machines, ships and guns. By 1900, Japan had become one of the strong nations of the world.

4. As the nation's strength grew, Japan set out to build a large empire. It took Formosa from China in 1895. In 1904-5, it defeated Russia and gained Korea. In 1931, Japan invaded China and took Manchuria. Fighting against us during World War II, the Japanese held much of Southeast Asia. However, Japan was defeated by the Allies and lost all its colonies. Atomic bombs had been dropped on its cities of Hiroshima and Nagasaki. When the war was over, a new government was started with the help of the United States. In time, Japan recovered from the war. Its goods are again being sold throughout the world.

5. A constitution was drawn up in 1957 giving Japan a parliamentary form of government. The chief lawmaking body is called the Diet. It is made up of two houses. Members of these houses are elected by all persons over twenty-one years of age. The chief officer is the prime minister, who is chosen by the Diet. The Jap-

473

anese still have an emperor or king, but he has no real power. Tokyo is the capital city.

6. Japan is one of the most thickly populated countries in the world, having 650 people for each square mile of land. About half the working people are farmers and fishermen. More than a third are factory workers. The rest are in professions or service occupations. There are many large cities: Tokyo, Osaka, Kyoto, Kobe, Nagoya and Yokohama. All except Kyoto are seaports. All are on the main island of Honshu. The large cities have crowds of busy people, traffic problems, neon lights, mostly Western-style dress, modern buses, subways and tall buildings.

7. The Japanese people have the highest standard of living in the Far East. Most people can read and write. Japanese children study much the same things American children do. English is also taught. Japanese boys and girls even enjoy many of the same sports Americans do, such as baseball, tennis and swimming. Most Japanese are Buddhists. Others are Shinto-ists. (This religion teaches that the emperor is a descendant of the sun goddess.) The Christian religion was brought to Japan about 400 years ago and also has many followers. The temples, shrines and churches of these religions can be seen throughout the islands.

8. The Japanese are very good farmers. Because there is so little farmland, each acre must produce enough to feed seven people. The farmers live in small villages on the coastal lowlands. These villages have radios, TV, electric lights, sewing machines, newspapers and schools. Many of the farmers have second jobs as fishermen or factory workers in order to support their families better.

9. Most Japanese farmers own their own land. Their fields are small and scattered. The work is done chiefly by hand, and the whole family shares in the work. The nearby hillsides are terraced to provide more farmland. In the warm southeast, the chief crop is rice. On the hillsides the farmer may also have tea bushes and mulberry trees. (Silkworms, you remember, feed on the leaves of the mulberry tree.) In the cooler north, wheat, barley and beans are grown. Despite their hard work, Japanese farmers cannot produce all the food the people need. Much food must be imported.

10. The Japanese are not a meat-eating people. (There are few dairy or beef cattle in the country because there is little grazing land.) Next to rice, fish is the most important food. There are many inlets along the coast, so it is

A Japanese family at home.

A classroom in Hokkaido. The Japanese are the most literate people in the Far East.

easy for village fishermen to put out to sea and return. Giant ship canneries roam all over the Pacific, and fish are processed on board as soon as they are caught. Since fish provides much the same nourishment as meat, the people of Japan enjoy a better-balanced diet than most of their

Far Eastern neighbors. In fact, the Japanese are the best-fed people in the Orient. Much fish is also exported to the United States in exchange for cotton, oil and wheat.

11. Compared with India and China, Japan is not rich in natural resources. The chief minerals are coal, gold, copper and sulfur. To keep its factories going, Japan imports such raw materials as oil, cotton, rubber, iron ore and manganese. Large forests cover the mountainsides. The wood is used for fuel and papermaking. However, so much wood has already been used that it must now be imported as well. The chief source of power is falling water, from the many streams that flow down the mountainsides. (These are fed by Japan's heavy rains and snows.)

12. Despite its need for food, raw materials and minerals, Japan is the most highly industrialized country in Asia. It was the first Far Eastern nation to build factories to supply its people with jobs and food. Japanese workers are known for their skill. There are great modern factories employing thousands of workers, as well as many small businesses made up of families working in their homes. Japan also leads the world in shipbuilding. It is the world's leading producer of silk goods. Steel manufacture is important, and Japanese cameras and instruments are known throughout the world.

13. Japan can easily be compared with Great Britain. Both are island nations. Britain's great

A modern shipyard in Yokohama, Japan.

power resource is coal; Japan's is water power. Both nations have developed a factory system that produces goods to trade for food and raw materials. Both have large merchant fleets. Both once ruled overseas empires to provide themselves with raw materials and markets. Now both must provide for their large populations through world trade. Japan's best customer is the United States. Its chief exports are fish, silk, tools, office machines, toys, metal products and clothing. Japan's imports are chiefly the foods and raw materials that it does not have—oil, wheat, raw cotton, rubber, iron, wool and tin.

14. Although it is the most modern nation of the Orient, Japan is not without problems. You have learned that its population is large and is growing larger. Japan must be able to provide more and more food for its people. The nation must also continue to carry on world-wide trade. It must sell goods to pay for its imports. Communist China is nearby and is growing in power. Many of Japan's markets for its goods are in Southeast Asia. Its supply of oil, rubber and tin comes from this area too. The spread of communism to Southeast Asia threatens this source of trade and raw materials. Finally, the Japanese are trying to build democracy within their homeland. They must have peace if their government is to grow in strength. The United States has promised to defend Japan against attack. It is important to us, too, that the Japanese people prosper in peace.

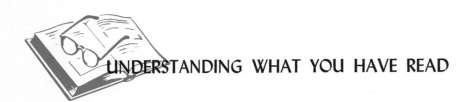

UNDERSTANDING WHAT YOU HAVE READ

1. **Which of the following questions are answered in this chapter?**
a. How is Japan governed?
b. How did the United States help Japan after World War II?
c. How do the Japanese make use of the waters around their islands?

2. **The main idea of *paragraphs 6 through 9* is to describe:**
a. how a small nation supports its people.
b. the farm life in a Japanese village.
c. the Japanese people and their work.

3. **The population of Japan is about:**
a. 50 million.   b. 75 million.   c. 96 million.

4. **Most Japanese are:**
a. Buddhists.   b. Christians.   c. Shintoists.

5. **There is intensive farming on the islands** of Japan because:
a. the Japanese know little of scientific farming.
b. farmers do not have machinery.
c. there is very little farm land.

6. **The Japanese depend a great deal upon manufacturing because they:**
a. must import raw materials.
b. must use finished goods to pay for imports.
c. need clothing for their armed forces.

7. **A *dense population* means that:**
a. the population is large.
b. people are crowded close together.
c. people live mostly near the seacoast.

8. **Canneries are places in which:**
a. foods are prepared for packaging.
b. fishermen prepare to catch fish.
c. tin goods are made.

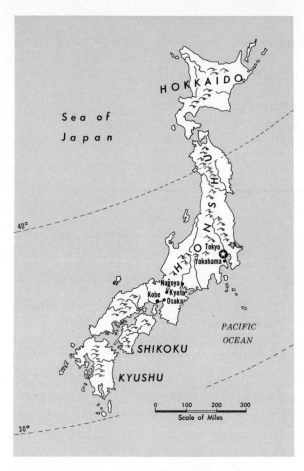

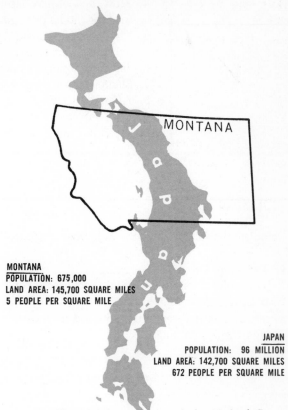

MONTANA
POPULATION: 675,000
LAND AREA: 145,700 SQUARE MILES
5 PEOPLE PER SQUARE MILE

JAPAN
POPULATION: 96 MILLION
LAND AREA: 142,700 SQUARE MILES
672 PEOPLE PER SQUARE MILE

Map # 55a and b—Japan and the United States

DEVELOPING IDEAS AND SKILLS

Map # 55a and b—Japan and the United States
Can you answer these questions?

1. Is Japan located in the high, middle or low latitudes?
2. What is the distance of the Japanese islands, from north to south?
3. On which of the islands are the largest cities located?
4. Osaka, Kobe, Yokohama and Nagoya are all large cities and have the same kind of location. What do they have in common?
5. How would you describe the topography of Japan?
6. What is the name given to a large number of islands surrounded by a large body of water?
7. Which is the more crowded nation, the United States or Japan?
8. Why do you think there are few rivers of great size on the Japanese islands?
9. If you traveled from your community to Tokyo, in which direction would you be traveling?
10. In which direction is the equator from Japan?

SUMMING UP

Do You Agree or Disagree?   Give the reasons for your answers.

1. The Japanese eat much the same foods we do.
2. Japan's islands are very mountainous; there is little lowland for farming.

3. Japan's huge population is crowded into narrow lowlands.
4. Most Japanese are farmers or fishermen; however, they do not produce enough food for the large population.
5. The Japanese depend on manufacturing and trade to pay for the food and goods they must import.
6. Japan has built a modern nation with few natural resources.
7. Shintoists would rather have a president than an emperor ruling Japan.
8. After World War II, Japan began to recover with the help of the United States.
9. Most Japanese cannot read or write.
10. Japan has more factories than any other nation in the Far East.

FOLLOW UP

Complete the following sentences in your notebook.

1. The capital of Japan is _____.
2. The chief food crop of the Japanese people is _____.
3. _____ visited Japan in 1853 and began trade with the United States.
4. There are _____ main islands in Japan.
5. The _____ is the lawmaking body of Japan's government.
6. The Japanese substitute _____ for meat in their diet.
7. _____ buys more goods from Japan than any other nation.
8. Because of the lack of farm land, the Japanese farmer practices _____ farming.

CHAPTER 13

India: The Land of Villages

PROBLEM: Why are so many Indians poor when their country has many advantages?

READING FOR A PURPOSE:
1. Where is the Ganges Plain?
2. Who was Mahatma Gandhi?
3. What are India's large cities?

1. South of the Himalaya Mountains of Asia is a large triangle-shaped peninsula. This large area, about half the size of the United States, is sometimes called a subcontinent. While it is occupied by two countries, India and Pakistan, the nation of India covers most of it. India is the seventh largest nation in the world, taking up about 1,300,000 square miles. With about 480 million people, it is the second most populous country in the world.

2. The Himalaya Mountains form the northern border of India. South of the mountains, a great plain stretches east and west across the subcontinent. The western part of the plain is drained by the Indus River. The eastern part is the valley of the Ganges and Brahmaputra Rivers. Many people live in this valley because the land is so fertile and well watered. South of the plains is the Deccan Plateau. On both sides of the plateau are long, narrow coastal lowlands or plains.

3. India lies mainly in the low latitudes. (Its latitude is about the same as that of Mexico and Central America.) Except in the highlands and mountains, the climate is generally hot and humid. (Because of the Himalayas in the north, the cold winds of central Asia do not reach India.) The rainfall varies throughout the country from the heaviest in the world to very small amounts. The rainfall is controlled by the seasonal winds called monsoons. In the summer (from June to September) the southwest winds bring rain to the land. In the winter the northeast monsoon takes over and blows from the land to the sea. Since it blows from the land, it brings little rain.

4. India had a long history before the Europeans came to its shores looking for tea, spices and jewels. When, in 1601, the British came, they built trading posts and in time ruled all of India. As they educated more people, a strong desire for freedom grew. One of the great leaders for Indian independence was a man called Mahatma Gandhi. He urged the people to fight against British rule, but not to use violence. He

Watering wheat fields in India with an old-fashioned wheel.

UNITED NATIONS

asked the people to refuse to buy British goods and to disobey British laws. He was put in jail many times, but this made him a greater hero to his people. It was largely because of Gandhi that the people of India gained their freedom from Great Britain in 1947.

5. The government of India is partly like that of Great Britain and partly like that of the United States. There is a written constitution. The chief lawmaking body is the Parliament, which has two houses. There is a president, but he has little power. The chief officer is the prime minister. He has the power to suggest laws and to carry them out when they are approved by Parliament. Like the United States, India has a federal government. The powers of the government are divided between the national government and the fifteen states. The capital city is New Delhi. The first prime minister and the leader of India through the first seventeen years of its independence was Jawaharlal Nehru.

6. India is one of the most crowded nations in the world, with about 350 people for each square mile of land. Its people speak many different languages, wear different clothing, eat

The old and new in India—a farmer and his bullocks work near electric power lines.

UNITED NATIONS

different foods and have different colored skins from one part of the country to another. Most of the people are poor farmers who live in thousands of small villages. The farms are owned mostly by large landholders; the farmer gives a share of his crops as payment to the owners. Farmers barely make a living and know little of the great modern world. Most work is done with a wooden plow and simple hand tools. The water buffalo often pulls the plow and the heavy carts. Cattle manure is used for fuel instead of fertilizer for the soil. When the cattle die, their hides are sold. In each village, there is a Hindu temple where the people worship.

7. The chief food crop of the Indian farmer is rice. The big rice areas are the rainy river valleys of the north. Indian farmers do not get as much rice from their land as do the Japanese farmers. There is not enough rice for the large population, so that more rice must be imported. On the drier Deccan Plateau, wheat and millet are grown. These cereals can withstand the drier climate. The chief cash crop of India is cotton. Much of it is grown near the city of Bombay. Indian farmers also grow jute, tea and rubber for export to other lands.

8. Although the nation is largely one of farmers, the number of people who live and work in the cities is growing. Bombay, the largest city of the country, is a seaport on the western coast. Calcutta, at the delta of the Ganges River, is the gateway to the fertile farming lands of the north and east. Madras is a seaport on the eastern coast. In the cities, old India and new India live side by side. The new India can be seen in the many cars and trucks, the Western style of dress, the modern office buildings and shops. Old India is seen in the buffalo carts, the sacred cows, the old bazaars and the many poor that crowd the streets.

9. For hundreds of years, the Indian people turned out wonderful handmade goods in their villages. Now factory production is growing in importance. The largest industry is textiles, made largely from the native cotton. However, iron- and steel-making is growing steadily, for India has many mineral resources. There are

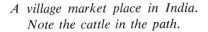

*A village market place in India.
Note the cattle in the path.*

Indian women draw water from a village pipe.

large deposits of iron in the Deccan Plateau. India also has coal, manganese and chromium. The Tata steel works near Calcutta are the largest mills in India. The rising industries—textiles, burlap bags (from jute), iron and steel goods—will gradually change the ways of living of millions of Indians.

10. India is trying very hard to make its government work. There are many problems, however. First, there is a huge population. One out of every seven persons in the world lives in India. There is not enough land to grow food for all the people. Half of the wheat in India comes from the United States, yet most Indians are underfed. India has too many cattle,

and these animals use valuable land. Second, much of India is dry for part of the year. Irrigation projects are needed to reclaim land so that more food can be produced.

11. In the third place, the village people live in "another world." Many of them have barely heard of Gandhi or Nehru. Many of them are sick and cannot read or write. So many different languages are spoken that Indians have a difficult time communicating with one another. Many are terribly poor. The caste system still divides the people, though it has been outlawed by the new government. Finally, India needs help and money to make better use of its resources.

UNDERSTANDING WHAT YOU HAVE READ

1. Which of the following questions are answered in this chapter?
a. Where are Kashmir and Goa?
b. What is the chief food crop of India?
c. What are India's farm problems?

2. The main idea of this chapter is to describe:
a. India's leaders.
b. the Indian farmer.
c. India's ways and peoples.

3. **India gained its freedom largely through the efforts of:**
a. Clive.   b. Churchill.   c. Gandhi.

4. **The winds that bring rain to India's farmers are the:**
a. monsoons.   b. easterlies.   c. hurricanes.

5. **Wheat is grown on the Deccan Plateau** because:
a. water is more plentiful.
b. it can grow better than rice in a drier climate.
c. machinery can be used.

6. **Cattle in India are a problem because:**
a. Moslems consider them to be sacred animals.
b. they graze on valuable land.
c. their meat is of a very poor grade.

DEVELOPING IDEAS AND SKILLS

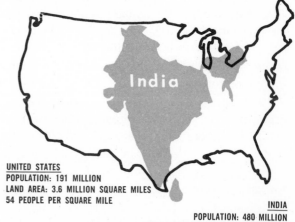

Map # 56a and b—India and the United States

UNITED STATES
POPULATION: 191 MILLION
LAND AREA: 3.6 MILLION SQUARE MILES
54 PEOPLE PER SQUARE MILE

INDIA
POPULATION: 480 MILLION
LAND AREA: 1.3 MILLION SQUARE MILES
380 PEOPLE PER SQUARE MILE

Map # 56a and b—India and the United States
Can you answer these questions?
1. Is India located in the high, middle or low latitudes?
2. How does India compare in size with the United States?
3. In which direction is the equator from India?
4. What are three important port cities of India?
5. How is India separated from Communist China?
6. The rivers of India flow in many directions. Why is this so?
7. What is the great river of northern India?
8. What nation borders India on two different sides?
9. How does the topography of northern India differ from that of the southern half of the country?
10. What is the approximate latitude and longitude of Bombay?
11. Which country is more crowded, India or the United States?
12. What word would you use to describe the land formation of India?

SUMMING UP

In the following, place before each statement the word that makes the statement correct: *Most, Some, A Few*

1. _____ Indians live in river valleys.
2. _____ of India's people live in small villages.
3. _____ people are able to read and write.
4. _____ cattle in India are used for their meat.
5. _____ people of India are poor.
6. _____ people of India work in steel mills.
7. _____ people speak the same language.
8. _____ large cities are seaports.
9. _____ powers of the government are in the hands of the president.
10. _____ parts of India lie in the low latitudes.

FOLLOW UP

I. *True or False*   Tell whether these statements are true or false. The underlined words make the statements true or false. If a statement is false, what word or words would you place in it to make it true?

1. India was once a colony of Great Britain.
2. The chief export crop of India is rice.
3. India's farmers grow jute, a fiber used in making sacks.
4. Most people of India are members of the Moslem religion.
5. The first prime minister of India was Mahatma Gandhi.
6. India's capital is located at New Delhi.
7. The drier southern part of India is known as the Deccan Plateau.
8. India shares the great peninsula with Burma.
9. India is thought to have great deposits of iron ore.
10. Bombay is India's great city near the delta of the Ganges River.

II. *Thinking*
Why are many millions of Indians living in poverty and poorly fed when the nation has so many advantages: large size, many people, fertile land, great numbers of cattle, reserves of iron and coal, much trade?

III. *Doing*
Prepare a diorama of a model village in India, showing these items:
a. the water wells.
b. kinds of roads and buildings.
c. kinds of homes.
d. work the people are doing.

CHAPTER 14

China: Land of the Red Dragon

PROBLEM: Can Red China become a leading industrial nation?

READING FOR A PURPOSE:
1. What is Red China's size and population?
2. How are the Chinese governed?
3. How are the Communists changing China?

1. Communist or mainland China is the largest country in the Far East—slightly larger than the United States. When we speak of Red China and its people, we are really speaking about the land along the eastern coast. This is where the majority of China's 700 million people live. There are high mountains in the south and west. In these mountains is the cold, empty plateau of Tibet. On the west and northwest are dry lands, including the Gobi Desert. On the north is the Soviet Union and on the east, the Pacific Ocean.

2. Unlike the high, dry areas of the west, southeastern China is lined with fertile river valleys and plains. This is the busy center of rice farming and trade. Canals by the thousands connect streams and have been the chief avenues of travel for hundreds of years. The major lowlands are the plains formed by the Hsi and Yangtze Rivers. The winds bring plenty of rain to the rice fields here. The climate of this part of China is the same as in our southeastern states. The largest cities are Shanghai and Canton.

3. The lands farther north are sometimes called North China. They include the valley of the Hwang Ho (Yellow River) and the fertile North China Plain. There is not as much rainfall here. The climate is cold, and there is a shorter growing season. For these reasons, this is the wheat-growing region of China. Most of the land is covered by a fine yellowish-brown dust called *loess*. As you know, the Hwang or Yellow River gets its name from the yellow loess it picks up. The Hwang Ho frequently overflows its banks, causing great damage to the nearby farmlands. The largest cities of North China are Peking and Tientsin. Peking is the capital of Communist China.

4. In the northernmost part of China is the province of Manchuria. The climate is humid continental, like that of our northeastern states. Mukden, the iron and steel center, is about the same distance from the equator as New York City. Here iron ore and coal are found near each other. This area has long been wanted by both Japan and the Soviet Union. Manchuria also has fertile farm land where wheat and millet take the place of rice as the chief food. Fewer people live here than in the warm southeast.

5. The government and life of the Chinese people have changed greatly in the last sixty years. You will recall from Chapter 5 that the republic in China never had a good chance to work. From 1920 to 1949, the Chinese people were invaded by Japan and also fought wars among themselves. In 1949, the Communist forces under Mao Tse-tung forced the Nationalist followers of Chiang Kai-shek to retreat to

Formosa. The Communists have ruled in China since that time.

6. The government of Communist China is much like that of the Soviet Union. This means that there are two governments, the "acting" government and the "real" government. Under the "acting" government, the chief lawmaking body is the National People's Congress. It meets yearly and has little power. The executive branch is the State Council or Cabinet, headed by a premier. The real rulers are the leaders of the Communist Party. There are about 13 million Party members, forming the largest Communist Party in the world. Party members hold the most important jobs and carry out government plans throughout the nation. Party-controlled newspapers and radio continually explain the plans of the Party to the people. The Party controls the army, the labor unions and the new youth groups. It decides what is to be taught in school. It controls most of the resources of the nation.

7. The Communists are changing the ways of living in China. For hundreds of years, the custom was for all members of a Chinese family to live together in the same house. The oldest male was the head of the home and the family worked for him. Most people could not read or write, so the village scholar was a respected person. Furthermore, most of the people practiced Buddhism, Confucianism, Taoism or Christianity. This way of life has been changed by the Communist rulers. Most children are now sent to school. Instead of loyalty to family and friends, loyalty to the Party is now taught. Religion is frowned upon. Instead of working for the family, people now work for the state. Women have been encouraged to work alongside men.

8. Farm life is also being changed by the Communist government. In China, as in other Asian lands, most people are farmers. More and more of their farm lands have been turned into "communes" or state farms. These communes are like factories in the fields; some are as large as 10,000 acres. The communes are different from the Soviet collective farms. On the Soviet collective farm, each member of the collective shares in the crop that is raised. In the commune, the workers are paid for the jobs they do, as on a Soviet state farm. Communes are directed by members of the Communist Party. On a rice commune, hand labor is still used. On a wheat commune there may be tractors and a mill to grind the grain. Most villages in the commune have electricity and schools. After several years of this system, Communist China is still importing food to feed her hungry millions.

9. The government of Red China owns the factories and mines as well as the farms. The Communist goal is to make China a great industrial power. Red China has coal and iron, manganese and tungsten. Only oil is lacking. The Chinese people are being pressed to build new factories and open new mines. Dams are being built to control floods and provide water for irrigation. Miles of railroad track are being laid. Trade with other nations of Asia is rapidly expanding.

10. In the Far East, the improvement in the standard of living of the millions of poor farmers is a goal of most governments. India and Japan are trying to follow the democratic way toward improvement. China is trying the Communist way. Millions in Asia are watching the

Mao Tse-tung, Chairman of the Central People's Government of China.

Chinese commune members divide newly harvested grain.

Eastfoto

work of communism very closely. The United States is watching as well, for it has a great interest in the outcome.

11. The United States is also worried about the growing military strength of Red China. China used its armies to support North Korea in the war with South Korea, 1950-1953. In 1962, Chinese soldiers invaded northern India; there were further misunderstandings between the two nations in 1965. China is now supporting the forces of North Vietnam. In 1964, Red China exploded an atomic bomb. China's growing power must have an effect on the newer nations of Asia and Africa. But this power has made enemies, too. India does not look upon Red China as a friend. What's more, the Soviet Union and Red China have "split" in their views of the goals of communism.

12. The Nationalist government of China still occupies the island of Formosa, about 100 miles east of the Chinese mainland. American troops are on the island, for the United States supports Chiang Kai-shek and his Nationalist government. Formosa is a crowded island of some ten million people. As in most of the Far East, the island is mountainous and the people live in the plains. Rice is the important product, although tea is grown for export.

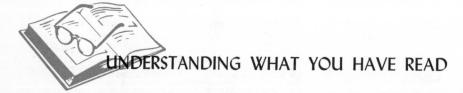

UNDERSTANDING WHAT YOU HAVE READ

1. Which of the following questions are answered in this chapter?

a. How did the Communists come into power?

b. Where do most of the people of China live?

c. Where is Hong Kong?

2. The main idea of *paragraphs 5 through 9* is to describe:

a. how the Communists are changing China.

b. how Red China differs from the Soviet Union.

c. the strength of Communist China today.

3. **The capital of Communist China is:**

a. Nanking.   b. Shanghai.   c. Peking.

4. **The chief area of fertile farm land in China is located in the:**

a. northwest.   b. northeast.   c. southeast.

5. **The Communists have changed the farm life of the people in that:**

a. large farms called "communes" have sprung up.

b. much farm machinery is seen everywhere on Chinese farms.

c. more people own their own land.

6. **Communist China is causing concern to the United States because:**

a. the Chinese now produce enough food to feed all their people.

b. China now produces enough steel for all its uses.

c. Chinese military strength is growing.

DEVELOPING IDEAS AND SKILLS

Map # 57a and b—Communist China and the United States

UNITED STATES
POPULATION: 191 MILLION
LAND AREA: 3.6 MILLION SQUARE MILES
54 PEOPLE PER SQUARE MILE

CHINA
POPULATION: 700 MILLION
LAND AREA: 3.7 MILLION SQUARE MILES
190 PEOPLE PER SQUARE MILE

Map # 57a and b—Communist China and the United States

Can you answer these questions?

1. Is Communist China in the high, middle or low latitudes?
2. Which is larger in size, the United States or Communist China?
3. From the map, can you tell where most of China's millions of people live?
4. How would you describe the topography of Communist China?
5. What is the big industrial city of Manchuria?
6. What countries border Communist China?
7. How far is it from Shanghai to the far western border of Red China?
8. What is the source of both the Yellow and Yangtze Rivers?
9. How far is Taiwan (Nationalist China) from the mainland of Red China?
10. What is the approximate latitude and longitude of Nanking?
11. If you flew from your community to Peking, in which direction would you be traveling?
12. What is the British-held city off the coast of southern China?

SUMMING UP

Do You Agree or Disagree? Give the reasons for your answers.
1. China is a small country with a large population.
2. Most of China is not good farm land.
3. Most of the people live in the fertile river valleys of the southeast.
4. Most transportation routes in Communist China have been waterways.
5. Mainland China is ruled by the Nationalist government of Chiang Kai-shek.
6. The Communists want to change China from a farming nation to a nation of mills and factories.
7. The people own the farm lands and factories of China.
8. Most young Chinese are now going to school.
9. China has large stores of all the important minerals.
10. Because of a strong army, the influence of Chinese communism is spreading throughout eastern Asia.

FOLLOW UP

I. Tell whether the following items refer to Communist China, India or to both countries. If an item applies to Communist China only, write C in your notebook; if it applies to India only, write I; if it applies to both countries, write B.

1. Not enough food is grown to feed all the people of the country.
2. More than half the people cannot read or write.
3. Rice is the chief food crop.
4. There is a population of more than 700 million people.
5. This nation is trying to have friendly relations with the United States.
6. This nation is larger in area than the United States.
7. There are fertile river valleys.
8. Farms are organized into communes.
9. Most people are farmers.
10. The government is similar to Great Britain's.

II. In many ways, the geography of Red China and the United States is similar. For example, the shape of China is very much like that of the U.S. Both are located about the same distance between the equator and the North Pole. Can you think of other geographic similarities between the two countries?

CHAPTER 15

Southeast Asia: New Nations With Problems

PROBLEM: How are the lands of Southeast Asia important to us?

READING FOR A PURPOSE:
1. What are the lands of Southeast Asia?
2. Who are the people of this region?
3. What are the special problems of these countries?

1. The world has long been interested in the lands of Southeast Asia. Early explorers sought a water route to the "Spice Islands," as part of Southeast Asia was once called. European nations were so eager for the resources of these lands that almost the entire region became colonies of nations of Europe. High as the interest of the world may have been in this area in past centuries, it was never greater than it is at this moment. Since independence came to most of the small countries of Southeast Asia, wars and the threat of Chinese communism have made the most news from this part of the world.

2. Southeast Asia includes the lands east of India and Pakistan and south of China and Japan. Part of this region lies on the continent of Asia, ending in the Malay Peninsula that extends southeast from the continent (see map, page 428). On the mainland of Asia are the nations of Burma, Thailand, Malaysia, Cambodia, Laos, North and South Vietnam and the city-state of Singapore. To the south and east are the archipelagoes of Indonesia and the Philippines and thousands of smaller islands. The total land area of Southeast Asia is about one half that of the United States, although it stretches across a greater distance from east to west.

3. In the entire region there are more than 220 million people, twice the number for each square mile of land as in the United States. The island of Java, part of Indonesia, has more than 1,000 people per square mile of land. This island alone has more than half of Indonesia's total population of 105 million.

4. Because so much of the region is water, and because it lies near the busy mainland of

A mother and her children in a Southeast Asian village.

Asia, it contains many important waterways. The Strait of Malacca, which separates the Malay Peninsula and the island of Sumatra, is one of the most important water passages in the world. The city of Singapore, located on the strait, is one of the world's leading ports. A huge amount of trade passes through the waters of Southeast Asia as goods are shipped to and from the Far East and the ports of Europe and America.

5. After the early explorers found the Spice Islands, European nations divided up almost the entire region among themselves. The Dutch held control over many of the islands, chiefly the ones that today make up Indonesia. Great Britain held Burma, the Malay Peninsula and Singapore. (That nation still has close ties with its former colonies.) The French colonized Indochina, now the countries of Cambodia, Laos and North and South Vietnam. Because of Magellan's voyage, the Spanish claimed the Philippines and ruled them until war with the United States in 1898. After that, the U.S. owned the Philippines until 1946, when freedom was granted. Only Thailand was ruled by its own kings for hundreds of years. Since 1946, all the nations here that were once colonies have gained their freedom.

6. This is a tropical region. Only the northern part of Burma lies outside the low latitudes. Yet because the lands are mountainous, almost any kind of climate may be found. The hardships are greatest in the lowlands where most of the people live. There are heavy rains, thick forests, poor soils in many places and the ever-present tropical diseases. Burma, Thailand, Vietnam and parts of the Philippines have the monsoon climate as in India. There may be little or no rain during the winter months, but from sixty to eighty inches of rain may fall from June to September. The archipelagoes of Indonesia and the Philippines were partly formed by volcanoes. On the Indonesian island of Java, the volcanic soils are fertile. Because much food can be grown, there is a huge population on the island.

7. Most of the people of Southeast Asia are "brown-skinned" Malays. However, in most countries there is a mixture of nationalities and religions. Chinese influence on these nations has been very strong. The Chinese are the largest minority group in Southeast Asia. In Malaysia, Chinese and Indians make up more than half the population. In the countries that border China, Buddhism is the largest religion. The Moslem religion has spread throughout the Malay Peninsula and Indonesia. In the Philippines, because of its Spanish settlement, more than ninety per cent of the people are Christians.

8. As you might expect, most of the people of Southeast Asia are farmers. They live in villages near their fields. This village life, in which

Teak rafts floating down to a sawmill in Rangoon, Burma.

people of different cultures live close together in peace, is a striking feature of life in this part of the world. One of the problems now in the region is the movement of people from the villages to the cities. The old family and village ties are breaking up. Cities are growing in size: Jakarta, Indonesia; Bangkok, Thailand; Saigon, South Vietnam; Rangoon, Burma; Manila, the Philippines; and Singapore. The outside world comes to Southeast Asia through the cities. Many are modern with wide, paved streets, tall buildings, electricity and air-conditioning. The wealth of Singapore is seen by the visitor in the grand homes and beautiful avenues of the city. Behind the main streets, however, are the slums that are a part of all Far Eastern cities.

9. The largest number of people make their living growing rice. The best rice-growing areas are the river valleys: the Irrawaddy in Burma, the Chao Phraya in Thailand and the Mekong in South Vietnam. The river valleys make these three nations the leading rice-exporting nations in the world. Most is exported to neighboring countries where it is badly needed. In areas of less rainfall, corn, millet, beans and sweet potatoes are grown.

10. Plantation farming is important in Southeast Asia. Plantation products are sold mainly to foreign countries. This kind of farming was begun by European and American businessmen. Each of the large farms specializes in one crop. The rubber plantations supply ninety per cent of the world's supply of natural rubber. Malaysia and Indonesia are the leading producers. Indonesia is also a large exporter of tea. More than half the world's coconut oil is produced in Malaysia and the Philippines. Palm oil, sugar, coffee and pepper are other plantation crops. Teak wood and quinine (used as a medicine in treating malaria) are products of the forests.

11. There are rich mineral resources, too. Southeast Asia produces half the world's supply of tin. Malaysia and the Philippines mine iron ore and manganese, a metal used in making fine steel. From Thailand we get tungsten, the long-burning metal in light bulbs. Oil is found in Indonesia, although it is a small part

A poor mountain village in Laos on the Red Chinese border.

of the world's supply. These minerals are mined for export. Because there is such mineral wealth in Southeast Asia, we can expect future development of industries in these countries.

12. The problems of the Southeast Asian nations are similar to problems of other underdeveloped regions around the world. Most of the people are poor, hungry, sick and illiterate. Indonesia, however, has made great gains in increasing the education of her people. The wealth of Southeast Asia is produced largely for the rest of the world. Very little of it is shared with the people who produce it. Furthermore, the people have had little experience in democratic government. They have lived far removed from the large cities, away from the ports and contact with world affairs.

13. Skilled workers and money are needed to start local industries. This will help to develop local buyers for the goods produced in Southeast Asia. The people must be able to share in the riches of their lands. Added to the problem of use of resources is the Communist desire to control the new, smaller nations of Asia. Wars in Laos and Vietnam have been caused by Communist influences. Indonesia's interest in friendship with Communist China presents further problems. The entire Free World looks with concern at the events in Southeast Asia.

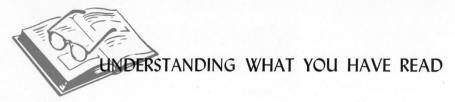

UNDERSTANDING WHAT YOU HAVE READ

1. Which of the following questions are answered in this chapter?

a. Why is the city of Singapore important?

b. How do people farm in Southeast Asia?

c. What countries are located on the mainland of Asia?

2. The main idea of *paragraphs 9 through 11* is to describe:

a. the chief products of Southeast Asia.

b. reasons for our interest in this region.

c. kinds of rice farming in Southeast Asia.

3. Most of the people of Southeast Asia live in:

a. large cities.

b. fertile lowlands.

c. hilly woodlands.

4. All of these are countries of Southeast Asia EXCEPT:

a. Malaysia.   b. Laos.   c. Iran.

5. All of these are important minerals of Southeast Asia EXCEPT:

a. mercury.   b. manganese.   c. tin.

6. All of these are large exports of Southeast Asia EXCEPT:

a. wheat.   b. rubber.   c. tea.

7. A reason why Southeast Asia is important in world affairs is that:

a. it has large deposits of coal.

b. its people have a high standard of living.

c. a great amount of trade passes in and around these lands.

8. A reason for poor transportation in Southeast Asia is that:

a. the lands are largely unexplored.

b. much of the land is forest.

c. narrow straits keep ocean-going ships from passing near the large land area.

DEVELOPING IDEAS AND SKILLS

Photograph Study

This photograph should help you to recall parts of the chapter you have just read. Can you explain the main idea of the photograph? Where in the chapter is it described?

UNITED NATIONS

SUMMING UP

Do You Agree or Disagree? Give the reasons for your answers.

1. The lands of Southeast Asia were ruled by one nation until 1946.
2. It would be unusual to find a Hindu temple or Moslem mosque in the villages of Southeast Asia.
3. Some of these lands were once known as the "Spice Islands."
4. Only since 1950 has the world become interested in Southeast Asia.
5. In some countries of this region, there is more than enough rice to feed the nation's people.
6. Mountains and large bodies of water have kept the people of Southeast Asia free from the influence of Communist China.
7. The countries of Southeast Asia can be called underdeveloped countries.
8. The tiny country of South Vietnam is of great interest to the people of the United States.

FOLLOW UP

Make a report on one of the countries of Southeast Asia. You may divide your report under these headings:

a. Land and Climate
b. The People
c. Progress in Farming and Industry
d. Leading Figures of the Country's History
e. Population Centers and Cities
f. Problems Faced by the Country
g. Plans for the Future

Groups in the class may study individual countries. Assemble pictures or bulletin-board displays of the nation you are studying. Current magazines, travel folders, government information agencies or magazines that deal with geography will provide you with information. Use the same headings for your display as for the written report.

BOOKS FOR UNIT 8

Author	Title, Publisher	Description
1. Bothwell, Jean	*The Missing Violin*, Harcourt	How Americans adjust to living in India.
2. Bro, Margueritte Harmon	*Su-Mei's Golden Year*, Doubleday	How a young girl saves a wheat crop in China.
3. Buck, Pearl	*The Big Wave*, Day	A tidal wave and its effects on a coastal village in Japan.
4. Clark, Roger	*Ride the White Tiger*, Little, Brown	The problems of a boy in war-torn Korea.
5. Dean, Vera and H. D. Harootunian	*Builders of Emerging Nations*, Holt, Rinehart	Brief pictures of the new leaders of Asia and Africa.
6. DeJong, Meindert	*House of Sixty Fathers*, Harper	The story of a little Chinese boy during the Japanese occupation of China in World War II.
7. Eaton, Jeanette	*Gandhi*, Morrow	A biography of the man who led India to freedom from Great Britain.
8. Fairservis, Walter	*Horsemen of the Steppes*, World	An exciting tale of the nomadic horsemen who overran great parts of Europe and Asia.
9. Kennedy, Jean	*Here Is India*, Scribner	The people and history of India by a person who grew up there.
10. MacGregor-Hastie, Roy	*The Red Barbarians*, Chilton	The life and times of Mao Tse-tung.
11. Potter, Jeffrey	*Elephant Bridge*, Viking	How a Burmese boy is adopted by an elephant herd.
12. Sommerfelt, Aimee	*The White Bungalow*, Criterion	The story of life in a small Indian village.
13. Uchida, Yoshiko	*Takao and Grandfather's Sword*, Harcourt	How a boy grows up in modern Japan.

UNIT 9

The Pacific World

CHAPTER 1

The World of Water

PROBLEM: How were the lands of the Pacific settled?

READING FOR A PURPOSE:
1. What do we mean by the Pacific World?
2. How was Australia settled?
3. How did World War II affect this region?

1. The Pacific World is the "world of water." In this region we find Australia, New Zealand and the thousands of islands of the Pacific Ocean. The Pacific World covers an area of 69 million square miles, more than all the land areas on the earth put together! The Pacific Ocean is the most important influence in the life of the people here. Australia, the island continent, is the largest mass of land in the region.

2. The entire region of the Pacific World is made up of islands. These range in size from the large continent of Australia to the tiny coral reefs or *atolls*. Except for Australia and New Zealand (and the islands of Indonesia that we studied with the Far East), these lands are governed by other nations. Their people have differ-

ent ways of making a living, from simple hunting, fishing and farming to the most modern kinds of manufacturing. Some of the people live very poorly, while others have a high standard of living.

3. It is thought that Australia was once connected to the mainland of Asia. Long ago, part of the land between them sank and the ocean waters covered it. All that remained above water were the islands of Indonesia and New Guinea. Over these island "bridges" from Asia came many of the animals and people who now live in the Pacific World. These early people were called *aborigines*. They lived by hunting, fishing and gathering fruits. They roamed freely until the Europeans came in the eighteenth century.

4. In 1770, long after our own New World had been found, Europeans discovered Australia. In that year an Englishman named Captain James Cook sailed along the eastern coast of Australia and claimed the land for Great Britain. The first English colony in Australia was started in 1788—years after the American Declaration of Independence from Great Britain! This colony was made up of convicts or prisoners. New Zealand was not settled until more than fifty years after that. Settlements did not grow quickly in the region because it was felt that the lands had few resources.

5. In the middle of the nineteenth century, whaling ships began to sail throughout the Pacific World in search of whales for oil. They stopped at the islands to get fresh water and food. In exchange for these items, they gave the natives such goods as cloth, tobacco and glass beads. At the same time, missionaries began to go to the islands. The ways of life of the natives began to change as contact with Westerners increased.

6. In 1851, gold was discovered in Australia. This was two years after our own gold rush in California. People hurried in great numbers to the southern continent. In less than seven years, Australia's population doubled. The Europeans pushed the native people farther inland.

7. Later in the nineteenth century, European nations took a new interest in the Pacific World.

Australia drew many people during the early gold rush days.

They wanted some of the raw materials of this area. They also wanted places of supply for ships sailing across the Pacific Ocean. When the west coast of the United States was settled after 1850, our nation also increased trade with the Far East. In 1898, the United States gained Hawaii. After the Spanish-American War we also acquired the Philippines and Guam. Our interest in the other Pacific islands and Australia grew as well.

8. After World War I, Japan was given many islands in the Pacific as "mandates" by the League of Nations. The Japanese fortified these islands with guns. After attacking Pearl Harbor in 1941, Japan overran other Pacific islands and lands in Southeast Asia. Bloody battles were fought throughout the Pacific before the war ended in August, 1945. The islands of Tarawa, Guadalcanal and Iwo Jima are familiar to Americans as battlegrounds in the Pacific during the war with Japan. After World War II, many of the islands were made a United Nations trust territory under the care of the United States. Other trust territories in the Pacific were assigned to some of the European nations.

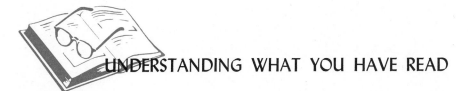

UNDERSTANDING WHAT YOU HAVE READ

1. Which of the following questions are answered in this chapter?
a. Who were Tasman and Bougainville?
b. What event in the nineteenth century caused an increase in the population of Australia?
c. Why were Europeans slow to settle in Australia?

2. The main idea of this chapter is to describe:
a. early settlements in New Zealand.
b. Australia's part in World War II.
c. important events in the history of the Pacific World.

3. Australia was claimed by Great Britain because of the voyages of:

a. Cook.　　b. Magellan.　　c. da Gama.

4. The first settlers in Australia were:

a. traders.　　b. farmers.　　c. convicts.

5. Europeans were slow to explore Australia because:

a. the natives were unfriendly.
b. Europeans thought it had no riches.
c. there were no good harbors.

6. The Europeans first came to this region in search of:

a. colonies.
b. spices and raw materials.
c. slaves.

7. The *aborigines* of Australia are like which people in the history of the United States?

a. Indians.　　b. Spanish.　　c. Negroes.

8. *Atolls* are:

a. early people of New Zealand.
b. small coral islands of the Pacific.
c. early whaling ships.

Map # 58—The Pacific World

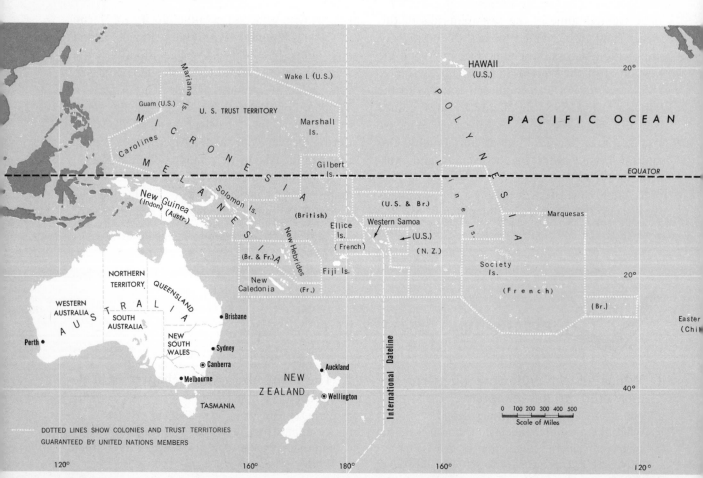

DEVELOPING IDEAS AND SKILLS

Map # 58—The Pacific World
Tell whether these statements are true or false.

1. The continent of Australia is occupied by many countries.
2. Micronesia and Polynesia are in the Atlantic Ocean.
3. New Zealand is northeast of Australia.
4. Australia is south of the equator.
5. The islands of Micronesia lie both north and south of the equator.
6. The Hawaiian Islands are the largest group in Polynesia.
7. Most islands in the Pacific are free.
8. The United States has a "trust territory" in the Pacific.
9. The Far Eastern region is closer to the "lands down under" than any other.
10. Most of Australia's people live on the western coast.

SUMMING UP

Do You Agree or Disagree? Give reasons for your answers.

1. Australia was settled long after our New World was found.
2. Nearly all people in the Pacific World do the same kind of work.
3. Most of the people of the Pacific islands govern themselves.
4. As a result of several wars, the United States now has a real interest in the Pacific World.
5. Before World War II, the most powerful nation in the Pacific World was Japan.
6. Between Australia and Asia there are many islands.
7. In the last few years, whaling ships have begun to visit the Pacific lands.
8. The United States has island possessions in the Pacific Ocean.

FOLLOW UP

Arrange these events *in the order in which they took place.*

1. Whaling ships and traders appear.
2. Aborigines come to Australia.
3. World War II ends.
4. The Spanish-American War is fought.
5. Voyages of exploration take place.
6. Gold rush to Australia brings settlers.
7. First colony in Australia is established.

CHAPTER 2

The Lands Down Under

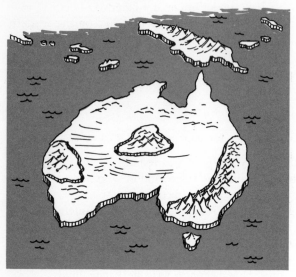

PROBLEM: What are the topography and climate of Australia and New Zealand?

READING FOR A PURPOSE:
1. Where is Australia located?
2. Where is Australia's desert?
3. What effect does the ocean have on the climate of New Zealand?

1. Australia is called the island continent. It is the only country to occupy an entire continent by itself. You could call Australia the smallest continent or the largest island on earth. With approximately three million square miles, it is the sixth largest country in the world. Australia is also called the "land down under," for it is entirely south of the equator. Therefore, its seasons are the opposite of ours. Australia's summer lasts from November to April; winter is from May to October.

2. Australia is located partly in the low latitudes and partly in the middle latitudes. Its location can be compared with that of Mexico and Central America, except that it is south of the equator instead of north. The large city of Melbourne, on the southeast tip of the continent, is 37° south—not as far south of the equator as Cincinnati, Ohio, is north. Australia is farther from the United States than any other major country. The airline distance from San Francisco to Sydney, Australia, is 7,500 miles!

3. Along Australia's east coast is a narrow coastal plain. A few miles inland, the land rises to become the eastern highlands or Great Dividing Range. These are the only mountains in Australia. They are not as high as some of the peaks in our Rocky Mountains. West of the mountains is a great central plain. This is called the "outback." Farther west, the land rises to form a vast, dry plateau. This plateau extends all the way to the western coast. Off the northeastern coast is a long coral reef called the Great Barrier Reef. It has been built up over the ages by millions of tiny sea animals.

4. Lack of water is a serious problem in most of Australia. There are no great rivers like the Congo, Mississippi or Amazon leading into the continent. The largest river is the Murray-Darling, which rises in the eastern highlands and flows southwest into the Indian Ocean.

5. Australia has a varied climate. The north and northeast have a savanna climate. In these areas there is a rainy season and a dry season. During the summer, the monsoons bring rain. During the winter, the wind shifts and the area is dry. It is always hot. The soil is poor because of the heavy rains. As you might guess, few people live in this part of the continent.

6. Most Australians live along the eastern coast. In general, this part of the country has a mild, damp climate. There is plenty of rainfall for farming. The largest cities are also located here. North of the city of Sydney, the climate is humid subtropical. South of Sydney, it is a marine climate as in our northwestern states.

7. Beyond the mountains to the west there is less rainfall. The winds that blow over the mountains have lost much of their moisture by the time they reach this area. This is a region of dry grasslands where the rainfall is from ten to twenty inches a year. It is a steppe climate. The

A highway through the "outback."

region is almost too dry for farming, but it is good for sheep grazing.

8. As you travel farther west, the land becomes drier and drier. The western half of Australia is a vast desert of sand and rock. (In fact, forty per cent of the country is desert!) Because of the mountains, no rain-bearing winds can reach this part of the continent. There are no regular winds blowing from the Indian Ocean to the east. South of the desert, the coastal areas have a Mediterranean climate—warm, dry summers and mild winters with some rain.

9. New Zealand lies about 1,200 miles southeast of Australia. It is located entirely in the middle latitudes. This country is made up of two main islands, North Island and South Island. Although they are each nearly 1,000 miles long, the islands are narrow, scarcely more than 200 miles wide. This means that the climate of the islands is affected by the ocean around them. These are mountainous islands; there are no deserts as in Australia. The winds blow from the west, so the west coast has more rain than the east coast. New Zealanders enjoy a marine climate, with mild and rainy summers and winters. The climate of New Zealand may be compared with that of its "mother country," Great Britain.

UNDERSTANDING WHAT YOU HAVE READ

1. **Which of the following questions are answered in this chapter?**
a. How do the people live in the northeast of Australia?
b. Why is it warm in Australia at Christmas time?
c. How do the mountains of Australia affect its climate?

2. **The main idea of this chapter is to describe:**
a. New Zealand's climate.
b. the desert area of Australia.
c. Australia's land and climate.

3. **New Zealand's climate is chiefly:**

a. marine.   b. desert.   c. rain forest.   c. high latitudes.

4. A great part of Australia cannot be used because it is:

a. too wet.   b. too dry.   c. too cold.

5. Seasons in Australia and New Zealand are the opposite of ours because these countries are in the:

a. northern hemisphere.

b. southern hemisphere.

6. The heart of Australia is dry because:

a. rain-bearing winds are blocked by eastern mountains.

b. there are few rivers.

c. the country is too near the equator.

7. The "outback" refers to:

a. the coral reefs along the Australian coast.

b. the dry central plain.

c. reservations where the aborigines live.

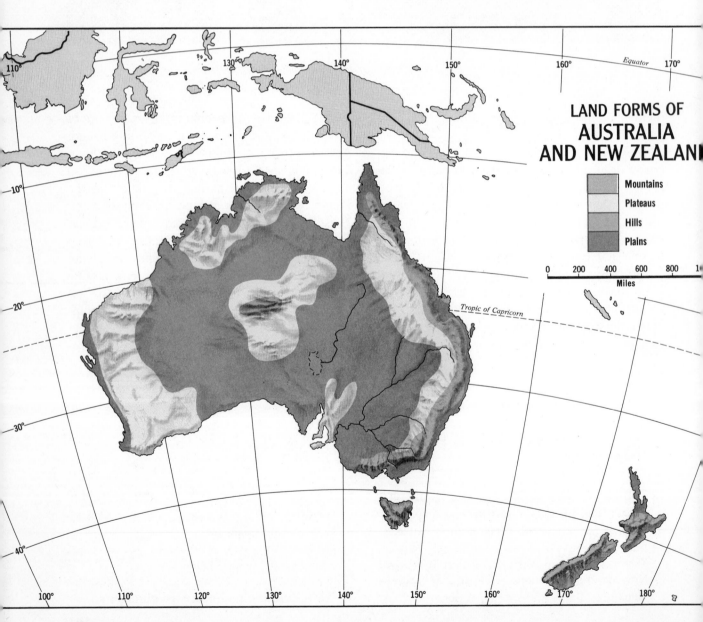

LAND FORMS OF
**AUSTRALIA
AND NEW ZEALAND**

Mountains
Plateaus
Hills
Plains

0   200   400   600   800   1
Miles

Equator

Tropic of Capricorn

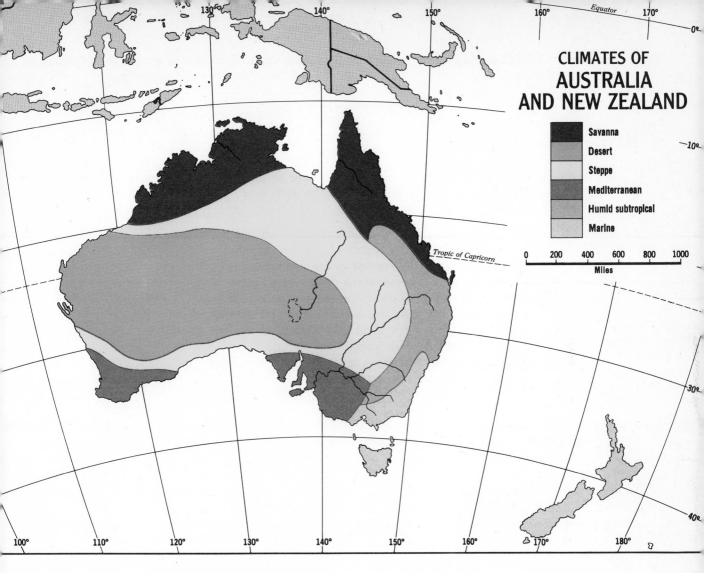

CLIMATES OF AUSTRALIA AND NEW ZEALAND

Savanna
Desert
Steppe
Mediterranean
Humid subtropical
Marine

0	200	400	600	800	1000

Miles

DEVELOPING IDEAS AND SKILLS

Map # 59—Land Forms of Australia and New Zealand

Tell whether these statements are *true* or *false*. Be able to explain your answers.

1. The striking feature of New Zealand is that it is chiefly a plateau.
2. The highest mountains in Australia are located along the southeastern coast.
3. Comparing the climate of Australia with its land forms, it is clear that most of Australia's desert is lowland.
4. Plains line the Australian coast on the south.
5. Most of the warm part of Australia is highland.
6. The eastern and western coasts of Australia have the same kinds of land forms.

Map # 60—Climates of Australia and New Zealand

Do You Agree or Disagree? Give reasons for your answers.

1. Both Australia and New Zealand have a great variety of climates.
2. The largest climatic region in Australia is desert.
3. Part of southern Australia is like southern California.
4. New Zealand has the same kind of climate as our northeastern states.
5. Only a small part of Australia has a climate like that of New Zealand.
6. As you travel northward along the eastern coast of Australia, temperatures become higher.

505

7. The heaviest rainfall in Australia is along the southwestern coast.

8. New Zealand's climate is strange for a country that lies largely in the middle latitudes.

SUMMING UP

Tell whether these statements are true or false. The underlined words make the statements true or false. If a statement is false, what word or words would you place in it to make it true?

1. As you travel north in Australia, the climate becomes warmer.
2. August is one of Australia's summer months.
3. Australia is the smallest of the continents.
4. Most of New Zealand is a great lowland plain.
5. New Zealand is located in the middle latitudes.
6. Most Australians live in the eastern part of the continent.
7. The largest single climate of Australia is the rain forest.
8. West of Australia is the Indian Ocean.
9. New Zealanders enjoy largely a marine climate.
10. Australia has a regular coastline.

FOLLOW UP

Plan a trip to Australia

1. How would you travel?
2. What time of year would you plan to go?
3. Which part of Australia would you like to visit?
4. What clothes would you take with you?
5. What languages would you study to prepare yourself?
6. What kind of people would you expect to find?

CHAPTER 3

The Modern People

PROBLEM: Who are the people of the "lands down under"?

READING FOR A PURPOSE:

1. How do most Australians earn a living?
2. Where do most Australians live?
3. What is the standard of living of the Australian people?

1. The populations of Australia and New Zealand are both small. Australia has about eleven million people (fewer than the state of New York or California) and New Zealand has about three million. These are mostly white people whose language, customs and ways of living are like those of Great Britain, Canada and the United States.

2. Australia is one of the most lightly populated countries in the world, with an average of only four people for each square mile of land. Because so much of the country is dry, most of the people live around the "rim" of the continent. In this respect, Australia is much like South America. The population is growing slowly. The Australians want people to come to their country, but they do not allow "non-

whites" from Africa and Asia to settle there. This lack of a rapidly growing population holds back the full development of the nation.

3. The first people of both Australia and New Zealand were the non-white aborigines. In Australia, these people are called Bushmen. They lived by hunting and gathering wild fruits. The Bushmen of Australia were pushed off their land by the white settlers in much the same way as the Indians were in North America. Today the aborigines make up less than one per cent of the people of Australia. Some are nomads on the "outback"; others live on government reservations or near the large cities.

4. In New Zealand the aborigines are Maoris. The Maoris are brown-skinned people. They fought against white men's settlement of the islands. After a while they accepted the new-comers and their ways of life. Today, there are about 300,000 Maoris in New Zealand; they enjoy the same rights as all other people in the country. They are educated, and many are lawyers, doctors and teachers.

5. While most of the land is used for raising sheep and cattle, most Australians live in cities where they work in factories, offices and shops. Most of the large cities are located in the southeast. (The port city of Perth on the west coast is the only large city outside the east.) The largest city is Sydney, which has more than two million people. Melbourne, in the mild marine climate of the southeast, is a seaport with more than one million people. Other large cities are Brisbane, Adelaide and Canberra, the capital.

A school in New South Wales. Many of the children are descendants of the aborigines.

Australian News & Information Bureau

A meeting of the Australian Parliament in Canberra, the nation's capital.

6. The cities of Australia are modern. They are remarkably clean and have very few areas that could be called slums. The people enjoy the comforts of modern living. Washing machines, refrigerators, radios and television sets are part of most city homes. The streets are wide and automobiles are everywhere. The Australians love to travel. If one considers the small population, Australia has more miles of highway and railroad track for its people than any other nation in the world. (However, the roads and railroads are found mostly in the populated areas.) Most of the major airlines also have routes to Australia. World travelers find Australia a wonderful place to visit.

7. Much of the success of the people of Australia and New Zealand can be traced to their governments. Both countries have a democratic form of government modeled after that of Great Britain. The chief lawmaking body in each is a parliament, elected by the people. The head of each government is the prime minister. They and the members of their cabinets lead their countries with the help of the parliaments. The governments of Australia and New Zealand were the first to pass many laws that have since been adopted by our own country: the secret ballot, the right of women to vote and pensions for workers. Both countries are members of the British Commonwealth of Nations.

8. The people of these two nations are among the most highly educated in the world. Children must attend school to the age of fifteen. It would be difficult to find an adult in either country who is not able to read and write. These nations wish to keep their high standards. As a result,

Most Australian cities are modern. This is Sydney, capital of the province of New South Wales.

their laws allow only people of a certain income or training to become citizens.

9. Both Australians and New Zealanders are great sports-loving people. In Australia, tennis is a favorite sport. Great tennis players have represented Australia in tournaments around the world. In track meets and swimming contests among nations, runners and swimmers from Australia have also become world-famous. Horse racing and cricket draw large crowds everywhere in the country.

10. In many ways, Australia is much like Canada. Both countries are very large but have small populations. Most of the people live along the "rim" of each country. In one case, the interior is largely a cold, watery wilderness; in the other, it is a dry, sandy desert. Both peoples have a high standard of living with most of them living in cities and working in offices, shops or factories. Despite their small populations, they are able to export foodstuffs and raw materials. Much of their trade is with either the United States or Great Britain.

UNDERSTANDING WHAT YOU HAVE READ

1. **Which of the following questions are answered in this chapter?**
   a. What are the large cities of New Zealand?
   b. How are the Maoris treated in New Zealand?
   c. How are the people of Australia governed?

2. **The main idea of this chapter is to describe:**
   a. the cities of the Pacific World.
   b. the ways of living of people "down under."
   c. the life of the aborigines.

3. **Most people in Australia work:**
   a. on farms and plantations.
   b. on ranches.
   c. in factories and offices.

4. **Both Australia and New Zealand have ways of life that have come from the:**
   a. Spanish.　　b. British.　　c. aborigines.

5. **The population of Australia is growing slowly because:**
   a. non-white immigrants are not welcome in the country.
   b. only a small part of the land can be used.
   c. the standard of living of the people is very low.

6. **Australia may be called a "hollow continent" because:**
   a. most people live along the coasts.
   b. it is shaped like a saucer.
   c. there are no rivers in the interior.

7. *Aborigines* **refer to the:**
   a. earliest people in a region.
   b. original plants and trees of a region.
   c. earliest European settlers.

DEVELOPING IDEAS AND SKILLS

Pictograph # 16—Population, Area and Standard of Living of the Pacific World

Can you answer these questions?

1. Is the standard of living of this region high or low compared with that of the United States? Is it a low-income or underdeveloped area?
2. Is the region as crowded as the United States?
3. Are the people of this region literate compared with the people of the United States?

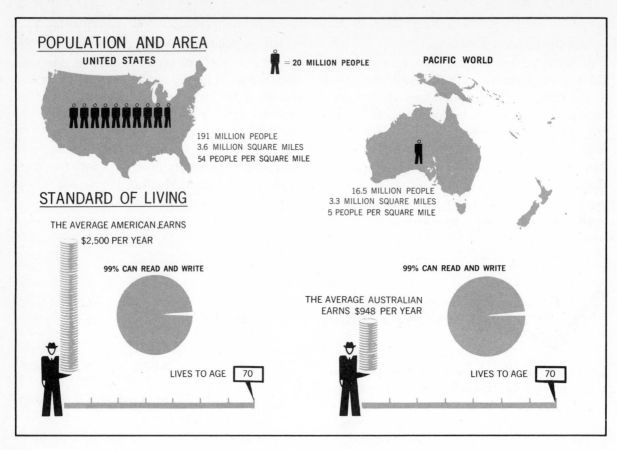

POPULATION AND AREA

UNITED STATES

= 20 MILLION PEOPLE

PACIFIC WORLD

191 MILLION PEOPLE
3.6 MILLION SQUARE MILES
54 PEOPLE PER SQUARE MILE

16.5 MILLION PEOPLE
3.3 MILLION SQUARE MILES
5 PEOPLE PER SQUARE MILE

STANDARD OF LIVING

THE AVERAGE AMERICAN EARNS
$2,500 PER YEAR

99% CAN READ AND WRITE

LIVES TO AGE 70

THE AVERAGE AUSTRALIAN
EARNS $948 PER YEAR

99% CAN READ AND WRITE

LIVES TO AGE 70

Pictograph # 16—Population, Area and Standard of Living of the Pacific World

4. How long may the average person in this region expect to live?
5. What facts tell you the standard of living of the people of the region?
6. How does this region compare with the United States in size?

SUMMING UP

Making Inferences   In our reading, many facts are given to us. From these facts we can draw conclusions. The following are some conclusions or inferences that you might make after reading Chapters 1, 2 and 3. Tell whether these conclusions are correct or incorrect. Give reasons for your answers.

1. The aborigines of Australia were never a farming people.
2. The early settlers of Australia did not travel far inland.
3. There are few highways on the "outback."
4. A visitor from a large city in the United States would find few things in an Australian city that would be familiar to him.
5. Automobiles would not be as important in New Zealand as in Australia.
6. Many railroad lines cross Australia from one coast to another.

7. The mountains of New Zealand give it a climate like that of Norway.
8. Athletes from the United States have been rivals of Australian athletes in many sports.

FOLLOW UP

Tell whether the following items refer to Australia, New Zealand or to both countries. If the item applies to Australia only, write A; if the item applies to New Zealand only, write N; if the item applies to both countries, write B.

1. Maoris fought against the white settlers.
2. The government is like that of Great Britain.
3. Women are allowed to vote.
4. It is largely a mountainous country.
5. There are a large number of English-speaking people.
6. It is sometimes called "land down under."
7. The country is only a little smaller than the United States.
8. The country lies partly in the low latitudes.
9. Much of the nation is desert.
10. The country is made up of long, narrow islands.
11. The discovery of gold helped to speed its settlement.
12. The people are highly educated.
13. The country has a pleasant marine climate.
14. Much of the land is used to raise sheep and cattle.

Wealth in a Dry Land

PROBLEM: How do the people of Australia make use of their resources?

READING FOR A PURPOSE:
1. Why is Australia good for raising sheep?
2. What is Australia's chief farm crop?
3. How has Australia been able to develop industries?

1. Much of Australia's land is too dry for farming. What's more, there are not enough people to work the land. Nevertheless, Australia produces more food than its population needs. It is one of the world's great food exporters and sends shiploads of meat and dairy products to Europe every year. Let us find out why.

2. Northern Australia is hot and rainy. It contains many plantations on which sugar cane and tropical fruits—pineapples, bananas and coconuts—are raised. Large amounts of these fruits are exported. The sugar cane lands reach almost to Brisbane, about halfway between northern and southern Australia. Sugar is another food export.

3. South of Brisbane, fruit and dairy farming takes place along the narrow coastal plains. The summers are cool and there is plenty of rain from the winds of the Pacific Ocean. As a result, there is good pasture land. The dairy farmers have good cattle and modern equipment and barns. They supply the people of nearby cities with many dairy products.

4. On the western side of the mountains are the wheat lands of Australia. Here the fields are large and the land is level. Therefore, machinery can be used. In this way, a few farmers can grow a great deal of wheat. Wheat is the chief farm crop of Australia. Next to wool, it is the most important export crop. Many wheat farmers also raise sheep.

5. Farther west it is too dry to grow wheat, but there is enough grass for sheep grazing. This is the area of the huge sheep ranches called *stations*. These stations are very large, because sheep have to roam far and wide to get enough to eat. The poorer the land, the larger the station. The few ranchers who live here are far apart. The nearest neighbor might be 100 miles away. Travel is difficult and water is scarce. It is not unusual for the sheep rancher to travel by jeep or airplane to look over his vast station. Most sheep are raised for their wool rather than their meat. Wool is Australia's chief export.

6. The sheep rancher has many problems. First, there is not enough water for the people and animals. This problem has been partly solved by digging deep wells called *artesian* wells. These wells are dug through a layer of rock. The water shoots to the surface. If it were not for the artesian water, many stretches of desert and "bush land" would have no drinking

A large sheep station near Canberra.

Australian News & Information Bureau

A large steel mill in New South Wales.

water at all for man or sheep.

7. Second, the sheep herder must fight all kinds of animal pests. There are wild dogs, rabbits, cattle ticks and kangaroos. The wild dogs or *dingos* were first brought to Australia as pets. They are hated because they kill the sheep—even more than they need for food. Rabbits are the worst enemies of the sheep herders, however. They eat the precious grass and the bark of the bushes. Rabbits limit the number of sheep that the pastures can feed. Another great pest is that unusual creature, the kangaroo. It was one of the first animals to come to Australia. Kangaroos like to eat the grass and brush too. The Australian is doing his best to fight the problems these animals cause.

8. In the northern plains, cattle are raised. The cattle feed on the coarse grass that grows during the rainy summers. From these cattle Australians get large amounts of hides and beef. The cattle ranches are far from railroads and seaports. Therefore, the animals must be driven to market across the country just as our cattle are herded great distances by cowboys.

9. Unlike Australia, New Zealand is a rainy country that is always green. The hills and lowlands of New Zealand are good for raising dairy cattle and sheep. The dairy farms are among the best in the world. New Zealand ranks high in the export of cheese, lamb, butter, wool and beef. Because of their exports, the people of New Zealand have a very high standard of living.

10. While sheep-herding and cattle-raising produce most of its exports, Australia is also a leading industrial nation. There are several reasons for this. First, because many machines are used on the farms and ranches, fewer people are needed there and they can go to work in the mills and factories.

11. Second, except for oil, Australia is rich in mineral resources. Broken Hill, in southeast Australia, is one of the richest mining areas in the world. Lead, zinc and copper are mined here. Nearby are large deposits of coal and iron. Australia's mills turn out steel for making automobiles, ships, airplanes and locomotives.

12. Third, Australia has two sources of power; coal and falling water. Despite the fact that there is a water shortage in much of Australia, water power is available in the eastern part of the country. The snow and rain from the Great Dividing Range cause many small streams to flow down the mountainsides toward the ocean. Australians have made good use of this power supply. Finally, good roads and railroads have been built so that raw materials from the mines and farms can easily be sent to the factories and seaport cities.

13. New Zealand does not have as many mineral resources as Australia. Therefore, it does not have as many large factories. Because much

Australian News & Information Bureau

of New Zealand is mountainous, power from falling water is used. Most of the factories make use of the products of New Zealand's farms; there are woolen and flour mills, meat-packing plants and dairies.

Life is very lonely in the "outback." Here children learn their lessons by short-wave radio. If they have a question for the teacher, they press a switch.

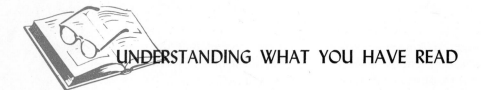

UNDERSTANDING WHAT YOU HAVE READ

1. **Which of the following questions are answered in this chapter?**
   a. How is water obtained in the "outback"?
   b. Why can Australia grow large amounts of wheat?
   c. What animals bother the sheep rancher?

2. **The main idea of *paragraphs 5 through 7* is to describe:**
   a. how the people of Australia use their resources.
   b. the sheep country of Australia.
   c. wheat-growing on the plains.

3. **Water is obtained in the "outback" through:**
   a. artesian wells.
   b. irrigation canals.
   c. dams.

4. **Australians are able to grow large amounts of wheat because:**
   a. the fields are large, flat and suited to the use of machinery.
   b. fields are far from the smoke-filled cities.
   c. they have a large labor supply and plenty of rainfall.

5. **Australia is good for raising sheep because:**
   a. there is plenty of grass throughout the country.
   b. the warm northern lowlands are ideal for raising sheep.
   c. much of the country is dry and sheep need little water.

6. **A good reason why Australia has been able to develop industries is that:**
   a. there is a large supply of workers.
   b. mineral resources are in good supply.
   c. oil is an important resource.

7. **An *artesian* well is:**
   a. dug on the side of a mountain.
   b. a spring in which water is pumped to the surface.
   c. dug deep in the soil through a layer of rock.

8. **The word *station*, as used in this chapter, refers to:**
   a. land and buildings used in raising sheep and cattle.
   b. a position in line.
   c. a regular stopping place on railroads.

514

DEVELOPING IDEAS AND SKILLS

Photograph Study

This photograph should help you to recall parts of the chapter you have just read. Can you tell the main idea of the photograph? Where in the chapter is it described?

Australian News & Information Bureau

SUMMING UP

Tell whether these statements are true or false. The underlined words make the statements true or false. If a statement is false, what word or words would you place in it to make it true?

1. The chief export of Australia is sugar.
2. Tropical fruits are grown in northern Australia.
3. Wheat farmers in Australia use mainly simple hand tools.
4. Pineapples are raised by some Australian farmers.
5. Many Australians work on sheep stations.
6. Many cattle ranches are found in the "outback."
7. Water is an important source of power in New Zealand.
8. New Zealand exports chiefly dairy products.
9. Australia and New Zealand carry on most of their trade with countries of Europe.
10. Rabbits are one of the pests that bother Australian ranchers.

FOLLOW UP

Reviewing Chapters 1 through 4. Which Does Not Belong?
Choose the item that *does not belong* with the others in each group.

1. Important animals of Australia: sheep, cattle, hogs, kangaroo
2. Mineral resources of Australia: coal, oil, copper, iron ore
3. Climates of Australia: desert, savanna, humid subtropical, taiga
4. Cities of Australia: Auckland, Melbourne, Sydney, Perth
5. Events in Australian history: colonies in Africa, discovery of gold, voyage of Capt. Cook, World War II
6. Farm products of Australia: wheat, sugar cane, citrus fruits, peanuts

CHAPTER 5

Life on the Islands

PROBLEM: What is life like on the Pacific islands?

READING FOR A PURPOSE:
1. How are the Pacific islands divided?
2. What is a "high" island?
3. What is a "low" island?

1. The great world of the Pacific Ocean is made up of thousands of islands. You will not be able to find most of them on a map. All of these islands are located in the tropics, north and south of the equator. The islands are divided into three parts: *Melanesia* or "black islands"; *Micronesia* or "small islands"; and *Polynesia,* which means "many islands."

2. The islands of Melanesia lie south of the equator and northeast of Australia. They extend southeastward as far as New Caledonia and the Fiji Islands. The largest island in the group is New Guinea, which covers about 300,000 square miles. Most of the people in Melanesia are Negroid or dark-skinned. None of these volcanic islands is independent. Great Britain, France, Australia and Indonesia each govern some of them.

3. Micronesia lies north of Melanesia. This group of islands is made up chiefly of coral atolls, barely above sea level. Their total land area is smaller than that of the state of Delaware. The chief island groups in Micronesia are the Marianas, the Carolines, the Marshalls and the Gilberts. All of these islands were the scenes of battles during World War II. Except for the Gilberts, the islands are a United Nations trust territory cared for by the United States. Guam, an old possession of the United States, is part of the Marianas. It has one of the finest harbors in the Pacific.

4. The eastern part of the Pacific World is known as Polynesia. Its total land area is not so large as that of the state of West Virginia. The largest island groups are Hawaii, Samoa, the Society Islands and the Marquesas. Hawaii, of course, is one of our states. Great Britain, New Zealand and France own other islands in this group. The Samoan islands are divided between the United States and Western Samoa, a new nation. Pago Pago, the capital city of American Samoa, has a very fine harbor.

5. All of the Pacific islands are near the equator. This means that the climate is warm throughout the year. The waters tend to keep the temperatures even, so that there is little change in temperature from one season to another. The average temperature on most of the islands is near 80°. There is plenty of rainfall. The winds blow from the east. If there are

Some natives of New Guinea.

A native house on a coral atoll.

A coral reef off the eastern coast of Australia.

mountains on the islands, the eastern or windward side is the part that receives the heaviest rain. This part of the Pacific often has severe storms called *typhoons*.

6. The Pacific islands fall into two groups, the "high" islands and the "low" islands. The "high" islands are usually larger. They are either the tops of underwater mountains or volcanoes that have been built up from the ocean floor. These islands contain more fertile land and support more people. The tribes that live on them have a higher standard of living than their "low"-island neighbors.

7. There are several reasons for this. First of all, "high" islands get more rainfall because their mountains can catch the winds. The rainy hillsides are covered with forests that are used to build boats and houses. Because of the rain and the fertile soil, a great variety of crops are grown: rice, yams, corn, coconuts, bananas, tobacco and taro (a starchy root made into a paste-like food called *poi*). The natives live in the valleys. Each valley supports a village. Many of the natives also raise pigs or cattle to use for food along with fish and fruit. Whatever they grow is needed for themselves; there is little to be sold.

8. The "low" islands are usually reefs or atolls. Many of them are barely above the surface of the water. The atolls are chains of small coral islands. They have been formed by millions of tiny coral animals that live in the ocean. These animals produce a limy shell that hardens to form the atoll. In the center of the atoll is a lagoon, a body of water like a pond. The coral reefs act as protection for the lagoon, and the heavy ocean waves do not enter it. During World War II, these lagoons were places where hundreds of ships lay at anchor. Because the atolls are hard-surfaced, they have been used as landing fields for airplanes.

9. Life on the "low" islands is much harder than on the "high" islands. There is little or no drinking water. The soil is thin for it is washed away or broken by wind and waves. People live on their own small farms. They use simple digging sticks to plant their crops. Their chief food crops are coconuts, taro and yams. They also catch fish from the sea.

10. The coconut palm is the chief resource of both "high" and "low" islands. It is grown in special pits free from salt water. It is a source of food, clothing and shelter for the natives. For the outside world, it is a source of *copra*. Copra is dried coconut meat. From the copra, oil is pressed out to make margarine, cooking and

517

salad oils, fine soaps and cosmetics. Coconut-shell charcoal is also exported for use in cigarettes and gas masks as a filter.

11. Along with subsistence farming and fishing, there are also plantations on many islands that grow crops for export. There are coconut or copra plantations. On New Caledonia, coffee and cocoa are raised; on Fiji, sugar cane; on Hawaii, pineapples. A number of "low" islands use the birds that have flown over them for thousands of years as a natural resource. As the birds fly over, their droppings fall on the islands. These droppings mix with the coral limestone and have changed it to a mineral called phosphate rock. This phosphate rock is important as a fertilizer. The countries that own these islands export phosphate rock to other lands.

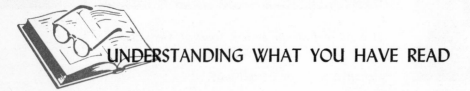

UNDERSTANDING WHAT YOU HAVE READ

1. **Which of the following questions are answered in this chapter?**
a. Why is life difficult on the "low" islands?
b. What are the many uses of the coconut?
c. How does the Pacific Ocean affect the climate of the islands?

2. **The main idea of *paragraphs 8 through 10* is to describe:**
a. life on the "low" islands of the Pacific.
b. export crops of the "low" islands.
c. the government of the "low" islands.

3. **The most valuable resource of the island peoples is:**
a. phosphate rock.   b. pineapples.   c. coconuts.

4. **Because they are surrounded by the Pacific Ocean, most of the islands:**
a. are coral atolls.

b. have plenty of rain.
c. trade with the nations of Latin America.

5. **Few people live on the "low" islands because:**
a. there is little fertile soil.
b. the Pacific winds are too strong.
c. the islands are too mountainous.

6. **The coconut is important in the life of the island peoples because it is:**
a. a source of oil for machinery.
b. used in building boats.
c. a source of food, shelter and clothing.

7. ***Copra* is the dried meat of:**
a. the coconut.   b. manioc.   c. sorghum.

8. **An *atoll* is built from:**
a. volcanoes.   b. glaciers.   c. tiny sea animals.

DEVELOPING IDEAS AND SKILLS

Photograph Study

The photograph on p. 519 should help you to recall parts of the chapter you have just read. Can you tell the main idea of the photograph? Where in the chapter is it described?

SUMMING UP

Tell whether the following refers to a "high" island (H) or to a "low" island (L):

_____ well watered	_____ volcanoes
_____ small in size	_____ little fertile soil
_____ fewer people	_____ mountainous
_____ higher living standards	_____ more minerals
_____ variety of crops	_____ people depend upon the coconut

FOLLOW UP

Do You Agree or Disagree?   Give the reasons for your answers.
1. The Pacific World consists only of islands.
2. All the Pacific islands are made of coral.
3. There are few islands in the Pacific in the high latitudes.
4. All the islands together make up a land area as large as the United States.
5. Most of the Pacific peoples are Negroid or brown-skinned.
6. We would call these islands an underdeveloped area.
7. The United States has had little interest in the Pacific Islands.
8. Most of the people make a living from subsistence farming and fishing.

519

CHAPTER 6

The Pacific World Today

IMPACT OF TRADE & WAR

PROBLEM: What is the future of Australia and the Pacific islands?

READING FOR A PURPOSE:
1. What are Australia's problems?
2. What is SEATO?
3. How did World War II affect the island people?

1. Australia is one of the largest countries in the world, yet it is one of the driest. A great desert occupies about forty per cent of the land area. There are few important lakes and rivers. The lack of water means that only a small part of the land can be farmed. In order to solve this problem, Australians are doing some remarkable things. One of the important projects under way is to change the course of the Snow River. This river rises in the eastern mountains and flows eastward. Australians are digging a tunnel through the mountains so that the water will flow to the western side where the water is most needed.

2. Parts of the Australian continent have hardly been explored. The great desert has separated the people of the eastern coast from other people in the country. Only one railroad crosses the continent to the city of Perth on the west coast. There is a need for more roads, railways and air routes spanning the continent. (Since air routes are easier to establish than railroads, air travel will probably increase in Australia in the future.)

3. Australia has the problem of defending itself. Before World War II, both Australia and New Zealand felt safe from invasion. They thought they were too far from the rest of the world. However, during the war, Japanese forces came close to the borders of Australia, capturing islands around the continent. Japan bombed the city of Darwin in the north. It was in the Battle of the Coral Sea that the American Navy stopped the advance of the Japanese and saved Australia from invasion.

4. After World War II, Australia and New Zealand realized that they needed allies or friends to help them keep their freedom. The United States joined these nations in a defense treaty in 1952. It was called ANZUS, after the first letters of the three nations. Its members agreed to help each other in case of war in the Pacific. In 1954, the ANZUS nations joined with Pakistan, the Philippines, Thailand, Great Britain and France in forming SEATO (Southeast Asia Treaty Organization). Each of these nations agreed to help the others in case of an attack on any member.

5. There is much to be done in the entire Pacific area, and there are few people to do it. While Australians would like more settlers, they do not admit "colored" peoples. This is resented by many in Southeast Asia, where most nations are over-crowded. Java, Indonesia, for example, is one of the most crowded places on earth. It is closer to Australia than Puerto Rico is to New York. Yet Javanese are not welcome as settlers. Red China is not very far away. Many of these nations probably look to their neighbor to the south for more room for their peoples. The nations of the Orient cannot feel too kindly toward a nation that refuses to admit people

UNATIONS (from Australian Govt.)

Change is coming to the islands. Here villagers are being taken to a health clinic for a check-up.

Australian News & Information Bureau

A government official explains to a group of natives about a coming election for a local council.

from their lands as citizens.

6. The lives of the people of the Pacific islands changed greatly during World War II. Many of the islands of Melanesia and Micronesia were occupied by United States and Australian troops. Many of the native people helped to build runways for airplanes and to load and unload ships. The people also sold food to feed the troops. Many of the island people received more money than they had ever had before. They bought Western clothing, tobacco, chewing gum, canned beef and other goods.

7. When the armed forces left after the war, there were no more such goods and jobs. But the people were no longer satisfied with jobs on coconut plantations where they work for low wages. Since then they have not been content with hard work that allows them to raise enough food for themselves only. They want to be able to buy goods from the outside world. They want better health, education and freedom to decide their own affairs.

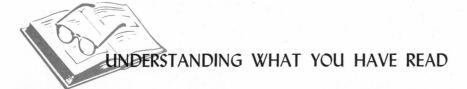

UNDERSTANDING WHAT YOU HAVE READ

1. **Which of the following questions are answered in this chapter?**
a. Why did Australia join SEATO?
b. Why does Australia have some fear of the lands to the north?
c. How are the Pacific islands prepared for self-government?

2. **The main idea of this chapter is to describe:**

a. how World War II changed the island peoples.
b. the problem of the peoples of the Pacific World.
c. the relationship between Asia and Australia.

3. **The lands to the north of Australia are:**
a. crowded.   b. small.   c. far away.

4. **Both Australia and New Zealand belong to the organization known as:**
a. OAS.   b. NATO.   c. SEATO.

5. Australia joined in a treaty with the United States because:

a. its population is small.
b. it has a fear of attack.
c. it needs to trade for food.

6. Few people have moved to Australia because:

a. there is no land upon which people can settle.
b. it is not open to "colored" peoples.
c. it is far from the western hemisphere.

7. **If a nation works with its *allies,* it is working with its:**

a. neighbors.   b. suppliers.   c. friends.

DEVELOPING IDEAS AND SKILLS

Cartoon (See p. 520.)
1. How has the Pacific World been changed?
2. What are some of the problems of the natives of this region today?

3. Why is this area important to us even though it is far away?
4. What is a trust territory?
5. What is a good title for this cartoon?

SUMMING UP

Fact or Opinion Which of these statements are facts and which are someone's opinion?

1. Most of Australia's problems would be solved if the country were opened to people of all lands.
2. Some day the atolls of the Pacific will be crowded with people.
3. American soldiers brought new goods and ideas to the people of the Pacific islands.
4. The Pacific islands should be given complete freedom to govern themselves.
5. Australia really has little to fear from the countries of Asia.
6. Many of the Pacific islands are too far away to concern the American people.
7. Many of the island people depend upon the sea for a living.
8. Japanese forces came close to invading Australia in World War II.

FOLLOW UP

Tell whether the following items refer to the United States, Australia or both countries. If the item applies to the United States only, write US; if it applies to Australia only, write A; if it applies to both countries, write B.

_____ An island country.
_____ High standard of living.
_____ Modern cities.
_____ Near the world's greatest trade routes.
_____ Few people live in center of the country.

_____ Many large, useful rivers.
_____ Cattle-raising is important.
_____ Large number of Negro people.
_____ Democratic government.
_____ Large supplies of oil.
_____ Desert region.
_____ More sheep than people.
_____ Women have equal rights with men.
_____ Smaller than Red China.
_____ Took part in World War II.

BOOKS FOR UNIT 9

Author	Title, Publisher	Description
1. Borden, Charles	*He Sailed With Captain Cook*, Crowell	A very human story of life aboard Cook's ship.
2. Burchfield, R. W. and E. M.	*New Zealand*, Macmillan	The story of the mountains and farmlands of New Zealand.
3. Cairns, G. O.	*The Land and People of Australia*, Macmillan	The story of animals, sheep stations and mining in Australia.
4. Fennimore, Stephen	*Bush Holiday*, Doubleday	An American visits the bush country of Australia.
5. Heyerdahl, Thor	*Kon-Tiki*, Rand McNally	The famous account of a voyage across the Pacific on a balsa raft.
6. Patchett, Mary	*Cry of the Heart*, Abelard-Schuman	Life in the Australian "outback."
7. Pease, Howard	*Jungle River*, Doubleday	Adventures in the rain forest of New Guinea.
8. Sperry, Armstrong	*Call It Courage*, Macmillan	A young man sets out to prove his courage in Polynesia.
9. Sperry, Armstrong	*Pacific Islands Speaking*, Macmillan	A brief account of the geography of the islands and their military value.

New Frontiers

PROBLEM: Where are we exploring today?

READING FOR A PURPOSE:
1. Why are the polar regions important?
2. When was the first spaceship launched?
3. What is a bathyscaphe?

1. You might think that the entire world has been explored as a result of the great voyages of discovery in the sixteenth century. But this is not so. There are still areas of South America and Africa that are a mystery to us. Also, there are many new frontiers for people who love adventure. These are the polar regions, the deep oceans and the spaces beyond the earth.

2. The polar regions, north and south, have become increasingly important for several reasons. First, the Arctic region in the north lies between the United States and the Soviet Union. Because of the airplane, our two nations are now very close to each other across the North Pole. Second, much of the weather we have in the middle latitudes is caused in part by cold air moving southward from the Arctic Ocean. This cold air sometimes blows as far south as Florida and the Gulf of Mexico. In the Antarctic, the southern polar region, it is believed that there are important mineral resources. As the world population continues to grow, our need for more and more resources is growing with it.

3. The Arctic, the northern polar region, is an ocean surrounded by land. An area of floating ice, it is surrounded by Alaska, Canada, Scandinavia and Siberia. The North Pole is located amid the ice-filled waters of the Arctic Ocean. The first people to explore this region were men looking for a water passage from the Atlantic to the Pacific Oceans. In 1888, a Norwegian explorer named Fridtjof Nansen became the first man to lead a party across the great ice-covered interior of Greenland. In 1909, Commander Robert E. Peary of the United States and his party became the first men to reach the North Pole.

4. In July, 1958, the United States atomic submarine *Nautilus* made one of the most amazing trips in sea history. This submarine, with a crew of 116 men, sailed under the Arctic ice cap all the way from Alaska to Greenland. At times the submarine was 400 feet beneath the surface of the ocean. The submarine traveled a total of 1,830 miles under water on this first voyage across the North Pole.

5. The Antarctic or southern polar region is largely a high, icy plateau 8,000 feet above sea level. This ice cap covers a continent of about six million square miles. (About half the continent is claimed by Australia.) Antarctica is one of the coldest lands on earth. It is colder than the Arctic because of the high elevation of the plateau and because of the thick layer of ice and snow that covers it. If the ice were to melt, the levels of all the oceans would rise and flood every coastal city in the world. Antarctica is really an icy desert. It is empty of people and land animals. The South Pole was first reached by man in 1911 when Roald Amundsen of Norway led an expedition there. Another famous explorer of the Antarctic was Admiral Richard Byrd of the United States.

6. One of the newest and most exciting fields for man's exploration is the space above the

earth. As early as 1919, an American named Robert Goddard suggested that man could build a rocket to go to the moon. (His doubting neighbors called him "Moon Mad" Goddard.) Ten years later, he flew one of the first liquid-fuel rockets. Rockets were also developed in other countries. During World War II, the Germans fired V-2 rockets on London from across the English Channel. A rocket is a new kind of engine in that it can run without air from the outside. The rocket carries its own air or oxygen in a tank. Thus, with the invention of the rocket it became possible to think of sending men into space, where there is no air.

7. Since the 1950's, scientists have been dealing with the problems of exploring space. In 1957, the Soviet Union sent the first spaceship, Sputnik I, into orbit around the earth. (That is, the spaceship moved around the earth in the same manner as the moon.) This opened up our space age. Shortly thereafter, the United States orbited its first spaceship or satellite, Explorer I. In 1961, the Soviet Union sent the first man into space, Major Yuri Gagarin. A year later, John Glenn of the U.S. made a successful orbit of the earth. Since then, dozens of manned and unmanned space flights have been launched by the two nations. The Soviet Union startled the world early in 1965 by sending two men into space. Two men had traveled in space before, but on this trip one of the spacemen left the ship and floated freely for a short time. United States astronauts have since achieved many more goals while floating in space. Furthermore, they have taken flights into space that have lasted as long as fourteen days. Even so, the "space race" has only just begun. The developments in this area in the years to come promise to be even more exciting than anything we have seen so far.

8. Man is also interested in finding out more about the waters of the earth. Three-fourths of our planet is covered by water. Yet this part of the earth is little known and its tremendous riches are hardly touched. The invention of the bathyscaphe, a ship that floats under the sea, has made it possible to learn more about our

Wide World Photos

Astronaut Ed White floats in space next to Gemini 4.

oceans. Two of the great underwater explorers are Henri Picard of Belgium and Jacques Cousteau of France. Because of their work, we are learning more about the oceans, our "silent world."

9. Ocean floors have vast plains and mountain ranges. Some of these mountains "stick their heads above water" and appear as islands. There are also deep trenches in the ocean floor. Near Guam, the Pacific Ocean reaches a depth of almost seven miles. Near Puerto Rico, the Atlantic Ocean is five miles deep.

10. The waters of the world will become more and more important as the years go by. Up to now, the oceans have been a source of food and salt. But soon we will turn to them for other things as well. The available supplies of fresh water must be increased. Scientists are trying to find an easy way to take the salt from sea water. If they succeed, man's supply of pure, fresh water will be almost endless. The demand for minerals is also growing. We are just beginning to realize what a valuable source of minerals the sea can be. Magnesium and oil are already being taken from sea waters.

CHAPTER 2

The World Is Your Neighborhood

PROBLEM: Why are all people in the world our neighbors?

READING FOR A PURPOSE:
1. When was the United Nations begun?
2. Where are the areas of great poverty?
3. Why must we use our resources wisely?

1. Throughout history, man has been cursed by war. World War II was the most terrible war known to man. More than sixteen million people were killed in battle and millions more died from starvation, bombings, wounds and persecutions. Because warfare has become so horrible, representatives of fifty nations met in 1945 to form a world organization to help keep peace in the world. A charter or constitution was drawn up to form the United Nations Organization. The headquarters of this organization is located in New York City. Since it began, the United Nations has been a strong force for peace in the world. The United States has always supported the United Nations in its efforts for peace.

2. Early in 1945, scientists developed a new and terrible weapon, the atom bomb. This bomb was dropped by the United States on the Japanese cities of Hiroshima and Nagasaki in August, 1945. More than 200,000 people were killed or injured in the bombings. Since that time even more powerful nuclear bombs have been exploded in tests. The United States, the Soviet Union, Great Britain, France and Red China have all tested these newer bombs. Except for Red China, they all have airplanes and missiles that can carry their bombs to targets thousands of miles away in a matter of minutes. It is within their power to destroy large areas of any nation in just seconds.

3. It is only a question of time before even more nations will be able to make atomic weapons. In 1963, the United States, the Soviet Union and Great Britain signed a treaty agreeing not to explode nuclear weapons under water or in the air. France and Red China did not sign this treaty. Nevertheless, the treaty may be the beginning of the control of atomic energy. Perhaps people can turn their attention to the use of this energy for the benefit of mankind. The search for peace in a world divided by atomic powers is one of our major problems.

4. Despite war and nuclear bombs, our vast world has still become a single neighborhood. Of course, to think of more than three billion people as your neighbors is not easy. Therefore, think instead of a small land with only 3,000 people. What might we find, if this land represented the world? One thousand of the 3,000 people would be white. They would be living on the best land and making use of its resources. Most of them would have a high standard of living and would look forward to a life of over seventy years.

5. Most of the other 2,000 people would be dark-skinned. More than half would go to bed hungry each night. More than half would not be able to read or write. Because of poor health services, their life span would be only thirty to thirty-five years. Most of these people would be found in Latin America, the Middle

A meeting of the U.N. Security Council in New York City.

East and North Africa, Sub-Sahara Africa, Southeast Asia and parts of Europe. (However, even the United States has areas of great poverty.) We cannot let this poverty around the world continue. People will not accept their poor conditions much longer, and they should not have to. The question facing America and the world is, how can we help poor people everywhere to realize their hopes for a better life for themselves and their children?

6. The people of the United States feel that they must help the underdeveloped countries. As you have learned, there are many reasons for doing so. We help people because all of us are human. Secondly, we do not believe that poverty is necessary in this world. The earth has too many riches for a large number of people to go hungry. Thirdly, when we help others, there are benefits for us—economic, political and social. As the underdeveloped nations raise their standard of living, they are better able to trade with us. And people who are well fed, clothed and housed are better able to resist wars and dictatorial governments.

7. Another problem facing the world is that of the growing population. This increase in population is especially heavy in the Far East, Latin America and Africa. The population of the world passed the three-billion mark some years ago. It is said that if the world keeps growing at its present rate, there will be almost seven billion people in the world in the year 2000. This growth is greatest in the underdeveloped

nations, as you might be able to guess.

8. In the past, the population of some countries was kept smaller because so many people were killed in wars or died of disease at a young age. Today, people are taught to care for their health; modern medicines are available to more people. We live longer, yet most of the people of the world are pressed into less

As the population continues to grow, the best use must be made of land for food.

than half the land area of the globe! Will there be enough food and resources to provide everyone with a decent standard of living?

9. While more and more resources are needed for the growing population, the world's forest and mineral resources are decreasing. Each year, man digs or pumps more minerals from the earth. Unlike water, these resources cannot be replaced. One wonders how long man can continue taking minerals from the earth. There are limits to the amount of coal, iron ore and oil to be found in the earth's crust. It is time that man thought very seriously about saving or conserving the gifts of nature.

10. Another of the world's problems is the treatment of people of different races. You have learned that people of many races live in the world. You have learned that there are more "colored people" in the world than there are white people. Many of the colored people have lived in colonies of Western nations. They have been ruled by white people. In Africa, chiefly, there has been a great deal of bad feeling against white people because they ruled there in years past. The whites still hold some of the best land. A question that Americans must answer to the world is this: Does our treatment of people of all races show that we recognize the importance of *each* person as a worth-while human being, regardless of his race?

Glossary

Glossary

The meanings given for the following words are the ones used in this book.

abacá	[ab a KA]	Hemp plant; its fibers are used to make rope.
aborigines	[ab o RIJ i neez]	First people to live in a land, as in Australia.
agriculture	[AG ri kul chur]	Farming; the use of land for raising plants, food crops and livestock.
alliance	[a LY ans]	An agreement among nations to help each other.
altitude	[AL ti tood]	Height above sea level.
aluminum	[a LOO mi num]	Light metal made from bauxite.
Antarctic Circle	[ant ARK tik]	Line of latitude 66½° south of the equator.
apartheid	[a PART hyt]	Policy of separating whites and Negroes in the Republic of South Africa.
archipelago	[ar ki PEL a go]	Any large group of islands.
Arctic Circle	[ARK tik]	Line of latitude 66½° north of the equator.
artesian well	[ar TEE zhun]	Well dug deep in the earth through a layer of rock that causes the water to shoot to the surface.
atmosphere	[AT mo sfeer]	"Blanket" of air that surrounds the earth.
atoll	[AT tol]	Small coral island; most often found in the South Pacific.
atomic energy	[a TOM ik EN ur jee]	Energy released through the splitting of an atom.
automation	[aw to MAY shun]	Use of machines in the manufacture of goods, often to do work once done by men.
axis	[AK sis]	Imaginary line through the earth at its poles, and upon which the earth spins.
basin	[BAY sin]	Low spot in the mountains; lowland area drained by a river.
bathyscaphe	[BATH i skayf]	Diving chamber used to explore the ocean depths.
bauxite	[BAWK syt]	Mineral ore from which aluminum is made.
bay		Body of water caused by an irregular place in the coastline and protected by the land around it.
bazaar	[ba ZAR]	Marketplace or shopping area in a Middle Eastern town.
Bedouins	[BED oo ins]	Nomadic tribe of the Middle East; herding camels and horses is their chief occupation.
Boers	[BORS]	Dutch settlers in South Africa.
cabinet	[KAB i net]	Group of men specially appointed to advise the head of a government.
cacao	[ka KAY o]	Tropical plant from whose seeds cocoa and chocolate are made.
canal	[ka NAL]	Waterway made by man to connect two bodies of water.
canneries	[KAN er eez]	Factories where fruit and fish are canned.

capital	[KAP i tal]	Seat of government in a country; or money and goods used to make more goods.
capitalism	[KAP i tal izm]	System under which people are free to own and develop their own property in order to make a profit.
cash crop		Crops raised for sale by a farmer; with profits from this crop he buys the goods his farm does not supply.
Caucasian	[kaw KAY zhun]	Member of the white race.
cinchona	[sin KO na]	Bark of a tree that grows in the rain forests of South America and Asia; used in making quinine.
citrus fruits	[SIT rus FROOTS]	Fruits like lemons, limes, oranges and grapefruit.
civil rights	[SIV il RYTS]	The rights and opportunities each person has as a citizen and human being, regardless of his race or religion.
climate	[KLY mat]	Average weather in a given region over a long period of time.
coast		The edge of land along the sea or ocean.
cold war		When nations oppose each other without carrying on a shooting war.
collective farm	[ko LEK tiv]	*Kolkhoz*—large farm owned by the Soviet government; the people work for a share of the crops.
colonialism	[ko LO ni al izm]	Ownership and governing of distant lands or colonies.
commercial farming	[ka MER shul]	Raising crops for sale.
Common Market		An agreement among six nations in Western Europe to lower tariffs and increase trade with each other.
commonwealth	[KOM un welth]	A group of nations who govern themselves but still show loyalty to a "mother country"; the British Commonwealth, for example.
commune	[KOM yoon]	Large state-owned farm in Communist China; the people work for wages as on a Soviet state farm.
communism	[KOM yoo nizm]	Form of government in the Soviet Union, Red China and Eastern Europe today. The people are controlled by the state and almost everything is owned by it.
competition	[kom pe TISH un]	When two businesses try to make and sell the same kinds of goods.
conservation	[kon ser VAY shun]	The practice of saving our natural resources.
constitution	[kon sti TOO shun]	Written plan of government.
consumer	[kon SOOM er]	Anyone who buys and uses any product.
consumer goods		Products made for people to buy and use, such as food, clothing, automobiles, radios, furniture.
continent	[KON ti nent]	One of the six largest bodies of land on earth: North America, Asia, Africa, etc.

cooperative	[ko OP er a tiv]	Group of farmers who agree to share all their gains and losses.
copra	[KO pra]	Dried "meat" or pulp of a coconut.
country		A nation and its land.
craftsmen	[KRAFTS men]	Workers skilled in making things by hand.
crop rotation	[ro TAY shun]	Growing different crops on a piece of land from year to year in order to keep the soil from "wearing out."
culture	[KUL chur]	Ways of living developed by a people.
current	[KUR ent]	Steady flow of water.
czar	[ZAR]	Former ruler of Russia.
dam		Wall built across a river to hold back the water for conservation or electric power.
degree	[di GREE]	Unit of measurement of temperature and of longitude and latitude.
delta		Area of land at the mouth of a river formed by the deposit of mud washed down by the river.
democracy	[de MOK ra see]	Nation or form of government in which the laws are made by the people or their elected representatives.
density of population	[DEN si tee, pop yoo LAY shun]	Number of people per square mile of land in an area.
desert	[DEZ ert]	Large, dry area where rainfall is less than ten inches each year.
dictatorship	[dik TAY ter ship]	Government ruled by one man or one party in which the people have little chance to choose what they want.
dike	[DYK]	Small mud wall built to control the flow of water in a rice field; also, a wall built to keep out the sea, as in the Netherlands.
distortion	[dis TOR shun]	Made crooked or twisted out of shape.
drift		Weak current or flow of water.
dry farming		Farming in areas of little rainfall. The farmer grows crops every other year, saving the little moisture that is collected in the soil.
dynasty	[DY nas tee]	Rulers of a nation from the same family.
earth	[URTH]	Land or soil; the name of our planet.
earthquake	[URTH kwayk]	Terrible shaking of the ground.
electricity	[ee lek TRIS i tee]	One form of power.
elevation	[el e VAY shun]	Height above sea level or above the surface of the earth.
empire	[EM pyr]	Group of lands under the rule of one person or one nation.
equal-area map	[EE kwal AIR ee a]	Map showing the correct size of land and water areas.
equator	[ee KWAY tor]	Imaginary line around the middle of the earth, halfway between the North and South Poles.
equinox	[EE kwi noks]	Time of the year when days and nights are of equal length all over the earth. At the equinox, the sun is directly overhead at the equator.

erosion	[ee RO zhun]	Wearing away of the soil through the action of wind, water or glaciers.
estancia	[es TAN si a]	Large cattle ranch in Latin America.
evaporation	[ee vap o RAY shun]	Process by which water is changed into water vapor.
exports	[EKS ports]	Goods sent out of a country.
extensive farming	[eks TEN siv]	Farming over large areas with machinery.
fazenda	[fa ZEN da]	Brazilian coffee plantation.
fellahin	[FEL a heen]	Peasants or small farmers of North Africa and the Middle East.
Fertile Triangle	[FUR til TRY an gle]	Rich farming area in the Soviet Union, shaped like a triangle.
feudalism	[FYOO dal izm]	System in which land is owned by a powerful lord and worked by people called serfs in exchange for the lord's protection.
fiord	[fee ORD]	Narrow inlet of the sea surrounded by steep cliffs, found especially in Norway.
foreign policy	[FOR in]	Plan or pattern of relations of one country with others.
Free World		Countries of the world that are not Communist.
gaucho	[GOW cho]	Cowboy on the pampas of Argentina.
geography	[jee OG ra fee]	Study of the earth and how people have adapted to all of its varying conditions.
glacier	[GLAY sher]	Large mass of ice and snow that moves slowly over the land.
globe		Round model or true map of the earth.
government	[GUV ern ment]	Persons who rule, that is, make and enforce the laws of, a country.
grazing	[GRAYZ ing]	Roaming or wandering over a pasture, eating the grass.
grid		Crisscrossing lines on a map that help to locate any place on earth.
growing season		Length of time from the planting of crops until they are harvested; length of time in which the weather is frost-free.
gulf		Body of water surrounded by land; usually larger than a bay.
hacienda	[ah see END ah]	Large plantation or farm in Latin America.
harbor		Body of water caused by an irregular place in the coastline and the land around it.
hardwood		Tough, heavy wood of such trees as oak, teak and mahogany.
heavy industry	[IN dus tree]	Manufacturing that uses heavy materials like iron and steel.
hemisphere	[HEM i sfeer]	Half the earth or globe.
herdsman		One who raises such animals as sheep, goats, cattle and camels for a living.
highland	[HY land]	Area of hills, mountains or plateaus; upland.
high latitudes	[LAT i toods]	That part of the earth between 66½° and 90° north and south of the equator.

hill		Elevated piece of land not higher than 1,000 feet above sea level.
humid	[HYOO mid]	Damp or wet.
humid continental	[kon ti NEN tal]	Climate found inland or on the eastern coast of continents, marked by cold winters, hot summers, and some rain throughout the year.
humidity	[hyoo MID i tee]	Amount of moisture in the air.
humid subtropical	[sub TROP i kal]	Climate on the eastern coast of continents in the middle latitudes, marked by long, hot summers, mild winters, and rain throughout the year.
ice cap		Mass of ice at the Poles that does not melt.
illiteracy	[il LIT er a see]	Lack of ability to read or write.
immigrants	[IM i grants]	People who come to a country from other lands.
imperialism	[im PEER ee al izm]	Rule of one nation over other lands.
imports	[IM ports]	Goods brought into a country.
industrial region	[in DUS tri al REE jun]	Area in which manufacturing is the chief kind of work.
Industrial Revolution	[rev o LOO shun]	The change from the making of goods at home with hand tools to the making of goods in factories with machines.
insecticide	[in SEK ti syd]	Liquid or powder used to kill insects.
intensive farming	[in TEN siv]	Growing crops in a small area with a great deal of hand labor that usually results in high yields.
International Date Line	[in ter NASH un al]	An imaginary north-south line in the middle of the Pacific Ocean; 180° longitude.
investment	[in VEST ment]	Spending of money in the hope of gaining a profit.
Iron Curtain	[KER tin]	A term used to describe the effort of the Soviet Union to close off its lands from communication and trade with the Free World.
irrigation	[ir i GAY shun]	Bringing water to dry land through canals or ditches.
island	[I land]	Body of land entirely surrounded by water.
isthmus	[IS mus]	Narrow strip of land joining two larger bodies of land.
jungle	[JUN gle]	Hot land covered all year with a dense growth of trees and plants.
jute	[JOOT]	Plant fiber used in making rope and burlap bags.
kibbutz	[ki BOOTS]	Farming community in Israel owned by the people who live and work on its land.
kraal	[KRAHL]	Village of an African tribe.
lake		Body of water surrounded entirely by land.
landlocked		Without a coastline or opening to the sea, such as Bolivia or Czechoslovakia.
Lapp		People who live and herd reindeer in the tundra region of northern Europe.
latex	[LAY teks]	Milky fluid from which rubber is made.

leaching	[LEECH ing]	Washing out minerals or nutrients from the soil.
League of Nations	[LEEG]	Organization formed after World War I to keep world peace. The United States did not join.
leeward	[LEE ward]	Away from the wind; the dry side of mountains that receives less rain.
legend	[LEJ end]	Key or guide to reading a map.
legislature	[LEJ is lay cher]	Lawmaking body.
light industry		Manufacturing that uses raw materials of light weight, such as fibers.
lines of latitude	[LAT i tood]	Imaginary lines running east and west around the earth and parallel to the equator; they measure in degrees the distance north and south of the equator.
lines of longitude	[LON ji tood]	Imaginary lines running north and south from Pole to Pole; they measure in degrees the distance east or west of the Prime Meridian that passes through Greenwich, England.
llama	[LAH ma]	Woolly South American mountain animal used by the Indians of the Andes for carrying burdens.
llanos	[LAH nos]	Lowlands of the Orinoco River in South America that are good for grazing cattle.
loess	[LO es]	Fine yellow dust or soil found in the Hwang River Valley in China.
lowland	[LO land]	Flat land near sea level; a plain.
low latitudes	[LO LAT i toods]	That part of the earth between 0° and 23½° north and south of the equator.
maize	[MAYZ]	Indian corn.
majority	[ma JOR i tee]	At least one more than half. For example, in the sentence, "A majority of the 100 members voted for the law," *majority* means that at least 51 voted for it.
mandate	[MAN dayt]	Authorization by the League of Nations to one nation to govern or care for other lands.
manioc	[MAN i ok]	Starchy food of a tropical plant, made into a bread by rain-forest peoples; also called cassava.
manufacture	[man yoo FAK cher]	Making of raw materials into useful goods by hand or machine.
map		Flat drawing that represents all or part of the earth by means of a scale.
marine climate	[ma REEN]	Wet climate on the western side of continents in the middle latitudes, marked by cool summers, mild winters, and rain throughout the year.
market	[MAR ket]	Anywhere that goods can be bought and sold, or anywhere that there is a demand for goods.
Marshall Plan	[MAR shal]	Plan to help European nations repair the damage to their homes, factories and farms that resulted from World War II.

536

mass production	[MASS pro DUK shun]	Method of making large amounts of goods at low cost.
Mediterranean climate	[med i ter RAY nee an]	Climate marked by hot, dry summers, mild winters, and little rain throughout the year, most of it in winter.
Mercator map	[mer KAY ter]	Map with straight grid lines, useful as a sailing chart.
merchant	[MER chant]	Person who buys and sells goods for profit; a trader.
meridian	[me RID ee an]	Line of longitude.
mesa	[MAY sa]	Upland with fairly flat top and steep sides.
mestizo	[mes TEE zo]	Person who is partly Spanish and partly Indian.
middle class		Group of people, such as professional men and skilled craftsmen, who are neither rich nor poor.
middle latitudes	[MID el LAT i toods]	That part of the earth between 23½° and 66½° north and south of the equator.
migratory farming	[MY gra tor ee]	Type of farming in which the farmer moves from place to place in search of better soil; practiced by primitive rain-forest peoples.
migratory workers		Field laborers who move from one farm to another to obtain work. They follow the seasons for harvesting a variety of crops.
mineral	[MIN er al]	Ore taken or mined from the earth: gold, lead, copper, etc.
missile	[MIS el]	An object shot into the air by the force of an explosion.
missionary	[MISH un air ee]	Person who brings his religion to those who are not members of his faith.
money crop		(See cash crop.)
Mongoloid	[MON go loyd]	Member of the "yellow" race.
monoculture	[MON o kul cher]	Country depending chiefly on its income from the raising of one crop, as in many countries of Latin America and Africa.
monotheism	[MON o thee izm]	Belief in one God.
Monroe Doctrine	[mon RO DOK trin]	Policy announced by President Monroe in 1823, warning European nations not to try to regain their colonies in the Americas.
monsoon	[mon SOON]	Winds that change direction each season. They bring a wet season when they blow from the water and a dry season when they blow from the land.
Moslem	[MOZ lem]	Follower of the religion of Islam.
mosque	[MOSK]	Moslem house of worship.
"mother country"		Country that has colonies.
nationalism	[NASH un al izm]	Strong feeling of pride in one's nation or government.
NATO	[NAY to]	North Atlantic Treaty Organization; an alliance of Western nations who have agreed to help each other in case of attack.

natural resources	[NACH er al ree SOR ses]	Those things given to us by nature in or on the land, such as soil, water, minerals, forests.
nitrate	[NY trayt]	Chemical used to make fertilizer or explosives.
nomad	[NO mad]	Person who wanders from place to place in search of better grazing land for his flock or herd.
North Pole		Northernmost point on earth.
oasis	[o AY sis]	Desert land where water can be found and some crops can be grown.
ocean		One of the largest bodies of salt water on the earth.
ocean current	[O shun KUR ent]	Swift-moving stream or "river" in the ocean.
oil palm	[OYL PAHM]	Tropical tree. The oil taken from its seeds has many commercial uses.
orbit	[OR bit]	Path or circle around the sun or around any body in space.
Orient	[OR i ent]	Countries of eastern and southeastern Asia.
outback	[OWT bak]	Dry, empty lands of Australia.
paddy	[PAD ee]	Small rice field, enclosed by dikes of mud.
pampas	[PAM pas]	Large grassy plains in the southeastern part of South America.
parallel	[PAIR a lell]	Line of latitude.
parliament	[PAHR li ment]	Lawmaking body, as in Canada or Great Britain.
peninsula	[pe NIN su la]	Piece of land almost entirely surrounded by water.
peon	[PEE on]	Poor farm worker of Latin America.
permafrost	[PERM a frawst]	Soil just below the earth's surface in the Arctic regions that never thaws or melts.
phosphates	[FOS fayts]	Salts found in the earth that are used in making fertilizer.
physical map	[FIZ i kal]	Map showing the land and water features of the earth.
plain		Broad stretch of level or almost level land.
planet	[PLAN et]	Body in space that revolves about a sun and gives off no light of its own.
plantation	[plan TAY shun]	A large farm on which one chief crop is grown.
plateau	[plat TO]	Large area of level highland, not so rough as mountains.
plaza	[PLAH za]	Public square in a Latin American village or town.
polar map	[PO ler]	Map in which the North or South Pole is the center.
port		Harbor or city around a harbor where ships deliver and pick up goods for trade or people who wish to travel.
prairie	[PRAIR ee]	Dry grassland or steppe.
Prime Meridian	[PRYM ma RID ee an]	First or beginning line of longitude, running through Greenwich, England; 0° longitude.

processing	[PROS sess ing]	Treating food or materials to make them ready for use.
province	[PROV ins]	Political subdivision of a country. Canada has provinces instead of states.
rainfall		Amount of water falling in a given time on a given region, measured in inches.
rain-forest climate		Year-round hot, rainy climate of the low forest lands near the equator.
ranch		Large area of land for raising cattle or sheep.
raw materials	[RAW ma TEER i als]	Natural resources, like wool, cotton, minerals, that can be turned into finished products.
refine	[ree FYN]	To remove the impurities from raw materials such as oil, sugar cane or minerals.
refugees	[REF yoo jeez]	People who flee from a country, usually because of religious or political persecution or war.
reincarnation	[ree in kar NAY shun]	Belief of the Hindu religion in which the spirit is said to take a new form after death.
republic	[ree PUB lik]	Nation in which the people elect representatives to make their laws.
reserves	[ree ZERVS]	Anything not yet used, as oil or mineral ores; or any place set apart, such as Negro settlements in the Republic of South Africa.
reservoir	[REZ er VWAHR]	Place where water is stored.
revolution	[rev o LOO shun]	Sudden change in government or in customs; also, the movement of the earth around the sun.
river		Large stream of water.
river mouth		Place where a river flows or empties into the sea.
river source	[SORS]	Where a river rises or begins.
rotation	[ro TAY shun]	Turning of the earth on its axis during a whole day; crops planted in turn on the same fields.
rural	[ROOR al]	Having to do with farms and villages.
satellite country	[SAT e lyt]	Nation under the control of a larger nation, such as the *satellites* of the Soviet Union.
savanna	[sa VAN a]	Hot climatic region of two seasons, rainy and dry, found north and south of the tropical rain forests.
scale of miles		A key that explains distance, or how far one place is from another on a map; also helps to show the size of an area.
sea		Large body of water, partly surrounded by land.
sea level	[SEE LEV el]	About the same height as the ocean; low point of land.
serf	[SURF]	A person who works for a lord or a large landowner, and who is bound to his lord's land and sold with it to any new owner.
sharecropper	[SHAIR krop er]	One who farms land belonging to another, and receives a share of the crop for his work.

sheik	[SHEEK]	Head man of a village or a tribe, chiefly in the Middle East.
slum		Old, crowded, poor section of a city.
South Pole		Southernmost point on earth.
soviet	[SO vi et]	Russian word for *council*.
state farm		*Sovkhoz*—large government-owned farm in the Soviet Union on which farmers work for wages.
steppe	[STEP]	Large treeless plain that has cold winters and hot summers, and receives from ten to twenty inches of rain a year; called a prairie in the United States.
strait		Narrow body of water that connects two larger bodies of water.
subcontinent	[sub KON ti nent]	An area of land almost as large as a continent; a land mass separated from the mainland by mountains, such as India.
subsistence farming	[sub SIS tens]	Farming in which the farmer grows only enough crops to feed himself and his family.
subtropical	[sub TROP i kal]	Between the temperate and the tropical zones.
surplus	[SUR plus]	Amount left over after needs are met, as a *surplus* of wheat or clothing.
tableland	[TAY bel land]	High plain or plateau; a mesa.
taiga	[TY ga]	Large cold forests of subarctic regions.
tariff	[TAIR if]	Tax on goods coming into a country.
temperature	[TEM per a cher]	Amount of heat or cold in the air, measured by degrees on a thermometer.
topography	[top OG ra fee]	All the features or land forms of the earth's surface: rivers, bodies of water, plains, mountains, valleys, plateaus; the general shape or form of the land.
trade		Exchange of goods between nations or persons.
treaty	[TREE tee]	Formal, written agreement between nations about boundaries, trade, etc.
tributary	[TRIB yoo tair ee]	Branch of a river.
Tropic of Cancer	[TROP ik, KAN ser]	Imaginary line of latitude 23½° north of the equator; the farthest point north that the sun appears directly overhead.
Tropic of Capricorn	[KAP ri korn]	Imaginary line of latitude 23½° south of the equator; the farthest point south that the sun appears directly overhead.
trust territory	[TER i tor ee]	Region placed under the care of one nation by the United Nations.
tsetse fly	[TSET see]	Insect found only in Africa whose bite causes sleeping sickness.
tundra	[TUN dra]	Level, treeless region of the Arctic that has long, severe winters and short summers. The ground is frozen nearly all year.
typhoon	[ty FOON]	Violent storm of the western Pacific Ocean.
underdeveloped	[UN der de VEL opt]	Not making full use of natural resources.

540

United Nations	[yoo NY ted NAY shuns]	Organization founded in 1945 to keep world peace.
urban	[UR ban]	Having to do with towns and cities.
valley		Lowland between hills and mountains.
veld	[VELT]	High grassy plain or tableland in South Africa, used for sheep and cattle grazing.
vertical climate	[VUR ti kal]	Climate of mountainous regions in which temperatures are warmer lower down and cooler higher up.
veto	[VEE to]	Power to prevent an action by refusing to agree.
Vital Triangle	[VY tal TRY an gle]	Area extending through Belgium, France and West Germany that is rich in coal and iron deposits and famous for its iron and steel products.
volcano	[vol KAY no]	Mountain that sometimes pours out smoke, fire and melted rock through a hole in its top.
water power		Physical force of water used to make electricity or to run machines.
weather	[WETH er]	Temperature of any area over a short period of time; the day-by-day changes in the condition of the air.
winds		Currents or streams of air.
windward		Toward the wind; the rainy or wet side of mountains.
wood pulp	[WOOD pulp]	Soft wood that has been crushed to make paper.

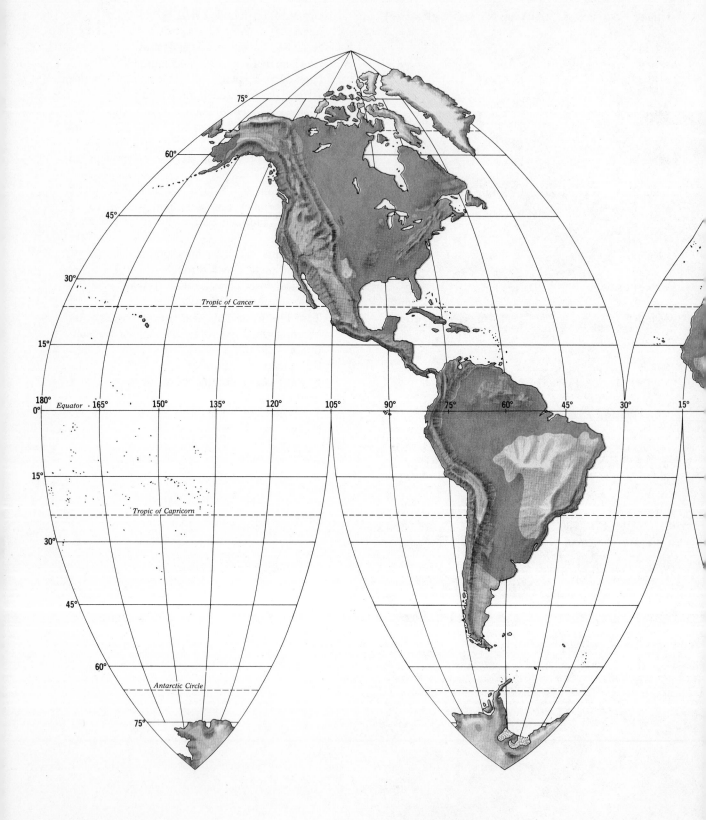

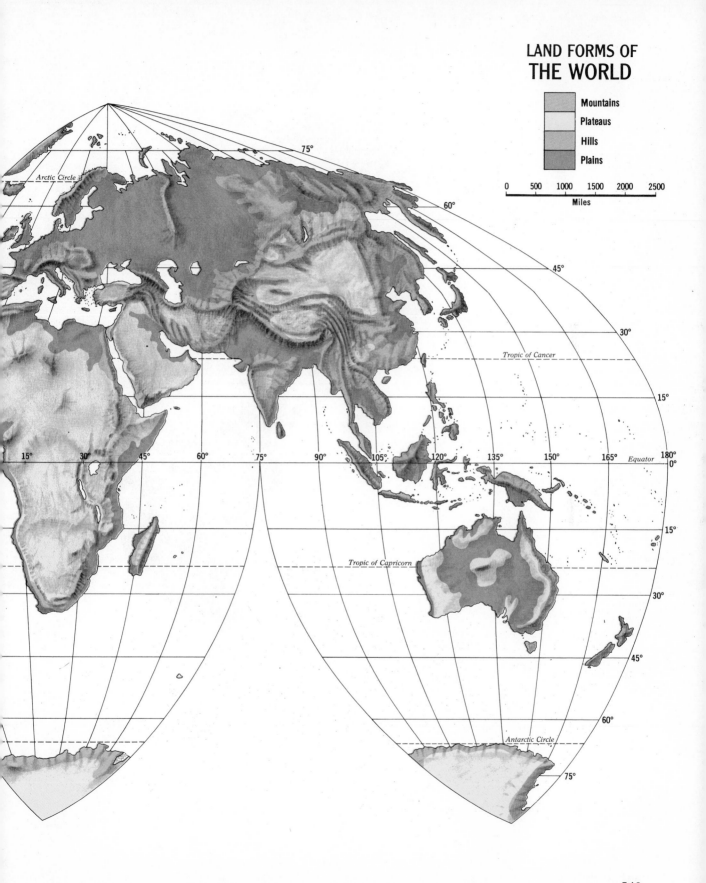

LAND FORMS OF
THE WORLD

Mountains
Plateaus
Hills
Plains

0 500 1000 1500 2000 2500
Miles

75°

Arctic Circle

60°

45°

30°

Tropic of Cancer

15°

15° 30° 45° 60° 75° 90° 105° 120° 135° 150° 165° Equator 180°
0°

15°

Tropic of Capricorn

30°

45°

60°

Antarctic Circle

75°

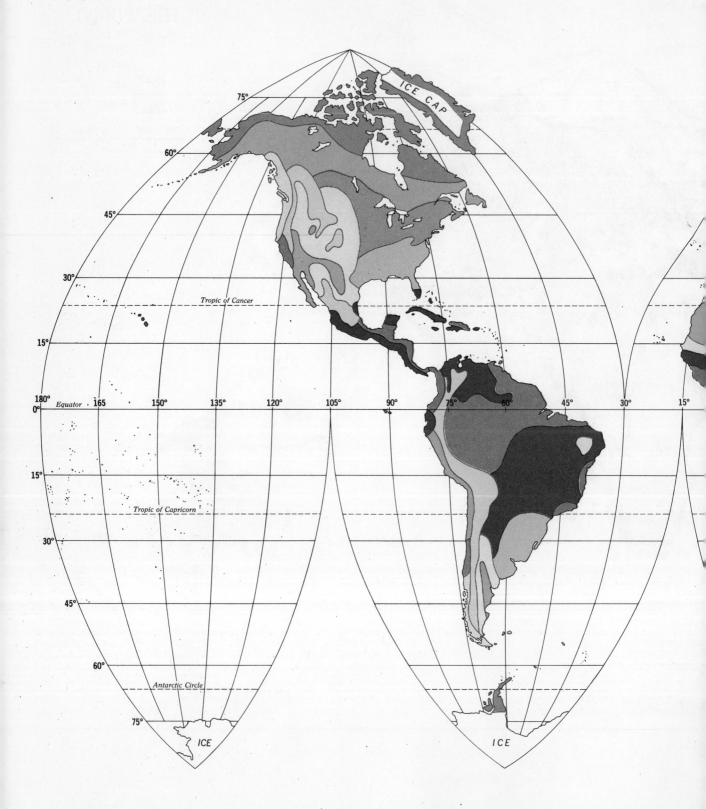

ICE CAP

75°

60°

45°

30°

Tropic of Cancer

15°

180° 165   150°   135°   120°   105°   90°   75°   60°   45°   30°   15°
0° Equator

15°

Tropic of Capricorn

30°

45°

60°

Antarctic Circle

75°

ICE   ICE

544

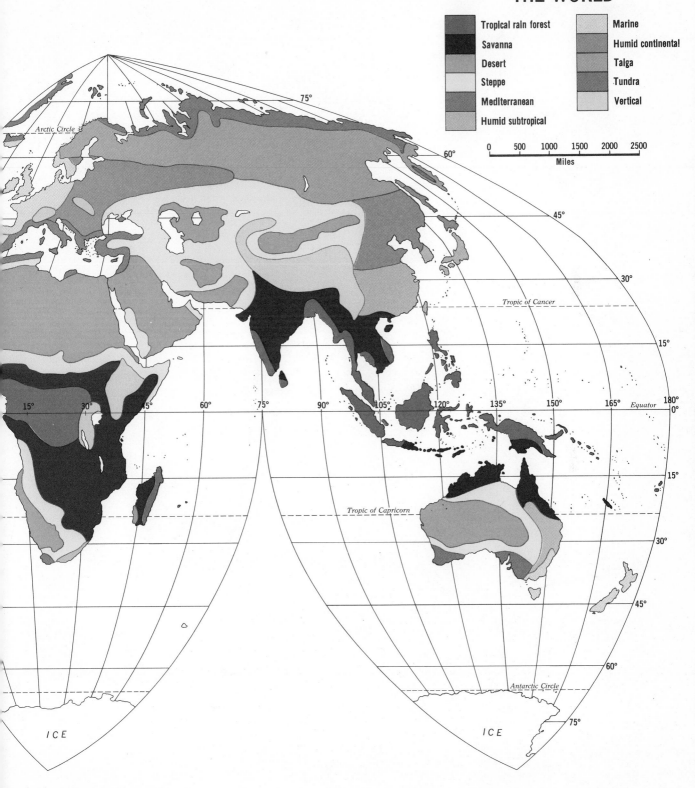

CLIMATES OF
THE WORLD

	Tropical rain forest		Marine
	Savanna		Humid continental
	Desert		Taiga
	Steppe		Tundra
	Mediterranean		Vertical
	Humid subtropical		

Miles
0   500   1000   1500   2000   2500

75°

Arctic Circle

60°

45°

30°

Tropic of Cancer

15°

15° 30° 45° 60° 75° 90° 105° 120° 135° 150° 165°   Equator   180°
0°

Tropic of Capricorn

15°

30°

45°

60°

Antarctic Circle

75°

ICE

ICE

545

The Countries of the World

ANGLO-AMERICA

COUNTRY	AREA	CAPITAL	COUNTRY	AREA	CAPITAL
Canada	3,851,809	Ottawa, Ontario	Missouri	69,674	Jefferson City
United States	3,615,210	Washington, D.C.	Montana	147,138	Helena
			Nebraska	77,237	Lincoln
Alabama	51,609	Montgomery	Nevada	110,540	Carson City
Alaska	586,400	Juneau	New Hampshire	9,304	Concord
Arizona	113,909	Phoenix	New Jersey	7,836	Trenton
Arkansas	53,103	Little Rock	New Mexico	121,666	Santa Fe
California	158,693	Sacramento	New York	49,576	Albany
Colorado	104,247	Denver	North Carolina	52,712	Raleigh
Connecticut	5,009	Hartford	North Dakota	70,665	Bismarck
Delaware	2,057	Dover	Ohio	41,222	Columbus
Florida	58,560	Tallahassee	Oklahoma	69,919	Oklahoma City
Georgia	58,876	Atlanta	Oregon	96,981	Salem
Hawaii	6,423	Honolulu	Pennsylvania	45,333	Harrisburg
Idaho	83,557	Boise	Rhode Island	1,214	Providence
Illinois	56,400	Springfield	South Carolina	31,055	Columbia
Indiana	36,291	Indianapolis	South Dakota	77,047	Pierre
Iowa	56,280	Des Moines	Tennessee	42,246	Nashville
Kansas	82,276	Topeka	Texas	267,339	Austin
Kentucky	40,395	Frankfort	Utah	84,916	Salt Lake City
Louisiana	48,522	Baton Rouge	Vermont	9,609	Montpelier
Maine	33,215	Augusta	Virginia	40,815	Richmond
Maryland	10,577	Annapolis	Washington	68,192	Olympia
Massachusetts	8,257	Boston	West Virginia	24,181	Charleston
Michigan	58,216	Lansing	Wisconsin	56,154	Madison
Minnesota	84,068	St. Paul	Wyoming	97,914	Cheyenne
Mississippi	47,716	Jackson	District of Columbia	69	

LATIN AMERICA

COUNTRY	AREA	CAPITAL	COUNTRY	AREA	CAPITAL
Argentina	1,072,745	Buenos Aires	Honduras	44,482	Tegucigalpa
Bolivia	416,040	La Paz	Jamaica	4,450	Kingston
Brazil	3,286,270	Brasília	Mexico	758,259	Mexico City
British Honduras	8,867	Belize	Nicaragua	57,143	Managua
Chile	286,397	Santiago	Panama	28,576	Panama
Colombia	455,335	Bogotá	Paraguay	157,000	Asunción
Costa Rica	23,421	San José	Peru	514,059	Lima
Cuba	44,206	Havana	Puerto Rico	3,435	San Juan
Dominican Republic	19,332	Santo Domingo	Surinam	55,400	Paramaribo
Ecuador	116,270	Quito	Trinidad and Tobago	1,960	Port-of-Spain
El Salvador	8,259	San Salvador	Uruguay	72,172	Montevideo
French Guiana	33,698	Cayenne	Venezuela	352,150	Caracas
Guatemala	42,042	Guatemala City	West Indies (Br., Dutch, Fr., U.S.)		
Guyana	83,000	Georgetown			
Haiti	10,714	Port-au-Prince			

547

WESTERN EUROPE

COUNTRY	AREA	CAPITAL	COUNTRY	AREA	CAPITAL
Andorra	191	Andorra	Luxembourg	999	Luxembourg
Austria	32,376	Vienna	Malta	95	Valletta
Belgium	11,775	Brussels	Monaco	370 (acres)	Monaco
Cyprus	3,572	Nicosia	Netherlands	15,764	Amsterdam
Denmark	16,619	Copenhagen	Norway	125,064	Oslo
Greenland	840,154	Godthaab	Portugal	35,464	Lisbon
Finland	130,165	Helsinki	San Marino	38	San Marino
France	212,659	Paris	Spain	195,504	Madrid
Greece	51,842	Athens	Sweden	173,378	Stockholm
Iceland	39,758	Reykjavik	Switzerland	15,944	Bern
Ireland	27,136	Dublin	United Kingdom of		
Italy	116,372	Rome	Great Britain	94,279	London
Liechtenstein	62	Vaduz	West Germany	95,931	Bonn

THE SOVIET UNION AND EASTERN EUROPE

COUNTRY	AREA	CAPITAL	COUNTRY	AREA	CAPITAL
Albania	11,097	Tirana	Poland	120,355	Warsaw
Bulgaria	42,796	Sofia	Rumania	91,584	Bucharest
Czechoslovakia	49,367	Prague	U.S.S.R.	8,655,890	Moscow
East Germany	41,645	East Berlin	Yugoslavia	98,766	Belgrade
Hungary	35,918	Budapest			

NORTH AFRICA AND THE MIDDLE EAST

COUNTRY	AREA	CAPITAL	COUNTRY	AREA	CAPITAL
Aden (Br.)	75	Aden	Morocco	172,104	Rabat
Afghanistan	250,000	Kabul	Muscat and Oman	82,000	Muscat
Algeria	920,000	Algiers	Qatar (Br.)	8,500	Doha
Bahrain (Br.)	250	Manama	Saudi Arabia	600,000	Riyadh and
Federation of South					Mecca
Arabia (Br.)	60,000	Al Ittihad	Syria	72,234	Damascus
Iran	628,060	Tehran	Trucial States (Br.)	32,300	Sharjah
Iraq	172,000	Baghdad	Tunisia	58,000	Tunis
Israel	7,993	Jerusalem	Turkey	296,500	Ankara
Jordan	37,500	Amman	United Arab		
Kuwait	5,800	Kuwait	Republic (Egypt)	386,198	Cairo
Lebanon	4,000	Beirut	Yemen	75,000	San'a
Libya	679,358	Tripoli and Benghazi			

AFRICA, SOUTH OF THE SAHARA

COUNTRY	AREA	CAPITAL	COUNTRY	AREA	CAPITAL
Angola (Port.)	481,351	Luanda	Cameroun	183,381	Yaoundé
Basutoland (Br.)	11,716	Maseru	Central African		
Bechuanaland (Br.)	275,000	Gaberones	Republic	238,000	Bangui
Burundi	10,747	Bujumbura	Chad	495,000	Fort-Lamy

COUNTRY	AREA	CAPITAL
Congo (Democratic Republic of the Congo)	904,757	Leopoldville
Congo (Congo Republic)	132,050	Brazzaville
Dahomey	44,290	Porto-Novo
Ethiopia	457,268	Addis Ababa
French Somaliland (Fr.)	8,800	Djibouti
Gabon	102,290	Libreville
Gambia	4,000	Bathurst
Ghana	91,843	Accra
Guinea	96,865	Conakry
Ivory Coast	127,520	Abidjan
Kenya	224,960	Nairobi
Liberia	43,000	Monrovia
Malagasy Republic	228,000	Tananarive
Malawi	37,374	Zomba
Mali	450,000	Bamako
Mauritania	418,810	Nouakchott
Mozambique (Port.)	297,731	Lourenço Marques

COUNTRY	AREA	CAPITAL
Niger	490,000	Niamey
Nigeria	356,669	Lagos
Portuguese Guinea	13,944	Bissau
Rhodesia	150,333	Salisbury
Rwanda	10,166	Kigali
Senegal	76,000	Dakar
Sierra Leone	27,925	Freetown
Somalia	246,205	Mogadishu
South Africa, Republic of	472,359	Pretoria and Capetown
South-West Africa (S.A.)	318,099	Windhoek
Spanish Sahara (Sp.)	106,000	El Aaiun
Sudan	967,500	Khartoum
Swaziland (Br.)	6,705	Mbabane
Tanzania	361,800	Dar es Salaam
Togo	20,400	Lomé
Uganda	93,981	Kampala
Upper Volta	105,900	Ouagadougou
Zambia	290,320	Lusaka

THE FAR EAST

COUNTRY	AREA	CAPITAL
Bhutan	18,000	Thimphu
Burma	261,789	Rangoon
Cambodia	71,000	Phnom-Penh
Ceylon	25,332	Colombo
Formosa (Taiwan, Nationalist China)	13,886	Taipei
India	1,261,597	New Delhi
Indonesia	735,865	Jakarta
Japan	142,688	Tokyo
Korea		
North	48,000	Pyongyang
South	37,427	Seoul
Laos	91,000	Vientiane
Malaysia	130,557	Kuala Lumpur

COUNTRY	AREA	CAPITAL
Maldive Islands	115	Male
Mongolian People's Republic	626,000	Ulan Bator
Nepal	54,362	Katmandu
Pakistan	365,529	Rawalpindi
People's Republic of China (Red China)	3,760,339	Peking
Philippines	115,758	Manila
Sikkim	2,745	Gangtok
Singapore	278	Singapore
Thailand	200,148	Bangkok
Vietnam		
North	63,000	Hanoi
South	63,000	Saigon

THE PACIFIC WORLD

COUNTRY	AREA	CAPITAL
Australia	3,258,270	Canberra
New Zealand	103,416	Wellington
Western Samoa	1,000	Apia

MAJOR RIVERS OF THE WORLD

RIVER	LENGTH IN MILES	RIVER	LENGTH IN MILES
Amazon (South America)	3,900	Mississippi-Missouri-Red Rock (North America)	3,860
Amur (Asia)	2,700	Missouri-Red Rock (North America)	2,683
Arkansas (North America)	1,450	Murray-Darling (Australia)	2,310
Brahmaputra (Asia)	1,800	Niger (Africa)	2,600
Colorado (North America)	1,450	Nile (Africa)	4,145
Columbia (North America)	1,214	Ob-Irtysh (Asia)	3,461
Congo (Africa)	2,718	Oder (Europe)	565
Danube (Europe)	1,770	Ohio-Allegheny (North America)	1,306
Dnieper (Europe)	1,420	Orange (Africa)	1,300
Don (Europe)	1,210	Orinoco (South America)	1,700
Donets (Europe)	735	Paraná (South America)	2,500
Elbe (Europe)	720	Plata-Paraguay (South America)	2,300
Euphrates (Asia)	1,675	Rhône (Europe)	500
Ganges (Asia)	1,560	Rio Grande (North America)	1,885
Hwang (Asia)	3,000	St. Lawrence (North America)	1,900
Indus (Asia)	1,900	Senegal (Africa)	1,000
Irrawaddy (Asia)	1,250	Tigris (Asia)	1,150
Lena (Asia)	2,680	Ural (Asia)	1,570
Loire (Europe)	625	Volga (Europe)	2,290
Mackenzie (North America)	2,635	Yangtze (Asia)	3,400
Madeira (South America)	2,000	Yenisei (Asia)	2,080
Magdalena (South America)	1,000	Yukon (North America)	1,800
Mekong (Asia)	2,600	Zambezi (Africa)	1,600
Mississippi (North America)	2,348		

Index

Index

Automobiles, 105, 224, 282, 296
Axis, of the earth, 20, 22
Aztec Indians, 155–156, 186

B

Babylonia, 327
Baghdad, Iraq, 323
Balkan Peninsula, 207
Balkash, Lake, 274
Baltic Sea, 206, 268
Baltimore, Maryland, 105
Bamboo, 462
Bananas, 168, 170, 187, 195, 393, 512, 517
Bangkok, Thailand, 491
Bantus, 388, 415
Barcelona, Spain, 249, 250
Barley, 227, 255, 291, 311, 340, 474
Bauxite, 47, 94, 124, 174, 195, 372, 400, 419, 465
Bedouin, 343
Belgium, colonies, 206, 224; in Congo, 305, 405–406; size, 202; steel, 223, 224. *See also* Common Market.
Benelux countries, 235
Ben-Gurion, David, 365
Bering Strait, 267, 277
Berlin, Germany, blockade, 239–240, 263, 303–304; longitude, 17; wall, 240, 263, 304
Birmingham, Alabama, 106
Black Sea, 268, 292, 300
Boers, 414
Bolívar, Simón, 157
Bolivia, 119, 150, 173
Bombay, India, 449, 480
Bonn, West Germany, 239
Boston, Massachusetts, 22
Brahmaputra River, 430, 479
Brasília, 179, 195
Brazil, 141; climate, 194; farming, 179, 195; government, 195; highlands, 145; history, 156, 194; people, 194–196; problems, 195; relations with U.S., 195; resources, 195; size and location, 194; topography, 145, 194. *See also* Amazon River.
Buddhism, 452, 453, 474, 490
Buenos Aires, Argentina, 146, 151, 162
Bulgaria, 279, 311–312
Bunche, Ralph, 356
Burma, 489, 490; freedom, 445; monsoons, 435–436; rice, 458, 491
Bushmen, 507
Butter, 396. *See also* Dairying.
Byrd, Admiral Richard, 524

C

Cabral, Pedro, 156
Cacao, 119, 170, 195, 394, 411, 419. *See also* Cocoa.
Cairo, Egypt, 331, 360

Calcutta, India, 430, 449, 470, 480, 481
California, 95, 110, 115, 277
Cambodia, 305, 445, 489, 490
Camels, 333, 343, 344
Canada, 54; climate, 75–77; compared with Australia, 509, with the U.S., 66–67; education, 87; farming, 126–127; foreign relations, 130–131, 134–135; forests, 123; government, 89–90; history, 80–82; industries, 122–124, 131; minorities, 133; people, 86–87; problems, 133–135; resources, 122–124, 130; size, 66; standard of living, 86; topography, 70–71; trade, 127; trade with the U.S., 130. *See also* Anglo-America.
Canadian Shield, 122, 123, 126. *See also* Laurentian Shield.
Canals, 114; Egypt, 359; Europe, 207, 223, 224; Far East, 440, 484. *See also* names of individual canals.
Canberra, Australia, 507
Capetown, South African Republic, 384, 385, 415
Capitalism, 99–101
Caribbean Sea, 28, 140
Caspian Sea, 274, 296
Caste system, 452, 481
Castro, Fidel, 183–184, 305
Catholics, Anglo-America, 85, 86; Latin America, 156, 160, 161, 190, 195; Europe, 214, 220; Spain, 249; Soviet Union, 283; Eastern Europe, 311. *See also* Christianity.
Cattle, Anglo-America, 105, 109, 114; Latin America, 169, 170; Brazil, 195; Western Europe, 227; Eastern Europe, 311; Africa, 380, 396, 397; India, 453, 457, 480, 481; Australia, 512, 513. *See also* Dairying, Grazing.
Caucasus Mountains, 24, 291
Central America, 140, 155
Central Plains, Anglo-America, 67, 70, 109, 110
Central Treaty Organization (CENTO), 245, 356
Central Valley, California, 71, 115
Ceylon, 426, 435; independence, 445; monsoons, 435–436; tea, 462
Charleston, South Carolina, 32, 151
Cheese. *See* Dairying.
Chemicals, 224
Chesapeake Bay, 105
Chiang Kai-shek, 427, 445, 484, 486
Chicago, Illinois, 21, 22, 105
Chickens, 228, 419
Chicle, 169
Chile, 21, 152, 173
China (Communist or Red China), 304, 307, 308–309; climates, 436, 484; communism, 427, 445, 467, 470, 485, 486; education, 469; farming, 458, 462–463, 485; government, 444–445, 485; history, 440–441, 444–445; location, 440, 484; military power, 308, 427, 486, 526; people, 448, 485, 490; relations with U.S., 444, 486; with Japan, 444, 445, 473; with

554

Soviet Union, 486; religions, 453–454, 485; resources, 466; size, 426, 484; topography, 484; transportation, 484, 485. *See also* rivers by name.

China (Nationalist), 427, 445, 484, 486

Chocolate, 394, 411

Christianity, Anglo-America, 85, 86; Western Europe, 202, 214, 215, 220, 254; Soviet Union, 283; Eastern Europe, 311; Middle East, 318, 328, 365, 366; Africa, 385; Far East, 454, 474, 490. *See also* Catholics, Protestants.

Chromium, 195, 348, 465

Cinchona tree, 169. *See also* Quinine.

Cinnamon, 462

Cities. *See* individual countries and regions, also cities by name.

Citrus fruits, 111, 115, 191, 210, 228, 365

Cleveland, Ohio, 22, 105

Climate, factors causing changes in, 32–33, 35–37; regions of, 39–42. *See also* regions and countries by name, also names of climatic regions.

Coal, 46; U.S., 95; Canada, 123; Latin America, 174; Europe, 223, 224; Britain, 244; Soviet Union, 294–296; Poland, 311; Turkey, 348; India, 465; China, 466, 484, 485; Japan, 475; Australia, 513

Cobalt, 400

Cocoa, 518. *See also* Cacao.

Coconuts, 419, 461, 491, 512, 517, 518

Coffee, Latin America, 170; Brazil, 195; Far East, 458, 461, 491; Pacific area, 518

Cold War, defined, 303; spread, 305

Collective farm, 290–291, 299, 485. *See also* Kolkhoz.

Colombia, 170, 179, 182

Colonialism, 216, 224, 243, 248, 405. *See also* individual countries.

Colorado River, 95, 115

Colored people, 52. *See also* Negro, Races.

Columbia Plateau, 114

Columbia River, 71, 95; power project, 122, 130

Columbus, Christopher, 155, 190

Commercial farming, 127, 458. *See also* Plantations.

Common Market, 216, 235–236

Commonwealth of Nations, 243, 244, 508

Communes, 458, 485

Communism, spread, 134, 135; Latin America, 184, 263, 305; Europe, 203, 240, 263, 303–304; Soviet Union, 263, 278, 283, 286–287, 299, 307; Eastern Europe, 311, 312; Asia, 304; China, 427, 445, 467, 470, 485, 486; Africa, 305. *See also* Communist Party.

Communist Party, 263, 278, 286–287, 290, 300, 301, 485

Confucianism, 452, 453–454

Congo Republic, 373, 400, 405–406

Congo River, 29, 376, 385; rain forest, 380

Conservation, 47, 134, 528. *See also* farming in individual countries.

Cooperatives, 228

Copenhagen, Denmark, 232

Copernicus, 215

Copper, 47; United States, 94; Chile, 173; Spain, 250; Finland and Norway, 255; Soviet Union, 294; Turkey, 348; Israel, 366; Africa, 372, 400; Japan, 475; Australia, 513

Copra, 517–518

Corn, United States, 109, 111, 165; Latin America, 170–171; Mexico, 187; Brazil, 195; North Africa and Middle East, 340; Africa, 396; China, 463; Pacific islands, 517

Corn Belt, 109

Cortez, Hernando, 156, 186

Cosmetics, 393, 518

Cotton, United States, 110, 111, 115; Latin America, 170–171; Mexico, 186; Brazil, 195; Soviet Union, 274, 291; North Africa, 340; Egypt, 359, 361; Far East, 462; India, 480

Cotton Belt, 110, 111

Crimean Peninsula, 274

Cuba, 140, 141, 160; Fidel Castro, 183–184; freedom, 182, 249; Soviet missile bases, 263; sugar, 169, 179

Czars, 277–278

Czechoslovakia, 279, 304, 311–312

D

Dairying, United States, 110, 115; Canada, 126; Puerto Rico, 191; Western Europe, 227, 228; Scandinavia, 255; Australia, 512; New Zealand, 513

Dams, United States, 95, 114; Soviet Union, 294, 295; North Africa and Middle East, 351; India, 465; China, 485. *See also* names of dams.

Danube River, 29, 207, 311

Dardanelles, 29, 268, 303, 318, 356

Dates, 115, 344

Dead Sea, 364, 366

Death Valley, 71

Deccan Plateau, 479, 480, 481

Democracy, 220; in Far East, 470, 485; Australia and New Zealand, 508. *See also* governments of individual countries: Canada, Japan, United States, Western Europe.

Democratic Revolution, 215–216

Denmark, 220, 227, 254

Denver, Colorado, 22, 106

Desert, climate, 39; United States, 71, 76, 115; Latin America, 151, 173; Soviet Union, 274; North Africa and Middle East, 322–323, 343–344, 380; Egypt, 359; Israel, 365, 366; Africa, South of Sahara, 381; China, 436; Australia, 503. *See also* deserts by name.

Detroit, Michigan, 21, 105

Diamonds, cutting, 366; Africa, 372, 400, 415

Diet, of Japan, 473

Directions, on map, 13